Studies in Church History

55

(2019)

CHURCHES AND EDUCATION

CHURCHES AND EDUCATION

EDITED BY

MORWENNA LUDLOW

CHARLOTTE METHUEN

ANDREW SPICER

PUBLISHED FOR

THE ECCLESIASTICAL HISTORY SOCIETY

BY

CAMBRIDGE UNIVERSITY PRESS

2019

Published by Cambridge University Press
on behalf of the Ecclesiastical History Society
University Printing House, Cambridge CB2 8BS, United Kingdom

First published 2019

ISBN 9781108487085

ISSN 0424–2084

SUBSCRIPTIONS: *Studies in Church History* is an annual subscription journal (ISSN 0424–2084). The 2019 subscription price (excluding VAT), which includes print and electronic access, is £110 (US $178 in the USA, Canada and Mexico) for institutions and £61 (US $98 in the USA, Canada and Mexico) for individuals ordering direct from the Press and certifying that the volume is for their personal use. An electronic-only subscription is also available to institutions at £86 (US $137 in the USA, Canada and Mexico). Special arrangements exist for members of the Ecclesiastical History Society.

Previous volumes are available online at www.cambridge.org/StudCH

Printed in the United Kingdom by Bell & Bain Ltd
A catalogue record for this publication is available from the British Library

Contents

Preface

Studies in Church History 55 takes as its theme 'Churches and Education'. It offers a collection of peer reviewed articles selected from the range of communications presented at the Ecclesiastical History Society's Summer Conference and Winter Meeting 2017–18, which took place at the University of Exeter and at the Institute for Historical Research, London under the presidency of Professor Morwenna Ludlow.

As is apparent from this rich collection of articles, Professor Ludlow's chosen theme, 'Churches and Education', generated considerable interest, and the resulting volume offers insights into a wide range of educational projects through which the Church has presented itself and its beliefs. We are grateful to Professor Ludlow for identifying this theme and also for the commitment she has shown to the society as its president during 2017–18. Our thanks go also to all those who contributed papers at the conferences, attended sessions and enhanced the quality of this volume by acting as peer reviewers. We thank particularly the authors of the articles which appear in this volume. We are particularly grateful to Dr Tim Grass for his careful editorial work and his engagement in so many aspects of the society's work, and to the Ecclesiastical History Society for funding his post.

The Summer Conference and Winter Meeting could not have taken place without the sterling work of the society's conference secretary, Dr David Hart, who was assisted by the conference teams at the University of Exeter and by staff at the IHR, and by the society's secretary, Dr Gareth Atkins, and treasurer, Simon Jennings. Our thanks, and those of all who participated, go to them all.

The Ecclesiastical History Society awards two prizes for articles accepted for publication in Studies in Church History. The Kennedy Prize, for the best contribution by a postgraduate student, has this year been awarded to Jennifer Bond for her article '"The One for the Many": Zeng Baosun, Louise Barnes and the Yifang School for Girls at Changsha, 1893–1927'. The President's Prize, for the best contribution by an early career scholar, goes to Dr Marina Xiaojing Wang for her article 'Western Establishment or Chinese Sovereignty? The Tientsin Anglo-Chinese College during the Restore Educational Rights Movement, 1924–7'. We are delighted to present these fascinating insights into the history of Christian education in China, and congratulate both authors.

Charlotte Methuen
University of Glasgow

Andrew Spicer
Oxford Brookes University

Contributors

Ruth Atherton
Postgraduate student, University of Birmingham

Frances Billinge
Honorary Associate Research Fellow, University of Exeter

Jennifer Bond
Postgraduate student, School of Oriental and African Studies

Caroline Bowden
Senior Research Fellow, School of History, Queen Mary University of London

Mark Chapman
Vice-Principal, Ripon College Cuddesdon; Professor of the History of Modern Theology, University of Oxford

Nicholas Dixon
Postgraduate student, Pembroke College, Cambridge

Jonathan Doney
British Academy Postdoctoral Fellow, University of Exeter

Inge Dornan
Lecturer in Politics and History, Brunel University

Robert A. H. Evans
Postgraduate student, University of Cambridge

Seb Falk
Rosamund Chambers Research Fellow, Girton College, University of Cambridge

Alena A. Fidlerová
Assistant Professor, Institute of Czech Language and Theory of Communication, Faculty of Arts, Charles University, Prague

Gail Ham
Dartmouth

Sarah Hamilton
Professor of Medieval History, University of Exeter

W. M. Jacob
Visiting Research Fellow, King's College London

Eleni Leontidou
House of European History, Brussels

Laurel Lied
Postgraduate student, Aarhus University

Morwenna Ludlow
Professor of Christian History and Theology, University of Exeter

Sophie Lunn-Rockliffe
Lecturer in Patristics, Faculty of Divinity, University of Cambridge; Fellow and College Lecturer in Theology and Religious Studies, Peterhouse

Caitriona McCartney
Postgraduate student, University of Durham

Laura M. Mair
Postdoctoral Research Fellow, University of Edinburgh

Ryan Mallon
Postgraduate student, Queen's University Belfast

Mary Clare Martin
Principal Lecturer and Research Lead, Department of Education and Community Studies, University of Greenwich

Grant Masom
Postgraduate student, Kellogg College, University of Oxford

Paul Moon
Professor of History, Auckland University of Technology

Hugh Morrison
Senior Lecturer, University of Otago

Judith Moss
Honorary Associate Research Fellow, University of Exeter

Julia Neville
Honorary Research Fellow, University of Exeter

Roger Ottewill
Southampton

Lucy K. Pick
Senior Lecturer in the History of Christianity, The Divinity School, University of Chicago

Fabio Pruneri
Associate Professor of the History of Education, University of Sassari

Mark Smith
Associate Professor in History, University of Oxford

Rebecca Springer
College Lecturer in History, Oriel College, University of Oxford

Jowita Thor
Postgraduate student, University of Edinburgh

Alexandra Walsham
Professor of Modern History, University of Cambridge

Marina Xiaojing Wang
Lecturer, Divinity School of Chung Chi College, Chinese University of Hong Kong

Martin Wellings
Oxford

Paula Yates
St Padarn's Institute, Cardiff

Abbreviations

ActaSS	*Acta sanctorum*, ed. J. Bolland and G. Henschen (Antwerp etc., 1643–)
ACW	Ancient Christian Writers, ed. J. Quasten et al. (New York, 1946–)
AHR	*American Historical Review* (1895–)
AHRC	Arts and Humanities Research Council
BAV	Biblioteca Apostolica Vaticana
BIHR	*Bulletin of the Institute of Historical Research* (1923–86)
BJRE	*British Journal of Religious Education* (1978–); previously *Religion in Education* (1934–61); *Learning for Living* (1961–78)
BL	British Library
BN	Bibliothèque nationale de France
Bodl.	Bodleian Library
CChr	Corpus Christianorum (Turnhout, 1953–)
CChr.CM	Corpus Christianorum, continuatio medievalis (1966–)
CChr.SL	Corpus Christianorum, series Latina (1953–)
CERC	Church of England Record Centre
CERS	Church of England Record Society
CHC	*Cambridge History of Christianity*, 9 vols (Cambridge, 2005–9)
ChH	*Church History* (1932–)
CHRC	*Church History and Religious Culture* (2006–)
CQR	*Church Quarterly Review* (1875–1968)
CRL	Cadbury Research Library, University of Birmingham
CRS	Catholic Record Society
CSEL	Corpus Scriptorum Ecclesiasticorum Latinorum (Vienna, 1866–)
DBI	*Dizionario biografico degli italiani* (Rome, 1960–)
EHR	*English Historical Review* (1886–)
EME	*Early Medieval Europe* (1992–)

ET	English translation
FOTC	Fathers of the Church (Washington DC, 1989–)
GH	*Gender and History* (1989–)
HBS	Henry Bradshaw Society
HE	*History of Education* (1972–)
HistJ	*Historical Journal* (1958–)
JEAH	*Journal of Educational Administration and History* (1968–)
JECS	*Journal of Early Christian Studies* (1993–)
JBS	*Journal of British Studies* (1961–)
JBV	*Journal of Beliefs and Values* (1979–)
JEH	*Journal of Ecclesiastical History* (1950–)
JEMH	*Journal of Early Modern History* (1997–)
JFH	*Journal of Family History* (1976–)
JFHS	*Journal of the Friends Historical Society* (1903–)
JICH	*Journal of Imperial and Commonwealth History* (1972–)
JMedH	*Journal of Medieval History* (1975–)
JRA	*Journal of Religion in Africa* (1967–)
JRH	*Journal of Religious History* (1960–)
JRL	John Rylands Library, University of Manchester
JSH	*Journal of Social History* (1967–)
JThS	*Journal of Theological Studies* (1899–)
JURCHS	*Journal of the United Reformed Church Historical Society* (1973–)
LCL	Loeb Classical Library
LMA	London Metropolitan Archive
LPL	Lambeth Palace Library
MGH	Monumenta Germaniae Historica inde ab a. *c.* 500 usque ad a. 1500, ed. G. H. Pertz et al. (Hanover, Berlin, etc., 1826–)
MGH AA	Monumenta Germaniae Historica, Auctores antiquissimi, 15 vols (1877–1919)
MGH BdK	Monumenta Germaniae Historica, Die Briefe der deutschen Kaiserzeit (1949–)

MGH Capit.	Monumenta Germaniae Historica, Capitula regum Francorum, 2 vols (1883–97)
MGH Capit. episc.	Monumenta Germaniae Historica, Capitula episcoporum (1984–)
MGH Conc.	Monumenta Germaniae Historica, Concilia (1893–)
MGH Fontes n.s.	Monumenta Germaniae Historica, Fontes Iuris Gemanici Antiqui n.s. (1933–)
MGH H	Monumenta Germaniae Historica, Hilfsmittel (1975–)
MGH L	Monumenta Germaniae Historica, Leges (1835–)
MGH LdL	Monumenta Germaniae Historica, Libelli de Lite Imperatorum et Pontificum, Saeculis XI et XII conscripti (1891–7)
MGH Poetae	Monumenta Germaniae Historica, Poetae Latinae Medii Aevi (1881–)
MGH Schriften	Schriften der MGH (1938–)
MGH SRG i.u.s.	Monumenta Germaniae Historica, Scriptores rerum Germanicarum in usum scholarum seperatum editi (1871–)
MGH SRM	Monumenta Germaniae Historica, Scriptores rerum Merovingicarum (1884–1951)
MGH SS	Monumenta Germaniae Historica, Scriptores (in folio) (1826–)
n.d.	no date
n.pl.	no place
NPNF II	A Select Library of Nicene and Post-Nicene Fathers of the Christian Church: A New Series, ed. Philip Schaff et al. 14 vols (New York, 1890–1900 and subsequent edns)
n.s.	new series
ODNB	H. C. G. Matthew and Brian Harrison, eds, *Oxford Dictionary of National Biography* (Oxford, 2004)
OECT	Oxford Early Christian Texts
OED	*Oxford English Dictionary*

OHA	Rowan Strong, gen. ed., *Oxford History of Anglicanism*, 5 vols (Oxford, 2017–18)
OHCC	Oxford History of the Christian Church
PH	*Paedagogica Historica* (1961–)
P&P	*Past and Present* (1952–)
PL	Patrologia Latina, ed. J.-P. Migne, 217 vols + 4 index vols (Paris, 1844–65)
QH	*Quaker History* (1962–)
RB	*Revue Bénédictine* (1890–)
RH	*Recusant History* (1951–)
RHE	*Revue d'histoire ecclésiastique* (1900–)
RO	Record Office
RS	*Rerum Britannicarum medii aevi scriptores*, 99 vols (London, 1858–1911) = Rolls Series
RSCHS	*Records of the Scottish Church History Society* (1923–)
s.a.	*sub anno* (under the year)
SC	Sources Chrétiennes (Paris, 1941–)
SCH	Studies in Church History
SHCM	Studies in the History of Christian Missions
TNA	The National Archives
TRHS	*Transactions of the Royal Historical Society* (1871–)
TTH	Translated Texts for Historians
VCH	Victoria History of the Counties of England (London, 1900–)
WHR	*Welsh History Review* (1960–)

Introduction

Education prompts certain fundamental questions about itself: who is (or should be) educated? By whom? By what means? About what should people be educated, and to what end? In the history of Christianity, these questions have been given a particular colour due to the fact that Christians trace their faith back to a teacher (rabbi), Jesus, and his disciples (*mathētai*).[1] Questions about who should be educated and how have become inextricable from the question of how the original teachings of Jesus were transmitted to later generations. This immediately brings to the fore problems regarding authority, interpretation and inclusivity (or exclusivity). As the articles in this volume show, Christians have responded to these issues in a wide variety of ways.

Besides internal disagreements about the scope, form and purpose of Christian teaching and about the authority of Christian teachers, questions about education have also been provoked by the complex relationship between Christianity and its various contexts. Some of these concern specific cultural influences: how have Christian approaches to education changed according to the use of different languages, different literary traditions and different modes of teaching? How have the churches responded to technical changes surrounding writing, book-making and communication? And to what extent has Christianity been interested in education towards ends which are not directly religious? Some of these questions reflect the complex relationship between Christianity, culture and political power. Most of our evidence of early Christianity, for example, relates to Christians in the Roman empire, where specifically Christian modes of education (catechetical, pastoral and ascetic) coexisted for a surprisingly long time alongside the traditional educational systems of Greek and Latin culture. Long after Constantine's reign, Christian parents continued to send their sons to schools which taught literacy and rhetoric through prolonged engagement with texts whose

[1] Of many examples one could cite, Jesus is addressed as 'Rabbi' (ῥαββί) by Peter (Mk 9: 5), Judas (Mk 14: 45), John's disciples (Jn 1: 38), Nathaniel (Jn 1: 49), Nicodemus (Jn 3: 2) and Mary Magdalene (Jn 20: 16). The designation 'disciples' (οἱ μαθηταὶ) is ubiquitous in the Gospels.

Studies in Church History 55 (2019), 1–5
doi: 10.1017/stc.2018.10

religious outlook was decidedly not Christian or even monotheist. Later, Christian foundations became the primary location for all kinds of formal education in most of Europe, although the situation remained much more complex in those regions where Christianity had taken root beyond the boundaries of the Roman empire. In some regions, Jews, Christians and Muslims continued to influence each other closely for centuries, not least in the content and modes of their education. Still later, under the dual drivers of mission and empire, Christians frequently found themselves in contexts where they were a numerical minority in terms of religion, language and culture, but where they were associated – explicitly or implicitly – with invasive European imperial power. As several articles in this volume demonstrate, questions regarding education become especially sharp when the Christian Church, or a Christian church, has been particularly closely associated with an empire or nation state. How does education function, for example, when Christianity is implicated with the efforts of those in power to shape those under their authority? Conversely, how has education been used by Christians to resist certain forms of power, whether that of formal political authority or that of social privilege? What motivates parents to educate their children in ways which are forbidden or discouraged by the state?

Bound up with such issues are questions about the form and location of education: were churches in a particular context concerned only with the education of people to be Christian disciples or also with their education in numeracy, literary and more complex intellectual or practical skills? How formalized were these forms of education? These issues have, of course, particular pertinence for the education of women, which for many centuries took place almost exclusively in a domestic sphere or in ascetic communities; they also relate to the education of those for whom much formal education was inaccessible due, for example, to poverty or disability, or to speaking a different mother tongue. While Christianity has at times actively restricted the scope of education – especially to men – several articles in the volume examine how some Christians have argued that it is a prime role of the Church to extend education as far as possible.

These articles arise from two conferences organized by the Ecclesiastical History Society, in July 2017, at the University of Exeter, and January 2018, at the Institute for Historical Research in London. The society invited a broad range of responses to the kind of questions noted above, and received a wonderfully stimulating selection of papers which ranged broadly in chronological range (from Late Antiquity to the 1970s) and geographical spread (from studies of English, Scottish and Welsh communities to examinations of Christian education across the globe in, for example, China, India, New Zealand, Sierra Leone, South Africa and the West Indies). We are delighted that this has resulted in such a rich edited volume. The purpose of this introduction will not be to summarize the content of each contribution, but rather to point the reader towards some notable themes emerging from the articles.

One of the interesting tensions to emerge is the relationship between the further education of those who were already educated and the elementary education of the majority. Our reliance on written evidence for our understanding of Christian education in Late Antiquity and the Middle Ages, together with low literary rates in those periods, perhaps explains the tendency of historians to focus on the (further) education of an educated elite, whether this is the education of the clergy in pastoral care (Leontidou, Hamilton, Springer) or the transmission of technical knowledge about astronomy (Falk) through monasteries. The study of form, as well as content, however, opens up questions about how people were educated, not least suggesting the possibility that some forms were appropriate for the less well trained, especially for those who could not read but who were experienced listeners. Pick and Evans show how specific literary forms – historiography, hagiography and dialogue – were used for Christian educational purposes in specific contexts. Ludlow and Lunn-Rockliffe's article, meanwhile, suggests that pleasure, including the pleasure of listening, was an important and under-appreciated educational mode in Late Antiquity, the legacy of which can be seen in Fidlerová's study of preaching and rhetoric in the Habsburg empire.

Given the strongly pedagogic bent of many of the Reformers and of their Catholic contemporaries, it is perhaps not surprising that articles examining the early modern period focus more intently on the education of the laity, especially through sermons and in catechisms, as shown in the articles by Atherton and Martin. Lied shows how works of fiction could have a catechetical function. Printed books and increasing literacy rates meant that Christian educational materials could be both officially sanctioned and available in the domestic sphere. In this period there is also much more evidence regarding Christian education for children and the specific aims of their educators. Walsham's article draws attention to the way in which families and institutions played complementary roles in forming children in a particular Christian tradition – in this case, Quakerism. By contrast, Bowden shows that the desire for a good Christian education sometimes cut across Protestant-Catholic dividing lines in surprising ways, as when Protestant parents sent their daughters to Catholic schools.

A popular theme for the two conferences was church-sponsored education of poor children: Jacob, Dixon and Mair examine English schools in the eighteenth, early nineteenth and mid-nineteenth centuries, respectively; the article by Billinge, Ham, Moss and Neville compares schools in three Devon communities; Yates studies the efforts of the circulating schools movement to make education accessible in remote parts of Wales. Thor explores the education of women in Scottish Magdalene Asylums. Examinations of these various institutions reveal intense debates about the effectiveness and the aims of the education provided: should philanthropic Christians aim to provide literacy and numeracy, or practical skills, or to further more spiritual (or even political) aims? A further set of articles analyses the relationship between churches, the state and education: Mallon considers the interactions between established and dissenting Presbyterian churches in debates about the state provision of education in mid-nineteenth-century Scotland; moving forward to the early twentieth century, Smith and Masom analyse debates in the Church of England about church-aided schools, and Doney studies recommendations from the British Council of Churches during the 1960s and 1970s regarding religious education in state schools.

Rapid cultural and technological changes during the late nineteenth and early twentieth centuries not only presented challenges but also new opportunities for Christian lay education, as is shown, from very different perspectives, by Ottewill's study of adult lay education in English Congregationalism and Pruneri's examination of Catholic responses to secularism in early twentieth-century Italy. Other articles study specific developments in church involvement in education, for example, changing perceptions of the role of Sunday School education (McCartney) and Methodist engagement with higher education in Oxford following the removal of restrictions placed on Nonconformists (Wellings).

Empires were, of course, important contexts for Christian educational enterprises; in this respect there are some continuities of theme between this volume and its predecessors, *Translating Christianity* and *The Church and Empire*. Several articles in the former volume showed how the introduction of Christianity from one context into another was preceded by, or led to, educational projects, some specifically linguistic (like the translation of the Bible or other religious texts), others more broadly cultural (like efforts to form a liturgical tradition in a new context or to use indigenous cultural forms such as theatre in Christian education). The broad theme of Church and empire is taken up in this volume by articles such as those by Dornan and Moon, which examine complex questions around the aims and means of education by Christians in various nineteenth-century colonial contexts: New Zealand, the British West Indies, Africa and India. Chapman argues that, for some influential Anglican missionaries, a movement from evangelizing to educating was underpinned both by a theological conviction that truth could be found beyond Christianity and by the much more problematic idea that the cultures of the East were, in the language of the day, 'higher civilizations' in comparison to those encountered in other mission fields. Morrison focuses on education, not of the recipients of mission, but of those children in Britain and elsewhere who were being educated by Sunday Schools, youth mission societies and magazines to support missionary effort: this did not just raise money, but was also aimed at forming children in various ways as young Christian world citizens. Finally, two fine prize-winning articles by Bond and Wang engage with Christianity, education and colonialism in the Chinese context. Each gives an especially subtle analysis of the interaction between local and Western agency in Chinese educational establishments during the late nineteenth and early twentieth centuries, Bond studying the Chinese educationalist Zeng Baosun and the Yifang School for Girls which she founded in Changsha in 1918, and Wang examining how the tensions which were perceived to exist between being Christian and being Chinese played out in the history of the Tientsin Anglo-Chinese College during the early twentieth century.

I would like to thank all participants in the two conferences, and especially those whose articles appear here, for their stimulating and scholarly contributions, which have greatly enhanced my own understanding of this topic. I am most grateful to my co-editors, Charlotte Methuen and Andrew Spicer, and the assistant editor, Tim Grass, for the care and professionalism which they have dedicated to this volume.

Morwenna Ludlow

Education and Pleasure in the Early Church: Perspectives from East and West

Morwenna Ludlow and Sophie Lunn-Rockliffe*
University of Exeter / University of Cambridge

Early Christian teachers and preachers were often cautious about, if not suspicious of, pleasure, but they also had a lively awareness of the psychological aspects of pedagogy, and of the power of pleasure and delight to persuade, move, instruct and even convert. This article explores the treatment of pleasure as a pedagogical tool, tracing this subject through the lens of sermons, letters, treatises and poetry written in Latin and Greek and drawing out both classical and biblical themes. It notes that, while most of the authors considered acknowledge pleasure as a potential problem in pedagogy, it is a problem they attempt to navigate. The article sketches out various approaches to the problem, noting especially the pleasure involved in reading, performing and expounding Scripture; pleasure used as a conscious educational strategy; and discussions which weigh up the dangers and gains of pleasure in education.

In the late fourth century, Maximus, bishop of Turin, returned to his congregation after a few days' absence, probably to attend a church council. He began his sermon by promising to preach 'something richer', to 'refresh' them 'with a sweet sermon', after returning from what he memorably calls 'such a swarm of bishops'. 'That's right', Maximus continued: 'I said "a swarm of bishops", since like the bee they produce delightful honey from the blossoms of divine scriptures, and whatever pertains to the medicine of souls they make by the skill of their mouth'.[1] The arresting image of bishops

* Morwenna Ludlow: Department of Theology and Religion, University of Exeter, Amory Building, Rennes Drive, Exeter, EX4 4RJ. E-mail: m.a.ludlow@exeter.ac.uk. Sophie Lunn-Rockliffe: Faculty of Divinity, West Rd, Cambridge, CB3 9BS. E-mail: sjl39@cam.ac.uk.

[1] Maximus of Turin, *Sermo* 89 (transl. Boniface Ramsey, ACW 50 [New York, 1989], 211). As Ramsey notes (348 n. 1), Maximus's apian imagery bears some resemblance to Ambrose's *In hexameron* 5.21, but the idea of bishops as busy bees is found in other Latin preachers of the period: see, for example, Augustine, *Epistula* 109 (*Letters*, 2: *Letters 83–130*, transl. Sr Wilfrid Parsons, FOTC 18 [Washington DC, 2008], 239), from Severus of Milevius, in which Severus addresses Augustine thus: 'O truly skilful bee of God, building

Studies in Church History 55 (2019), 6–34
doi: 10.1017/stc.2018.12

working like busy bees to distil the Bible into delicious sweetness introduces the subject of this article: the role of pleasure in education in the late antique, post-Constantinian church. The so-called 'Fathers of the Church' sometimes appear rather austere. Ambrose, bishop of Milan in the late fourth century, counselled his fellow clergy to avoid all kinds of jokes; although at times honourable and pleasant, they were, he said, 'quite at odds with the rule of the church'.[2] But Christian teachers and preachers also had a lively awareness of the psychological aspects of pedagogy, and of the power of pleasure and delight to persuade, move, instruct and even convert. This article will explore the treatment of pleasure as a pedagogical tool through the lens of sermons, letters, treatises and poetry written in Latin and Greek.

In doing so, we will bring to the fore a theme which runs in and out of discussions of Christian discourse in Late Antiquity like a golden thread. Scholars have followed the Christian authors' own tendency to ponder the dangers of physical pleasures and the task of nurturing spiritual desire, attentive especially to the complex relationship between the two. The pleasure of words has been less of a scholarly focus, although there have been treatments of (for example) Gregory of Nazianzus's use of pleasure as a poetic device, the pedagogy of 'leading the soul through words' in John Chrysostom and Augustine's treatment of delightful speech in *De doctrina Christiana*.[3] Such discussions acknowledge the influence of classical arguments (beginning at least as early as Socrates) about the power of pleasure to persuade. They perhaps pay somewhat less attention

a honeycomb filled with divine nectar'. On Maximus, see Pauline Allen, 'Impact, Influence and Identity in Latin Preaching: The Cases of Maximus of Turin and Peter Chrysologus of Ravenna', in A. Dupont et al., eds, *Preaching in the Patristic Era: Sermons, Preachers and Audiences in the Latin West* (Leiden, 2018), 135–58.

[2] Ambrose of Milan, *De officiis* 1.23.102–3 (transl. Ivor J. Davidson, 2 vols, OECS [Oxford, 2002], 1: 177). In this, Christians shared much in common with other philosophers; for examples, see David Rylaarsdam, *John Chrysostom on Divine Pedagogy: The Coherence of his Theology and Preaching* (Oxford, 2014), 277–8.

[3] See, for example, Stratis Papaioannou, 'Gregory and the Constraint of Sameness', in Jostein Børtnes and Tomas Hägg, eds, *Gregory of Nazianzus: Images and Reflections* (Copenhagen, 2006), 59–81; Rylaarsdam, *John Chrysostom on Divine Pedagogy*, 13–54, 228–82 (chs 1, 6); and (two very different examples in a large literature) Rowan Williams, 'Language, Reality and Desire in Augustine's *De doctrina*', *Literature and Theology* 3 (1989), 138–50; Michael Roberts, *The Jeweled Style: Poetry and Poetics in Late Antiquity* (Ithaca, NY, 1989), 125–32.

to assumptions, common across the ancient world, about the power of poetry and music to soothe and penetrate the soul. A notable exception is Carol Harrison's absorbing treatment of the *Art of Listening*: although pleasure is not the dominant theme of her analysis, her work is an important perspective on pleasure as both a problematic and a positive response to Christian speech.[4]

In what follows, then, we hope to begin to draw some of these threads together, highlighting pleasure's specifically educational role and drawing out both classical and biblical themes. We will note that, while most of the authors discussed here acknowledge pleasure as a potential problem in pedagogy, it is a problem they attempt to navigate. We will sketch out various approaches to the problem and will seek to identify in them any shared understanding of the function of pleasure in education. We begin first by outlining the parameters of what we mean by 'education' in a specifically Christian late antique context.

The subjects taught by late antique bishops and others varied widely depending on their audience and context. For adult converts in the catechumenate, the programme of teaching was carefully and deliberately staged.[5] As Ambrose explains in his treatise on *The Mysteries*, delivered to an audience of catechumens, he had up to that point addressed moral topics connected to lessons from the Old Testament; but at this point in Lent, he turned to the 'mysteries', that is, the meaning of the sacraments, a topic which was not profaned by being shared with all and any listeners but only revealed to catechumens close to the point at which they were to be baptized at Easter.[6] Another climactic point of teaching in Lent was the exposition of the Creed and the Lord's Prayer, whether just to catechumens or to mixed audiences, with the Creed itself cast as an

[4] Carol Harrison, *The Art of Listening in the Early Church* (Oxford, 2013); Patricia Cox Miller, *The Corporeal Imagination: Signifying the Holy in Late Ancient Christianity* (Philadelphia, PA, 2009), 42–81 (chs 2–3); Roberts, *Jeweled Style*. See also, on a broader range of authors, Ruth Webb, *Ekphrasis, Imagination and Persuasion in Ancient Rhetorical Theory and Practice* (Farnham, 2009), 21, 76, 99–100.

[5] See Everett Ferguson, 'Catechesis and Initiation', in Alan Kreider, ed., *The Origins of Christendom in the West* (New York, 2001), 229–68; William Harmless, *Augustine and the Catechumenate* (Collegeville, MN, 2014).

[6] Ambrose, *De mysteriis* 1.1–2; see also Augustine, *De catechizandis rudibus* and Peter Chrysologus's catechetical *Sermones* 56–72. In the East, catechetical works by Cyril of Jerusalem (*Catechetical Lectures* and *Mystagogical Lectures*) and John Chrysostom (*Baptismal Instructions*) survive.

epitome of Scripture for beginners.[7] For those attending church services, the main 'teaching' moment in church was the sermon, which usually revolved around exegesis of the lessons read during the service, but which also often had distinctive moral and even polemical dimensions. Other forms of text – particularly hymnody, composed for performance within the liturgy by writers such as Ephrem, Ambrose and Paulinus – also had clearly educational functions, whether expanding on the content of Scripture or expounding the mysteries of faith.[8] Outside the ecclesiastical context, elite and intellectually ambitious Christians could pursue private scriptural and linguistic study, either in house groups, such as the women's groups patronized by Jerome in Rome, or virtual groups made possible through the exchange of letters. They could listen to or read devotional and instructive poetry by writers such as Proba, Prudentius, Sedulius and Gregory of Nazianzus.[9]

[7] See the characterizations of Nicetas of Remesiana, book 5 of whose *Instructio ad competentes* comprised an explanation of the Creed; Augustine, *De fide et symbolo* 1, idem *De symbolo ad catechumenos* 1. Christian teachers also offered explanations of the Creed for more advanced audiences, particularly in polemical contexts, such as Rufinus of Aquileia, *Commentarius in symbolum apostolorum*, written for bishop Laurentius. For a sermon on the Creed addressed to a mixed audience of baptized Christians and catechumens, see Peter Chrysologus, *Sermo* 62. Gregory of Nyssa wrote series of sermons on the Lord's Prayer and on the Beatitudes for a general audience.

[8] On Ambrose's hymnody, see Brian Dunkle, *Enchantment and Creed in the Hymns of Ambrose of Milan* (Oxford, 2016), 13–51 (ch. 1), with useful comparative discussion of other authors from Ephrem to Hilary and Augustine.

[9] On early Christian poetry, see especially Jaś Elsner and Jesús Hernández Lobato, eds, *The Poetics of Late Latin Literature* (Oxford, 2017); Karla Pollmann, *The Baptized Muse: Early Christian Poetry as Cultural Authority* (Oxford, 2017), especially 37–75, 161–75 (chs 2, 7) for Prudentius, 101–19 (ch. 4) for Proba. On Proba, see also Elizabeth A. Clark, 'The Virgilian Cento of Faltonia Betitia Proba', *Studia Patristica* 17/1 (1982), 412–16; Martin Bazil, '"Rem nulli obscuram repetens". Les Stratégies intertextuelles dans l'exorde du *Cento Probae*', *Graecolatina Pragensia* 20 (2004), 15–25; Sigrid Schottenius Cullhed, *Proba the Prophet: The Christian Virgilian Cento of Faltonia Betitia Proba* (Leiden, 2015). On Prudentius, see, for example, Anne-Marie Palmer, *Prudentius on the Martyrs*, Oxford Classical Monographs (Oxford, 2006); Brian Dunkle, 'Ambrosian Imitation in Sedulius and Prudentius', in idem, *Enchantment and Creed*, 186–213. On Sedulius, see, for example, Carl P. E. Springer, *The Gospel as Epic in Late Antiquity: The* Paschale Carmen *of Sedulius*, Supplements to *Vigiliae Christianae* 2 (Leiden, 1988); Sedulius, *The Paschal Song and Hymns*, transl. Carl P. E. Springer, Writings from the Greco-Roman World 35 (Atlanta, GA, 2013); Dunkle, 'Ambrosian Imitation'. On Gregory of Nazianzus, see, for example, Neil B. McLynn, 'Among the Hellenists: Gregory and the Sophists', in Børtnes and Hägg, eds, *Gregory of Nazianzus*, 213–38; Suzanne Abrams Rebillard, 'The Autobiographical *Prosopopoeia* of Gregory of Nazianzus', *Studia Patristica* 47 (2010), 123–8; eadem, 'Historiography as Devotion: *Poemata de seipso*', in Christopher

As well as educating their congregations, bishops were involved in the formation of other clerics in and beyond their dioceses, both their peers in the episcopate and lower orders of clergy. Thus Gregory of Nyssa's so-called *Catechetical Oration* is a text teaching other clerics how to teach, with particular attention paid to how to present what is taught: 'the same method of instruction' is not 'suitable in the case of all who approach the word', therefore 'the method of recovery must be adapted to the form of the disease'.[10]

As these comments suggest, this discussion concerns in part texts composed by and for a fairly well-educated elite. The letters to fellow clerics found in the letter collections of Ambrose, Augustine or the 'Cappadocians', for example, assume a confidently literate audience, who could respond in kind.[11] Moreover, much poetry, even if heard rather than read, assumed an audience sophisticated enough to appreciate its skill and beauty. However, as Harrison has reminded us, literacy in the ancient world did not necessarily entail the ability to read confidently by oneself.[12] Someone with a middling education would have had a degree of familiarity with classics by Homer or Vergil or (in a Christian context) with the most cited books of the Bible, simply by repeated hearing. Theatre was a very popular and reasonably accessible medium in Late Antiquity and spread knowledge of certain traditional myths as well as certain stock characters.[13] Finally, many of the Christian texts discussed in this article were first communicated

A Beeley, ed., *Re-Reading Gregory of Nazianzus: Essays on History, Theology, and Culture* (Washington DC, 2012), 125–42; Brian Dunkle, 'Introduction' to *Poems on Scripture: St Gregory of Nazianzus*, Popular Patristics Series 46 (Crestwood, NY, 2012).

[10] 'The presiding ministers of the "mystery of godliness" have need of a system in their instructions, in order that the Church may be replenished by the accession of such as should be saved, through the teaching of the word of Faith being brought home to the hearing of unbelievers': Gregory of Nyssa, *Oratio catechetica*: Preface (NPNF II 5; references to this series use the online versions at: <http://www.ccel.org/fathers.html>).

[11] The term 'Cappadocians' conventionally designates the literary circle of Basil, his brother Gregory of Nyssa and Basil's friend Gregory of Nazianzus (and sometimes some of their associates).

[12] Harrison, *Art of Listening*, especially 4.

[13] According to Agnieszka Kotlińska-Toma, theatre was 'the most accessible and egalitarian form of mass entertainment' in the Hellenistic period: *Hellenistic Tragedy: Texts, Translations and a Critical Survey* (London, 2015), 2–3, 7, 25, 28. Blake Leyerle has argued, from the style and content of John Chrysostom's preaching, that a broad section of his congregation had a familiarity with various forms of theatre: *Theatrical Shows and Ascetic Lives: John Chrysostom's Attack on Spiritual Marriage* (Berkeley, CA, 2001), especially 13–16, 20–1, 160.

by being spoken (sermons preached, then written up from notes) or read aloud, and to congregations containing those whom preachers characterized as of limited literacy.[14] Consequently, one should not assume that the use of pleasure as a pedagogical tool would have been aimed just at the highly educated elite (for example, those educated enough to compose sophisticated texts). A modestly educated tradesman, for example, could certainly have had enough familiarity with certain texts, themes and characters to respond with pleasurable recognition when a preacher alluded to them. This is quite apart from the different question of the extent to which certain kinds of sweet or pleasant style had a broad appeal: assertions that certain biblical texts could give pleasure even to children certainly suggest that this was what various ecclesiastical writers thought, even though their belief would be difficult for us to test.[15]

It is very difficult to reconstruct the audience for fourth-century Christian sermons and one must concede, at least, that audiences would have differed according to context. Paulinus, writing about visitors to the shrine to St Felix at Nola, frequently characterized them as rustics preoccupied by the rhythms of agricultural life and the rumblings of their bellies, and the 'birthday hymns' (*natalicia*) which he composed for this congregation to mark the annual feast-day of their saint were markedly simple in their diction.[16] By contrast, from what we know of aural literacy and the theatre, it is plausible to assume that the urban congregations of Ambrose, Basil and John Chrysostom, for example, would have included those who, whilst not a highly educated elite, nevertheless had the kind of cultural sensibility which could respond to certain ideas and certain literary and rhetorical techniques with pleasure.[17]

Through letters, and through copying and disseminating treatises and sometimes sermons, bishops sought and shared insights into the

[14] Nicetas of Remesiana, *Instructio* 5.13, expressed the value of learning and explaining the Creed as encapsulating the message of salvation for those who 'are unable, or too busy with their worldly affairs, to read the Scriptures'.

[15] See further, pp. 18, 26.

[16] On Paulinus's context, see Dennis Trout, 'Christianizing the Nolan Countryside: Animal Sacrifice at the Tomb of St Felix', *JECS* 3 (1995), 281–98; on the style and register of his poetry, see R. P. H. Green, 'Paulinus of Nola and the Diction of Christian Latin Poetry', *Latomus* 32 (1973), 79–85.

[17] To what extent the reflections in this article apply to other contexts, especially non-urban ascetic communities, is a question which would require further research.

content of their teaching and the most effective modes of engaging with their pupils. Thus, for example, among Ambrose's extensive correspondence with other priests and bishops, we find him writing to Sabinus of Piacenza in the 390s, sending Sabinus works such as the *Hexameron* (his massive cycle on creation), accompanied by letters which he wrote late at night (as he emphasizes, not by dictation but in his own hand), begging Sabinus to weigh their contents and particularly to comment on their style and to flag up any 'vain flattery and persuasiveness', words which had delighted him, the author, but which were actually empty and worthless.[18] In some of these contexts, writers explain a pedagogical technique which we shall address directly: the use of pleasure.

The Delights of Scripture and its Performance

One of the most important subjects to be taught in and out of church was biblical exegesis.[19] In the first generations after Constantine it was a pedagogical priority to provide converts with clear, persuasive and attractive explanations of the many meanings of Scripture, whether literal, historical, spiritual, allegorical or other. For many adult converts to Christianity – especially for the well-educated – the Bible was a novel, puzzling, unwieldy and stylistically underwhelming set of sacred texts: as Jerome remarked to Paulinus, newly made bishop of Nola, the simplicity and poor vocabulary of Scripture was due either to the faults of translators or to deliberate purpose.[20] Augustine recalled how, in the period preceding his baptism, Ambrose suggested he read Isaiah, but he did not understand the opening of the book and laid it aside for when he had acquired

[18] Ambrose, *Epistula* 23.3 (*Letters*, transl. Mary Beyenka et al., FOTC 26 [Washington DC, 2001], 125). Compare Gregory of Nyssa's *Epistula* 29, accompanying the first part of his treatise against Eunomius, asking for feedback on words which he feared were written in too much anger.

[19] On this massive subject, see Frances Young, *Biblical Exegesis and the Formation of Christian Culture* (Cambridge, 1997).

[20] Jerome, *Epistula* 53.10. Comments such as these have sometimes been taken by scholars to indicate that the Old Latin translations were simply bad; more recent research suggests that, although awkward, they were not ignorant and their style may have reflected a specific translation method: see Philip Burton, *The Old Latin Gospels: A Study of their Texts and Language* (Oxford, 2000); see also Clark, *Christianity and Roman Society*, 83–4.

'more practice in the Lord's style of language'.[21] The regular assertions made by Christian teachers in the fourth and fifth centuries AD of the riches and delights of the Bible were, therefore, not just a repetition of a widely accepted proposition but perhaps more of a defensive strategy provoked by criticisms of the content and style of Scripture.[22]

The imagery used to characterize Scripture was insistently nutritive: drink for the thirsty and food for the hungry. Nor was this fare said merely to be sustaining; it was also delicious. The characterization of Scripture as food and drink drew in part on sacramental notions of the word of God as bread and wine. Drawing analogies between food and text, and between their preparation and consumption, was also a long-established classical rhetorical manoeuvre, allowing the writer to appeal to his listeners' or readers' tastebuds, and transferring qualities of gastronomic taste (bitterness, sweetness and so on) onto twin literary and moral domains.[23] Nicetas of Remesiana, a bishop in Dacia writing in praise of psalmody, cast the delights of singing and listening to Scripture in church in terms of eating: 'Like guests at table enjoying a variety of dishes, our souls feast [literally 'are fattened', *saginantur*] on the rich banquet of lessons and hymns.'[24] Nicetas focuses on the delightfully nourishing quality of the scriptural feast, drawing on the long-established belief that textual *varietas* is a hallmark of quality and enjoyment.[25] For Gregory of

[21] Augustine, *Confessiones* 9.5.13 (transl. Henry Chadwick [Oxford, 1991], 163). In *De doctrina Christiana*, Augustine wrote more positively about biblical writers than Jerome, but nonetheless acknowledged that 'they used our eloquence side by side with a rather different eloquence of their own' (4.6.9), before analysing in formal rhetorical terms two passages from 2 Corinthians and Amos, to demonstrate their stylistic virtues. He concluded of Paul's writing that a 'knowledgeable person' recognizes that it is the 'commata, cola and periods' of his writing, 'deployed with tasteful variety, which produces the beauty of this style, which pleases and moves even the uneducated, like a pleasant face': ibid. 4.7.13 (*On Christian Teaching*, transl. R. P. H. Green [Oxford, 1997], 108–9).

[22] Indeed, their understanding of biblical style was often more sophisticated than their defensive remarks imply: Morwenna Ludlow, 'Christian Identity and Rhetoric about Literary Style', in Richard Flower and Morwenna Ludlow, eds, *Rhetoric and Religious Identity in Late Antiquity* (Oxford, forthcoming 2020).

[23] John Bramble, *Persius and the Programmatic Satire: A Study in Form and Imagery* (Cambridge, 1974), 45–59; Emily Gowers, *The Loaded Table: Representations of Food in Roman Literature* (Oxford, 1993).

[24] Nicetas of Remesiana, *De utilitate hymnorum* 12 (A. E. Burn, *Niceta of Remesiana: His Life and Works* [Cambridge, 1905], 74).

[25] William Fitzgerald, *Variety: The Life of a Roman Concept* (Chicago, IL, 2016).

Nyssa, the 'teachings of the gospel' are like an apple (as described in the Song of Songs) which 'fattens the body and pleases the taste'.[26] The singing of psalms, he says, is 'a side dish of the meal with which the nourishment of the teaching is sweetened as if with sauces'.[27]

As well as food for the hungry, Scripture was also drink for the thirsty. Ambrose, writing to a new bishop called Constantius, patched together a series of watery metaphors drawn from different parts of the Bible to describe Scripture itself as a sea containing deep meanings, 'sweet and transparent streams' and 'cool fountains'; he praised the 'agreeable sentences' which refreshed the minds of the hearers with spiritual drink and soothed them with the sweetness of their moral precepts.[28] Greek writers associated fresh or sweet (*glukus*) water with the sweet (*glukus*) words of God.[29] Thus, in one of his early letters, Gregory of Nazianzus chides Gregory of Nyssa for having given up being a reader in the church for a career in rhetoric: 'What is wrong with you …', he complains, 'that you have thrown away those holy, thirst-quenching books you once proclaimed to the people … ? Why have you turned your hand to salty, undrinkable literature?'[30] Preaching was also regularly characterized in terms of the liquid nourishment provided through milk to infants, as a staging post on the way to more substantial and more taxing solids: Ambrose was one of many teachers to draw on the imagery of 1 Corinthians 3: 2 ('I fed you with milk, not solid food') to characterize sermons as 'milk'.[31]

These appeals to the spiritual senses might have been primarily metaphysical, but the notion that Scripture provided pleasurable

[26] Gregory of Nyssa, *Homiliae in Canticum Canticorum* 4 (*Homilies on the Song of Songs*, transl. Richard A. Norris Jr, Writings from the Greco-Roman World 13 [Atlanta, GA, 2012], 137).

[27] Gregory of Nyssa, *In inscriptiones Psalmorum* 1.3 (25) (*Gregory of Nyssa's Treatise on the Inscription of the Psalms*, transl. Ronald E. Heine, OECS [Oxford, 1995], 92).

[28] Ambrose, *Epistula* 15.3 (transl. Beyenka, 77–8).

[29] See Ps. 18: 10 (LXX): God's judgments are 'sweeter (γλυκύτερα) than honey'. Some modern European languages preserve the connection between fresh water and sweetness better than English: for instance, French *eau douce*, German *Süßwasser*, Italian *acqua dolce*.

[30] Gregory of Nazianzus, *Epistula* 11 (transl. Daley, 173). Elsewhere, he boasts that as a poet he will not 'send forth both sweet and briny water': 'On Silence at the Time of Fasting', *Carmina* 2.1.34, line 97 (transl. Carolinne White, *Gregory of Nazianzus: Autobiographical Poems*, Cambridge Medieval Classics 6 [Cambridge, 1996], 173).

[31] Ambrose, *Epistula* 15.6 (transl. Beyenka, 78). On this theme as part of a broader discussion of nourishment, see John Penniman, *Raised on Christian Milk: Food and the Formation of the Soul in Early Christianity* (New Haven, CT, 2017).

and satisfying spiritual and ethical refreshment nonetheless engaged the audience's bodies and particularly their bellies.[32] For the pre-modern congregations of large cities and agricultural communities alike, the poorer of whom would have been regularly hungry and perhaps thirsty, the evocation of delicious refreshment would have been particularly tantalizing; early Christian teachers regularly acknowledged the oscillation between hunger and satiety which characterized the rhythms of pre-industrial life, and which were further heightened by Christian practices of feasting and fasting.[33] Indeed, homilists repeatedly commended Scripture as a delicious spiritual feast while condemning Christians' excessive enjoyment of physical feasting and promoting the virtues of fasting, especially, but not only, in Lent.[34] A similar paradox can also be seen in the erotic language of some of the patristic treatises promoting virginity.

A noteworthy aspect of these appeals to Scripture as nourishment is that they do not always apply to the parts of the Bible which are the most obviously 'pleasant', such as the poetry of the Psalms or the Song of Songs. In his *Homilies on the Hexameron*, Basil revels in the sheer attractiveness of the text of Genesis:

[32] See Paul Gavrilyuk and Sarah Coakley, eds, *The Spiritual Senses: Perceiving God in Western Christianity* (Cambridge, 2012), especially 1–70.

[33] See Peter Garnsey, *Famine and Food Supply in the Graeco-Roman World* (Cambridge, 1988), 3–7, 'Famine and Shortage'. For a medieval comparison between the norm of scarcity and the privilege of overeating, see Caroline Walker Bynum, *Holy Feast and Holy Fast: The Religious Significance of Food to Medieval Women* (Berkeley, CA, 1988), 3–5. For allusions in sermons to the impact of feasting and fasting, see Allen, 'Impact, Influence and Identity'.

[34] See, for example, Augustine *Sermo* 28 on fasting at Pentecost, comparing the words of Scripture to food; ibid. 205E on fasting at Lent, suggesting that the word of God will sustain his congregation in spirit while they fast in body. Compare Gregory of Nazianzus contrasting the luxuries of the Christian feast of the nativity – 'the words and the divine law and the narratives' – with the luxuries of traditional Greek midwinter celebrations ('On the Theophany, or Birthday of Christ', *Orationes* 38.5), or Basil's severe instructions that ascetics must clear away sensuous pleasures to make way for the sweetness of Scripture: Basil, *Regulae fusius tractatae* 6; idem, *Regulae brevius tractatae* 174, 180. Penniman's *Raised on Christian Milk* is an important study of how food was used to symbolize education and formation; he discusses the erotics present in some of this discourse (especially ibid. 138–64 [ch. 5]) and the pleasure with which a child suckles at the breast (ibid. 165–200 [ch. 6]), but the pleasure of nourishment (and its implications for spiritual pedagogy) is not a major theme. For food as a symbol of pedagogy, see also Everett Ferguson, 'Divine Pedagogy: Origen's Use of the Imagery of Education', in idem, *The Early Church at Work and Worship*, 2: *Catechesis, Baptism, Eschatology, and Martyrdom* (Cambridge and Eugene, OR, 2014), 254–68.

> Our discussion yesterday treated of the works of this [the first] day, and divided the narrative so as to give you food for your souls in the morning, and joy in the evening. To-day we pass on to the wonders of the second day. And here I do not wish to speak of the narrator's talent, but of the grace of Scripture, for the narrative is so naturally told that it pleases and delights all the friends of truth. It is this charm of truth which the Psalmist expresses so emphatically when he says, 'How sweet are thy words unto my taste, yea, sweeter than honey to my mouth'.[35]

In its appeal to the senses, the Bible was not presented as inert text to be enjoyed with the physical eyes 'on the page'; it came alive when read aloud in church and outside, pleasing by its very sound and conjuring up delightful mental images. Indeed, preachers such as Ambrose and John Chrysostom emphasized the capacity of the performance of Scripture to soothe, charm and instruct, all at once. 'You have heard the Apostolic voice!' Chrysostom proclaims, comparing the sound of Paul's words to a trumpet that simultaneously rouses the troops and dismays their enemy. It is also like a lyre which soothes anxieties and 'with pleasure instils into us much profit'. He attributes to Paul the literary virtues of *enargeia* (vividness) and *varietas* together with the theological virtue of bearing good spiritual fruit: Paul's words create a pleasant image in the mind's eye which has a spiritual impact.

> For as in a meadow, I perceive in what has been read a great diversity of flowers; a multiplicity of roses and violets and copious fruit of the Spirit is scattered around, as well as an abundant fragrance … . The reading of the divine Scriptures is not a meadow only, but a paradise; for the flowers here have not a mere fragrance only, but fruit too, capable of nourishing the soul.[36]

[35] Basil, *In hexaemeron* 3.1 (quoting Ps 118: 103 LXX). Gen. 1:1 is 'food for your souls in the morning'; Gen. 1: 2–5 provides 'joy in the evening' (NPNF II 8).

[36] John Chrysostom, *De statuis ad populum Antiochenum* 1.1–2, cited in George Kennedy, *Greek Rhetoric under Christian Emperors* (Princeton, NJ, 1983), 247. In addition to being a classical motif, for Christians the lyre would evoke David soothing Saul (1 Sam. 16: 14–23); fruitfulness perhaps alludes to Matt. 7: 15–20. Chrysostom ingeniously attributes *varietas* to what others might condemn as the somewhat piecemeal structure of 1 Timothy. For *enargeia* and Christian adaptation of the *varietas* idea (applied to meadows), see Michael Roberts, *Jeweled Style*, 39–40, 50–1, 76; Cox Miller, *Corporeal Imagination*, 73–7 (making the connection to paradise). *Ekphrasis*, the bringing of a detailed scene to the mind's eye, aimed to have an emotional impact on the hearer: whether it caused pleasure or indignation, it helped to persuade: Webb, *Ekphrasis*, 21, 76, 99–100.

John Chrysostom's appreciation of Paul was not unique: Peter Chrysologus, bishop of Ravenna in the early fifth century, describes the rhythm of services as divided between three readings from, and homilies on, the Psalms, the Gospel and Paul: as he put it, the chanting of Psalms fills and delights the ear with delightfulness (*dulcedine*), and similarly 'doctrine' (by which he means Paul) unfolds the mystery of the Gospel 'more pleasantly' (*libentius*) and 'with the greatest sweetness' (*suavitate maxima*).[37] Peter Chrysologus was perhaps working against the grain here in promoting Paul's writings in comparative and superlative terms (as *more* pleasant and *most* sweet), since, as we will see, it was more common for preachers and teachers to emphasize the book of Psalms as the greatest repository of musical and poetic delights.

At the start of his homily on Psalm 1, Basil emphatically defends both the usefulness and the sweetness of the Psalms.[38] Although humans are distracted by pleasure (*hēdonē*), it is precisely pleasure which the Psalms use to redirect humans towards the good and truthful, an idea which Basil expresses with the classic analogy of 'wise physicians who, when giving the fastidious rather bitter things to drink, frequently smear the cup with honey'.[39] The emotional effect of the Psalms is to soothe and bring peace. In sum, the Psalter 'effaces, as far as is possible, the passions … with a certain harmonious persuasion (*psuchagōgias*) and pleasure (*hēdonēs*) which produces sound thoughts'.[40] The meaning of the term *psuchagōgia* lies somewhere between 'persuade' and 'entertain', so it was inextricable from pleasure. In the *Phaedrus*, Plato warns that rhetoric's power of leading the soul through words (*psuchagōgia dia logōn*) must be carefully

[37] Peter Chrysologus, *Sermo* 116 (*St Peter Chrysologus, Selected Sermons; St Valerian, Homilies*, transl. George E. Ganss, FOTC 17 [Washington DC, 2004; first publ. 1953], 194).

[38] On patristic traditions of commentary on the Psalms, see Brian Daley, 'Finding the Right Key: The Aims and Strategies of Early Christian Interpretation of the Psalms', in idem and Paul Kolbet, eds, *The Harp of Prophecy: Early Christian Interpretation of the Psalms* (Notre Dame, IN, 2015), 11–28. Daley discusses Christian commentators' adaptation of classical ideas of the role of 'sweetness' in instruction for their exegesis of the Psalms: ibid. 14–15.

[39] Basil, *Homilia in Psalmos* 1.1 (*Exegetic Homilies*, transl. Agnes Clare Way, FOTC 46 [Washington DC, 1963], 152). On the general point, see Plato, *Leges* 2.659e–660a (educators use song to make good teaching pleasant, just as physicians recommend healthy food which tastes pleasant); for the 'honeyed cup', see Lucretius, *De rerum natura* 1.936–8; Themistius, 'An Exhortation to the Nicomedians', *Orationes* 24.302.

[40] Basil, *Homilia in Psalmos* 1.1.

reined in by the speaker learning philosophy. The word *psuchagōgia* was often used in tension with the truth: Basil uses it, for example, to warn against historians who make up stories to entertain their readers and, more ambivalently, for the pleasure of recalling events which were painful, but whose sting is soothed by the presence of a friend and the passage of time.[41] It is all the more striking, then, that he also uses *psuchagōgia* to describe the method used by the Psalms.

Basil draws attention especially to the Psalms' use of music, a very direct means of pleasure: listeners learn 'something profitable' because, 'what enters the mind with joy and pleasure somehow becomes more firmly impressed upon it'.[42] In his *Treatise on the Inscriptions of the Psalms*, Gregory of Nyssa follows his brother's cue, repeatedly asserting that the Psalms evoke pleasure (*hēdonē*) and echoing Basil's conclusions about music: 'The great David combined singing with the philosophy concerning the virtues, thereby pouring the sweetness (*hēdonēn*) of honey, as it were, over these sublime teachings. In this singing, nature reflects on itself in a certain manner and heals itself.'[43] In his commentary on Psalm 1, Ambrose explained that 'while what is sung gives delight (*cantatur ad delectationem*), at the same time instruction is being imparted. … [W]hat you will drink in with sweetness (*suavitate*), once it is infused into the heart, is not likely to slip away.'[44] That is, singing the Psalms was thought to be both a pleasurable and almost stealthy way of embedding the text deeply into the singer's body, specifically into the heart, the seat of cognition and emotion.[45] Ambrose's commentary undoubtedly owed much to Basil's; but while Basil justified the pleasure of the Psalms by stressing their usefulness, Ambrose's emphasis is more insistently on their delight.[46] Indeed, Ambrose

[41] '[I]s not rhetoric the art of leading the soul by words?' (τέχνη ψυχαγωγία τις διὰ λόγων): Plato, *Phaedrus* 261a, cf. 271c; compare Basil, *Ad adolescentes* 4; Basil, *Epistula* 127.1.

[42] By contrast, 'a forceful lesson does not always endure': Basil, *Homilia in Psalmos* 1.2 (transl. Way, 153).

[43] Gregory of Nyssa, *In inscriptiones Psalmorum* 1.3 (23); cf. ibid. (17) (transl. Heine, 91, 87–8).

[44] Ambrose, *Enarrationes in xii Psalmos Davidicos* 1.10 (*Commentary of St Ambrose on Twelve Psalms*, transl. Íde Ní Riain [Dublin, 2000], 5).

[45] On the heart in Augustine and its relation to classical philosophical thought, see Sarah Catherine Byers, *Perception, Sensibility and Moral Motivation in Augustine: A Stoic-Platonic Synthesis* (Cambridge, 2012), 35 and n. 88.

[46] Jan den Boeft, 'Delight and Imagination: Ambrose's Hymns', *Vigiliae Christianae* 62 (2008), 429–30; Dunkle, *Enchantment and Creed*, 43.

invoked the value of psalm-singing for young Christians: 'Children look forward to a psalm; infants – unwilling to learn other things – delight in practising a psalm. It is a kind of game by which we learn more of doctrine than we would by formal instruction.' He concluded that 'treasured with delight (*voluptate*), the psalms are understood without pain or labour'.[47] Nicetas of Remesiana also explicitly promoted the virtues of singing hymns and psalms in church services,[48] arguing that singing psalms was edifying, consoling, and pleasing to God. Sung psalms were sweet in their melody, and entered the soul because they were pleasant. Within his treatise, there is a hint that not all his Christian contemporaries agreed with this position, since he reports that unnamed critics (also cast as 'heretics') objected to such practices and apparently counselled silent prayer.

Nonetheless, the idea that singing was a powerful tool for teaching underpins the development and popularity of Christian hymnody – that is, of poetic texts expanding on Scripture, to be chanted or sung. Christian hymns seem to have been first composed and disseminated in the Syriac East: Ephrem the Syrian composed a vast corpus of hymns, and disclosed in passing that he was responding to the hymnic output of the heretical Bardaisan, whose hymns are cast as disguising bitterness with sweetness, and their recipients as sick people who chose unhealthy food.[49] The practice of composing and singing hymns was subsequently translated across the Roman empire, including Ambrose's Milan: Augustine, reflecting on the period immediately after his baptism at Milan, remembered weeping during hymns and songs, moved 'by the music of the sweet chants of your Church'. His summary of how such singing 'worked' echoes Ambrose's account: 'The sounds flowed into my ears and the truth was distilled into my heart.'[50]

The Delights of Expounding Scripture for Teachers and Pupils

In his *Homilies on the Hexameron*, Basil dwells on the beauties of the natural world, amassing countless details about trees, plants and

[47] Ambrose, *Enarrationes* 1.9 (transl. Ní Riain, 5).
[48] Nicetas of Remesiana, *De utilitate hymnorum* 1–2.
[49] On Ephrem's composition of hymns to counter the influence of Bardaisan's heretical hymns, see Ephrem, *Hymni contra haereses* 53.5.1–5.
[50] Augustine, *Confessiones* 9.6.14 (transl. Chadwick, 164). On Ambrose's hymnody, see Dunkle, *Enchantment and Creed*.

animals. His discourse is beautiful, rich and varied. At the end of his eighth homily he apologizes to his congregation that his sermon has been unconventionally long: he has kept them from their meal or from less innocent amusements. 'Do you love enjoyment and pleasures?' he asks: 'behold the oracles of the Lord, which, for a healthy soul, are "Sweeter than honey and the honeycomb"'.[51] But he is also talking about the attractiveness of his preaching:

> I have still many observations to make on the products of the sea, for the admiration of my attentive audience … although this honourable assembly is pleased by my speech, and the recital of the marvels of the Master is grateful to the ears of His servants, let me here bring the ship of my discourse to anchor … .

He closes by recommending that his audience talk about his sermon as they eat their evening meal, so that when they sleep their thoughts will still be full of the memory of his preaching and they will continue to 'enjoy the pleasure of the day' as they sleep.[52]

We have some (albeit scarcely unbiased) evidence that Basil's preaching did indeed give pleasure. In his eulogy on Basil, Gregory of Nazianzus emphasizes that Basil's 'writings and labours' were not merely effective, but gave 'charm', 'pleasure' and 'delight', which outdid all rival attractions, secular or religious.[53] Indeed, Gregory's description of reading Basil's theology can only be a description of the effects of *psuchagōgia*: 'Whenever I handle his *Hexameron*, and take its words on my lips, I am brought into the presence of the Creator, and understand the words of creation, and admire the Creator more than before.' Basil's works, Gregory says, vividly bring Bible stories to his mind's eye; they embolden his preaching; they deepen his understanding of Scripture. Basil's stories of saints cause him to 'despise the body' and follow their example. His moral treatises 'purify soul and body, making me a temple fit for God, and an instrument struck by the Spirit, to celebrate by its strains the glory and power of God. In fact, [Basil] reduces me to harmony and order, and changes me by a Divine transformation'.[54] Although Gregory does not mention pleasure directly here, his words do

[51] Basil, *In hexaemeron* 8.8, quoting Ps. 18: 10 LXX (NPNF II 8).
[52] Ibid. 7.6 (NPNF II 8).
[53] Gregory of Nazianzus, *Orations* 43.66 (NPNF II 7).
[54] Ibid. 43.67 (NPNF II 7).

seem calculated to prove that Basil's words amply fulfil the requirements of good Christian pedagogical writing, which Gregory defines at the beginning of the eulogy: 'To the admirers of virtue a discourse is at once a pleasure and an incentive to virtue'.[55]

Many preachers were anxious that, far from delighting their audiences, they were boring or off-putting. Ambrose reminded his clerical readers of the importance of getting the length and style of one's discourse just right:

> Our exposition should not be excessively lengthy, but nor should it be broken off too soon: it ought to leave behind neither a sense of distaste nor an impression of carelessness and inattention. Our language should be pure, simple, clear, and plain, full of seriousness and dignity; it should not be studied with elegance, but nor should it be bereft of a touch of appeal.[56]

Peter Chrysologus regularly expressed concern about his congregation's ability to tolerate the length of his sermons, and indeed postponed portions of preaching in order not to weary them.[57] Augustine, in a treatise on catechizing written for a deacon of Carthage called Deogratias, sympathized with Deogratias's confession that he sometimes bored himself when he was teaching catechumens. Augustine admitted that he too was almost always displeased by his own speech; his tongue fell so short of the abilities of his mind, and the speed of his internal thought processes was slowed down by physically enunciated words. However, Augustine noted that, despite this anxiety, his words still seemed able to elicit delight (*delectatio*) in his audience, who thereby profited from them. He reassured Deogratias that his discourse was not as displeasing to others as it was displeasing to him, and emphasized that teachers were listened to with greater satisfaction when they themselves took joy in their work. He concluded that it was thus the duty of the one who catechized to take pleasure in his

[55] Ibid. 43.1 (NPNF II 7).
[56] Ambrose, *De officiis* 1.22.101 (transl. Davidson, 177).
[57] For example, Peter Chrysologus, *Sermo* 74 (*St Peter Chrysologus, Selected Sermons*, vol. 2, transl. William B. Palardy, FOTC 109 [Washington DC, 2004], 127), finished by stating that 'in order not to be tedious, we shall explain later what our faith contains'; at the end of *Sermo* 96 (transl. Palardy, 156), he postponed the remainder of what he had planned to say in order that 'this work … may be lighter for us all'; in *Sermo* 122 (transl. Palardy, 209), he admitted that he had previously postponed some discussion because 'weariness begets aversion'.

work, 'for the more he succeeds in this the more appealing [literally "sweeter", *suavior*] he will be'.[58] In these introductory paragraphs, Augustine outlined a powerful psychology of the central role of pleasure in both teaching and learning. To be a good teacher, you must enjoy the content and process of what you are teaching. To learn well, you must enjoy your education.

This tallies with Augustine's own account of his conversion, written only a little earlier. When Augustine arrived at Milan as a teacher of rhetoric in 384, he was not a Christian, but a Manichee. Nonetheless, he recalls in *Confessions* that he went to hear Ambrose, the bishop of the city, preach. He confesses that he had no interest in the content of his sermons, but wished rather to test whether the bishop's famous oratorical skills lived up to their reputation. He recalls how, to start with, he was bored by and contemptuous of Ambrose's subject matter, but 'was delighted by the sweetness of his speech' (*delectabar suavitate sermonis*). He then explains that the pleasure he took in Ambrose's eloquence meant that the subject matter came to make an entry into his mind, as the two could not be separated, and, in Augustine's telling, the delight he took in Ambrose's eloquent teaching thus advanced him one step further in his conversion.[59] Augustine presents himself as converted as if by stealth, delighted by the beauty of Ambrose's language; this of course coincides with Ambrose's own account of the pedagogical efficacy of the beauty of the Psalms, discussed above.

Augustine expounded the role of pleasure and delight in teaching and learning at much greater length in his *De doctrina christiana*, the first two and a half books of which were written in the period 396–7, and to which he returned in 426, finishing book 3 and adding book 4. In the earlier phase of writing, Augustine explained how lessons that could be taught in plain statements, on topics such as membership of the Church and the life of faith, gave more pleasure if they were presented in beautiful imagery such as that in Song of Songs, although he admitted that it was unclear why this was so.[60]

[58] Augustine, *De catechizandis rudibus* 1–2 (Augustine, *Instructing Beginners in Faith*, transl. Raymond Canning, ed. Boniface Ramsey, Augustine Series 5 [Hyde Park, NY, 2006], 8). On this passage, see Harmless, *Augustine*, 160–2. See also Gregory of Nazianzus, *Orations* 4.17, cited by Papaioannou, 'Gregory and the Constraint of Sameness', 68.

[59] Augustine, *Confessiones* 5.8.23–5.14.24 (transl. Chadwick, 87–8).

[60] Augustine, *De doctrina* 2.6.7–8 (transl. Green, 32–3).

However, by the 420s, Augustine had developed a fuller account of the pleasures of making sense of figurative language in Scripture. In a treatise against telling lies, he explained:

> Those things are veiled in figures, in garments as it were, in order that they may exercise the mind of the pious inquirer, and not become cheap for being bare and obvious. Although we have learned their meaning stated openly and plainly in other places, still, when they are dug out of obscurity, they are somehow recreated in our knowledge and thus become sweet (*dulcescunt*). A student is not hindered because they are shrouded in this way. On the contrary, they are rendered more acceptable; for being remote they are more ardently (*ardentius*) desired, and for being desired they are more joyfully discovered.[61]

Here, Augustine built on the Ciceronian notion that metaphor, although first introduced by necessity, was developed through 'pleasure and delight' (*iucunditas delectatioque*), and extended Cicero's figurative language about how metaphor was a form of clothing.[62] However, where Cicero had written about the *invention* of metaphor, like a garment first worn to keep off the cold but then developed into adornment, Augustine was concentrating on the process of *interpreting* metaphor.[63] Augustine's account was also, albeit implicitly, much more erotic than Cicero's: if metaphor was a way to keep meaning decent, hiding its naked form from the casual looker, then the process of understanding metaphor involved stripping those garments away, with the consequent delight of discovery described in the burning language (*ardentius*) of erotic love.

[61] Augustine, *Contra mendacium* 24 (transl. Mary Sarah Muldowney, in Augustine, *Treatises on Various Subjects*, ed. Roy J. Deferrari, FOTC 16 [Washington DC, 2002; first publ. 1952], 154).

[62] '"The third method in our list, the use of metaphor, is of wide application; it sprang from necessity due to the pressure of poverty and deficiency, but it has been subsequently made popular by its agreeable and entertaining quality. For just as clothes were first invented to protect us against cold and afterwards began to be used for the sake of adornment and dignity as well, so the metaphorical employment of words was begun because of poverty, but was brought into common use for the sake of entertainment"': Cicero, *De oratore* 3.155 (*Cicero, De oratore Book III, together with De fato, Paradoxa stoicorum, De partitione oratoria*, transl. H. Rackham, LCL 349 [Cambridge, MA, 2014; first publ. 1942], 121–3): At this point in the dialogue, the speaker, Crassus, is making an extended comparison between the inventions of metaphor and clothing.

[63] See Rita Copeland, *Rhetoric, Hermeneutics and Translation in the Middle Ages: Academic Traditions and Vernacular Texts* (Cambridge, 1991), 155–8, on Augustine redefining the rhetorical category of *inventio* as a hermeneutical tool.

Pleasure as a Deliberate Strategy in Educating

Augustine returned to his *De doctrina* in 426, adding a substantial fourth book about the duties of the Christian teacher expounding Scripture in which he argued that wisdom was more important than eloquence, but that eloquence also had a role in Christian instruction, using the common analogy of eloquence as a sweetness which made bitter medicine more acceptable. He made the gustatory quality of learning explicit: 'Learning has a lot in common with eating: to cater for the dislikes of the majority even the nutrients essential to life must be made appetizing.'[64] Augustine then cited the famous Ciceronian maxim that the eloquent should speak to 'instruct, delight and move listeners', and stated explicitly of the second of this list that '[a] hearer must be delighted so that he can be gripped and made to listen'.[65]

Well-educated Christians like Basil and Gregory of Nazianzus had similar cultural assumptions to Augustine. If good words could instruct, delight and move, then good literature was both pleasant and useful. Indeed, most literature (with some careful interpretation) could be made useful.[66] Therefore, in his advice on the education of young men, Basil compares the works of poets such as Homer and Hesiod to attractive flowers and uses the honey trope to urge his readers to engage with the texts more deeply: 'For just as bees know how to extract honey from flowers which to humans are agreeable only for their fragrance and colour, even so here also those who look for something more than pleasure and enjoyment in such writers may derive profit for their souls.'[67] Although Basil appears unaware of the difference between honey and nectar, his clever metaphor successfully conveys the idea that Christian readers must neither take something from every flower, nor drink everything from just one bloom. However, although the flowers of Greek literature are pleasurable and can

[64] Augustine, *De doctrina* 4.11.26 (transl. Green, 117).

[65] Ibid. 4.12.27 (transl. Green, 117–18), citing Cicero, *De oratore* 69.

[66] For Christians, this assumption turned into a belief in the 'catechetical end of all literature': Dunkle, 'Introduction', to *Poems on Scripture*, 17.

[67] Basil, *Ad adolescentes* 4 (transl. Frederick Morgan Padelford, *Essays on the Study and Use of Poetry by Plutarch and Basil the Great*, Yale Studies in English 15 [New Haven, CT, 1902], online at <http://www.tertullian.org/fathers/basil_litterature00.htm>, accessed 6 July 2018. Compare Gregory of Nazianzus: 'The ancients sang instruction in their verse, | Making delight the vehicle of beauty, | Forming the heart for virtue by a song': 'On his own Verses', *Carmina* 2.1.39 (transl. Daley, 165).

lead the young to the 'honey' of teachings about virtue, Basil also warns about the dangers of lack of discrimination: one must guard against the possibility that one might 'drink in poison with honey'.[68]

Furthermore, if all literature could be useful then poetry could have a role in Christian pedagogy, and it was not just hymns or liturgical poetry that were acceptable. One explanation for the numerous attempts at Christian poetry in the late fourth century may have been the decree of the emperor Julian in 362 that those who taught classical texts (such as Homer) in schools should themselves uphold traditional religion, a move which was interpreted as expressing Julian's desire to keep Christians away from teaching the 'pagan' classics.[69] Christians responded, it is argued, by writing their own classics, putting Christian ideas in Greek forms.[70] That may be one explanation, but another explanation is staring us serious-minded scholars in the eye: perhaps Christians wrote Christian poetry because it was fun and because they thought it would give others pleasure too, all the while educating them into the bargain.

Gregory of Nazianzus's poem *On his own Verses* expresses this particularly clearly. After professing to eschew the temptations of fame, the poet gives four reasons for writing verse rather than prose: first, Gregory hoped that the effort of writing verse would force him to write less; secondly, he would show that Christian literature could rival that of others.[71] Whilst these reasons perhaps hint at the pleasure Gregory's verse might give an audience, the next invoke pleasure

[68] Basil, *Ad adolescentes* 4 (transl. Padelford).

[69] This issue has provoked much scholarly controversy. For a brief but subtle assessment, see Gillian Clark, *Christianity and Roman Society* (Cambridge, 2004), 89–90; see also John McGuckin, *St Gregory of Nazianzus: An Intellectual Biography* (Crestwood, NY, 2001), 117. For a challenge to the scholarly consensus, with helpful analysis of various interpretations, see Neil McLynn, 'Julian and the Christian Professors', in Carol Harrison, Caroline Humfress and Isabella Sandwell, eds, *Being Christian in Late Antiquity: A Festschrift for Gillian Clark* (Oxford, 2014), 120–34.

[70] See, for example, Dunkle, *Poems on Scripture*, 18–20; (more subtly) John McGuckin, 'Gregory: The Rhetorician as Poet', in Børtnes and Hägg, eds, *Gregory of Nazianzus: Images and Reflections*, 193–212, at 212.

[71] Gregory of Nazianzus, 'On his own Verses', *Carmina* 2.1.39 (transl. Daley, 163–4); this poem is 'a sketched out program of Christian paideia': McGuckin, 'Rhetorician as Poet', 209–10. Gregory does not specify who these others are: referring to them as 'strangers' (τοὺς ξένους: PG 37, 1333:1), he seems to be making a distinction between poets who are Christian and those who are not, but it is unclear whether he is referring to contemporary or classical works. Readers of Gregory's vast corpus of poetry might raise an eyebrow over the first reason.

specifically: not only has writing poetry consoled him in his illness, Gregory writes, but its qualities can attract young people to God. To press the point home Gregory blends the trope of the honeyed cup with the ancient belief in the soothing qualities of the lyre:

> And of the folk who find such joy in words:
> My verse could be for them a pleasant potion,
> Leading them towards the Good by mild persuasion,
> Sweetening by art the bitter taste of law.
> Verse helps us to relax the tightened string,
> If we but will, even if it be not more
> Than lyric songs, musical interludes.
> I write them simply, then, for your delight,
> Lest other pleasures steal you from true Beauty.[72]

Even in his so-called *Poemata arcana* (poems of the mysteries), which tend towards an epic rather than a pastoral style, Gregory announces that he will 'mix a little enjoyment with my poem'.[73] He describes with pleasing bravura the brilliance of a rainbow and the violence of a raging river, and playfully echoes Homeric tropes in his first lines: 'We shall sing first of the Son'; 'Sing also the praise of the Spirit'.[74] His autobiographical works, although sometimes tending to gloomy introspection, sparkle with wit – not least, caustic remarks about his enemies. Gregory's pedagogical method is to draw the audience into the narrative through emotion, inducing his audience to respond to and with him.[75] In another collection of poems Gregory plays with rhythm, acrostics and other mnemonic effects so that young believers can memorize key facts and digest key truths of the gospel. He describes

[72] Gregory of Nazianzus, 'On his own Verses', *Carmina* 2.1.39 (transl. Daley, 164). For the 'pleasant potion' see also Himerius, *Orations* 16.2–19, alluding to *Odyssey* 4.219–32.

[73] Gregory of Nazianzus, 'From the extempore Oration given when discord arose within his School', *Poemata arcana* 7.53 (transl. D. A. Sykes, ed. C. Moreschini [Oxford, 1997], 37).

[74] Ibid. 6.1–7, 27–32 (transl. Sykes, ed. Moreschini, 27, 29); for the opening lines of poems 2 and 3, cf. Homer, *Iliad* 1.1; Homer, *Odyssey* 1.1; Virgil, *Aeneid* 1.1. The *Iliad* and the *Odyssey* were well known even to schoolboys: these allusions were not especially erudite.

[75] Suzanne Abrams Rebillard analyses precisely how Gregory of Nazianzus's autobiographical poetry, which is 'universally agreed to be pedagogical', affects its audience: 'Historiography as Devotion', 127–8, 134, 136.

this kind of poem as a 'helpful plaything for children'.[76] In sum, whatever their precise theme and audience, Gregory appears to ascribe to his own poems something of the pleasant usefulness which Basil saw in the Psalms: as Neil McLynn argues, his poetry had a 'constructive' purpose and Gregory was not merely 'aiming to impress'.[77]

The notion that poetry was an easier medium through which to teach than prose can also be found in Latin Christian writing. Sedulius, writing in the early fifth century, produced five volumes of poetry in dactylic hexameters about Old Testament miracles and the miracles of Christ which were to prove incredibly popular. However, in stark contrast to the common homiletic presentation of Scripture, and especially the Psalms, as a delightful and inexhaustible feast discussed earlier, and pointedly comparing his own work unfavourably with the 'splendid meals offered by noble men of learning', Sedulius Sedulius characterized his work as modest fare to the dinner guest-cum-reader, 'a few greens from a poor man's garden'.[78] However, in an accompanying letter to the dedicatee, a presbyter called Macedonius, Sedulius's rationale for writing in verse drew repeatedly on the pleasure principle. He was mindful of the fact that 'there are many for whom instruction in worldly letters is all the more attractive because of the delights of poetry (*poeticas … delicias*) and the pleasures of verse (*carminum voluptates*)'. He continues: 'what they see honeyed with the allurement of verse they take up with such eagerness in their hearts that by repeating it again and again they become sure of it and store it up in the depths of their memory'. That is, poetry allures its readers into recitation and repetition, which in turn lodges it deep within. Sedulius concludes that making use of this habit might allow them to be 'won for God of their own will'. Consequently, the desire to convert learned readers by retelling the central stories of Scripture in poetry is, he tells Macedonius, not frivolous but appropriate.[79]

The Dangers and Gains of Pleasure in Education

The relationship between pleasure and persuasion, between delight and education, in patristic thought was not solely negative or positive,

[76] Dunkle, *Poems on Scripture*, 22.
[77] McLynn, 'Among the Hellenists', 234.
[78] Sedulius, *Paschale carmen* (*Paschal Song*, transl. Springer, 3).
[79] Sedulius, *Epistola ad Macedonium* 1 (*Paschal Song*, transl. Springer, 213).

but rather relational. In introductory remarks to his commentary on Psalm 1, Ambrose emphasized the double-edged quality of *delectatio* (delight or enjoyment): 'Enjoyment of future bliss was the highest motive God put to us for the practice of virtue. Enjoyment, too, was the furious spur by which the devil plotted our downfall.' He went on to outline how God had placed Adam in paradise to enjoy eternal delight, and how he had been deceived by the serpent by means of delight. After listing some of the delights of nature, from birds singing melodiously in some lovely spot, to breast-feeding infants being caressed, he concludes that 'it belongs to our very nature to love what gives pleasure'.[80] So, on the one hand, there was a well-developed suspicion of elegant and persuasive language being used to move man to sin, grounded in the scriptural narrative of the fall, in which the serpent seduced the first humans through speech; this was woven together with anxieties about how false teachers, especially heretics (like Satan before them) could flatter and delight their audiences into embracing bad doctrine. On the other hand, there was also a strong interest in how the beauty of language was connected to (albeit perhaps inadequate to describe) the beauty of God's good creation, and Christian teachers repeatedly pointed out that Scripture was full of beautiful and pleasing phrases and images, and recommended that Christian teachers should make use of pleasing and sweet language in their own discourses to please, persuade and instruct their congregations. It is notable how much of the vocabulary of pleasure and delight (*delectatio*, *dulcitudo*, *suavitas*, *voluptas* in Latin, *hēdonē*, *glukasma*, *terpsis*, *chara* in Greek) has strong sensory and sensual associations with the body and its appetites – often thought to be gateways to demonic suggestion – and yet could also be deployed to spiritual ends.[81]

A key example of this tension can be found in Gregory of Nyssa's *Homilies on the Song of Songs*. In the preface, Gregory defends his allegorical method, which is to find spiritual edification in the attractively erotic language. There is danger, he acknowledges, in 'more fleshly folk' being led astray by the text into sensory pleasure; but really the text is about 'spiritual welfare'.[82] It is also emphatically about

[80] Ambrose, *Enarrationes* 1.1–2 (tr. Ní Riain, 1–2).

[81] That is, ἡδονή (enjoyment, pleasure, especially sensual pleasures), γλύκυσμα (sweetness clearly alluding to a sweet taste or smell), τέρψις (enjoyment, delight), χαρά (joy).

[82] Gregory of Nyssa, *Homiliae in Canticum Canticorum*, Preface (transl. Norris, 3). Although 'fruit' here 'certainly means teaching', it must be received by 'the soul that has trained its organs of sense': 4 (transl. Norris, 131).

teaching: Gregory repeatedly refers to the bride in the Song as 'the teacher'.[83] She is the one who is first seduced by the divine Word and then uses her own words to point the way to him.[84] In Gregory's interpretation, she is rarely a soul on an introspective ascent to the divine; instead she is a symbol of the teaching role of the Church and its members, she is compared to Paul or other apostles[85] and she teaches with authority.[86]

Gregory's interpretation is stimulated by the fact that, like the Psalms, the Song of Songs was easy to regard as pleasurable to read. To Gregory, trained in rhetoric, its speeches sounded like ancient *encomia*, speeches of praise which evoke the audience's pleasure. The divine Word is the 'herald and portraitist of [the bride's] beauty'. He declaims like a classical rhetorician, dwelling on her features in loving detail; his words of praise give pleasure through repeated comparison and analogy: 'Behold you are beautiful. Your eyes are like doves'.[87] Commenting on how the Word highlights the pleasantness of spring with certain literary techniques, Gregory concludes that he 'gives pleasure in [his] account of springtime's beauty, both casting out gloom and dwelling fondly upon accounts of things that are sweeter'.[88] Not only are God's words pleasantly beneficial; so are those of the Church. When Gregory describes how the bride (the Church) receives teachings from the groom (the Word) and passes them on to others, he stresses that these teachings are sweet and should continue to give pleasure. For example, in Homily 10 the bride calls down the Holy Spirit on her garden, the members of the Church, asking the Spirit to 'prepare them, as you pour out the sweet savour of the doctrines, to let sweet-smelling prophecy and the

[83] Ibid. 2, 4, 13, 15 (transl. Norris, 51, 147, 399, 403, 463).

[84] Ibid. 15 (transl. Norris, 463). See Morwenna Ludlow, 'Texts, Teachers and Pupils in the Writings of Gregory of Nyssa', in Lieve van Hoof and Peter van Nuffelen, eds, *Literature and Society in the Fourth Century AD: A Magic Stronger than the Governors' Power* (Leiden, 2014), 83–102, at 99–102.

[85] Gregory of Nyssa, *Homiliae in Canticum Canticorum* 10 (transl. Norris, 319).

[86] Ibid. (transl. Norris, 317; in Greek, this echoes Mk 1: 22 and parallels). This emphasis on the bride as teacher seems not to be a strong feature of Latin exegesis of the psalm, to judge from Karl Shuve, *The Song of Songs and the Fashioning of Identity in Early Latin Christianity* (Oxford, 2016).

[87] Gregory of Nyssa, *Homiliae in Canticum Canticorum* 7 (transl. Norris, 227). Gregory analyses how the groom praises the bride: ibid. 3 (transl. Norris, 89) and how the bride gives a pleasurable account of the groom: ibid. 14 (transl. Norris, 451–3).

[88] Ibid. 5 (transl. Norris, 159).

saving teachings of the faith flow freely from their mouths in every type of language'.[89]

Gregory does not shrink totally from the association of pleasure with the body: for him, the language of sensory pleasure indicates the fact that the Church can talk of Christ precisely because of the Word's incarnation in a real human body.[90] Although his preface shows that he is aware of the dangers of the Song's sensory language, he clearly believes that the Song (and his interpretation of it) should render the right kind of pleasure because it has been inspired by the divine Word.

Nevertheless, Gregory and his contemporaries are clearly anxious about the fact that there is a very narrow line between the appropriate and the inappropriate use of pleasure in their discourse. For example, they apologize for getting caught up in the flow of their own eloquence as if they fear they are enjoying their own words too much.[91] They are anxious, too, about the tone of their speech: attacks on heretics could bring a kind of pleasure, but Gregory of Nyssa, for example, expresses his concern that his vituperative attacks on Eunomius went beyond the pale.[92] The teacher who used humour walked an especially tricky tightrope. As we saw above, Ambrose took a generally dim view of clerical jokes. The Cappadocians certainly use amusing absurdities to refresh the congregation with a moment of pleasure and prod them to take note of what has just been said. But humour 'which lacks moderation' could also become

[89] Ibid. 10 (transl. Norris, 319): the prophets, Paul and the four evangelists are cited as examples of those who pass on the 'sweet savour of Christ': ibid. The 'sweet throat' of Song 5: 16 signifies 'the servants and interpreters of the Word, in whom Christ speaks. The blessed Paul gave proof of the Christ speaking in him, and, having lent Christ his own voice, he gave voice to sweetness': ibid. 14 (transl. Norris, 451).

[90] '[The bride] leads her virgins to the theophany that came to us through the medium of the flesh … . So the bride says to them: "My kinsman is white and ruddy … his head is as fine gold"': ibid. 13 (transl. Norris, 405).

[91] Among countless examples, see Basil, *In hexaemeron* 8.8 ((NPNF II 8; despite declaring himself 'ashamed to see that my discourse oversteps the accustomed limits', Basil is certain he has pleased his audience); Gregory of Nazianzus, 'On his own Verses', *Carmina* 2.1.39 (transl. Daley, 163); Gregory of Nyssa, *Contra Eunomium* 3.10.45 ('I am aware that my book is getting somewhat disorderly. It does not stay in its correct course, but like a hot and headstrong foal is being carried away': transl. Stuart G. Hall, in Johan Leemans and Matthieu Cassin, eds, *Gregory of Nyssa, Contra Eunomium III: An English Translation with Commentary and Supporting Studies*, Supplements to *Vigiliae Christianae* 124 [Leiden, 2014], 235).

[92] Gregory of Nyssa, *Epistula* 29.

unpleasant, as Gregory of Nazianzus points out in a passage which itself uses humour to illustrate his point:

> Even in regard to sweet honey, too much and too often can make us sick. As Solomon says (and I agree with him), 'there is a season for everything' … just as a flower is quite out of season in winter, and just as man's clothing does not look right on a woman, or vice versa. Just as uproarious laughter would be seriously out of place at a funeral, or bitter tears shed at a party … .[93]

Precisely because it brought pleasure, there was anxiety that good teaching could cross the dividing line between edification and entertainment. John Chrysostom is famously grumpy on this count. He complains that his congregation are applauding his sermons for the wrong reasons: they are childish; they are not really listening; and it encourages vanity in the preacher. On one occasion, the congregation even applauds his suggestion that they should ban applause! Notably, John identifies pleasure as the heart of the problem: 'you desire not to hear a discourse calculated to lead you to compunction, but one that may delight you from the sound and composition of the words, as though you were listening to singers and minstrels'.[94] A preacher who panders to his audience, he says, is just like a parent who vainly tries to please a sick child by giving them cake and fizzy drinks, when such food will only make them sicker. John admits that he has given way to the temptation 'when we idly busy ourselves about beautiful expressions, and the composition and harmony of our sentences, in order that we may please, not profit: (when) we make it our aim to be admired, not to instruct; to delight, not prick to the heart; to be applauded and depart with praise, not to correct men's habits!' When people applaud him, Chrysostom confesses, he is 'delighted, and give[s] way to the pleasurable feeling'; but then he goes home and weeps, reckoning that as soon as the congregation applauded,

[93] Gregory of Nazianzus, *Orationes* 27.5, quoted in John McGuckin, 'St Gregory the Comic', in Christopher A. Beeley, ed, *Re-Reading Gregory of Nazianzus: Essays on History, Theology, and Culture* (Washington DC, 2012), 269–76, at 275. Humour is, of course, contextual and some images seem offensive or bizarre to us today, while other gentler attempts simply pass us by.

[94] All remaining quotations in this paragraph: John Chrysostom, *In Acta Apostolorum* 30 (PG 60: 225–6).

they had forgotten what he had said.[95] Augustine revealed a similar anxiety when preaching away from home at the bidding of another bishop; he explained that 'the time my satisfaction, my joy, is really solid and unalloyed is when I am listening, not when I am preaching. Then, you see, I can enjoy myself without a qualm. That pleasure has no side to it; where there is only the solid rock of truth, there's no need to fear the precipice of pride.'[96]

Conclusion

The Christian writers we have surveyed were fully aware of the dangers of pleasant speech. Indeed, they have many negative things to say about pleasure: while we have not dwelt on them here, it is evident how concerns about pleasure affect discussions of how good speech could both educate and delight. As we have just seen, writers such as Ambrose and Gregory warned against the dangers of misusing or misunderstanding delightful speech because of its connection with sensory and worldly pleasures. They were ostensibly defending Scripture itself (and, as we have seen, there was general agreement that Scripture was pleasant nourishment and sweet refreshment). But they were surely also making a space in Christian education for their own forms of sweet persuasion. Of all the prose writers we have considered, Ambrose and Gregory were perhaps the ones who were most unabashed at luxuriating in the sheer pleasure of a pedagogical language which was both sensuous and edifying. Augustine's prose often shares these qualities, but he is somewhat more careful and deliberate in his defence of delight as a literary strategy. He has a teacher's sensitivity to the need for both good, plain speech and for the kind of pleasure which rendered good argument gripping and ultimately persuasive. A related, but slightly different strategy was evident in the poets we have discussed: for them, pleasure was the justification for their choice of the elaborations of poetry over plainer

[95] Somewhat beyond the time-frame of our study here, the Byzantine literary critic Michael Psellos provides a vivid example of how an author could get stuck at the surface level of a text, seduced by its beauty: 'Psellos, the reader, indulges in the material pleasures of writing', using eroticized imagery to convey his pleasure: Stratis Papaioannou, *Michael Psellos: Rhetoric and Authorship in Byzantium* (Cambridge, 2013), 96.

[96] Augustine, *Sermo* 179.3 (transl. Edmund Hill, ed. John E. Rotelle, Works of St Augustine 3/5 [Charlottesville, VA, 2001; first publ. 1992], 299); and, for the effect of praise on him, *Confessiones* 10.36.59.

prose: as both Sedulius and Nazianzus comment, 'honeyed words' make their work more attractive and thus more educational. In addition, both poets point to another pedagogical advantage: poetry pleasantly seeps into the memory, whether by encouraging repetition, or by the use of entertaining mnemonic devices.

Basil's attitude to pleasure seems somewhat cautious, weighing pleasure up against the usefulness of a text, whether it was a psalm or one of the Greek classics. Nevertheless, we have seen how, in his *Homilies on the Hexameron*, he clearly delights in the process of exegesis. This is something rather different from the enjoyment of a particular literary tone; rather, the pleasure is more active, consisting in chewing a text over and digesting it. A similar pleasure in hermeneutical activity was also evident in Augustine's vivid, erotically suggestive account of 'uncovering' biblical metaphors. In addition, these writers saw teaching not only as merely conveying information or demonstrating a practice, but as a performance. This was clearly a divisive idea: Augustine actively recommends that Deogratias should enjoy his teaching of catechumens, for then they too will enjoy listening and learn more. On the other hand, Augustine also reveals that listening was for him a greater joy than preaching, since it kept him safe from the dangers of proud display. John Chrysostom similarly fears the entry of pride and superficiality into his preaching (a much more public performance). If his audience claps, are they really learning? And if he enjoys preaching, is he merely enjoying their praise?[97] The ancients often distinguished between public speaking (associated with theatre and the forum) and private teaching (associated with schools and more private contexts). It is possible that in expressing anxieties about applause and praise, John Chrysostom is wondering whether one could recalibrate the Christian sermon so that it was associated less with showy public performance and more with the exposition of texts to a committed audience. Both public and private teaching could bring pleasure to the audience, but perhaps Augustine's and Chrysostom's comments suggest that there was something more dangerous in the pleasures brought by public display.

While there are clear differences in approach among the authors considered here, there seem also to be some common notions about good and bad uses of pleasure in Christian education. Good

[97] John Chrysostom, *In Acta Apostolorum* 30.

pleasure not only attracts the audience, but draws what they are learning deep into their soul. A bad use of pleasure, however – even if it is used to enhance truthful teachings – distracts the audience away from what they are meant to learn. There appears to be a distinction here between depth and superficiality: pleasure which remains on the surface is not really doing its job. This explains the popularity of gustatory metaphors in pedagogy: one needed to properly ingest and digest what one was learning. But it also raised the stakes, for a teacher of falsehood who used pleasurable words could do untold damage to a pupil's soul.

Finally, the writers we have examined here all seem fully aware of the question of pleasure in education. Whether they guarded against the overuse or misuse of pleasure, weighed it up against a text's utility, devised careful strategies for its employment or revelled in its power – in one way or another, like Paul and the Psalmist, they all used 'honeyed words'.

Dialogue in the Monastery: Hagiography as a Pedagogical Model

Lucy K. Pick*
The Divinity School, University of Chicago

This article explores the reasons why dialogue has been such a key part of religious education by examining several texts from the medieval period: Gregory the Great's Dialogues, *Petrus Alfonsi's* Dialogue against the Jews *and three hagiographical narratives from tenth-century Spanish manuscripts. It will argue that when read or listened to, the dialogue of the text was meant in turn to cue an internal dialogue, a response within the self, and a transformation. While meditative religious reading of all kinds was thought of as producing this inner reflection and debate, the dialogue format was an especially effective didactic tool for inculcating in beginners a mode of internal reflection and questioning, inspired by an outside source. Finally, although the content and even the message of the dialogue that is written or overheard may be fixed and clear, its effect on those who read or hear it remains open and provisional. It is up to readers or listeners to draw their own conclusions and absorb their own lessons from it.*

Dialogue is everywhere in the Middle Ages. It is found as a central device in numerous literary genres: pedagogy, scholastic texts and narrative hagiography, to name but a few. Dialogue was a fact in texts because it was a fact in life: in the practice of scholastic disputation, in the rituals of court whose scripts are royal diplomata, and above all in the liturgy. Dialogue also has an ancient role in education, including religious education. We think of Platonic dialogues, of course, and some college classrooms still aspire to the Socratic method. Dialogue has retained a central role in religious education in traditions as disparate as Buddhism and Judaism. Dialogue in the Middle Ages continued to be a technique of pedagogy, whether the dialogue was between two adversaries, or between a master who instructed and a student or disciple who questioned and learned.

* The Divinity School, 1025 E 58th St, Chicago IL 60637, USA. E-mail: lucypick@uchicago.edu.

Studies in Church History 55 (2019), 35–55
doi: 10.1017/stc.2018.13

Dialogue might be something that happened in a schoolroom or monastery, or it might be read, silently or aloud, from a written text.[1] But why has dialogue been such a key part of religious education? What advantages does it offer over other potential modes of instruction, such as the lecture or the treatise? The task of this article is to begin to answer these questions.

I will argue that when read or heard, the dialogue of the text was meant in turn to cue an internal dialogue, a response within the self, and a transformation. The written dialogues themselves are often explicit about this intent. While meditative religious reading of all kinds was thought of as producing this inner reflection and debate, the dialogue format is thought to be especially effective for inculcating in beginners a mode of internal reflection and questioning, inspired by an outside source. Finally, although the content and even the message of the dialogue that is written or overheard may be fixed and clear, its effect on those who read or hear it remains open and provisional. It is up to them to draw their own conclusions and absorb their own lessons from the dialogue.

The primary examples of the way dialogue serves a pedagogical function will be taken from a series of hagiographical texts, copied in tenth-century Spain and used in women's monastic contexts. I begin, however, by introducing the important precedent set by Gregory the Great's *Dialogues* for the use of dialogue in a didactic context during the medieval period. Petrus Alfonsi's *Dialogue against the Jews*, a popular example of the likewise popular genre of inter-religious dialogues between Christians and Jews, will offer a different model of the didactic intent and effect of a dialogue format. By starting with these more obviously didactic texts and discussing how they use dialogue to teach with, it will more easily become apparent that the dialogues in my hagiographical texts likewise serve more than a strictly narrative function. Dialogue in these hagiographies invites the reader into a process of engagement with the text, the goal of which is her own self-transformation.

[1] The most important recent work on dialogue and disputation as pedagogy in the Middle Ages is Alex J. Novikoff, *The Medieval Culture of Disputation: Pedagogy, Practice, and Performance* (Philadelphia, PA, 2013). See also Marie Anne Polo de Beaulieu, ed., *Formes dialoguées dans la littérature exemplaire du moyen âge* (Paris, 2012); Simon Goldhill, ed., *The End of Dialogue in Antiquity* (Cambridge, 2008); Seth Lerer, *Boethius and Dialogue: Literary Method in the* Consolation of Philosophy (Princeton, NJ, 1985).

Gregory the Great's *Dialogues* exemplifies the dialogue format. It was ubiquitous in libraries in the medieval Latin West, and its influence was felt particularly early in Spain.[2] The text unfolds as a private conversation between Gregory and a student, the deacon Peter, about whether the age of saints has passed. Peter suggests to Gregory that there are no longer men in Italy who are famed for virtue, as there were in the early church, and moreover miracles are no longer performed.[3] Gregory takes four books to show him that this is not the case. Peter intervenes, albeit briefly, throughout, expressing wonder, asking for clarification and, most of all, pointing out biblical parallels for the miracles Gregory describes. For example, after hearing some of the miracles of St Benedict, Peter says:

> The things you report be strange, and much to be wondered at: for in making the rock to yield forth water, I see Moses; and in the iron, which came from the bottom of the lake, I behold Elisha; in the walking [of Maurus] upon the water, I perceive Peter; in the obedience of the crow, I contemplate Elijah; and in lamenting the death of his enemy, I acknowledge David: and therefore, in my opinion, [Benedict] was full of the spirit of all good men.[4]

We might question why Gregory needs Peter at all. Why was he moved to describe the deeds of the saints in a dialogue, when he could simply have described their deeds and miracles, and then made the biblical parallels himself? And why have named figures in the text at all? Why not simply present the ideas and stories in it from the perspective of a distant third-person narrator?

The people make the dialogue a drama, and the drama connects ideas to embodied practice or exercise, and thence to the reader. Peter, the student who questions his master face to face, stands in this text in the place of the reader. Readers who wish to learn from Gregory's text identify with his student Peter, model themselves on him and learn alongside him as he passes from foolishness to wisdom. It is a dialogue between scriptural texts that Peter knows and cites and

[2] Ann Elizabeth Kuzdale, 'The Dialogues of Pope Gregory the Great in the Literary and Religious Culture of Seventh- and Eighth-Century Europe' (PhD dissertation, University of Toronto, 1995), 79–178. Kuzdale estimates that there were at least 79 known partial or complete manuscripts of the *Dialogues* between the seventh and tenth centuries: personal communication, 22 September 2017.

[3] Gregory the Great, *Dialogues*, Prol. 7 (SC 251, 260, 265; 1: 14).

[4] Ibid. 8 (2: 164, 166). Translations into English are my own, except where noted.

the contemporary lives of the saints that Gregory relates, connecting the two and showing that the good days are not all behind us. It is a dialogue that teaches its readers how to read the Bible, and to read the events and lives of their own day through the light of the Scriptures. The reading or hearing of written dialogue becomes a tool of formation, education and cultivation of the devotional self in the monastery.

In this respect, this dialogue has a great deal in common with the numerous Christian dialogues that describe conversations between a Christian and a Jew.[5] These are often criticized by modern standards for giving short shrift to the Jew, for not allowing him to speak much and for not allowing him to make the arguments a 'real' Jew would have made, for instance, in response to accusations that Jews read only the letter of the Old Testament, while Christians understand the spirit. The *Dialogue against the Jews* of the twelfth-century Jewish convert to Christianity Petrus Alfonsi is a case in point. Educated in Islamic Spain, where he received a broad education, Petrus was baptized as a Christian in 1106 in the city of Huesca, at the time ruled by the king of Aragón, before travelling as a teacher to England and northern France. His *Dialogue* explains his adoption of Christianity to his unconverted self, the character Moses.[6] Moses does little more in the text than pose questions and ask for clarification, despite the fact that Petrus, above all people, would have known genuine Jewish objections to the Christian positions, as well as Jewish defences against the points he makes; had he wished, he could have articulated them through the persona of Moses.[7] But this text and

[5] The bibliography on this subject is vast, but see, for example, Bernhard Blumenkranz, *Les Auteurs chrétiens latins du moyen âge sur les juifs et le judaïsme*, Études juives (Paris, 1963); Amos Funkenstein, 'Basic Types of Christian Anti-Jewish Polemics in the Later Middle Ages', *Viator* 2 (1971), 373–82; Jeremy Cohen, *The Friars and the Jews: The Evolution of Medieval Anti-Judaism* (Ithaca, NY, 1982); Robert Chazan, *Daggers of Faith: Thirteenth-Century Christian Missionizing and Jewish Response* (Berkeley, CA, 1989); Gilbert Dahan, *Les Intellectuels chrétiens et les juifs au moyen âge* (Paris, 1990); Samuel Krauss, *The Jewish-Christian Controversy from the Earliest Times to 1789* (Tübingen, 1996); Novikoff, *Medieval Culture of Disputation*, 172–221.

[6] John Tolan, *Petrus Alfonsi and his Medieval Readers* (Gainesville, FL, 1993), 9–11, 183.

[7] Petrus Alfonsi, *Diálogo contra los judíos*, ed. Klaus-Peter Mieth, transl. Esperanza Ducay, Larumbe 9 (Huesca, 1996); idem, *Dialogue against the Jews*, transl. Irven M. Resnick, FOTC Medieval Continuation 8 (Washington DC, 2006). On the role played by Moses, see Anna Sapir Abulafia, 'Moyses in Service of Petrus in Petrus Alfonsi's *Dialogus*', in Carmen Cardelle de Hartmann and Philipp Roelli, eds, *Petrus Alfonsi and his* Dialogus*: Background, Context, Reception*, Micrologus' Library 66 (Florence, 2014), 111–28, at 114, 117–24.

the many other *dialogi*, *altercationes* and *disputationes* that precede and follow it were not written to present an accurate depiction of the Christian-Jewish debate. They were written for the most part in Latin, and thus for a learned Christian audience. They took Christian readings of the Bible, especially the Old Testament, but also of events such as the fall of Jerusalem to the Romans and the destruction of the Temple, and the meaning of the Roman empire, and contrasted them with readings labelled 'Jewish' of the same texts and events in a dialogue format to show the truth of the Christian readings and the falsity of the Jewish ones.

This Jew who serves as a sparring partner for Christian theology has been called a hermeneutical Jew, a Jew who may only poorly overlap with real Jews, but who was a crucial tool in Christian self-understanding and definition.[8] Whereas the Christian reader identifies with Peter in Gregory's *Dialogues* and learns alongside him, when reading Christian-Jewish dialogue, the Christian reader learns by aversion. The perspective that is Jewish is already automatically labelled as wrong, and the Christian learns what errors to avoid.

On the other hand, whilst polemic is part of Petrus Alfonsi's purpose, it is not his whole purpose. Some of what he teaches bears little on Christian-Jewish debate, but demonstrates a different way in which these dialogues served a didactic purpose. Book 1 of his *Dialogue* treats of the nature of God and his unity. But a good part of it is given over to recounting astronomical information about the shape of the world, its divisions, the way the sun passes over its surface and so forth, complete with diagrams. Petrus uses biblical authority as a support for these observations, but they have only tangential relevance to his intention to explain his conversion. Moses's interventions in these sections are simply to ask for clarification and to demonstrate that he has understood Petrus's explanations. This is ironic because it was while he was still Moses, the Spanish Jew, that Petrus had learned what he knew about astronomy, information he now shares with his Christian world, which stands with Moses, reading and learning.[9] Knowledge which had come to Christian Europe from Jewish and Muslim sources has been repackaged as inherently Christian.

[8] Jeremy Cohen, *Living Letters of the Law: Ideas of the Jew in Medieval Christianity* (Berkeley, CA, 1999), 3 n. 3.
[9] Petrus Alfonsi, *Diálogo* 1.16–23.

Why is this a part of the *Dialogue*? If we take Petrus at his word in his preface that his intention in writing is to explain the reasons why, as he puts it, '[t]he Christian law is superior to all others', this astronomy is a pointless digression.[10] But if we see the *Dialogue* more broadly as a teaching text, then it makes perfect sense. Our clue to his intentions here is found in another text by Petrus, the so-called 'letter to the peripatetics' addressed to the wandering scholars of France who sought out the best masters in the subjects that interested them. Called an apologia for astronomy, it is really an advertisement for Petrus's own expertise in the subject:

> It has come to our ears that some of those who investigate wisdom … prepare to traverse distant provinces and exile themselves in remote regions in order to acquire a fuller knowledge of astronomy. To them I reply without hesitation that since the truth is what they desire to see, they will soon have what they wish, and that which they prepare to seek in remote places is close at hand, unless they have some doubt that we are somewhat gifted in this art.[11]

Petrus's contribution to Christian thought was not that he came up with definitive arguments against Jews. Rather it was as a teacher, a conduit of knowledge from the non-Christian world about Jewish exegetical traditions, but also about such little-related subjects as astronomy. Above all, we must remember the device of Petrus Alfonsi literally speaking to himself, to his alter ego Moses, representing on the page the kind of internal dialogue in which the reader is meant to engage. This highlights the importance of voice and of who is speaking what parts in this dialogue. Who voices a given perspective or discloses particular information is as important as the perspective or information itself.

We move now from considering these placeless, plotless, explicitly didactic dialogues to examining how dialogue is used within a collection of narratives about holy women. Here too, more unexpectedly, dialogue does not merely further the plot of the narrative; it also plays a didactic role. Five manuscripts copied in medieval Spain during the tenth century transmit all or part of a collection of eight Latin lives of female holy women: El Escorial, Real Biblioteca del Monasterio de San Lorenzo, MSS a.II.9 and a.I.13; Madrid, Biblioteca Nacional

10 Ibid., Prol. 7.

11 Tolan, *Petrus Alfonsi*, 166–7, 175 (Tolan's translation).

de España (hereafter: BNE), MS 10007; Madrid, Biblioteca de la Real Academia de la Historia (hereafter: BAH), MS 13; and Paris, BN, nouv. acq. lat., MS 2178. The women are Constantina, Helia, Melania the Younger, Castissima, an anonymous virgin, Egeria, Pelagia and Mary of Egypt. I class these under the rubric of hagiography, using that term loosely to describe narrative accounts of holy women, intended as models of right thought and behaviour. Taken individually, a couple of them, like the dialogue of the anonymous virgin or the life of Helia, might not seem to fit the genre understood more strictly, as they are about women for whom no cult is attested. However, as I will argue, they must be read together as a corpus and interpreted within the context of the lives that travel with them and the manuscripts that contain them and what all that may tell us about how they were intended to be used.[12] No manuscript transmits only these lives; the bulk of the codices are filled with additional texts, hagiographic, monastic or both. At least one, El Escorial, MS a. I.13, was copied for a religious community of women.[13]

The whole collection of eight lives is worthy of further attention. A large amount of documentary evidence exists showing women before 1100 in Spain who entered the religious life under vows, but we have found very little to this point that would help us understand what religious life meant to them, what they feared and dreamed of, or how they hoped to be transformed by it. This corpus offers a chance to shed light on that question. Here, I will introduce three of the eight: the *Life of Constantina*, the *Life of Helia* and the *Dialogue of the Virgin*, a conversation between an anonymous virgin and an old man. Hagiography (both the *passio* or martyrdom account and the *vita* or saint's life) conventionally includes dialogical elements, but

[12] BN, nov. acq. lat., MS 2178, fol. 207^r; and BAH, MS 13, fol. 287^v have separate tables of contents which list them together as a collection within the larger manuscript.

[13] Two of the four manuscripts (El Escorial, Real Biblioteca del Monasterio de San Lorenzo, MS a.II.9 and BN, nouv. acq. lat. MS 2178) copy the full collection of eight lives, while the other three (El Escorial, MS a.I.13; BNE, MS 10007; BAH, MS 13) transcribe different subsections of the collection: Virginia Burrus and Marco Conti, eds, *The Life of Saint Helia*, OECT (Oxford, 2013), 6–9. Joyce E. Salisbury, *Church Fathers, Independent Virgins* (London, 1991), begins the work of considering them as a collection, discussing the contents of the eight lives, with a consideration of the manuscript tradition on pp. 129–33. Guillermo Antolín, 'Estudios de códices visigodos. Códice a.II.9 de la Biblioteca del Escorial', *Boletín de la Real Academia de la Historia* 54 (1909), 55–67, 117–28, 204–46, 265–315, discusses El Escorial, MS a.II.9 in detail and provides partial transcriptions.

I will argue that these three texts, in different ways, use dialogue not merely to advance the narrative but as a form of pedagogy intended to help form its audience through a kind of internal cultivation of the self. As we shall see, the *Life of Constantina* melds new dialogues to an older hagiographic tradition to expand greatly on the late antique story of Constantina, and the text on the anonymous virgin is wholly constructed from inter-nested conversations. I begin, however, with the *Life of Helia*.

The story of 'St Helia' is unusual not only because it recounts the story of a woman for whom we have no other evidence of a cult, but even more because it was written as a series of dialogues strung together with only enough narrative to provide them with the barest of a frame. The dialogical elements are so important to the text that the different speeches are marked out with character cues, as we would find in the script of a play (Fig. 1).[14] It is divided into three books. The first involves a debate between Helia ('The Virgin') and her mother over whether it is better to marry or to remain a virgin, as the mother attempts to persuade her daughter into marriage. They continue their debate in the second book, until the mother decides that dialogue is not working on her recalcitrant daughter, and moves to physical punishment to convince her of the error of her position. Helia escapes to the local bishop, whom she persuades, with another speech, to take up her cause. He hides her and debates with her furious mother. In the third book, after her paternal aunt has raised a peasant army in support of her niece and been defeated by the emperor, Helia is summoned to a public trial and debates with the civic judge. The account ends with no clear resolution, but Helia gets the last word in a speech that asserts her ability as a woman to gain salvation by means other than having children, and a poem that affirms the biblical foundation of her identity as a virgin.[15]

Even before the mother uses physical punishment on Helia, their conversation is acrimonious. The mother opens their debate by asking:

[14] Many manuscripts of Gregory the Great's *Dialogues* use character cues (*praenotatio nominum*) in the same way: Bruno Judic, 'Le recueil fondateur. Les *Dialogues* de Gregoire le Grand', in Polo de Beaulieu, ed., *Formes dialoguées*, 69–87, at 80–2.

[15] See the excellent edition by Burrus and Conti, *Life of Helia*, 76–173. I use their translation in what follows.

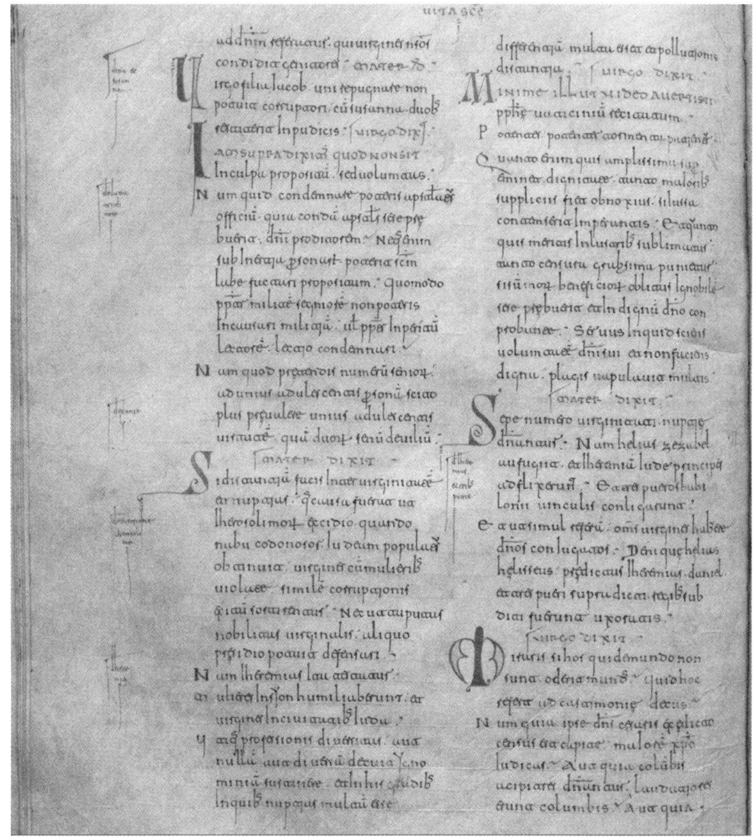

Fig. 1. El Escorial, Real Biblioteca del Monasterio de San Lorenzo, MS a.II.9, fol. 78v, *Vita Sancte Helie*. © Patrimonio Nacional.

> Why, being forgetful of our discipline, do you oppose the doctrine of your fathers and follow the path of a new superstition? Abandon your devotion to this empty religious observance and comply with the wishes of your parents, before you experience the severity of your mother's judgment and suffer the shame of your most grave error.[16]

Before she turns on her daughter with switches, the mother calls her '[v]erbose girl, profaner of the divine laws, insolent towards maternal

[16] Ibid. 86–7.

admonitions, oblivious of our favors, rebellious, reckless, presumptuous, irresponsible, inconsiderate, foolish-talking, and unrestrained.'[17] Not all dialogue will be civil, and founded in reason and evidence alone.

The *Life of Saint Helia* exists somewhere between the two poles that are dialogue between master and student and dialogue between religious antagonists. In Gregory's *Dialogues*, Peter and Gregory are on the same 'team', as it were, each at different stages of the same path of spiritual growth. In the numerous Christian dialogues that feature a Christian and a Jew, like that between Petrus Alfonso and Moses, the two sides are positioned on opposite sides – faith versus infidelity; the spirit versus the letter – although the intent remains both exegetical and transformative for the reader. All the characters in the *Life of Helia* are Christians, albeit perhaps of different sorts. Still, it has in common with both Gregory's *Dialogues* and the Christian-Jewish debate deep attention to problems of biblical interpretation. Helia and her mother, her mother and the bishop, and finally Helia and the judge all cite biblical verses to support their positions and use biblical exegesis against each other, and the debate turns on which one is reading the Bible correctly, especially the commandment to obey one's parents.[18] Helia herself even embodies biblical dialogue, as when, committed to the virginal life but unsure of how to pursue it, she paraphrases to herself Mary's dialogue with the angel at the Annunciation (Luke 1: 34): 'How will this be done, since I do not know the order?'[19] Moreover, the mother presents a challenge to Helia and the reader, in that her arguments in favour of marriage are not weak ones but are drawn from the same Bible from which Helia draws her own counter-arguments in favour of virginity. It is up to the reader to sift and discern what a right reading might be, to internalize the correct possible readings of the Scriptures and their application to lived life, and to choose virginity for herself.

Even the more narrative elements of the *Life* have a strong dialogical quality. The dialogue of the narrative is with those who stand outside the text, reading or hearing the *Life*. In the prologue, the narrator addresses the man who commissioned the *Life*, his own master, improbably named Macedonius, promising this spiritual father the

[17] Ibid. 134–5.
[18] Ibid. 132–3.
[19] Ibid. 84–5. The *Life* has *ordinem* where the Vulgate has *virum*.

obedience Helia refuses to her physical mother.[20] At the opening of the first book, he addresses a second audience, of female virgins, who are expected to benefit from the image he paints them of Helia and her debates, and who reward him with their powerful prayers on his behalf: 'The painting of this living tablet will benefit you in no small measure, O blessed virgins, if only you may procure for us divine approbation through your prayers, by imploring the Lord plainly.'[21] The text that reveals Helia becomes a portrait at which the virgins may gaze, to measure their own performance. This audience is imagined as one not of readers but of listeners, encountering this text as an oral performance, as suggested by the direction that follows the author's address to them: 'Thus if it now pleases the one who is here to speak the life of Saint Helia, let the discourse begin to be disclosed.'[22] And although the dialogue itself ends without explicit resolution, the text as a whole concludes with a prayer in the first person in which St Helia and her audience of virgins become one, a single 'I' who is a virgin, and whose life is modelled on the Bible:

> I am Christ's virgin; to know a husband
> I desire not, because I desire to possess paradise.
> I who should follow the Lord have heard
> How numerous are the rewards of virginity
> Established by lofty promise, not of this time
> But immortality extending to heaven.
> I hear that *those who are pure of heart are blessed,*
> *because they can see God* [Matt. 5: 8].
> They possess blessed life *who have*
> *castrated themselves for the kingdom of God* [Matt. 19: 12].
> Nor is there any doubt that those who have remained chaste
> and virginal are made *equal to the angels* [Luke 20: 36].[23]

The virgin who can speak the 'I' of this poem becomes one with Helia, and also with the Scriptures.

The second text to be discussed from this collection, which I refer to as the *Dialogue of the Virgin*, is a brief exchange between an

[20] Ibid. 76–9.
[21] Ibid. 80–1.
[22] Ibid.
[23] Ibid. 172–3.

anonymous virgin and an old man, in which he enquires about the events that led her to seek a life of virtue, and she answers him by relating a series of nested dialogues that explain the transformation of her life.[24] She tells him how her parents modelled different ways of life for her before their deaths. Her father was ill most of the time, and spoke so little you might think he had no voice, while her mother was so talkative you might think she was all tongue.[25] The mother fought with everyone, and lived a life of drunken luxury and adultery. After their deaths, the virgin had an internal dialogue about which mode of life she should follow: her father's suffering seemed to show he was disfavoured by God, while her mother's happiness implied God's favour. The virgin tells the old man that, resolving to follow the ways of her mother, she then fell asleep and experienced a vision of a man of magnificent appearance. The virgin recounts the conversation she had with this man, and how he showed her the fates after death of her virtuous father and wicked mother. Within this vision, she then speaks to her parents. Her father calls her 'daughter' and promises her that his reward of peace and comfort will be hers if she follows his ways, while her mother, suffering the tortures of the damned, begs the girl to release her from her torments.

The internal dialogues within the text conclude with a second-person imperative admonition directed outside the text, to its reader. This urges its audience:

> Despise all transitory things. Have no care for the world, as if you were dead. Despise in living what you will not be able to have after death. Behold, a way of living has been given to you; you have an orderly law which you ought to follow. You already know what it is to live rightly. Take care, lest what you learn by reading, you despise in living. Fulfil through deeds what you have learned by seeing.[26]

This admonition recalls *Helia*'s author's address to the virgins at the opening of that text, and the identification of the virgin who listens to or reads the text with Helia in its concluding poem.

The *Dialogue of the Virgin* is a variation on a passage with the incipit *Narravit quidam senex* ('A certain old man recounted'). It is found

[24] The text is transcribed from El Escorial, MS a.II.9, fol. 116, in Antolín, 'Códices visigodos', 279–82.
[25] Ibid. 279.
[26] Ibid. 282.

in the *Verba seniorum* (*Sayings of the Fathers*), said to be a translation of apophthegmata from Greek into Latin, attributed to John the subdeacon, who may be Pope John III (561–74).[27] The *Verba seniorum* forms part of the *Vitae patrum* (*Lives of the Fathers*) tradition. This particular passage is found in numerous medieval manuscripts.[28] The version in El Escorial, MS a.II.9 makes important changes to the original, however. In the original version, the content of what here are nested dialogues is all related by the old man who is named first and who questions the virgin, who is herself also old.[29] In our version, the virgin, whose age is not mentioned, speaks for herself and is named first, putting the focus on her experiences and her first-person speech, rather than on the old man's account of her story.[30] Likewise, the admonition directed outside the text toward its reader that is in our version is wholly missing from the original. These changes heighten the dialogic qualities of the text that are designed to draw in the reader, especially the female reader, and encourage a process of self-transformation alongside the woman at the heart of the story.

The dialogues of the virgin with her father and mother, with the old man, with herself and with the splendid man of her vision become a dialogue between the text and the reader in which the reader is asked to perform an act of internal reflection and transformation that matches the transformation of the virgin in the text. The text plays with paradox. The father's silence is rewarded and the mother's loquacity punished, but it is only through dialogue that the daughter herself is saved. The reader must consider options and choose wisely, but what any reader's actual response will be remains an open question. The text highlights a gap between text and lived life, a gap that is bridged by correct reading.

Constantina, daughter of Emperor Constantine, is the subject of the *Life of Constantina*, the only text discussed here whose subject is securely historically attested. Constantina, or Constantia as she is sometimes known, appears as a supporting character in a number of early saints' lives. She is a recipient of a healing miracle that

[27] *Verba seniorum* 1.15 (PL 73, cols 995C–998A).

[28] Some of these can be identified by searching for the incipit in 'Monastica', online at: <http://monastica.ht.lu.se>.

[29] *Verba seniorum* 1.15 (PL 73, cols 995C–D).

[30] Antolín, 'Códices visigodos', 279.

leads her to a life of consecrated virginity in the fifth-century *Passio* of St Agnes, in whose name she builds a basilica and near whose tomb she establishes her own mausoleum.[31] In the intertwined *Passiones* of Gallicanus and of John and Paul, she is sought as bride by the pagan, Gallicanus, her father's general. She refuses to give him an answer right away, but sends her servants, John and Paul, on campaign with him, while she educates his two daughters, Attica and Artemia. She persuades the girls to adopt a life of Christian virginity, while her servants convert Gallicanus. After she and her father die, and Julian the Apostate becomes emperor, Gallicanus, John and Paul are all martyred.[32] These stories are related by (among others) Aldhelm in his *Carmen de virginitate*, which was known in ninth-century Spain.[33]

The *Life of Constantina*, preserved, in whole or in part, in four of the five Spanish manuscripts discussed here, takes the *Passiones* of Agnes, Gallicanus, and John and Paul and compiles them into a tale that makes Constantina the heroine.[34] It accomplishes this by adding significant new material to the corpus, which has not yet received sufficient attention. A large part of this new material is dialogical in nature, and bears a close relationship in theme and concerns to the dialogues of Helia and of the anonymous virgin. Like the other two texts, the narrator of this new material has a strong authorial presence and directly addresses an audience made up of virgin readers or listeners: 'O how blessed are you, virgins of Christ, who strive to follow the example of Constantina Augusta.'[35] Likewise, it speaks in several places of what the virgins who will read the text may learn from the example of Constantina.[36]

[31] *Passio S. Agnetis, ActaSS* Ian. 2, 351–4; Hannah Jones, 'Agnes and Constantia: Domesticity and Cult in the Passion of Agnes', in Kate Cooper and Julie Hillner, eds, *Religion, Dynasty, and Patronage in Early Christian Rome 300–900* (Cambridge, 2007), 115–39, at 115–20.

[32] *ActaSS* Iun. 5, 37–9, 159–61; Jones, 'Agnes and Constantia', 118–19; Conrad Leyser, '"A Church in the House of the Saints": Property and Power in the Passion of John and Paul', in Cooper and Hillner, eds, *Religion, Dynasty, and Patronage*, 140–62, at 147–52.

[33] Aldhelm, *Carmen de virginitate*, lines 1927–74, 2051–2120, in *Opera Omnia*, MGH AA 15, 432–4, 437–40; Andrew Breeze, 'The Transmission of Aldhelm's Writings in Early Medieval Spain', *Anglo-Saxon Studies* 21 (1972), 5–20, at 9–10.

[34] El Escorial, MS a.II.9, fols 59^{r}–72^{r}; ibid., MS a.I.13, fols 109^{v}–125^{v}; BAH, MS 13, fols 288^{r}–293^{v}; BN, nouv. acq. lat., MS 2178, fols 207^{r}–219^{v}.

[35] El Escorial, MS a.I.13, fol. 111^{r}.

[36] For example, 'Ad edificationem uirginum christi conscribimus ut ex paucis multa noscuntur': ibid., fol. 110^{r}; 'Set reuertamur ad Constantinam augustam ut tu, uirgo christi, que studio edificationis tuę lectionis huius hystoriam discis': ibid., fol. 111^{v}.

In its newly expanded form, the longest part of the *Life* concerns Constantina's efforts to educate Attica and Artemia about the truth of Christianity and the value of virginity. The dialogues in which this takes place are introduced by Constantina's own prayer to God that her efforts to convert the girls be successful, a kind of dialogue between herself and God, in which God's response is shown in the success of her project.[37] The girls themselves engage in an epistolary dialogue with their aunt, Octavia, who, like Helia's mother, is Christian, but thinks that they ought to be married. In support of her position, Octavia adduces the Old Testament examples of Abraham and Sarah, Isaac and Rebecca and the other patriarchs, as Helia's mother had done.[38]

Constantina then plays host to a full-fledged three-day symposium with all the virgins who live with her, 'not just noble but wise', on the nature of the highest good and the ultimate evil for humankind.[39] Constantina asks the virgins to write a few sentences on what each believes to be the highest good and ultimate evil, and she then addresses each woman's argument in turn. The first virgin suggests the highest good is the law that teaches us to do what profits us, while the ultimate evil is the one who does not wish us to know that law. The second says that life is the highest good and death is the ultimate evil; another says the highest good is a clear conscience and the ultimate evil is guilt; a fourth opposes peace and war, and so on. Constantina responds to each one, every time turning their arguments around to argue that the highest good is virginity and the ultimate evil is concupiscence.

Her symposium is not notable for its philosophical acuity, but the author's decision to present arguments in favour of virginity using the device of a formal debate, which the text calls a *convivium* and *colloquium*, is a strikingly unusual choice in this time and place (i.e., in Spain any time between the Visigothic period and the early tenth century, when the text appears in its earliest manuscript). Its closest parallel is Methodius's late third-century *Symposium* in Greek, which features ten women who compete to offer speeches in praise of virginity.[40] In Methodius's work, we only hear the words of the women as

[37] Ibid., fols 112^{r}–^{v}.

[38] Ibid., fol. 112^{r}; Burrus and Conti, *Life of Helia*, 110–15.

[39] El Escorial, MS a.I.13, fol. 113^{v}.

[40] Methodius of Olympus, *The Symposium: A Treatise on Chastity*, ACW 27 (Westminster, MD, 1958), 38–162; Jason P. König, 'Sympotic Dialogue in the First

mediated through the conversation of the two female figures Euboulion and Gregorion, avatars of Methodius and his female patron.[41] However, as in the dialogue of the virgin above, there is no intermediary reporting the symposium in the *Life of Constantina*, so that the reader is the immediate audience for the debate. Constantina's symposium is so similar in form, yet so completely different in content to Methodius's, that it is tempting to speculate that the author of the former knew about the latter but was perhaps unable to read its Greek.

The narrator of the dialogues that form the symposium repeatedly stresses its mood of affability and openness. In El Escorial, MS a.I.13, the *Life of Constantina* is immediately preceded by a short passage from Gregory the Great's *Pastoral Rule*, which foreshadows the emphasis of the narrator of the *Life* on friendly dialogue as a means of instruction:

> It means this, when the Lord speaks to Moses, saying: 'If a man go in all innocence with his friend into the forest to chop wood, and the wood of the axe fly from his hand, or the iron slip from the handle and strike his friend and slay him, let him flee to one of the aforesaid cities and live; lest by chance the next of kin to him whose blood has been shed, goaded by grief, pursue him, and overtake him and strike him, killing him' (Deut. 19: 5–6). For indeed we go with a friend into the wood as often as we turn ourselves towards looking into the delinquencies of subordinates. And we chop wood in all innocence, when with pious intention we cut off the vices of delinquents. But the axe flies from the hand when rebuke is drawn on to asperity more than is necessary. And the iron leaps from the handle, when out of reproof issues speech too hard. But he who, chopping, kills his friend, must needs fly to three cities, that in one of them he may live; since if someone turns to penance, he is hidden under hope, faith and charity in sacramental unity, and he is not held guilty of the homicide he committed. And the next of kin to the slain man will not kill him when he finds him because, when the strict Judge comes, who has joined himself to us by sharing in our nature, he without doubt does not require the penalty of his fault

to Fifth Centuries CE', in Simon Goldhill, ed., *The End of Dialogue in Antiquity* (Cambridge, 2008), 85–113, at 85, 102–6.

[41] Methodius, *Symposium*, 184 n. 3.

> from him whom faith, hope and charity hide under the shelter of his pardon.[42]

This lesson in the powers of peaceable dialogue and the dangers of 'immoderate reproof' harmonizes with the irenic course of Constantina's symposium. Both the symposium and the passage from Gregory focus responsibility for the success or failure of a dialogue with the master (or mistress) who initiates and guides it. The placement of this passage in the manuscript serves to emphasize the pedagogical aims and intent of the saints' lives that follow it.

The disposition towards friendly debate provides a sharp contrast, however, to the violence and acrimony of Helia's *Life*. This pushes us to consider another dialogue experienced by the audience of these texts: that of the different texts with each other. The reader must adjudicate, not only between different sides in a debate, but also between modes of debating. These texts likewise exist alongside the entire world of texts, spoken and read, that would be familiar to a woman vowed to religious life and dedicated to liturgical observance. We should think of these texts being read as part of a regime of spiritual exercises within the context of the dramatic and embodied performance of monastic liturgy.

My reading of these texts and the dialogues in them assumes the existence of a notion of a self in the Middle Ages, and of a reader who is self-conscious and can engage in inner dialogue in relationship to a text, who can be transformed through contemplation of a text.

[42] 'Illut autem quid significat quod dominus ad Moysen loquitur dicens: *Si quis abierit cum amico suo simpliciter ad silbam ad ligna cedenda et lignum securis in manu fuerit, ferrumque lapsum de manubrio amicum eius percusserit et occiderit, hic ad unum supradictum urbem fugiat et uibat ne forte proximus cuius effusus est sanguis, doloris stimulo, persequatur et adpreendat eum et occidat anima eius.* (Deut. 19: 5) Ad silbum quippe cum amico imus, cotiens ad intuenta subditorum delicta conuertimur. Et ligna simpliciter cedimus cum delinquentium uitia pia intemtione resecamus. Set securis manum fugit quam sese correptio plus quam ne[ce]sse est in asperitatem protrayt; ferrumque lapsum de manubrio prosilit, cum de correptione sermo durior exit. Et amicum eius percutiens occidit qui auditorem suum prolata contumelia ab spiritu dilectionis interficit. Set his que amicum suum percutiens occidit, ad tres necesse est ut urbes confugiat ut sub una earum uiuat quia, si quis ad penitentiam conuersus in unitate sacramenti sub spe fide et caritate absconditur, reus perpetrati omicidii non tenetur. Quem extincti proximus cum inuenerit non occidet quia, cum districtus iudex aduenerit qui sese nobis per natura consortium iunxit, ab eo procul dubio culpe reatum non expetit, que sub eius ueniam, spes, fides, et caritas abscondit': El Escorial, MS a.I.13, fol. 109^{v}; Gregory the Great, *Pastoral Rule* 2.10 (SC 381–2, 2: 250, 252).

Augustine crystallized these notions for medieval readers, but they have a long pre- and post-history; among others, the Desert Fathers and their monastic successors connected transformation of the self with disciplined life and meditative reading.[43] It is in that light that the works discussed in this article are especially interesting. We can posit a reading or hearing self who is transformed when she encounters Gregory and Peter speaking to each other in the closed circuit of Gregory's *Dialogues*, or any other text in which speakers turn towards each other and the reader reads or hears read their speech to each other from the outside, as a witness or, better, an audience. We can posit it, and we are right to do so. But the hagiographical texts discussed are of special interest because at the same time as their characters speak to each other, the texts in various ways break the fourth wall, so to speak, between actors and audience. The transformation of the audience or readers is not concealed beyond or outside the text; it is invited on stage.

How does this happen? Enormous work is done in the texts by the use of, and shifts in, point of view or perspective. If you want to tell a story, you need plot, characters, setting and story. If you want to tell a story to someone, the point of view you choose is critical, because it creates the relationship with the story's audience. Gregory's *Dialogues* would not provide the same experience for the reader if Gregory had told us about Benedict and the other saints as, for example, an omniscient or absent third-person narrator, or in the form of a first-person memoir in the voice of the saints. It is what it is because of the 'I' and 'you' of the dialogue between Gregory and Peter. The fact that teachings about astronomy in the *Dialogue against the Jews* are put in the mouth of the Christian Petrus, rather than the Jew Moses, changes how the reader is supposed to view this science. And it is in the way the hagiographical texts layer and embed dialogue, and shift point of view, that they show the most creativity. We find in them multiple layers of dialogue, including between two characters in the text; between the scriptural account of the past, the now of the text and the now of the reader; between the lived life of the audience and

[43] Brian Stock, *Augustine the Reader: Meditation, Self-Knowledge, and the Ethics of Interpretation* (Cambridge, MA, 1996), 1–3, 14–18; John Dagenais, *The Ethics of Reading in Manuscript Culture: Glossing the* Libro de Buen Amor (Princeton, NJ, 1994), xvii, 6–8, 15–16, 21; Mary Carruthers, *The Craft of Thought* (Cambridge, 1998), 3–5, 107–12.

the model in the text; and between the self of the reader and the desired, idealized or transcendent self. The characters speak to each other, the narrator speaks to us, and at times we read along with the first-person 'I' of the saint. The characters describe earlier dialogues to each other. The characters speak through written letters, and in formal disputation with an audience inside and outside the text.

The stakes of this reading work were high for the readers of these hagiographical dialogues. They sought to address the problem of what kind of Christian the reader was going be and to help the reader answer such questions as the best way of being a Christian. The Christian readers of these texts thought of themselves as engaged in an ongoing process of conversion, and these texts were self-consciously part of that process. A Christian life involved the development of discernment, but how could one learn to discern as a Christian before one was capable of discernment? This was a paradox of being and becoming that reading the right kinds of texts and meditating on them was meant to overcome.[44]

These texts are also of special interest because they are both about and directed towards women, inviting women through dramatic dialogue to embody the lessons of the texts in their own practice. It may be no accident that these texts that stage themselves so creatively have both female performers and audience. There may be a special affinity and interest of women religious for modes of devotion and transformation that involved drama; in particular women religious seem to have been concerned not just with dialogue as text but dialogue specifically as drama.[45] We see this in particular in contemporary Ottonian Germany. The dialogue of the nuns and Agius on the death of Hathumoda of Gandersheim is an early example.[46] More famous, from the same monastery, are the plays of Hrotsvit of Gandersheim, which form the second part of her collected writings in the only manuscript to transmit them. The first part consists of

[44] On Augustine and the stages of transformation through reading, see Stock, *Augustine the Reader*, 199–200.

[45] The topic of nuns and drama needs further attention, but see, for example, Katie Normington, *Medieval English Drama* (Cambridge, 2009), 26–31; Elissa B. Weaver, *Convent Theatre in Early Modern Italy* (Cambridge, 2002), 49–95; and the work of the Medieval Convent Drama Project at the University of Fribourg, online at: <http://medievalconventdrama.org>.

[46] Agius of Corvey, *Dialogus* (MGH Poetae 3, 369–88).

poems, the last of which relates the passion of Agnes, although it omits the role played by Constantina in promoting her cult.[47] The first of the plays is about Gallicanus, and Constantina (here called Constantia) plays a role in the conversion of her would-be suitor, although this play does not include the epistolary debate of his daughters with their aunt or the extended symposium.[48] It is significant that Hrotsvit, like the hagiographer who wrote the *Life of Constantina* copied in the Spanish manuscripts, found dramatic inspiration in the story of Gallicanus, Constantina, John and Paul. Moreover, there is an additional suggestive parallel between Hrotsvit's writing and the women religious of Christian Spain. Hrotsvit's poem about St Pelagius concerns the titular saint of the Leonese royal female monastery, founded in the tenth century.[49]

The editors of the *Life of Helia* suggest that it may be situated in a context of fourth-century Iberian Priscillianist asceticism.[50] Questions of the provenance of this particular text cannot be answered, however, without considering *Helia* in the context of the other lives with which it is transmitted in this corpus of manuscripts. Moreover, such questions of origins may in the end prove to be no more interesting than understanding how all of these texts were used in dialogue with each other. The reader must sort through the differences between them, such as the way the antagonistic dialogues in the *Life of Helia* contrast with the irenic debate in *Life of Constantina*, and the admonition in the passage from Gregory's *Pastoral Rule* that masters should be careful when they instruct. We need to consider not only when these texts were written and (as far as we can know) by whom, but also who collected them together and what governed their choices of what to include and exclude. We have a corpus of lives that dates in its origins to Late Antiquity,[51] but which was added to and modified between the sixth and tenth centuries, then

[47] Hrotsvit, *Agnes*, in *Opera Omnia*, ed. Walter Bershin (Munich, 2001), 114–30.
[48] Hrotsvit, *Gallicanus*, in *Opera Omnia*, ed. Bershin, 136–63. Jane Chance, *Literary Subversions of Medieval Women* (New York, 2007), 23–8, argues that Hrotsvit may have known of the stories of Agnes and Constantina either directly or indirectly through Ælfric's Old English *Lives of the Saints*, but because of their relative dates and because Ælfric's work was in Old English, if Hrotsvit had an Anglo-Saxon inspiration it was more likely to have been Aldhelm, *De virginitate*.
[49] Hrotsvit, *Pelagius*, in *Opera Omnia*, ed. Bershin, 63–77.
[50] Burrus and Conti, *Life of Helia*, 15–28.
[51] Salisbury, *Independent Virgins*, 129–30.

copied and recopied. We need to ask who copied the collection, and for whom. What was the history of the manuscript copies we have, who might have read them, and how were they used in the monastic communities that produced them?

Even at this early stage of research, however, it is possible to make some preliminary observations. The authors of these texts showed a striking creativity and originality in their use of dialogue within the genre of hagiography. The goals of these dialogues were both exegetical and pedagogical. Finally, in all three of the texts I have concentrated on here, the dialogues do not merely exist within the frame of the saint's life. Dialogue slips the bonds of the text, to engage the one who reads or hears the text read and by so doing to transform its audience.

'Instructing readers' minds in heavenly matters': Carolingian History Writing and Christian Education

Robert A. H. Evans*
University of Cambridge

This article explores the ways in which histories were used in the moral and doctrinal education of Christian elites in the West from the late Roman to the Carolingian periods. In the sixth century, Cassiodorus wrote that histories, whether Christian or not, were useful for 'instructing the minds of readers in heavenly matters'. How far was this characteristic of the period? Traditionally, scholars have emphasized either the apologetic purpose or the moral of specific histories, such as Orosius's Historiae *or Bede's* Historia Ecclesiastica. *Few modern scholars, however, have examined the long-term development of history writing as a vehicle for Christian education during the transformation of the Roman world. Those who have done, such as Karl-Ferdinand Werner and Hans-Werner Goetz, have emphasized continuity rather than change. The article sketches some of the changes and continuities across the period. In particular, it demonstrates that there was a shift from the apologetic concerns of the fifth-century historians, writing to educate Christians from pagan backgrounds, to the doctrinal (as much as moral) concerns of Frankish historians, emerging from the Carolingian Renaissance.*

The empire of Charlemagne and his successors in the late eighth and ninth centuries witnessed two highly significant and related cultural developments. Both had a lasting impact on the culture of western Europe. The first, and broader of the two, was a revival of Christian education, which was directly encouraged by the Carolingian rulers.[1] In a famous letter to Baugulf, abbot of Fulda,

* 9 Amhurst Court, Grange Rd, Cambridge, CB3 9BH. E-mail: rae32@cam.ac.uk. I wish to thank the audience at the Ecclesiastical History Society's Winter Meeting in January 2017 for their helpful observations, my supervisor Rosamond McKitterick for her feedback on early drafts of this article, and the anonymous peer reviewers for their stimulating comments. Any mistakes remain, of course, my own.

[1] Rosamond McKitterick, *The Frankish Church and the Carolingian Reforms, 789–895* (London, 1977); John J. Contreni, *Carolingian Learning, Masters and Manuscripts* (Aldershot, 1992); Giles Brown, 'Introduction: The Carolingian Renaissance', in

Studies in Church History 55 (2019), 56–71
doi: 10.1017/stc.2018.14

Charlemagne wrote that 'everyone ought to learn', so that 'the mind might understand what ought to be done' and the 'tongue might charge ahead in praises to Almighty God'.[2] Fulda, to take the example of Baugulf's own monastery, could boast a rapidly expanding library with the resources of which its pupils were trained.[3] It would be here that many great Carolingian theologians were educated, including Hrabanus Maurus, Lupus of Ferrières and the controversial Gottschalk of Orbais.

The second, a more specific but related development, was an explosion in the preservation of older histories and the writing of new ones.[4] Even in Baugulf's time, his monastery possessed a copy of Eusebius-Jerome's chronicle,[5] and it later acquired extremely rare copies of certain Roman histories.[6] During the ninth century, the monastery also produced the *Annals of Fulda*, which were an outstanding example of the Carolingian enthusiasm for narrating their own recent past.[7] These annals were just one example of the many historical narratives being written and read in the Carolingian empire. This article considers the relationship between these two developments, by asking how these histories might have served Christian educational purposes.

Although these histories were often (although not exclusively) written in an ecclesiastical context, their narratives had much wider relevance. Annals such as those of Fulda, for example, recounted

Rosamond McKitterick, ed., *Carolingian Culture: Emulation and Innovation* (Cambridge, 1994), 1–51.

2 '[D]ebet ergo quisque discere … quid agere debeat intelligat anima, quanto in omnipotentis Dei laudibus…cucurrerit lingua': MGH Capit. 1, 79 (*Epistola de litteris colendis*). All translations are my own except where noted otherwise.

3 Rosamond McKitterick, *The Carolingians and the Written Word* (Cambridge, 1989), 169–70.

4 Yitzhak Hen and Matthew Innes, eds, *The Uses of the Past in the Early Middle Ages* (Cambridge, 2000); Rosamond McKitterick, *History and Memory in the Carolingian World* (Cambridge, 2004); Helmut Reimitz, *History, Frankish Identity, and the Framing of Western Ethnicity 550–850* (Cambridge, 2015); Clemens Gantner, Rosamond McKitterick and Sven Meeder, eds, *The Resources of the Past in Early Medieval Europe* (Cambridge, 2015).

5 McKitterick, *Written Word*, 170.

6 Timothy Reuter, *The* Annals of Fulda*: Ninth Century Histories 2*, Manchester Medieval Sources (Manchester, 1992), 5; Gavin Kelly and Justin Stover, 'The *Hersefeldensis* and the *Fuldensis* of Ammianus Marcellinus: A Reconsideration', *Cambridge Classical Journal* 62 (2016), 108–29.

7 *Annales Fuldenses* (hereafter: *AF*; MGH SRG i.u.s. 7).

the military and political experiences of the wider Carolingian elites.[8] They reflected how boundaries between monastic and lay worlds were far more porous than earlier scholarship recognized.[9] For instance, Fulda's abbots sometimes led Frankish armies into battle alongside lay aristocrats and had close connections to the royal court.[10] Moreover, the extent to which the Carolingian lay elite was both literate and interested in improving itself has been substantially and positively re-evaluated in recent years.[11] As Mayke de Jong has put it, 'this was not an elite in which military men proudly left the business of letters to women and priests'.[12] Despite the very limited evidence of how histories were read by contemporaries, it is necessary to consider how far these works sought to shape and inform attitudes and behaviour.

It will be argued in what follows that Carolingian historians were especially invested in shaping their readers' attitudes to God's agency, and so represent an educational enterprise. The significance of divine agency in early medieval historiography is being recognized increasingly. Sarah Foot has argued that such histories 'essentially recorded the workings of God's will on earth'.[13] Matthew Innes sees early medieval views of history as 'a confusing mass of events which could only be understood in terms of divine agency'.[14] Nonetheless, the versatility and purpose of God's agency in historical narrative remains understudied. As Andrew Marsham notes, there was a 'spectrum of perspectives' on how to integrate religion into

[8] Reuter, *Fulda*, 8; Matthew Innes and Rosamond McKitterick, 'The Writing of History', in eadem, ed., *Carolingian Culture*, 193–220, at 201.

[9] Matthew Innes, 'Memory, Orality and Literacy in an Early Medieval Society', *P&P* 158 (1998), 3–36.

[10] For example, Sigihart of Fulda: *AF*, 76 (*s.a.* 872).

[11] McKitterick, *Written Word*, 210–70; Mayke de Jong, 'The Empire as *ecclesia*: Hrabanus Maurus and *biblical historia* for Rulers', in Hen and Innes, eds, *Uses of the Past*, 191–226; Patrick Wormald and Janet L. Nelson, eds, *Lay Intellectuals in the Carolingian World* (Cambridge, 2007); Rachel Stone, *Morality and Masculinity in the Carolingian Empire* (Cambridge, 2011); W. C. Brown et al., eds, *Documentary Culture and the Laity in the Early Middle Ages* (Cambridge, 2013).

[12] Mayke de Jong, 'Carolingian Political Discourse and the Biblical Past: Hraban, Dhuoda, Radbert', in Gantner, McKitterick and Meeder, eds, *Resources of the Past*, 87–102, at 89.

[13] Sarah Foot, 'Annals and Chronicles in Western Europe', in eadem and Chase Robinson, eds, *The Oxford History of Historical Writing*, 2: *400–1400* (Oxford, 2012), 346–67, at 364.

[14] Innes, 'Memory, Orality and Literacy', 13.

medieval historiography.[15] This article captures some shades of that spectrum in the specific context of Carolingian education.

We begin not with the histories themselves but with the educational handbooks which Carolingian historians were reading. This will highlight the place and purpose of historiography in Carolingian education. We shall then consider how the Carolingians adapted the histories which these handbooks recommended to their own context, in a way which shows both continuity and sensitivity to changing educational challenges. The remainder of the article discusses two case studies from Carolingian historical narratives and what these might have taught their readers, whether clerical or lay, about discharging their military and political duties.

Educational Handbooks and Carolingian Education

Where did historiography sit in Carolingian education? Early medieval writers say frustratingly little about history's place in the educational curriculum. The Latin word *historia* did not denote a clearly defined genre or educational subject.[16] Historians and historiography had, however, appeared in various works from which the Carolingians obtained their ideas about education, and these educational handbooks, composed in Late Antiquity, exerted an enormous influence on Carolingian patterns of reading and book collection.[17]

Jerome and his continuator, Gennadius of Marseilles, for example, mention several historians in their bibliographical guide to Christian literature, *On Famous Men*, which shows that histories were seen as important alongside exegetical and doctrinal works.[18] Jerome wrote that Hegesippus, whose works are now lost, 'gathered many things *useful* to the reader'.[19] The reason for this utility, however, is rarely mentioned.

[15] Andrew Marsham, 'Universal Histories', in Foot and Robinson, eds, *Oxford History of Historical Writing* 2, 431–45, at 441.

[16] Deborah M. Deliyannis, 'Introduction', in eadem, ed., *Historiography in the Middle Ages* (Leiden, 2003), 1–12.

[17] McKitterick, *Written Word*, 165–210.

[18] Jerome, *De viris illustribus* (ed. W. Herding, *Hieronymus,* Liber de viris inlustribus. *Gennadius,* De viris inlustribus [Leipzig, 1924]). For Carolingian interest in *De viris*, see McKitterick, *Written Word*, 201.

[19] '[M]ultaque ad utilitatem legentium pertinentia hinc inde congregans': Jerome, *De viris* 22 (Herding, ed., *Hieronymus*, 24; italics in translations mine). For the reception of Hegesippus, see Richard Pollard, 'The *De Excidio* of "Hegesippus" and the Reception of Josephus in the Early Middle Ages', *Viator* 46 (2015), 65–100.

Jerome simply listed the titles of Eusebius and his own chronicle, rather than explaining why they were worth reading.[20] Gennadius did the same for Rufinus and Orosius.[21] Hegesippus and Orosius, nonetheless, were seen as useful against paganism. For Jerome, Hegesippus wrote one history 'arguing against idols … he showed the error from which they had first grown'.[22] For Gennadius, Orosius wrote 'against the enemies of Christians'.[23] As the Carolingians read and copied these texts, they would have learned that history had educational value because of its support for arguments against paganism.

In addition to Jerome and Gennadius, the Carolingians also derived ideas about education from Isidore of Seville's *Etymologies*, written in seventh-century Spain.[24] Isidore treated history as part of grammar, a subject which he introduced as being about learning (*disciplina*).[25] Isidore's book on grammar concluded with a discussion of history, in which he wrote that 'history of peoples' was 'no impediment to those who wish to read useful works'.[26] Indeed, histories were written 'for the instruction of the living'.[27] Like Jerome and Gennadius, Isidore only alluded to history's educational utility. He was more interested in the rules of historiography, such as its chronological scope and the need for witnesses, than why it was useful. Although its place in Isidore's discussion of grammar granted history a formal role in the Carolingian organization of knowledge, this role was small and undeveloped.

Alongside Jerome, Gennadius and Isidore, however, the Carolingians were also reading Cassiodorus's *Institutes of Secular and Divine Learning*, which significantly influenced medieval ideas about education.[28] Indeed, several of the great monastic libraries of

[20] Jerome, *De viris* 22, 81 (Herding, ed., *Hieronymus*, 24, 50–1).

[21] Gennadius, *De viris* 17, 40 (Herding, ed., *Hieronymus*, 78–9, 88–9).

[22] '[A]dversum idola disputans, quo primum errore crevissent … ex qua ostendit': Jerome, *De viris* 22 (Herding, ed., *Hieronymus*, 24).

[23] '[A]dversus querulos Christiani nominis': Gennadius, *De viris* 40 (Herding, ed., *Hieronymus*, 88).

[24] Isidore, *Etymologiae* 1.41–4 (*Etymologiarum siue Originum libri XX*, ed. W. M. Lindsay, vol. 1, Oxford Classical Texts [Oxford, 1911]; this volume is unpaginated); cf. McKitterick, *Written Word*, 201; Deliyannis, 'Introduction', 3–4.

[25] '[D]isciplina a discendo nomen accepit': Isidore, *Etymologiae* 1.1.

[26] 'Historiae gentium non inpediunt legentibus in his quae utilia dixerunt': ibid. 1.43.

[27] '[A]d institutionem praesentium': ibid.

[28] Cassiodorus, *Institutiones* (*Cassiodorus senatoris Institutiones*, ed. R. A. B. Mynors [Oxford, 1937]); cf. Matthew Innes and Rosamond McKitterick, 'The Writing of History', in Rosamond McKitterick, ed., *Carolingian Culture: Emulation and Innovation* (Cambridge, 1994), 193–220, at 193.

the Carolingian period were in part gathered and organized according to Cassiodorus's recommendations.[29] The *Institutes* provided a comprehensive guide to what literary Christians needed to read and supplied a series of bibliographical essays on every aspect of Christian learning, including exegesis, rhetoric, medicine, geometry, astronomy, music and history.

The *Institutes*' first sixteen chapters concern the reading of Scripture, together with recommendations of what to read from the Fathers.[30] For Cassiodorus and his Carolingian successors, Scripture was the indisputable basis of Christian education.[31] The seventeenth chapter, however, at the head of the section dealing with extra-biblical Christian learning, considers historiography. This was a highly privileged position within the text as a whole and Cassiodorus's subsequent comments made clear that this was not accidental: 'Christian studies … also have the relators of times … who, since they relate ecclesiastical matters and describe the changing happenings through different times, always instruct readers' senses in heavenly matters.'[32] Having the Bible was not enough for serious Christian students; histories were also necessary. The reference to enlightenment in 'heavenly matters' further suggests that historiography was educationally foundational for the Christian because of its moral and spiritual significance.

For Cassiodorus, however, this heavenly instruction depended on a specific feature of Christian historical narrative. He explained that 'these historians strive to ascribe nothing to fortuitous causes, nothing to the gods' infirm power, as the Gentiles did, but ascribe everything truly to the Creator's will'.[33] Histories taught Christian students that events happened because God willed them, as opposed to pagan attributions of power to the gods or to fortune. This was similar to the commendations of Hegesippus and Orosius found in Jerome-Gennadius, but located the value of historical narrative specifically in what it taught readers about God, and about God's agency in history.

[29] McKitterick, *Written Word*, 194.

[30] Cassiodorus, *Institutiones* 1.1–16 (ed. Mynors, 2–55).

[31] For Carolingian attitudes to Scripture, see de Jong, 'Empire as *ecclesia*'.

[32] '[H]abent etiam … relatores temporum et studia Christiana … qui cum res ecclesiasticas referant, et vicissitudines accidentes per tempora diversa describant, ut sensus legentium rebus caelestibus semper erudiant': Cassiodorus, *Institutiones* 1.17.1 (ed. Mynors, 55).

[33] '[Q]uando nihil ad fortuitos casus, nihil ad deorum potestates infirmas, ut gentiles fecerunt, sed arbitrio Creatoris applicare veraciter universa contendunt': ibid.

Adapting Orosius's *Seven Books*

Carolingian readers had access to numerous earlier Christian narratives which depicted God's agency in history. Most of these, especially those recommended by Jerome, Gennadius and Cassiodorus, were written in contexts where paganism presented a serious cultural and educational threat. This is reflected in the anti-pagan note sounded by these educational handbooks (with the exception of Isidore). Although the Carolingians had to contend with Vikings and Slavs, these groups were never depicted as a cultural threat in the way that late antique paganism had been. How did the Carolingians' educational view of history adapt to this change in context?

There is insufficient space to consider the Carolingian reception of divine agency from earlier histories, such as those of Gregory of Tours and Bede. I shall focus instead on the specific example of Orosius's *Seven Books of History against the Pagans*,[34] which Cassiodorus and Gennadius had heartily recommended.[35] As Peter Van Nuffelen has argued convincingly, Orosius was engaged in a systematic assault on history's role in the pagan education system, while using the rhetorical techniques taught by that system to full effect.[36] The Romans were brought up to hunger for glory and power by reading the histories of Sallust, Livy and others.[37] Orosius used his history to deprogramme a Roman elite indoctrinated by this pagan system of education.[38] He did this in part by showing the horror of the pasts presented so attractively by earlier Roman historians, but also by showing the hand of the Christian God in the pagan past. A typical example concerned a miraculous hailstorm which saved Rome from Hannibal. Orosius demanded of his readers: 'Now let the despisers of the True God respond to me: whether Roman fortitude or divine mercy prevented Hannibal from capturing and ruining

[34] Ibid.

[35] Orosius, *Historiae* (*Orosius, historiarum adversum paganos libri VII accredit eiusdem liber apologeticus*, ed. Karl Zangemeister [Vienna, 1882]).

[36] Peter Van Nuffelen, *Orosius and the Rhetoric of History* (Oxford, 2012), 186–207; although see the recent response by Hans-Werner Goetz, 'Orosius und seine "Sieben Geschichtsbücher gegen die Heiden". Geschichtstheologie oder Rhetorik?', *Archiv für Kulturgeschichte* 96 (2014), 187–98.

[37] Van Nuffelen, *Orosius*, 68–9.

[38] Ibid. 17–18.

Rome?'[39] Orosius's purpose in mentioning God's agency supported Cassiodorus's juxtaposition of 'Gentile' and Christian understandings of history. This approach was educational in that it sought to re-educate audiences who were used to thinking in non-Christian terms about history and human experience.

How was Orosius useful to Christian audiences in the Carolingian empire which did not face such pagan threats? An intriguing manuscript from Tours, which contains an epitome of the *Seven Books*, offers some clues.[40] The scribe removed Orosius's asides to his imagined pagan audiences, such as that concerning Hannibal. The scribe nonetheless continued to ascribe certain important events to God's agency. The emperor Theodosius, for example, was described as reforming the Roman empire 'with God supporting him'.[41] The Roman general Mascezel was described as learning from Theodosius's example when he landed an army in Caprari. The scribe wrote, closely following Orosius, that Mascezel, 'knowing from Theodosius how much the prayer of man through faith in Christ might obtain from God's mercy', prayed for and 'merited' a bloodless victory over his enemies.[42] This showed how a particular character within the narratives learned about the personal implications of God's agency. History was still important to the extent that it educated its readers in responding correctly to God's agency, as Mascezel had. This lesson was clearly seen as relevant to this scribe's audience in a way that attacks on pagan understandings of history were not.

Learning from Carolingian Annals

The remainder of this article considers how two Carolingian historians taught their readers about the relevance and implications of God's

[39] '[R]espondeant nunc mihi obtrectatores ueri Dei hoc loco: Hannibalem a capessenda subruendaque Roma utrum Romana abstinuit fotitudo an diuina miseratio': Orosius, *Historiae* 4.17.8 (*Orosius*, ed. Zangemeister, 252–3).

[40] Leiden, Universiteitsbibliotheek, VLQ MS 20. I have discussed this manuscript elsewhere, with Rosamond McKitterick, in 'A Carolingian Epitome of Orosius from Tours: Leiden VLQ 20', in Helmut Reimitz, Rutger Kramer and Graeme Ward, eds, *Historiographies of Identity*, 4: *Historiography and Identity towards the End of the First Millennium, a Comparative Perspective* (Vienna, forthcoming).

[41] '[D]eo sibi adminiculante': VLQ MS 20, fol. 139^v; cf. Orosius, *Historiae* 7.35.23.

[42] '[M]asezel iam inde ad theodosium sciens quantum in rebus desperatissimis oratio hominis per fidem Christi a clementia dei impetraret … uictoriam meruit': VLQ MS 20, fol. 139^v; cf. Orosius, *Historiae* 7.36.5.

agency for their own contexts. These texts were written by and for Christians, but this did not make their authors any less concerned to train and educate their audiences in a Christian worldview, which ascribed events purely to God's agency.

Divine agency, as the example of Orosius shows, was not a new element in Christian historiography. It had also played an important role (albeit with different emphases) in the histories produced by Gregory of Tours and Bede, which were also available to the Carolingians.[43] My intention here is to demonstrate how Carolingian historians carefully constructed their own narratives to press the practical implications of God's agency upon their ninth-century readers, both lay and clerical. Many of these examples are military, and the relationship between religion and war has been widely discussed in modern scholarship.[44] I am more concerned to explore how Carolingian historians brought a broader theological belief – that God governed history – to bear on the specific challenges facing their audiences, which often included military conflict.

The Annals of Metz

The *Annals of Metz*, in their earliest redaction, recounted Frankish history from 678 to 805, and were probably completed around 806.[45] Their authorship and purpose have attracted considerable discussion in recent years, with some suggesting the authorship of Abbess Gisela, sister of Charlemagne, at Chelles, and others defending anonymous authorship at Metz.[46] Whatever the case, the work seems to have been written to defend Charlemagne's succession

[43] For Gregory, see Reimitz, *History, Identity, Ethnicity*, 27–125, with discussion of Christianity at 65–70; for Bede, see N. J. Higham, *(Re-)reading Bede: The* Ecclesiastical History *in Context* (London, 2006), especially 148–67.

[44] For summary of recent scholarship, see Robert A. H. Evans, 'Christian Hermeneutics and Narratives of War in the Carolingian Empire', *Transformation: A Holistic Journal of Mission Studies* 34 (2017), 150–63, at 152–4.

[45] *Annales Mettenses Priores* (hereafter: *AMP*; MGH SRG i.u.s. 10); Paul Fouracre and Richard Gerberding, *Late Merovingian France: History and Hagiography 640–720* (Manchester, 1996), 330–49; Yitzhak Hen, 'The *Annals of Metz* and the Merovingian Past', in idem and Innes, eds, *Uses of the Past*, 175–90; idem, 'Canvassing for Charles: The *Annals of Metz* in Late Carolingian Francia', in Richard Corradini, ed., *Zwischen Niederschrift und Wiederschrift. Hagiographie und Historiographie im Spannungsfeld von Kompendienüberlieferung und Editionstechnik* (Vienna, 2010), 139–46.

[46] For a summary of the debate, see Hen, '*Annals of Metz*', 176–7.

plan of 806, and to support the primacy of Charles the Younger (d. 811) among the ageing emperor's sons. It might well have been written to educate Charles about the realities of kingship and military command.[47]

The *Annals of Metz* ascribe numerous events in the narrative to God's will. The hero of the early part of the narrative was Pippin II (d. 714), Charlemagne's great-grandfather, who achieved de facto rule of the Frankish world in the late seventh century. Pippin defeats his various enemies 'with the Lord cooperating',[48] and governs the Franks 'with Christ granting it'.[49] The author, therefore, consistently teaches her (or his) readers to view the history of Carolingian success as dependent on God. This was something which this annalist appears to have learned from other Carolingian historians. The *Annals of Metz* also incorporates an earlier narrative known as the *Royal Frankish Annals*, which was written around 790x800 and cover Frankish history from 741 to its present.[50] The *Royal Frankish Annals* had also framed recent history with consistent reference to God's agency.[51] The author of the *Annals of Metz* took this language and projected it onto the earlier past of the late seventh century, which suggests that the annalist learned from the earlier work how to write God into her narrative.

It is especially significant that the *Annals of Metz* describes the young Pippin being taught about divine agency in his education.[52] His saintly aunt Begga, for example, instructed Pippin that 'in his coming rule, he should keep himself, with the Lord helping, among his teenage lessons'.[53] Begga herself is described as educating him 'with the Lord providing'.[54] His aunt Gertrude also taught Pippin 'heavenly discipline', while 'filled with God's grace'.[55]

[47] Janet Nelson, 'Gender and Genre in Women Historians of the Early Middle Ages', in J.-P. Genet, ed., *L'Historiographie médiévale en Europe* (Paris, 1991), 149–63, at 159.

[48] 'Domino cooperante': *AMP*, *s.a.* 688 (MGH SRG i.u.s. 10, 5).

[49] 'Christo largiente': *AMP*, *s.a.* 691 (MGH SRG i.u.s. 10, 13).

[50] *Annales Regni Francorum* (hereafter: *AMP*; MGH SRG 6); see Reimitz, *History, Identity, and Ethnicity*, 335–45, for the most recent discussion.

[51] Evans, 'Christian Hermeneutics', 154–5.

[52] For the role of women in Carolingian education, see Janet Nelson, 'Les Femmes et l'évangélisation au IXe siècle', *Revue du Nord* 68 (1986), 471–86.

[53] '[U]t sese regno futuro inter adolescentiae erudimenta … Domino adiuvante servaret': *AMP*, *s.a.* 678 (MGH SRG i.u.s. 10, 3).

[54] '[P]restante Domino': *AMP*, *s.a.* 688 (MGH SRG i.u.s. 10, 2).

[55] '[G]ratia Dei repleta caelesti disciplinae': ibid. (MGH SRG i.u.s. 10, 4).

Pippin, 'gifted with divine grace, went beyond all his relatives' salutary admonitions'.[56] This shows the importance of divine agency in education itself, but is also significant if these annals were indeed written by an abbess in order to educate a Carolingian prince. Begga and Gertrude may be representing Gisela's perception of her own role in teaching Charles the Younger. If this was the case, these passages suggest that the writing and reading of the *Annals of Metz* were themselves seen as acts willed by God for the education of Christians.

The narrative depicts Pippin putting his teenage lessons into practice on various occasions. The most significant and well-constructed episode concerns the battle of Tertry in 687, traditionally seen as the starting point of Carolingian supremacy.[57] The *Annals of Metz* does not simply ascribe Pippin's triumph to God. Instead, it presents the respective combatants as examples of good and bad responses to divine agency. The annalist compared Pippin to Theuderic III (d. 691), ruler of the Frankish kingdom of Neustria and opponent of Pippin, who led the rival kingdom of Austrasia. Theuderic and Pippin approach the battle differently, 'with unequal plans'.[58] The reader is invited to consider the contrasting attitudes, either of which were possibilities for contemporary Carolingian commanders.

The annalist begins with Theuderic, the proud and oppressive king of Neustria. Theuderic 'boasted more in his multitude of innumerable people than in the counsel of prudence'.[59] The annalist uses language intended to denote pride, as in the description of Theuderic's forces as 'his multitude of innumerable people'. Theuderic tells his men that Pippin had sought peace because Pippin was terrified of the Neustrian king. Theuderic even believes that Pippin 'had been handed over to him'.[60] This use of the passive is significant. God could be the implied agent here, but it also makes Theuderic the centre of attention. The boast was itself groundless, because Theuderic was in fact trusting in his own strength.

[56] '[G]ratia divine preditus cunctas salubres suae genitricis ammonitiones ... preveniebat': ibid. (MGH SRG i.u.s. 10, 3).
[57] Fouracre and Gerberding, *Late Merovingian France*, 24.
[58] '[N]on paribus consiliis': *AMP*, *s.a.* 690 (MGH SRG i.u.s. 10, 10).
[59] '[I]n innumerabilis populi multitudine magis quam in consiliis prudentiae confidens ... gloriabatur': ibid.
[60] '[T]raditum sibi iam Pippinum': ibid.

Pippin, by contrast, describes himself as fighting 'for love of him who has the power to save *those hoping in him* [Ps. 16: 7]'.[61] As Begga and Gertrude had taught him, he defines himself in terms of his trust in God rather than his own strength. He also now teaches these lessons to his men, telling them 'to commend themselves with prayers and offerings … to the omnipotence of God, who gives honour and victory to *all fearing him and guarding his precepts* [Ps. 118: 36]'.[62] While the annalist could simply have ascribed Pippin's victory to God, she prefers to demonstrate the correct attitude to God's agency through the direct speech of her hero. The vocabulary of hoping in and fearing God, as opposed to boasting, emphasizes the importance of attitudes and beliefs as much as actions. It is no coincidence that Pippin's speech also describes God's faithfulness and power (using language from the Psalms), precisely those attributes which evoked this kind of trust.

Readers could easily have identified themselves with Pippin's army, especially if they were among the higher echelons of the Carolingian elite. Pippin's speech is as much a challenge to these readers as it was to the characters within the narrative. The annalist then uses the narrative to demonstrate the efficacy of such an attitude. Pippin attacked, 'superior in arms and counsel', and Theuderic was routed.[63] Pippin subsequently 'bestowed ample spoils to his followers', an important measure of his success, while also 'giving thanks to God'.[64] Throughout the text, the author uses the words and attitudes of Pippin and his men both to demonstrate God's agency and to show the proper human response.

The Annals of Fulda

The *Annals of Metz*'s demonstration of correct attitudes to God's agency can also be found in the *Annals of Fulda*, introduced above. These exist in several different versions, involving different authors and continuations from the 830s until the early tenth century, and between them

[61] '[Q]uod pro eius amore gerebat, *qui* potestatem habet *salvos facere sperantes in* se': ibid. (MGH SRG i.u.s. 10, 10–11).

[62] '[S]ese votis et orationibus Dei omnipotentiae … commendarent, qui dat honorem et victoriam *omnibus timentibus eum et custodientibus precepta* eius': ibid. (MGH SRG i.u.s. 10, 10).

[63] '[P]restantior consilio et armis': ibid. (MGH SRG i.u.s. 10, 11).

[64] '[S]polia ampla, Deo gratias referens, suis fidelibus impertitur': ibid. (MGH SRG i.u.s. 10, 12).

cover Frankish history from 714 until 901.[65] For most of their history, they were linked to the monastery of Fulda and the archbishopric of Mainz, with one other continuation being written in Bavaria.[66] Just as the *Annals of Metz* were deeply relevant to the concerns of the Carolingian elite in the early 800s, so the *Annals of Fulda* address the east Frankish elites of the late ninth century.[67]

As various scholars have argued, the entry for 869 was the work of a new author, who continued the narrative until 882.[68] This author was clearly passionate about God's agency, and took a very different approach from that of his predecessor. Up to this point, the annals had been remarkably reticent about ascribing events to God's will.[69] By contrast, the entry for 869 depicted God's agency in almost every episode. A rebel army, for example, was defeated 'with the Lord dealing out a worthy reward for [their] treachery', while King Louis the German (d. 876) lay ill but 'merited to be cured by the Heavenly Doctor' by distributing alms.[70] This pattern continued, albeit slightly less intensely, for the remainder of this author's section into the 880s. The different treatments of divine agency show how different historians, apparently all monks at Fulda, could write about God very differently. The later author wanted to teach his readers that God was active in their recent past.

This annalist's account of campaigning on the eastern border of Louis' kingdom in 869 shows that it was not simply the frequency of God's intervention that taught these lessons but the whole shape of the narrative. Whereas the *Annals of Metz* had contrasted the different attitudes of its characters to divine agency, the description of the Bohemian rebellion in the *Annals of Fulda* shows how the correct attitude had played out in recent events. The entry for 869 begins dramatically, with the annalist writing that 'constant' Bohemian raids 'infested' the frontier, the raiders burning settlements and taking

[65] Reuter, *Fulda*, 1–14; Simon MacLean, *Kingship and Politics in the Late Ninth Century: Charles the Fat and the End of the Carolingian Empire* (Cambridge, 2003), 23–47.
[66] MacLean, *Kingship and Politics*, 24–7.
[67] For the east Frankish kingdom, see Eric Goldberg, *Struggle for Empire: Kingship and Conflict under Louis the German, 817–876* (Ithaca, NY, 2006)
[68] Sigemund Hellmann, 'Die Entstehung und Überlieferung der Annales Fuldenses. I', *Neues Archiv* 33 (1908), 705–17; Reuter, *Fulda*, 8–9.
[69] For a few exceptions, see *AF*, *s.aa.* 850, 854, 857 (MGH SRG i.u.s. 7, 41, 45, 48)
[70] 'Domino illi infidelitatis suae condignam mercedem retribuente … unde et a caelesti medico … curari promeruit': *AF*, *s.a.* 869 (MGH SRG i.u.s. 7, 68–9).

women captive.[71] Although these raiders were checked, more tribes joined them. The Bohemians then 'devastated many places and killed those rashly assembling against them'.[72] The historian thus raises the stakes within the narrative by emphasizing the threat facing the Franks. As King Louis made a plan of campaign against the particular threat posed by Rastiz, ruler of the Moravians, further disaster struck: Louis fell ill. At the crisis point of the narrative, with the king dying and the Bohemians overrunning the kingdom, Louis, 'forced by necessity, gave command of his army to Charles, his youngest son'.[73] Although Charles the Fat (d. 888) was actually thirty years old, the annalist here implies his inexperience. The annalist seeks to stress to the fullest extent the catastrophe facing the kingdom: as its fate hung in the balance, the least experienced prince marched out to face the foe.

At this point of crisis, the historian notes, Louis also 'commended the result of this affair to the Lord'.[74] In the light of what follows, this is the turning point of the narrative. Charles came to Rastiz's fortifications, which were described as 'vast' and 'unlike any older ones', a further threat.[75] He and his army, however, attacked, 'relying on God's help'.[76] All Rastiz's fortresses were burned, his treasures looted and his followers routed. In other words, Charles's victory was comprehensive. Just as the annalist had stressed the threat facing the kingdom, so he also describes the extent of Charles's victory in lavish detail. The annalist then concludes the account with Charles meeting his brother Karlmann (d. 880), with both 'rejoicing together in the victories given to them by heaven'.[77]

The historian took his readers carefully from threat and danger to hope and finally success. In many respects, such a structure is a basic form of storytelling, which has been discussed at length by literary scholars.[78] There is an inciting incident (the Bohemian rebellion), a

[71] '[C]rebris incursionibus infestant': ibid. (MGH SRG i.u.s. 7, 67).

[72] '[P]lurima loca devastant et quosdam sibi incaute congredientes interficiunt': ibid.

[73] '[U]nde necessitate conpulsus Karolum filiorum suorum ultimum eidem exercitui praefecit': ibid. (MGH SRG i.u.s. 7, 68–9).

[74] 'Domino exictum rei commendans': ibid. (MGH SRG i.u.s. 7, 69).

[75] '[I]neffabilem … munitionem et omnibus antiquissimis dissimilem': ibid.

[76] 'Dei auxilio fretus': ibid.

[77] '[D]e victoria sibi caelitus data gratulantes': ibid.

[78] See Patrick O'Neill, 'Narrative Structure', in David Herman, Manfred Jahn and Marie-Laure Ryan, eds, *Routledge Encyclopedia of Narrative Theory* (London, 2005), 366–70.

further complication (the illness of Louis) and finally a reversal and resolution (military victory). The resolution comes, however, as a result of God's agency within the narrative. The characters' response to the unfolding events is to recognize that the resolution of the story depends on God. Louis commends the result of the campaign to God from his sickbed. Charles advances against the huge fortresses 'relying on God's help'. The story concludes with the recognition by Charles and Karlmann of God's hand in their success. The Fulda historian is presenting a carefully constructed vision of how the world works, which commends the behaviour of Louis the German and his sons. When its readers faced similar crises and challenges, the logic of the narrative would have encouraged them to depend on God.

Conclusion

Both these historians were sensitive to the practicalities of campaigning, especially the importance of leadership. Each narrative, nonetheless, ultimately ascribes responsibility for the course of events not to human efforts but to God, just as Cassiodorus had recommended. This supports recent conclusions that these and other Carolingian educational texts were read by the laity.[79] These narratives were too carefully constructed to have been written simply to teach novice monks facts and dates. Rather, the men who ran the Carolingian empire continued to need training and educating in the correct response to battles against the odds.

It is noteworthy that both sets of annals emphasize attitude as much as behaviour. Carolingian armies often undertook certain ritual actions before and after battle, such as fasting and the praying of litanies.[80] Charlemagne himself described such rituals in a letter to his queen, Fastrada, in 791.[81] An older generation of scholarship used to present such ritual rather mechanistically, as a *quid pro quo* intended

[79] For example, Marios Costambeys, Matthew Innes and Simon MacLean, *The Carolingian World* (Cambridge, 2011), 302–3; Stone, *Morality and Masculinity*, 45–50.

[80] Michael McCormick, 'The Liturgy of War in the Early Middle Ages: Crisis, Litanies, and the Carolingian Monarchy', *Viator* 15 (1984), 1–25; for a survey of recent literature, see Evans, 'Christian Hermeneutics', 153–4.

[81] See Rosamond McKitterick, *Charlemagne: The Formation of a European Identity* (Cambridge, 2008), 43–8, especially for the links between this letter and contemporary histories.

to obtain God's favour.[82] Elements of this could have been read from Orosius, such as his reference to how Mascezel's fasting 'merited' victory. While Carolingian historians occasionally described similar rituals, their emphasis is much more on the attitudes which these actions reflected. Pippin urges his men not only to make offerings to God but to fear and trust him. The Fulda annalist describes Charles the Fat's dependence on, and celebration of, God's help, rather than the specific ritual actions this may have involved. Theuderic, by contrast, failed to perceive God's agency correctly and relied on his own strength, which proved insufficient. These narratives were, therefore, educating their audiences in the faith and its implications, showing that God was a trustworthy and powerful source of help.

These histories thus presented practical examples of the relevance of deeply held Christian beliefs. Their approach was inspired by the examples of Cassiodorus, Orosius and others, but the authors also developed their works much further. As a result, history writing can be seen as representing what was fundamental about the Carolingian renewal of Christian education: the practical application of correct doctrine in a changing political context.

[82] For example, Michael Wallace-Hadrill, *Early Medieval History* (Oxford, 1975), 72–3; Janet Nelson, 'On the Limits of the Carolingian Renaissance', in Derek Wood, ed., *Renaissance and Renewal in Christian History*, SCH 14 (Oxford, 1977), 51–69; James Campbell, *Essays in Anglo-Saxon History* (London, 1986), 14.

Penitential Manuscripts and the Teaching of Penance in Carolingian Europe

Eleni Leontidou*
Brussels

This article discusses the educational value of penitential literature in Carolingian Francia. In particular, it looks at manuscripts which were not simple penitential handbooks but were compiled as educational tools for priests. Apart from penitential works, these manuscripts included monastic rules, moral and ascetic works providing moral instruction, and, in some cases, school texts and glossaries.

This article is an exercise in the study of penitentials in their manuscript context: it focuses on Carolingian miscellanies of a didactic nature, which include fragments of penitential texts, in an effort to decipher what their exact purpose and audience may have been. It will argue that two distinct categories of 'educational penitentials' can be discerned in books produced during the period of cultural growth of the late eighth and ninth century known as the Carolingian Renaissance. The first comprised collections of a morally educative character; in the context of these manuscripts, the penitentials resemble moral treatises. The second were more obviously school books, since they also included texts such as glossaries and treatises on the seven liberal arts; some of them were used to educate future confessors, while others reflect the need to include moral education about sin in Carolingian school curricula.[1] In these educational manuscripts, penitentials were often excerpted and presented in a more succinct matter, sometimes as lists of sins, in the systematic fashion of a school text. The article will also argue that lists of sins in the context of educational penitentials often functioned as mnemonic schemes.

The promotion of penitential ideals was part and parcel of the Carolingian programme of reform. The Carolingian reformers were

* House of European History, Rue Belliard / Belliardstraat 135, 1000 Brussels, Belgium. E-mail: elenileontidou@live.com.

[1] Due to the tendency to regard manuscripts comprising a variety of texts belonging to different genres as 'miscellanea', these manuscripts are rarely studied in much detail.

Studies in Church History 55 (2019), 72–82
doi: 10.1017/stc.2018.15

preoccupied with the concept of religious and moral *correctio*. School subjects such as grammar were taught with an emphasis on spiritual and moral betterment: for example, those who knew how to read well could engage with the Gospels and those who were aware of the basics of harmony could participate in ecclesiastical hymnody.[2] In the context of Carolingian society, penance was therefore extremely important since a Christian society ought to have mechanisms in place for dealing with sin. Penitential handbooks of Irish origin were available and known on the European mainland from the sixth century, but in the ninth century Frankish penitentials also emerged and there was an upsurge in the production of penitential manuscripts.[3] In addition, texts widely utilized in the Carolingian education system often included a strong moral and penitential component: Carolingian students learned how to read by using the Psalms, often committing them to memory. Alcuin of York, one of the protagonists of the Carolingian programme of reform, was the first to comment on the seven penitential psalms as a distinct group, in his *Exposition on the Penitential Psalms*.[4] Alcuin also wrote a text which sheds light on the importance of penance, addressed to the young monks of St Martin at Tours. This text, entitled *Ad pueros sancti Martini*, is interesting in its dismissal of feelings of shame, presented in a discussion of the physiological symptom of blushing, which, according to Alcuin, often kept students from confessing their sins.[5] This discussion of penance in a school context shows that there was an educational aspect to the theological discussion about the sacrament. Throughout Alcuin's oeuvre, sins and virtues are perceived as being constantly in battle with one another, with each vice having its antidote: this echoes

[2] For an important general overview of the Carolingian Renaissance, see John J. Contreni, 'The Carolingian Renaissance: Education and Literary Culture', in Rosamond McKitterick, ed., *The New Cambridge Medieval History*, 2: c.*700*–c.*900* (Cambridge, 1995), 709–57; see also Thomas M. Buck, *Admonitio und Praedicatio. Zur religions-pastoralen Dimension von Kapitularien und kapitulariennahen Texten (507–814)* (Frankfurt am Main, 1997), 67–156.

[3] For an overview of penance and penitential reforms under the Carolingians, see Rob Meens, *Penance in Medieval Europe, 600–1200* (Cambridge, 2014), 106–39.

[4] Donald A. Bullough, *Carolingian Renewal: Sources and Heritage* (Manchester, 1991), 160–240 ('Alcuin and the Kingdom of Heaven'), at 173–4.

[5] On blushing, see Abigail Firey, 'Blushing before the Judge and Physician: Moral Arbitration in the Carolingian Empire', in eadem, ed., *A New History of Penance* (Leiden. 2008), 173–200.

Prudentius's *Psychomachia*, another influential work often used as a school text.[6]

Penitential handbooks were important texts throughout the Middle Ages and remain invaluable sources for the study of a range of aspects of medieval history, from episcopal power to personal religiosity and attitudes towards gender and sexuality.[7] In addition, the notion that some penitentials may have had an educational aspect to them has not been left entirely unexplored: the idea that specific manuscripts may have been used for educational purposes, either for the laity or for ministers hearing confessions, has been suggested by Rob Meens who, in his study of the so-called 'Tripartite penitentials' (those drawing on three traditions, Irish, Anglo-Saxon and Frankish) noted eight 'educational' manuscripts.[8] However, Meens hesitated to suggest an audience for these educational books.[9] Four of them contain extracts from the Carolingian penitential of Halitgar of Cambrai, one of the so-called 'reform penitentials' written to counterbalance what were thought to be inconsistencies between the penitential handbooks which were in circulation at the time.[10]

The presence of this type of book in Carolingian monastic or cathedral libraries can be examined in the context of the debate surrounding the use of penitential handbooks before 1215, when the promulgation of the canon *Omnis utriusque sexus* at the Fourth Lateran Council made annual confession compulsory.[11] Following research by Franz Kerff, Alexander Murray asserted that the penitentials were mainly used by bishops in a judicial context, as guides to the

[6] Sinead O'Sullivan, *Early Medieval Glosses on Prudentius' Psychomachia: The Weitz Tradition* (Leiden, 2004), 23–130.

[7] On the question of individuality and personal religiosity, see Peter Von Moos, 'L'Individu ou les limites de l'institution ecclésiale', in Brigitte M. Bedos-Rezak and Dominique Iogna-Prat, eds, *L'Individu au Moyen Âge. Individuation et individualisation avant la modernité* (Paris, 2005), 271–88. On medieval sexuality and penitential discipline, see Pierre J. Payer, *Sex and the Penitentials: The Development of a Sexual Code 500–1150* (Toronto, ON, 1984).

[8] Rob Meens, *Het tripartite boeteboek. Overlevering en betekenis van vroegmiddeleeuwse biechtvoorschriften (met editie en vertaling van vier tripartita)* (Hilversum, 1994), 259–60.

[9] Ibid. 264.

[10] For a thorough study of Halitgar's Penitential, see Raymund Kottje, *Die Bussbücher Halitgars von Cambrai und des Hrabanus Maurus. Ihre Überlieferung und ihre Quellen* (Berlin, 1980).

[11] Norman P. Tanner, ed., *Decrees of the Ecumenical Councils*, 2 vols (London, 1990), 1: 245.

imposition of penalties.[12] In contrast, Raymund Kottje, after examining the vocabulary and terminology of the texts, concluded that most were actually used in a pastoral context by priests, for the administration of penance.[13] It has also been suggested that there was a move from the use of penitentials in a pastoral context in the ninth century to a juridical or episcopal context in the tenth and eleventh centuries.[14] Determining the audience for what I will refer to as 'educational penitentials' is helpful for the ongoing rewriting of the existing grand narratives regarding the use of penitential handbooks and consequently regarding the practice of penance. Most of the educational penitentials occupy an awkward position between pastoral and judicial manuscripts, sharing some common characteristics with each category but defying precise categorization as either. It is worth noting, however, that by contrast with judicial manuscripts, the tariffs in educational penitentials are in most cases presented as remedies for sin, rather than as punishments for sinners.[15] Their nature is more informative than preventative: often the tariffs for sins are not included in the manuscript, as seen in the many books which include only the opening chapters of Halitgar's penitential, which provide definitions of sins and their corresponding virtues. When the tariffs are included, they are presented more as remedies than as punishments: for example, in the rubrics of the penitential texts in a Vatican Library manuscript discussed below, BAV, MS Pal. Lat. 485, the word 'remedy' is used frequently in the titles of the penitential texts included and at one point a text is called 'salutary medicine for the soul'.[16] For these reasons, therefore, 'educational

[12] Franz Kerff, 'Mittelalterliche Quellen und mittelalterliche Wirklichkeit. Zu den Konsequenzen einer jüngst erschienenen Edition für unser Bild kirchlicher Reformbemühungen', *Rheinische Vierteljahrsblätter* 51 (1987), 275–86; idem, '*Libri paenitentiales* und kirchliche Strafgerichtsbarkeit bis zum Decretum Gratiani. Ein Diskussionsvorschlag', *Zeitschrift der Savigny-Stiftung für Rechtsgeschichte, Kan. Abt.* 75 (1989), 23–57; Alexander Murray, 'Confession before 1215', *TRHS* 6th ser. 3 (1993), 51–81.

[13] Raymund Kottje, 'Buße oder Strafe? Zur "Iustitia" in den "Libri Paenitentiales"', in *La giustizia nell'alto medioevo (secoli V–VIII)*, Settimane di Studio del centro italiano di studi sull'alto medioevo 42 (Spoleto, 1995), 443–74.

[14] Rob Meens, 'The Frequency and Nature of Early Medieval Penance', in Peter Biller and Alastair J. Minnis, eds, *Handling Sin: Confession in the Middle Ages* (Woodbridge, 1998), 35–61; idem, 'Penitentials and the Practice of Penance in the Tenth and Eleventh Centuries', *EME* 14 (2006), 7–21.

[15] See the discussion in Kottje, 'Buße oder Strafe?'.

[16] Vatican City, BAV, Pal. Lat. 485, fol. 101v.

penitentials', even though they form their own distinct category, can be seen as part of the same movement that led to the proliferation of pastoral manuscripts in the ninth century.

As mentioned above, I have made a broad distinction between books that read like collections of moralizing texts with an emphasis on penitential themes and books resembling school manuscripts. Moralizing collections including penitentials may have been a Carolingian innovation, but their transcription and proliferation was not limited to the ninth century: a large number of these manuscripts were actually produced during the tenth and eleventh centuries. For example, the tenth-century Zurich, Zentralbibliothek, MS Rh. 102 also contains texts from Augustine, Jerome, Isidore, Bede, Alcuin and Gennadius.[17] This particular manuscript addresses theological questions and includes a creed, an epistle by Jerome regarding the assumption of Mary, and extracts from Isidore of Seville's *Etymologies* concerning God, the Holy Spirit and the Trinity. It was, perhaps, intended for the basic theological education of young priests or monks. Similarly, the tenth-century Paris, BN, MS 2077 focuses on theology, with a specific interest in heresiology, including texts such as Augustine's works against the Manichees and Arians, as well as other patristic extracts, notably by Fulgentius of Ruspe and Gregory the Great.[18]

Books that belong in the second category of educational penitentials resemble miscellanies more closely: they are essentially school books, including such items as glossaries and computus texts, as well as penitentials. The penitentials themselves are often excerpted. This article focuses on these books, since they constitute a unique but understudied category of manuscripts.[19] Most of the manuscripts discussed here date from the second half of the ninth century and their conception can be examined in the context of the Carolingian Renaissance.[20] There are more educational manuscripts with

[17] Bernhard Bischoff, *Katalog der festländischen Handschriften des neunten Jahrhunderts (mit Ausnahme der wisigotischen)*, 3 vols (Wiesbaden, 1998–2017), 3: 542.

[18] Ibid. 60.

[19] My sources for the choice of manuscripts discussed here were Meens's list of educational manuscripts (*Het tripartite boeteboek*, 259–60) and the lists of manuscripts including individual penitential books in the appendices of his *Penance in the Early Middle Ages*, 226–37. Raymund Kottje's comprehensive presentation of manuscripts containing Halitgar's penitential was also useful: *Die Bussbücher*, 14–82.

[20] There is however, an early tenth-century manuscript which belongs in this category: Paris, BN, MS 614A. It includes penitential and liturgical material, but also the *Interrogationes de littera et de singulis causis*, a school text: see Nicholas Everett, 'The

penitentials than the few examples following indicate; I have focused on those including works which were Carolingian schoolbooks par excellence.

One example of a miscellany including both educational and penitential texts is Vatican City, BAV, MS Pal. Lat. 485, a late Carolingian compilation from Lorsch. According to Frederick Paxton, this book functions as 'a manuscript tool needed to translate the goals of the reform into reality'.[21] The manuscript contains votive missal formulae, collectively known as the 'Lorsch confession', a computus and calendar, *Instructiones cryptographicae*, a manual for dream analysis, interpretations of Hebrew and Greek names, pseudo-Alcuinian expositions on the mass and an epistle of Jesse of Amiens on baptism, along with canons and various penitential works (including penitentials by pseudo-Egbert and Cummean). This manuscript, in short, combines penitential works with liturgical material and other texts intended to have a practical use, such as the computus, as well as reference works on dreams and Greek and Hebrew names and expositions on the sacraments. Overall, the tome appears as a compendium which could function simultaneously as a reference work, a teaching manual and a book to be used during the liturgy. The inclusion of capitularies addressed to the clergy, texts providing education on basic sacramental theology and information on the meaning of Greek and Hebrew words shows beyond doubt that the manuscript was used for the education of priests. This collection of texts is indicative of the expectations placed upon clergy by Carolingian reformers and of the pivotal role that education was considered to play in the fulfilment of their ministry.

Another educational miscellany, St Gall, Stiftsbibliothek, MS Cod. Sang. 184 (codicological unit 2), is a particularly interesting manuscript, the purpose of which only becomes clear upon closer inspection.[22] Bound with another, slightly later book, it contains texts by Augustine and the beginning of Halitgar's penitential

---

Interrogationes de littera et de singulis causis: An Early Medieval School Text', Journal of Medieval Latin 16 (2006), 227–75, at 254. Further research is needed to establish whether similar books continued to be transcribed well into the tenth century.

[21] Frederick S. Paxton, '"Bonus liber": A Late Carolingian Clerical Manual from Lorsch (Bibliotheca Vaticana MS Pal. lat. 485)', in Laurent Mayali and Stephanie A. J. Tibbetts, eds, *The Two Laws: Studies in Medieval Legal History dedicated to Stephan Kuttner* (Washington DC, 1990), 1–30.

[22] Bischoff, *Katalog*, 3: 312 (no. 5642).

(under the title *De octo principalibus vitiis*, 'On the eight principal sins'), as well as computistical and astronomical texts. The first text in the collection, Augustine's sermon *De disciplina christianorum*, makes the purpose of the compilation clear: in it Augustine uses the word 'discipline' in the sense of learning.[23] The 'learning' to which Augustine refers is Christian instruction and teaching, the knowledge of how to 'live well', essential for Christians who wish to inherit eternal life.[24] Learning is seen, in Augustine's text, as a means to fulfil God's plan on earth. This hints that the collection has a moral educational value, with Halitgar's penitential extract having a preventative as well as an educational function in the context of the manuscript. The penitential fragment therefore, fits well with the computistical texts, schemata, tables and glossaries which were also included in the manuscript, as each had its own part to play in providing a complete Christian education. The make-up of this collection suggests that learning about capital sins and their corresponding virtues was essential for educated Christians, and especially priests and those being prepared for the monastic life.

A third example of a penitential used in a school environment can be found in BAV, MS Reg. lat. 215, possibly written in Tours. This book includes an excerpt from Halitgar's penitential, along with letters by, and excerpts from works by, the Church Fathers Jerome and Isidore, glosses on the Gospels, a list of synonyms attributed to Cicero (*Synonyma Ciceronis*) and Isidore's *Chronicle*. The manuscript also contains the *Scolica grecarum glossarum*, which are considered to be lecture notes from a Greek class.[25] The excerpts from Halitgar's penitential are once again the chapters on the cardinal virtues, consisting entirely of passages borrowed from Julianus Pomerius and Alcuin's *De vitiis et virtutibus*. Moreover, the same passage from Halitgar's penitential is excerpted in another manuscript, the ninth- or tenth-century BN, MS Lat. 242 (codicological unit 3), another school

[23] '[D]isciplina a discendo dicta est': St Gall, Stiftsbibliothek, MS Cod. Sang. 184 (codicological unit 2), fol. 189.

[24] 'Propter hoc discitur bene vivere, ut perveniatur ad semper vivere': ibid.

[25] M. L. W. Laistner, 'Notes on Greek from the Lectures of a Ninth-Century Monastery Teacher', *Bulletin of the John Rylands Library* 7 (1923), 421–56; see also Patrizia Lendinara, 'The *Scholica graecarum glossarum* and Martianus Capella', in Mariken Teeuwen, Sinéad O'Sullivan, eds, *Carolingian Scholarship and Martianus Capella: Ninth-Century Commentary Traditions on* De nuptiis *in Context* (Turnhout, 2011), 301–62.

book, containing among other texts the aforementioned *Synonyma Ciceronis*.[26] In these collections, penitentials, works by Church Fathers and glossaries enhanced and complemented one another, all considered as works possessing significant educational value for Christians.

The emphasis on the enumeration and description of sins, as seen in the excerpted passages from Halitgar's penitential and found in two of the three manuscripts mentioned above, provides a systemization that would be useful in an educational context. A school manuscript which demonstrates this is one that does not contain a penitential text: Leiden, Universiteitsbibliotheek MS Voss. Lat. F. 48, a copy of the famous late antique tract on the seven liberal arts, *The Marriage of Philology and Mercury*, with the addition of extensive glosses, is one of the best-known ninth-century school books.[27] The final pages of this manuscript are dedicated to diagrams and notes. One, in particular, seems out of place. It reads:

> These are the twelve abuses of the world: the wise man without works, the old man without religion, the young man without obedience, the rich man without charity, the woman without modesty, the nobleman without virtue, the argumentative Christian, the proud pauper, the unjust king, the neglectful bishop, the community without order, the people without a law.[28]

This is the beginning of a sixth- or seventh-century Irish moral tract which lists, as its title proclaims, the twelve 'abuses' committed by

[26] This text circulated in different versions and variant forms: see Giorgio Brugnoli, *Studi sulle* Differentiae verborum (Rome, 1955), 27–37; Birger Munk Olsen, *L'Étude des auteurs classiques latins aux XIe et XIIe siècles*, 1: *Documents, études et répertoires publiés par l'Institut de Recherche et d'Histoire des Textes* (Paris, 1982), 133–5, 340–50.

[27] Bischoff, *Katalog*, 2 : 51 (no. 2191); K. A. De Meyier, *Codices Vossiani latini*, 1: *Codices in Folio* (Leiden, 1973), 100–3; Claudio Leonardi, 'Raterio e Marziano Capella', *Italia medioevale e umanistica* 2 (1959), 73–102; Jean Préaux, '*Les Manuscrits principaux du* De nuptiis Philologiae et Mercuri de Martinus Capella', in Guy Cambier, Carl Deroux and Jean Préaux, eds, *Lettres latines du moyen âge et de la renaissance* (Brussels, 1978), 76–128, at 79, 101, 123; Mariken Teeuwen, *Harmony and the Music of the Spheres: The Ars Musica in Ninth-Century Commentaries on Martianus Capella* (Leiden, 2002), 72–3, 88–98.

[28] 'Duodecim abusivis sunt saeculi: sapiens sine operibus, senex sine religione, adolescens sine oboedientia, dives sine elemosyna, femina sine pudicitia, dominus sine virtute, Christianus contentiosus, pauper superbus, rex iniquus, episcopus neglegens, plebs sine disciplina et populus sine lege': Pseudo-Cyprian, *De duodecim abusivis saeculi* (CSEL 3/3, 152).

specific categories of people.[29] This text has attracted interest in modern scholarship mainly because of the ninth abuse, the 'unjust king', which has been considered as a precursor of, or an example for, the Carolingian 'mirrors of kingship'.[30] This text has no obvious connection to the rest of the notes and diagrams, nor does it seem to be related to the original text and the glosses: its position between diagrams connected to the disciplines of harmony and mathematics may be connected to medieval theories on the philosophical resonance of numbers and the order of a Christian universe.[31] However, the complete text was also often transmitted with penitential literature, as can be found in two ninth-century manuscripts, St Gallen, MSS Cod. Sang. 277 and 570, which combine *De duodecim abusivis* with the penitential of Halitgar. This is not entirely unexpected, since *De duodecim abusivis* is, essentially, a list of sins. What is more, it could be used as a mnemonic device similar to the lists of vices in penitentials.[32]

In a moralizing movement with a perfect society as its ultimate goal, such as was the Carolingian Renaissance, precise catalogues of moral entities, transmitted by the clerical elite, were used to convince penitents of the importance of discretion and restraint. It was important to define the sins, to discuss them at length and then to exercise the self-control needed to refrain from them. The notion of self-control as the root of sinlessness and as something to be taught can be found in the Church Fathers whose early lists of principal sins were very influential on penitential literature, especially in the works of Gregory the Great and John Cassian, written primarily with a monastic audience in mind but by the Carolingian period definitely reaching the laity. In them the reader is warned that sinners often rationalize their behaviour and claim to be innocent. Gregory's definition of sin is based on lack of reason: reason helps the Christian not

[29] Ibid. 152–73. On the text, see Aidan Breen, 'The Evidence of Antique Irish Exegesis in Pseudo-Cyprian, *De duodecim abusivis saeculi*', *Proceedings of the Royal Irish Academy* 87C (1987), 71–101; On the text's popularity in Carolingian Europe, see Hans H. Anton, 'Pseudo-Cyprian: *De duodecim abusivis saeculi* und sein Einfluss auf den Kontinent, insbesondere auf die karolingischen Fürstenspiegel', in Heinz Löwe, ed., *Die Iren und Europa im früheren Mittelalter*, 2 vols (Stuttgart, 1982), 2: 568–617.

[30] Rob Meens, 'Politics, Mirrors of Princes and the Bible: Sins, Kings and the Well-being of the Realm', *EME* 7 (1998), 345–57.

[31] See Contreni, 'Carolingian Renaissance', 739–40.

[32] See also Jennifer Solivan, 'Depictions of Virtues and Vices as Mnemonic Devices', *Imago Temporis: Medium Aevum* 11 (2017), 159–92.

to become a slave to his or her passions and also to avoid making absurd rationalizations which would lead to more sinning.[33] Penitential education was required to cultivate this kind of reason.

Educational penitentials should probably be understood in the context of Carolingian efforts to reform and educate the clergy, both secular and monastic. They are an expression of the ideal combination of liberal arts and divine learning, as promoted in such formative works as Cassiodorus's *Institutions* and Augustine's *On Christian Doctrine*. The manuscripts described here were probably used in a 'school' setting, where pupils were studying under a master. Some were used as reference works, books which could be referred to for information when needed, or as core texts in the library of their respective foundation. They were transcribed for the needs of these pupils, who were probably either future clergymen or oblates.[34] Lay students of possibly 'external' monastic schools or cathedral schools are a more unlikely choice for an 'audience' of educational penitentials, due to the overall lack of evidence for an existence of a regular, institutionalized form of education for lay people during the Carolingian period, especially during the mid-to-late ninth century when internal struggles and Viking attacks took their toll on education.[35]

In conclusion, there is a specific category of books that can be considered 'educational penitentials'. These can be studied separately from pastoral and judicial penitentials, since their use and purpose are entirely different. They were not conceived as handbooks with lists of penalties or as confessors' manuals; instead, their purpose was to inform and instruct. Some of them were conceived as collections of morally edifying texts, while others were transcribed to be used as handbooks for the education of priests and future confessors. The excerption of the penitential texts and the layout of these

[33] Carole Straw, 'Gregory, Cassian, and the Cardinal Vices', in Richard Newhauser, ed., *In the Garden of Evil: The Vices and Culture in the Middle Ages* (Toronto, ON, 2005), 35–58; eadem, *Gregory the Great: Perfection in Imperfection* (Berkeley, CA, 1988), 107–27.

[34] On clerical and monastic schools, see Contreni, 'Carolingian Renaissance', 713–15.

[35] 'External' monastic schools were located outside the precincts of the monastery, and were intended for the education of children not destined for the monastic life. The external school of the monastery of St Gall is an example often cited to argue for the widespread existence and operation of such schools during the Carolingian period, but M. M. Hildebrandt, *The External School in Carolingian Society* (Leiden, 1992), argues that it was neither typical nor regular in the ninth century. On complaints about the disarray of late Carolingian education, see Contreni, 'Carolingian Renaissance', 715–16.

manuscripts points to the desire of the compilers to promote memorization, but only to a degree: it was important to keep the contents of the manuscripts in mind rather than learning them by heart. This is made apparent by the fact that many of the excerpted penitentials are accompanied in the manuscripts by common reference works, such as computistical texts, schemata, tables and glossaries. Students needed to keep the harmful effects of sinning in mind, but they could always refer back to the book for more detailed information.

Despite their seemingly miscellaneous nature, these manuscripts show a remarkable passion for cohesion and organization. In fact, many of their attributes can be related to values formulated and established during the Carolingian Renaissance: the passion for the collecting, rewriting and rearranging of texts, the attempt to organize thought processes, and the emphasis on proper conduct and discipline. It is also easy to trace the creation of these collections back to the higher echelons of clerical hierarchy, who were interested in the formation of a clergy that could properly administer the sacraments. Perhaps these attributes can be seen as authentically Carolingian; more importantly, they provide evidence that there was almost always an undeniable purpose behind medieval 'miscellaneous' collections. The purpose, in this case, was to serve as useful handbooks for the moral cultivation and education of a priesthood that would be able to fulfil God's plan on earth.

Educating the Local Clergy, *c.*900–*c.*1150

Sarah Hamilton*

University of Exeter

Scholars interested in those medieval clergy charged with the delivery of pastoral care have highlighted the flourishing of reforming movements in the ninth and thirteenth centuries. Thus the period between the fall of the Carolingian empire and the beginnings of the so-called pastoral revolution is generally viewed as one of episcopal neglect. Focusing on case studies drawn from the Carolingian heartlands of north-east Frankia and Lotharingia, as well as what had been the more peripheral regions of northern Italy and southern England, this article offers a revised interpretation of the education of the local clergy in the post-Carolingian world. Exploring the ways in which higher churchmen sought to innovate on the texts they inherited from their Carolingian predecessors, it demonstrates how they paid considerable attention to the preparation and ordination of suitable candidates, to the instruction and monitoring of local clergy through attendance at diocesan synods and local episcopal visitations, and to the provision of suitable texts to support local churchmen in the delivery of pastoral care.

Much about the lives of the men who served the local churches and communities across the medieval West is obscure.[1] Compared to the apparent richness of the evidence for their monastic counterparts, that surviving for the lower ranks of the secular clergy makes for slim pickings.[2] Thus we learn about the life of the village priest called Brihtric

* Department of History, Amory Building, Rennes Drive, Streatham Campus, Exeter, EX4 4RJ. E-mail: s.m.hamilton@exeter.ac.uk.

[1] The research for this paper was conducted with the support of the Humanities in the European Research Area funded project, 'After Empire: Using and Not Using the Past in the Crisis of the Carolingian World, *c.*900–*c.*1050' (UNUP), funded from the European Union's Research and Innovation Horizon 2020 programme under grant agreement no. 649387.

[2] See especially the evidence of monastic customaries edited in the series Corpus Consuetudinum Monasticarum (Siegburg, 1963–); on customaries, see Susan Boynton and Isabelle Cochelin, *From Dead of Night to End of Day: The Medieval Customs of Cluny / Du Coeur de la nuit à la fin du jour. Les Coutumes clunisiennes au moyen âge*, Disciplina Monastica 3 (Turnhout, 2005); Carolyn Marino Malone and Clark Maines, eds, *Consuetudines et Regulae: Sources for Monastic Life in the Middle Ages and the Early Modern Period*, Disciplina Monastica 10 (Turnhout, 2014).

Studies in Church History 55 (2019), 83–113
doi: 10.1017/stc.2018.16

in the mid-twelfth-century village of Haselbury Plucknett in southern Somerset only from incidental references in the *vita* of the anchorite, Wulfric, who was enclosed in a cell attached to Brihtric's church. The *vita*'s author regarded Brihtric favourably, describing him as a devout and devoted servant of God: he 'much resembled the blessed Wulfric in simplicity and humility, serving God day and night like him with psalms and prayers; and in so far as his ministry allowed him, he kept perpetual watch in his church', riding to and from his house on horseback so as to maximize the time he spent in the church.[3] However, we are told, whilst he knew the psalms and prayers, the English Brihtric was unable to communicate with his Norman bishop in either Latin or French: thus when Wulfric cured a mute man and gave him the ability to speak French, Brihtric complained: 'You have never given me the use of French and when I come before the bishop and the archdeacon I have to stand as mum as any mute.'[4] We are also told that Brihtric was seemingly married, in contravention of church law at the time, and had a son, Osbern, who in time succeeded him as priest.[5] Further details reveal that Osbern seems to have served a practical apprenticeship: Osbern told Wulfric's biographer how as a boy he used to enter the holy man's cell to serve when Wulfric celebrated mass. Osbern also assisted his father: 'one Sunday when Master Brihtric went to bless the water in the church the aspersorium was missing. His son Osbern had accidentally taken it home and now the troubled lad did not know what to do.' (He therefore borrowed Wulfric's *aspersorium* and thus came to witness the holy man having a vision.)[6]

[3] 'Fuit enim in simplicitate et humilitate beato Wulfrico simillimus, psalmis et orationibus sicut et ille die ac nocte inserviens et quantum ministerii sui ratio sinebat, perpetuas in ecclesia sua excubias celebrabat': John of Ford, *Vita Wulfrici* 16 (*Wulfric of Haselbury, by John, Abbot of Ford*, ed. Maurice Bell, Somerset Record Society 47 [Frome, 1933], 30–1). For an English translation, see *John of Forde: The Life of Wulfric of Haselbury, Anchorite*, transl. Pauline Matarasso, Cistercian Fathers 79 (Collegeville, MN, 2011), 116–17. On this text, see H. Mayr-Harting, 'Functions of a Twelfth-Century Recluse', *History* 60 (1975), 337–52.

[4] 'Nam homini alienigenae cui satis erat linguam ad loquendum aperuisse ad geminum linguae officium deuotus ministrasti et mihi qui cum ad episcopum et archidiaconum uenio quasi mutus silere compellor, Gallici usum sermonis non dedisti': John of Ford, *Vita Wulfrici* 14, 29 (*Life of Wulfric*, transl. Matarasso, 115).

[5] John of Ford, *Vita Wulfrici* 35 (Osbern described as Brihtric's son: 'quod filius eius Osbernus'), 74 (Osbern succeeds Brihtric), 82 (reference to Godida, 'Godida mater Osberni presbyteri'), 52–3, 102–3, 109.

[6] Ibid. 35, 52–3 (*Life of Wulfric*, transl. Matarasso, 139, 187). For Osbern serving Wulfric in his cell while he celebrated mass, see also ibid. 74, 102.

This master-apprentice model for the vocational training of those charged with responsibility for delivering pastoral care is likely to have been the most common model of training for the local priesthood, but it is one which, understandably, has left relatively little trace.[7] Education could also be found in monasteries, cathedrals and religious houses, but, in the words of William Dohar, 'the curricula of those schools were not especially pastoral, though a student could certainly obtain the foundations for whatever education he needed in the cure of souls as well as advanced instruction in practical and speculative theology'.[8] The haphazard nature of the education available generated considerable anxiety, albeit only intermittently, about the state of learning and education of local priests amongst the diocesan bishops charged with responsibility for their oversight.

This anxiety has manifested itself at various points in the history of the church in the Latin West. Some of these points are well known. Although it was not until 1563 that the Council of Trent prescribed the establishment of seminaries in each diocese 'to maintain, to educate religiously and to train in ecclesiastical discipline', the curriculum the Tridentine fathers defined would have been familiar to their medieval predecessors.[9] The council required of those who were to be priests:

> [T]hey shall learn grammar, singing, ecclesiastical computation, and the other liberal arts; they shall be instructed in sacred Scripture;

[7] See the study of thirteenth- and fourteenth-century priestly education by William J. Dohar, '*Sufficienter litteratus*: Clerical Examination and Instruction for the Cure of Souls', in Jacqueline Brown and William P. Stoneman, eds, *A Distinct Voice: Medieval Studies in Honor of Leonard E. Boyle, OP* (Notre Dame, IN, 1997), 305–21, at 305: 'a more common-place school for pastoral care in the Middle Ages was the master-apprentice association formed, with varying degrees of success, between local curates and the interested youth of the parishes'. On father-son succession in local churches in this period, see Julia Barrow, *The Clergy in the Medieval World: Secular Clerics, their Families and Careers in North-Western Europe* c.*800*–c.*1200* (Cambridge, 2015), 338–41.

[8] Dohar, '*Sufficienter litteratus*', 305. See also Barrow, *Clergy*, 222: 'much education went on at a lower level, without attention to rhetoric and dialectic'; Jeffrey H. Denton, 'The Competence of the Parish Clergy in Thirteenth-Century England', in Caroline M. Barron and Jenny Stratford, eds, *Church and Learning in Later Medieval Society: Essays in Honour of R. B. Dobson*, Harlaxton Medieval Studies n.s. 11 (Donington, 2002), 273–85, at 284: 'There is little evidence to suggest that … university training and parish duties had much, directly and in practice, to do with each other.'

[9] Council of Trent: The Twenty-Third Session, canon 18, in J. Waterworth, ed. and transl., *The Canons and Decrees of the Sacred and Oecumenical Council of Trent* (London, 1848), 187.

> ecclesiastical works; the homilies of the saints; the manner of administering the sacraments, especially those things which shall seem adapted to enable them to hear confessions; and the forms of the rites and ceremonies.[10]

Previous church councils had prescribed the establishment of diocesan schools: thus canon 18 of the Third Lateran Council (1179) enjoined that in 'every cathedral church a master is to be assigned some proper benefice so that he may teach the clerics and the poor scholars', and this provision was repeated by the Fourth Lateran Council (1215).[11] These canons are testament to the wider interest shown in clerical education and the quality of the pastoral ministry in the thirteenth century, which, alongside promotion of support for the friars as preachers, led also to increased documentation of episcopal visitations of local priests, for example, as well as the composition of pastoral manuals for guidance and training, especially in how to hear confessions.[12] Whilst this pastoral revolution has long attracted the interest of modern scholars, in recent decades researchers, including Rosamond McKitterick, have also drawn attention to the significance attached by Frankish rulers and their bishops in the ninth century to pastoral education.[13] This episcopal interest is manifest both in their

[10] Ibid. 188.

[11] Lateran III, canon 18, and Lateran IV, canon 11, in Norman P. Tanner, ed., *Decrees of the Ecumenical Councils*, 2 vols (London, 1990), 1: 220, 240.

[12] Dohar, '*Sufficienter litteratus*'; Helen Birkett, 'The Pastoral Application of the Lateran IV Reforms in the Northern Province, 1215–1348', *Northern History* 43 (2006), 199–219; Leonard E. Boyle, *Pastoral Care, Clerical Education and Canon Law, 1200–1400* (London, 1981); idem, 'The Fourth Lateran Council and Manuals of Popular Theology', in Thomas J. Heffernan, ed., *The Popular Literature of Medieval England* (Knoxville, TN, 1985), 30–43; Joseph Goering, 'The Internal Forum and the Literature of Confession', *Traditio* 59 (2004), 175–227; idem, 'The Changing Face of the Village Parish II: The Thirteenth Century', in J. A. Raftis, ed., *Pathways to Medieval Peasants* (Toronto, ON, 1981), 323–33.

[13] Rosamond McKitterick, *The Frankish Church and the Carolingian Reforms, 789–895* (London, 1977). Nor is this a phenomenon novel to the Carolingians; I should like to thank Morwenna Ludlow for drawing my attention to a passage in the preface to Gregory of Nyssa's *Catechetical Oration* which suggests that as early as the fourth century bishops composed catechetical texts as handbooks for training their clergy: 'The presiding ministers of the "mystery of godliness" have need of a system in their instructions, in order that the Church may be replenished by the accession of such as should be saved, through the teaching of the word of Faith being brought home to the hearing of unbelievers': *Selected Writings and Letters of Gregory, Bishop of Nyssa*, transl. William Moore and Henry A. Wilson, NPNF II 5 (London, 1893), online at the Christian Classics

legislation, especially in the issuing of episcopal statutes (*capitula*), and in the investment the bishops made in composing treatises to train priests in elementary canon law and liturgy. Susan Keefe, Yitzhak Hen, Rob Meens, Niels Rasmussen, Carine van Rhijn and Monika Wenz, amongst others, have drawn attention to the existence of collections of pastoral texts seemingly made for local clergy during the eighth and ninth centuries.[14] This article investigates the period between these two great flourishings in pastoral care. It is not my intention to suggest that the tenth and eleventh centuries witnessed as formal or as widespread a movement as those of the ninth or thirteenth centuries, but rather to argue that the wealth of material suggests a lively and continuing interest in the education of local clergy in the post-Carolingian world on the part of both bishops and the clerics themselves.

Ethereal Library: <http://www.ccel.org/ccel/schaff/npnf205.xi.ii.ii.html>, accessed 7 June 2018.

[14] Susan Keefe, *Water and the Word. Baptism and Education of the Clergy in the Carolingian Empire*, 2 vols (Notre Dame, IN, 2002); Carine van Rhijn, *Shepherds of the Lord: Priests and Episcopal Statutes in the Carolingian Period* (Turnhout, 2007); eadem, 'The Local Church, Priests' Handbooks and Pastoral Care in the Carolingian Period', *Chiese locali e chiese regionali nell' alto medioevo*, Settimane di studio del Centro italiano di studi sull'alto medioevo 61 (Spoleto, 2014), 689–710; eadem, 'Carolingian Rural Priests as (Local) Religious Experts', in Steffan Patzold and Florian Bock, eds, *Gott handhaben. Religiöses Wissen im Konflikt um Mythisierung und Rationalisierung* (Berlin, 2016), 131–46; eadem, 'Manuscripts for Local Priests and the Carolingian Reforms', in Steffen Patzold and Carine van Rhijn, eds, *Men in the Middle: Local Priests in Early Medieval Europe*, Ergänzungsbände zum Reallexikon der Germanischen Altertumskunde 93 (Berlin, 2016), 177–98; eadem, 'Pastoral Care and Prognostics in the Carolingian Period: The Case of El Escorial, Real Biblioteca di San Lorenzo, MS L III 8', *RB* 127 (2017), 272–97; Yitzhak Hen, 'Knowledge of Canon Law among Rural Priests: The Evidence of two Carolingian Manuscripts from around 800', *JThS* n.s. 50 (1999), 117–34; idem, 'Educating the Clergy: Canon Law and Liturgy in a Carolingian Handbook from the Time of Charles the Bald', in idem, ed., *De Sion exibit lex et verbum Domini de Hierusalem: Essays in Medieval Law, Liturgy and Literature in Honour of Amnon Linden* (Turnhout, 2001), 43–58; idem and Rob Meens, eds, *The Bobbio Missal: Liturgy and Religious Culture in Merovingian Gaul* (Cambridge, 2004); James McCune, 'The Sermon Collection in the Carolingian Clerical Handbook, Paris, Bibliothèque nationale de France Lat. 1012', *Mediaeval Studies* 75 (2013), 35–91; Rob Meens, 'The Frequency and Nature of Early Medieval Penance', in Peter Biller and A. J. Minnis, eds, *Handling Sin: Confession in the Middle Ages* (Woodbridge, 1998), 35–62; Niels K. Rasmussen, 'Célébration épiscopale et célébration presbytériale. Un essai de typologie', in *Segni e riti nella chiesa altomedievale occidentale*, Settimana di studio del Centro italiano di studi sull'alto medioevo 33 (Spoleto, 1987), 581–603; Monika Wenz, 'Bücher für Priester auf dem Land. Ausbildung von Experten religiösen Wissens im Karolingerreich' (PhD thesis in progress, University of Tübingen).

This article will investigate the evidence for the education of local clergy in three main sections. It will begin by considering the education for their preparation and ordination, go on to examine the instructions arising from local visitations and synods, and conclude with a consideration of some of the books which seem to have been made to support the work and education of the clergy. It focuses on evidence from three regions: late Anglo-Saxon England, tenth- and eleventh-century Italy, and north-east Frankia and Lotharingia in the same period. This last region constituted the heartlands of Carolingian authority, and witnessed the production of many of the texts associated with the ninth-century pastoral reforms, allowing us an insight into the extent of continuity in the changed political world of the tenth and eleventh centuries.[15] Although the kingdom of (northern) Italy was also under Carolingian rule, it seems to have been rather more peripheral in questions of clerical education.[16] Whilst Anglo-Saxon England had never formerly been under Carolingian rule, it came under Carolingian cultural influence in both the ninth and tenth centuries.[17]

Church law emphasized that bishops should ensure the suitability of candidates for ordination to the priesthood. Regino of Prüm compiled a collection of canon law for the archbishops of Trier and Mainz in the early tenth century; his avowed intention was to compile a handbook of all the texts a bishop might need when visiting his diocese.[18] In it he

[15] As indicated, for instance by the distribution of Carolingian episcopal *capitula* outlined in van Rhijn, *Shepherds of the Lord*, 229–32 (Appendix 2).

[16] On Carolingian Italy in general, see Paolo Delogu, 'Lombard and Carolingian Italy', in Rosamond McKitterick, ed., *The New Cambridge Medieval History*, 2: c.*700*–c.*900* (Cambridge, 1995), 290–319. On the absence of penitentials in the ninth century, see *Paenitentialia Italiae Saeculi XI–XII*, CChr.SL 156C, xi. On the absence of episcopal *capitula*, see van Rhijn, *Shepherds of the Lord*, 229–32.

[17] On relations in the ninth century, see Janet L. Nelson, 'England and the Continent in the Ninth Century I: Ends and Beginnings', *TRHS* 6th ser. 12 (2002), 1–21; eadem, 'England and the Continent in the Ninth Century II: The Vikings and Others', *TRHS* 6th ser. 13 (2003), 1–28; eadem, 'England and the Continent in the Ninth Century III: Rights and Rituals', *TRHS* 6th ser. 14 (2004), 1–24; eadem, 'England and the Continent in the Ninth Century IV: Bodies and Minds', *TRHS* 6th ser. 15 (2005), 1–28. For the tenth century, see David Rollason, Conrad Leyser and Hannah Williams, eds, *England and the Continent in the Tenth Century: Studies in Honour of Wilhelm Levison (1876–1947)*, Studies in the Early Middle Ages 37 (Turnhout, 2010).

[18] Regino of Prüm, *Libri duo de synodalibus causis et disciplinis ecclesiasticis*, abridged edn in *Das Sendhandbuch des Regino von Prüm*, ed. Wilfried Hartmann (Darmstadt, 2004), 20–2.

included a canon on 'how the bishop ought to conduct the ordination', pertaining to the ordination of both priests and candidates for other orders. The bishop should call all the candidates for ordination to come to the city four days before their ordination; he should direct

> priests and other prudent men with knowledge of divine laws and experienced in ecclesiastical sanctions diligently to investigate the life of the ordinands, their family, their native land, age, institution, the place where they were educated, whether they are well educated, whether they are instructed in the law of the Lord. Above all, whether they hold the catholic faith firmly, and if they can explain it with simple words. … For three continuous days they should be examined and on the Saturday the examiners who investigated them should represent them to the bishop.[19]

There are no surviving earlier precedents for this particular canon, although it is consistent with the provisions made in earlier church law.[20] For example, Regino also cited a canon from the fifth-century collection, the *Statuta ecclesia antiqua*, which describes in greater detail what candidates for ordination were expected to know. The bishop or his delegate should examine the ordinand and investigate his character, education, training and knowledge. The ordinand should be prudent, temperate, educated, instructed in divine law, aware of the different senses of Scripture, trained in ecclesiastical dogmatics and able to explain the Creed in simple words.[21]

It would be easy to dismiss such restatements of canon law as belonging to a closed textual world bound up with authority and precedent, rather than being an accurate reflection of reality, but Regino

[19] '*Qualiter episcopus debeat ordinationem facere* … Et tunc episcopus e latere suo dirigere debet sacerdotes et alios prudentes viros gnaros legis divinae et exercitatos in ecclesiasticis sanctionibus, qui ordinandorum vitam, genus, patriam, aetatem, institutionem, locum ubi educati, si bene sint literati, si in lege Domini instructi, diligenter investigent; ante omnia, si fidem catholicam firmiter teneant et verbis simplicibus asserere queant. … Igitur per tres continuos dies diligenter examinentur, et sic sabbato, qui probati inventi sunt, episcopo repraesententur': ibid. 1.453 (ed. Hartmann, 228–30).

[20] Although Regino cites his authority as a council of Nantes, there is no known source for this canon. Wilfried Hartmann suggests that the attribution of canons to otherwise unknown sources in Regino generally reflects ninth-century canon law and practice, and probably reflect the proceedings of now lost councils: 'Die *Capita incerta* im Sendhandbuch Reginos von Prüm', in Oliver Münsch and Thomas Zotz, eds, *Scientia Veritatis. Festschrift für Hubert Mordek zum 65. Geburtstag* (Stuttgart, 2004), 207–26.

[21] Regino, *Libri duo* 1.455 (ed. Hartmann, 230–2).

organized his law collection in a very systematic and practical way to support the work of the bishop. For example, he included a list of the questions he should ask of both the priest and the local community to establish the extent to which the priest and his flock conformed to current orthodoxy and orthopraxy.[22] Regino's collection circulated fairly widely in the Ottonian Reich and was incorporated into the twenty-book collection compiled by Burchard, bishop of Worms, in the early eleventh century.[23] Book 2 of Burchard's *Decretum* is devoted to holy orders.[24] In addition to Regino's material, he also copied provisions from the episcopal statutes issued by Haito of Basle on 'what ought to be necessary for priests to learn and to know'.[25] Haito specified '[t]he necessary (books) for priests to acquire knowledge of: a sacramentary, a lectionary, an antiphonary, the baptismal rite, a computus, penitential canons, a psalter and appropriate homilies for days throughout the whole year on Sundays and important feast days'. If he lacks knowledge of any of these things, he can hardly be called a priest because 'so great are the dangers of which the Evangelist speaks: If a blind man is led by a blind man, they both fall into the ditch' (Matthew 15: 14).[26] The focus here is on knowledge

[22] Ibid. 1: *Inquisitio*, 2.1–5 (ed. Hartmann, 24–38, 234–50). On these texts, see Walter Hellinger, 'Die Pfarrvisitation nach Regino von Prüm', *Zeitschrift der Savigny-Stiftung für Rechtsgeschichte. kanonistische Abteilung* 48 (1962), 1–116; Wilfried Hartmann, *Kirche und Kirchenrecht um 900. Die Bedeutung der spätkarolingischen Zeit für Tradition und Innovation im kirchlichen Recht*, MGH Schriften 58, 56–7, 311–13; Sarah Hamilton, *Church and People in the Medieval West, 900–1200* (Harlow, 2013), 12–13.

[23] Regino, *Libri duo* 7. For a more extensive guide to the Regino manuscripts and literature, see Lotte Kéry, *Canonical Collections of the Early Middle Ages (*ca.*400–1140): A Bibliographical Guide to the Manuscripts and Literature* (Washington DC, 1999), 128–33. For Burchard's use of Regino, see Hartmut Hoffmann and Rudolf Pokorny, *Das Dekret des Bischofs Burchard von Worms. Textstufen – Frühe Verbreitung – Vorlagen*, MGH Hilfsmittel 12. The most easily accessible edition is Burchard of Worms, *Decretum*, PL 140, cols 537–1065; on the manuscripts, see Kéry, *Canonical Collections*, 133–55; on the principles behind Burchard's compilation, see Greta Austin, *Shaping Church Law around the Year 1000: The* Decretum *of Burchard of Worms* (Farnham, 2009).

[24] Burchard, *Decretum* (PL 140, cols 617–66).

[25] 'Quae presbyteri necessario discere et scire debeant', ibid. 2.2 (PL 140, col. 625).

[26] 'Sexto, quae ipsis sacerdotibus necessaria sunt ad discendum, id est sacramentarium, lectionarius, antiphonarius, baptisterium, compotus [*sic*], kanon, paenitentialis, psalterium, homeliae per circulum anni dominicis diebus et singulis festivitatibus aptae. Ex quibus omnibus, si unum defuerit, sacerdotis nomen vix in eo constabit, quia valde periculosae sunt evangelicae minae quibus dicitur: "Si caecus caeco ducatum praestet, ambo in foveam cadunt"': Haito of Basel, *Capitula* 6 (MGH Capit. episc. 1, 211). Of the ninth-century episcopal statutes, Haito's is, in Carine van Rhijn's view, the 'most

of the liturgy as much as church law. Burchard's aspirations to be comprehensive mean that it is difficult to make too much of his inclusion of such material. Other evidence, however, reinforces the suggestion that some bishops at this time took the examination of candidates for the priesthood seriously.

Turning to the ordination rites themselves, they suggest that churchmen should use the occasion as an opportunity for education. The rites are generally found in those collections of rites reserved to bishops which are known to modern scholars as pontificals.[27] In recent years scholars have increasingly recognized that the relationship between textual record and the enactment of the liturgy is far from straightforward. Rites are not simple guides as to how to conduct a service, but rather more complex records of the 'ought world' of medieval liturgists: how they thought their liturgical world should be.[28] It is, however, clear that ordination rites recorded across northern Europe and the former Carolingian empire stabilized fairly early.[29] It is striking, therefore, that there is a distinct group of four pontificals copied in late Anglo-Saxon England which suggest that their compilers were giving considerable thought to the rite of ordination itself.[30] It was usual for the ordination rites for the various

explicit on the subject of (liturgical) knowledge and understanding': *Shepherds of the Lord*, 107–8.

[27] On pontificals, see Niels Krogh Rasmussen, *Les Pontificaux du haut moyen âge. Genèse du livre de l'évêque*, Spicilegium sacrum lovaniense. Études et documents 49 (Leuven, 1998); for a review of recent work, see Sarah Hamilton, 'Interpreting Diversity: Excommunication Rites in the Tenth and Eleventh Centuries', in Helen Gittos and Sarah Hamilton, eds, *Understanding Medieval Liturgy: Essays in Interpretation* (Farnham, 2016), 125–58, at 126–7.

[28] On this point, see the brief observations by Helen Gittos, 'Researching the History of Rites', in eadem and Hamilton, eds, *Understanding Medieval Liturgy*, 13–37, at 20–2; Hamilton, 'Interpreting Diversity', especially 128; eadem, 'The Early Pontificals: The Anglo-Saxon Evidence reconsidered from a Continental Perspective', in Rollason, Leyser and Williams, eds, *England and the Continent*, 411–28; Henry Parkes, *The Making of Liturgy in the Ottonian Church: Books, Music and Ritual in Mainz, 950–1050* (Cambridge, 2015), 10–12.

[29] Roger E. Reynolds, *Clerics in the Early Middle Ages: Hierarchy and Image*, Variorum Collected Studies 669 (Aldershot, 1999); idem, *Clerical Orders in the Early Middle Ages: Duties and Ordination*, Variorum Collected Studies 670 (Aldershot, 1999), especially XI, 'The Ordination of Clerics in the Middle Ages'. For a helpful summary, see Barrow, *Clergy*, 28–9, 34–9.

[30] Paris, BN, MS Lat. 10575, the 'Egbert Pontifical': *Two Anglo-Saxon Pontificals (the Egbert and Sidney Sussex Pontificals)*, ed. H. M. J. Banting, HBS 104 (London, 1989), 15–31; BN, MS Lat. 943, fols 45r–61r, the 'Dunstan' or 'Sherborne' Pontifical with

grades of clergy in use across the Latin West to be preceded by two texts. One, generally entitled 'Capitulum Sancti Gregorii' (the Chapter of St Gregory), reminds the bishop that he should not ordain anyone before they reach the age of maturity or before they have been examined.[31] The other is a text belonging to the genre that Roger Reynolds termed 'Ordinals of Christ'.[32] These texts list the various grades of clerical orders – generally seven – and justify them by linking them to the events in Christ's life; they therefore give 'dominical sanction', in Reynolds's phrasing, to ecclesiastical grades which had not been recorded in the New Testament.[33] The 'Ordinals of Christ' seem to have served two fundamental purposes: to inspire clerics to imitate Christ, and at the same time to serve as a mnemonic device for the seven clerical orders.[34]

In the Anglo-Saxon group of manuscripts – the earliest of which is the pontifical made for Archbishop Dunstan in the 960s – this list of orders has been linked to a statement of the duties for each grade, as well as to events in Christ's life. The link to the events of Christ's life

digitized copy, online at: <http://gallica.bnf.fr/ark:/12148/btv1b6001165p.r=sherborne?rk=21459;2>, accessed 25 February 2018; Rouen, Bibliothèque municipale MS 368 (A.27), the 'Lanalet Pontifical': *Pontificale Lanaletense (Bibliothèque de la Ville de Rouen A.37, Cat. 368): A Pontifical formerly in use at St Germans Cornwall*, ed. G. H. Doble, HBS 74 (London, 1937), 49–59; London, BL, Add. MS 57337, fols 36^{v}–51^{v}, the 'Anderson Pontifical' with digitized copy, online at: <http://www.bl.uk/manuscripts/Viewer.aspx?ref=add_ms_57337>, accessed 6 June 2018, transcribed by Marie A. Conn, 'The Dunstan and Brodie (Anderson) Pontificals: An Edition and Study' (PhD thesis, University of Notre Dame, 1993), 231–45. See Roger Reynolds, 'Christ as Cleric: The Ordinals of Christ', in *Clerics in the Early Middle Ages*, II, 15.

[31] For a full version of this text, see that in Claudius Pontifical I, edited in *The Claudius Pontificals (from Cotton MS. Claudius A.iii in the British Museum)*, ed. D. H. Turner, HBS 97 (London, 1971), 33–4; for an abbreviated version, see that in the 'Egbert Pontifical', in *Two Anglo-Saxon Pontificals*, ed. Banting, 16.

[32] Roger E. Reynolds, *The Ordinals of Christ from their Origins to the Twelfth Century*, Beiträge zur Geschichte und Quellenkunde des Mittelalters 7 (Berlin, 1978); idem, 'Christ as Cleric'.

[33] Reynolds, 'Christ as Cleric', 4.

[34] This is my interpretation. Reynolds suggests these possibilities: 'From their origins the Ordinals of Christ fulfilled a variety of functions. On the humblest level they could be used as space-fillers, practice pieces, and probationes pennae. At a slightly higher level they also served as wit sharpeners or puzzles for monks or clerics … [they have] affinity with erotematic literature. … They were used in the education and inspiration of clerical ordinands, and when a cleric was ordained, he could be asked about the origins and duties of the grade he was to receive in terms of an Ordinal of Christ': 'Christ as Cleric', 10–11.

is thus well known, but this description of the pastoral duties of the priest is peculiar to Anglo-Saxon texts.

> [Christ] was a priest when he accepted bread in his holy hands and similarly the chalice, gazing to God his Father in heaven, giving thanks and blessing the priests, appointed moreover deservedly and it is understood by wisdom, not age, and the priest ought to bless, to offer and to lead well, to preach and to baptize and to communicate because he is the senior of all these aforesaid grades and stands in place of the bishop in his church. For not on account of the decrepitude of old age but on account of wisdom they are called priests.[35]

This text owes a good deal to patristic writings, particularly the works of Isidore of Seville.[36] What is also striking, however, is the emphasis on wisdom as fundamental to the conduct of the sacerdotal ministry, distinguishing the priest from other clerical orders. The rite itself includes an admonition to candidates for the priesthood and for the diaconate about their future behaviour: they must be assiduous, not fall asleep in the vigil, be sober not drunk, be chaste, guard the gifts of the faithful carefully, not leave anything putrid in the sacristy, and so forth.[37] In addition, this particular text has been amended in the Dunstan Pontifical manuscript to allow for the possibility of ordaining more than one candidate at once.[38] Such changes are not of themselves evidence of practical usage. Although Dunstan's pontifical was clearly a personal book made for him, as is evidenced by the inclusion at the beginning in the same script as that of the main text a copy of the

[35] 'Presbiter fuit quando accepit panem in suis sanctis manibus similiter et calicem respiciens in caelum ad deum patrem suum gratias agens et benedixit presbiteros autem merito et sapientia dici non aetate intelligendum est presbiterum autem oportet benedicere offerre et bene preesse predicare et baptizare atque communicare quia his supradictis gradibus senior est et uicem aepiscopi in aecclesia facit. Non enim propter decrepitam senectutem sed propter sapientiam presbiteri nominantur': BN, MS Lat. 943, fol. 46^{r}. Compare the texts in the 'Egbert Pontifical', in *Two Anglo-Saxon Pontificals*, ed. Banting, 18; in the 'Lanalet Pontifical', in *Pontificale Lanaletense*, ed. Doble, 49; and in the 'Anderson Pontifical', in Conn, 'Dunstan and Brodie (Anderson) Pontificals', 232.

[36] Reynolds, 'Christ as Cleric', 15.

[37] BN, MS Lat. 943, fols 49^{v}–50^{r}.

[38] The digitized copy shows the inclusion of interlinear alternatives, such as 'uel uobis' above 'tibi': ibid., fol. 49^{v}: <http://gallica.bnf.fr/ark:/12148/btv1b6001165p/f104.image.r=sherborne>, accessed 25 February 2018. See similar interlinear alternatives to allow for plural ordination in the Anderson Pontifical: BL, Add. MS 57337, fols 42^{v}–46^{r}: <http://www.bl.uk/manuscripts/Viewer.aspx?ref=add_ms_57337_fs001r>, accessed 7 June 2018; and in the Lanalet Pontifical: *Pontificale Lanaletense*, ed. Doble, 55–7.

papal letter granting him the pallium, the fact that the succeeding rite for the ordination of a bishop has been similarly amended with an interlinear reading in the plural is probably suggestive of a copyist with an interest in ensuring that the text of each of the ordination rites supports correct delivery in both the singular and the plural, rather than reflecting amendments for a particular occasion.[39] Minor and consistent changes like these ones in the Dunstan Pontifical therefore suggest an ongoing interest in ordination rites and the expectations of clerical office on the part of the compilers of such collections.[40]

Nor were such concerns confined to England. One Italian pontifical, copied for the Tuscan see of Arezzo in the late eleventh century, testifies to a similar anxiety in its revisions to the ordination rite. Its compilers laid striking emphasis upon the behaviour and duties of the priest, using the occasion to emphasize the practical and moral requirements of the priesthood rather than as an opportunity for more theological reflection.[41] In addition to the 'Ordinals of Christ', this pontifical includes a text enjoining those examining candidates for the priesthood and diaconate to explore the candidates' morals, knowledge and nature. They should also check whether candidates have committed any serious sins, whether they are penitents and whether they are married.[42] The emphasis is on ensuring compliance with the canonical requirements of office.

Ordination rites inform us about what should happen. However, there is another category of texts of relevance to this investigation: these set out the questions which should be asked of candidates prior to their ordination, often referred to as 'priests' exams'.[43]

[39] BN, MS Lat. 943, fols 54^v–59^r.

[40] Ibid., fols 7^r–8^v; on this manuscript as one of several pontificals made for a particular bishop in this period, see Hamilton, 'Early Pontificals', 422–7; on the use of the first person in the rubric for the rite for church dedication as evidence for Dunstan's reforming interests, see Helen Gittos, *Liturgy, Architecture, and Sacred Places in Anglo-Saxon England* (Oxford, 2013), 224–8.

[41] Oxford, Bodl., MS Canon. Lit. 359, fols 24^v–33^v. For a description, see *A Summary Catalogue of Western Manuscripts in the Bodleian Library at Oxford*, 4, ed. Falconer Madan (Oxford, 1897), 390–1 (no. 19444). Although known to musicologists and liturgical scholars, it has not been the subject of sustained study: see entry in the Bodleian Library's bibliographical database, online at: <https://medieval.bodleian.ox.ac.uk/catalog/manuscript_3041>, accessed 7 June 2018.

[42] Bodl., MS Canon. Lit. 359, fol. 26^r.

[43] Ernest Vykoukal, 'Les Examens du clergé paroissial à l'époque carolingienne', *RHE* 14 (1913), 81–96; Carine van Rhijn, 'Karolingische priesterexamens en het probleem van correctio op het platteland', *Tijdschrift voor Geschiedenis* 125 (2012), 158–71; eadem,

They first emerge around 800 and seem to have been composed in response to the Frankish rulers' concerns about the standards of education amongst local priests, as part of a wider programme to ensure that lay Christians led correct and righteous lives.[44] Various examples of priests' exams are extant: there are nine different texts surviving in twenty-two different manuscripts from the ninth century.[45] These priests' exams were not widely copied in later periods. Of the nine Frankish priests' exam texts identified, only two appear to have been copied after the ninth century: that attributed to Bishop Waltcaud of Liège (d. 831), and the early ninth-century southern French text, 'Dic mihi pro quid'.[46] This temporal pattern is all the more surprising when contrasted with that for episcopal statutes, with which they have often been confused by modern editors: Bishop Theodulf of Orléans's early ninth-century *capitula*, for example, survive in more tenth- and eleventh-century copies than in copies made in the ninth century.[47] Studies by Wilfried Hartmann and

'"Et hoc considerat episcopus, ut ipsi presbyteri non sint idiothae": Carolingian local *Correctio* and an unknown Priests' Exam from the Early Ninth Century', in Rob Meens et al., eds, *Religious Franks: Religion and Power in the Frankish Kingdoms. Studies in Honour of Mayke de Jong* (Manchester, 2016), 162–80.

[44] On the wider programme, see especially Charlemagne's *Admonitio generalis* (789) and the text known to modern readers as the *Instructio pastoralis* and attributed to Archbishop Arn of Salzburg: *Die Admonitio generalis Karls des Grossen*, MGH Fontes n.s. 16, 220 (§68); Raymond Étaix, 'Un manuel de pastorale de l'époque Carolingienne (Clm 27152)', *RB* 91 (1981), 105–30. For a recent overview of the Carolingian material, see van Rhijn, '"Et hoc considerat episcopus"'.

[45] For details of the nine texts and the number of ninth-century copies, see van Rhijn, '"Et hoc considerat episcopus"', 165 n. 12.

[46] Waltcaud survives in a copy variously dated to the late ninth or the first half of the tenth century: Cologne, Erzdiöcesan- und Dombibliothek, MS 120 (s. $ix^{4/4}/x^{in}$), (MGH Capit. episc. 1, 24, 44, which dates it to s. x^1; for dating to the last quarter of the ninth century, see Bernhard Bischoff, *Katalog der festländischen Handschriften des neunten Jahrhundert*, 1: *Aachen-Lambach* [Wiesbaden, 1998], 400). For a full description of this manuscript, see Klaus Zechiel-Eckes, *Die Concordia canonum des Cresconius. Studien und Edition*, Freiburger Beiträge zur mittelalterlichen Geschichte Studien und Texte 5, 2 vols (Frankfurt am Main, 1992), 2: 319–21. 'Dic mihi pro quid' survives in six ninth-century manuscripts, one from the twelfth century and three from the tenth and eleventh centuries plus one fragment: Barcelona, Biblioteca de la Universidad de Barcelona, MS 228 (s.x^{ex} / s.xi^{in}); Florence, Biblioteca Riccardiana, MS 256 (s. xi); BN, MS lat. 1008 (s. ix/x); BN, MS lat. 13092 (s. xi) (fragment), identified by van Rhijn in '"Et hoc considerat episcopus"', 175–6.

[47] According to its most recent editor, Peter Brommer, it survives in some seventeen ninth-century and nineteen tenth- and eleventh-century copies: MGH Capit. episc. 1, 75–99.

Carine van Rhijn suggest these ninth-century priests' exams were generally copied into priests' handbooks alongside other forms of pastoral and didactic material, such as handbooks of penance; expositions of the Lord's Prayer, the creed and the baptismal liturgy; sermons; and texts on the clerical grades.[48] In later periods, however, priests' exams seem to have been copied in much more monastic contexts.[49]

Although the later period was not much interested in priests' exams, one new text was copied in England. It is included in a collection copied at Worcester towards the end of the eleventh century: Oxford, Bodleian Library, MS Junius 121.[50] This manuscript contains a variety of pastoral texts, in both Old English and Latin, including statutes, homilies, penitentials and other didactic texts, many of which focus on the duties of priests and bishops. The codex probably belonged to the late eleventh-century bishop of Worcester known as St Wulfstan (1062–95), but several of the texts it contains are associated with his predecessor, the early eleventh-century bishop of Worcester and concurrently archbishop of York, Wulfstan I (1002–23).[51] Amongst these texts is a priest's exam in Old English.[52] Whilst its provisions broadly echo the contents of the ninth-century Frankish

48 Van Rhijn, '"Et hoc considerat episcopus"', 168–9; Wilfried Hartmann, 'Neue Texte zur bischöflichen Reformgesetzgebung aus den Jahren 829/31. Vier Diözesansynoden Halitgars von Cambrai', *Deutsches Archiv* 25 (1979), 368–94.

49 For instance, 'Dic mihi pro quid' was copied alongside Gregory's *Dialogues* in a twelfth-century manuscript, El Escorial, Real Biblioteca del Monasterio de San Lorenzo, MS Q. III. 10: see the description in Susana Zapke, ed., *Hispania Vetus: Musical-Liturgical Manuscripts from Visigothic Origins to the Franco-Roman Transition, Ninth to Twelfth Centuries* (Bilbao, 2007), 368–9.

50 On this collection, see Neil R. Ker, *Catalogue of Manuscripts containing Anglo-Saxon* (Oxford, 1957), 412–16 (no. 338); Helmut Gneuss and Michael Lapidge, *Anglo-Saxon Manuscripts. A Bibliographical Handlist of Manuscripts and Manuscript Fragments written or owned in England up to 1100* (Toronto, ON, 2014), 495–8 (no. 644).

51 Helen Foxhall-Forbes is currently researching this collection. See her 'Affective Piety and the Practice of Penance in late Eleventh-Century Worcester: The Address to the Penitent in Oxford, Bodleian Library, Junius 121', *Anglo-Saxon England* 44 (2015), 309–45; eadem, 'Making Books for Pastoral Care in late Eleventh-Century Worcester: Oxford, Bodleian Library, Junius MS 121 and Hatton MSS 113 + 114' (forthcoming); I am extremely grateful to her for generously letting me read her research ahead of publication and follow here her conclusion that this manuscript is a collection compiled to support the education of local priests.

52 D. Whitelock, M. Brett and C. N. L. Brooke, eds, *Councils and Synods with other Documents Relating to the English Church*, 1: *871–1066* (Oxford, 1981), 422–7 (no. 57). This text is discussed by Foxhall-Forbes, 'Making Books', 15–16, eadem, *Heaven and Earth in Anglo-Saxon England: Theology and Society in an Age of Faith* (Farnham, 2013), 40, 49; Barrow, *Clergy*, 34.

Latin texts, it is not a straight translation of any of them, but seems rather to have been compiled independently by a more pragmatic author, almost certainly Archbishop Wulfstan himself.[53] Unlike the Carolingian exams, this text is presented as a sermon, and begins with an extract translated from Haito's ninth-century *Visio Wettini*, which warns priests of the punishments awaiting them if they do not keep the commitments made at their ordination, before lamenting the fact that 'there are too many who desire the high order more than they should', and suggesting that prelates should therefore be more cautious in accepting candidates for higher orders than they have been in the past.[54] Other aspects, however, suggest that it was compiled by a pragmatic realist. The demand that anyone desiring to enter holy orders should come before the bishop a full month before he wishes to be ordained so that he may be examined is not found in the Frankish tradition; the request that the candidate should bring his own supplies so as not to be a burden on those examining him is also novel.[55] Further testimony to the pragmatism of its compiler is the provision that the candidate should present a token from his teacher, testifying to his standard of education.[56] The content of the exam itself is more traditional. It begins by asking the candidate to explain his faith in clear terms to other men; then asks him to explain 'how he knows his ministry, and how he understands baptism, and how he comprehends the symbolism of the mass and also of the other church services', and whether he knows the canons and his computus so 'he can divide the course of the year'.[57] Some of the

[53] On Wulfstan's likely authorship, see Joyce Tally Lionarons, *The Homiletic Writings of Archbishop Wulfstan: A Critical Study* (Woodbridge, 2010), 39–40. On Wulfstan's conception of the bishop as teacher of teachers, see Jay Paul Gates, 'Preaching, Politics and Episcopal Reform in Wulfstan's early Writings', *EME* 23 (2015), 93–116.

[54] Whitelock, Brett and Brooke, eds, *Councils and Synods*, 1: 423 (§§6–8). On its manuscript context, see Foxhall-Forbes, 'Making Books', 15–16.

[55] Whitelock, Brett and Brooke, eds, *Councils and Synods*, 1: 424 (§9). Compare the four days in Regino of Prüm, *Libri duo*, 1.453 (ed. Hartmann, 228–30, at 228), copied by Burchard, *Decretum* 2.1 (PL 140, col. 625); this canon, attributed by both Regino and Burchard to the Council of Nantes, is one of Regino's 'capitula incerta' for which there is no known source: Hartmann, 'Die *Capita incerta*'. The closest parallel in the Frankish priests' examinations is the requirement in the Halitgarian 'Primitus cum venerint' that the bishop should check whether the candidate is lettered and well taught, whether priests and good witnesses will testify for him, and whether he knows the documents of the faith: Hartmann, 'Neue Texte', 392.

[56] Whitelock, Brett and Brooke, eds, *Councils and Synods*, 1: 424 (§10).

[57] Ibid. 424–5 (§§11–13).

Frankish ninth-century texts go into more detail, demanding that the candidate also be grilled about his knowledge of how to baptize, and whether he can use the correct Latin forms for masculine and feminine, plural and singular candidates for baptism, his knowledge of the different texts of the creed, and of the exorcism, as well as his knowledge of the gospels, homilies, books of pastoral care and canons.[58] However, the Anglo-Saxon author was more pessimistic – or realistic – than his Frankish predecessors, for MS Junius 121 continues:

> If he is certain in all these things, he is then the better worthy of orders. If he knows too little of these things, he is first to learn, and afterwards receive orders. And nevertheless, if one must out of necessity ordain a half-educated man, who knows all too little, one is then to do so, if there is great necessity, on condition that he find surety for himself that he will learn afterwards as eagerly as ever he possibly can.[59]

Unlike the Frankish texts, the Worcester exam goes into further detail about how the teacher or examiner should present the candidate to the bishop and give an account of his learning, before handing him over to be ordained and receiving him back afterwards.[60] It concludes by enjoining those who are ordained as mass-priests to celebrate thirty masses for the bishop, whilst those who are ordained deacon should sing thirty psalms, and both should pray zealously for the bishop for their whole lifetime.[61] For the author of this text, ordination clearly establishes a bond of confraternity between the ordinand and the bishop.

The final piece of evidence for episcopal anxiety about the quality of the candidates they appointed to the priesthood is to be found in the *epistolae formata*.[62] These are letters of reference written by bishops on behalf of members of the lower clergy, usually addressed to the

[58] For knowledge of correct baptismal prayers for both sexes, plural and singular: 'Primum omnium', ed. in Vykoukal, 'Les Examens du clergé paroissial', 85. For knowledge of creeds, see, for example, Waltcaud of Liège, *Capitula* 2 (MGH Capit. episc. 1, 46); and the Halitgarian 'Primitus cum venerint', ed. in Hartmann, 'Neue Texte', 393; for creeds, exorcism, gospels, homilies, and books of pastoral care (the editor suggests this is possibly an allusion to Gregory the Great's *Regula pastoralis*) and canons, see *Capitula Frisingensia prima* 1–2, 5, 11–14 (MGH Capit. episc. 3, 204–5).

[59] Whitelock, Brett and Brooke, eds, *Councils and Synods*, 1: 425 (no. 57, §§14–16).

[60] Ibid. 425–6 (§§17–20).

[61] Ibid. 426–7 (§21).

[62] For a helpful introduction, see Richard Fletcher, 'An *Epistola Formata* from León', *BIHR* 45 (1972), 122–8.

bishop of another diocese, and testifying to such matters as the subject's education, ordination, suitability for pastoral office, or possession of permission to travel outside his diocese.[63] They survive sporadically both in formulary collections and accidentally across the Latin West from the ninth to eleventh centuries, attesting to their widespread use.[64] The correspondence of Ratbod, archbishop of Trier (883–915), preserves two such letters; one, dated 906, from Ratbod to the bishop of Metz testifying to the education that the priest Gislemarus has received in his diocese; another from the bishop of Verdun to Ratbod vouching for the priest Adruinus.[65] The continued use of templates such as these testifies that education of the priesthood – at least of those sufficiently close to the bishop to obtain his support when moving to a different diocese – remained valued in the tenth century. However, they were only ever probably in use for the few: what of the many?

Pessimism is depressingly common amongst modern commentators on contemporary education, and tenth-century bishops were no exceptions to what seems to be a more universal trait. In a letter addressed to his diocesan clergy written during Lent in 966, Bishop Rather of Verona grumbled that he had summoned his clergy three times to the synod and found them to be ignorant.[66] In a letter

[63] On the importance such letters in canon law, see the restatement of practice by the Council of Ravenna in 998: *Die Konzilien Deutschlands und Reichsitaliens 916–1001*, 2 vols, MGH Conc. 6/2, 546.

[64] For example, see *Formulae Merowingici et Karolini Aevi*, MGH L 5, 162, 218, 383, 387, 408–9, 519, 557–68; Eugène de Rozière, *Recueil général des formules usitées dans l'Empire des Francs du Ve au Xe siècle*, 3 vols (Paris, 1859–71), 3: nos 645, 647–8.

[65] PL 129, col. 1396. On the letter of Ratbod concerning Gislemarus, see van Rhijn, *Shepherds of the Lord*, 176.

[66] 'Quia mirari vos scio, immo murmurare, quod est peius, non nescio, quod tertio iam vos vocavi et quasi nihil vobiscum egi, ne frustra hoc me fecisse putetis, fateor, quia explorandi vos causa hoc feci, et quales vos me inventurum estimavi, tales, pro nefas, inveni': *Die Briefe des Bischofs Rather von Verona*, MGH BdK 1, 124–5 (no. 25) ('I know that you are surprised – or rather [which is worse] I know that you grumble – that I have summoned you three times now and yet seem to have done nothing with you. So you should not think that I have done this to no purpose, I admit that I have done it in order to examine you, and I have found you to be such, alas, as I thought that I would find you to be': *The Complete Works of Rather of Verona*, transl. Peter L. D. Reid, Medieval and Renaissance Texts and Studies 76 [Binghamton, NY, 1991], 444 [no. 43]). For consideration of Rather's attempts at reform of the Veronese clergy, see Fritz Weigle, 'Ratherius von Verona im Kampf um das Kirchengut 961–68', *Quellen und Forschungen aus italienischen Archiven und Bibliotheken* 28 (1937–8), 1–35; Louis F. Lumaghi, 'Rather of Verona: Pre-Gregorian Reformer' (PhD thesis, University of Colorado at Boulder, 1975), 69–71;

written later that year Rather related the background to his diocesan letter. He recounts how he had sent his archpriest and archdeacon together with the cathedral canons to conduct a two-day visitation of the parishes and 'make examination' (*discuterent*) and report back to him 'all that had to be corrected' (*emendenda omnia*).[67] He complained that those conducting the visitation had focused on whether the priests knew the Psalms 'and such', and had found that they did; however, when he probed, Rather discovered that 'many of them did not even know' the Apostles' Creed.[68] He had therefore composed his letter to all the diocesan clergy, instructing them to learn the three creeds and to recite them by heart when they were next summoned if they wished to remain priests in his diocese.[69] He went on to provide simple instruction on why the Lord's day is so called and how it should be observed, writing:

> I grieve that you do not all know this and things like this, in fact I lament that you do not care about them at all; as your pastor I instruct you to hasten to learn them, and earnestly try, I beg, to teach God's people by good example because you do not know how to do so by words.[70]

Rather then went on to quote the text of a synodal address, known to modern commentators as the *Admonitio synodalis*, which circulated widely in the tenth century.[71] He enjoined the parish priests in his diocese that the creeds, in particular, should be 'written down and memorized', but was disappointed to discover that the cathedral

---

Maureen C. Miller, *The Formation of a Medieval Church: Ecclesiastical Change in Verona, 950–1150* (Ithaca, NY, 1993), 45–50. None of these works pay sustained attention to this text.

[67] MGH BdK 1, 144 (no. 26); *Complete Works of Rather*, transl. Reid, 473 (no. 47).

[68] 'De psalmis et huiusmodi … Sciscitatur utque de fide, illorum inveni plurimos neque ipsum sapere symbolum, qui fuisse creditur apostolorum': MGH BdK 1, 144–5 (no. 26); *Complete Works of Rather*, transl. Reid, 473 (no. 47).

[69] 'Quicumque vult ergo sacerdos in nostra paroechia esse aut fieri aut permanere, illas tres memoriter nobis recitet, cum proxime a nobis huc vocatus fuerit': MGH BdK 1, 125 (no. 25); *Complete Works of Rather*, transl. Reid, 445 (no. 43).

[70] 'Ista et illis similia quia vos penitus nescire doleo, immo de talibus nil curare gemisco pastoraliter ut addiscere festinetis, praecipio, et quia sermone ignoratus, bono exemplo Dei populum erudire, quaeso, studeatis': MGH BdK 1, 129 (no. 25); *Complete Works of Rather*, transl. Reid, 448 (no. 43).

[71] MGH BdK 1, 130–5 (no. 25); cf. *Admonitio synodalis*, ed. Robert Amiet, in 'Une "Admonitio synodalis" de l'époque carolingienne. Étude critique et édition', *Mediaeval Studies* 26 (1964), 12–82.

canons, in particular, objected to the singing of the Athanasian Creed, despite the willingness of parish priests to do so.[72] Rather had a stormy and difficult relationship with the clergy of Verona and with the local count, which resulted in his being ejected from the see some two years after this synod.[73] His account has therefore to be read in the light of his unsuccessful attempts to impose his authority upon the diocese.

Nonetheless this encounter is interesting for what it reveals about the difference in interpretation of the inherited Carolingian clerical standards between the Veronese higher clergy and their Lotharingian-educated bishop. Rather's expectations of the education of the clergy in his diocese conform to those of his Frankish predecessors. In the *Admonitio generalis* (789), Charlemagne and his advisors set out what local priests should know:

> To priests. Let the bishops diligently examine the priests throughout their parishes, their faith, their baptism, and their celebrations of masses, that the priests might hold upright faith and observe catholic baptism and understand well the prayers of the Mass. And that the psalms might be sung in a fitting manner according to the division of the verses and that the priests themselves might understand the Lord's prayer and preach for the understanding of all … .[74]

For Charlemagne and his bishops knowledge of the faith, encompassed in knowledge of the various creeds, sat alongside knowledge

[72] MGH BdK 1, 145–6 (no. 26); *Complete Works of Rather*, transl. Reid, 474 (no. 47).

[73] See the works listed in n. 66; cf. also Hubertus Siebert, 'Rather von Verona, Abt von Lobbes, Bischof von Verona (931–34, 946–8, 961–68) und Lüttich (953–55)', *Neue Deutsche Biographie*, 25 vols (Berlin, 1953–2012), 21: 176–8; Hans Martin Schaller, 'Rather, Bischof von Verona und Lüttich (d. 974)', *Lexikon des Mittelalters*, 9 vols (Munich, 1977–99), 7: 457–8.

[74] 'Sacerdotibus. Ut episcopi diligenter discutiant per suas parrochias presbyteros, eorum fidem, baptisma et missarum celebrationes, ut et fidem rectam teneant et baptisma catholicum observent et missarum preces bene intellegant, et ut psalmi digne secundum divisiones versuum modulentur et dominicam orationem ipsi intellegant et omnibus praedicent intellegendam': MGH Fontes n.s. 16, 220 (§68); transl. in P. D. King, *Charlemagne: Translated Sources* (Kendal, 1987), 216. On the role of subdivision of psalms into smaller parts, verses and half-verses to support the performance of choral psalmody in the Carolingian period, and the challenges caused by variations in division, see Susan Rankin, 'Singing the Psalter in the Early Middle Ages', in Daniel J. DiCenso and Rebecca Maloy, eds, *Chant, Liturgy, and the Inheritance of Rome: Essays in Honour of Joseph Dyer*, HBS Subsidia 7 (London, 2017), 270–89.

of baptism, the mass, the Psalms and the Lord's Prayer.[75] Whilst Rather chose to stress the importance of knowing all three creeds, the Veronese higher clergy's focus on priests' knowledge of 'the psalms and such' also fits with these earlier Carolingian regulations.[76] Indeed, Bishop Waltcaud of Liège in his early ninth-century *capitula* adapted the precepts of the *Admonitio generalis* into questions which stressed the need for memorization, emphasising that priests should understand the Athanasian and Apostles' Creeds, and also that they memorize the Psalms.[77] Half a century later, Archbishop Hincmar of Reims in his *capitula* in 852 also stressed the importance of memorizing certain texts, including the Psalms: Priests should learn the Creed and the Lord's Prayer, but should also

> understand, have learnt by memory and deliver distinctly the prefaces and canon of the mass and should be able to read well the prayers of the mass and the epistle and gospel lessons and know also by heart how to pronounce the words and distinctions of the psalms according to rule with the usual canticles.[78]

Nor were such requirements reserved to local parish priests. Churchmen in the post-Carolingian centuries continued to attach importance to memorizing key liturgical texts. Indeed, monastic customaries from the tenth and eleventh centuries specify the role of

[75] For example: 'Et hoc consideret episcopus, ut ipsi presbyteri non sint idiothae, sed sacras scripturas legant et intellegant, ut secundum traditionem Romane ecclesiae possint instruere, et fidem catholicam debeant ipsi agere et populos sibi commissos docere, missas secundum consuetudinem caelebrare, sicut romana traditio nobis tradidit': Arno of Salzburg (*c.*798), §4, in Raymond Étaix, 'Un Manuel de pastorale de l'époque Carolingienne (Clm, 27152)', *RB* 91 (1981), 105–30, at 117; 'Fidem catholicam sancti Athanasii et cetera quaecumque de fide, symbolum etiam apostolicam, orationem dominicam ad intellegendum pleniter cum expositione': Waltcaud of Liège, *Capitula* 2 (MGH Capit. episc. 1, 46).

[76] On early medieval psalmody, see Rankin, 'Singing the Psalter'.

[77] 'Psalmos vero, quomodo a presbiteris tenentur vel intelleguntur': Waltcaud of Liège, *Capitula* 2 (creeds), 14 (Psalms; MGH Capit. episc. 1, 46, 48).

[78] 'Ut unusquisque presbiterorum expositionem symboli atque orationis dominicae iuxta traditionem ortodoxorum patrum plenius discat et exinde predicando populum sibi commissum sedulo instruat. Praefationem quoque canonis et eundem canonem intellegat et memoriter ac distincte proferre valeat et orationes missarum, apostolum quoque et evangelium bene legere possit. Psalmorum etiam verba et distinctiones regulariter ex corde cum canticis consuetudinariis pronuntiare sciat. Nec non et sermonem Athanasii de fide, cuius initium est "Quicumque vult salvus esse", memorie quisque commendet et sensum illius intellegat et verbis com munibus enuntiare queat': Hincmar of Rheims, *Capitula* 1.1 (MGH Capit. episc. 2, 34–5).

memorization in the education of young boys. Their curriculum consisted essentially of training in the liturgy; between services, the oblates were to practise reading and singing in groups; readings, in particular, were usually to be performed from memory.[79] Rather's critique of the visitation undertaken by his senior clergy revealed conflicting interpretations of this Carolingian legacy within mid-tenth-century Verona rather than, as he implied, demonstrating the negligence of his senior clergy.[80]

Carolingian precedents cast a long shadow over tenth- and eleventh-century Europe. Turning to England, we find widespread copying and citation of Frankish legislation about the duties expected of local priests; such copies turn up both in canon law collections and in pontifical manuscripts.[81] However, late Anglo-Saxon England is unique in Europe for its widespread use of the vernacular, Old English. One of the reasons for this is explained in an admonitory

[79] Susan Boynton, 'Training for the Liturgy as a Form of Monastic Education', in George Ferzoco and Carolyn Muessig, eds, *Medieval Monastic Education* (London, 2000), 7–20; eadem, 'The Liturgical Role of Children in Monastic Customaries from the Central Middle Ages', *Studia Liturgica* 28 (1998), 194–209, especially 199–200. From the eleventh century onwards, there is evidence that adult novices were expected to memorize psalms and hymns through silent reading of books: eadem, 'Orality, Literacy and the early Notation of the Office Hymns', *Journal of the American Musicological Society* 56 (2003), 99–168, at 149–57.

[80] Rather's contemporary, Bishop Atto of Vercelli (924–61), also attached importance to knowledge of the Creed: 'Ut omnes fidem catholicam memoriter teneant. Primo omnium fidem catholicam omnes presbiteri et diacones seu subdiacones memoriter teneant': Atto of Vercelli, *Capitula* 4 (MGH Capit. episc. 3, 266–7). For reasons of space it has not been possible to consider Atto's work here, but see Suzanne Fonay Wemple, *Atto of Vercelli: Church, State and Christian Society in Tenth-century Italy*, Temi e Testi 27 (Rome, 1979).

[81] Capitula by Ghaerbald of Liège I, Theodulf of Orléans I and II and Radulf of Bourges are found in manuscripts of canon law associated with Archbishop Wulfstan of Worcester and York: Cambridge, Corpus Christi College, MS 265, 20–2, 51–8, 113–42; Bodl., MS Barlow 37, fols 14^{v}–15^{r}, 19^{r}–21^{v}, 25^{r}–26^{v}, 27^{r}–31^{r} (MGH Capit. episc. 1, 8–10); other copies of Theodulf are in Corpus Christi College, MS 201, 179–269; Bodl., MS Bodley 865, fols 97–112; Ghaerbald I is found in legal collections such as BL, MS Cotton Nero A.i (B), fols 127^{v}–129^{v}; Bodl., MS Bodley 718, fols 3^{r}–5^{r}, as well as in the 'Dunstan', 'Egbert' and 'Lanalet' pontificals: BN, MS lat. 943, fols 149^{r}–150^{v}; Pontifical, BN, MS lat. 10575, fols 6^{v}–9^{r}, Rouen, Bibliothèque municipale, MS 368, fols 178^{v}–180^{v} (MGH Capit. episc. 1, 8, 10). For a summary of recent scholarship on these manuscripts, see Gneuss and Lapidge, *Anglo-Saxon Manuscripts*. For consideration of these texts within their wider manuscript context, see Patrick Wormald, *The Making of English Law: King Alfred to the Twelfth Century*, 1: *Legislation and its Limits* (Oxford, 1999), 198–219. On the relationship between Ghaerbald's Capitulary and Wulfstan's episcopal statutes, see Michael Elliot, 'Ghaerbald's First Capitulary, the *Excerptiones Pseudo-Ecghberhti* and the Sources of Wulfstan's Canons of Edgar', *Notes and Queries* 57 (2010), 161–5.

letter written on behalf of Archbishop Wulfstan to his priests by Abbot Ælfric of Eynsham *c.*1006.[82] This letter thus belongs to the same genre, although it is written in a more measured tone than Rather's splenetic letter on the same theme. It begins: 'It befits us bishops that we reveal to you priests the written instructions which our canon teaches us, and also the gospel, in the English language; for not all of you can understand the Latin', and goes on: 'I know for certain that this our admonition will displease far too many of you. Yet one or other will be so inspired by God that he will desire to hear the holy teaching and to correct himself for the benefit of his soul.'[83] Its contents repeat precepts about the conduct, duties and knowledge expected of priests, taken from Carolingian legislation. It specifies the books a priest should own, and that his vestments should be clean, his chalice made of imperishable material, and his altar kept clean and free from mouse-droppings.[84] But the very act of translation from Latin into Old English brings into stark relief how the higher elite conceived of priestly office, describing books and communion vessels as a priest's tools, and comparing the knowledge required for the priestly ministry to the skills of worldly craftsmen:

> Why should you be less competent than worldly craftsmen (*woruldcræftan*) in your spiritual ministry for God's services, in that you do not have the weapons for the spiritual conflict, namely the things which we have now told you of? The smith gets for himself hammer and anvil and tongs and bellows and every sort of tool; the carpenter also axe and auger and all the tools which belong to woodwork. The fisherman and the huntsman provide nets for themselves, and all men

[82] 'Ælfric's First Old English Pastoral Letter for Wulstan, Archbishop of York', *Die Hirtenbriefe Ælfrics*, ed. B. Fehr, Bibliothek der angelsachsischen Prosa 9 (Hamburg, 1914), repr. with a supplement to the introduction by Peter Clemoes (Darmstadt, 1966), 68–145; available with transl. in Whitelock, Brett and Brooke, eds, *Councils and Synods*, 1: 255–302 (no. 46). On this correspondence, see Malcolm Godden, 'The Relations of Wulfstan and Ælfric', Joyce Hill, 'Archbishop Wulfstan: Reformer?', in Matthew Townend, ed., *Wulfstan, Archbishop of York: The Proceedings of the Second Alcuin Conference* (Turnhout, 2004), 353–74, 309–24 respectively; eadem, 'Monastic Reform and the Secular Church', in Carola Hicks, ed., *England in the Eleventh Century: Proceedings of the 1990 Harlaxton Symposium*, Harlaxton Medieval Studies 2 (Stamford, 1992), 103–17.

[83] 'Ælfric's First Old English Pastoral Letter', §§2, 4 (Whitelock, Brett and Brooke, eds, *Councils and Synods*, 1: 260–1).

[84] Ibid., §§157–64 (Whitelock, Brett and Brooke, eds, *Councils and Synods*, 1: 291–3).

> skilled in worldly crafts (*woruld-cræftige men*) make their tools; and the husbandman does not plough unless he knows how to plough. Take heed for yourself now, I pray you, that you may be better in your spiritual craft (*gastlicum cræfte*) for Christ's services, as it befits you that you should be, than the laymen in their worldly crafts (*woruldcræftum*).[85]

Cræft here reflects the range of the Latin *ars*, that is art, skill or trade,[86] and the comparison with lay professions makes explicit how the work and learning of a priest is viewed not so much as academic learning for learning's sake, but rather as a craft, based on the acquisition of skills and requiring physical tools.[87]

Foremost amongst the tools that Wulfstan specified a priest needed were books. In the words of the letter: 'You must be equipped with books as befits your order. A mass-priest must have a missal and a book of the epistles, and a hymn-book and a reading-book and a psalter and a manual and a penitential and a computus; and they are to be well-corrected.'[88] Similar lists of the books a priest should be owned can be traced back to the early ninth-century Carolingian episcopal capitula. The early ninth-century list of works which are necessary for priests to know specified by Haito, bishop of Basle (806x812/13) included 'a sacramentary, a lectionary, an antiphonary, the baptismal rite, a computus, the penitential canons, a psalter, homilies for days throughout the year on Sunday and important feast days'.[89] The contents of such lists often varied somewhat. That of Archbishop Ruotger of Trier (915x929), for example, included a collection of homilies: 'That priests have their own necessary and corrected books, that is a psalter, a lectionary, a gospel book, a missal,

[85] Ibid., §§165–71 (Whitelock, Brett and Brooke, eds, *Councils and Synods*, 1: 293–4).

[86] Angus Cameron et al., eds, *Dictionary of Old English: A to H Online* (Toronto, ON, 2016), online at: <http://www.doe.utoronto.ca>, accessed 2 March 2018.

[87] Compare the allusion to how no craftsmen can work well without tools in reference to a schoolboy who comes to his lesson without writing implements, in *Anglo-Saxon Conversations: The Colloquies of Ælfric Bata*, ed. Scott Gwara, transl. David W. Porter (Woodbridge, 1997), 112–13. This passage and also the description of the monk's calling as an *ars* or *cræft*, similar but superior to that of a blacksmith, other metal-smith, carpenter or worker, in Ælfric's *Colloquy*, are discussed by Julia Crick, 'Learning and Training', in eadem and Elisabeth van Houts, eds, *A Social History of England, 900–1200* (Cambridge, 2011), 352–72, at 358–9.

[88] 'Ælfric's First Old English Pastoral Letter', §§157–8 (Whitelock, Brett and Brooke, eds, *Councils and Synods*, 1: 291–2).

[89] Haito of Basle, *Capitula* 6 (MGH Capit. episc. 1, 211). See n. 26 above for the Latin.

capitula, 40 homilies and a martyrology.'[90] That quoted by Rather in 966 was more minimalist: 'Let each church have a full missal, lectionary, and antiphonary.'[91] Such lists seem to go back to early ninth-century lists such as that of Gharbald of Liège's *Capitula* (*c.*801/2x809), which listed: 'a missal, a lectionary, a martyrology, a penitential, psalter and other books'.[92] As Gharbald emphasizes, it was the priest's responsibility to ensure *secundum possibilitatem* (according to his means or status) that his church was properly equipped. Whilst local priests were generally answerable for possession of 'the necessary books' in episcopal capitula, inventories and estate surveys make clear that local churches were endowed with basic book collections from the ninth century onwards.[93] In practice, therefore, the holdings of local priests often became elided with those of their church.

In recent decades scholars have begun to identify codices which contain combinations of such pastoral texts and to suggest that they were intended either for use by, or to train, local priests.[94] To date, most attention has been paid to ninth-century collections. In 2002 Susan Keefe identified some eighteen ninth-century manuscripts made as 'instruction-readers' for local priests, together with a further twenty-nine codices whose make-up and contents suggest they were made for schools to educate local clergy, and thirteen made for bishops as pastoral manuals or reference collections.

[90] 'Ut sacerdotes libros sibi necessarios correctos habeant, psalterium scilicet, lectionarium, evangelium, missalem, capitula, XL omelias et martyrologium': Ruotger of Trier, *Capitula* 5 (MGH Capit. episc. 1, 63).

[91] 'Missalem plenarium, lectionarium et antiphonarium unaquaque ecclesia habeat': MGH BdK 1, 131 (no. 25).

[92] 'Ut unusquisque secundum possibilitatem suam certare faciat de ornatu ecclesiae, scilicet in patenam et calicem, planetam et albam, missalem, lectionarium, martyrologium, paenitentialem, psalterium vel alios libros, quos potuerit, crucem, capsam, velut diximus iuxta possibilitatem suam': Ghaerbald of Liège, *Capitula II* 9 (MGH Capit. episc. 1, 39–40).

[93] Carl I. Hammer, 'Country Churches, Clerical Inventories and the Carolingian Renaissance in Bavaria', *ChH* 49 (1980), 5–17. On book ownership by local priests and local churches, see Yitzhak Hen, 'Priests and Books in the Merovingian Period', in Patzold and van Rhijn, eds, *Men in the Middle*, 162–76; van Rhijn, 'Manuscripts for Local Priests'.

[94] For England, see the evidence of the holdings of local churches assembled by Michael Lapidge, 'Surviving Booklists from Anglo-Saxon England', in idem and Helmut Gneuss, eds, *Learning and Literature in Anglo-Saxon England: Studies presented to Peter Clemoes on the Occasion of his Sixty-Fifth Birthday* (Cambridge, 1985), 33–89.

Subsequent research has identified other examples.[95] Keefe concluded from her study of baptismal instruction manuscripts that the Carolingian reform movement had been largely an episcopal undertaking, with variations between dioceses.[96] The copying of similar manuscripts from the tenth and eleventh centuries, albeit on a smaller scale, points to the sporadic continuation of such efforts in this period, as illustrated by three manuscripts compiled in northern France, Rome and southern England.[97]

Taking these in chronological order, the first codex, now London, BL, Add. MS 19725, is a medium-sized, eminently portable codex: it survives as 129 folios measuring 175–180 × 150 mm.[98] It was written at the turn of the ninth and tenth centuries in a centre somewhere in north-east Frankia under the influence of a scribe trained at Rheims. Although known to scholars, it has never, to my knowledge, been considered as a collection in its own right. Various pastorally orientated texts are gathered together including:

> a Bedean martyrology (including a selection of local saints which suggests it was compiled at a church under the influence of Lobbes);[99]
> a computus;
> a penitential *ordo*;[100]

[95] Keefe, *Water and the Word*, 1: 22–38, 160–3. Further manuscripts are identified in MGH Capit. episc. 4, 9. At a workshop on priests' books held at the University of Utrecht on 4 November 2016, Carine van Rhijn suggested there might be as many as thirty-three manuscripts of the type classified by Keefe as 'instruction-readers' and some forty of those she identified as 'school books'.

[96] Keefe, *Water and the Word*, 1: 143–55.

[97] See also van Rhijn's point that annotations and additions in later hands testify to the use of ninth-century books in later centuries: 'Pastoral Care and Prognostics', 273.

[98] Bernhard Bischoff, *Die südostdeutschen Schreibschulen und Bibliotheken in der Karolingerzeit*, 2 vols (Wiesbaden, 1960–80), 2: 230, for attribution to north-east Frankia; for description, see Reinhold Haggenmüller, *Die Überlieferung der Beda und Egbert zugeschriebenen Bußbücher* (Frankfurt am Main, 1991), 70.

[99] Henri Quentin, *Les Martyrologes historiques du moyen âge. Etude sur la formation du martyrologe romain* (Paris, 1907), 26–7.

[100] Ludger Körntgen, *Studien zu den Quellen der frühmittelalterlichen Bußbücher*, Quellen und Forschungen zum Recht im Mittelalter 7 (Sigmaringen, 1993), 239–41; idem, 'Bußbuch und Bußpraxis in der zweiten Hälfte des 9. Jahrhunderts', in Wilfried Hartmann, ed., *Recht und Gericht in Kirche und Welt um 900* (Munich, 2007), 197–215, at 206–7.

> Gennadius of Marseilles's *De ecclesiasticis dogmatibus*;[101]
> a collection of episcopal capitula from the ninth century;[102]
> a history of the early church.[103]

To these initial texts various others were added in different hands over the course of the tenth to twelfth centuries. These additions include a prayer for Palm Sunday, which is only otherwise found in manuscripts compiled under a north-east Frankish influence;[104] an exorcism rite in an eleventh-century hand; and various medical recipes for curing both human illnesses, including gout, and animal diseases, including swine fever.[105] Finally the text of a letter purporting to have come direct from heaven about how Sunday should be observed was added on a blank leaf in a twelfth-century hand.[106] In other words, the contents of this manuscript suggest a codex made for a local church serving a rural community in north-east Frankia: remember that a martyrology, computus and penitential are amongst the sort of books that a local priest, as we have seen, was supposed to own. In this particular case, the only two obits added to the martyrology are for two women, suggesting it may have been used, at least at one time, by a priest serving a female community.[107] These

[101] C. H. Turner, 'The "Liber Ecclesiasticarum Dogmatum" attributed to Gennadius', *JThS* 7 (1905), 78–99; idem, 'Supplenda', *JThS* 8 (1906), 103–14. Although written in the context of fifth-century debates about heresy, Gennadius's text focuses on the significance and conduct of pastoral rites for baptism, the eucharist and penance, making it a useful teaching aid.

[102] MGH Capit. episc. 1: 34–5, 83; 3: 22–3; 4: 89.

[103] This text is a compendium, including Rufinus's *Historia Monachorum* 1.4.4, 1.5.2, 7.1, 7.6, 9.4.1, 9.5.1, 11.9.1; and Bede's *Historia Ecclesiastica* 5.12, 5.13-14. I should like to thank Robert Evans for his help in identifying the elements of this text.

[104] BL, Add. MS 19725, fol. 1^{r}: '*Oratio in ramis palmarum*: Deus qui temporibus noae famuli tui …'. The text is found in the sacramentary-pontifical made for Ratoldus, abbot of Corbie (972–86): *The Sacramentary of Ratoldus (Paris, Bibliothèque nationale de France, lat. 12052)*, ed. Nicholas Orchard, HBS 116 (London, 2005), 185 (no. 810); it is also extant in the pontifical-benedictional copied in early eleventh-century England, apparently from a north-east Frankish exemplar, and associated with Archbishop Wulfstan: Turner, ed., *Claudius Pontificals*, 63.

[105] Franz Kerff, 'Frühmittelalterliche pharmazeutische Rezepte aus dem Kloster Tegernsee', *Sudhoffs Archiv* 67 (1983), 111–16.

[106] Dorothy Haines, ed. and transl., *Sunday Observance and the Sunday Letter in Anglo-Saxon England*, Anglo-Saxon Texts 8 (Cambridge, 2010), 204–5.

[107] BL, Add. MS 19725, fols 7^{r} (Odrada), 14^{r} (Osanna). Another possibility is that a female house evolved into a house of secular canons, along the lines of the female house of Antoing near Tournai, which had transformed into a house of secular canons

amendments suggest that the modes of delivery of pastoral care may have been more complex than those envisaged by those modern scholars, who tend to project a model of a local church served by a local priest onto the post-Carolingian centuries.

The second codex is now in the Vatican Library: BAV, Archivio S. Pietro H. 58. This is a slightly larger (285 × 200 mm) and more complex codex; it is copied in two hands: one hand copied folios 81–121 in Rome *c.*1000; the other folios 1–80 and 122–150, probably also in Rome but slightly later.[108] Quite when the two parts were joined together is unclear, but, as I argued in a paper delivered to this society in 2000, there are good reasons for believing that they were brought together early on, for the contents fit with the duties enjoined on priests in the *Admonitio synodalis* (see Table 1).[109]

The manuscript also includes three collections of canons, as well as miscellaneous canons from Greek councils and early papal letters; a didactic poem on the duties of the priest, falsely attributed to Sedulius; the hagiographical Passion of St Lucy and lections for St Eustratius; and a sermon by Haymo of Auxerre. The didactic poem on the 'Vita pastoralis' sets out the duties and behaviour of a priest. He is to guard his sheep carefully; read and study; know the seven canonical hours and when they should be observed; remember the importance of attending the synod; know the significance of baptism, and of the mass and how it is celebrated; refrain from accepting money for his services, carrying arms or marrying; and know the importance and significance of penance and the rites for the dying.[110] Written in simple Latin, this poem would seem to have a pedagogic function. This book has been tentatively attributed to the community of canons serving SS. XII Apostoli in Rome, on the grounds of the hagiography it contains; it is therefore possible that this community had a role in training boys to become priests using

---

by the mid-tenth century following its transfer to the male monastery of Lobbes in the late ninth century: Steven Vanderputten, *Dark Age Nunneries: The Ambiguous Identity of Female Monasticism, 800–1050* (Ithaca NY, 2018), 74–6.

[108] See now the description of this manuscript in *Paenitentialia Italiae Saeculi XI–XII*, CChr.SL 156C, xlvii–lii.

[109] Sarah Hamilton, 'The Rituale: The Evolution of a New Liturgical Book', in R. N. Swanson, ed., *The Church and the Book*, SCH 38 (Woodbridge, 2004), 74–86; the table is drawn from Appendix 2 (ibid. 85–6).

[110] Edited by Bernhard Bischoff, 'Ein karolingische "Vita Pastoralis": "Sedulius, Carmen alpha"', *Deutsches Archiv für Erforschung des Mittelalters* 37 (1981), 559–75.

Table 1.

Admonitio synodalis	**BAV, Archivio S. Pietro, H. 58**
§87 Let him understand well the prayers of the Mass and the canon, and if not, let him be able to quote them from memory.	Ordo missae (fols 1–4) Missa in dominica ad palmos (fols 4–9)
§90 Let him be able to utter distinctly and individually the exorcisms and prayers for making catechumens, for blessing the waters also, and the rest of the prayers over the male and female, plural and singular.	Litany and blessing of holy water and salt on Holy Saturday (fols 10–12) Ordo ad cattecumenum faciendum (fols 34–40) Ordo ad cattecumenum faciendum (fols 34–40)
§91 Likewise he must at least know how to say the order for the baptism and visitation of the sick and according to the manner canonically reserved for it the order of reconciling and anointing of the sick, and the prayers also relating to that necessity.	Ordo ad visitandum infirmum vel ingendum (vel communicandum) (fols 29–34) Ordo ad visitandum infirmum II (fols 41–2)
§92 That he should visit the sick and reconcile them spontaneously and not for money but through charity, and say the prayers and seven special psalms over them.	Ordo ad visitandum infirmum vel ingendum (vel communicandum) (fols 29–34) Ordo ad visitandum infirmum II (fols 41–2)
§93 Likewise that he know the orders and prayers for making the obsequies of the dead.	Ordo in agenda mortuorum (quando anima egreditur de corpore) (fols 12–29)
§94 Likewise the exorcisms and benedictions of salt and water he should know by heart.	Blessing of holy water and salt on Holy Saturday (fols 10–12) Blessings various (fol. 40)
§95 He should know the lesser compute, that is, the epacts, and the Easter chronology and the rest, if possible.	Paschal table (fol. 79) Computus (fol. 80)
§96 That he should have a martyrology and a penitential.	Bede's martyrology (fols 59–79) Penitential (fols 109–21) Halitgar's Penitential, books III–V (fols 138–43)
§98 That everyone should have this little book and frequently read it and observe what is in it.	

(amongst other didactic tools) simple, mnemonic texts such as this one.[111]

The final codex is a slightly different sort of collection: now Cambridge, Corpus Christi College, MS 422, and known as the 'Red Book of Darley' after its sixteenth-century provenance.[112] It is rather smaller than the other two manuscripts: it now measures 194 mm × 129 mm.[113] It is generally dated to around 1061 on the grounds of both the Easter tables and palaeography.[114] Where it was written is uncertain, but current opinion favours Sherborne; by the end of the sixteenth century it was in the hands of a family in Darley Dale, Derbyshire, although it may have been acquired by the church there as early as the twelfth century.[115] Its contents are much more focused on liturgical rites than the two previous books considered. It includes a calendar, Easter tables and other computus, the canon of the mass, various votive mass texts, rites for blessing marriage and candles at Candlemas, prayers for matins and for the sinner, ordeals by water, fire and bread and cheese, rites for baptism, visiting the sick, burial and funeral masses, together with those for various

[111] For attribution, see Pierre Salmon, 'Un "Libellus Officialis" du XIe siècle', *RB* 87 (1977), 257–88; for doubts about this, see Paola Supino Martini, *Roma a l'area grafica Romanesca (secoli X–XII)*, Biblioteca di scrittura e civiltà 1 (Alessandria, 1987), 73–4 n. 75.

[112] A digital copy can be viewed at Parker Library on the Web, online at: <parker.stanford.edu>, accessed 9 March 2017.

[113] See descriptions online (n. 112 above) and in Ker, *Catalogue*, 119–21 (no. 70); Mildred Budny, *Insular, Anglo-Saxon and early Anglo-Norman Manuscript Art at Corpus Christi College, Cambridge: An Illustrated Catalogue*, 2 vols (Kalamazoo, MI, 1997), 1: 645–66.

[114] Ker, *Catalogue*, 120; Christopher Hohler, 'The Red Book of Darley', *Nordiskt Kollokvium i Latinsk Liturgiforskning* 2 (Stockholm, 1972), 39–47, at 40.

[115] For this assessment of the current scholarship and for what follows, I am indebted to Helen Gittos, 'Is there any Evidence for the Liturgy of Parish Churches in Late Anglo-Saxon England? The Red Book of Darley and the Status of Old English', in Francesca Tinti, ed., *Pastoral Care in Late Anglo-Saxon England* (Woodbridge, 2005), 63–82. For the suggestion that it constitutes one piece of evidence amongst many that monasteries in later Anglo-Saxon England were supportive of, and involved in the delivery of, pastoral care, see Francesca Tinti, 'Benedictine Reform and Pastoral Care in Late Anglo-Saxon England', *EME* 23 (2015), 229–51, at 243–4. For a more recent account of scriptorium and provenance, see Gneuss and Lapidge, *Anglo-Saxon Manuscripts*, 118–19 (no. 111). For the attribution to Sherborne on the grounds of the mention of the local cult of Wulfsige in the calendar, see Simon Keynes, 'Wulfsige, Monk of Glastonbury, Abbot of Westminster (*c.*990–3), and Bishop of Sherborne (*c.*993–1002)', in Katherine Barker, David A. Hinton and Alan Hunt, eds, *St Wulfsige and Sherborne: Essays to celebrate the Millennium of the Benedictine Abbey 998–1998* (Oxford, 2005), 53–94, at 75–6.

offices.[116] In Helen Gittos's words, it contains 'almost everything that the putative parish priest required', or indeed a local parish priest: a computus, a sacramentary, and occasional offices for baptism and burial.[117] The only major elements missing are lectionary, gospel book, homiliary and penitential. Moreover, the rites for both baptism and the visitation of the sick include rubrics in Old English, although the prayers and responses remain in Latin.[118] Thus the rite for baptism includes rubrics on the role of the godparents in Old English. Similarly that for the visitation of the sick makes provision for the priest to address the sick person in Old English, although the priests' prayers and chants are in Latin. What Gittos has described as this 'casual bilingualism' suggests this is a world in which Old English had high status; it could be and was used where appropriate to explain to priests with poor Latin how to administer rites.[119] Its use is therefore a reflection of a lively and ongoing interest in the education of the local clergy in southern England.[120]

The absence of formal structures for the education of the local clergy remained a source of anxiety amongst bishops in the post-Carolingian world. This study suggests that in regions both in the Carolingian heartlands and on their periphery, higher clergy gave time and thought to the education of the clergy before ordination, through the revision of ordination rites, priests' exams and letters

[116] For a detailed description of the contents, see M. R. James, *A Descriptive Catalogue of the Manuscripts in the Library of Corpus Christi College, Cambridge*, 2 vols (London, 1912), 2: 315–22; also available, together with a modern bibliography, at Parker Library on the Web; for a recent summary, see Gittos, 'Red Book', 68–9. On the ordeal by bread and cheese, see Sarah Larratt Keefer, 'Ut in omnibus honorificetur Deus: The Corsnæd Ordeal in Anglo-Saxon England', in Joyce Hill and Mary Swan, eds, *The Community, the Family and the Saint: Patterns of Power in Early Medieval Europe* (Turnhout, 1998), 237–64.

[117] Gittos, 'Is there any Evidence?', 69.

[118] Ibid. 70–5; R. I. Page, 'Old English Liturgical Rubrics in Corpus Christi College, Cambridge MS 422', *Anglia* 96 (1978), 149–58; T. Graham, 'The Old English Liturgical Directions in Corpus Christi College, Cambridge, MS 422', *Anglia* 111 (1993), 439–46.

[119] Gittos, 'Red Book', 76; the phrase originates with Susan Kelly: 'Anglo-Saxon Lay Society and the Written Word', in Rosamond McKitterick, ed., *The Uses of Literacy in Early Medieval Europe* (Cambridge, 1990), 36–62, at 50.

[120] For an example of another bilingual collection of liturgical and penitential texts compiled at Worcester Cathedral for the education of the pastoral clergy, see Victoria Thompson, 'The Pastoral Contract in Late Anglo-Saxon England: Priest and Parishioner in Oxford, Bodleian Library, MS Laud Miscellaneous 482', in Tinti, ed., *Pastoral Care*, 106–20.

formata. They were also dedicated to raising standards for those in post through visitations and synods. More informally, several codices point to the ongoing commitment to pastoral education demonstrated not only by bishops but also by communities of local clergy and local priests.

In highlighting bishops' commitment to the education of the local clergy, I do not mean to suggest that the tenth and eleventh centuries witnessed a pastoral project on the scale of those of either the ninth or thirteenth centuries. This intermediate period visibly lacked the overall leadership, direction and urgency provided by the Frankish rulers and the thirteenth-century popes in council. That said, the work of Susan Keefe and Yitzhak Hen on priestly manuals has drawn attention to the absence of evidence for the implementation of any unified reform movement in the ninth century, highlighting instead the degree of variation in the texts produced between dioceses in the execution of the Frankish reforms, and the significance of local episcopal agency.[121] At the same time, researchers working on the thirteenth-century church have begun to highlight the different ways in which individual bishops approached the reform of their clergy.[122] The picture outlined in this study is one which was also a consequence of local episcopal agency: the bishops of the tenth and eleventh centuries are rather more comparable to both their predecessors and their successors in this regard than has often been acknowledged. Despite the introduction of some innovations, across all three regions their debt to their Frankish predecessors remained substantial. The continued commitment by bishops in these three very different regions to enforcing and raising standards amongst their pastoral clergy, both before and even more after ordination, was not expressed through the uncritical repetition of pre-existing precepts, but was rather the result of continued reflection upon, reworking of, and development of earlier texts. In this way, the higher clergy in Frankia, England and Italy sought to ensure that local priests had the necessary training in the tools and skills needed to conduct their craft.

[121] Keefer, *Water and the Word*, 1: 143–55; Yitzhak Hen, *The Royal Patronage of Liturgy in Frankish Gaul: To the Death of Charles the Bald (877)*, HBS Subsidia 3 (London, 2001).
[122] Robert Brentano, *Two Churches: England and Italy in the Thirteenth Century* (Princeton, NJ, 1968); Adam J. Davis, *The Holy Bureaucrat: Eudes Rigaud and Religious Reform in Thirteenth-Century Normandy* (Ithaca, NY, 2006).

Prelacy, Pastoral Care and the Instruction of Subordinates in Late Twelfth-Century England

Rebecca Springer*
Merton College, Oxford

Historians of the Middle Ages usually associate the phrase 'pastoral care' with the sacraments and religious services performed by parish priests on behalf of lay people. But late twelfth-century writers primarily attributed pastoral care to prelates. Closely following the tradition of Pope Gregory I's Pastoral Rule, *they held that prelates bore the responsibility to govern, guide and (perhaps most importantly) instruct their subordinate clergy or religious. Prelates did this by preaching, and they were supposed to validate their words with the example of their own righteous lives. But although commentators assumed that prelates would be reasonably well educated, late twelfth-century writers did not attribute good preaching to intellectual aptitude, or to the availability of preaching treatises or model sermon collections, as historians often assume. In an age of intellectual vibrancy and flourishing schools, ensuring that prelates instructed their subordinates remained firmly a moral, rather than an educational, question for the English church. Only by instructing subordinates could a prelate ensure their, and by extension his own, eternal salvation: neglect of preaching was tantamount to murder. This article uses the little-studied writings of Alexander of Ashby, Bartholomew of Exeter and Thomas Agnellus to uncover new links between ideas about prelacy, pastoral care and the instruction of subordinates in the high Middle Ages.*

The history of pastoral care, and more broadly of clerical ministry to the laity, in the high and later Middle Ages is tied up with the history of education at virtually every level, from the development of practical theology at the university of Paris in the second half of the twelfth

* 270 Harrison Avenue #303, Jersey City, NJ, 07304, USA. E-mail: rebeccaspringer4@gmail.com. I am grateful to Ian Forrest for his supervision of the research underpinning this article, to those who offered comments and questions at the Ecclesiastical History Society Summer Conference, and to the society for supporting my conference attendance. All translations in this article are my own.

Studies in Church History 55 (2019), 114–128
doi: 10.1017/stc.2018.17

century,[1] to the provisions for clerical education in the Third and Fourth Lateran Councils in 1179 and 1215[2] and the proliferation of instructional treatises for parish priests.[3] This story is well known; here I want to highlight a part of it which has been less emphasized. My interest is not so much in the actual practice of religious ministry, but rather in the way in which pastoral care was conceptualized: in particular, by four little-known writers active in England during the second half of the twelfth century. Drawing on ideas which had percolated through ecclesiastical literature since the time of Gregory the Great (d. 604), these writers asserted that 'prelates', that is, those who bore the burden of pastoral care, were responsible for spiritually instructing their 'subjects' by word and example. The approach of these authors was not to provide detailed instructions for the holders of specific ecclesiastical offices, but rather to emphasize the moral imperative that, in their view, defined the relationship between pastoral care and education.

The texts studied here have been chosen in part because they have not received much attention from scholars. Alexander of Ashby was prior of the Augustinian canons of Canons Ashby in Northamptonshire, and

[1] Paul Anciaux, *La Théologie du sacrement de pénitence au xiie siècle* (Louvain, 1949); Bernhard Poschmann, *Penance and the Anointing of the Sick* (New York, 1964); John Baldwin, *Masters, Princes, and Merchants: The Social Views of Peter the Chanter and his Circle*, 2 vols (Princeton, NJ, 1970); Gilbert Dahan, ed., *Pierre le Mangeur ou Pierre de Troyes, maître du XIIe siècle. Études réunies* (Turnhout, 2013); Jacques Le Goff, *The Birth of Purgatory*, transl. Arthur Goldhammer (Chicago, IL, 1984); G. R. Edwards, 'Purgatory: "Birth" or "Evolution"?', *JEH* 34 (1985), 634–46; Joseph Goering, *William de Montibus (c.1140–1213): The Schools and the Literature of Pastoral Care* (Toronto, ON, 1992); Rob Meens, *Penance in Medieval Europe, 600–1200* (Cambridge, 2014), 190–214; Ian P. Wei, *Intellectual Culture in Medieval Paris: Theologians and the University,* c.*1100–1330* (Cambridge, 2012).

[2] Norman P. Tanner, ed., *Decrees of the Ecumenical Councils*, 2 vols (London, 1990), 1: 220, 240.

[3] Leonard Boyle, 'The "Oculus sacerdotis" and some other Works of William of Pagula', *TRHS* 5th ser. 5 (1955), 81–110; idem, '*Summae confessorum*', in *Les Genres littéraires dans les sources théologiques et philosophiques médiévales: definition, critique et exploitation. Actes du colloque international de Louvain-la-Neuve, 25–27 mai 1981*, Textes, études, congrès 5 (Louvain, 1982), 227–37; Pierre Michaud-Quantin, *Sommes de casuistique et manuels de confession au moyen âge (XII–XVI siècles)*, Analecta Mediaevalia Namurcensia 13 (Louvain, 1962); Joseph Goering and Pierre J. Payer, 'The "Summa penitentie Fratrum Predicatorum": A Thirteenth-Century Confessional Formulary', *Mediaeval Studies* 55 (1993), 1–50; Catherine Rider, 'Lay Religion and Pastoral Care in Thirteenth-Century England: The Evidence of a Group of Short Confession Manuals', *JMedH* 36 (2010), 327–40.

died in 1208x1214. He was a frequent papal judge-delegate,[4] and authored, among other works, *De artificioso modo predicandi*, a preaching treatise with five model sermons attached.[5] Bartholomew of Exeter was bishop of Exeter from 1161 to 1184, a noted canonist and probably a one-time Parisian master.[6] He is remembered as the author of a widely copied penitential,[7] but here I focus on the volume of one hundred and twenty-five sermons which he bequeathed to the Exeter Cathedral library.[8] Robert of Cricklade was the prior of another Augustinian house, St Frideswide's Priory in Oxford, from 1141 to 1174,[9] and authored a collection of *Homiliae super Ezechielem*, conceived as a continuation of Gregory the Great's homilies on the same book.[10] Finally,

[4] Greti Dinkova-Bruun, 'Alexander of Ashby: New Biographical Evidence', *Mediaeval Studies* 63 (2001), 305–22.

[5] All of Alexander's works known are edited in Alexander of Ashby, *Alexandri Essebiensis opera omnia*, 2 vols; CChr.CM 188, 188A. *De artificioso modo predicandi* is at 1: 22–71. See also Franco Morenzoni, 'Aux origines des "Artes praedicandi". Le "De artificioso modo predicandi" d'Alexandre d'Ashby', *Studi Medievali* 3rd ser. 32 (1991), 887–985.

[6] For biographies of Bartholomew, see Adrian Morey, *Bartholomew of Exeter, Bishop and Canonist: A Study in the Twelfth Century* (Cambridge, 1937); Bartholomew of Exeter, *Bartholomaei Exoniensis contra fatalitatis errorem*, CChr.CM 157, Introduction; Frank Barlow, 'Bartholomew (*d.* 1184)', *ODNB*. For his importance as a canonist, see Charles Duggan, *Twelfth-Century Decretal Collections and their Importance in English History* (London, 1963), 77–123.

[7] Bartholomew's *Liber penitentialis* is edited in Morey, *Bartholomew of Exeter*. See also Leonard E. Boyle, 'The Inter-Conciliar Period 1179–1215 and the Beginnings of Pastoral Manuals', in Filippo Liotta, ed., *Miscellanea Rolando Bandinelli Papa Alessandro III* (Siena, 1986), 45–56, at 47; Meens, *Penance*, 205–9; Albrecht Diem, 'Virtues and Vices in Early Texts on Pastoral Care', *Franciscan Studies* 62 (2004), 193–223, at 202; Jason Taliadoros, 'Bartholomew of Exeter's Penitential: Some Observations on his Personal Dicta', in Péter Erdö and Anzelm Szuromi, eds, *Proceedings of the Thirteenth International Congress of Medieval Canon Law*, Monumenta Iuris Canonici 14 (Vatican City, 2010), 457–73.

[8] Oxford, Bodl., MS 449; Audrey M. Erskine, 'The Growth of Exeter Cathedral Library after Bishop Leofric's Time', in Frank Barlow et al., eds, *Leofric of Exeter: Essays in Commemoration of the Foundation of Exeter Cathedral Library in A.D. 1072* (Exeter, 1972), 43–55, at 49. The sermons are in Bodl., MS 449. See also Johannes Baptist Schneyer, *Repertorium der lateinischen Sermones des Mittelalters für die Zeit von 1150–1350*, 11 vols (Munich, 1969–90), 1: 424–35. In what follows I give the Schneyer numbers in parentheses for unpublished sermons.

[9] John Blair, 'Saint Frideswide reconsidered', *Oxoniensia* 52 (1987), 71–127; R. W. Hunt, 'English Learning in the Late Twelfth Century', *TRHS* 4th ser. 19 (1936), 19–42, at 31–3.

[10] Cambridge, Pembroke College, MS 30; Hereford Cathedral, MS O.III. Robert recalls Gregory's complaint at the end of his *Homiliae in Ezechielem*, and begins his collection with Ezekiel 41, where Gregory left off: 'Quod et ipse [Gregorius] plangit in fine undecime omelie dicens, "O iam cogor linguam ab expositionis sermone retinere, quia tedet

Thomas Agnellus was archdeacon of Wells from *c.*1168 to *c.*1195.[11] His forty-eight sermons survive only in a single manuscript.[12]

There is another feature, besides their being relatively unknown, which unifies these works. Although they vary in their format and intended audiences, they all draw on a common rhetorical model of pastoral care, as shown below. This was not true of all pastoral texts produced in late twelfth-century England; for example, the better known writings of William de Montibus, head of the school at Lincoln Cathedral from the 1180s to 1213, are much more practical and pedagogical in their approach,[13] including numerous verse and prose treatises on subjects such as penance, virtues and vices, and logic, intended for the use of students of theology. As Joseph Goering has observed, theologians trained by William de Montibus might go on to instruct other lay people or clergy, perhaps parish priests,[14] and several of William de Montibus's works, notably *Peniteas cito*, contain what might be considered advice about pastoral care in practice. But William's writings do not comment on the moral imperative of pastoral care or on the role of the pastor more generally, nor do they discuss the danger of pastoral failure; they are meant to inform, not to inspire.[15] By contrast, although some of the writers studied in this article, particularly Alexander of Ashby, do offer practical advice to pastors, they also put forward a vision in which the prelate's responsibility to teach his subjects is a moral imperative: that is, they are less concerned with practical instruction than with exhortation.

---

animam meam uite mee"': Pembroke College, MS 30, fol. 1[ra]; Gregory the Great, *Homiliae in Hiezechihelem prophetam* (CChr.SL 142, 397); Schneyer, *Repertorium*, 5: 171–6.

[11] *English Episcopal Acta*, 10: *Bath and Wells, 1061–1205*, ed. Frances M. R. Ramsey (Oxford, 1995), lvii–iii, 218; J. Armitage Robinson, *Somerset Historical Essays* (London, 1921), 80–5.

[12] Bodl., MS Laud Misc. 71; Schneyer, *Repertorium*, 5: 709–11.

[13] Goering, *William de Montibus*. For William's biography, see ibid. 3–28.

[14] Ibid. 66–7.

[15] It should be noted that the sermon collection which Goering ascribes to William de Montibus, 'the one sermon collection that William manifestly intended as a pastoral aid', was actually written by Alexander of Ashby: Goering, *William de Montibus*, 515–66, quotation at 566; F. Morenzoni, '"Sermones breues et leues composui". Les Sermons d'Alexandre d'Ashby', *Studi Medievali* 3rd ser. 42 (2001), 121–64.

Prelacy and Pastoral Care

Much scholarship has focused on innovation in twelfth-century religious thought: the influence of Aristotelian logic, the scholastic method and the turn toward practical theology.[16] But the writers studied here relied heavily on much older ideas. They conceptualized pastoral care as a bipartite relationship between contrasting groups, which we might generalize as prelates and subjects. In this model, a prelate, bearing the weight of pastoral care, guides and governs subjects; the prelate takes primary, if not exclusive, responsibility for the subjects' spiritual welfare. The precedents for this kind of thinking stretched back for centuries. Latin writers of Late Antiquity had occasionally mentioned solicitous bishops acting 'with pastoral care' or being constrained by pastoral care,[17] but it was Gregory the Great's formulation of pastoral care as a burden set on the shoulders of prelates – so solemn and ponderous in its requirements that even Gregory himself was 'unequal to it in merit' – which was to shape the thinking and language of ecclesiastical writers down to the thirteenth century.[18] By the time of Bede, pastoral care was associated with abbots and priors as well as with bishops, and the phrase *cura animarum* was used interchangeably with *cura pastoralis*. In fact, these two phrases

[16] Most influential have been Charles H. Haskins, *The Renaissance of the Twelfth Century* (Cambridge, MA, 1927); R. W. Southern, *The Making of the Middle Ages* (New Haven, CT, 1953); Giles Constable, *The Reformation of the Twelfth Century* (Cambridge, 1996); Baldwin, *Masters*; Joseph Goering, 'The Internal Forum and the Literature of Penance and Confession', in W. Hartmann and K. Pennington, eds, *The History of Medieval Canon Law in the Classical Period, 1140–1234: From Gratian to the Decretals of Pope Gregory IX* (Washington DC, 2008), 379–428. Recent contributions include Wei, *Intellectual Culture*; Tomas Zahora, *Nature, Virtue, and the Boundaries of Encyclopaedic Knowledge: The Tropological Universe of Alexander Neckam (1157–1217)* (Turnhout, 2014). For this and the following paragraph, see also Rebecca Springer, 'Local Religious Life in England, *c.*1160–1210' (DPhil thesis, University of Oxford, 2017), 10–11, 61–2.

[17] Augustine of Hippo, *Epistula* 178 (PL 33, col. 773); Gregorius Turensis, *Liber de virtutibus sancti Martini* 1.10 (MGH SRM 1.2, 145); *Synodus Romana 502* 13 (MGH AA 12, 449); Ennodius, *Praeceptum de cellulanis* (PL 63, col. 256).

[18] Gregory the Great, *Registrum epistularum* 1.24, 41; 3.29 (2 vols, CChr.SL 140, 140A, 1: 22, 31–2, 47, 174, quotation at 22). See Vera Paroneto, 'Connotazione del "pastor" nell'opera di Gregorio Magno teoria e prassi', *Benedictina* 31 (1984), 325–43; Conrad Leyser, *Authority and Asceticism from Augustine to Gregory the Great* (Oxford, 2000), 142, 160–2; Lorenzo Dattrino, 'Gregorio Magno *Pastor et Praedicator*', *Lateranum* 75 (2009), 355–70; George E. Demacopoulos, 'Gregory's Model of Spiritual Direction in the *Liber regulae pastoralis*', in Bronwen Neil and Matthew Dal Santo, eds, *A Companion to Gregory the Great* (Leiden, 2013), 204–24, at 210.

became so synonymous with the office of prelacy that chroniclers across Europe from the eighth century on described elections, institutions, deaths and resignations of both abbots and bishops in shorthand by stating that they 'took up' or 'gave up' the *cura pastoralis* or *cura animarum*.[19] The office of a prelate, then, conferred the burden of pastoral care: a responsibility to govern and instruct subject souls.

The late twelfth-century English writers studied in this article draw heavily on this Gregorian model of prelacy and pastoral care, but they were not only concerned with the duties of bishops and abbots. When modern scholars speak of 'prelates' they are referring to men who held high ecclesiastical offices, generally bishops and heads of male religious houses. *Prelatus*, the Latin cognate, could have the same meaning in late twelfth- and early thirteenth-century England, but as the past passive participle of *preferre* (literally 'the one set in front') it could also refer to any leader or important person, secular or ecclesiastical.[20] That is, prelacy was a function, as well as a category, of office. The four writers studied here distinguish between two contrasting groups, one which bears pastoral care and one which is subject to it. They refer to the former group, which we might generalize as 'prelates', variously as prelates, preachers, pastors or priests (*sacerdotes*),[21] and to the latter as subjects, subordinates, listeners, the people or the flock. In practice, this prelate-subject dichotomy usually

[19] A few examples of many: Altfrid, bishop of Münster, *Vita Liudgeri Mimigardefordensis* 14 (MGH SS 2, 408); *Annales Alamannici, Continuationes Sangallenses tres (860–926, 1185)* (MGH SS 1, 50); *Annalista Saxo (741–1139), s.a.* 970 (MGH SS 6, 623); Anonymous of Herrieden, *De episcopis Eichstetensibus* 27 (MGH SS 7, 261); Anson of Lobbes, *Vita Ursmari episcoporum et abbatum Lobbiensis* 2.8 (MGH SRM 6, 460); Bernold of Constance, *Apologeticus* 10 (MGH LdL 2, 69); *Chronica Boemorum, Continuatio monachi Sazavensis (932–1162)*, 'De exordio Zazovensis monasterii' (MGH SS 9, 150); *Chronicon Sancti Michaelis monasterii in pago Virdunensi* 11 (MGH SS 4, 82); *Collectaneum exemplorum et visionum Clarevallense e codice Trecensi 946* 4.36 (CChr.CM 208, 323); Abbot Folcwin of Laubes, *Gesta abbatum Sancti Bertini Sithiensium* 109 (MGH SS 13, 630); Sigebert of Gembloux, *Gesta abbatum Gemblacensium* 15 (MGH SS 8, 531).

[20] Richard Ashdowne, David Howlett and Ronald Latham, eds, *Dictionary of Medieval Latin from British Sources*, 3 vols (Oxford, 2018), *s.v.* 'praeferre', §7.

[21] This varied language, like so much writing about prelacy and preaching, reflects the thought of Gregory the Great, whose elusive references to *rectores*, *praedicatores*, *sacerdotes*, *pastores* and *prelati* have caused historians to ponder whether he intended the *Regula pastoralis* for an audience wider than bishops, perhaps even including secular rulers: Leyser, *Authority*, 157–8; Robert A. Markus, 'Gregory the Great's *Rector* and his Genesis', in Jacques Fontaine, Robert Gillet and Stan Pellistrandi, eds, *Grégoire le Grand, Chantilly, Centre culturel Les Fontaines, 15–19 septembre 1982, actes*, Colloques internationaux du

referred to the holder of a high ecclesiastical office and the clergy or religious directly under his governance, such as an abbot over his monks or a bishop over his cathedral and diocesan clergy. But it could also refer by analogy to a priest over his parishioners. The ambiguity of the language employed by these writers indicates that the state of having been 'set in front', and the responsibilities which that status incurred, were far more important than the particular office which an individual held.

A brief discussion of the intended audiences of the works studied here will reveal this 'functional' definition of prelacy at work. We may begin with Alexander of Ashby. In a rhetorically florid prologue, Alexander dedicates *De artificioso modo predicandi* to an unnamed acquaintance, an abbot, who has since forsaken the duty of preaching. Alexander frames his treatise as an attempt to encourage his friend to begin preaching once more; whether this abbot was a rhetorical construction or a real acquaintance, it is clear that *De artificioso modo predicandi* is pitched for prelates. Yet Alexander seems to imagine that such prelates will preach to clerical or religious audiences and to lay people, since the model sermons he appends to the treatise address both types of audiences.[22] This means that when Alexander writes of *prelati* and *subiecti*, it is not always clear whether he is thinking of prelates and clerical or religious subordinates, or parish priests and lay people, or prelates and lay people; or, indeed, whether he is talking about any, or even all, of these pairs. He often uses *prelatus* and *sacerdos* interchangeably.[23] In other words, Alexander sees prelacy in numerous different relationships in which one party has the pastoral care of another, and is unconcerned to distinguish among those relationships.

The two sermon collections of Bartholomew of Exeter and Thomas Agnellus may be grouped together. Both gather sermons written for a variety of different preaching occasions, and which address a range of identifiable audiences. Although many of

Centre national de la recherche scientifique (Paris, 1986), 137–46; R. Reydillet, *La Royauté dans la littérature latine* (Rome, 1981), 463.

[22] Alexander included the first of the five appended sermons as a demonstration of how to preach to *eruditi* and *simplices* simultaneously, while the third, fourth and fifth sermons all address the duties of *prelati*, including how prelates should teach *minores sacerdotes* to perform sacraments correctly: *De artificioso modo predicandi* (*Opera omnia*, 1: 38, 48–71).

[23] Ibid. 24, 49–50, 61–2.

Bartholomew's sermons are not obviously aimed at any particular audience, drawing routine moral lessons from biblical stories, some are specific enough that the audience may be identified as lay people,[24] religious,[25] religious women,[26] clerics in general[27] and priests or prelates.[28] I shall draw on sermons directed at the last category. Similarly, Thomas Agnellus preached to prelates,[29] mixed groups of prelates and lesser priests,[30] mixed groups of secular clergy and religious,[31] religious only,[32] priests or clergy in general[33] and the canons of the collegiate church of St Andrew in Wells (later Wells Cathedral) specifically.[34] Of course it was natural to preach about pastoral care to those who had it; therefore I draw on sermons of Bartholomew and Thomas which address prelates or priests. Bartholomew tends to prefer *pastores* as a general term for this group, while Thomas uses *prelati*; both are working broadly within the Gregorian prelate-subject dichotomy, and rarely offer enough specific details to indicate exactly what sort of people they are thinking about.[35] Such sermons might have been preached to parish clergy during episcopal or archidiaconal visitations, to cathedral clergy, or to gatherings of ecclesiastical dignitaries.

Robert of Cricklade's *Homiliae super Ezechielem* provide a final example. Deliberately modelled on Gregory the Great's *Homiliae in Ezechielem*, these homilies constitute a unified treatise rather than a collection of sermons written for specific preaching occasions. Internal references to a *lector* and to gathered *fratres* suggests that Robert intended the homilies to be read aloud to a clerical or religious community such as the regular canons of St Frideswide's Priory in

[24] Bodl., MS 449, fols 23rb–24ra (30), 26rb–^{vb} (34), 33vb–34vb (45), 47ra–^{vb} (60), 49rb–^{vb} (63).

[25] Ibid., fols 1va–2rb (2), 21vb–22rb (28), 24ra–^{vb} (31), 53ra–^{b} (70), 61va–62rb (84), 62rb–63ra (85).

[26] Ibid., fols 54vb–55rb (73).

[27] Ibid., fols 3va–4va (5), 8vb–9va (12), 11rb–12rb (15), 20ra–21ra (26), 32vb–33vb (44), 39ra–^{vb} (49), 56va–57ra (76), 70rb–^{vb} (97).

[28] Ibid., fols 34vb–37ra (46), 57vb–58rb (78), 58rb–^{vb} (79).

[29] Bodl., MS Laud Misc. 71, fols 1va–5va (1), 70vb–73va (20).

[30] Ibid., fols 90rb–93vb (24).

[31] Ibid., fols 13vb–18va (4), 29va–34rb (8), 100va–104ra (28).

[32] Ibid., fols 41vb–44va (11), 66rb–73va (19).

[33] Ibid., fols 5va–13vb (2), 53rb–5vb (15), 58vb–66rb (17).

[34] Ibid., fol. 49rb (13).

[35] An exception is one passage in which Thomas Agnellus moves directly from a discussion of (bad) *prelati* into one of a (bad) *presbiter*: ibid., fol. 54ra (15).

Oxford.[36] Although the canons do seem to have been interested in ministering to lay people in the middle of the twelfth century,[37] we do not need to focus on how relevant Robert's advice would have been to the day-to-day activities of the canons. His primary aim was biblical exegesis, not practical instruction, and he lumps together various appellations – prelates, bishops, doctors and preachers – as a single category, representing in this way an enlightened group which instructs an equally indistinct group of subjects.

The idea of 'functional' prelacy is crucial to understanding how these four writers conceptualized pastoral care. Despite addressing different audiences, they employed a simple dichotomy between prelates and subjects, and were content to let this idea stand for a range of pastoral relationships. It is possible that they used such ambiguous language as *prelati* and *subiecti* because they wanted their work to appeal to as wide an audience as possible. More immediately, as the rest of this article argues, these writers believed that the moral responsibility of prelacy, the prelate's responsibility to instruct and guide his subjects, was more important than the practicalities of actually carrying out that instruction. Therefore, it did not matter whether the 'prelate' in question was a bishop, an abbot, a regular canon or a secular parish priest; the pastoral mandate was the same.

Teaching by Word and Example

In the high Middle Ages, the phrase *docere verbo et exemplo*, 'to teach by word and example', was frequently used by ecclesiastical writers describe the responsibility of prelates to educate their subjects.[38] This was another idea traceable to Gregory the Great, and its importance for the writers studied here is difficult to overestimate. Sometimes, it was a handy cliché, a shorthand nod toward familiar conceptions of good prelacy or preaching in a general sense.[39] 'The prelate should instruct his subjects by his own word of doctrine

[36] Pembroke College, MS 30, fols 6va (2), 54rb (12).

[37] *The Cartulary of the Monastery of St Frideswide at Oxford* 22, ed. S. R. Wigram, 2 vols, Oxford Historical Society 28, 31 (Oxford, 1895–6), 1: 27.

[38] Caroline Walker Bynum, *Docere verbo et exemplo: An Aspect of Twelfth-Century Spirituality*, Harvard Theological Studies 31 (Missoula, MT, 1979), 15. For this section, see also Springer, 'Local Religious Life', 64–8, 70–1.

[39] Alexander, *Collectio secundo* 1; *Sermones uarii* 19 (*Opera omnia*, 1: 220, 368, 374); Pembroke College, MS 30, fol. 10rb (2).

and example of life', Alexander of Ashby writes, and does not need to elaborate.[40] However, clichés often point to widespread and influential assumptions. The phrase also represented a specific conviction that the verbal instruction of subordinates had to be backed up with demonstrable personal virtue. That in turn required the prelate to cultivate both doctrinal understanding and a moral life superior to that of his subjects. In a sermon on the theme 'Get you up to a high mountain, you who bring good tidings to Zion [Isa. 40: 9]', Alexander explains that the preacher must 'ascend the mountain' by living a moral life in order to be seen and heard more clearly by those to whom he preaches, as if the mountain were a raised pulpit.[41] Thomas Agnellus uses a similar metaphor, in which the mountain represents the priest himself: he is the first to receive the light of wisdom, and 'may rise above the life of his subjects as if gazing down on those below him'.[42]

The idea of teaching by word and example was also malleable, and the writers studied here frequently altered it to reflect their own priorities. For example, Bartholomew, a bishop who was particularly committed to the provision of intercessory prayer in his cathedral and diocese,[43] emphasized the prelate's duty to pray for his subjects in addition to teaching them by word and deed. In a sermon for St Peter's feast day, he describes three ways in which 'each and every pastor should feed the elect committed to him like the sheep of Christ: by example, by word, and by prayer. By example, as those who pasture them live well; by word, as they commend good living to them with blessed speech; by prayer, as they pray for their subordinates'.[44] Robert, prior of an Augustinian house at which public sermons were delivered,[45] replaced *verbo* with the more specific and forceful

[40] 'Prelatus subiectos sibi instruere debet uerbo doctrine et exemplo uite': Alexander, *Sermones uarii* 4 (*Opera omnia*, 1: 275).

[41] Alexander, *De artificioso modo predicandi* 5 (*Opera omnia*, 1: 61–71).

[42] 'Sic honestate preemineat subditorum uitam tamquam inferiorem aspiciat': Bodl., MS Laud Misc. 71, fol. 9ra (2).

[43] Exeter, Cathedral Archives, D&C 802; Roger de Wendover, *Flores Historiarum*, *s.a.* 1161, ed. H. G. Hewlett, 3 vols, RS 84 (London, 1886–9), 1: 18–20; Bodl., MS 449, fol. 72ra (98).

[44] 'Tribus autem modis unusquisque pastor electos sibi commissos tanquam oues Christi pascere debet: exemplo scilicet, uerbo, et oratione. Exemplo, ut qui eas pascunt bene uiuant; uerbo, ut bonam uitam sancto sermone commendent; oratione, ut pro subditis orent': Bodl., MS 449, fol. 57vb (78).

[45] Bodl., MS Wood empt. 13, fols 74^{r}–76^{v}, 93^{r}–97^{r}; *ActaSS* Oct. 8: 47, 579.

praedicatio when he praised 'the blessed preachers by whose example and preaching we are stirred up to praise God'.[46] And Alexander, closely connected with the school based at St Andrew's Priory, Northampton,[47] associates the phrase with lecturers in the schools. The penitent should judge his own life and sins, he writes, like a judge, or bishop, or 'a doctor in his chair, teaching others by word and example the path to a better life'.[48] In another sermon Alexander goes so far as to affirm that 'any good men who are able to enlighten others by word and example can be called "the light of the world"', implying, perhaps, that even a layman might usefully instruct his neighbours or family.[49]

In spite of these variations, it was clear that all four writers believed that subjects would benefit more from instruction 'by example' than from instruction 'by word'. Alexander, in a sermon appended to his preaching treatise, cites Gregory's *Regula pastoralis*: 'The flock is better led by example than by word'. For this reason, Alexander writes, 'the example of a good deed should precede words of wisdom'.[50] Bartholomew and Robert also advised would-be preachers to focus on their morality first and their preaching second. 'For first we should chastise ourselves and tame our carnal vices and luxury', Bartholomew writes. 'Then we should observe and imitate the life of the good men who came before us; then we should correct our subordinates and defend them with our staff, that is, our counsel and our

[46] 'Sancti predicatores quorum exemplo et predicatione ad laudandum deum excitamur': Pembroke College, MS 30, fol. 10[rb] (2).

[47] Alexander, *De artificioso modo predicandi* 1, 3, *Collectio primo* 22 (*Opera omnia*, 1: 33–40, 53, 203–7); H. G. Richardson, 'The Schools of Northampton in the Twelfth Century', *EHR* 56 (1941), 595–605.

[48] 'Debet eciam sedere quasi doctor in cathedra, docendo alios uerbo et exemplo uiam uite melioris': Alexander, *Sermones uarii* 19 (*Opera omnia*, 1: 368).

[49] Alexander, *Opera omnia*, 1: 220. This was not an anomalous view. Bartholomew's *Liber penitentialis* encourages that 'filios suos debent ad scolam siue ad monasteria siue foras presbiteris ut fidem catholicam recte discant et orationem dominicam, ut domi alios edocere ualeant' ('they [lay people] should send their sons out to a school or monastery or priest to learn correctly the Creed and Lord's Prayer, so that they can teach the rest of their household'): Morey, *Bartholomew of Exeter*, 2, 176. Robert asserts that 'electi quique … uerum etiam uerbo et exemplo eam [ecclesiam sacram] subleuant'('any of the elect … truly may uplift the sacred church by their word and example'): Pembroke College, MS 30, fol. 49[ra] (10).

[50] 'Precedere enim debet exemplum boni operis uerba sapientie, quia ut ait beatus Gregorius: grex per exempla melius quam per uerba gradietur': Alexander, *De artificioso modo predicandi* (*Opera omnia*, 1: 30).

word'.[51] Robert similarly upholds 'the preachers who should first nourish virtue in themselves with great zeal, so that they can demonstrate an abundance of virtues'.[52] It was particularly clear that audiences were likely to see through a hypocritical preacher, with disastrous consequences. Thomas warned that 'doctrine cannot be easily sold to listeners if it comes from a master held in contempt. If his life is despised, consequently his preaching will be easily held in contempt. Thus the guilt of the priest is the ruin of the people.'[53] He was alluding to an often repeated line from Gregory's letters which Alexander copied verbatim,[54] elaborating an inversion of the *docere verbo et exemplo* principle: 'Bad priests are the cause of the ruin of the people. We should dread this, and to increase our dread it would be good for us to investigate why it is so. Priests are the cause of the ruin of the people in three ways: indiscriminate silence, undisciplined word, and bad example.'[55]

It is clear, however, that *exemplum* did not have to precede *verbum* only to head off potential claims of hypocrisy. It was important for prelates to lead virtuous lives because the failure to preach was itself considered a moral failure: a good prelate would surely preach. The implications of this idea are made clear in Alexander's *De artificioso modo predicandi*. As mentioned above, this preaching treatise purports to address an unnamed abbot whom Alexander had known 'in the schools'. Alexander's friend had been a promising student, but he gave up intellectual pursuits after becoming a regular canon, despite the suitability of the religious life to study: 'You have become like an uneducated man or a despiser of learning, pursuing neither reading nor doctrine, even though your many fellow canons were frequently bringing you illustrious documents for your edification',

[51] 'Nam prius debemus castigare nosmetipsos et in nobis domare uicia carnis et luxuriam, et post inspicere et imitari uitam bonorum uirorum qui ante nos fuerunt, deinde alios nobis subditos corrigere et defendere nostro baculo, id est nostro consilio et nostro uerbo': Bodl., MS 449, fol. 36va (46).

[52] 'Et [Abraham] significat predicatores qui ut possint aliis uirtutum copiam monstrare, in se primum oportet multo studio nutrire': Pembroke College, MS 30, fol. 13vb (3).

[53] 'Doctrina namque auditoribus non facile produci si ceperit a magistro contempni. Cuius si uita despicitur, consequens est ut et predicatio facile contempnatur. Vnde culpa sacerdotum, ruina populi', Bodl., MS Laud Misc. 71, fol. 10rb–^{va} (3); cf. ibid., fol. 47vb (13).

[54] Gregory the Great, *Registrum epistularum* 11.46 (CChr.SL 140A, 943).

[55] Alexander, *De artificioso modo predicandi* 4 (*Opera omnia*, 1: 58).

Alexander writes.[56] But he is primarily concerned about his friend's lack of study because he believes it is connected to a more significant failing: the abbot has ignored 'the office of preaching':[57]

> If you take away the food of life, will you not be judged to have inflicted death upon them? Do you really not know that the law sentences to death the priest who enters the temple without the sound of bells attached to the edge of his hyacinth tunic? … It is also said to you by the prophet: if you will not announce to my people their wickedness, I will consider their blood to be on your hands.[58]

Alexander's solution to the moral problem of a prelate's failure to preach is instructive, and perhaps unexpected. There is nothing in his letter to indicate that the abbot is neglectful because he lacks the skills or tools to preach; indeed, Alexander says he was a good scholar who had ample access to books. The preaching treatise which Alexander sent him gives advice on how to structure a sermon using principles from Ciceronian rhetoric, principles which would have been familiar to anyone who had studied the *trivium*.[59] It also gives advice on how to tailor a message to varied audiences, much of which is lifted

[56] 'Factus es quasi homo ilitteratus aut litterarum contemptor, nec lectioni, nec doctrine insistens, cum plures concanonici tui preclara ad edificacionem te sepius audiente proferent documenta': Alexander, *De artificioso modo predicandi* (*Opera omnia*, 1: 23).

[57] 'Et elegisti in silentio potius et quiete legem perfecte addiscere, quam imperfectus docere. Hac ratione tibi tunc officium predicandi dissimulare licuit, cui nunc in cathedra collocato non dissimulare licebit' (And you chose rather to learn the law completely in silence and quiet while you were still unprepared to teach. For this reason you were permitted to ignore the office of preaching, which, now that you are seated on the throne, you are not permitted to ignore'): Alexander, *De artificioso modo predicandi* (*Opera omnia*, 1: 23).

[58] 'Quibus si subtraxeris cibum uite, nonne iudicaberis mortem intulisse? Numquid ignoras quod legis censura sacerdotem occidit qui tabernaculum ingreditur sine sonitu tintabulorum extremis horis tunice iacinctine inherentium? … Postremo tibi per prophetam dicitur: si non annunciaueris populo meo scelera eorum, sanguinem eorum de manu tua requiram': Alexander, *De artificioso modo predicandi* (*Opera omnia*, 1: 24); cf. Ezek. 32: 8. In Exod. 28: 33–5, Moses orders priests to wear garments with bells sewn on when they enter the innermost room of the tabernacle (often known as 'the holy of holies'), or risk God's wrath. This was allegorized by Gregory the Great, who connects the sound of the bells to preaching: Gregory, *Pastoral Rule* 2.4 (1: 190, 192).

[59] Marianne G. Briscoe, *Artes praedicandi*, Typologie des sources du Moyen Âge occidental 61 (Turnhout, 1992), 258–9; Matthew Kempshall, *Rhetoric and the Writing of History, 400–1500* (Manchester, 2011), 14–15.

directly from Gregory's *Pastoral Rule*, undoubtedly also familiar.[60] In short, Alexander is not trying to educate his friend, but to spur him on, to drive home the import of the prelate's responsibility to preach by acting out that import himself: that is, by writing a treatise about it. Alexander assumes that his friend's recent neglect of study is a symptom of his lack of appreciation for the gravity of the prelate's office. More specifically, Alexander is responding to a conviction about what is required of prelates, writing with the Day of Judgement in mind, at which he and other prelates, standing alongside the apostles themselves, would be held to account for the souls under their care. In another sermon he cautions prelates to 'strive through preaching to acquire many whom you will be able to present to the Lord on the day of judgement, when Peter will present the Jews, Paul the Greeks, Andrew Achaea, Matthew Ethiopia, and so on'.[61]

Conclusion

For the four writers studied in this article, prelacy and pastoral care were fundamentally defined by a moral imperative to educate others. Specifically, 'prelates' were held – and expected – to teach their 'subjects' primarily by modelling virtuous living, and secondarily by instructing them verbally, especially by preaching. So important was this responsibility that it sat at the heart of what it meant to be a prelate in the first place. Pastoral care, the prelate's spiritual burden, was, to put it simply, an instructional and governance relationship between a superior and an inferior. This functional framework was both sufficiently flexible and sufficiently evocative to be useful for writers working in a range of contexts, such as crafting a preaching aid for prelates, writing sermons for delivery to clergy or penning

[60] The *Regula pastoralis* was often read in monastic refectories at mealtimes: Tessa Webber, 'Public Reading and its Books: The Framework of Norms', Lyell Lecture series, University of Oxford, 3 May 2016. Guibert of Gembloux, Hildegard of Bingen's secretary, advised a contact whom he considered to be a 'useless prelate' to mend his ways by reading just two books, Bernard of Clairvaux's *De consideratione* and Gregory's *Regula pastoralis*: Guibert de Gembloux, *Guiberti Gemblacensis epistolae* 50 (2 vols, CChr.CM 66, 66A; 2: 509).

[61] 'Studeatis predicando multos adquirere quos positis in die iudicii Domino presentare, quando presentabit Petrus Iudeos, Paulus Grecos, Andreas Achaiam, Matheus Ethiopiam, et sic alii alios': Alexander, *De artificioso modo predicandi* 3 (*Opera omnia*, 1: 53).

an exegetical treatise for reading aloud to regular canons. It allowed them to look beyond concrete practicalities, instead drawing attention to what they perceived to be more important: the prelate's responsibility to teach his subjects. As Alexander of Ashby's writings demonstrate, these writers also felt confident that any prelate who fully grasped this responsibility, and his ultimate accountability to God, would take care to work out the practicalities of ministering to his flock.

It remains to offer some thoughts on how this distinctive strain of pastoral writing might fit into broader narratives. Collectively written between perhaps 1161 at the earliest and 1214 at the latest, these texts in one sense represent a fifty-year historical period. They circulated little, or not at all, and therefore probably did not shape the thinking of many readers or listeners, especially when compared with, for instance, William de Montibus's *Peniteas cito*. However, in another sense, these writings attest to the continued influence of centuries-old clichés and concepts of pastoral care at the end of the twelfth century. Historians crave both specificity and novelty; by contrast, the prelate's responsibility to instruct his subordinates was an old idea, and indeed one that tended to obscure, or lump together, a variety of lived experiences. It may be that these ideas were more pervasive – geographically, chronologically or across genres – than previously realized. It is clear that by the end of the twelfth century a more practical and applied type of pastoral literature, epitomized by William de Montibus and (not long after) Thomas of Chobham and the earliest post-Lateran synodalia, was emerging.[62] There was, it seems, a growing consensus in the thirteenth century that offering specific instructions on how to fulfil the duties of pastoral care was more valuable than simply trying to motivate zealous and virtuous pastors. This should not blind us, however, to the emphasis placed by some English writers on prelacy, pastoral care and the instruction of subordinates in the second half of the twelfth century.

[62] Goering, *William de Montibus*; Thomas of Chobham, *Thomae de Chobham summa confessorum*, ed. F. Broomfield, Analecta mediaevalia Namurcensia 25 (Louvain, 1968); idem, *Summa de arte praedicandi* (CChr.CM 82); F. M. Powicke and C. R. Cheney, eds, *Councils and Synods with other Documents relating to the English Church*, 2: *A.D. 1205–1313*, 2 vols (Oxford, 1964), 2: 57–96, 125–37.

'I found this written in the other book': Learning Astronomy in Late Medieval Monasteries

Seb Falk*
Girton College, Cambridge

Recent histories have challenged narratives of a late medieval decline in monastic scholarship. This article extends that work to the natural sciences, showing how monks could learn astronomy and mathematics through their scholarly labour of reading, copying and glossing. Although the processes of learning are often poorly documented, and are often conflated with teaching, it is possible, through close reading of annotations and reconstruction of mathematical processes, to get a glimpse of an individual in the moment of acquiring scientific skills. Focusing on a piece of adaptive copying carried out by an English Benedictine monk c.*1380, this article explores the devotional motivations underlying his work, and argues that it was through such copying and compilation that he acquired the expertise necessary to invent an astronomical instrument some years later.*

Medieval learning can be hard to trace. We certainly have good evidence of medieval teaching: one celebrated teaching text from the science of astronomy is Geoffrey Chaucer's guide to the astrolabe, ostensibly written for his ten-year-old son, through which, he writes, 'I purpose to teche the a certein nombre of conclusions aperteynyng to the same instrument'.[1] Much, too, is known about techniques of memorization.[2] Yet we do not know how 'little Lewis' read his father's instructions, or how he came to understand the instrument in his hands. This is a common problem, since documents of learning contexts, generally produced by teachers, tend to reflect the transmission of didactic material rather than its reception.[3] Thus when

* Girton College, Huntingdon Rd, Cambridge, CB3 0JG. E-mail: sldf2@cam.ac.uk.

[1] Geoffrey Chaucer, *A Treatise on the Astrolabe*, Prologue 11–13, in *The Riverside Chaucer*, ed. Larry Benson (Oxford, 1987), 662.

[2] Mary Carruthers, *The Book of Memory: A Study of Memory in Medieval Culture*, 2nd edn (Cambridge, 2008).

[3] Alain Bernard and Christine Proust, eds, *Scientific Sources and Teaching Contexts throughout History: Problems and Perspectives* (Dordrecht, 2014), 1–15.

Studies in Church History 55 (2019), 129–144
doi: 10.1017/stc.2018.18

historians discuss 'medieval learning' they are often referring to the delivery of knowledge – or, worse, simply knowledge itself – rather than the processes by which it was absorbed.[4]

Recent historical work has, however, begun to trace learning processes. Research within the field of history of science has focused on the practices of scientists, including learning practices, though this 'practice turn' is less popular for pre-modern science and rarely extends to the poorly documented practices of scientific non-elites.[5] Meanwhile, historians of monasticism, seeking to challenge assumptions about a late medieval decline in monastic scholarship, have begun to uncover the opportunities monks had to learn in almonry schools, at university and within the cloister itself.[6] This article brings the two fields together through its exploration of the astronomical study of a monk who, although he was immersed in the scholarly practices of well-resourced Benedictine houses, may not have attended university, and never attained either prominence within scientific circles or a position of authority within the cloister.

The 'monastic renaissance' we find in at least some wealthier and better-connected monasteries extended to the sciences, which were not just practised by experts in universities.[7] In particular, astronomy was an important subject of study, enshrined in the *quadrivium* of mathematical sciences and central to monastic concerns such as time-keeping and healthcare. It was studied through a range of Christian and non-Christian sources, including some texts that were explicitly intended as beginners' primers. However, such textbooks were not indispensable to learning, and this article will show how monastic scholarly practices could facilitate learning (and indeed may have been implicitly intended to do so) in ways that obviated the need for the guidance of a teacher. Close reading of the texts and objects

[4] See, for example, John Murdoch and Edith Sylla, eds, *The Cultural Context of Medieval Learning* (Dordrecht, 1975), 1–30.

[5] Karine Chemla, 'Observing Mathematical Practices as a Key to Mining our Sources and Conducting Conceptual History', in Lena Soler et al., eds, *Science after the Practice Turn in the Philosophy, History, and Social Studies of Science* (New York, 2014), 238–68.

[6] See, for example, James Clark, *The Benedictines in the Middle Ages* (Woodbridge, 2011), who sets himself against the views of David Knowles, *The Religious Orders in England* (Cambridge, 1957).

[7] James Clark, *A Monastic Renaissance at St Albans: Thomas Walsingham and his Circle, c.1350–1440* (Oxford, 2004).

produced in monasteries can reveal the processes by which those sciences were learned and in turn developed and disseminated.

Monasteries had been centres of astronomical scholarship before the foundation of universities and continued to be so, if in a reduced capacity, thereafter. Such scholarship went well beyond the practical timekeeping and calendrical calculation developed by Bede (*c.*673–735): by 1100 Walcher, prior of Great Malvern, had carried out observations and computed lunar tables that far surpassed what was necessary to find the date of Easter.[8] Moreover, Benedictine abbeys in Catalonia, France and southern Germany had been at the forefront of the reception of mathematical knowledge from the Islamic world, producing some of the earliest Latin translations of texts on instruments such as the astrolabe.[9] Such scholarly commitment was underpinned by a range of motivations. Precise timekeeping symbolized order and authority, and had the practical benefit of regulating monastic routines; it is not surprising that monasteries possessed a range of time-telling devices.[10] A second practical driver could have been the use of astrology for medical purposes: the largest astrological libraries in this period were in religious houses, and the Benedictines had particular rules governing the dress to be worn and the biblical verses to be intoned when carrying out surgical procedures such as phlebotomy.[11] Monks were also, it seems, attracted to astronomy by devotional motivation – the desire to approach the mind of God by learning about his creation – as well, perhaps, as simple intellectual curiosity.[12]

[8] Bede, *The Reckoning of Time*, ed. Faith Wallis, TTH 29 (Liverpool, 1999); Stephen McCluskey, *Astronomies and Cultures in Early Medieval Europe* (Cambridge, 1998), 180–4.

[9] Charles Burnett, 'King Ptolemy and Alchandreus the Philosopher: The earliest Texts on the Astrolabe and Arabic Astrology at Fleury, Micy and Chartres', *Annals of Science* 55 (1998), 329–68.

[10] Catherine Eagleton, 'John Whethamsteade, Abbot of St Albans, on the Discovery of the Liberal Arts and their Tools: Or, Why were Astronomical Instruments in Late Medieval Libraries?', *Mediaevalia* 29 (2008), 109–36, at 122.

[11] Hilary Carey, *Courting Disaster: Astrology at the English Court and University in the Later Middle Ages* (Basingstoke, 1992), 41–2; Cornelius O'Boyle, 'Astrology and Medicine in Later Medieval England: The Calendars of John Somer and Nicholas of Lynn', *Sudhoffs Archiv* 89 (2005), 1–22, at 14–15.

[12] On this issue, see Andrew Cunningham, 'The Identity of Natural Philosophy: A Response to Edward Grant', *Early Science and Medicine* 5 (2000), 258–78; Edward Grant, 'God and Natural Philosophy: The Late Middle Ages and Sir Isaac Newton', ibid. 279–98; Andrew Cunningham, 'A Last Word', ibid. 299–300.

With the rise of the European universities in the twelfth century, monasteries lost some of their importance as centres of scholarship, but they remained significant intellectual institutions. Several recent histories have argued against earlier accounts of late medieval monastic stagnation. Historians have naturally focused on traditional monastic interests such as theology, history and canon law, but the point applies equally, and in some cases with even greater force, to the mathematical sciences. From the late thirteenth century, the chapters of English Benedictines enacted statutes to promote study, and in 1336 the papal bull *Summi magistri* ordered Benedictine houses to send one monk in every twenty to university; although some were later reprimanded for not doing so, others, like Westminster and St Albans, sent far more than required.[13] Few monks stayed long enough to graduate, and they were required to focus on theology and canon law, but they would have studied the introductory arts course, unless they had already done so at their monastery.[14] That meant at least some of the mathematical sciences: arithmetic, geometry, astronomy and music. On their return to the cloister, some monks brought their scientific interests, or at least their scientific books, with them. Many astronomical texts surviving from monastic libraries were produced at universities. Even if the monks who brought them back deposited them in the monastic library and never looked at them again, they were available for other monks to study.[15] They include the most widespread primers such as John of Sacrobosco's *On the Sphere*, as well as a range of more recondite texts. These fed into an active internal network of learning, in which monks were encouraged to busy themselves with the gamut of scholarly tasks: 'studying, reading, and writing books; glossing, correcting, illuminating, and also binding', as the 1351 constitutions of Thomas de la Mare (abbot of St Albans 1349–96) put it.[16] The abbots of St Albans were clearly aware of the advantages of university

[13] David Wilkins, ed., *Concilia Magnae Britanniae et Hiberniae* (London, 1737), 595; Alban Léotaud, 'The Benedictines at Oxford, 1283–1539', in Henry Wansbrough and Anthony Marett-Crosby, eds, *Benedictines in Oxford* (London, 1997), 20–36, at 25–6.

[14] Joan Greatrex, 'From Cathedral Cloister to Gloucester College', in Wansbrough and Marett-Crosby, eds, *Benedictines in Oxford*, 48–60, at 54–6.

[15] Wilbur R. Knorr, 'Two Medieval Monks and their Astronomy Books: MSS. Bodley 464 and Rawlinson C.117', *Bodleian Library Record* 14 (1993), 269–84.

[16] Thomas Walsingham, *Gesta abbatum monasterii Sancti Albani*, ed. Henry T. Riley, 3 vols, RS 28 (London, 1867–9), 2: 433 (my translation).

education, as they were consistently generous benefactors to Gloucester College, Oxford.[17] As well as the benefits of learning which monk-students brought back to St Albans and which trickled down through the monastery, such munificence must have contributed to the abbey's reputation for scholarship at this time; and this in turn may have attracted new monks to the house, sometimes directly from Oxford.[18]

One monk who made that move was Richard of Wallingford. He had studied at Oxford for six years before making his profession, and after only three years in St Albans returned to the university for a further nine years, during which he completed his most important work.[19] He had been back in the monastery for only a few weeks in autumn 1327 when abbot Hugh of Eversden died, and following some energetic lobbying Richard was elected to succeed him.[20] Succeeding generations of monks recalled his efforts to restore the abbey finances neglected by previous abbots, and the leprosy that cut short his tenure, but above all they celebrated his achievements as an astronomer. Both the surviving images of him (in the abbey chronicle and book of benefactors) show him with astronomical instruments of his own invention.[21] In his most important and celebrated work, the *Treatise on the Albion* (1326), he prayed of his Albion instrument, a multifunctional planetary computer of unprecedented refinement and complexity, that 'its place among other instruments will not be undistinguished, especially since its design could direct the minds of many people to higher things'.[22] The Albion was certainly distinguished in its capacity to simplify and speed up the difficult calculations involved in astronomy and astrology, such as predicting eclipses and the positions of celestial bodies, as well as timekeeping and calendrical computation; in addition, any student who worked through the treatise, which comprised geometrical proofs as well as explanation of the instrument's construction

[17] Léotaud, 'Benedictines at Oxford', 27–8.

[18] Walsingham, *Gesta abbatum*, ed. Riley, 3: 410–11; Clark, *Monastic Renaissance*, 15.

[19] Walsingham, *Gesta abbatum*, ed. Riley, 2: 182.

[20] John North, *God's Clockmaker: Richard of Wallingford and the Invention of Time* (London, 2005), 77–9.

[21] London, BL, Cotton MSS Claudius E.IV, 'Deeds of the Abbots of St Albans', fol. 201^{r}; Nero D.VII, 'Book of Benefactors', fol. 20^{r}.

[22] Richard of Wallingford, 'Tractatus albionis', in J. D. North, ed., *Richard of Wallingford: An Edition of his Writings*, 3 vols (Oxford, 1976), 1: 340 (my translation).

and uses, would learn a great deal about the heavens. There is no sense in monastic accounts that Richard's scientific interests detracted from his piety; rather, the monks took pride in his contribution to the abbey's reputation for learning.[23] It was surely to preserve and perhaps enhance this reputation, as well as to honour his memory, that fresh copies were made of Richard's most significant work: at least three of the nine more-or-less faithful copies of the *Albion* (that is, those not following John of Gmunden's popular fifteenth-century edition) were produced at St Albans.[24] It is clear that his successors valued his achievements in advancing learning at the monastery and promoting its reputation as a centre of scholarship. The abbey chronicle stresses Richard's 'many books and instruments of Astronomy, and Geometry, and other particular sciences, in which he excelled beyond all his contemporaries'; his fifteenth-century successor abbot John Whethamsted (himself a great supporter of monastic learning, who built and stocked the library at Gloucester College) wrote that 'the albion contains in itself the functions of all the other instruments. Richard of Wallingford, formerly abbot of the monastery of Alban, first discovered it – a man so learned in the art of astronomy that, from his time to the present, there has been no Englishman like him.'[25]

Reverence for Richard of Wallingford was undoubtedly a motivating factor in the production of the manuscript that is the principal subject of this article, Bodleian Library MS Laud Misc. 657. The codex comprises eighty leaves, still in their medieval binding, of which twenty-six were initially left blank (four of these were filled by a slightly later hand). In the first two-thirds of the book, a single hand copied two of Wallingford's works: the *Albion* and another instrument treatise, the *Rectangulus*, also written in 1326. This copy of the *Rectangulus* has little to distinguish it from others. *Albion*, however, presents a different case, as its scribe explained on the first page:

23 BL, MS Cotton Nero C.VI, fol. 149ʳ; Walsingham, *Gesta abbatum*, ed. Riley, 2: 207.

24 Oxford, Bodl., MS Laud Misc. 657, fols 2ʳ–45ʳ; MS Ashmole 1796, fols 118ʳ–159ᵛ; Oxford, Corpus Christi College, MS 144, fols 44ʳ–78ᵛ; North, ed., *Richard of Wallingford*, 2: 127–30.

25 Walsingham, *Gesta abbatum*, ed. Riley, 2: 207 (my translation); BL, MS Cotton Nero C.VI, fol. 149ʳ (my translation). On Gloucester College and John Whethamsted, see Léotaud, 'Benedictines at Oxford', 28.

> It should be known that Master Richard, abbot of the monastery of St Albans, first composed this book; and through it he devised and made that marvellous instrument which is called Albion. But afterwards a certain Simon Tunsted, professor of sacred theology, changed certain things not only in the book but also in the instrument, as will be clear to scholars in this book. Also, he added certain things.
>
> Master John of Westwyke gave this book to [the priory of] God and the blessed Mary and St Oswyn, king and martyr, at Tynemouth; and to the monks serving God there. May the soul of the said John and the souls of all the faithful, through the mercy of God, rest in peace. Amen.[26]

The life of this John Westwyk has been partially reconstructed in a recent article by Kari Anne Rand: he was evidently first a monk of St Albans before moving to Tynemouth around 1380.[27] He was there for no more than three years before leaving to take part in the 1383 crusade to Flanders led by Bishop Henry le Despenser. Later he returned to St Albans, where he probably died soon after 1397; it was there or perhaps in London that he wrote the Middle English instrument treatise known as *The Equatorie of the Planetis*, long attributed to Chaucer.[28] There is no evidence that Westwyk studied at university. Yet his composition of the *Equatorie* in 1393 demanded no little scientific expertise. Assuming that he acquired this expertise within the monastery, his learning processes can be observed in his production, shortly before his move north to Tynemouth, of MS Laud Misc. 657.

Westwyk's prefatory note, quoted above, makes it quite explicit that he is collating two versions of the treatise, those of Richard of Wallingford and Simon Tunsted (a Franciscan active at Oxford in the 1350s and 1360s), and that he is studying them alongside an actual Albion instrument. For the most part his copy is identical to other early copies of Richard of Wallingford's treatise. Where it differs, it is not always immediately clear how much is copied directly from Tunsted, since no other copy survives of his version.

26 Bodl., MS Laud Misc. 657, fol. 1^{v} (my translation).

27 Kari Anne Rand, 'The Authorship of *The Equatorie of the Planetis* revisited', *Studia Neophilologica* 87 (2015), 15–35.

28 Cambridge, Peterhouse, MS 75.I. The attribution was proposed by Derek Price, ed., *The Equatorie of the Planetis* (Cambridge, 1955); see also Kari Anne Rand Schmidt, *The Authorship of the Equatorie of the Planetis*, Chaucer Studies 19 (Woodbridge, 1993); eadem, 'Authorship revisited'.

Wallingford's editor John North suggested that all substantive changes were Tunsted's; conversely, James Clark argued that Westwyk had produced a 'more advanced' version of Tunsted's text.[29] Careful reading, however, makes it clear that while most changes were probably made by Tunsted, some represent original writing by Westwyk.[30]

Throughout the text Westwyk is clear about his elucidatory editorial task. For example, where he writes out two versions of the same description of a part of the instrument, he interposes himself: 'Concerning the circle on the first face of the first disc, I found this written in the other book.'[31] Elsewhere he makes his use of a physical Albion instrument explicit, noting that 'this conclusion is void, because this statement supposes that the circle of the year of the Sun, with the days of the months, is inscribed on the second limb just as on the first; which is not the case on our instrument, nor is it necessary, so it is best omitted.'[32] Collating rather than editing, he bracketed the void conclusion, but did not delete it.

In his later *Equatorie of the Planetis* treatise, Westwyk was to show himself attentive to the relationship between the size and accuracy of instruments: the treatise begins by advising the reader that 'the largere that thow makest this instrument … the ner the trowthe of thy conclusiouns'.[33] In his collation of the *Albion* we see him learning the importance of size. Where the original treatise stated that the Albion was to be at least 12 inches in diameter, Westwyk's version changes this to 16; but he then drew a caret, with the marginal addition 'or 12'.[34] A marginal gloss in an early fifteenth-century hand in another St Albans copy of the *Albion*, which refers in the present tense to 656 divisions in the margin of the spiral disc of 'the abbot's Albion', suggests that the writer had seen Richard of Wallingford's own instrument; the number of divisions suggests that it was probably around 15 inches in diameter.[35] It could well be the same

29 North, ed., *Richard of Wallingford*, 2: 130; James Clark, 'Intellectual Life at the Abbey of St Albans and the Nature of Monastic Learning in England, *c.*1350–*c.*1440: The Work of Thomas Walsingham in Context' (DPhil thesis, University of Oxford, 1997), 142.

30 This is also more or less the conclusion drawn by Rand, 'Authorship revisited', 12–13.

31 Bodl., MS Laud Misc. 657, fol. 21r (my translation).

32 Ibid., fol. 22v (my translation).

33 Peterhouse, MS 75.I, fol. 71v.

34 Bodl., MS Laud Misc. 657, fol. 10v.

35 Corpus Christi, MS 144, fol. 59v; North, *Richard of Wallingford*, 2: 181.

instrument studied by Westwyk, who perhaps revised the text to reflect the size of the instrument he was using, before deciding to reinsert Wallingford's original specification. Certainly on the following page access to the instrument made a difference to Westwyk's scribal practice, as he wrote: 'note that the figure of the circles of the first limb of the first face should be in this space, but it is very plainly inscribed on the instrument, so it is omitted here'.[36] Following this is a partially complete diagram; the circles have been traced out, but the scales have not been filled in (Fig. 2; cf. Fig. 1). Manuscripts of the *Albion*, particularly those from St Albans, generally include a high proportion of Richard of Wallingford's diagrams (perhaps reflecting a devotional motivation for their production), unlike many medieval treatises, where copyists were often reluctant to do the geometry, so Westwyk's omission is more significant than it might appear.

On occasions Westwyk's collation of the two versions of the *Albion* tested the limits of his abilities. In one remarkably frank note, he wrote: 'the abbot works with the circle of iomyn for the equation of days. But Simon works in another way, as is taught in the 18th use; and also in many other places which seem inconsistent.'[37] The implication is clear: he has noted multiple differences between the work of Richard of Wallingford and Simon Tunsted, but he is not always able to disentangle their implications or decide which is better.

Westwyk's attempts to work out the treatise as he collates it are in general quite successful. However, some mistakes are apparent. Close examination of his diagrams suggests that while he was able to copy simple figures with care and a reasonable level of accuracy, more complex constructions caused him greater difficulty. We see this, for example, in his copy of the diagram illustrating the hour lines of lunation on the first face of the first disc. The explanation in the treatise is quite explicit, but a comparison (Figs 3–4) with the best extant version of this diagram, in Corpus Christi MS 144, shows that Westwyk did not follow it effectively. The instructions require that, after completing the inner and outer graduated rings, an eccentric circle is to be drawn touching the outside of the inner graduated ring at the top, and the inside of the outer graduated ring at the bottom; a further concentric circle is then to be drawn, of a medium size such that it

[36] Bodl., MS Laud Misc. 657, fol. 11r (my translation).

[37] Ibid., fol. 45r (my translation). The circle of iomyn (from the Arabic for 'day') was a part of the Albion used to convert between mean and true time.

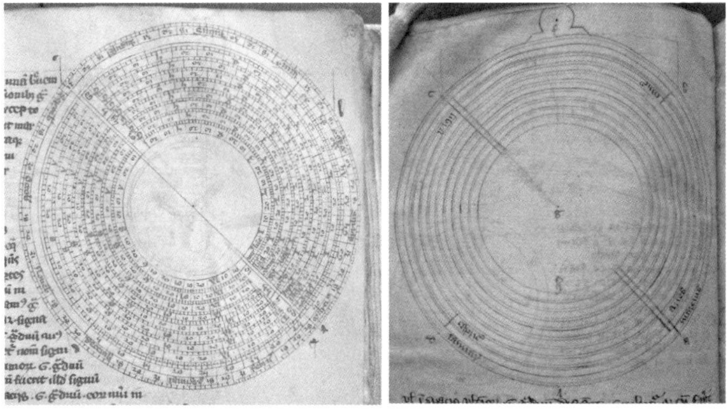

Figs 1–2: The first limb of the first face of Richard of Wallingford's Albion. Fig. 1 is a complete diagram of that part of the instrument; John Westwyk explained his choice not to complete this diagram in his copy (Fig. 2). Oxford, Corpus Christi College, MS 144, fol 55^{r}; Bodl., MS Laud Misc. 657, fol 11^{v}. Reproduced by permission of the President and Fellows of Corpus Christi College, Oxford, and the Bodleian Libraries, University of Oxford.

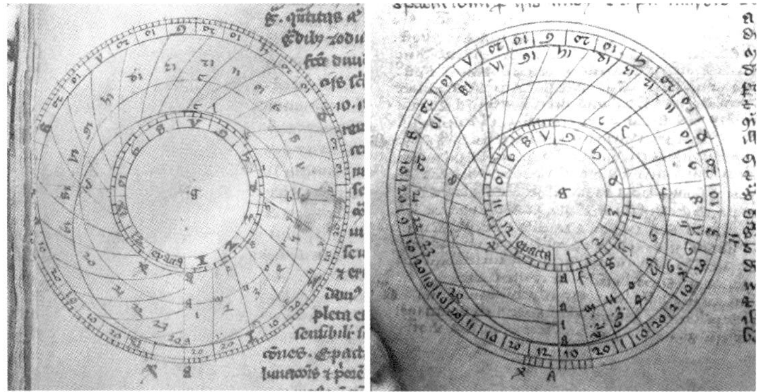

Figs 3–4: The hour lines of lunation on the first face of the first disc of Richard of Wallingford's Albion. The two medium-sized circles should intersect on the horizontal diameter DGB; this has been done successfully in Fig. 3 (left), but in Fig. 4 (John Westwyk's copy) the intersection is clearly too low. Westwyk also did not divide the inner, middle and outer circles evenly into the correct number of parts. Oxford, Corpus Christi College, MS 144, fol 58^{v}; Bodl., MS Laud Misc. 657, fol 15^{v}. Reproduced by permission of the President and Fellows of Corpus Christi College, Oxford, and the Bodleian Libraries, University of Oxford.

intersects the eccentric circle on the horizontal diameter DGB. This was accomplished successfully in Corpus Christi 144, but Westwyk drew the medium-sized circle rather too large, so it clearly does not intersect the eccentric circle in the correct place. Moreover, the inner, middle and outer circles were to be divided into 20, 22 and 24 parts respectively; Westwyk divided them rather unevenly into 23, 24 and 25 (comparison of the lower-left quadrants of figures 3 and 4 should make the difference clear).

Westwyk's attempts to learn from the treatise are clearest in the long section he added to the end of it, which draws on a range of diverse sources in Islamic and Jewish astronomy. Wallingford advertised his invention as bringing together the functions of several other instruments, and Westwyk appended a two-page summary of the relationship between those instruments.[38] This is separated from the main treatise and is somewhat disjointed in style, quite different from the earlier text, so it is very likely to be an original addition by Westwyk himself. He first compares the Albion with the saphea of the eleventh-century Andalusian astronomer al-Zarqālī, whom he knew as Arzachel; Wallingford had deliberately not given full details of the saphea since 'it has its own treatise', and it appears Westwyk was hoping to mitigate Richard's omission with some helpful detail from that treatise.[39] He then moves on to the astrolabe, noting a few features common to all astrolabes before exploring some distinctive attributes of the Albion's astrolabe plate. Here his discussion draws on the canonical text attributed to the eighth-century Persian Jewish astronomer Māshā'allāh, which was in the library at St Albans.[40] Finally, after the astrolabe plate, Westwyk focuses his attention on the Albion's rather complex plate for lunar and solar eclipses. Here, too, he draws on his reading of other sources to supplement the *Albion*'s theoretical content. Richard of Wallingford had cited Albategni, the tenth-century Syrian al-Battānī, and Westwyk apparently followed up this citation in order to expand on Wallingford's

[38] Ibid., fols 43^{r}–44^{r}.

[39] Richard of Wallingford, 'Tractatus albionis' 3.36, in North, ed., *Richard of Wallingford*, 1: 380 (my translation).

[40] Collated with Richard of Wallingford's collected works in Bodl., MS Ashmole 1796, fols 40^{v}–55^{v}. Arzachel's tables and canons were also there (now Dublin, Trinity College, MS 444); his saphea treatise is not represented in surviving manuscripts or catalogues from the monastery, but it may well have been there, since it was a popular companion work for the sorts of instrument treatises that interested the St Albans monks.

discussion of lunar eclipses with al-Battānī's explanation of three reasons why the quantity of eclipse varies.[41]

The learning process visible through MS Laud Misc. 657 extends to its mathematical tables. It was unusual for medieval astronomical treatises, especially instrument treatises, to include tables; although tables circulated in enormous quantities and variety, they were normally somewhat independent from texts, and astronomers tended to compile their own sets to suit their individual purposes. The *Albion*, however, did have its own tables, which Richard of Wallingford had drawn up specifically to aid in the construction of the instrument.[42] John Westwyk copied the complete set, with great accuracy: a comparison of a sample table (4.17) in five copies of the *Albion* shows that Westwyk's copy has no scribal errors at all, whereas three of the other four have rather more.[43] His accuracy is remarkable, particularly since the opaque content of tables normally leads to a higher incidence of scribal errors than is found in texts.

Apart from copying them, Westwyk made two important additions to the *Albion* tables. First, he added a table of lunar elongations at the end of the treatise, because, as he explained, 'the Lord Abbot put the mean longitude of the Moon on his spiral; but Master Simon put the elongation of the Moon from the Sun on his spiral … so I wrote this table, so that anyone can make it that way if he likes'.[44] Tunsted's redesign had made Wallingford's original table useless; Westwyk, in contrast, is at pains to make his copy useful, adding a *signe-de-renvoi* so that the new table can be read alongside the original one (where he marked a corresponding sign).[45] Westwyk's statement that 'I wrote' (*scripsi*) the table does not mean that he computed it personally; its inconsistent values suggest that it was derived from

[41] Bodl., MS Laud Misc. 657, fol. 43ʳ. Al-Battānī's *zīj* was translated into Latin twice in the twelfth century; there is no record of his work at St Albans, but he is cited in the *Albion*, where Richard of Wallingford gave an indication of his reputation by placing him alongside Ptolemy: Al-Battānī, *Opus astronomicum*, ed. Carlo Nallino (Milan, 1899), 57–8; Richard of Wallingford, 'Tractatus albionis' 3.24.

[42] Richard of Wallingford, 'Tractatus albionis' 2.10.

[43] Bodl., MS Laud Misc. 657, fol. 42ʳ; Corpus Christi MS 144, fol. 78ᵛ (the only other perfect copy); BL, MS Harley 80, fol. 54ʳ; MS Harley 625, fol. 164ʳ; Bodl., MS Ashmole 1796, fol. 159ʳ; see Sebastian L. D. Falk, 'Improving Instruments: Equatoria, Astrolabes, and the Practices of Monastic Astronomy in Late Medieval England' (PhD thesis, University of Cambridge, 2016), 172.

[44] Bodl., MS Laud Misc. 657, fol. 45ʳ (my translation).

[45] Ibid., fol. 39ᵛ.

two pre-existing tables rather than drawn up from scratch. It contains a large number of copying errors, and since, as we have established, Westwyk was normally a very accurate copyist, it was most likely copied from a corrupt exemplar.

However, the second additional table was certainly computed by Westwyk himself. The design of the Albion called for at least one scale of oblique ascensions (the arc of the ecliptic that rises with a given arc of the equator – that is, in a given time), in order to help find the ascendant and divide the astrological houses. The first such scale was to be inscribed in the innermost circle on the limb of the second face of the mater, for the latitude of a place 'where we intend to stay for a long time and make many observations; additional scales could also be inscribed on the plates for other latitudes'.[46] To assist in this, the final table in the *Albion* treatise was a table of oblique ascensions for latitude 51° 50′, the latitude of Oxford. (St Albans was close to the same latitude, which may partially account for the survival of so many books of Oxford astronomy at the abbey.) Westwyk copied that table, but also added another, for latitude 55°; to make his intention clear, he wrote 'tynemuth' [*sic*] just below the table header.[47]

Tynemouth was a dependent house of St Albans. Set on a cliff overlooking the North Sea, and strategically close to the Scottish border, it was in every sense an outpost. Ambitious monks went there to prove themselves (including Thomas de la Mare, who had been prior when elected to the abbacy of the mother house);[48] wayward monks were sent there as punishment.[49] We cannot be sure why Westwyk went, but we know he was there for only three years before joining the ill-fated crusade of the bishop of Norwich to Flanders.[50] In any case, he took MS Laud Misc. 657 with him. Its quality of parchment and (as we have seen) varied sources mean that it was clearly produced at St Albans; but Westwyk's addition of the table for 55° shows that it was intended as a gift for the northern cell: the addition represents an act of charity in distributing the fruits of learning in St Albans to a

[46] Richard of Wallingford, 'Tractatus albionis' 2.18, in North, ed., *Richard of Wallingford*, 1: 324–5.

[47] Bodl., MS Laud Misc. 657, fol. 42^{v}.

[48] Walsingham, *Gesta abbatum*, ed. Riley, 2: 380–1.

[49] Ibid. 1: 258.

[50] Ibid. 2: 416; for the date of Westwyk's arrival at Tynemouth, see Rand, 'Authorship revisited', 7.

daughter house, but also an act of devotion to the memory and reputation of Richard of Wallingford.

Computing the table required some sophisticated spherical trigonometry. The table header, which Westwyk copied from Wallingford's original, explains that 'it was calculated and composed as explained in the canons in the second book of the *Almagest*'.[51] However, when we deconstruct the tables for 51° 50′ and 55° using modern software, we find that although Wallingford cited Ptolemy's *Almagest*, the most important work of ancient astronomy, as a source, he used a value for the table's crucial underlying parameter – the obliquity of the ecliptic – that was different from Ptolemy's: 23° 33′ 30″, rather than 23° 51′ 20″.[52] Yet Westwyk did use a Ptolemaic value in his calculations. Having no way of knowing what Wallingford had done, he simply followed the lead Wallingford had given in the table header. The great labour of calculation meant that tables like this were far more often copied than computed from scratch; it is therefore rare to find a table for an unusual latitude like Westwyk's. Its production was perhaps in part an act of charity towards the monks of Tynemouth, but it was also undoubtedly an exercise in mathematical learning. His faithfulness to Ptolemy's methods, greater than that of his source, can be seen as a learner's uncertainty about how closely to follow unfamiliar instructions.

In 1393, some thirteen years after his collation of MS Laud Misc. 657, John Westwyk wrote *The Equatorie of the Planetis*, drafting a

[51] Bodl., MS Laud Misc. 657, fol. 42^{v}. In Book 2 of the *Almagest* Ptolemy provided tables of rising times (equivalent to oblique ascensions) for a range of latitudes. These may be computed from the right ascensions (explained in *Almagest* 1.16), which were found by a method mathematically equivalent to the modern formula: $\sin \alpha = \tan \delta \times \cot \varepsilon$, where α is right ascension, δ is declination and ε is the obliquity of the ecliptic (the formula for declination also incorporated obliquity). The size of the obliquity also underlies the ascensional difference γ, for which Ptolemy outlines a method equivalent to the modern formula: $\sin \gamma = \tan \delta \times \tan \varphi$, where φ is the observer's latitude. The oblique ascension can be found by subtracting γ from α: see Olaf Pedersen, *A Survey of the Almagest*, rev. Alexander Jones (New York, 2011), 96–7, 110–13.

[52] The methods of analysis are explained in Seb Falk, 'Copying and Computing Tables in Late Medieval Monasteries', in Matthieu Husson, Clemency Montelle and Benno van Dalen, eds, *Editing and analysing Numerical Tables: Towards a Digital Information System for the History of Astral Sciences*, Ptolemaeus Arabus et Latinus (Turnhout, forthcoming 2019). They are based on Benno van Dalen, 'Ancient and Mediaeval Astronomical Tables: Mathematical Structure and Parameter Values' (PhD thesis, University of Utrecht, 1993), 67, 185.

description of a planetary instrument he had apparently designed himself and compiling astronomical tables to aid in its use. The *Equatorie* is a thoroughly pedagogical work. Although Westwyk was still himself learning as he wrote it (Seneca's dictum 'while men teach, they learn' may well have been familiar to him), he writes with the authoritative voice of a teacher.[53] His instructions for the construction of the equatorium make use of many of the techniques Chaucer had pioneered in his *Treatise on the Astrolabe*: direct, informal address to the reader, didactic repetition and anticipating a student's misunderstandings. He warns his reader against a mistake that will make the instrument inaccurate, and immediately gives a tip for undoing such a mistake, writing 'yif thow myshappe in this cas i shal teche the a remedie'.[54] The resulting set of instructions is remarkably easy to follow, and can be used to make a fully functioning instrument; this is rarely true of medieval treatises, which often read more like thought experiments.[55] The act of charity implied by the composition (or perhaps translation) of this text in Middle English is matched by Westwyk's earlier devotion to the brothers of Tynemouth, and to the memory of Richard of Wallingford, expressed through his copying of the *Albion* and *Rectangulus* treatises. Yet his production of MS Laud Misc. 657 was also a learning experience. John had probably come to St Albans abbey from the nearby village of Westwick, and although he may have studied at the grammar school sponsored by the abbey, he is unlikely to have gone to university. Nevertheless, in part because of the learning brought by those monks who did attend university, John could have obtained an astronomical education (with or without supervision) through the monastic labour of 'studying, reading, writing, glossing [and] correcting' enjoined by his abbot Thomas de la Mare.

That scholarly labour could certainly include astronomy, embracing not only texts by English monks but also the great works of Islamic and Jewish astronomy. Although recent research has revealed

[53] Seneca, *On Crowds* 7.8, in *Epistles, vol. 1*, transl. Richard Gummere, LCL 75 (Cambridge, MA, 1917), 34. The popularity of Seneca at that time is discussed by Grace Wilson, '"Amonges Othere Wordes Wyse": The Medieval Seneca and the "Canterbury Tales"', *Chaucer Review* 28 (1993), 135–45.

[54] Peterhouse, MS 75.I, fol. 73^{v}.

[55] A virtual model of the equatorie, created by Ben Blundell and Seb Falk following Westwyk's instructions, can be found online at: <https://cudl.lib.cam.ac.uk/view/MS-PETERHOUSE-00075-00001>.

the hitherto unappreciated range of monastic scholarship, more remains to be done to gain a fuller understanding of their scientific interests; many manuscripts remain unedited and poorly catalogued. Likewise, the networks, outside elite university circles, through which scientific ideas circulated and developed remain largely unmapped. The loss of so many texts, as well as library catalogues and other supporting documents, makes it hard to catch a glimpse of such networks and their processes of communication and learning. Yet with careful reading we can uncover some of their practices. At any rate, we can be sure, despite Richard of Wallingford's concern that through such practices he had 'strayed from the study of pious things', that the theories and methods he helped develop were valued, and learned with devotion and pride, by late medieval monks.[56]

[56] Richard of Wallingford, 'Tractatus albionis' 3.42, in North, ed., *Richard of Wallingford*, 1: 389 (my translation).

Peter Canisius and the Development of Catholic Education in Germany, 1549–97

Ruth Atherton*
University of Birmingham

The Jesuit Peter Canisius (1521–97) became widely respected as a catechist, pedagogue and preacher who worked tirelessly on behalf of the Catholic faith. Canisius's set of three catechisms – the Large, Small *and* Smaller *– were the most popular and widely available Catholic catechisms in sixteenth-century Germany: by his death, at least 357 editions had appeared, in a number of languages. Employed in Catholic schools, churches and homes across the Holy Roman Empire, his catechisms have been interpreted as a direct response to the Protestant attack on Catholicism in Germany. However, the boundaries between Catholicism and heresy were not always clear to the laity. Drawing on examples from his catechisms and his approach to the Index of Prohibited Books, this article suggests that Canisius sought to promote a policy of inclusion among his fellow Catholics in a time of conflict and uncertainty. In recognizing the distinct nature of German Catholicism, Canisius advocated a tailored educational approach to contentious doctrines and practices. Directed towards the German laity, this approach taught the lesson of compromise and acceptance among those who identified as Catholic. The article adds to existing scholarship on Jesuit education, Canisius's contribution to the development of a German religious identity, Jesuit casuistry and the dissemination of religious knowledge in German society.*

With a career spanning five decades, Peter Canisius (1521–97) was instrumental in the protection of Catholicism in the Holy Roman Empire. In 1583, Canisius observed in a letter to Claudio Acquaviva that 'most Germans are by nature straightforward, simple and good-natured, born and educated in the heresy of Lutheranism,

* 100 Bloomfield Rd, Gloucester, GL1 5BP. E-mail: R.K.Atherton@bham.ac.uk. I would like to thank Charlotte Methuen for her help and guidance, as well as the anonymous reviewers for their insightful feedback. I have included the original text for my own translations; in cases where the translation is taken from a secondary source, original and translated sources are both referenced.

Studies in Church History 55 (2019), 145–160
doi: 10.1017/stc.2018.19

they imbibe what they have learned partly in school, partly in church and partly in heretical writings, and that is why they have gone astray'.[1] To save the erring from damnation, Canisius centred his career on the education of German society. This article examines the nature of the education that he promoted. The first part focuses on Canisius's German-language catechisms, while the second explores his response to the Index of Prohibited Books. The overall impression given by his activities and literary works is that Canisius fought to establish an educational programme influenced by, and designed for, German Catholics, as opposed to implementing the universal Catholicism advocated by the Council of Trent. The outcome was that he promoted an inclusive approach to religion for those identifying as Catholics, while remaining utterly opposed to Protestants.

Education was a crucial method by which the minds of the laity could be shaped. Attitudes towards education began to change in the early sixteenth century, when it came to be seen as vital for the formation of well-rounded, pious Christians.[2] Pedagogical techniques developed and, in particular, catechisms for children grew in popularity, featuring prominently on curricula across the empire. Indeed, in 1516 Erasmus commented that 'nothing makes so deep and indelible a mark as that which is impressed in those first years'.[3] The drive to influence the minds of children coincided with growing efforts to teach the laity as a whole, and Canisius was but one of the many pedagogues of early modern Germany. Significant figures include Martin Luther, whose catechisms influenced the content and structure of other catechetical texts, as well as his colleague and friend, Philip Melanchthon, who formulated the Augsburg Confession of 1530 and whose educational efforts in schools and universities earned him the name 'teacher of Germany'.[4] Canisius shared similar

[1] 'Errant ut plaerique Germani, natura simplices, rudes, faciles ad ea imbibenda, quae in haeresi Luterana nati et educati, partim in scholis, partim in templis, partim in scriptis haereticis didicerunt': *Beati Petri Canisii, Societatis Iesu, Epistulae et acta*, ed. Otto Braunsberger, 8 vols (Freiburg im Breisgau, 1896–1923), 8: 131.

[2] Gerald Strauss, *Luther's House of Learning: Indoctrination of the Young in the German Reformation* (Baltimore, MD, 1978), 34–5.

[3] *Erasmus: The Education of a Christian Prince, with the Panegyric for Archduke Philip of Austria*, ed. Lisa Jardine (Cambridge, 1997), 5.

[4] Sachiko Kusukawa, 'Melanchthon', in David Bagchi and David C. Steinmetz, eds, *The Cambridge Companion to Reformation Theology* (Cambridge, 2004), 57–67, at 57.

pedagogical ambitions with these Lutheran educators: each sought to teach the tenets of Christian doctrine to the German laity, as well as the clergy, in an accessible and simple format.

Modern scholarship views Canisius in two opposing ways. The first stems from a nineteenth-century interpretation of Canisius, viewing him as a man ahead of his time with regard to ecumenical dialogue.[5] Julius Oswald argues that Canisius engaged with Protestants in a 'friendly manner', and tried to 'settle theological differences objectively'.[6] Similarly, Rita Haub argues that Canisius relied on 'objectivity, gentleness and understanding', and suggests, in particular, that his catechisms were not polemical.[7] In contrast, Hilmar Pabel views Canisius as a 'typical Catholic controversialist' who was 'disposed to display hostility, more than good will to Protestants' and argues persuasively that to see Canisius as ecumenical in his dealings with Protestants 'distorts historical vision'.[8] Indeed, it is evident from his wider literary career that Canisius was not gentle towards Protestants. Therefore, rather than focusing on his treatment of Protestants, this article examines his attitude towards his fellow Catholics, arguing that he adopted an inclusive pedagogical approach to those Catholics living on the fringes of orthodoxy. This did not extend to non-Catholics, but it permitted those who identified as Catholics to remain as such. In part, this was because Canisius had to engage with the political objectives of the emperor and the Bavarian dukes, particularly Duke Albrecht V (r.1550–79). Though Catholic, these rulers were influenced by political considerations in their dealings with Protestants and the Roman Curia, leading to the implementation of policies designed to minimize

[5] Johannes Janssen, *Geschichte des deutschen Volkes seit dem Ausgang des Mittelalters*, 8 vols (Freiburg im Breisgau, 1885), 8: 382–3; Peter Lippert, 'Petrus Canisius, der Heilige (Zu seiner Heiligsprechung 21. Mai 1925)', *Stimmen der Zeit* 109 (1925), 161–72; Max Pribilla, 'Canisius und die Protestanten', ibid. 396–400.

[6] Julius Oswald, 'Ringen um die Einheit der Kirche, Petrus Canisius und Philipp Melanchthon', in idem and Rita Haub, eds, *Jesuitica. Forschungen zur frühen Geschichte des Jesuitenordens in Bayern bis zur Aufhebung 1773* (Munich, 2001), 20–40, at 37.

[7] Rita Haub, *Petrus Canisius. Botschafter Europas* (Limburg an der Lahn, 2004), 49, 65.

[8] Hilmar Pabel, 'Peter Canisius and the Protestants: A Model of Ecumenical Dialogue?', *Journal of Jesuit Studies* 1 (2014), 373–99, at 373, 376. Hallensleben asks whether we should view Canisius as an early ecumenist: Barbara Hallensleben, 'Kirche in der Sendung. Die Antwort des Petrus Canisius auf die Erfahrung des "draußen"', in Rainer Berndt, ed., *Petrus Canisius SJ (1521–1597). Humanist und Europäer* (Berlin, 2000), 347–63, at 363.

confessional tensions. Furthermore, Canisius recognized the realities of being a Catholic in a time of religious heterogeneity, leading him to adopt a policy of inclusion regarding wavering Catholics in his German catechisms and his interactions with the laity. This is not to imply that Canisius was an 'ecumenicist before his time', as Pabel accuses modern historians of suggesting, but to suggest that Canisius promoted a brand of Catholic orthodoxy to ordinary Germans that was influenced by the political and religious climate of Germany.[9]

In acknowledging Canisius's agenda, this article suggests that there was a difference between the developing Tridentine Catholicism and the Catholicism that was emerging in sixteenth-century Germany. It contributes to discourse on the nature of Jesuit political thought, as well as the development of German confessionalism in the sixteenth century, and enhances our understanding of early modern German education.[10] It engages with R. J. W. Evans's interpretation of 'aulic Catholicism': a form of Catholic doctrine and practice which developed at a pace set by the Austrian authorities, rather than by Rome.[11] Moreover, aspects of Canisius's pedagogical approach resonate with Howard Louthan's examination of the imperial court in the later sixteenth century, at which Viennese peacemakers searched for compromise between opposing confessions.[12] By viewing Canisius's catechetical activities in the light of these broader themes, his attitude towards education can be better understood.

Born in Nijmegen in 1521, Canisius rejected his father's ambition for him to study law and get married, instead electing to join the Society of Jesus in 1543. Founded by Ignatius Loyola in 1540, the society's purpose was to strengthen Catholicism across Europe and beyond.[13] After a series of wars and political setbacks, Emperor Charles V had lost his fight to prevent the spread of Lutheranism,

[9] Pabel, 'Canisius', 373.

[10] Harro Höpfl, *Jesuit Political Thought: The Society of Jesus and the State, c.1540–1640* (Cambridge, 2004).

[11] R. J. W. Evans, *The Making of the Habsburg Monarch 1550–1700: An Interpretation* (Oxford, 1979), 59–61; Elaine Fulton, 'Wolves and Weathervanes: Confessional Moderation at the Habsburg Court of Vienna', in Luc Racaut and Alec Ryrie, eds, *Moderate Voices in the European Reformation* (Aldershot, 2005), 145–61.

[12] Howard Louthan, *The Quest for Compromise: Peacemakers in Counter-Reformation Vienna* (Cambridge, 1997).

[13] John W. O'Malley, *The First Jesuits* (Harvard, MA, 1995).

and the Peace of Augsburg confirmed its legal status in the empire in 1555. This development was not welcomed by Catholics, with Canisius informing Cardinal Truchess in January 1556 that, in Austria and Bavaria, many people continued to 'pester and attack rulers' to adopt the 'Confession, or rather, Confusion of Augsburg'.[14] The peace made the containment of Lutheranism a far harder task for the Catholics and in despair Charles abdicated, leaving his brother Ferdinand to succeed as emperor. Unfortunately, the pope did not recognize Ferdinand's succession because Charles had not asked for permission to abdicate.[15] This slight to Ferdinand's pride caused Canisius to worry that the new emperor might make 'dangerous concessions' to the Lutherans.[16] Political considerations remained important to Canisius for the remainder of his life and, along with his concerns regarding the spread of heresy, featured prominently in his publications and activities.

Canisius's publications can be categorized broadly into two groups. One sought to challenge Protestant doctrines: his most polemical treatises were his works on John the Baptist (1571) and the Virgin Mary (1577). These were intended as a Catholic response to the *Magdeburg Centuries*, a thirteen-volume history of the Christian Church written in Magdeburg by a group of theologians under the direction of Matthais Flacius Illyricus and published between 1559 and 1574. In his polemical works, Canisius rejected the claims of 'the corrupters of the word of God'.[17] Personal correspondence echoed his disdain for Protestants: in a letter to the archbishop of Cologne written in August 1572, Canisius declared that if the leading Protestant figures 'were all crushed up with a mortar, they would not produce one ounce of theology'.[18] Such views earned Canisius the nickname 'hammer of heretics', as well as the scorn of Protestant leaders.[19]

However, the second category of Canisius's publications – those directed either to a general audience or to his secular patrons –

[14] 'Urgent et infestare pergunt Principes … Augustanae confessionis aut potius confusionis': *Beati Petri Canisii*, ed. Braunsberger, 1: 595.

[15] James Brodrick, *Saint Peter Canisius* (Chicago, IL, 1980), 354.

[16] Ibid. 424.

[17] Pabel, 'Canisius', 389.

[18] 'Qui onnes si in mortario contunderentur, non exprimeretur, inquit, vna uncia verae Theologiae': *Beati Petri Canisii*, ed. Braunsberger, 7: 73.

[19] Pabel, 'Canisius', 374.

stand in marked contrast to his polemical activities: his German catechisms refrained from intense polemic on disputed points, while his response to the Roman Index cautioned against banning all Germans from reading prohibited material in order to avoid antagonizing secular patrons and German students. This second category is all the more noteworthy because of the difference in approach compared to his other literary endeavours. It represents Canisius's understanding that a tailored response was needed to address the religious strife in Germany. This was summed up in a letter to Acquaviva in January 1583, in which Canisius warned that understanding the cause of the religious problems in Germany was the only way they could be addressed.[20] Twenty-five years earlier, he had declared in a letter to Duke Albrecht that 'we must forget Italy and Spain and devote ourselves only to Germany … . Here we must work with all [our] strength and with the greatest enthusiasm'.[21]

Soon after arriving in Germany in 1549, Canisius informed Loyola's secretary, Juan Alfonso de Polanco, that 'it is useless to look for practical interest in religion among present-day Germans', noting that they rarely attended church sermons, did not fast during Lent and read heretical books.[22] To combat this apathy and the spread of heresy, Canisius advised that 'various seminaries' ought to be established.[23] Children, too, were not to be overlooked: in a sermon delivered at Innsbruck in 1572, Canisius declared that children 'are the best part of Christianity, the noblest provision of the Church'.[24] His educational programme was intended not only to encompass the training of future clerics drawn from Germany to serve Germany, but also the general education of German children. The most popular tool Canisius used in his ambitious educational programme was the catechism.[25]

[20] *Beati Petri Canisii*, ed. Braunsberger, 8: 139.

[21] 'Italiens und Spaniens müssen wir vergessen und uns Deutschland allein hingeben, nicht auf einige Zeit, sondern für das ganze Leben. Hier müssen wir aus allen Kräften und mit dem größten Eifer arbeiten': Otto Braunsberger, *Entstehung und erste Entwicklung der Katechismen des seligen Petrus Canisius aus der Gesellschaft Jesu* (Freiburg im Breisgau, 1893), 126.

[22] 'Oltre di questo, communemente il zelo de la religione non bisogna cerear hora nelli Tedeschi': *Beati Petri Canisii*, ed. Braunsberger, 1: 308.

[23] Ibid. 7: 358.

[24] 'Sunt optima portio Christianismi – Der edelste uorrat der Kirchen': ibid. 7: 630.

[25] For the development of his catechisms, see Braunsberger, *Entstehung und erste Entwicklung*. For their popularity, see Paul Begheyn, 'The Catechism (1555) of Peter

Canisius produced three versions of his catechism: the *Large*, the *Small* and the *Smaller*. The *Large Catechism*, aimed at university students and the clergy, was published in Latin in 1555 and a German translation followed in 1556.[26] The *Smaller Catechism*, intended for young children, appeared later in 1556, and the *Small Catechism*, designed for older school children and 'simple' adults, in 1558.[27] In his *Testament*, Canisius recalled that the *Small* and *Smaller* catechisms were used 'in the schools for the first instruction of the children, and also in the churches, so that from them the faithful can be brought closer to the rudiments of Catholic piety'.[28] The 1596 edition of Canisius's *Smaller Catechism* was 'divided from syllable to syllable, so that [children may] with little difficulty learn to read quicker, which will then serve them well for writing'.[29] In a similar manner to Melanchthon's pedagogical approach, Canisius merged educational and religious texts to teach the basics of religious doctrine and to offer direction on civic duty and obedience.[30]

The reality of early modern Catholic obedience should be noted: while in theory the papacy expected secular authorities to be subordinate to them, in practice this goal was incompatible with the secular interests of the princely powers in the context of imperial policy.[31] The result was that Christians owed obedience to two sets of

Canisius, the most published Book by a Dutch Author in History', *Quaerendo* 36 (2006), 51–84.

[26] Peter Canisius, *Summa doctrinae christianae* (Vienna, 1555); idem, *Frag und Antwort Christlicher Leer* (Vienna, 1556).

[27] Peter Canisius, *Catechismus Minimus* (Ingolstadt, 1556); a German translation of this catechism appeared as idem, *Der Klein Catechismus sampt kurtzen Gebeten für die ainfältigen* (Ingolstadt, 1556); idem, *Parvus catechismus* (Dillingen, 1558).

[28] 'Und man benützt sie in den Schulen fur die erste Unterweisung der Kinder und auch in den Kirchen, damit die Anfangsgründe der katholischen Frömmigkeit von da aus besser den Gläubigen nahegebracht warden können': *Das Testament des Petrus Canisius. Vermächtnis und Auftrag*, ed. Julius Oswald and Rita Haub (Frankfurt am Main, 1997), 86–7.

[29] 'Der lieben Jug-end zum Nu-ßen ha-be ich die-sen Ka-te-chis-mum von Sil-ben zu Silben ab-getheilt ver-fer-ti-get, da-mit sie mit leich-ter Mü-he de-sto ge-schwin der le-sen ler-nen, wel-chet ih-nen als dann zum Schrei-ben be-stens die-nen wird': Peter Canisius, *Kleiner Catechismus* (Freyburg im Uchtland, 1596), 3.

[30] Bert Roest, 'Rhetoric of Innovation and Recourse to Tradition in Humanist Pedagogical Discourse', in Stephen Gersh and Bert Roest, eds, *Medieval and Renaissance Humanism: Rhetoric, Representation and Reform* (Leiden, 2003), 115–48, at 147.

[31] Joachim Whaley, *Germany and the Holy Roman Empire*, 1: *Maximilian I to the Peace of Westphalia, 1493–1648* (Oxford, 2013), 38–9, 339–42.

authorities with potentially conflicting demands.[32] In Germany, this can be seen clearly in the actions of Duke Albrecht V, who ignored instructions from Trent that did not support his political ambitions. For example, while Philipp Apian, a Protestant, was expelled from Ingolstadt in 1568 for refusing to swear the *professio fidei tridentinum*, in other instances Albrecht allowed dynastic ambitions to undermine Tridentine decrees.[33] In 1564 and 1567 Albrecht installed his eleven- and three-year-old sons as bishops of Freising and Regensburg respectively, in direct defiance of Trent's efforts to outlaw the appointment of minors to ecclesiastical benefices.[34] It was under conditions such as these that Canisius adopted a policy of inclusion rather than exclusion in his educational programme.

In 1568, rumours began to circulate that Canisius had converted to Protestantism. In response, he began to include a confession of faith at the end of some of his publications.[35] This 'author's confession' rejected the doctrines of Luther and Calvin, declaring that Canisius had 'nothing in common' with any heretic, and affirmed his adherence to the 'one holy, Catholic, apostolic and Roman Church'.[36] Canisius evidently was a 'hammer of heretics' but the question is, when, in his eyes, did one cease being a Catholic and become a heretic?[37] The answer is not always clear in the catechisms. Instead, Canisius tailored his material to suit his audience: he was operating in Germany at a time when Lutheranism was a legal alternative to the Catholic faith; the Bavarian dukes and the emperor were making concessions to Lutherans; and he had first-hand experience of confessional diversity in Germany. To prevent the loss of those who identified as Catholics, Canisius forebore to attack those whose devotional practices verged on heresy but did not become heretical.

[32] Höpfl, *Jesuit Political Thought*, 54.

[33] Jürgen Helm, 'Religion and Medicine: An Anatomical Education at Wittenberg and Ingolstadt', in idem and Annette Winkelmann, eds, *Religious Confessions and the Sciences in the Sixteenth Century* (Leiden, 2001), 51–70, at 53.

[34] Philip M. Soergel, *Wondrous in his Saints: Counter-Reformation Propaganda in Bavaria* (Berkeley, CA, 1993), 79.

[35] Hilmar M. Pabel, 'Augustine's Confessions and the Autobiographies of Peter Canisius, SJ', *CHRC* 87 (2007), 453–75, at 470.

[36] 'Ich will nichts mit denen gemein haben': Canisius, *Testament*, 91; 'Non noui Lutherum, Caluinum respuo, haereticis omnibus dico anathema: nihil mihi cum his commune esse volo … cum vna sancta Catholica, Apostolica, & Romana Ecclesia': Peter Canisius, *Summa doctrinae christianae* (Antwerp, 1574), unpaginated.

[37] '[H]aereticorum malleum': *Beati Petri Canisii*, ed. Braunsberger, 8: 447.

In 1558, Albrecht V ordered a visitation of the Bavarian dioceses. The results were disappointing, revealing a lack of Christian knowledge amongst the people, an alarming degree of clerical concubinage, the use of Lutheran practices and the inclusion of Lutheran hymns in churches, specifically Luther's *Aus tiefer Not*, which rejected works of penance through its emphasis on repentance and faith in God's word.[38] In early 1558, Canisius spent six weeks in the Bavarian city of Straubing, which had witnessed the successful infiltration of Lutheranism. Canisius openly acknowledged the heretical faith and lack of Catholic devotion in his sermons there.[39] In the same year, in response to Duke Albrecht's removal of a schismatic preacher in Straubing, Canisius counselled him to 'act confidently in the matter of religion, do not allow wolves to rage in either the churches or in the schools'.[40] Canisius did not accept Protestantism and strove to protect Catholicism, but the bounds of Catholic orthodoxy were not rigid. Indeed, in 1562, Canisius delivered a sermon in Augsburg which addressed the question of dancing on Sundays.[41] Despite dancing and other such activities being 'accompanied by many sins', Canisius declared that he would 'consider it an impertinence were anyone to judge, condemn and despise his neighbour because he indulged in such recreations'.[42] Here he was teaching a lesson of coexistence, and this can be detected in his catechisms.

In 1563, a Bavarian territorial diet approved the granting of the chalice to the laity as part of a package of conciliatory measures designed to reconcile dissenters with the Catholic Church. Emperor Ferdinand pushed for a similar concession for the rest of Germany and, in 1564, Pope Pius IV allowed bishops in five German provinces, including Bavaria, to administer the sacrament in both kinds.[43] Canisius's 1563 German edition of the *Large*

[38] Alexander J. Fisher, *Music, Piety, and Propaganda: The Soundscape of Counter-Reformation Bavaria* (Oxford, 2014), 35–6; Anton Landersdorfer, *Das Bistum Freising in der bayerischen Visitation des Jahres 1560* (St Ottilien, 1986).

[39] *Beati Petri Canisii*, ed. Braunsberger, 2: 816.

[40] 'Et oro, ut Christi gratia fauente pietas tua confidenter agat in negotio Religionis, nec sinat usquam grassari lupos [siue in] templis, siue in scholis': ibid. 284.

[41] As Susan Karant-Nunn notes, dancing and other festivities, such as feasting and drinking, were discouraged by both Protestants and Catholics, although Catholic clergy were more tolerant of such pastimes: *The Reformation of Feeling: Shaping the Religious Emotions in Early Modern Germany* (Oxford, 2010), 62.

[42] Brodrick, *Canisius*, 831; *Beati Petri Canisii*, ed. Braunsberger, 3: 648–9.

[43] Michael A. Mullett, *The Catholic Reformation* (London, 1999), 57.

Catechism appears to have predicted this papal concession because it did not forbid the chalice to lay people.[44] Analysis of the precise wording employed in the *Large Catechism* reveals that there was a limited degree of flexibility in the Jesuit's discussion of communion in both kinds.

On the question on whether communion should be offered to the laity in one or two kinds, Canisius explained:

> The faithful laity … are not obliged [*verbunden*] by the command of God to receive the sacrament in two kinds … the custom (that the laity receive under one kind) was established by the Church and the Holy Fathers, not without reason and has been so long held, [that] it is to be regarded as a law which may not be overturned or the Church's authority changed at the behest of a single person.[45]

Here, Canisius challenged the Protestant argument that divine law requires communion in both kinds, drawing on church teachings to argue that communion in one kind 'is established not without reason'.[46] He expressed astonishment regarding those who conspired with the 'new despisers of the Church' regarding communion in both kinds and he taught that the fruits of the sacrament are available only to those who 'persist in the unity of the Church', emphasizing that those who insisted on 'the external signs of the sacrament' would make themselves unworthy partakers and would not receive its fruits.[47] Nonetheless, he taught that divine law did not 'oblige' the laity to receive communion under both kinds. In contrast, the *Tridentine Catechism* explicitly forbade the laity to receive the chalice. This is a subtle difference: Canisius defended the practice of administering only the bread to the laity without expressly forbidding them to receive the wine.

[44] Peter Canisius, *Catholischer Catechismus oder Sumārien Christlicher Lehr Inn frag uñ anntwort / der Christlicher jugent / unnd allen einfaltigen zu nuz und heil gestelt* (Cologne, 1563), unpaginated.

[45] 'Die glaubigen Leien … sein nit verbunden auß dem gebot Gottes zu der empfahung des Sacraments under zweierlei gestalt … die gewonheit (den Leien zu peisen unter einerlei gestalt) von der Kirchē und heiligen Vattern nit on ursach eingefurt und gar lang gehaltē ist / ist si fur ein gesaz zubehalten / welchs nit mag um̄ gestollen / oder an der Kirchen Authoritet nach eins jeden wolgefallen verkert werden': ibid.

[46] 'Nit on ursach eingefurt': ibid.

[47] 'Die eusserlichen zeichen dieses Sacraments … Mit den newn verachtern der … bestendigen in der einigkeit der Kirch': ibid.

Secondly, Canisius taught that the 'law' of communion in one kind could not be changed 'at the behest of a single person'. While this was probably a direct challenge to Luther and other reformers, it may also reflect Canisius's context. The policies adopted by the emperor and the Bavarian dukes indicate that there was a demand for the chalice from the laity. Moreover, the legalization of Lutheranism in the empire after the Peace of Augsburg meant that Catholics could find themselves living in areas where they had little choice but to receive communion in both kinds. Thus the question of audience becomes significant. Canisius's *Large Catechism* was intended primarily for the clergy and was designed, in part, to provide them with a defence against Protestant doctrines. Therefore Canisius provided a robust defence of communion in one kind, which could be used to support a priest in their administering of communion to the laity, but which stopped short of expressly forbidding communion in two kinds. The *Small Catechism*, however, was designed for the laity, some of whom could be living in Lutheran territories, or in a Catholic area where receiving communion in two kinds had been declared the normal practice. David Luebke has demonstrated that in Westphalian Haltern, for instance, which lay on the border between the Hochstift Münster and Recklinghausen Vest, the priest permitted those who wished to receive communion in both kinds to do so.[48] Luebke argues that lay people 'were fully equipped to pick and choose among the ritual offerings available to them', despite their adherence to an otherwise orthodox Roman Catholicism.[49] In the *Small Catechism*, Canisius taught that unbelievers, sectarians and heretics would not receive the sacrament worthily, so that only a Catholic would be a worthy partaker.[50] However, Canisius was faced with a conundrum: if he excluded those Catholics who received communion in both kinds by prohibiting the lay chalice, this could potentially exclude otherwise loyal Catholics from the fold. Therefore, in not expressly forbidding communion in both kinds in the *Small Catechism*, Canisius left open the possibility that an individual who identified as a Catholic and participated in the sacrament as a

[48] David M. Luebke, *Hometown Religion: Regimes of Coexistence in Early Modern Westphalia* (Charlottesville, VA, 2016), 93.
[49] Ibid. 101.
[50] Peter Canisius, *Der kleine Catechismus, oder kurtze Summa des wahren Christlichen und Catholischen Glaubens* (Dillingen, 1574), 107.

repentant believer would receive the fruits of that participation. In this way, Canisius's *Small Catechism* seems to have been designed to promote inclusivity within Catholicism.

More broadly, this indicates that catechisms could offer a more fluid expression of confessional identity than existing scholarship has recognized.[51] Canisius's audience was Catholic, but the practical expression of Catholic faith was not uniform across Germany. The subtleties in Canisius's catechisms acknowledge this confessional fluidity within German Catholicism, which arose from the political and social realities of being a Catholic in a bi-confessional empire, as well as from the pre-existence of local practices that were not all consistent with the developing Tridentine Catholicism of the later sixteenth century. Canisius's approach to communion in both kinds suggests that he tailored his catechisms to include as many as possible of those who identified as Catholic. In so doing, he made space to accommodate the experience of those Catholics living in areas where receiving the chalice was an established practice.

Despite Albrecht's conciliatory measures, in 1563 Graf von Ortenburg led an unsuccessful Lutheran conspiracy to overthrow Catholicism in Bavaria. As a result, in February 1564 Canisius informed Laynez that the duke was taking a much firmer position against the Protestants, and in April he asserted that 'little by little' Catholicism was strengthening in the duchy.[52] Demonstrating this growing strength, in 1565 a territorial decree was issued that prohibited the sale or inheritance of books that were not printed in approved German cities.[53] In the following year, the duke forbade books to be sold in Bavaria that were not included in his catalogue of permitted material.[54] This catalogue was different to the Index of Prohibited Books, which had been issued by the pope in 1559. Canisius had immediately expressed doubts regarding the nature of the Roman Index, and in a letter to Laynez he confided that he would rather have a list of approved rather than prohibited texts.[55] Despite official endorsement of censorship, enforcing the law was not straightforward

[51] Lee Palmer Wandel, *Reading Catechisms, Teaching Religion* (Leiden, 2016).
[52] *Beati Petri Canisii*, ed. Braunsberger, 4: 447, 406.
[53] John Frymire, *The Primacy of the Postils: Catholics, Protestants, and the Dissemination of Ideas in Early Modern Germany* (Leiden, 2010), 339.
[54] Allyson F. Creasman, *Censorship and Civic Order in Reformation Germany, 1517–1648: 'Printed Poison & Evil Talk'* (Farnham, 2012), 58.
[55] *Beati Petri Canisii*, ed. Braunsberger, 2: 358.

and Canisius continued to push for a settlement that was suited to the political and religious conditions in Bavaria.

In October 1559, Canisius informed Laynez that he wanted to 'obtain grace from the pope on behalf of our confessors, that they may not be kept from conferring absolution to students who have any impure' texts.[56] In other missives sent to Laynez that year, Canisius reported that the Catholics of Germany, Bohemia and Poland considered the 'Index intolerably severe, nor can we obtain that which it prescribes'.[57] He warned 'we do not see how we are to maintain our classes and schools if we must obey this strict decree to the letter'.[58] Certainly, Canisius was aware that his students possessed heretical books: while teaching at the University of Ingolstadt in 1549, his pupils had surrendered their copies of prohibited books over Christmas on the understanding that they would be returned in the new year.[59] In 1561, the pope provided a dispensation for Germany, lifting the ban on classical texts and books that had been annotated or published by heretics, leaving prohibited only those books with expressly heretical content.[60]

Canisius's letters reflect the complex relationship between his obligations and the realities of being Catholic in early modern Germany. As a Jesuit, he owed allegiance to the pope and was expected to protect papal authority and interests. Concurrently, while in Germany he owed allegiance to the emperor, and while in Bavaria to the dukes. Each of these superiors demanded obedience from Canisius and his fellow Jesuits, but their individual policies and objectives did not always reflect the conditions facing Catholics in their daily lives. Canisius's responses to censorship mark him out as a keen defender of Catholicism, but his approach was inclusive rather than exclusive. Essentially, those who declared themselves Protestant would have no quarter from Canisius, but those who identified as Catholic could be treated with more discretion. This approach is exemplified in his

[56] 'Tum apud nouum Pont. impetrari gratiam velim Confessarijs, vt ne rigore Cathalogi arceantur ab absolutione conferenda studiosis ratione librorum, si quos habent impuros': ibid. 533.

[57] 'Accedit durities Cathalogi, ut isti interpretantur, intollerabilis; nec videmus obtineri posse, quod praescriptum est': ibid. 380.

[58] 'Certo non vedemo modo di potere intratenere le nostre classe et schole se dovemo andare secondo la lettera della stretta prohibitione': ibid. 446.

[59] Brodrick, *Canisius*, 138.

[60] Ibid. 468.

evaluation of a library of books inherited by a member of the powerful Fugger family of Augsburg in 1577.

Canisius first became acquainted with the Fuggers when he converted Ursula Fugger to the Roman faith in 1559. Simone Laqua-O'Donnell comments that Canisius saw this conversion as particularly important because her elite status meant that she was a powerful tool in the promotion of post-Tridentine Catholicism in Augsburg.[61] It was important, therefore, to ensure Ursula and her family were taught how to be good Catholics and acted in a manner that supported Trent's vision of Catholicism. However, in his examination of Philip's library, Canisius discovered texts that were annotated by heretics or contained material that was not strictly orthodox. Describing his findings in a letter to Scipione Rebiba, Canisius declared that 'since the Index of Prohibited Books has not been published in Germany and since reading books on religious matters and using German Bibles is encouraged here … I thought it fit not to condemn books that have become familiar to Catholics here in their daily confrontations with heretics'. Moreover, 'most Catholics here are used to reading just about everything that is not utterly impious'. While Canisius was no friend to heretics, Philip Fugger was not a heretic: he 'is a good Catholic and he has inherited most of the books from his father'.[62] Canisius knew that Fugger was a powerful ally to Catholicism, and therefore proposed that Fugger be granted a dispensation. In doing this, Canisius was acknowledging the nature of German Catholicism and the realities of living as a Catholic in a bi-confessional city. This was a radically different response to that shown by Canisius to members of his own family in 1565 when he burned their non-Catholic books, or when he wrote in 1583 that heretical books should be burned or removed from the empire.[63] Canisius would have preferred heretical books to be expunged from the empire, but he knew that this was an unrealistic goal and recognized the dangers of excluding otherwise loyal Catholics from the fold.

[61] Simone Laqua-O'Donnell, 'Family Matters: Peter Canisius as Confessor and Spiritual Guide in Early Modern Augsburg. A Case Study', *Journal of Jesuit Studies* 2 (2015), 606–23, at 607.
[62] Paul Begheyn and Vincent J. C. Hunink, 'Two Unpublished Letters by Peter Canisius (1521–97) to Cardinal Scipione Rebiba, 1577', *Lias: Sources and Documents relating to the Early Modern History of Ideas* 34 (2007), 3–10, at 4 (Letter 2).
[63] Pabel, 'Canisius', 379.

Canisius's experience of confessional diversity was not limited to Germany: the ageing Jesuit spent his final years in Fribourg, a member city of the Swiss Confederation which had a strong Lutheran and Reformed presence. While Fribourg remained Catholic, the structure of the Swiss Confederation rested on a series of alliances, with bi-confessional territories developing in areas that were jointly ruled by Catholic and Reformed states.[64] In his final sermon, delivered in Fribourg on 5 August 1596, Canisius reflected that one objective of the Jesuits was to 'to bring [people] back from the error of heresy'.[65] His activities in Germany were in line with this intention, and on his death in December 1597 he left a pedagogical legacy that was to last centuries.

Canisius's *Testament* expressed the hope that he had 'remained within the limits of an orthodox teacher'; of that there is little doubt.[66] However, although his activities and publications in the educational sphere reveal Canisius to be a skilful pedagogue, they also show how far he was prepared to go in the defence of his faith. He avoided taking unpopular actions, such as endorsing the Roman Index when it was practically and politically inexpedient; he minimized polemic in his German-language catechisms; and his teaching was conditioned by his daily interactions with ordinary Germans living on the brink of heresy. Recognizing the limits of a universal approach to education, Canisius explained to Cardinal Morone in 1576 that 'it is not easy for any to understand the poor state and needs of Germany, except those who see it with their eyes and learn from long experience'.[67] This experience led Canisius to develop a version of Catholic education that was suited to the needs of Germans.

[64] Daniela Hacke, 'Confessional Cultures and Sacred Space: Towards a History of Political Communication in Early Modern Switzerland', in Melissa Calaresu, Filippo de Vivo and Joan Pau Rubiés, eds, *Exploring Cultural History: Essays in Honour of Peter Burke* (Farnham, 2010), 169–90, at 174; Amy Nelson Burnett and Emidio Campi, eds, *A Companion to the Swiss Reformation* (Leiden, 2016).

[65] 'Reducendi ab haereseos erroribus in viam': *Beati Petri Canisii*, ed. Braunsberger, 8: 881.

[66] 'Dass ich innerhalb der Grenzen eines rechtgläubigen Lehrers geblieben bin': Canisius, *Testament*, 82.

[67] 'Non facile quiuis assequi uel compraehendere potest Germaniae miserum statum et necessitates, nisi qui eas suis oculis uidet et longa experientia didicit': *Beati Petri Canisii*, ed. Braunsberger, 7: 362.

The concept of identity and meaning is central to an understanding of the actions and events in early modern Germany and wider Europe. What did it mean to be a Catholic in Augsburg, or a Catholic in Straubing? Studies have demonstrated that identity and meaning varied across Germany, but how was this variety provided for in educational material intended for a wide readership?[68] Focusing on education as a way to bridge the gap between orthodoxy and the reality of confessional pressures might be one way to address these questions. Rather than beginning with the hypothesis that education facilitated confessional division, it may enhance our understanding of early modern German education to see it instead as part of a broader process of accommodation or, for the seventeenth and eighteenth centuries, negotiated decision-making based on a pragmatic handling of religious pluralism.[69]

[68] Simone Laqua-O'Donnell, 'Catholic Piety and Community', in Alexandra Bamji, Geert H. Janssen and Mary Laven, eds, *Ashgate Research Companion to the Counter-Reformation* (Farnham, 2013), 281–97, at 286.

[69] Robert James Bast, *Honor your Fathers: Catechisms and the Emergence of a Patriarchal Ideology in Germany, 1400–1600* (Leiden, 1997), 231; Wandel, *Reading Catechisms*; Benjamin Kaplan, *Divided by Faith: Religious Conflict and the Practice of Tolerance in Early Modern Europe* (Harvard, MA, 2010).

Nature and Nurture in the Early Quaker Movement: Creating the Next Generation of Friends

Alexandra Walsham*
University of Cambridge

This article explores the place of education within the early Quaker movement in England. It examines how Quaker attitudes towards human nature shaped their views on the role of nurture in the creation of a community of believers, and probes the theological assumptions that underpinned this, notably their repudiation of conventional Protestant ideas about original sin and predestination. It also traces the evolution of Quaker views on spiritual direction in domestic and institutional settings against the backdrop of the transformation of the Society of Friends from a radical evangelical sect to a more sober and disciplined movement in the later seventeenth century. Particular attention is paid to the part that education played in ensuring that Quakerism was passed down to the next generation, once the heady excitement of its initial conversionary phase had waned.

In 1670, two leading Quakers, George Fox and Ellis Hookes, published *A Primmer and Catechism for Children.* Designed as a handy guide to teach the young how to read and spell, together with a didactic dialogue between a scholar and a master, it incorporated various other useful appendices, including an ABC; a guide to pronouncing proper names in Scripture; a discussion of dipthongs, consonants, syllables, vowels, spelling and other points of grammar; a list of weights, coins and measures; a page of proverbs; and various multiplication tables. A further addition was a dictionary of 'hard words used in our English tongue'. One of its entries was 'Education', which was defined as 'bringing up'.[1]

This article explores the place of education in the early Quaker movement, from its beginnings in the 1650s to the mid-eighteenth

* Trinity College, Cambridge, CB2 1TQ. E-mail: amw23@cam.ac.uk. I am grateful to the Leverhulme Trust for funding the research underpinning this article, and to Naomi Pullin and the anonymous reviewers for helpful comments.

[1] G[eorge Fox] and E[llis] H[ookes], *A Primmer and Catechism for Children* (London, 1670), 103.

Studies in Church History 55 (2019), 161–176
doi: 10.1017/stc.2018.35

century.[2] By contrast with previous scholarship on this topic, which has focused largely on formal instruction in schools, it offers fresh insight into Quaker practices of child-rearing within the forum of the home. By focusing particular attention on printed texts prepared for parental use, it traces the evolution of the sect's views on the nurture and instruction of the young from the radical and anarchic evangelicalism that marked its early phases to the more disciplined, inward-looking and endogamous community that it progressively became. It deepens our understanding of the inherent tensions within Quaker thinking on this topic and explores how this dynamic subtly changed as the Society of Friends was steadily transformed from a body of voluntary converts into one dominated by people who had inherited the faith from their mothers and fathers. In the process, it illuminates the complementary roles families and institutions played in perpetuating Quakerism as it moved into its second and third generations. More broadly, this article offers a case study in how education is implicated in the transition of evangelical movements into tolerated churches and the domestication of Dissenting groups as denominations. As membership of the sect became a function less of a blinding moment of insight than of passive birthright, Quakers ironically found it necessary to rely on methods that their founders had insisted had no efficacy in the mysterious work of becoming one of the Children of Light.

[2] Previous treatments of this topic include W. A. Campbell Stewart, *Quakers and Education as seen in their Schools in England* (London, 1953); Harold Loukes, *Friends and their Children: A Study in Quaker Education* (London, 1958); Howard H. Brinton, *Quaker Education in Theory and Practice* (Wallingford, PA, 1967; first publ. 1940); Paul A. Lacey, *Growing into Goodness: Essays on Quaker Education* (Paoli, PA, 1998). See also Dorothy G. B. Hubbard, 'Early Quaker Education in England, 1647–1903' (MA thesis, University of London, 1939); L. John Shroud, 'The History of Quaker Education in England, 1647–1903' (MEd thesis, University of Leeds, 1944); these are summarized in Russell S. Mortimer, 'Quaker Education', *JFHS* 39 (1947), 66–70. Considerable attention has been paid to Quaker education in America: see, for example, Thomas Woody, *Early Quaker Education in Pennsylvania* (New York, 1920); Sydney V. James, 'Quaker Meetings and Education in the Eighteenth Century', *QH* 51 (1962), 87–102. For general overviews, see Elizabeth Ann O'Donnell, 'Quakers and Education', in Stephen W. Angell and Pink Dandelion, eds, *The Oxford Handbook of Quaker Studies* (Oxford, 2013), 405–19; Stephen W. Angell and Clare Brown, 'Quakers and Education', in Stephen W. Angell and Pink Dandelion, eds, *The Cambridge Companion to Quakerism* (Cambridge, 2018), 128–46. Quakers are barely mentioned in Rosemary O'Day, *Education and Society 1500–1800: The Social Foundations of Education in Early Modern Britain* (London, 1982); or Helen M. Jewell, *Education in Early Modern England* (Basingstoke, 1998).

Early Quakerism was a religion rooted in the overpowering emotional experience of regeneration and rebirth. Its founders and earliest adherents were men and women who felt an extraordinary internal transformation as they discerned the workings of the 'Light within' their hearts and minds. They thought of themselves as the children of God and as a special generation appointed by the Lord to usher in his rule on earth.[3] They were filled with heady excitement about the end of the world and the anticipated second coming of Christ.[4] This sense of urgency manifested itself in the provocative forms of proselytism in which they engaged in the 1650s, including running naked through the streets as a sign, disrupting church services and engaging in protests and 'testimonies' of other kinds.[5] Quaker ministers, both men and women, roused their hearers to experience the same kind of spiritual turmoil and to recognize the seed of salvation that lay within them.

The consequence was a movement marked by family conflict and intergenerational friction. Many early Quakers were young people who took pride in abandoning what they described as their 'carnal' ties to their mothers, fathers, sisters and brothers and found surrogate parents and siblings in the guise of fellow Friends. Thomas Ellwood recalled the violent rage into which his father had fallen when he became a Quaker, impounding his horse, confiscating his allowance in an effort to prevent him from attending meetings, and flying at him with both fists in fury at his disobedience. He found asylum in the home of Isaac and Mary Penington, who were 'tender nurses to me in this time of my religious childhood'.[6] As Nicholas Gates

[3] See Hilary Hinds, *George Fox and Early Quaker Culture* (Manchester, 2011), 13–32 (ch. 1); Martha Paxson Grundy, 'Learning to be Quaker: Spiritual Formation and Religious Education among Early Friends', *Quaker Studies* 11 (2007), 151–65; Douglas Gwyn, 'Seventeenth-Century Context and Quaker Beginnings', and Hilary Hinds, 'Unity and Universality in the Theology of George Fox', in Stephen W. Angell and Pink Dandelion, eds, *Early Quakers and their Theological Thought 1647–1723* (Cambridge, 2015), 13–31, 48–63.

[4] See T. L. Underwood, 'Early Quaker Eschatology', in Peter Toon, ed., *Puritans, the Millennium and the Future of Israel: Puritan Eschatology 1600 to 1660* (Cambridge, 1970), 91–103; Douglas Gwyn, 'Quakers, Eschatology and Time', in Angell and Dandelion, eds, *Oxford Handbook of Quaker Studies*, 202–17.

[5] On the early years of the movement, see Barry Reay, *The Quakers and the English Revolution* (1985); Rosemary Moore, *The Light in their Consciences: Early Quakers in Britain 1646–1666* (University Park, PA, 2000).

[6] Thomas Ellwood, *The History of Thomas Ellwood written by himself* (London, 1885), 53–66, 77. On the emphasis on household division and youthful rebellion in the first

recounted in his *Tender Invitation to all, to embrace the Secret Visitation of the Lord to their Souls* (1708) he too had become an 'Alien to my Father's House' and had been many times threatened with being 'Cast off'.[7] When Edward Burrough's mother and father, 'the old man and old woman … according to the flesh', died within ten days of each other, he disdained to attend their funeral, saying 'it is only pertaining to outwards, and I feel no freedom to it at present'.[8] As Richard Vann has argued, in this atmosphere of eschatological expectancy and youthful zeal the education and upbringing of future generations hardly seemed a priority.[9]

Early Quakers were also vehement in their repudiation of 'humane learning' and its institutions. They disparaged the ancient universities for teaching the 'Heathen Arts' and insisted that such institutions could make neither true ministers nor real Christians. They attacked the study of theology and classics and called for them to be ejected from the curriculum. Convinced that Jesus alone was the word of God, they insisted that only through the revelatory workings of the indwelling Light did the canonical text of Scripture become a source of spiritual truth.[10] They also fiercely rejected 'teachers': this was a derogatory term which Friends used to disparage the clergy of the Church of England, whose 'brain knowledge', for all its Latinate erudition, was superficial and empty, a mere earthly wisdom.[11] The pretension of university learning was likewise repudiated. The only 'teacher' and 'schoolmaster' that human beings required was Christ, who alone could nurture and water the seed within them and, in the words of Fox and Hookes, 'open the eyes of the

generation of Friends, see also Naomi Pullin, 'Children of the Light: Childhood, Youth and Dissent within early Quakerism', in Lucy Underwood and Tali Banner, eds, *Childhood and Religious Minorities* (forthcoming).

7 Nicholas Gates, *A Tender Invitation to all, to embrace the Secret Visitation of the Lord to their Souls* (London, 1708), 27.

8 Quoted in Elisabeth Brockbank, *Edward Burrough: A Wrestler for Truth 1634–1662* (London, 1949), 132.

9 Richard T. Vann, 'Nurture and Conversion in the Early Quaker Family', *Journal of Marriage and Family* 31 (1969), 639–43, at 641; idem, *The Social Development of English Quakerism 1655–1755* (Cambridge, MA, 1969), 168.

10 See George Fox, *A Paper sent forth into the World from them that are scornfully called Quakers* (London, 1654), 2; Thomas Lawson, *A Mite into the Treasury* (London, 1680), 39–46.

11 The phrase 'brain knowledge' is ubiquitous, but for one example, see George Fox, *The Great Mistery of the Great Whore unfolded* (London, 1659), 78.

blind'.[12] What early Quakers called 'convincement' was a supernatural process of revelation involving the Holy Spirit in which the intellect and reason had no part to play. 'Education' in a formal institutional sense was irrelevant to the mystery of salvation. The inspiring figures whose preaching brought many into the arms of the sect were catalysts rather than conduits of this.

At the same time Quaker theology had two features that made it more open to acknowledging the salutary effects of nurture and upbringing, at least in theory. The first was its insistence that all people held within them the capacity to be saved. Quakers strongly rejected the Calvinist doctrine of predestination, by which God had elected a minority to salvation and the majority to reprobation. Denying that the Lord had made decisions about the fate of believers before the beginning of time, they believed in the possibility of redemption in an ahistorical present and stressed the presence of 'an Evangelical and Saving Light and Grace in all'.[13] Secondly, they condemned traditional Protestant teaching on original sin as an 'invented and unscriptural barbarism'. They stepped back from neo-Augustinian pessimism about human nature. Men and women were tainted as a result of the fall, but Adam's guilt was not transmitted to his posterity until they had committed acts of disobedience themselves. His evil and corrupted seed was not imputed to infants until they actively embraced it. In short, Quaker soteriology was predicated on the possibility of human perfectibility and universal salvation.[14] Children were innocent creatures but the root of sin could still easily germinate within them.[15]

This is the context in which the various primers and catechisms prepared by George Fox and other leading Quakers in the first decades of the movement must be assessed. Fox's *Catechisme for Children, that they may come to learn of Christ the Light* was published in 1657 and John Perrot's *A Primer for Children* appeared in 1660.

[12] Humphrey Smith, *To all Parents of Children upon the Face of the whole Earth* (London, 1660), 22: 'let the Lord God be the Teacher of your Children'; Fox and Hookes, *Primmer and Catechism*, 60.

[13] Robert Barclay, *An Apology for the True Christian Divinity, as the same is held forth, and preached, by the People, called in scorn, Quakers* ([London?], 1678), 67–8.

[14] Ibid. 57–67 (quotation at 67). On original sin, see also Stephen Crisp, *A New Book for Childern to learn in* ([London, 1681]), 58–67.

[15] See Jerry W. Frost, 'As the Twig is Bent: Quaker Ideas of Childhood', *QH* 60 (1971), 67–87.

William Smith wrote *A New Primmer* in 1662 and his *New Catechism* appeared in 1667. Stephen Crisp's *New Book for Childern* dates from 1681.[16] As Kate Peters has shown, in the 1650s Quakers creatively utilized the printing press to combat their enemies and to win new converts, confident that reading a written text could be as efficacious as hearing a Quaker minister preach.[17] To their opponents within and beyond the Church of England, the importance they attached to their own writings, usurping the pre-eminent place of the sacred canon of Scripture, was arrogant, presumptuous and blasphemous: a satirical image in the Baptist minister Benjamin Keach's *The Grand Imposter Discovered* (1675) depicted a set of scales on which the Bible outweighed a pile of Quaker books (Fig. 1). The portable, pocket-sized library of educational textbooks they produced in the late seventeenth century reflected Friends' continuing investment in the printed book as a didactic device and as a vital tool in building their movement.

Although many were explicitly addressed to children and those young in years, these works were also clearly intended to be read by adults who were novices in the Quaker faith and who had yet to recognize the stirrings of grace within them. The figures of 'Father' and 'Child' in these dialogues invoke forms of spiritual as well as biological kinship. The terms are arguably deployed as much metaphorically as they are literally; it was common for early Quakers to describe newly convinced Friends as 'new begotten babes'.[18] Their aim is to prepare their readers to perceive the Light within their souls and to experience the inner direction of the Spirit. In short, they are devised for people who are not yet Friends themselves. William Smith's primer includes passages in which the Child asks: 'must I be born again', and how he or she will know when this has happened. The reply is: 'by diligent waiting in the

[16] George Fox, *A Catechisme for Children* (London, 1657); William Smith, *A New Primmer wherein is demonstrated the New and Living Way, held forth by way of Question and Answer, as from a Child's Enquiry after Truth, to be informed by the Father* (London, 1662). No copy of Perrot's book is extant. For a brief discussion of these works and some of their eighteenth-century successors, see David Blamires, 'Early Quaker Educational Books for Children', *JFHS* 63 (2012), 20–30.

[17] Kate Peters, *Print Culture and the Early Quakers* (Cambridge, 2005), especially 15–42 (ch. 1).

[18] See, for example, London, Library of the Society of Friends (hereafter: LSF), MS VOL 62/5, 7–8 (Richard Moore to Charles Lloyd, 6th day of 3rd month, 1662).

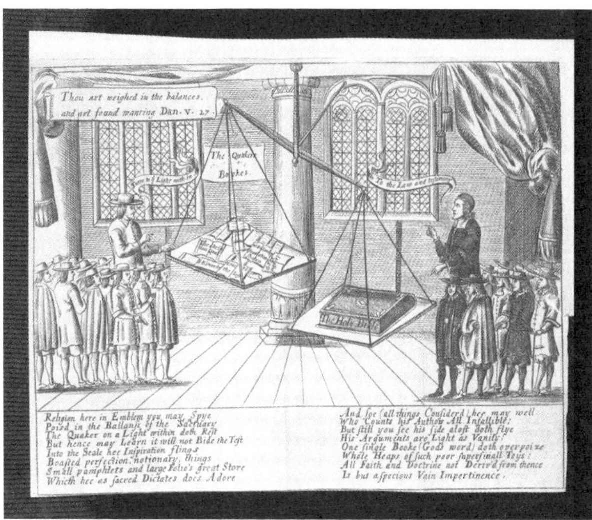

Fig. 1: The Quakers' books weighed in the balance: Benjamin Keach, *The Grand Imposter Discovered* (London, 1675), facing p. 193. Reproduced by permission of the Bodleian Libraries, University of Oxford, shelfmark 8° Z 46 (2) Th.

Light, whereby thou wilt come to feel the effectual working of God's Power'. By the end the Child is better informed, but is still a probationer in the faith who has yet to be sincerely convinced.[19] Such texts seek to cultivate the conditions in which the immortal seed within people might begin to sprout and in which they will cast off the old man and be reborn as new creatures. They are not envisaged as instruments of that salvation themselves. The Herefordshire Quaker Humphrey Smith's *To all Parents of Children* (1660) insisted that no amount of education could bring children to Christ without the Light. They would come to be heirs of the promise of God only by divine regeneration, not by human effort. Yet it is indicative of the tensions within Quaker thinking that Smith's tract also advertised itself as an attempt to prevent iniquity from passing 'by tradition from Parents to Children, and so from one Generation to another'.[20]

These little books also serve to explain and instruct their readers in Quaker principles and values: the sect's controversial teachings

[19] Smith, *New Primmer*, 27.
[20] Smith, *To all Parents*, 23–4 and title page.

regarding tithes and oaths; its refusal of hat honour and flattering titles; its use of the informal pronouns 'thee' and 'thou' instead of 'you' (a denial of deference to social superiors that scandalized contemporaries as impolite and disrespectful); its rejection of pagan names for the months and days of the week; and its denunciation of Anglican baptism and communion as 'the Pope's inventions'.[21] They teach antagonism towards churches as steeple houses and false teachers, preachers, priests and professors as 'blind Guides' and deceiving Antichrists.[22] They also foster hostility to those who scorn and deride the people called 'Quakers', in the process happily embracing the derogatory nickname levelled against them as a linguistic weapon as a badge of honour.[23] In this sense they serve as mechanisms for Quaker socialization, for the inculcation of cultural habits that were already becoming emblems of identity and tokens of differentiation. This included the deployment of a vivid scriptural vocabulary, suffused with words such as 'abomination', 'caterpillar', 'drowsiness', 'filthiness', 'heritage', 'lasciviousness', 'pestilent', 'reprobate' and 'zealous', which Fox and Hookes taught children to spell out in syllables in the ABC that prefaced their *Primmer and Catechism*.[24]

Thirdly, these works are devices for instructing readers in useful forms of knowledge. They are presented as edifying alternatives to the profane and frivolous books that poured from contemporary presses. Stephen Crisp presented his little textbook as 'a fruit of the Plant of Righteousness', published to counteract the poison 'sprung forth of the corrupt Tree' of conventional Christianity.[25] Fox's own concern with how children were trained up by 'customary teaching' found expression in an admonitory pamphlet addressed to schoolmasters and schoolmistresses in 1657, which accused these 'fleshly' teachers of fostering a culture of 'filthy jesting', backbiting, and

[21] See, for example, Fox and Hookes, *Primmer and Catechism*, 75–83; Smith, *New Primmer*, 38–9, 44–5, 46–53. On Quaker plain language, see Richard Bauman, *Let your Words be Few: Symbolism of Speaking and Silence among Seventeenth-Century Quakers* (Cambridge, 1983), 43–62 (ch. 4).

[22] Fox, *Catechism*, 9, 25–6, 31, 58, 60–1.

[23] Fox and Hookes, *Primmer and Catechism*, 75–6. On the sect's active appropriation of its hostile nickname, see Peters, *Print Culture*, 91–123 (ch. 4).

[24] Fox and Hookes, *Primmer and Catechism*, 3–14. On Quaker language, see T. Edmund Harvey, *Quaker Language* (London, 1928).

[25] Crisp, *New Book*, 'A short Epistle', unpaginated.

railing, 'brazen-facedness', immodesty and boldness that corrupted the tender minds and manners of their pupils and drowned so many in 'the deep Ditch' and 'Pit' of vanity and lust.[26] Quaker educational texts prioritize instruction in literacy and basic arithmetic and serve as aids to Bible reading.[27] They embody the dual conviction that education cannot in and of itself bring one to Christ but that it can assist in the formation of practical skills that have utility in secular life. In a famous letter written to his wife and children in 1682, William Penn recommended 'the useful parts of mathematics, as building houses or ships, measuring, surveying, dialling, navigation', but reserved pride of place for agriculture, which he saw as 'industrious, healthy, honest and of good example'. Penn instructed his spouse to 'keep an ingenious person in the house to teach them' rather than send them to schools, 'too many evil impressions being commonly received there'.[28]

Penn's worries aside, the emphasis on 'useful knowledge' served as an incentive to the movement's early foundation of schools for both boys and girls. Fox provided the stimulus for establishing one for each sex at Waltham Abbey and Shacklewell respectively in 1668, and by 1671 there were at least fifteen under the care of Quarterly Meetings.[29] Alongside mathematics and agriculture, natural science and modern languages featured prominently in the academic curriculum; in keeping with the vocational spirit of Quaker educational thinking, theology and the classics were conspicuous by their absence.[30] The vital importance that Friends attached to teaching and training the young is also reflected in the proliferation of unlicensed Quaker schoolmasters and tutors[31] and their precocious commitment to educating the children of the poor. In 1662 Friends imprisoned in the Ilchester Friary began a school instructing

[26] George Fox, *A Warning to all Teachers of Children, which are called School-Masters and School-Mistresses* (London, 1657), 2, 5.

[27] Fox and Hooke's *Primmer and Catechism* was frequently republished under the title *Instructions for right Spelling, and plain Directions for reading and writing true English* (London, 1673 and later edns).

[28] William Evans and Thomas Evans, eds, *The Friends' Library: Comprising Journals, Doctrinal Treatises, and other Writings of Members of the Religious Society of Friends*, 14 vols (Philadelphia, PA, 1837–50), 5: 167.

[29] See William C. Braithwaite, *The Second Period of Quakerism* (Cambridge, 1961), 525–33; Arnold Lloyd, *Quaker Social History 1669–1738* (London, 1950), 66–74 (ch. 13).

[30] See Greaves, 'Early Quakers', 27–30; Braithwaite, *Second Period*, 528.

[31] See Adrian Davies, *The Quakers in English Society 1655–1725* (Oxford, 2000), 122–6.

local boys in the rudiments of reading, writing and bookkeeping; elsewhere they funded teachers for the offspring of the needy and indigent.[32] The society felt a moral imperative to step in where fathers and mothers could not afford to provide suitable instruction for their young. It acted *in loco parentis*. Indeed, the meetings conceived of themselves as a second, supplementary family that shared in the sacred responsibility of child-rearing.[33]

The later seventeenth century saw further educational developments. In 1695 John Bellers issued a set of proposals for 'raising a college of industry' to train Friends in manufacturing trades and husbandry. Designed to bring profit to the rich, succour the poor and educate Quaker youth, this novel experiment in social welfare was a remedy for idleness akin to both a workhouse and a commune, as well as a response to Bellers's perception that few private persons had the resources or energy to give their children an 'exact Education at Home'. This was a process which he compared with cultivating the soil in which plants grew: a sound instructor was akin to 'a good Seeds-man'.[34] It also reflected a precocious piece of political arithmetic: in a supplementary petition to Parliament he calculated that the true annual cost of idleness was somewhere in the region of £5,200,000.[35]

As the sect acquired the trappings of institutionalization, the emphasis on upbringing and nurture became more pronounced, Quakerism moved into its second and third generations and as its adherents themselves moved into a new phase of the lifecycle, the duties and responsibilities of parenthood acquired growing importance. The relationships of spiritual kinship that the sect served to forge became closely entangled with biological ties. The encompassing celestial family of Friends increasingly overlapped with those

[32] Christine Trevett, *Women and Quakerism in the Seventeenth Century* (York, 1991), 125, 127.

[33] Sydney V. James, 'Quaker Meetings and Education in the Eighteenth Century', *QH* 51 (1962), 87–102; Frost, 'As the Twig is Bent', 67; Naomi Pullin, *Female Friends and the Making of Transatlantic Quakerism, 1650–c.1750* (Cambridge, 2018), 93–151.

[34] John Bellers, *Proposals for raising a Colledge of Industry of all useful Trades and Husbandry, with Profit for the Rich, a plentiful Living for the Poor, and a good Education for Youth* (London, 1695); idem, *An Epistle to Friends concerning the Education of Children* (London, 1697), quotations at 1, 2.

[35] John Bellers, *To the Lords and Commons in Parliament assembled: A Supplement to the Proposal for a Colledge of Industry* ([London, 1696]?).

bound by blood. By the mid-eighteenth century, 80 to 90 per cent of Quakers were the children of Friends.[36]

Adult Quakers naturally yearned for ways to ensure that their own offspring would find the Light within themselves. John Field's *Friendly Advice … unto believing Parents and their tender Offspring* (1688) was a sign of the times. It stressed the necessity of 'Christian education' of children as a blessing of God, taking note of the grief that unruly sons and daughters caused to mothers and fathers who 'cockered' and 'fondly' indulged them, as well as underlining the importance of keeping them away from evil influences. It concluded with the warning that parents who neglected this imperative task would have their children's blood on their hands.[37] John Banks's *An Epistle to Friends* (1692) provided similar words of good counsel and wholesome advice to parents and children. Urging parents to labour to restrain the wild and wanton nature of their offspring and to beget a love of the truth and of other Friends, it encouraged attendance at meetings and education at home through reading Scripture and Friends' books. Banks firmly underlined the godly duty of parents to train up their children, who were to wait in the fear of the Lord until they felt him at work in their hearts. He acknowledged that convincement could not be taught, but implied that the groundwork could be laid by education and nurture.[38] Bellers too thought that unless 'more Care, and a better Method' were taken too many Quakers would 'leave the service, and lose the Blessing of Upholding the Profession of Truth in succeeding Ages to the Families of Strangers, whilst the Posterity of the present Professors of it, may have little Share in it'.[39] Growing stress on the role of the family in the economy of salvation and upon the home as a key locus of religious instruction had the

[36] Vann, *Social Development*, 166, and see 158–96 (ch. 5). On growing importance of family, see also Frost, *Quaker Family*, especially 64–88 (ch. 4); Jack D. Marietta, 'Quaker Family Education in Historical Perspective', *QH* 63 (1974), 3–16; Pullin, *Female Friends*, especially 33–92 (ch. 1).

[37] J[ohn] F[ield] and R. S., *Friendly Advice in the Spirit of Love unto believing Parents and their tender Offspring in relation to their Christian Education* (London, 1688), sig. A3^{r}, 16.

[38] John Banks, *An Epistle to Friends shewing the great Difference between a Convinced Estate and a Converted Estate* (London, 1692).

[39] Bellers, *Epistle*, 1.

consequence of raising the profile of Quaker 'mothers in Israel' as spiritual educators, as Naomi Pullin has demonstrated.[40]

This was accompanied by an evolving preoccupation with the 'rising generation'. Increasingly Quakers were created not through the enthusiastic conversionary zeal that had marked the sect's first phase but by carefully cultivating the faith of one's offspring. Friends' concern with upbringing in the setting of the family and classroom intensified.[41] The Welsh schoolmaster John Kelsall noted in his diary many meetings at which the matter of bringing up the 'young generation … in the service of the truth' was stressed as an imperative of the sect in the early eighteenth century. Visiting Quaker ministers, both women and men, earnestly pressed this upon their listeners, lamenting how frequently parents fell short of expectations in this respect. The future of the sect increasingly seemed to lie in and with its children, who were regarded as 'the heritage of the Lord'.[42] As Anthony Benezet wrote to Samuel Fothergill in 1758, 'next to our more immediate duty to God', the education and training of youth ought to 'be the chief concern of everyone that really desires the welfare and enlargement of the borders of Zion'.[43]

It is also significant that in 1737 the London Yearly Meeting formalized the status of the children of Quakers in the rules drawn up regarding removal and settlement. The result was to make membership of what later became known as the Society of Friends a privilege of birth.[44] Declaring that 'the right education of children, and the nurture of the young, is of very great consequence to them, and to the succeeding generation', in 1760 the Yearly Meeting 'pressingly' exhorted all parents and heads of families to procure useful learning for their children and to

40 Pullin, *Female Friends*, 33–92 (ch. 1).

41 On this trend, see also Pullin, 'Children of the Light'.

42 LSF, MS S 185, Transcript of John Kelsall's diary, vol. 1, 1701–12, 65, 11; cf. ibid. 14, 26–7, 31, 39, 41, 67, 101, 104–5, 118–19, 139.

43 Evans and Evans, eds, *Friends' Library*, 9: 220–2. On Benezet, see William C. Kashatus, 'A Reappraisal of Anthony Benezet's Activities in Educational Reform, 1754–1784', *QH* 78 (1989), 24–36.

44 *Extracts from the Minutes and Advices of the Yearly Meeting of Friends held in London, from its First Institution* (London, 1783), 214; see also Walter Joseph Homan, *Children and Quakerism: A Study of the Place of Children in the Theory and Practice of the Society of Friends, commonly called Quakers* (Berkeley, CA, 1939), 99–118 (ch. 4); Vann, *Social Development*, 143–4.

> labour to bring them acquainted with the holy seed, which is sown by the divine hand in every heart for that gracious end: that they may, through the Lord's blessing upon such pious and paternal endeavours, be induced to place their affections upon it, and cleaving thereto in faithful obedience, come to experience it to be unto them, Christ within the hope of their glory … .[45]

In 1766, it reiterated 'the great and lasting importance of religious education to their offspring'. Directing the young 'into the path of purity, by which they may obtain the pearl of great price' was to be preferred over supplying them with 'superfluous and uncertain riches', which were all too 'frequently the sorrowful means of their declension and ruin'. A year later the Meeting renewed the call to Quaker parents to take every opportunity to impress 'a sense of the Divine being' upon their children in 'their tender years', saying that 'though virtue descendeth not by lineal succession, nor piety by inheritance, yet we trust the Almighty doth graciously regard the sincere endeavours of their parents, whose early and constant care is over their offspring for their good; who labour to instruct them in the fear of the Lord'.[46] Such statements reflected the conviction and hope that although saving faith was not hereditary, a salutary environment might be conducive to instilling in children a sincere and lifelong commitment to Quakerism.

In this task parents were to be aided by professional educators. The London Yearly Meetings repeatedly emphasized the need to recruit schoolmasters and mistresses who were faithful Friends, and their proliferation flew in the face of official efforts to maintain an Anglican monopoly on education through the continuing harassment of Quaker teachers, especially following the Schism Act of 1714.[47] Sending one's children to Quaker schools became a way of keeping them uncontaminated by contact with the wider world and protecting them from 'the wiles of Satan'. Parents were advised against allowing their offspring to enrol for training and apprenticeship with those outside the society. The Yearly Meeting repeatedly stressed the need for children to be given 'a suitable and guarded education … by

[45] *Extracts from the Minutes and Advices*, 77.

[46] Ibid. 77–9.

[47] On the continuing prosecution of Quaker teachers, see David L. Wykes, 'Quaker Schoolmasters, Toleration and the Law, 1689–1714', *JRH* 21 (1997), 178–92.

which they may be prevented from mixing with others not of our religious persuasion'. By the 1770s, schools were envisaged as places of quarantine from the 'hurtful habits' of the world.[48]

These are telling symptoms of the rise of birthright Quakerism, a trend that, paradoxically, had intensified after the Act of Toleration of 1689. Just at the moment when Quakers had more room for manoeuvre, they also turned inward to focus ever more attention on consolidation within the forum of the family through intermarriage and by preventing the haemorrhage of the young. Catechisms and primers became instruments of indoctrination in a theology that was solidifying, especially through the Scottish Quaker Robert Barclay's *Apology,* into written form.[49] Experiences of regeneration themselves changed between the first and second generations, as Nikki Coffey Tousley has shown, with confident assurance giving way to greater doubt in the sphere of discernment.[50]

However, the inherent tensions within Quaker attitudes to education continued to rear their heads. There was growing anxiety about the fact that 'mere education' was taking the place of the tumultuous emotional experience of rebirth and regeneration: it was becoming an ersatz substitute for the empowering zeal felt by the sect's founders and first converts. Like the plain testimonies of simple dress, hat honour and levelling language, it was congealing into custom. It is telling that some of the frictions that led to schismatic divisions within the movement in North America during the 1690s centred on unease about these very developments. A hallmark of this group, which was led by George Keith, was its insistence that the children of Friends should themselves be obliged to demonstrate their own sincere convincement when they came to years of discretion. Their parents were required to register the dates of their 'Spirituall Birth' as well

[48] *Extracts from the Minutes and Advices*, 175, 180, 219–20. For the contribution of female educationalists to this project, see Elizabeth Bouldin, '"The Days of Thy Youth": Eighteenth-Century Quaker Women and the Socialization of Children', in Michele Lise Tarter and Catie Gill, eds, *New Critical Studies on Early Quaker Women, 1650–1800* (Oxford, 2018), 202–20.

[49] Barclay, *Apology*; Barclay's influential *Catechism and Confession of Faith* (London, first publ. 1673) was frequently reprinted.

[50] Nikki Coffey Tousley, 'The Experience of Regeneration and Erosion of Certainty in the Theology of Second-Generation Quakers: No Place for Doubt?', *Quaker Studies* 13 (2008), 6–88; eadem, 'Sin, Convincement, Purity, and Perfection', in Angell and Dandelion, eds, *Oxford Handbook of Quaker Studies*, 172–85.

as their 'outward birth' in the Monthly Meeting register.[51] John Hands's *Seasonable Epistle* of 1705 included a section addressed specifically to 'those that are Friends by Education, but not by Conversion', seeking to rouse them to a true realization of the seed within, while John Crook called upon the children and servants of believing parents and masters to examine themselves and assess whether they had derived their religion simply 'by Tradition, only because of your outward Relations', rather than by the 'inward Work of God' upon their souls.[52] The compelling criticism that Barclay had levelled against the early church – that when men and women became Christians 'by birth and education, and not by conversion, and renovation of Spirit', then 'Christianity came to be lost', 'and nothing remained but a shaddow and image' – had come home to roost among the Friends themselves.[53] In this way, Quakerism faced some of the same problems that beset New England puritanism in the wake of the Halfway Covenant of 1662, which extended the right of baptism to the children of visible saints, a decision that provoked anguish in some quarters even as it offered comfort to worried parents.[54] Although Friends repudiated the exclusivist doctrine of election and reprobation that underpinned congregational ecclesiology, they too drifted towards the view that faith could be passed down the generations. Biological kinship and spiritual kinship converged steadily.

By the early eighteenth century, education in the guise of a devout and careful upbringing was increasingly perceived as key to the survival of the society, but the deep-seated ambivalence about learning

[51] J. William Frost, *The Quaker Family in Colonial America: A Portrait of the Society of Friends* (New York, 1973), 68; idem, 'As the Twig is Bent', 73; George Keith, 'Gospel Order and Discipline', *JFHS* 10 (1913), 70–6, at 73–5. For Keith's critique of puritan covenant theology, which incorporated the children of believers into the visible church, see *The Presbyterian and Independent Visible Churches in New-England and else-where, brought to the Test* (Philadelphia, PA, 1689), 84–6.

[52] John Hands, *A seasonable Epistle to believing Parents, and their Children* (London, 1705), 5–7; John Crook, *The Design of Christianity* (London, 1701), 319–20.

[53] Barclay, *Apology* (1678 edn), 184; see also Robert Barclay, *Truth Triumphant through the spiritual Warfare, Christian Labours, and Writings of that able and faithful Servant of Jesus Christ* (London, 1692), 406.

[54] See Edmund S. Morgan, *The Puritan Family* (New York, 1966), 177–82; Robert G. Pope, *The Half-Way Covenant: Church Membership in Puritan New England* (Princeton, NJ, 1969); Anne S. Brown and David D. Hall, 'Family Strategies and Religious Practice: Baptism and the Lord's Supper in Early New England', in David D. Hall, ed., *Lived Religion in America: Towards a History of Practice* (Princeton, NJ, 1997), 41–68.

that had been at the heart of Quakerism from the beginning persisted. Quaker theology was conducive to recognizing the power and agency of nurture, both through its repudiation of predestination in favour of the theoretical possibility of universal salvation and through its resistance to Augustinian teaching on original sin and its stress on childhood as a state of innocence. This partly helps to explain why Friends placed so much emphasis on the merits of utilitarian education and vocational training. However, the sect's radical insistence on feeling the emotional upheaval of an internal conversion experience wrought in the soul by the only true 'teachers', the Light of Christ and the Holy Spirit, ultimately rendered human strategies for spiritual instruction ineffectual and futile. Eighteenth-century Quakerism was thus caught between a rock and a hard place.

Convent Schooling for English Girls in the 'Exile' Period, 1600–1800

Caroline Bowden*
Queen Mary University of London

Following the Reformation, Catholic families seeking to educate both sons and daughters in their faith faced many challenges. The penal laws proscribed the creation of Catholic schools in England and forbade parents to send children abroad for education. However, such was the determination to provide Catholic schooling that families were prepared to break the laws and meet the expense of fees and travel. The convents established schools for several reasons. For some orders it was part of their religious purpose to educate girls, others saw it as a means of educating future members, and all needed to secure their convents financially and be self-sufficient. Schooling provided varied significantly. This article, drawing mainly on manuscript sources from convents and some of the families with daughters attending convent schools, considers the scope of the provision of girls' education in the 'exile' period and offers some preliminary insights into the experience of pupils.

> Mrs Cornwallis (as she has often told us) together with her Companion Mrs Austin, was instructed [by F. Prasset] in the Rudiments of Greek and Hebrew, Geography and Astronomy, which occasioned a certain Chamber, in which they studied to be called the *Globe Room*. A name which likely as long as the House stands, will perpetuate the memory of the wise method he took to train up two young Gentlewomen, and to fit them for the task they had undertaken of qualifying young Ladies with a suitable Education.[1]

* 5 Merthyr Terrace, London, SW13 8DL. E-mail: c.bowden@qmul.ac.uk.

[1] London, Westminster Diocesan Archives (hereafter: WDA), A Series, vol. 39 (1700–1734), no. 134, 'Some Account of Hammersmith School from 1669', (*c*.1715), 3–4; for the Hammersmith context, see Denis Evinson, *Pope's Corner* (London, 1980). Mrs Cornwallis: Cecily Cornwallis, entered Hammersmith 1669, d. York 1723, superior at Hammersmith *c*.1685–1715: 'Who were the Nuns? A Prosopographical Study of the English Convents in Exile 1600–1800', online database, at: <https://wwtn.history.qmul.ac.uk/>, UID MW055. Mary Austen: d. Hammersmith 1687: 'Who were the Nuns?', MW008. Where identities are given from this database, the first date given, unless

Studies in Church History 55 (2019), 177–204
doi: 10.1017/stc.2018.27

> My design is to model, raise and continue a school which may educate young Gentlewomen til their Parents think it proper to send them abroad, and give a Christian Institution to others whom the foundress or circumstances of their Parents will not suffer to cross the Seas.[2]

Although the word 'exile' is used in the title of this article, both these quotations come from archives of the school established by the Mary Ward Sisters at their convent in Hammersmith, then just outside London. This points to some of the complexities relating to the study of convent schooling for English girls in the period between 1600 and 1800. The convent in Hammersmith was opened by Frances Bedingfield in 1669 in contravention of the laws that forbade the presence of convents or Catholic schools in England.[3] Indeed, until the re-migration of the enclosed convents, together with some of their schools, at the time of the French Revolution, the Mary Ward Sisters provided the only Catholic schooling for girls on English soil. The first quotation demonstrates the standard of education associated with the convent school in Hammersmith: the teachers, Cecily Cornwallis and Mary Austen, had themselves been educated to an unusually high level by the convent's Jesuit chaplain. Such standards equipped them to deliver high-quality education to their pupils, although it would have been difficult to replicate this in a small community over time. The second quotation tells us more about the purpose of the school, which aimed to provide a Catholic education on home soil as an alternative to schooling in exile. It also indicates the

---

otherwise specified, is for profession. F. Prasset was Jeremiah or John Pracid SJ (1639–86), chaplain at Hammersmith 1675–8; he died in York: Geoffrey Holt, ed., *The English Jesuits, 1650–1829: A Biographical Dictionary*, CRS 70 (London, 1984), 205. Spelling in all quotations in this article follows the original.

2 WDA, A Series 39, no. 138, 'The Rules to be observed by the Mistress of the School', [*c.*1703].

3 In 1581, statute 23 Eliz. cap. 1 instituted a fine for keeping a non-churchgoing or unlicensed schoolmaster; in 1585, statute 27 Eliz cap. 2 fined parents for sending children abroad for education or to join a religious house. These were confirmed by James I in 1604. Further laws increased the number of offences for which fines had to be paid: for instance, in 1662 the penalty for being or keeping an unlicensed schoolmaster could be up to three months' imprisonment. In 1700, the penalty for being an unlicensed schoolteacher was raised to imprisonment for life: see A. C. F. Beales, *Education under Penalty: English Catholic Education from the Reformation to the Fall of James II* (London, 1963), 172–3. Frances Bedingfield (1616–1704): superior at Hammersmith 1669–85, at York 1686–99 and then at Munich until her death: 'Who were the nuns?', MW017.

cautious approach of the sisters in their unwillingness to challenge the authorities too directly about the Catholic nature of the religious instruction that was undertaken in the school: here they refer to 'Christian' rather than 'Catholic'. A boarding school was started at Hammersmith by Frances Bedingfield around 1677 and functioned there until 1771, under the noses of the authorities, attracting the daughters of many prominent Catholic families, including the Petres, Talbots, Brownes, Giffords and Shelleys.[4] Records show that some girls went on to join other religious institutions or schools on the Continent, although for many the school at Hammersmith was their only school experience. The school, like the convent, breached the regulations which forbade parents to educate their daughters as Catholics either at home or abroad, and from the outside, the buildings at Hammersmith (and from 1686 also at York) looked like a row of ordinary houses, to avoid attracting attention.[5] Such was the determination of some English families to bring up their daughters in the Catholic faith that parents seeking to provide their daughters with a Catholic education flouted the law.[6]

Considering the importance of girls' education, very little research has been undertaken on schooling for English girls in the early modern period. In 1999, Kenneth Charlton published an important survey of girls' education in early modern England, which focused mainly on Protestant girls.[7] My doctoral research studied parental attitudes to girls' education in order to explore reasons for the wide variations in the educational experience of English girls and led to the publication of two articles on convent education.[8] I concluded that

[4] Names taken from list of Hammersmith pupils held at York, Bar Convent Archives, MS C44.

[5] The buildings at York appear on the cover of my copy of Sister Gregory Kirkus's pamphlet history, *Five Houses of the Mary Ward Institute not to be forgotten* (York, n.d.).

[6] The penal laws remained in force, although they were not always rigorously enforced; indeed, by the mid-eighteenth century they were rarely enforced at all. But anxiety remained and anti-Catholic sentiment continued to flare up from time to time, for example during the Gordon Riots of 1780.

[7] Kenneth Charlton, *Women, Religion and Education in Early Modern England* (London, 1999), particularly 126–53; idem, 'Women and Education', in Anita Pacheco, ed., *Companion to Early Modern Women's Writing* (Oxford, 2002), 3–21.

[8] Caroline Bowden, 'Girls' Education in the Late Sixteenth and Early Seventeenth Centuries in England and Wales: A Study of Attitudes and Practice' (PhD thesis, University of London, 1996); eadem, 'Community Space and Cultural Transmission: Formation and Schooling in English Enclosed Convents in the Seventeenth Century', *HE* 34 (2005), 365–86; eadem, '"For the glory of God": A Study of the Education of

differences in fathers' attitudes to the future roles of their daughters were crucial to decisions being made regarding their schooling and that wide variations were to be found in both Catholic and Protestant families. The penal laws applying to the Catholic community from the reign of Elizabeth until Catholic emancipation in 1828 not only hindered access to Catholic schooling but also imposed such severe financial penalties for those practising Catholicism that some families would not have been able to afford to pay school fees and travel costs.[9]

Convent Schooling

Most of the convent schools discussed in this article were located on the Continent, identified in the section on 'Schools and Pupils' below and listed in the Appendix. In addition to the English schools, some space is given to French Ursuline schools, whose pupils included a few English girls amongst their number, such as Christina Dennett, who later became a reforming head teacher at the Sepulchrine school at Liège, and Charlotte Jerningham, part of a family of letter-writers who provide a vivid account of schooling at the Ursuline convent in Paris at the end of the eighteenth century.[10]

New convents for English women were established initially in the southern Netherlands from 1598, and from 1634 in France. They committed themselves to accepting only English members and remaining financially independent.[11] This commitment to being

English Catholic Women in Convents in Flanders and France in the First Half of the Seventeenth Century', *PH* 35 supplement 1 (1999), 77–95. An early pioneer researching Catholic education who included girls was William F. Hastings, 'The Education of English Catholics 1559–1800' (MA thesis, London University, 1923). My thanks go to Fr Peter Harris for drawing my attention to this thesis and permitting me to read his copy.

[9] See Martin J. Havran, *The Catholics in Caroline England* (Stanford, CA, 1962), 1–17, 'The Letter of the Law'.

[10] All the letters are included in the microfilm, *Aristocratic Women: The Social, Political and Cultural History of Rich and Powerful Women*, Part 2: *The Correspondence and Diaries of Charlotte Georgiana, Lady Bedingfield (formerly Jerningham), c.1779–1833 … from Birmingham University Library* (Marlborough, 1998), reels 1–14.

[11] See, for instance, Claire Walker, *Gender and Politics in Early Modern Europe: English Convents in France and the Low Countries* (Basingstoke, 2002); Caroline Bowden, 'Introduction' to eadem, gen. ed., *English Convents in Exile 1600–1800*, 6 vols (London, 2012–13), 1: xi–xxvii.

self-supporting meant that members of the convent communities had to devise means of raising revenue, for instance taking in boarders, making lace or, in most cases, establishing schools. These schools had to be incorporated into convent property without encroaching on the enclosure of the choir nuns.

The majority of pupils went to school at one of the enclosed communities in exile, but, as I have already suggested, in any discussion of girls' education it is essential also to recognize the significant role and influence of the Mary Ward Sisters, also known as the Institute of Mary, whose way of life and schools were distinctive, being based on a Jesuit model.[12] Reflecting her determination to educate girls, Mary Ward quickly established schools when she opened houses on the Continent, including St Omer, Rome and Munich.[13] It was through the success of the school in Munich that, with the support of the elector of Bavaria, her work survived the institute's suppression by the papacy in 1631 and became the only community to establish houses on English soil during the period under consideration here.[14] Mary Ward Sisters did not wear habits: they dressed as respectable lay spinsters. In England they had to be particularly careful not to draw attention to themselves because of the penal laws, for instance, by using appropriate titles such as 'Mistress' as lay women. They provided as much teaching as they could themselves, hiring additional teachers when necessary. Unlike most girls' schools in England during the period, which tended to be short-lived, the school at Hammersmith operated successfully for over a century. However, such was the demand for convent schooling that most English girls attending a convent school between 1600 and 1800 had to cross the Channel.

The English convents varied in the way they arranged and managed teaching in their schools. Orders such as the Benedictines and Poor Clares, who were contemplatives, generally saw teaching primarily as part of the preparation of future members, to be combined with

[12] Other names by which the order was known during this period included the Jesuitesses and (by the end of the eighteenth century) the Institute of the Blessed Virgin Mary.

[13] For an account of this period, see Mary Wright, *Mary Ward's Institute: The Struggle for Identity,* Sydney, 1997), 1–13; Margaret Mary Littlehales, *Mary Ward: Pilgrim and Mystic* (London, 1998), 61, 116–18, 157–8.

[14] This is discussed at greater length by Henriette Peters, *Mary Ward: A World in Contemplation* (Leominster, 1994); Mary Oliver, *Mary Ward 1585–1645* (New York, 1959), 225–9 (Appendix II). The school in Munich survives, still known locally as the school of the 'Englische Fräulein'.

the formation of candidates.[15] The rule for the Canonesses created a combination of the contemplative and active religious life, with the teaching of girls being a core part of the canonesses' daily routine. Although Canonesses were enclosed, like the contemplative orders, their performance of a reduced office went some way to accommodate their teaching roles. Their schools tended to be larger, and the curricula broader, while still retaining significant religious elements. The schools of the contemplatives were generally small and more likely to be based round devotions because the nuns' own lives focused on prayer, reading and writing. Teaching was an incidental part of this work and it was given less time in the structure of the choir nuns' day, in contrast to the Canonesses' daily timetable. Like the Canonesses, the Mary Ward Sisters had teaching girls at the heart of their religious life: Mary Ward planned to establish two schools connected to each house, one a boarding school, the other a free school for poorer girls.[16]

As I have already suggested, it is important to include the schools of the French Ursulines in a study of convent education for English girls. Founded in 1535 by Angela Merici, the Ursulines decided in 1612 to accept enclosure as required by the Tridentine reforms, rather than close down their schools.[17] By the end of the eighteenth century they had around four hundred convents and schools in France, with a wide-ranging curriculum, and were providing most of the schooling for women. Some English convents, including the Canonesses at Bruges, sent a number of their own postulants to the Ursulines so that they could immerse themselves in a French religious

[15] For an overview of Tridentine Catholicism, see, for instance, Ronnie Po-Chia Hsia, *The World of Catholic Renewal, 1540–1770*, 2nd edn (Cambridge, 2005).

[16] The area of curriculum studies in convent schools still needs considerable research before definitive conclusions can be drawn; very little has survived in convent archives. For research on the schools at the Bar Convent, see M. Gregory Kirkus, *Education in the Bar Convent in the 18th Century* (York, n.d.); Susan O'Brien, 'Women of the "English Catholic Community": Nuns and Pupils at the Bar Convent, York, 1680–1790', in Judith Loades, ed., *Monastic Studies 1* (Bangor, 1990), 267–82; Kathy J. Wilson, 'Catholic Female Education and British National Identity, 1760–1870' (MA thesis, University of York, 2004); Jack Kitching, 'The History and Development of Catholic Education in the North and East Ridings of Yorkshire and the City of York from 1571 to 1870' (MEd thesis, University of Durham, 1956).

[17] The work of the Ursulines and Mary Ward Sisters is further discussed by Laurence Lux-Sterritt, *Redefining Female Religious Life: French Ursulines and English Ladies in Seventeenth-Century Catholicism* (Aldershot, 2005), especially 75–102.

environment and learn French more quickly. In addition, several contemporary accounts record that English parents (both Catholic and Protestant) from south-east England sent their daughters to boarding schools in Channel ports such as Boulogne. These were said to be less expensive than girls' boarding schools in England.

An item on the front page of a 1766 issue of the *St James' Chronicle* claimed to be a 'Copy of a letter from an English Gentleman in Paris on his travels to a friend in London'.[18] The article covered education for boys and girls, and made the claim, as yet uncorroborated, that thirty Protestant girls from the Dover area of Kent were boarding at a French convent school in Boulogne (probably the Ursuline school) and a further forty-seven at Calais.[19] There were several reasons why Protestant parents might send their daughters to a French convent boarding school apart from cost: for instance, admiration of French language skills and French manners, and the opportunity to mingle with well-bred French girls. Additionally, Ursuline schools were held in high esteem for the quality of their teaching. However, one point exercising the anonymous author was his view that Protestant girls were being subjected to Catholic religious propaganda which they could pass on to their families once they married. He was also concerned that the girls were being given only a 'partial History of England: and taught to believe that the true King of England is in Exile in Rome'.[20] While the piece contains a number of factual errors and is unreliable as evidence regarding pupil numbers, it nevertheless offers an interesting contemporary insight into the perceived influence of convent schools.

Sources

The search for material regarding convent schools and the identification of pupils and their families proved to be a complex process, often yielding only fragmentary evidence. The primary purpose of the religious communities was the religious life of their members. It is

[18] Printed in Aidan Bellenger and Jeremy Black, 'The Foreign Education of British Catholics in the Eighteenth Century', *Downside Review* 105 (1987), 310–16. They suggest that the school at Calais used by English parents was probably the French Benedictine convent of Our Lady of Pity: ibid. 315.

[19] Ibid. 310.

[20] Ibid. 311. James, son of James II, died in exile in Rome in January 1766.

understandable that when faced with catastrophes such as fires and floods, or disasters such as having to deal with French revolutionaries hammering at the door, when nuns had to make extraordinarily difficult decisions about what they could keep, school records were not the top priority.[21] Several communities were barely able to escape with their lives and what they could carry in their pockets. However, a mixture of good fortune and careful planning led to the survival of a surprising amount of material from the exile period, particularly about the members, although it is harder to piece together details about schooling. Fortunately, some letters between families and the convents have survived which provide glimpses of the experience of attending school. By piecing together convent material with letters and other personal documents from family archives, it is possible to begin producing a cultural history of the education of girls in early modern English convent schools. The names of the English girls who attended French Ursuline schools remain elusive, although enough material survives to suggest that further research would make a significant contribution to understanding the full range of convent education available to English girls. Even for the English convent schools, research is still in its early stages and this overview can only touch briefly on some important areas of interest. It is essential to acknowledge how much remains to be done, particularly regarding the curriculum and teaching. For the foreseeable future, research into convent schooling will remain a work in progress.

Parental Attitudes to Convent Education

Surviving evidence shows that, like Protestant parents, Catholic parents were identifying the importance of girls' education to their roles in the family as wives and mothers; however, unlike Protestant parents, Catholic parents had the religious life as an alternative for their daughters. Both these paths for women could help to secure the future of English Catholicism. The parents of daughters who saw their future outside the convent aimed to create potentially model wives whose marriages would fit familial expectations, reflect well on their parents and ensure the survival of a beleaguered minority.

[21] I am indebted to the communities who granted me generous access to their archives, and to archivists and librarians who are the present custodians of manuscripts and books from convents which have recently closed or downsized.

Within the overarching parental ambitions for their daughters were wide variations about desirable intellectual outcomes, even amongst families of similar social backgrounds and levels of income.[22] As a result, amongst the English aristocracy and landed gentry – both Catholic and Protestant – there were women who found writing letters challenging whilst others could translate from Latin and French and were accomplished authors or musicians. Such disparities and uneven standards can also be seen in the education of pupils who attended convent schools. Nevertheless schooling, even of an elementary nature, was viewed by parents (with some justification) as providing the basis for later improvement.[23] Educated girls might become mothers who were able in turn to play a significant role in the upbringing of children, and to provide a sound moral example especially to their daughters. In many cases parents were prepared to make considerable personal sacrifices to achieve those ends.

One Catholic parent who gave his opinion on girls' education was Sir Thomas Strickland of Sizergh Castle, Westmorland, who in 1692 wrote a letter of advice to his son:

> It is hard for a young man to know how to Chuse or value a virtuous Woman … therfor endeavor to Chuse a Woman whose Education and character is virtuous, and modest, and let not fortune be the sole ame of Marriage, though I know they Condition will much require it and there are good Women with great fortunes. But let the main ground of they Marriage be grounded in the fear of God and trew affection and that will sweeten all the troubles of married life.[24]

[22] Letter collections providing evidence of parental interest in girls' education include the papers of the Blundell, Throckmorton and Thimelby families: see Geoff Baker, *Reading and Politics in Early Modern England: The Mental World of a Seventeenth-Century Catholic Gentleman* (Manchester, 2010); Janet E. Hollinshead, *Women of the Catholic Community: The Blundells of South Lancashire during the Seventeenth and Eighteenth Centuries* (Wigan, 2010); Geoffrey Scott, 'The Throckmortons at home and abroad, 1680–1800', in Peter Marshall and Geoffrey Scott, eds, *Catholic Gentry in English Society: The Throckmortons of Coughton from Reformation to Emancipation* (Farnham, 2009), 171–211; Kate Gibson, 'Marriage Choice and Kinship among the English Catholic Elite, 1680–1730', *JFH* 42 (2016), 144–64. For the Thimelby family, see Claire Walker, 'Exiled Children: Care in English Convents in the 17th and 18th Centuries', *Children Australia* 41 (2016), 168–77, at 174.

[23] I developed this argument in 'Women in Educational Spaces', in Laura Knoppers, ed., *The Cambridge Companion to Early Modern Women's Writing* (Cambridge, 2009), 85–96.

[24] Sir Thomas Strickland of Sizergh Castle to his son Walter, 1692: Henry Hornyold, *Genealogical Memoirs of the Family of Strickland of Sizergh* (Kendal, 1928), 136–8

Sir Thomas also commented specifically on his wife Winifred's capabilities, both as a manager and a mother: 'I am Confident she will have Care of that poor temporall estate I shall leave her, and will bring the[e] up in the fear of God and his Catholic Church'. She must have been educated to fulfil these obligations.

Increasingly, research on lived religion in the early modern period is showing that divisions between Catholics and Protestants in England were not nearly as sharply defined as has previously been thought.[25] For instance, some families chose to intermarry; at parish level neighbours managed to get along for most of the time, and, as we have seen, some Protestant girls were sent to Catholic boarding schools. Like better-off Catholic parents, some Protestant parents wanted to secure an education for their daughters in boarding schools, away from worldly influences, and they were attracted by the reputation of the Catholic schools they chose.

Schools and Pupils 1600–1800

What do we know about pupils who faced the challenges and undertook what were often hazardous journeys in search of a convent education? Finding names and family details of pupils in convent schools is challenging: lists that survive exist in a range of formats, with some only fragmentary. Young women arrived at convents either to try out the religious life or as schoolgirls; some changed from one category to another. Numbers must therefore be treated with caution. In compiling lists of names, I focused on girls known to have arrived at a convent for schooling: these numbers are still provisional. It is evident

(quotation at 137). Thomas's wife, Winifred Trentham, died in 1725 at the Poor Clares, Rouen.

[25] William J. Sheils, '"Getting On" and "Getting Along" in Parish and Town: Catholics and their Neighbours in England', in Benjamin Kaplan et al., eds, *Catholic Communities in Protestant States: Britain and the Netherlands,* c.*1570–1720*, Studies in Early Modern European History, Britain and the Netherlands 16 (Manchester, 2009), 67–83. See also the 'Introduction' to the updated edition of the 'Who were the Nuns?' database, Katharine S. B. Keats-Rohan, ed., *English Catholic Nuns in Exile 1600–1800: A Biographical Register*, Prosopographica et Genealogica 15 (Oxford, 2017), xliii. In response to his bishop's enquiries in 1738, the rector of Somerton reported: 'The Protestants and papists by long living together in ye same Parrish are so blended and united together, having for several years married one among another': 'Catholicism in Somerton', online at: <http://somertonoxon.co.uk/st-james-church/catholicism-in-somerton/>, accessed 21 July 2018.

from the sources that school careers were generally very short, and many schoolgirls only spent a couple of years at most at a convent school.

Mary Ward Institute Schools (in England)

The Mary Ward schools at Hammersmith and in York provided a choice for Catholic parents who preferred to keep their daughters nearer home or were unable to afford the cost of sending them abroad. A few English girls were sent to continental schools belonging to the institute, including those at Paris and Munich, but most English girls attending Mary Ward schools did so in England. The legal position of the schools made the sisters act cautiously in public, but it did not seem to deter parents.[26] For the Bar Convent, York, which opened its school in 1686, more than eight hundred eighteenth-century names have been listed.[27] Numbers entering the school at Hammersmith remained relatively constant at around ten a year, even as numbers entering community dwindled; the names of 841 girls attending the school between 1669 and 1771 were recorded.[28] The school finally closed in 1781. Some names on the list were annotated, indicating pupils who left to marry, some who moved to York and others who went on to the religious life in continental convents. In its way, Hammersmith was a feeder institute.

Canonesses

In Liège, the Sepulchrine Canonesses opened a school when the convent was founded in 1642, but this remained small. However, following restructuring and reforms from October 1770 to May 1794, initiated by Christina Dennett, 350 pupils of six different nationalities passed through the school, several of whom spent more than five

[26] Denis Evinson, 'The Catholic Revival in Hammersmith', *London Recusant* 7 (1977), 19–45, at 22.

[27] Susan O'Brien, 'Women of the "English Catholic Community"', 270; Wilson, 'Catholic Female Education', A1–A31; Mary C. E. Chambers, *The Life of Mary Ward*, ed. H. J. Coleridge, 2 vols (London, 1882–5), 1: 389–416. The list for York covers the period 1710–1886.

[28] A version of the register is held in Bar Convent Archives, MS C44; see also Thomas Faulkner, *The History and Antiquities of the Parish of Hammersmith* (London, 1839), 251–3.

years there.[29] In Bruges, the Augustinian Canonesses listed 695 names of girls attending their school between the mid-seventeenth century and 1793.[30] By contrast, no trace of a list of names of those attending the school of the Augustinian Canonesses in Louvain has yet been found, although a building for a school appears on the contemporary plan of the convent.[31] The school of the Paris Augustinian Canonesses has only a partial listing of pupils, which includes 123 names for the period from 1676 to 1720; this is supplemented by an undated notebook containing the names of many of the French pupils, which is still to be fully deciphered.[32]

Poor Clares

All four convents had small schools, although nothing has so far been found about pupils at Dunkirk and Gravelines. The little evidence that survives suggests that pupils arrived as a result of recommendations passed mainly through family networks. The only comments about the school at Aire appear in letters from the printer and bookseller J. P. Coghlan. In 1779, he removed his daughters from the Benedictine school at Cambrai after he had been advised that they were backward in reading, and transferred them to Aire. By 1782, he commented that his daughter Elizabeth was very much improved and he was impressed by the school, 'as the best of any, either for duty to God or instruction for worldly business … as I have known anything of'.[33]

[29] Colchester, Archives of the Canonesses of the Holy Sepulchre (hereafter: ACHS), cupboard 5, box D, MS 7 (n.d. but in nineteenth-century hand).

[30] Bruges, Archives of the Priory of Nazareth of the Augustinian Canonesses Regular of St John Lateran, 'The Names of the young Ladies and Gentlewomen Pensioners at the Monastery of the English Canonesses Regular of the Holy Order of St Augustine at Bruges, from the Year 1629 to 1908', typescript transcription of original list.

[31] See Adam Hamilton, ed., *The Chronicle of the English Augustinian Canonesses Regular of the Lateran, at St Monica's in Louvain, 1548–1644*, 2 vols (Edinburgh, 1904–6), 2: facing p. 13.

[32] London, WDA, Augustinian Convent, Paris, Notebook 32, 'List of Pupils received into the School 1633 till 1881' (many missing); Antony Allison, 'The English Augustinian Convent of Our Lady of Syon: Its Foundation and Struggle for Survival during the First Eighty Years, 1634–1713', *RH* 21 (1992–3), 451–96, at 485–7 (Appendix I, 'The School').

[33] Frans Blom et al., eds, *The Correspondence of James Peter Coghlan (1731–1800)*, CRS 80 (Woodbridge, 2007), 78, 95, 121.

The convent at Rouen also had a small school. There is no convent list; however, Ann Forster provisionally listed 103 names for the period from 1646 to 1770.[34] Occasionally schoolgirls are discussed in the convent chronicles. For instance, Mary Strickland arrived there in 1713, aged ten, brought by her father, Walter Strickland.[35] Mary exhibited model behaviour and entranced the nuns. She was sent to a French Benedictine convent to improve her language skills, but became ill and returned to Rouen. She died in the convent aged thirteen. The account of her life in the convent annals contains nothing about schooling and is similar to a hagiography of a young and devout religious made particularly appealing because of her youth and tragic death. Another pupil, Harriet Goldie, later wrote her own version of her life as a schoolgirl at Rouen: this is included as one of the case studies below.[36]

Franciscans

From the community's foundation, the Franciscan sisters established a small school focused primarily on devotional teaching. By the time they moved to the Prinsenhof in Bruges in 1662, the school had two mistresses, who were 'to instruct the pupils in all piety and devotion, not permitting any vaine secular discourse contrarie to virtue'.[37] The pattern of the day was linked to the liturgical rhythms of the convent set by the performance of the office. It was described by the author of the convent history as 'turning girls into devout Catholic maidens, ready to take up their role as nuns or as obedient wives keen to instruct their future children in the faith'. Here is a contemplative community which clearly saw a double purpose in the education they provided.

Benedictines

The situation regarding the existence of schools seems to have been different in each of the Benedictine convents, and so far little is

[34] Ann M. C. Forster, 'The Chronicles of the English Poor Clares of Rouen II', *RH* 18 (1986), 149–91, at 182–5.

[35] Bowden, ed., *English Convents in Exile*, 1: 217, 219, 222–5, 228 (the volume is an edition of the 'Rouen Chronicles').

[36] See p. 199–201 below.

[37] S[ister] M[ary] F[rances], *Hidden Wheat: The Story of an Enclosed Franciscan Community, 1621–1971* (n.pl., [1971]), 75–8, at 77.

known about arrangements for schoolgirls. A brief reference in the convent history to the fact that 'our Sisters ... had always occupied themselves with education' points to the presence of a school at Dunkirk. We also know the names of two pupils (Margaret and Katharine Ireland) who were sent to school at Dunkirk around 1670, when their newly widowed father decided to become a Jesuit.[38] Brussels was known to have a school from the early days of its foundation, with a few pupils named from 1609, although there are no sign of any school buildings on plans of the convent.[39] Little evidence has been found regarding schoolgirls at Ghent.[40] Eighty-five names of schoolgirls between 1625 and 1725 are included amongst the lists of religious and aspirants from Cambrai, but no other information about the school has yet been found.[41] From Pontoise, the names of 240 *Pensionnaires* aged between five and seventeen who attended between 1658 and 1782 have survived.[42] However, it seems that the community was unable to make enough money from their boarders: although the pupils paid fees, Pontoise failed financially and was sold at auction in 1786.

The Conceptionists (familiarly known as the Blue Nuns):

The names of 155 pupils have survived for a period between 1733 and 1792.[43] This Paris school became well known, and the pupils include many names from elite French and English families, among them Charlotte Jerningham's mother, Frances. There are hints in several sources that this school was akin to a finishing school, with a focus on accomplishments and manners as well as learning to move in the right social circles. For instance, Lucy Rothe arrived as a schoolgirl in August 1757, her parents paying £25 per annum, and she

[38] *A History of the Benedictine Nuns of Dunkirk* (London, 1957), 136, 70.
[39] *Chronicle of the first Monastery founded at Brussels* (East Bergholt, 1898), 73–5, plan between pp. 40 and 41.
[40] The school and a few pupils are mentioned in *Annals of the English Benedictines of Ghent* (East Bergholt, 1898).
[41] Cecilia Heywood and Joseph Gillow, eds, 'Records of the Abbey of Our Lady of Consolation Nuns at Cambrai 1620–1793', in *Miscellanea 8*, CRS 13 (1913), 1–81.
[42] Jacques Grimbert, 'Histoire du clos des Anglaises à Pontoise', *Mémoires de la Société Historique et Archeologique de Pontoise, du Val-d'Oise et du Vexin* 81 (1998), 267–388.
[43] Egerton Castle, ed., *The Jerningham Letters (1780–1843)*, 2 vols (London, 1896), 2: 404–8.

brought a maid for whom she paid £15 per annum. The Jerningham letters offer us insights into the experience of attending this school at the end of the eighteenth century.[44]

A small Dominican school at the Spellikans, near Brussels, which took mainly French and Flemish girls has been identified by Whelan, but no further details are currently known.[45] No evidence of schools has yet been found at the Bridgettines in Lisbon, or from three houses of Carmelites in the southern Netherlands. All these were contemplative convents. Geography may have played a role here: the journey to Lisbon would have been hard and expensive to arrange, particularly for young girls. However, the contemplative life must have represented an additional obstacle. Carmelite houses were small and Carmelites spent long periods of time in solitary prayer in their cells, a discipline which would not easily have accommodated teaching.

Pupils appear in the school records at all ages from five upwards, with a few even younger. Of necessity far from home and in exile, these girls were boarders who might have long gaps between parental visits or opportunities to return home. In addition, the position of these schools within the convent precincts must have influenced the behaviour of young girls trying to fit in to the quiet of monastic life. Rules governing enclosure were strictly laid down and exactly followed in the English convents in exile. The reputation which helped to attract new members depended on exactly following the rule which governed every aspect of life in the convent. It stipulated where candidates for membership could go and how they fitted into the community, but schoolgirls were a separate category and needed their own spaces and different rules. Such complications affected decision-making about creating and managing schools.

Even with the best of intentions, having young children in a convent must have disturbed the peace of the enclosure and increased the need for lay sisters to look after them. When in 1674 two daughters of the earl of Powis, Lucy and Winefrid Herbert, aged five and four, became pupils with the Pontoise Benedictines, they paid extra to have a lay sister to wait on them.[46] Their parents held appointments

[44] *Aristocratic Women*, Part 2, reels 1–14.

[45] Basil Whelan, *Historic English Convents of Today* (London, 1936), 257, 259.

[46] Cergy-Pontoise, Archives départementales Val-d'Oise, 68H10, Bénédictines anglaises de Pontoise, 'Promesse d'obediences d'abbesses, liste de religieuses, registre de vêtures, 1652–1779' (1674).

at the Jacobite court of James II in exile at St Germain, outside Paris. The school career of three Stafford (Howard) girls can be traced through three separate convents. In 1725, following the death of their mother, Anne, that year, the younger two were placed by their father, William Stafford-Howard, with the Mary Ward Sisters in Hammersmith, where the eldest was already a pupil. Two years later, the three sisters, now aged seven, five and three, were taken in by the Poor Clares at Rouen at their father's request. In May 1733, the eldest, Mary, was sent to the Blue Nuns in Paris, where two of Lord Stafford's sisters had been professed and where he was a generous benefactor. Following his death in 1733, there appears to have been something of a tussle between the Poor Clares and the Blue Nuns over the girls' future, but finally in 1735 the younger sisters, Anastasia and Ann, left Rouen, much to the nuns' grief and affliction.[47] The loss of either parent always destabilized families; it was particularly disruptive for Catholics trying to avoid losing their children to a Protestant parent-substitute as required by officials under the penal laws.[48]

Teaching and Learning

The evidence outlined above has drawn attention to the wide range of ages and experience of pupils and to the diversity of the provision of schooling. There was a degree of interconnectedness between the convents, with the movement of girls carrying with them their experiences from one school to another and reporting back to parents in their letters. It is not possible from the sources currently available to study the curricula on offer in the schools. What was feasible depended largely on the qualities of the choir nuns at a particular time, the charism of the convent, the structure of the religious life and the number and ages of the pupils.

[47] Their presence in Hammersmith is confirmed by the pupil lists. For Rouen, see Bowden, ed., *English Convents in Exile*, 1: 99–101, 102, 115–16. For the Blue Nuns, see Joseph Gillow and Richard Trappes-Lomax, eds, *Diary of the 'Blue Nuns', or, Order of the Immaculate Conception of Our Lady, at Paris, 1658–1810*, CRS 8 (1910), 96, 97, 98.

[48] See Havran, *Catholics in Caroline England*, 1–17; for the text of the 1606 'Act for the better discovering and repressing of Popish Recusants' particularly relevant here, see J. R. Tanner, ed., *Constitutional Documents of the Reign of James I, 1603–1625* (Cambridge, 1930), 100, 102.

Convent schools appear to have accommodated parents' wishes as far as they could, and provided a personal experience. The image of the Blue Nun with a single pupil, her hand held by a choir nun, actually represents reality in some schools.[49] Girls might arrive at any time of the year, there was a wide range of ages at entry and it was possible that only four pupils might come over a whole year. There was flexibility, too, over the length of stay: some girls stayed only a few weeks, whereas others remained several years. Even where numbers were growing, we can see that school mistresses focused on the individual experience. For instance, the Sepulchrines at Liège kept a book from 1785 in which they noted parental requirements for their daughters, such as the language to be used in letters home, extras to be taught, whether the pupil had had smallpox and whether she had been confirmed. The first page concerns the Misses Dillon, who arrived on 10 December 1785: 'They take all the common lessons. Three of dancing every week – The same of Music – They are to write to their father once a month in French. They are never to go out. They must attend particularly to French. They have never been confirmed.'[50] They are noted in the register as having left in September 1786: if the parental request regarding not going out had been followed they would have spent nine months within convent walls. During 1787, fifteen pupils arrived over the course of the year, each with her own page of special instructions.

Across Europe, the eighteenth century saw the gradual spread of new ideas regarding girls' schooling, as well as changes in parental attitudes towards girls' education. Several convents appointed reforming heads who introduced changes which transformed learning experiences in their schools. For instance, a broader curriculum including geography, history and languages can be seen in the changes introduced by Sepulchrine Canoness Christina Dennett (1730–81) at Liège. She was determined to include the education of girls in her reforms of the community, and had experienced a broader curriculum herself as a schoolgirl with the Ursulines. Her contemporary biographer wrote about her plans: 'She set her heart on giving Catholic girls the same advantages which they would have had in the great schools

[49] See Caroline Bowden and James Kelly, eds, *The English Convents in Exile, 1600–1800: Communities, Culture and Identity* (Farnham, 2013), plate 27, 'Blue Nun Teaching'.

[50] Colchester, ACHS, MS M1, 'Young Ladies who entered as Pensioners 1785–1807, including Recommendations given by Parents', unpaginated.

in England.'[51] Dennett's ambition chimes closely with the aim of Sir Thomas Gascoigne nearly a century earlier, when he financed the foundation of the Bar Convent School, York, in 1686.[52]

The Sepulchrines had run a school since their foundation, but it remained very small. Dennett's ambitious plans required new school buildings and she emphasized that she wanted to teach girls who would become wives and mothers, as well as those who wished to enter religious life. The curriculum included reading, writing, French, Italian, letter-writing for every occasion, arithmetic, double-entry book-keeping, history (both secular and religious), geography, globes and presentations. Masters were to be employed for extras such as dancing, painting and music. It was a scheme which appealed to parents: within four years, sixty boarders were in residence and further buildings were needed.[53] A similar curriculum is reflected in the accounts for the schoolgirls at York, in which payments for globes, equipment for painting and drawing and extra masters for music and dancing are visible.[54]

This breadth of studies can also be seen in the Ursuline schools in France attended by a number of English girls. From the beginning of the eighteenth century, the Ursulines had expanded their educational programme, adding secular and religious history, biographies of famous people, dictionaries, geography, astronomy, geology and natural history to the studies of their pupils. However, the content of the lessons was only part of the girls' education. At the same time, the convents were teaching the pupils good manners and instructing them as to how to comport themselves well and speak correctly as part of developing body and mind.[55]

[51] Caroline M. K. Bowden, 'Dennett, Mary [*name in religion* Christina] (1730–1781)', *ODNB*; *A History of the New Hall Community of Canonesses Regular of the Holy Sepulchre* (Roehampton, 1899), particularly 80.

[52] See the material in the new (2017) Bar Convent museum, showing the origins of the schools at the Bar Convent.

[53] Hastings, 'Education of English Catholics', 252–3, 257, 260; *New Hall Community*, 58.

[54] For instance, Bar Convent Archives, MS E4, 'Copies of the Young Ladies' Bills', August 1770.

[55] Marie Chantal Gueudré, *Histoire de l'ordre des Ursulines en France*, 3 vols (Paris, 1957–63), 2: 229, 234, 235, 237, 241, 244, 253, 257, 259. For further discussion of teaching at the Ursuline schools, see Lux-Sterritt, *Redefining Female Religious Life*, particularly 75–102.

Life as a Convent School Pupil

The convent schools had no terms: holidays fitted the liturgical calendar. Schoolgirls did not go home for the holidays, although they did write letters to their parents giving them news of life at school.[56] Some of them remained at the convent without a break for their whole time in the school, up to three years in a few cases. Some schools permitted visitors and exeats; others were more restrictive and only permitted pupils to talk to their families at the grate like the nuns, otherwise keeping them confined to their part of the enclosure. Unlike the membership of the convents, which was almost entirely English, in the schools there were pupils of different nationalities. This was particularly true of Sepulchrines in the 1770s and 1780s after Christina Dennett's reforms. The Paris schools had many local pupils, as did the English convent in Bruges in the second half of the eighteenth century, and there was often a substantial number of Irish pupils also.[57] Table 1 gives one of the few examples from the period setting out the pattern of the school day, indicating how the Mary Ward Sisters integrated elements of the religious life with school studies. The pattern of the day for schoolgirls at enclosed contemplative convents tended to allocate more time for them to follow the divine office with the community. At Hammersmith, pupils were in chapel only twice a day.

As the size of the community of sisters reduced, the school at Hammersmith employed additional lay teachers to teach French and supplement the instruction given by the sisters. A manuscript setting out the duties of officials in the house includes a section headed 'The Office of the Mistress of the School'. From this, it is apparent that considerable thought had gone into how teaching was carried out and the kind of teachers that were wanted. For instance:

> Mistresses … ought to be Persons of extraordinary Genius, Patience and Discretion; and never give themselves the Liberty of committing any of those Faults, which they should correct in their Scholars. A

[56] For examples of letters home, see Arundel Castle, Howard Letters 1687–1735, Letters 42, 43, 53, Ann Howard to her father Bernard, 1733–5; letters from the Throckmorton girls are discussed in Walker, 'Exiled Children'.

[57] Names of pupils taken from lists in convent archives. The incomplete nature of the lists makes any detailed observations or analysis unsatisfactory at present.

Table 1. A School Day, reconstructed from details in a Hammersmith manuscript.[58]

6.30 or 7.30	Pupils to rise and give hearts to God. Dress themselves in silence with strict regard to rules. Go to school for morning prayer.
8.00	Breakfast.
8.30	In twos to chapel to hear mass or perform devotions.
9.15	Start school exercises, spelling or reading English or Latin for half an hour. Then all have the same lesson in the same book, pronouncing the same words. Divide the class if they are not all the same standard. Learn marking,[59] plain work, embroidery, writing, casting accounts, or (under a master) dancing and music.
12.15	Learn Catechism and repeat it to their mistress.
1.00	Dinner, during which silence kept or speak in low voice. Pupils by turn to say grace and read a chapter of a spiritual book or life of a saint. Must take their places according to when they arrived in school. Must behave like young gentlewomen. File out to recreation in the presence of a mistress.
3.00	Return to school exercises: first hour for things that need the best light, second in reading and spelling and the rest in easier works.
6.30	Beads and other prayers in chapel. At 6.00 on Wednesday, go to school to say the Catechism and hear it expounded.
7.00	Supper, followed by recreation in sight of a mistress in school or garden.
8.30	Night prayers, then retire in silence, short prayers by bedside. They should think pious thoughts till they fall asleep.

fond Partiality ought particularly to be avoided, because it makes the Favourite odious, and the Mistress despicable to the Rest.[60]

There were enough pupils to divide them into classes of different levels and we can imagine the atmosphere and procedure in the class room from the following instruction:

Each Class shall have their Lesson out of the same Book, whether English or Latin, and being seated before the Mistress shall in silence

[58] London, WDA, A Series 40, no. 159, n.d., 19–21. For other examples of school days, see Whelan, *Historic Convents*, 256, 258; Allison, 'English Augustinian Convent', 485–7.
[59] According to the *OED*, in 1713 'marking' was listed as part of the curriculum of a girls' school in Lambeth, and involved marking either clothing or linen with initials.
[60] London, WDA, A Series 39, no. 135*, 27.

> attend to their Lesson, till they are calld up to say all or a part of it, or to spell or pronounce some word, which another seems not able to do.[61]

Learning was reinforced by repetition: on Mondays the girls had to repeat the previous week's lessons. The pupils were to be constantly watched, partly to ensure that their manners and deportment at all times were correct: any punishments should be appropriate to the offence. The development of character is also covered: for instance, children should learn how to become good Christians by learning how to work and avoid idleness. They must report scandalous behaviour, but not trivial vexations, so as not to be a gossip or talebearer.[62]

Family Archives and Convent Schooling: Two Case Studies

Documents in these families illustrate aspects of life in eighteenth-century convent schools. These are rare, chance survivals which allow readers to approach the lived experience of schooling and to begin to understand how families made choices regarding girls' education. Space permits only brief consideration; nevertheless, they reveal a range of experiences from the latter part of the exile period.

The Huddleston Family

The Huddleston family owned an estate and a substantial country house at Sawston, near Cambridge. Ten Huddleston girls attended the school run by the Augustinian Canonesses at Bruges between 1688 and 1781, and at least four moved to school in Paris in the 1780s.[63] Four Huddleston women were professed as choir nuns at Bruges and could provide support which might serve to soften the school experience for individual pupils. Letters from Sister Justina Huddleston (d. 1787) reveal the importance of having family members at hand for girls boarding far from home.[64] Furthermore, the

[61] Ibid. 28–9.

[62] Ibid. 29–32.

[63] Names from the typescript list in Bruges, Archives of the Priory of Nazareth; Cambridge, Cambridgeshire Archives, Huddleston Papers (hereafter: CA, HP), Correspondence, MS 488/C1; five of these letters edited by Victoria Van Hyning appear in Bowden, ed., *English Convents in Exile*, 3: 295–306. For the nuns, see 'Who were the Nuns?'

[64] For Justina Huddleston, see 'Who were the Nuns?', BA113.

letters demonstrate that Sister Justina enjoyed the contact, to the extent of keeping an eye out for her great-nieces even after they left Bruges, reporting back to their parents on their academic progress and manners. Outside the convent, the young Huddlestons, both girls and boys, were taken under the wing of their aunt, Mary Bostock, who lived in Paris and acted *in loco parentis* while they were at school. Mary Bostock took care of Polly when it was decided she should change schools and her husband acted as an interim teacher so that Polly's progress should not be lost. He commented on Polly's French: 'Our neice Polly's French letter is in a manner entirely her own, with but little correction on my [part] I wish I may be able to bring her to a more regular formed hand-writing, & at the same time that it may become a more free, easy hand-writing.'[65]

Polly was taken away from the convent school at Bruges on the grounds that she was unhappy there, and sent to the Augustinian school in Paris.[66] Mrs Bostock reported her opinion on schools in Paris compared with Bruges:

> my brother in his letter to Mr B says he hopes Jenny[']s education here will not exceed 40 pounds a year[.][67] I fear it will come to much more, the pension is not more then in Flanders, what runs away with the money is the masters who are paid very high endead, the same dancing master who is as he ought to be for his price a very good one teaches all the young ladys in their schole, the other masters wee have desired may be got as reasonable as possible. The French master wanted each a guinea a month but, how ever he [h]as agread to take that for both of them, these are all the masters they have at present. Polly wishes to learn to paint in water colours & wee are desirious she should, musick she does not seem to have much turn for, Jenny has learnd to draw at Bruges[.] she wishes to have a master to continue to learn that & allso her musick[.] every one seems to think she will have a strong good voice, on the other side I will give you a list of the prices of all the masters which the superior Mrs Lancaster[68] gave me for your

[65] Cambridge, CA, HP, MS 488/C1/MH18, postscript to letter of Mary Bostock, 3 March 1784.

[66] Polly's name appears in the register of pupils for 1778.

[67] Forty pounds (if it is sterling) was considerably more than the cost of attending other convent schools at that time, which was typically £20–25.

[68] Frances Louisa Lancaster (1750–1808), superior at the Augustinian Convent, Paris, professed 1765: 'Who were the Nuns?', PA100.

> information & then you can determine whither you chuse Jenny should learn the musick & the drawing[.] their cousin who is now with us tells me the nuns doe not chuse to take more young ladys then a limited number that they can attend properly too, that several have been refused, but th[at] Mrs Lancaster told her she would not refuse any of the Huddlestons. It is a house where they are clever & therefore very desireable, very expensive to be sure, but you will have some thing for your money, whereas at Bruges laterly you have had very little[.] their schole is crouded with Flemish dowdys & the time takeing up in teaching them English, their duty excepted they learn very little … .[69]

I have quoted at length because the letter makes some significant points about convent schooling. We see how pupils moved between schools, the importance of the masters who taught the extras, what the extras were, comparative costs and evidence of considerable care being taken over the choice of school. Members of the Huddleston family were aware of variations in the quality of teaching across the schools and were trying to make informed decisions.

Once Polly and Jenny were at school in Paris with the Augustinians, they were allowed out of the convent on occasion for expeditions. One letter they wrote home reported that the mother superior had allowed them to go to an exhibition of pictures and to see a procession of a hundred captives redeemed from Algiers, still wearing the same clothes they had worn on their release at Marseille.[70] The letters that Huddleston school girls wrote in English to their parents suggest that the teaching that they received allowed them to write fluently and easily. They wrote affectionately about their families and all of them married after they left school. Convent schooling seems to have broadened their experiences and expanded their horizons.

Harriet Goldie (1781–1845)

Two years before she died, Harriet Goldie began writing a memoir of her childhood and her days at two convent schools, which she entitled

[69] Cambridge, CA, HP, MS 488/C1/MH19, Mary Bostock to her sister, 8 July 1784. The nuns were all too aware of Joseph II's policies towards contemplative convents, which he ordered to be closed on the ground that they were not useful. The prioress took in more Flemish pupils (called here 'dowdys') partly to demonstrate the importance of the service they provided to local people.

[70] Ibid., MS 488/C1/MH68, Mary Huddleston to her mother, 29 October 1785.

'Days of Yore'.[71] The manuscript is thought to have been destroyed during World War II, but fortunately a typescript had already been made. The memoir provides rare personal insights into one girl's experience of convent schooling at the end of the eighteenth century. Harriet (also known as Henrietta) was the daughter of a Protestant Edinburgh banker and his wife Sophia Macdowell. Mr Goldie died in 1785, when the children were still very young, and their mother took Harriet and her brother George to live in the country outside Edinburgh, where she taught them herself. In 1788, the Goldies went to stay with Catholic friends, Cecilia and Gerard Strickland at Sizergh Castle, Westmorland.[72] Following the death of her first husband, Charles Strickland, in 1770, Cecilia had decided to educate her daughter in convent schools. Mary Cecilia was sent in 1772 to the Bar Convent, York, then to the Poor Clares at Rouen, and finally from 1778 to the Sepulchrines at Liège for four years.[73] Through the Stricklands, Mrs Goldie became interested in the Catholic faith and, perhaps influenced by her friend's experience of the school, decided around 1790 to take her children to the Poor Clares at Rouen, where the family were, one after another, received into the Catholic Church. Harriet attended lessons in the convent and also took extra classes outside. The nuns taught the girls catechism and religious studies; feminine accomplishments were gained from masters and, together with her brother George, Harriet also undertook more advanced studies with other masters in the town. Harriet wrote that there were about fifteen or twenty students in the school, English, French and Portuguese.

In a somewhat haphazard fashion Harriet managed to learn a range of subjects and skills: Latin (with her brother), French translation, dancing, plain work and music, including the harp, piano and singing. Harriet's experience indicates the individuality of convent education at this period. She benefited from the presence of her mother and brother in Rouen, and from her mother's determination to facilitate her studies and expand her educational opportunities. The Goldies were caught

[71] I am indebted to Mark Goldie for introducing me to this important document and for allowing me to read his personal copy and make extensive notes; he is currently editing the memoir for publication. No page references are given because of the document's internal pagination complications.

[72] For the Strickland family, see also p. 185–6 above.

[73] Mary Cecilia (1766–1817), daughter of Charles Strickland and Cecilia Townley: Hornyold, *Genealogical Memoirs*, 171–2.

up in the events of the French Revolution and endured imprisonment with the nuns in the convent, but they were able to return to England in December 1794. Mrs Goldie spent the first months of 1795 trying to find suitable schools for her children. After visiting several, she decided to send Harriet to the Sepulchrine school newly opened at Dean House, outside Salisbury. Although Harriet was writing fifty years later, she clearly differentiates her year with the Sepulchrines from her time in Rouen, making clear the difference between schooling with a primary religious focus and the revised curriculum of the Sepulchrines following Christina Dennett's reforms.[74] Dean House continued the broader curriculum brought from Liège, which was more suited to those who had no intention of entering the convent as nuns. Harriet was its first pupil,[75] and in her memoir she recorded her time and the members of the community with affection. Mother Agatha Laurenson, responsible for the school, was clearly highly educated and determined to develop her pupils' learning.[76] Harriet comments on how clever Mother Laurenson was, knowing five languages, teaching interesting history, writing a new history text book for them[77] and showing Harriet how to make presentations. These (as in the Mary Ward schools) were regarded as part of the learning process and were performed by pupils to important visitors such as potential parents and benefactors.

Conclusion

These two case studies illustrate the points made earlier regarding the individuality of the experience of convent education during this period and the ways in which families and nuns adapted the programmes on offer. Girls from these families made the most of their opportunities and wanted more than devotional reading and catechism, needlework and feminine accomplishments from their schooling: others had very different attitudes and experiences. These girls had parents who recognized the importance of education for girls, sought advice and chose institutions that were recommended to them. We see how each pupil's

[74] *New Hall Community*, 58, 121, 122.
[75] Colchester, ACHS, MS M1, 'Young Ladies who entered as Pensioners'.
[76] Mary Agatha Laurenson (1774–1834): 'Who were the Nuns?', LS131.
[77] Published anonymously as *A General History of Modern Europe, being from the Beginning of the Sixteenth Century to the Year 1854*, 4th edn (London, 1854).

timetable could be tailor-made according to parental wishes; but we can see also that this was expensive and thus beyond the reach of many families. Even the two boarding schools in England were too expensive for many parents, although travel costs were lower. The level of parental involvement in their daughter's schooling in these examples is considerable, and it is hard to imagine that this could be widely replicated, given the complications of cross-Channel contacts and arrangements.

The case studies illustrate a range of variables. There is the initially Protestant Goldie family, headed by a widow, all three of whom converted to Catholicism while Harriet was attending school in Rouen. The Huddleston correspondence shows the transnational contacts made by Polly, Jenny, Harriet and Charlotte through their encounters with local fellow pupils at Bruges. The case studies bear witness to the broad curriculum introduced for girls at the schools of the Canonesses and the Mary Ward Sisters, rather than schooling which focused primarily on religious instruction. These girls were sent away in their teenage years, suggesting their mothers were responsible for their early childhood education and upbringing. Like many convent schoolgirls, none of these girls entered religious life, and Harriet Goldie never married. The evidence shows mothers closely involved in the choice of school and Mrs Goldie (unusually) accompanying her daughter to Rouen; other children were sent over with chaperones. This was possibly due to her circumstances as a widow and her interest in receiving religious instruction. Other parents chose to travel from England to visit their children when they were at school abroad.[78]

Taken overall, the evidence demonstrates that convent schooling for English girls could be made to fit a range of aspirations and appears to have been very flexible to suit parental wishes. It has also been argued that, in a survey of convent schooling for English girls, it is important to include girls who attended the French Ursuline boarding schools. The Mary Ward Sisters' schools at Hammersmith and York, operating through much of the exile period in spite of the penal laws, provided education with a formal structure and a broad syllabus for girls in schools nearer at hand, representing schooling that would provide Catholic girls with similar opportunities to those then available in Protestant schools. Christina Dennett's

[78] See, for example, accounts of parental visits in Frank Tyrer, ed., *The Great Diurnal of Nicholas Blundell*, 2: *1712–1719*, Record Society of Lancashire and Cheshire 112 (Chester, 1970), 172–205, July 1716–August 1717.

reforms at Liège enabled the Sepulchrine school to flourish and to establish a successful school when they migrated to England. Piecing together sources over this long timespan, we can start to uncover what is meant by convent schooling during the exile period. The aim here has been to provide enough pointers to suggest directions for future research and to introduce readers both to individuals who experienced life in convent schools and to some of the members of convents who were influential in managing them. Set against a backdrop of penal laws intended to prevent the survival of Catholicism, the creation of girls' schools on this scale is a remarkable achievement. The easing of the application of the penal laws in the eighteenth century and changes in attitudes towards girls' schooling are reflected in the growth in size of Catholic schools and reforms in their curricula that gave rise to the experiences described in the case studies.

Appendix: Foundations of English Convents, grouped by Order

Those known to have schools are marked*.

*Louvain, Augustinian Canonesses, 1609, arrived in England 1794.
*Bruges, Augustinian Canonesses, 1629, in England 1794–1802, still in Bruges.
*Paris, Augustinian Canonesses, 1634, in Paris until 1911.

*Liège, Sepulchrine Canonesses, 1642, arrived in England 1794.

*Gravelines, Poor Clares, *c.*1606, arrived in England 1795.
*Dunkirk, Poor Clares, 1625 (temporary), 1652 (permanently) from Gravelines, arrived in England 1795.
*Aire, Poor Clares, 1629, offshoot of Gravelines, arrived in England 1799.
*Rouen, Poor Clares, 1644 from Gravelines, arrived in England 1795.

*Brussels, Franciscans, 1619, to Nieuport 1637, to Bruges 1662, arrived in England 1794.
*Paris, Franciscans / Conceptionists ('Blue Nuns'), 1659, arrived in England by 1799, died out 1838.

*Brussels, Dominicans, 1660, arrived in England 1794.

*Brussels, Benedictines, 1599, arrived in England 1794.
*Cambrai, Benedictines, 1623, arrived in England 1795.
*Ghent, Benedictines, 1624, from Brussels, arrived in England 1794.
Paris, Benedictines, 1653, from Cambrai, arrived in England 1795.
*Pontoise, Benedictines, *c.*1658, started in Boulogne 1652, offshoot of Ghent, closed 1786.
*Dunkirk, Benedictines, 1662, from Ghent, arrived in England 1795.
Ypres, Benedictines, 1665, became Irish convent and remained until 1914.

Antwerp, Carmelites, 1618/19, arrived in England 1794.
Lierre, Carmelites, 1648, from Antwerp, arrived in England 1794.
Hoogstraten, Carmelites, 1678, from Antwerp, arrived in England 1795; some left in 1790 to found a convent in Maryland.

*St Omer, Mary Ward Sisters, 1609, suppressed 1630/1.
*Liège, Mary Ward Sisters, 1616, suppressed 1630/1.
*Paris, Mary Ward Sisters, 1650–1705.
*Hammersmith, Mary Ward Sisters, 1669–1795.
*York, Bar Convent, Mary Ward Sisters, 1686, still open.

Lisbon, Bridgettines, 1594. The Bridgettines were the only community founded before the Reformation (at Syon). They returned to England under Mary Tudor and went into exile a second time in 1558, moving round the Southern Netherlands, and then leaving for Rouen in 1580. Most returned from Lisbon to England in 1809.

Preachers or Teachers? Parish Priests and their Sermons in the Late Enlightenment Habsburg Empire

Alena A. Fidlerová*
Charles University, Prague

*This article explores the role parish priests were expected to play in educating the populace of the Habsburg empire at the end of the eighteenth century, and especially how this was manifested in the form and content of their sermons. Emperor Joseph II took a keen interest in the education of future priests and expected them to be good shepherds (*pastores boni*) and educators to their parishioners. To this end, together with his mother, he carried out several reforms in their education (such as changing theology faculty curricula, introducing pastoral theology as a new subject and establishing general seminaries) and even issued a special decree on 4 February 1783, providing detailed instructions for preachers. The article outlines how future priests were taught to educate their parishioners through their sermons, concentrating on how they followed these instructions in their homiletic practice, which changed the form and content of sermons radically. It is based on archival material concerning the education of future priests (such as court decrees, governmental orders and university curricula), pastoral theology textbooks used at the Prague faculty of theology, and selected printed sermons.*

Throughout the history of the Christian Church, the spiritual education of parishioners through preaching and catechesis has been one of the priest's principal duties. However, the conception of what pertains to such education, how it should be achieved, the relative importance of the sermon within it and the sermon's desired form and content varied greatly. The three traditional canonical goals of persuasion were those of *docere*, *movere* and *delectare* (teaching, moving and delighting).[1] The Enlightenment period brought about an important

* Pod Pekařkou 31, 14700 Praha 4, Czech Republic. E-mail: alena.fidlerova@ff.cuni.cz.
This article was prepared with support from the Grant Agency of the Czech Republic, project 17-06507S, 'Bohemical Hagiography of Czech Saints from Tridentine to Enlightenment Reforms', and the Charles University project Progres Q09, 'History: Key for the Understanding of the Global World'.

[1] For their classical origin, see, for example, Cicero, *Brutus* 185.

Studies in Church History 55 (2019), 205–224
doi: 10.1017/stc.2018.28

change: the Baroque style of preaching, with its predilection for *movere* with the help of *delectare*, still survived,[2] but it made way for a new style, focusing on *docere* (and by means of it, *movere*); the emphasis on salvation and eternal life (or eternal punishment) was replaced by a focus on the earthly life of a Christian as a loyal subject aware of his or her duties.[3] Combined with the changing concept of a parish priest and the character of eighteenth-century culture, portrayed by Karl Barth as a culture of pedagogy prone to perceiving the church as an educational institution (*Erziehungsanstalt*),[4] this made the preacher virtually a teacher of adults.

This article explores the new role parish priests were expected to play in educating the masses in the Cisleithanian part of the Habsburg empire[5] at the end of the eighteenth century, concentrating on how change manifested itself in the required and actual form and content of clerical sermons, as compared with previous Baroque practice[6] and especially the *concetto* or 'metaphysical' preaching style.[7]

[2] According to John W. O'Malley, the emphasis on *movere* is typical for the Jesuit tradition: *The First Jesuits* (Cambridge, MA, 1993), 96. *Delectare* was emphasized, for example, by the Austrian Augustinian preacher Abraham a Santa Clara (1644–1709): Udo Sträter et al., 'Predigt', in Grigor Kalivoda et al., ed., *Historisches Wörterbuch der Rhetorik*, 12 vols (Tübingen, 1992–2015), 7: 45–96, at 86–7.

[3] For the general characteristics of Baroque and Enlightenment homiletics, see Johann Baptist Schneyer, *Geschichte der katholischen Predigt* (Freiburg, 1969), especially 267–302, 305–26; Werner Schütz, *Geschichte der christlichen Predigt* (Berlin and New York, 1972), especially 140–5, 159–71; Joris van Eijnatten, 'Reaching Audiences: Sermons and Oratory in Europe', in Stewart J. Brown and Timothy Tackett, eds, *CHC*, 7: *Enlightenment, Reawakening and Revolution 1660–1815* (Cambridge, 2008), 128–46; O. C. Edwards Jr, 'Varieties of Sermon: A Survey of Preaching in the Long Eighteenth Century', in Joris van Eijnatten, ed., *Preaching, Sermon and Cultural Change in the Long Eighteenth Century* (Leiden and Boston, MA, 2009), 3–53, especially 5–11; Sträter et al., 'Predigt', 65–96.

[4] Karl Barth, *Die protestantische Theologie im 19. Jahrhundert. Ihre Vorgeschichte und ihre Geschichte* (Zürich, 1947), 41, 43.

[5] Cisleithania was an unofficial designation for the northern and western parts of the Habsburg empire, partly divided from the Hungarian lands (Transleithania) by the river Leitha.

[6] For the characteristics of various preaching styles and types of Baroque homiletics, see Hilary Dansey Smith, *Preaching in the Spanish Golden Age: A Study of some Preachers of the Reign of Philip III* (Oxford, 1978); Peter Bayley, *French Pulpit Oratory 1598–1650: A Study in Themes and Styles with a Descriptive Catalog of Printed Texts* (Cambridge, 1980).

[7] About *concetto* rhetoric, see Florence Vuilleumier, 'Les conceptismes', in Marc Fumaroli, ed., *Histoire de la rhétorique dans l'Europe moderne* (Paris, 1999), 517–37; Mercedes Blanco, *Les Rhétoriques de la pointe. Baltasar Gracián et le conceptisme en Europe* (Geneva, 1992).

It is based on an analysis of state legislation concerning the tasks and education of priests, and explores the changes in content of this education, as manifested in the legislation and in selected printed sermons. The article focuses specifically on Bohemia and Moravia, and in particular on curriculum changes at the University of Prague, the textbooks used there and the Czech sermons given by clerical alumni. The results can be taken as typical for the whole Cisleithanian part of the empire because individual provinces were expected to follow closely the legal and educational guidelines imposed by Vienna. Developments in the empire, however, differed significantly from those in other European countries, due to the specific character of the Austro-Habsburg Enlightenment; this was introduced from above, took root relatively late and only reached its most characteristic form (known as Josephinism) in the last decades of the eighteenth century.[8] The homiletical principles within these developments are still largely *terra incognita*. Not only is this topic under-researched in general,[9] but there is even less consideration of how peasants and townspeople rather than educated elites were addressed. Moreover, the sociocultural situation of the Czech-speaking population in this period means that Czech sermons represent precisely this least researched branch of homiletics.

The goal of the article is twofold. First, it aims to introduce the late Enlightenment sermon as a valuable subject of study for the history of both homiletics and education. Due to the common misconception that the Enlightenment was essentially secular,[10] and that its late, full-fledged phase tended to be derivative and thus uninteresting,[11] the sermons of this period have rarely been studied.[12] However, Czech

[8] About Josephinism, see Eduard Winter, *Der Josefinismus. Die Geschichte des österreichischen Reformkatholisizmus* (Berlin, 1962).

[9] Literature on Enlightenment homiletics does not generally mention any preachers from the Habsburg empire, irrespective of the language(s) they used. The only brief account mentioning some German-language sermons I could find was Rainer Bendel, 'Liturgie, Predigt und Gebet', in Michael Pammer, ed., *Handbuch der Religionsgeschichte im deutschsprachigen Raum*, 6: *1750–1900* (Paderborn, 2007), 133–57, at 144–51.

[10] Sträter et al., 'Predigt', 75; Pasi Ihalainen, 'The Enlightenment Sermon: Towards Practical Religion and a Sacred National Community', in van Eijnatten, ed., *Preaching, Sermon and Cultural Change*, 219–60.

[11] Barth, *Die protestantische Theologie*, 146.

[12] Of the specialized works, the most important is Reinhard Krause, *Die Predigt der späten deutschen Aufklärung (1770 –1805)* (Stuttgart, 1965). Besides this, there are studies of outstanding figures such as Franz Volkmar Reinhard, by Christian-Erdmann Schott,

Catholic Enlightenment sermons not only played an important role in popular education but were also the heralds of a cultural reorientation of the Czech Lands from a southern to a western European model which represented an early instance of the convergence of Catholic and Protestant religious cultures after the period of confessionalization.[13] Second, the article goes beyond existing methodological approaches to the question of homiletics as education. So far, published homiletic texts have mostly formed the primary subject of such research, together with major theoretical works of famous preachers. I shall argue that in addition to, and to some extent even preceding, analysis of these texts, legal regulations and the education of future priests must be taken into account. These shaped the sermons profoundly; what looks like a spontaneous change in preaching style may in fact represent their influence. This article therefore addresses the theme of church and education in two ways: in addition to describing the role of priests in the education of their parishioners through their sermons, it also discusses the role of university homiletical education in enabling future priests to fulfil this task. Undoubtedly, other archival sources such as visitation records or priests' diaries could contribute further to the picture, but there is not space for this here. The contemporaneous development of Czech Protestant homiletics must also be set aside. During the Baroque period, only the Catholic church was officially permitted to function in the Habsburg empire. Although (some) non-Catholic denominations were finally legalized by the Toleration Patent of 1781, their communities were scattered and weak, and their clergy were not educated at Czech universities; consequently, they had little opportunity to influence their Catholic contemporaries.

Möglichkeiten und Grenzen der Aufklärungspredugt, dargestellt am Beispiel Franz Volkmar Reinhards (Göttingen, 1978); or Johann Michael Sailer, by Chrisostomus Schreiber, *Aufklärung und Frömmigkeit. Die katholische Predigt im deutschen Aufklärungszeitalter und ihre Stellung zur Frömmigkeit und zur Liturgie. Mit Berücksichtigung von Johann Michael Sailer* (Munich, 1940).

[13] I use here the concept of confessionalization defined as a complicated process through which the adherents of Lutheran, Reformed and Catholic confessions developed distinct confessional cultures with a strong sense of group identity, active popular piety and strong churchly character (*Kirchlichkeit*): see Marc R. Forster, 'With and without Confessionalization: Varieties of Early Modern German Catholicism', *JEMH* 1 (1997), 315–43; idem, *Catholic Revival in the Age of the Baroque: Religious Identity in Southwest Germany, 1550–1750* (Cambridge, 2004).

State Regulations concerning Preaching and Preacher Education

According to Barth, eighteenth-century Christianity sought to transform theology in four respects: to make it state-controlled, bourgeois or moralistic, scientific or philosophical, and individual or interiorized.[14] Although Barth made this observation about German Protestantism, it also holds true generally for the reform Catholicism championed by the enlightened Habsburg monarchs Maria Theresa and (especially) Joseph II. Among other changes, these developments brought about a shift in the concept of the priest. In accordance with the Josephinian concept of the state church,[15] the priest was now understood as a civil servant. Even though he was still answerable to his bishop or the superior of his religious order, these were answerable to the monarch rather to Rome in all issues except questions of faith.[16] The dissolution of numerous monasteries, the reform of parish organization and a series of educational reforms strengthened the position of the secular priest at the expense of the monastic clergy. His main duties now included the promotion of 'modern' religious views (tolerance, morality, ethics), of agricultural, hygienic or medical improvements,[17] of civic virtues and of obedience to the state. The parish priest was to educate his parishioners and to influence not only their religious beliefs but also the practical aspects of their lives.[18]

However, not everybody in the empire subscribed to the new approach. The dissolution of the Jesuit order in 1773 facilitated these changes because it was no longer necessary to negotiate educational reforms with the Societas Jesu,[19] but less progressive clergy and

[14] Barth, *Die protestantische Theologie*, 65.

[15] Cf. Max Vögler, 'Religion und Politik', in Pammer, ed., *Handbuch der Religionsgeschichte*, 6: 59–101, at 63–5.

[16] Karl Otmar Freiherr von Aretin, 'Einleitung', in idem, ed., *Der Aufgeklärte Absolutismus* (Köln, 1974), 11–51, at 33.

[17] For example, from 1804 priests in the empire were obliged to preach several times a year about the beneficial effects of vaccination: Rainer Bendel, 'Liturgie, Predigt und Gebet', 146–7.

[18] See Jiljí Chládek, *Počátkowé Opatrnosti Pastýřské* (Prague, 1780/1), 29–30, Knihopis K03309, Knihopis = KPS – Knihopis Database, online at: <http://www.knihopis.cz/knihopis-eng.html>.

[19] Compare the objections of Jesuit provincials against the 1752 reforms of the gymnasia summarized in Karl Wotke, *Das oesterreichische Gymnasium im Zeitalter Maria Theresias*, 1: *Texte nebst Erläuterungen*, Monumenta Germaniae paedagogica 30 (Berlin, 1905), xv–xvi.

laity still had to be educated to adopt the reforms. This could not be achieved by means of school reforms alone, because it was not only children and young people who were to be educated in this way; the edification of adults was also necessary. Since adults no longer attended school (if they ever had) and most of them did not read edifying periodicals or books regularly (if at all), the only people to whom this task could be entrusted were parish priests. Their main vehicle was the sermon. Consequently, directives regarding their education as preachers and their subsequent preaching activities were some of the most prominent aspects of legislation and school reform.

It is well known that Joseph II took a keen personal interest in the work and education of parish priests.[20] Using diverse types of state regulations such as court decrees (*Hofdekret*), governmental orders (*Gubernialverordnung*) and patents (*Patent*), the education of future priests and their pastoral work were defined by precise rules. Some of these decrees explicitly referred to the preachers as 'teachers of the people' (*Lehrer des Volks*, *Volkslehrer*),[21] thus indicating the general context for their activities. In a court decree of 4 February 1783, the emperor provided detailed instructions for preachers. These were mostly concerned with the specific topics to be treated in sermons ('unnecessary doctrinal controversies' were banned, as was speaking out against state laws and regulations), but some were more general. Preachers were advised to stick to the truth of the gospel, to avoid any ambiguous expressions or inappropriate allusions and not to include unnecessary, incidental themes. The practical teaching of Christianity, together with its application in daily life, was to be covered every year, in an appropriate order. The sermon should not only enlighten the minds of its hearers, but should also (and primarily) improve their hearts, sowing and promoting virtue. To achieve this goal, preachers should 'in their sermons, especially in rural areas, adopt the tone of a friendly discussion rather than that of an orator'.[22]

[20] Winter, *Der Josefinismus*, 123–4.
[21] Court decree, 7 October 1784: Peter Karl Jaksch, *Gesetzlexikon im Geistlichen, Religions- und Toleranzsache, wie auch in Güter-, Stiftungs-, Studien- und Zensursachen für das Königreich Böhmen von 1601 bis Ende 1800. Aus den Originalakten des k. k. Gubernialarchivs ausgezogen und geordnet*, 6 vols (Prague, 1828), 4: 509; court decree, 28 December 1788: ibid. 527.
[22] 'In den Predigten, besonders auf dem Lande, mehr den Ton eines freundschaftlichen Gespräches, als eines Redners annehmen': ibid. 507–8.

A number of court decrees related to the curricula of theological faculties and general seminaries.[23] These stipulated that candidates for the priesthood were to be trained in homiletics, not only theoretically but also through practical exercises in their classes[24] and occasional preaching in the seminary church under the guidance of its rector.[25] Although theoretical education was deemed important – only those who had successfully completed their courses in biblical studies, dogmatic theology, morals and homiletics were to be allowed to preach[26] – practical exercises and the emulation of appropriate models were not to be neglected, either during or after the young men's studies. This can be seen from a court decree of 28 December 1788,[27] which listed the works to be read and followed by young priests in the 'priests' houses' (*Priesterhäuser*) where they were expected to live between completion of their seminary studies and appointment to their first position. Besides the Church Fathers, these included French neo-classical Catholic homileticians (Louis Bourdaloue, Jean-Baptiste Massillon and Guillaume de Segaud), contemporary German Protestants (Johann Lorenz von Mosheim) and English Anglicans (John Tillotson), together with late eighteenth-century German Protestant Enlightenment preachers known as the neologians (*Neologen*; Johann Friedrich Wilhelm Jerusalem, Johann Joachim Spalding and Georg Joachim Zollikofer). The high proportion of contemporary non-Catholic preachers offered as models differed significantly from previous practice, but this was not illogical, because these preachers and theologians counted Jacques-Bénigne Bossuet, Bourdaloue and Massillon

[23] General seminaries were centrally established schools for the education of all future Catholic priests, which replaced a variety of monastery and episcopal schools and were managed by the emperor himself. They were established by the decree of 30 March 1783, with teaching commencing that November, and abolished shortly after the emperor's death in 1790. The students were to enter them after completing their philosophical studies, and were to complete a six-year theological course and one year of practical training: Winter, *Der Josefinismus*, 134–62.

[24] A court decree of 1 June 1779 gives detailed instructions for class exercises: Jaksch, *Gesetzlexikon*, 4: 512–13.

[25] Court decree, 7 October 1784: ibid. 509.

[26] Governmental order, 18 July 1800: ibid. 510. Rhetoric is not mentioned here, because it was taught at secondary school (gymnasium) and in the philosophical faculty, but not in the faculty of theology or the general seminary.

[27] Ibid. 527.

among their models,[28] and in their preaching they put emphasis on themes deemed accessible to their audiences and morally and practically edifying.[29] The reliance of Joseph II on Protestant models in his fight against Baroque piety was clear to his contemporaries,[30] and his sympathies with the neologians may have been strengthened by their support for religious tolerance and the existing social order.[31] However, whilst both the imperial decree and the neologians refer to preachers as teachers of religion, sometimes in quite similar terms,[32] their approaches are not identical. Habsburg legislation saw the preacher's position as closer to that of the school teacher, inasmuch as both were understood predominantly as civil servants answerable to the state. For the neologians, in contrast, the idea of the educator was closer to that of the preacher and acquired part of the preacher's dignity: 'The term "teacher" has never achieved such high standing as in this period'.[33]

The Habsburg court decrees show that, unlike in other periods, the education and activities of Enlightenment preachers in the empire were regulated directly by state legislation which was based on and recommended not only Catholic but also Protestant models. These directives shaped the education of future priests, to which we now turn.

Pastoral Theology at the University of Prague and Instruction in Homiletics

Both during the co-regency of Joseph II with his mother Maria Theresa and during Joseph's own reign, several reforms of priestly education were carried out. The most important was launched in 1774, after the dissolution of the Jesuit order which until then had

[28] Krause, *Die Predigt*, 15.
[29] Albrecht Beutel, *Kirchengeschichte im Zeitalter der Aufklärung* (Göttingen, 2009), 114.
[30] Fritz Valjavec, *Der Josephinismus. Zur geistigen Entwicklung Österreichs im achzehnten und neunzehnten Jahrhundert*, 2nd edn (Munich, 1945), 106–8.
[31] Werner Schütz, 'Die Kanzel als Katheder der Aufklärung', *Wolffenbütteler Studien zur Aufklärung* 1 (1974), 137–71, at 147–8, 153–4.
[32] For example, both Johann Otto Thieß (*Anleitung zur Amtsberedsamkeit der öffentlichen Religionslehrer des neunzehnten Jahrhunderts* [Altona, 1801], 50–3, 175) and this decree (Jaksch, *Gesetzlexikon*, 4: 527) emphasized that the preacher should be a teacher of the people, teaching 'in a popular way'.
[33] 'Nie wieder hat das Wort Lehrer einen so hohen Rang bekommen wie in dieser Zeit': Schütz, 'Die Kanzel', 143.

controlled faculties of theology and philosophy.[34] The proposal for the reform of theological studies, entitled *Entwurf einer besseren Einrichtung theologischer Schulen in den k. k. Erblanden* (*Draft of an improved Establishment of Theological Schools in the Monarchical Imperial Dominions*), was drafted by Franz Stephan Rautenstrauch (1734–85), Benedictine abbot at Břevnov and Broumov and director of the faculty of theology in Prague and later in Vienna.[35] From our point of view, its most important innovation was the establishment of a new subject of study: pastoral theology, comprising instruction in pedagogy (catechesis, homiletics and private instruction), the administration of the sacraments and the exemplary life of a priest.[36] This is not to suggest that homiletics had not been taught before, but it had been treated as a branch of rhetoric, as the art of speaking ornately and convincingly, rooted in a gift of God rather than human instruction.[37] Now, homiletics was set apart from general rhetoric as a teachable and learnable set of rules belonging to pastoral care, and more specifically to its pedagogical aspect.

In Prague, the language both of instruction and of textbooks of pastoral theology varied during the last decades of the eighteenth century and the first decades of the nineteenth. From 1775/6, Franz

[34] Josef Petráň, *Nástin dějin Filozofické fakulty Univerzity Karlovy v Praze (do roku 1948)* (Prague, 1983), 83–94; Marie Pavlíková and Ivana Čornejová, 'Filozofická fakulta', in Ivana Čornejová, ed., *Dějiny Univerzity Karlovy II, 1622–1802* (Prague, 1996), 102–5. See also Ivo Cerman, 'The Enlightenment Universities', in idem, Rita Krueger and Susan Reynolds, eds, *The Enlightenment in Bohemia: Religion, Morality and Multiculturalism* (Oxford, 2011), 55–67; Harm Klueting, 'The Catholic Enlightenment in Austria or the Habsburg Lands', in Ulrich L. Lehner and Michael Printy, eds, *A Companion to the Catholic Enlightenment in Europe* (Leiden, 2010), 127–64, at 138–9.

[35] Vienna, 1782; 2nd revised edn 1784. A brief synopsis was published as [Franz Stephan Rautenstrauch], *Theologiae pastoralis et polemicae delineatio tabellis proposita* (Vienna, 1778); and [idem], *Tabellarischer Grundriß der in deutscher Sprache vorzutragenden Pastoraltheologie* (Vienna, 1778), repr. as [idem], 'Tabellarischer Grundriß der Pastoraltheologie', in Josef Dobrovský, ed., *Böhmische und mährische Litteratur auf das Jahr 1780*, 2/i (Prague, 1780), 12–25. For Rautenstrauch, see Alois Kříšťan, *Počátky pastorální teologie v českých zemích* (Prague, 2004), 34–9; Karel Beránek, 'Teologická fakulta', in Čornejová, ed., *Dějiny Univerzity Karlovy II*, 69–98, at 94–5.

[36] For the beginnings of pastoral theology in Prague, see Kříšťan, *Počátky*. See also Josef Müller, *Der pastoraltheologisch-didaktische Ansatz in Franz Stephan Rautenstrauchs 'Entwurf zur Einrichtung der theologischen Schulen'* (Vienna, 1969).

[37] This opinion was shared by the neo-classicists and the advocates of *concetto*: see, for example, the textbook by the Czech Jesuit Bohuslav Balbín, *Verisimilia humaniorum disciplinarum seu Judicium privatum de omni litterarum (quas humaniores appellant) artificio* (Prague, 1666), 239.

Christian Pitroff had been teaching homiletics in Latin, but between 1778/9 and 1804/5, parallel German and Czech lectures were held, the latter given by the Premonstratensian Jiljí (Aegidius) Chládek.[38] During this period, Czech and German textbooks by Pitroff, Chládek and Giftschütz were used,[39] but as they all had to conform to the framework set by Rautenstrauch's *Entwurf*, they were very similar in content. Rautenstrauch defined homiletics as 'the skill and rules for writing and preaching sermons appropriate for the education of the people', which sought to teach 'the skill of preaching in a popular manner'.[40] The term *populär* here meant preaching in such a way that the sermon achieved its main goal of instructing even the simplest members of the preacher's congregation in matters of faith and life.[41] To this end, both the content and the form of the sermon had to be adapted, imposing considerable restrictions on their complexity; however, this did not mean that such a sermon was easy to prepare.

To characterize the preaching style taught in the context of pastoral theology, I will briefly summarize selected recommendations of the textbooks. At the beginning of the relevant section, Chládek devoted a long passage to outlining the history of Christian eloquence, the nadir of which he saw in the *concetto* preaching style. He described this as a type of eloquence which had originated in Italy and Spain; in his view, it had destroyed all remnants of correct homiletics, for it preferred to quote pagan authors and secular historians and poets rather than Scripture and the Church Fathers, and sought embellishment from fables, gossip, worthless rhetorical

[38] Hermann Zschokke, *Die theologischen Studien und Anstalten der katholischen Kirche in Österreich. Aus Archivalien* (Vienna and Leipzig, 1894), 198–200; Beránek, 'Teologická fakulta', 95; Křišťan, *Počátky*, 73.

[39] Franz Christian Pitroff, *Anleitung zur praktischen Gottes Gelahrheit nach dem Entwurfe der Wiener Studien-Verbesserung verfasset, und zum Gebrauche akademischer Vorlesungen eingerichtet* (Prague, 1783 first publ. 1778/9); Chládek, *Počátkowé*; Franz Giftschütz, *Leitfaden für die in den k. k. Erblanden vorgeschriebenen deutschen Vorlesungen über die Pastoraltheologie* (Vienna, 1785); Franz Giftschütz and Václav Stach, *Počátkowé k Weřegnému w Cýs. Král. zemjch předepsanému wykládanj Pastýřské Theologie* (Prague, 1789/90), Knihopis K02705, KPS – Knihopis Database, online at: <http://www.knihopis.cz/knihopis-eng.html>.

[40] '[D]ie Art, und Regeln ..., gute, dem Volksunterrichte angemessene Predigten zu verfassen, und vorzutragen ... die Kunst ... populär zu predigen': Rautenstrauch, *Entwurf*, 106–7.

[41] Ibid. 107.

questions and witty formulations based on verbal play.[42] As the forefathers of the rebirth of homiletics, Chládek named a number of French neo-classical Catholic preachers: Bossuet, Esprit Fléschier, Bourdaloue and Massillon. He concluded by remarking that it was superfluous to mention excellent contemporary preachers by name, because students should already know them.

Pitroff and Giftschütz seem to have been less fierce opponents of the *concetto* preaching style (they do not mention it), but more in favour of contemporary Protestant developments than Chládek. They too acknowledged the French neo-classicists, and as contemporary models they recommended selected French Jesuits and Protestant adherents of the Enlightenment, most often the neologians.[43] Of these, Giftschütz in particular listed names such as Johann Andreas Cramer, August Friedrich Wilhelm Sack, Wilhelm Abraham Teller, Georg Friedrich Seiler and Friedrich Gabriel Resewitz, besides those already mentioned. The appearance of these names both in the textbooks and in the court decree of 28 December 1788 offers good evidence that the convergence of Catholic and Protestant approaches to homiletics in the Enlightenment Habsburg empire occurred at least partly as a result of an intentional educational strategy, supported by the monarch, state officials and enlightened clergy.

The heritage of classical rhetoric was not rejected in the textbooks but was adapted to their pedagogical goals. Chládek's directions as to how to prepare a sermon are divided according to the classical rhetorical scheme into *inventio*, *dispositio*, *elocutio*, *memoria* and *pronunciatio*.[44] Under *inventio*, he treats the theme or the main truth of a sermon: it should be connected to the Gospel reading of the day, suitable for the spiritual education of the congregation and easy to understand.[45] Another requirement, often not met by Baroque sermons, is that the theme be 'true', meaning provable and free of any exaggeration: for instance, instead of the theme 'St Augustine is the most learned of all saints and the greatest of all scholars', the theme 'St Augustine is a great saint and great teacher' should be chosen.[46]

[42] Chládek, *Počátkowé*, 73–116, at 81.
[43] Pitroff, *Anleitung*, 353–6; Giftschütz, *Počátkowé*, 144–8.
[44] Chládek, *Počátkowé*, 91.
[45] Ibid. 91–3.
[46] Ibid. 92.

The final requirement is that the theme be simple, consisting of one subject and one predicate only: for instance, 'repentance is necessary for salvation', rather than 'repentance and prayer are necessary for salvation'.[47] After this, the *divisio* should follow, if necessary, but it should be logical and never into more than two or three parts.[48] A fitting quotation from Scripture, illustrating the theme well, should then be chosen.[49] Finally, suitable arguments should be found which speak to both reason and will (or only to the will, if the subject is well known); these should be supported by examples. If quotations from Scripture appear here, they should normally be interpreted literally; spiritual interpretation is appropriate only if already intended by the text itself.[50] If the preacher wants to affect the will of his listeners, he should choose the strongest arguments, which concern the present rather than the future and this world rather than the next.[51] There must always be sufficient such arguments, not merely one or two, so that they may speak to the widest range of listeners.[52] The preacher should not forget to arouse passions or emotions (*affects*),[53] but only at suitable points of the sermon, for a short time, and when he himself is able to feel them.[54]

The section dealing with *dispositio* mentions the classical constituent parts of a sermon: *exordium*, *propositio*, *divisio*, *narratio*, *confirmatio*, *applicatio* and *epilogus*. Of these, *applicatio* should never be omitted, as it teaches listeners how to apply what they have heard to their daily lives.[55] The *exordium* should serve the mental preparation of the audience; at its best, it explains the Scripture text and its

[47] Ibid. 92–3.
[48] Ibid. 94–5.
[49] Ibid. 95–6.
[50] Ibid. 97.
[51] Ibid. 98.
[52] Ibid. 98–9.
[53] This requirement is usually interpreted as a 'remnant of baroque rhetorical theory' in Chládek's homiletical concept: Zdeněk Nešpor, 'Výchova kněží a jejich působení na přelomu 18. a 19. století', *Lidé města* 8/2 (2006) [online journal], at: <http://www.lidemesta.cz/archiv/cisla/8-2006-2/vychova-knezi-a-jejich-pusobeni-na-prelomu-18.-a-19.-stoleti.html>, last accessed 22 November 2018. However, it is in full agreement with Rautenstrauch's recommendations that sermons should touch listeners' hearts and capture their imagination and that the preacher should be moved himself (*selbst gerührt*): Rautenstrauch, *Entwurf*, 110–12.
[54] Chládek, *Počátkowé*, 99–102.
[55] Ibid. 102.

relation to the theme of the sermon. It should not be too long and should have a natural relation to the theme.[56] The *propositio* should be as short and as comprehensible as possible, leaving not a single unclear word unexplained.[57] Concerning argumentation, Chládek, following Erasmus, stresses that only a rhetorical, and not a philosophical, form of argumentation should be used; it is not necessary to include Latin quotations or to mention the precise location in the Bible of the texts quoted.[58] The *epilogus*, on the other hand, is where the preacher should demonstrate his strength and art, using the most powerful figures and the most unusual words. It should normally consist of repetition of what has already been said and should arouse the emotions. It should be short and adorned with appropriate figures: for repetition, *interrogatio*, *apostrophe* and *prosopopoeia* are recommended; for emotional impact, *exclamatio*, *hypotyposis* and *interrogatio* should be used.[59]

Enlightenment Sermons compared to the previous Tradition

To demonstrate the effects of this preacher education, I offer a short comparison of two Czech-language sermons preached on the feast of St Wenceslaus by two famous preachers of the time. The first, representing the *concetto*-influenced preaching typical of Czech Baroque,[60] was preached by Chrysostomus Xaverius Ignatius Táborský (1696–1748), a Premonstratensian who served as parish priest in the Moravian villages of Bohuňovice and Kněhnice.[61] It was published in his postil *Tria tabernacula in Monte Thaboreo exstructa … seu Sermones LXI. de Sanctis* (Olomouc, 1738).[62] The second was by Vojtěch Nejedlý (1772–1844), a poet of the Czech National Awakening period who served in several Czech parishes and later as

[56] Ibid. 103.
[57] Ibid. 104.
[58] Ibid. 104–7.
[59] Ibid. 109–10.
[60] Miloš Sládek, *Slovo ze srdce jejich aneb Nedělní kázání v pobělohorských bohemikálních postilách a tradiční perikopní systém* (Prague, 2017), 53. The same opinion was shared by Enlightenment critics of Czech Baroque homiletics.
[61] See Václav Pumprla, *Knihopisný slovník českých, slovenských a cizích autorů 16.–18. století* (Prague, 2010), 1106; Sládek. *Slovo ze srdce jejich*, 277–84.
[62] Knihopis K16037, KPS – Knihopis Database, online at: <http://www.knihopis.cz/knihopis-eng.html>.

dean in his native town of Žebrák.[63] This sermon was printed in Nejedlý's postil *Swátečnj Kázanj na celý rok*, vol. 2 (Prague, 1807).[64] Both Táborský and Nejedlý seem to have been above average in the level of their education and the effort they invested in their published work. The dedication and preface suggest that Táborský published his postil himself; for Nejedlý, this is confirmed by the testimony of a younger contemporary.[65] The printed versions probably were not identical with spoken versions even when (as in these cases) they were published by their authors; the spoken sermons may have been less complicated and adapted to the reactions of the listeners, and the printed texts were expanded and polished. However, the early modern version of classical rhetoric did not make 'any real distinction between written and spoken style'[66] and in their printed postils the authors endeavoured to produce texts corresponding to their concept of an ideal sermon. Thus these sermons offer exemplary material for analysis, even if parishioners did not actually hear them.

Joris van Eijnatten has commented that the *concetto* sermons typically 'exploited unusual chains of thought, antitheses, word play and novel imagery in an intricate oratorical design replete with digressions and byways'.[67] Such sermons often started with an introduction based on a question, a contrast, a comparison or a gradation; they placed the emphasis on the main proposition or *narratio*, featuring a free and varying sequence of argumentation replete with comparisons, gradations, contrasts or dialogues with moralistic applications; and they ended with a summary, an exhortation to the congregation and a prayer.[68] To show erudition and attract attention, preachers frequently adorned their sermons with Latin quotations and allusions to ancient and medieval emperors and kings, heroes, mythological and literary figures or sages and poets, quoting not only from the Bible or Church Fathers but also from other text genres, including poetry,

[63] See Mojmír Otruba, 'Nejedlý, Vojtěch', in Jiří Opelík et al., eds, *Lexikon české literatury*, 4 vols (Prague, 2000), 3/1: 461–3; Václav Pumprla, *Knihopisný slovník*, 774.
[64] Knihopis K06124, KPS – Knihopis Database, online at: <http://www.knihopis.cz/knihopis-eng.html>.
[65] Antonín Rybička, 'Vojtěch Nejedlý. Kněz a básník', in idem, ed., *Přední křisitelé národa českého*, 2 vols (Prague, 1884), 2: 315–32, at 318.
[66] W. Pierre Jacoebee, 'The Classical Sermon and the French Literary Tradition', *Australian Journal of French Studies* 19 (1982), 227–42, at 231.
[67] Van Eijnatten, 'Reaching Audiences', 140.
[68] Schneyer, *Geschichte der katholischen Predigt*, 270.

legends, and manuals of geography, natural history and medicine.[69] The goal was to help listeners 'grasp religious truths by leading them to the intended destination along unexpected paths'.[70]

On the feast of St Wenceslaus, the prince and martyr murdered by his brother in 936, and the most important Czech patron saint, venerated as the eternal ruler of the Czech Lands, every preacher was supposed to celebrate the saint in as appealing a manner as possible, usually using means such as name-giving (*nominatio*), comparison (*comparatio*) and distribution (*distributio*).[71] Táborský constructs his sermon[72] mostly around comparisons of similar and dissimilar figures, connected by the basic theme of violently spilled (innocent) blood. He starts with a sequence of nine stories about such personages from the Bible and classical and European literature and history, repeating constantly that this is not the person he is going to talk about. This rather entertaining passage, which includes stories about sensational executions and the mutilation or killing of adulterous women, also shows his erudition; in the printed version he always provides bibliographical notes. Only thereafter does he approach his main theme, the comparison of St Wenceslaus and Abel. Most of the sermon is devoted to the narration of the stories of these two men, both of whom were murdered by their brothers, supplemented with ample references to other related stories from the Bible or ancient history and mythology. In this way, the preacher demonstrated that Wenceslaus and Abel were equal in every respect except that Abel's blood had called to God for revenge, whilst that of St Wenceslaus, who had been purified in baptism and communion by contact with the blood of Jesus, calls for mercy and clemency. Táborský then appealed to his listeners to follow Wenceslaus in his mercy and generosity to widows, orphans and the poor, his quietness, his veneration of the eucharist and his humility. He finished with passionate exclamations addressing the blood of St Wenceslaus. The text is full of rhetorical questions, exclamations, direct speeches by

[69] Ibid. 270–1.

[70] Van Eijnatten, 'Reaching Audiences', 140.

[71] For characteristics of Baroque sermons for saints' days, see the afterword in Werner Welzig, *Lobrede. Katalog deutschsprachiger Heiligenpredigten in Einzeldrucken aus den Beständen der Stiftsbibliothek Klosterneuburg* (Vienna, 1989); for a short summary, see Edwards, 'Varieties of Sermon', 22–7.

[72] Chrysostomus X. I. Táborský, *Tria tabernacula in Monte Thaboreo exstructa … seu Sermones LXI. de Sanctis* (Olomouc, 1738), 799–814, with a lengthy Latin title.

individual characters, vivid descriptions, Latin quotations and exhortations to the audience.

The sermon of Vojtěch Nejedlý has a Czech title referring to St Wenceslaus as martyr and 'heir' of the Czech Lands, and begins with a quotation from Wisdom 10: 10, which affirms that the righteous are led by wisdom in right paths and shown the kingdom of God.[73] This is one of the pericopes appointed to be read on the saint's day. An introduction and two parts, indicated by the headings 'Part One' and 'Part Two', follow. The introduction announces the theme of the sermon, which is that wisdom is necessary for everybody to amend his or her life, and illustrates this theme with examples. Only biblical figures are mentioned here and no bibliographical notes (not even references to individual biblical books) are given. Wenceslaus is finally mentioned as the paragon of wisdom, and the author contemplates the question of whether everybody should strive to advance in wisdom and the means of reaching such wisdom. As the foundation of wisdom, Nejedlý identifies the daily effort to sharpen one's mind, improve one's inclinations of heart and strengthen one's virtues, illustrating this with examples from everyday life (for instance, a gardener tending a tree) and emphasizing the necessity of working hard at self-improvement. He also narrates several stories demonstrating the harmful effects of foolishness on material and physical wellbeing, especially warning against faith in superstitions and magical practices, denying the existence of witches and urging his listeners to believe in modern medical practices such as vaccination rather than magical rituals. Further, he criticizes the superficial, ritualistic Christianity of unwise people, void of real virtue and morality. Nejedlý contrasts this to the way of life of wise and virtuous people, naming his contemporary, the farmer, reeve and village scholar František Vavák, as an example. At the very end of the sermon, St Wenceslaus and his wise and virtuous deeds are mentioned briefly, together with the deeds of another wise Czech king, Charles IV. In the brief second part, Nejedlý urges parents to educate their children and send them to school, and to attend public sermons and catechetical exercises, where they can not only receive Christian education but also acquire agricultural, housekeeping and social skills; they can learn to read Scripture aloud to the members of their household and discuss what has been read, to hold discussions with old and wise people, and

[73] Vojtěch Nejedlý, *Swátečnj Kázanj na celý rok*, 2 vols (Prague, 1807), 2: 139–62.

above all to examine everything with their own reason. The sermon is written in plain, informative prose; direct speech and exclamations are rare, but there are direct appeals to the audience, rhetorical questions and quotations which are always biblical, directly illustrating the point and only in Czech. There is no prayer or exhortation at the end.

As we have seen, the goal of Táborský's sermon was to praise the saint through narrating selected episodes from his life and comparing him to other personages, and thus to move the audience to imitate his virtues. Nejedlý also aimed to improve his parishioners' souls and lives, but he chose very different means and his goal was not the same as Táborský's. Nejedlý's sermon renounced most of the techniques used by Táborský, following the prescriptions of Chládek's textbook quite closely and conforming well to the conception of Rautenstrauch and Joseph II. When using examples, Nejedlý always preferred to use them to edify rather to entertain or to astonish. His sermon was more practical and less rhetorical than required. It virtually lacked any *epilogus*, in which the author was supposed to show his skills in rhetoric. However, it provided plenty of examples from daily life, and was aimed at the education of listeners in the broadest sense (moral, religious, intellectual and practical), including not only factual information but also practical advice. All this left little space for rhetoric adornment and almost completely replaced the praise of the saint which had represented the foundation of Táborský's sermon.

Conclusion

Werner Schütz declares the Enlightenment and the sermon 'identical concepts', and the pulpit 'the teacher's desk of the Enlightenment'.[74] Pasi Ihalainen is more wary, but also stresses that sermons were 'important contribution to the Enlightenment debate and the emergence of modernity'.[75] This article has shown, using the example of Czech-language Enlightenment sermons, that this emerging modernity manifested itself in Catholic homiletics through an altered preaching style and that it was intimately connected to the changing conception of the priest. From the Baroque reverend father entitled to

[74] 'So werden Aufklärung und Predigt geradezu identische Begriffe': Schütz, 'Die Kanzel', 143.

[75] Ihalainen, 'Enlightenment Sermon', 217.

perform sacred rituals and inspire the audience to the adoration of the Almighty, the priest's role became that of a person teaching wise and virtuous living, primarily through his sermons. Thus the preacher and the school teacher, both understood as civil servants, were to perform very similar tasks, with the difference that the former was responsible for the education not merely of the youth but of all his parishioners.

To achieve this goal, a new preaching style was required, modelled on the approach of the German Protestant neologians. The transition to this style was generally neither spontaneous nor gradual, but was instilled by careful theoretical and practical university instruction in homiletics. Under its influence, young priests embraced the new approach and renounced the previous tradition, despite its literary values and possibly also its popularity with the audience. The result was a substantial unification of the form and content of sermons. These changes were supported by some enlightened members of the church hierarchy, but most importantly they were enacted by state legislation. In this 'century of education', the monarch who expected the priests to become disseminators of edification ensured that they received the necessary guidance at the beginning of, and during, their careers. Thus, in comparison to the previous period, a major change is visible in the role of the state. Although state regulation had played an important role in the period of confessionalization, during the eighteenth century in particular religious culture was 'created at the intersection of church reform, state policy, and popular needs and desires',[76] and the religious orders, parish priests and the laity often took the initiative.[77] In contrast, during the Enlightenment the monarch and his advisers influenced the activities of parish preachers directly, regardless of the opinions of the church hierarchy, religious orders or the laity. The intention of Joseph II, voiced in court decrees and other legislation, was elaborated in Rautenstrauch's *Entwurf*, which in turn was realized in the approach implemented at the faculty of theology. Consequently, the new priests were no longer living in the same religious and spiritual world as the wider population did, unlike their predecessors.[78] Their regard for the needs and preferences of common people, great as it was intended to be, did not make them willing to

[76] Forster, 'With and without Confessionalization', 343.
[77] On the important role of popular religious practice, see Forster, *Catholic Revival.*
[78] Forster, 'With and without Confessionalization', 331.

accommodate popular desires manifested in practices like pilgrimages, processions, saints' feasts or confraternities. We do not know whether the seemingly appropriate approach of their sermons was more successful than the older one, and we cannot simply assume it. Expectations of their listeners must have played a decisive role. If listeners desired moral and practical instruction and were open to new medical or agricultural developments, they were probably satisfied, but if they were looking for entertainment and deep emotional experience, they were probably disappointed.

Printed Czech Enlightenment sermons, as exemplified by that of Nejedlý, demonstrate that preaching of this period followed the requirements of textbooks and state legislation. Although still based on classical rhetoric, Nejedlý's sermon deliberately gave up many of its aspects. This does not mean that the preachers renounced all their rhetorical and literary ambitions. Perceiving themselves as teachers of the people, they strove to affect not only the reason but also the emotions of the audience, but in a dramatically different way from the *concetto* preachers as exemplified by Táborský. Instead of seasoning their sermons with fables, comic or terrifying stories and anecdotes, historical and mythological allusions or witty comparisons, they sought to catch the attention of parishioners by narrating stories close to everyday life. Instead of using rhetorical means aiming at achieving a psychosomatic reaction,[79] these sermons were increasingly aimed at the cognitive faculty. Nejedlý tried to tailor his sermon to his audience, comprising mainly common people, to catch their attention and help them to learn. In this strong emphasis on the listener and his or her needs and abilities, the closeness of Enlightenment homiletics to emerging modern pedagogy is clearly visible. The sermon thus became close to popular edifying prose with persuasive elements. In fact, this stylistic convergence may be seen as one of the factors facilitating the contemporary rise of secular prose concerning practical ethics or social life (the duties of the rich to the poor and vice versa), hitherto usually treated in sermons or spiritual literature.

Despite the many similarities to, and the strong influence of, the neologians, Enlightenment preachers in the Habsburg empire cannot be seen simply as their followers or imitators, not least because especially those preaching in Czech may not have known the neologians'

[79] Sträter et al., 'Predigt', 86.

work first-hand. Rather, these preachers were educated to use the style by university instruction in homiletics, which in turn followed state legislation shaped by the emperor himself. Thus they should be regarded as representatives of an original version of Christian Enlightenment, typical for the Habsburg lands and featuring a Catholic reinterpretation of Protestant impulses.

Danish Catechism in Action? Examining Religious Formation in and through Erik Pontoppidan's *Menoza*

Laurel Lied*
Aarhus University

In 1737 Erik Pontoppidan, a Danish bishop of pietist leanings, published a Lutheran catechism, Sandhed til Gudfrygtighed *(*Truth unto Godliness*), which became the Church of Denmark's official catechism for the following fifty years, with new editions being printed in Norway into the twentieth century. For a figure largely overlooked by modern scholarship, he has enjoyed an extraordinarily lengthy influence over Christian formation in Scandinavia and in Norwegian immigrant communities in the USA. Pontoppidan not only left behind this 'official' programme of Christian education, but also an unofficial blueprint,* Menoza *(1742–3). This* opbyggelse *('edifying') novel recounts the conversion of an imaginary Indian prince, Menoza, and his subsequent travels around Europe.* Menoza *might even be said to offer its readers an alternative or additional Lutheran catechism in literary form. This article examines Menoza's Christian formation in the light of Pontoppidan's official catechism. Which topics of the catechism receive emphasis or are downplayed? Does the progression and linking of doctrinal topics match the catechism's layout or does the author restructure Christian theology for pedagogical purposes? The article also considers the non-doctrinal elements of the characters' catechesis, especially in relation to pietist expectations regarding conversion. What indoctrination, intentional or unintentional, into the vocabulary and experience of pietist culture did Pontoppidan offer his Scandinavian readers?*

In 1737 Erik Pontoppidan, a Danish Lutheran bishop of pietist leanings, published a catechism, *Sandhed til Gudfrygtighed* (*Truth unto Godliness*). This became the Church of Denmark's official catechism for the next fifty years, with new editions being printed in Norway

* Emmasvej 28 3TV, 8220 Brabrand, Denmark. E-mail: laurel.lied@cas.au.dk. Research for this article received funding from the European Union's Horizon 2020 research and innovation programme under Marie Skłodowska-Curie grant agreement no. 676258.

Studies in Church History 55 (2019), 225–240
doi: 10.1017/stc.2018.29

even into the twentieth century.[1] Henrik Horstbøll writes of the catechism's publication that 'the manual became one of the 18th century's largest book projects'.[2] Thus, for a figure largely unknown to wider modern scholarship, Pontoppidan has enjoyed an extraordinarily enduring influence over Christian formation and the lives of the faithful, not only in Scandinavia but also in Norwegian immigrant communities in the USA. More significantly for the theme of this volume, Pontoppidan left behind not only his 'official' programme of Christian education, but also an unofficial blueprint in *Menoza* (1742–3). This *opbyggelse* ('edifying') novel recounts the conversion to Christianity of an imaginary Indian prince named Menoza and his subsequent travels around Europe. *Menoza* might be said to offer its readers an alternative or additional Lutheran catechism in literary form, intertwined with the novel's larger project of offering a pietist commentary on the contemporary European religious scene.

This article examines the nature of conversion(s) in *Menoza* in the light of Pontoppidan's official catechism. Which topics of the Lutheran catechism receive emphasis, are elaborated upon or are downplayed? Does the progression and linking of doctrinal topics match the order of the catechism or does Pontoppidan restructure Christian theology for pedagogical purposes? I shall also explore the non-doctrinal elements of the periods of catechesis undergone by Menoza and other characters, especially in relation to pietist expectations regarding conversion.[3] What indoctrination, intentional or

[1] Printing continued into the twentieth century, although Hallgeir Elstad writes that Pontoppidan's book was phased out towards the end of the nineteenth: 'Til erstatning for Pontoppidan. Et blikk på noen opplysningskatekismer i Danmark og Norge', *Dansk teologisk tidsskrift* 72 (2009), 161–80, at 180. More recently Dag Thorkildsen has again articulated the importance of the work for generations of Norwegians in shaping their understanding of Christianity: 'Lutherdom og nasjonal identitet i Norden', *Teologisk tidsskrift* 1 (2017), 42–54, at 51.

[2] Henrik Horstbøll, 'Pietism and the Politics of Catechisms: The Case of Denmark and Norway in the Eighteenth and Nineteenth Centuries', *Scandinavian Journal of History* 29 (2004), 143–60, at 146. It is unclear if Horstbøll is referring here to the catechism as one of the largest book projects in Denmark, in Scandinavia or in the whole of Europe. He might also have in mind the large annual standing order for about ten thousand copies from a single publishing house in Copenhagen: ibid. 151. Horstbøll's statement aims to impress upon his readers that the book was not only intended to reach every corner of Denmark and Norway but that probably it actually did so: ibid. 151–2.

[3] For more detailed discussion of conversion and pietism, see the recent study by Jonathan Strom, *German Pietism and the Problem of Conversion* (University Park, PA, 2017), which seeks to complicate the narrative of an established conversion paradigm

unintentional, into the vocabulary and experiences of pietist culture did Pontoppidan offer his Scandinavian readers? First, however, I shall briefly outline the historical context of Pontoppidan's two works and their complex publication histories, particularly in Scandinavia and the USA. At the close of the article, I shall return to this bibliographic information, which offers some evidence about contemporary attitudes towards these texts.

Danish pietism, often more narrowly termed state pietism (*statspietism*),[4] was an early eighteenth-century phase of the history of the Danish church. It was heavily influenced by German pietism, which emerged as a movement in the 1680s and 1690s. As a reform movement, the term 'pietism' is generally applied to a variety of interrelated religious movements. Its hallmarks were (and are) a focus on lay readership of the Bible, church reform, the priesthood of all believers and an emphasis on the 'new birth' of the believer. In the Danish context, the variety of religious expression within German pietism had to adapt the stricter boundaries of Danish religious life, particularly in relation to the official censorship of books printed in Denmark and in Danish. Nonetheless, the movement engendered a comprehensive education system and improved general literacy levels when confirmation was made mandatory in 1736, since the decree establishing this required primary schooling or regular instruction by a church official.[5]

As the official catechism used in Denmark-Norway for confirmation preparation, the number of editions of *Sandhed til Gudfrygtighed* or of works based on extracts from it is impressive.[6] Horstbøll writes:

within German pietism. This article seeks rather to read Pontoppidan's texts in the light of one another, drawing out the similarities in order also to find differences of emphasis.

[4] The term 'state pietism' refers to official political support for pietism during the reign of Christian VI (1730–46). However, pietism was present in Denmark before and after this: Carsten Bach-Nielsen and Per Ingesman, eds, *Kirkens Historie*, 2 vols (Copenhagen, 2012), 2: 304–16.

[5] Thomas Munck, 'Literacy, Educational Reform and the Use of Print in Eighteenth-Century Denmark', *European History Quarterly* 34 (2004), 275–303, at 299. Munck discusses some of the practical difficulties and results of the decree. The history of literacy and book culture in Scandinavia has also been discussed in Charlotte Appel, *Læsning og bogmarked i 1600-tallets Danmark* (Copenhagen, 2001); Gina Dahl, *Books in Early Modern Norway* (Leiden, 2011).

[6] In 1771, a Danish priest, Peder Saxtorph, edited and simplified the text, reducing Pontoppidan's work to about a hundred pages; by comparison, the 1752 edition of *Sandhed til Gudfrygtighed* is 208 pages. This edited work, *Udtog af Dr. Erich*

'from the 1700s, over 40 different editions of Pontoppidan's exposition of the Church catechism have been preserved'.[7] During the nineteenth century, in Norway alone over one hundred editions or abridgements of the text were published.[8]

Pontoppidan's catechism also had a lasting popularity in the USA. At least six Norwegian editions of his catechism were printed in Iowa from 1873, and a loose English translation was printed in Chicago in 1877, with a second edition in 1895.[9] Another shortened English translation was published in the US in 1900 by the Lutheran Free Church. This went through at least ten editions by 1933.[10]

Menoza does not have as extensive a publishing history as *Sandhed til Gudfrygtighed*. The Danish Royal Library holds four editions of the Dutch translation and five of the German, alongside four Danish editions published in Denmark and two Swedish editions. The Norwegian National Library Catalogue reveals that editions were published in Norway in 1847, 1880 and 1931, and the Danish Royal Library supplies a fourth, published in Norway in 1881. The publishing dates for the Danish editions (1742–3, 1745–51, 1763–4 and 1860) are earlier than those of the editions published in Norway, another indication that Pontoppidan had a longer literary life in Norway.

Since there is not space for an exhaustive study of Pontoppidan's catechism and novel, this article will focus on the theme of conversion[11] as presented in the novel. Besides the conversion to

Pontoppidans Forklaring, til de Eenfoldiges Nytte (*Extracts of Doctor Erik Pontoppidan's Explanation, for the Use of the Simple*), was also widely used in Norway.

[7] Horstbøll, 'Pietism and the Politics of Catechisms', 152.

[8] Mogens Brøndsted, 'Historien om Pontoppidans "Forklaring" i Danmark og Norge', *Fund og Forskning I Det Kongelige Biblioteks Samlinger* 12 (1965), 47–65, at 65.

[9] See <https://www.worldcat.org>.

[10] Harald Ulrik Sverdrup, *Luther's Small Catechism: Explained in Questions and Answers* (Minneapolis, MN, 1900), online at 'Project Gutenberg': <http://www.gutenberg.org/ebooks/36081>, accessed 28 December 2017. The translator's preface from this edition names Pontoppidan's *Explanation.* For information linking various editions of the work, see 'Luther Seminary Catalog', online at: <https://luthersem.on.worldcat.org/oclc/854308792> and Worldcat, at: <http://www.worldcat.org/title/luthers-small-catechism-explained-in-questions-and-answers/oclc/747742676/editions?referer=di&editionsView=true>, both accessed 28 December 2017.

[11] Jonathan Strom names three types of conversion: from one religious tradition to another, from one Christian confessional group to another, and an 'inward change of heart' in a Christian. The last is most associated with pietism, but he observes that all

Christianity of Menoza himself, I will draw on several other accounts of conversion, including those of a young woman in Montpellier, a young German count and an older Viennese woman. In the novel, these and similar episodes are referred to using terms such as 'conversion' (*omvendelse*) or 'awakening' (*opvækkelse*), and Pontoppidan's catechism reveals how closely these terms are linked in his thought to the larger idea of new birth.[12]

Menoza's actual conversion occurs long after he has come to hold many of the classical theistic beliefs to be true, but also after he has developed an aversion to religion's 'dry external existence'[13] and to the hypocritical behaviour of believers, and has come to trust implicitly in his conscience or inward guide (*rettesnor*). He initially hears the gospel from several Catholic missionaries, but it is from Danish Lutheran missionaries that he receives his final catechesis before being baptized. The actual conversation begins with a discussion of reason and revelation, where revelation is never to be set against reason but rather deals with that which is beyond reason. The bulk of the dialogue between Menoza and the Danes revolves around questions about Christ and his identity, especially his fulfilment of the Old Testament prophecies and his role as Saviour, atoning for sin. The middle section of the conversation deals with justification, the need

three would be recognized by pietists. Moreover, he writes that despite the large body of research on conversion, 'at present, there is no systematic understanding of conversion for early modern Europe': 'Pietist Experiences and Narratives of Conversion', in Douglas H. Shantz, ed., *A Companion to German Pietism, 1660–1800*, Brill's Companions to the Christian Tradition 55 (Leiden, 2014), 293–318, at 293–4. This article deals with conversion stories of all three types, but the third type is present in each example.

[12] 'Hvad er genfødelsen eller den nye fødsel? Det samme som en levende tros meddelelse eller opvækkelse af den åndelige død, omvendelse og oversættelse fra mørket til lyset, fra Satans magt til Gud' ('What is rebirth or the new birth? The same as the awakening from spiritual death to a living faith, repentance and movement from darkness to light, from the power of Satan to God'): Pontoppidan, *Sandhed til Gudfrygtighed udi en eenfoldig og efter Mulighed kort dog tilstrekkelig Forklaring over Sal. Doct. Mort. Luthers Liden Catechismo* (Copenhagen, 1752), 119. Translations from Danish or Norwegian editions of Pontoppidan's texts are my own.

[13] 'Udvortes tørre Væsen': Erik Pontoppidan, *Menoza. En asiatisk Prinds, som drog Verden omkring og søgte Christne, særdeles i Indien, Spanien, Italien, Frankrig, England, Holland, Tydskland og Danmark, men fandt lidet af det, han søgte* [*Menoza, an Asian Prince, who travelled around the world seeking Christians, especially in India, Spain, Italy, France, England, the Netherlands, Germany and Denmark, but found little of what he sought*], 3 vols (Copenhagen, 1860), 1: 33.

for sanctification and finally the reasonableness of the resurrection.[14] Finally the outward elements of the Christian faith, the sacraments of baptism and the eucharist, are explained. These final elements of Christianity trouble Menoza the most because of their external nature, which in his eyes veers close to superstition. The variation in baptismal rites also suggests to Menoza that baptism is not an eternal and unchanging truth.[15] He is reassured by historical reasoning concerning the origin of the sacraments and the practical grounds for variations in the baptismal rites. Shortly afterwards, during a severe illness, he prays for and receives the 'sweet taste of [the Lord's] grace, which I [Menoza] rightly considered the pouring out of [Christ's] love in my heart'.[16] This spiritual reassurance acts also as a physical cure and he is subsequently baptized.

Let us now examine this story in the light of the typical Lutheran catechism layout present in *Sandhed til Gudfrygtighed* (*Truth unto Godliness*), which is intended as an explanation of the Lutheran *Small Catechism*: introduction, the Ten Commandments, the Apostles' Creed, the Lord's Prayer, and the sacraments of baptism and the eucharist. Menoza's informal catechesis begins apart from the church and the Scriptures, but he describes himself as 'awakened by God's prevenient grace to seek further light'.[17] His search begins along theistic lines, related to those covered briefly in the catechism's section on the first article of the Creed, initially skipping the explication of the Ten Commandments. Menoza's introduction to Christ gives more space to the exegesis of Old Testament prophecies than does *Sandhed til Gudfrygtighed*, something that might speak to the passion for biblical scholarship often displayed by pietists. The catechism defines justification in the section on the Creed (question 503 under the third article).[18] Sanctification is also dealt in this section, although it is renamed, or at least merged with, renewal (*fornyelse*), a term which itself connects with the pietist emphasis on the new man and allows for sanctification to be sought continually in this

[14] Ibid. 1: 75–87 (letter 7).

[15] Menoza is referring to the difference between full immersion (and possibly naked) baptism and a baptism by affusion or aspersion: ibid. 1: 95.

[16] 'Sød Smag af sin Naade, som jeg ret holdt for hans Kjærligheds Udøselse i mit Hjerte': ibid. 1:101.

[17] 'Af Guds forekommende Naade opvakt til at søge mere Lys': ibid. 1: 8.

[18] Pontoppidan, *Sandhed til Gudfrygtighed* (Copenhagen, 1752), 125.

life but never fully achieved.[19] Baptism and the sacrament of the Lord's table are the final themes in both Menoza's education and Pontoppidan's catechism, although they are treated quite differently. In *Menoza*, Pontoppidan seems to be on the defensive when dealing with the external elements of the Christian religion.[20] Similarly, the section of his catechism on baptism, after discussing the sacrament, turns to the nature of conversion or repentance and the new man (questions 673–99).[21] Likewise, the section on the eucharist deals with the themes of sorrow for sin and self-examination (questions 744–52).[22] However, although these themes of sorrow and repentance are not as strong in Pontoppidan's depiction of Menoza's catechesis, they find their place in the novel's other tales of conversion.

Menoza's first opportunity to act as a spiritual counsellor occurs in Montpellier, after his rousing defence of the priesthood of all believers causes uproar in the town.[23] Several young ladies are stricken with melancholy, and eventually he is called to one who has been confined to bed by sorrow and sickness. She declares that Menoza's words have moved and troubled her and she implores him: 'if [you] can lead me to land again, then shall my duty to you be greater than to any person on earth'.[24] This depth of feeling is repeated as she describes how earlier she had tried to force herself to feel sorrow and repentance for her sins, but now 'the sorrow in my heart is an entirely different quality … . Now I see and feel what I have to grieve for, and even in my most bitter sorrow I find a wonderfully sweet taste'.[25] In the face of the protestations of the young woman's mother, Menoza supports the young woman. When her mother insists that her daughter is already very pious, avoiding lavish dress and only reluctantly attending

[19] Ibid. 128. Note that renewal here is a daily task, not a single event. Earlier in the catechism, Pontoppidan notes that rebirth, justification and renewal can all be understood by the term 'sanctification', although usually sanctification refers specifically to renewal: 'Hvad forstås ved det ord helliggørelse? I en vidtløftig mening begriber det i sig disse tre uadskillelige ting, genfødelsen, retfærdiggørelsen og fornyelsen. Ellers betegner det ofte alene den daglige fornyelse': ibid. 119.

[20] Pontoppidan, *Menoza*, 1: 95.

[21] Pontoppidan, *Sandhed til Gudfrygtighed*, 169–77.

[22] Ibid. 188–92.

[23] Pontoppidan, *Menoza*, 1: 124–5.

[24] 'Kan I føre mig vel til Lands igjen, da bliver min Forpligtelse mod Eder større end imod noget Menneske paa Jorden': ibid. 125.

[25] 'Har Sorgen i mit Hjerte en Ganske anden Art … . Nu seer og Føler jeg, hvad jeg har at sørge for, og I min bitterste Sorrig selv finder jeg en underlig sød Smag': ibid. 126.

dances, the daughter declares that until now, her very nature has been hypocritical: she had avoided some evils but desire for God was not her only motivation.[26] Menoza's words, she says, have awakened her to the truth which is now 'so living and powerful in my heart'.[27] Menoza ends the encounter with a short evangelizing speech in which he explains that the work of justifying faith only begins when the truth triumphs over the world and he emphasizes the necessity of drawing closer to Christ, who is the true giver of the grace and power that leads to sanctification. In reply the young woman declares vehemently: 'O yes, my Jesus! Draw me after you'.[28] Examining this short episode, several themes stand out. There is sorrow, an unbidden sense that one's previous identity had been fundamentally hypocritical, and a strong emotional desire and longing for Christ. These recur in the following instances.

The second convert is a young German count whom Menoza meets in Venice during carnival in 1718.[29] This festive backdrop gives Menoza much to grieve over, as it confirms to him that 'Christ is driven out from among the Christians and that to a great degree they have forgotten the mind of Christ'.[30] The count is described as a Lutheran who has received a good Christian upbringing and education but is beset by temptations brought about by his European journey. The count and his stories can be read as a foil to Menoza, who is also a man of noble birth on a world tour. The count seeks out Menoza's support and expresses his desire to follow Christ while lamenting society's expectation that the nobility should attend balls and dances.[31]

For the count, knowledge of the particularities of Christian doctrine is not the issue, for he is well educated; rather the process of formation is the focus. His conscience or nagging heart plague him when attending various 'frivolities' (as Menoza regards them), even though

[26] Ibid. 127.
[27] 'Saa levende og kraftig i mit Hjerte som nu': ibid. 128.
[28] 'Ak ja min Jesu! drag mig efter dig': ibid.
[29] The name of the count is given as W***, a literary practice of the period that could either shelter the author from legal liability if the character was an actual person or be used as a literary trope to suggest this count was a real person. The count's story perhaps fits more closely the other English translation of *omvendelse*, 'repentance'.
[30] 'Christus udryddes iblandt de Christne, og at man I høj Grad har glemt hans Sind': Pontoppidan, *Menoza*, 1: 168.
[31] Ibid. 170.

he declares he has no desire to dance or gamble. The conversation between the count and Menoza that follows reveals the complexity of moral dilemmas and purposes inherent in situations that 'in their nature seem innocent, yet through misuse become sinful'.[32] Danish pietists, like English puritans earlier, were instrumental in closing Danish theatres for a time, and here Pontoppidan associates dances, comedies and operas with the sin of luxuriousness, 'which meek and vigilant Christians should never consider themselves safe from'.[33] After this argument, and an exhortation to sobriety and against the frivolous mood displayed in dancing as unworthy for a serious Christian, the count returns several days later and attests to Menoza's wisdom.[34] Their second conversation dwells on the subject of play, broadly considered. Here Menoza gives a more nuanced understanding of human entertainments and joys, arguing that in God's wisdom it was not only the necessities that were created for humans, but also much that 'delights and amuses the taste, the mind or the other senses'.[35] The danger comes when these amusements become the primary focus, or a type of addiction which leads to what Menoza terms a half-life, or more correctly a half-death.[36] The count acknowledges that his gambling is itself a type of theft, from his own tenants or farmers.[37] In the end, the count, in distress over his misdeeds, seeks God's help and vows he will never gamble again.[38] The episode ends with Menoza secretly paying off the count's gambling debt and gaining him as a travelling companion for a time.

The final convert is also a card player, this time a woman in Vienna. Pontoppidan describes her as a well-known card player with a heavily made-up face, but also as a zealously devout Catholic anxious for Menoza's soul. The conversation between them is presented as a theological examination of Menoza set up by

[32] 'Ting, som i sin Natur synes uskyldig, og dog ved Misbrug bliver syndig': ibid.
[33] '[E]n ydmyg og aarvaagen Christen aldrig bør holde sig sikker nok': ibid. 171. This type of Christian watchfulness is also commanded by Pontoppidan in his catechism: *Sandhed til Gudfrygtighed*, 46, 65.
[34] Pontoppidan, *Menoza*, 1: 171–3.
[35] '[T]il at fornøje og for lyste Smagen, Sindet eller de øvrige Sandser': ibid. 173.
[36] Ibid. 175; see also Pontoppidan, *Sandhed til Gudfrygtighed*, 66.
[37] Pontoppidan, *Menoza*, 1: 177. The reference is to his poor farmers, presumably tenants on his family's estate, whose rent he has squandered.
[38] Ibid. 177–8.

the woman together with the Jesuits, whom she ensures are present. Menoza thus begins by portraying himself as a person who seeks only Christ and the truth, rather than thinking according to sectarian positions.[39] The second section of the conversation is a debate over the eucharist, with Menoza seeming to catch out a Jesuit over the possibility that Christ was bodily present in a dual manner during the Last Supper. What is at stake here is the question of who has the right to read and interpret the Bible, and the role of reason in such interpretation. A second meeting a few days later between Menoza and the lady leads to a more personal conversation. He suggests that her blind trust in religious authorities is a type of superstition. A condensed catechesis follows about the narrow path of following Christ, and the lady is brought to tears. She confesses how earlier her confessor suppressed her doubts and she sobs that 'all her existence has hitherto been of the world and not of the Father, who by his word of truth gives us birth as new creatures'.[40] Menoza leaves Vienna not long afterwards, but expresses the hope that the lady has been led towards conversion to the truth.

There are marks of sorrow and distress present in all four of these episodes. Menoza and the young lady are both afflicted in a physical fashion, she being confined to bed and he with an illness. Each conversion involves an element of education: Menoza's is understandably the most extensive, but the conversation with the count, who is explicitly described as having received a thoroughly Christian upbringing, also contains a didactic section detailing the pleasures permitted to Christians, such as the enjoyment of natural beauty, and explaining the reasons why certain types of 'play' are forbidden: they generally lead to some form of addiction, accompanied by anger or jealousy.[41] The three European episodes each serve as a condemnation of Christian hypocrisy. The young lady's conversion is the most explicit, for she calls her previous existence hypocritical, even though her mother declares she has been a model of piety. The Viennese lady's vanity and gambling are tacitly shown to be at odds with her apparent outward piety, but Menoza goes even further,

[39] Ibid. 199.
[40] '[A]lt hendes Væsen havde hidindtil været af Verden og ikke af Faderen, som ved sit Sandheds Ord føder os til nye Kreaturer': ibid. 209.
[41] See ibid. 173–5.

declaring that she is not yet a true Christian.[42] Similarly, the count's ostensibly pious intentions stand in conflict with his actions.[43]

All these conversions resonate most clearly with the teachings included under the topic of baptism in Pontoppidan's catechism. This defines conversion or repentance: 'to convert is to know deeply, feel, repent and hate the sins one has committed, yes, all the perversity of one's sinful nature, and inwardly to long for God's grace in Christ, and soberly to intend to improve one's life'.[44] Later in the same section, Pontoppidan explicitly denies the possibility of conversion without regret or shame. True regret for sins is, he says, 'a spiritual pain and sadness that crushes the heart, which will probably sting and even bring tears to the sinner's eyes now and then'.[45] In *Menoza*, these teachings take shape through the characters.

Despite Menoza's sickness, which precedes that 'sweet taste of grace' and his baptism, his story is not primarily one of repentance. Trygve Skarsten has described Menoza as the perfect pietist post-conversion,[46] but from the beginning his journey is characterized differently from that of the other converts. Menoza longs for God[47] and is described as 'asking the way to heaven'.[48] In his story, his imperfect or incomplete knowledge acts as his sin, and thus as a source of sorrow.[49] However, the themes of repentance and sorrow are rather more clearly found in the stories of the Christian conversions, or reconversions.

Pontoppidan's novel thus allows him to explore a type of noble savage drawn by, and longing for, God.[50] There is an element of idealization in Menoza's catechesis which makes it possible for Pontoppidan to present large sections of his catechism in the opening

[42] 'Madame, De er endnu ingen Christen': ibid. 206.

[43] Ibid. 169.

[44] 'At omvende sig, er, hiertelig at kiende, føle, fortryde og hade sin begangne Synder, ja al sin syndige Naturs Vanart, inderlig længes efter Guds Naade i Christo, og alvorlig faae i Sinde, at forbedre sit Levnet': Pontoppidan, *Sandhed til Gudfrygtighed*, 170 (Q. 675).

[45] 'En aandelige Smerte og Bedrøvelse, der sonderknuser Hiertet, og kommer det ligesom til at svie, ja undertiden trykker Graad og Taare af Synderens Øyne': ibid. 171 (Q. 682).

[46] Trygve Skarsten, 'Erik Pontoppidan and his Asiatic Prince Menoza', *ChH* 50 (1981), 33–43, at 40.

[47] Pontoppidan, *Menoza*, 1: 21.

[48] '[A]t spørge Vej til Himlen': ibid.

[49] Ibid. 20.

[50] Ter Ellingson, *The Myth of the Noble Savage* (Berkeley, CA, 2001) 374; he argues that the noble savage as a rhetorical device was already present in the seventeenth century.

chapters. However, this approach, set up in the novel as a search for truth, sets aside some of the moral instruction found in the catechism, although the theme of disdaining hypocritical behaviour is found in both works. In the novel, such behaviour is generally that of others and not Menoza's. The other converts offer something different to their readers, rectifying this omission in Menoza's story. They warn his audience that to be a true Christian, it is not enough to be baptized and confirmed. In a variety of ways, these figures reveal how Christendom has betrayed the true understanding of what it is to be a Christian. They offer a framework for conversion, a type of pietist cultural education.

Of course, this reading of *Menoza* is dependent on the assumption that readers have turned to the novel as a source of moral instruction and devotional engagement.[51] One must ask whether Pontoppidan's work had an audience who viewed the text in this fashion. Several editions include forewords which, if not revealing readers' attitudes and reading patterns, suggest that editors often saw *Menoza* as a devotional or edifying text. Pontoppidan's own address to the reader of *Menoza* is entitled 'a few words for useful consideration by the sensible reader'.[52] It explores the theme of truth as single (that is, there is only one truth) and thus strong and enduring, compared to the multiplicity intrinsic to lies. This is an interesting beginning to a fictional narrative, which contains a variety of conversion stories, suggesting that for Pontoppidan fiction is not inimical to the truth. Pontoppidan also decries the many contemporary Danish writings that he feels promote the 'false words of Satan' which deceive and confuse the simple, observing that 'one of the most ancient ways to

[51] The plot of Menoza fits quite well with Tera Pettella's description of eighteenth-century novels that rely upon familiar patterns set up by earlier texts, including devotional texts. She writes of *David Simple*: '[I]t incorporates a number of formal characteristics that become even more marked in novels as the century progresses: meandering plots, monotonous successions of inset narratives, calamitous trials, as well as irksome (to modern sensibilities) didacticism. These characteristics are familiar to eighteenth-century readers because they appear in a variety of popular texts throughout the late seventeenth and early eighteenth centuries, including epic and heroic romance. Likewise, devotional texts possessed a remarkable number of the formal features that are associated with novels, such as emphatic, intrusive narrators, affective engagement, and elaborate introductory material that framed occasions for instruction': 'Devotional Readings and the Novel Form: The Case of *David Simple*', *Eighteenth-Century Fiction* 24 (2011–12), 277–99, at 280. She argues for a 'stability of established religious reading practices': ibid. 279.

[52] 'Faa Ord til den fornuftige Læsers tjenlige Efterretning': Pontoppidan, *Menoza*, 1: 3.

teach is to portray truth, not only in clear, dry and bare rules, but also, for the sake of our make-up as human beings, through examples, stories, parables and fables, which catch the eye quickly and yet remain longest in the memory'.[53] For the author, then, these ideas represent the novel's 'foundation, method and context'.[54]

The 1931 Norwegian translation of *Menoza* gives some indication of the reputation of the novel nearly two centuries later. The publisher helpfully informs readers that the novel 'is especially lively and interesting and has therefore been widely read up to the present … . It contains Christian wisdom of enduring worth and is a lovely memorial of the rich spiritual life of pietism at its best.'[55] A similar vein of thought is also expressed in the Danish edition of 1860, albeit with a slightly more critical edge:

> Nevertheless it is obvious that a book such as this one is not reprinted as an edifying book for contemporary Christians, but rather in part as a memorial of a historic personality and a past period in our church, and in part as a useful and enjoyable read for people who understand the distinction between pious reflections and articles of faith … .[56]

The publisher, Vilhelm Birkedal, also recognizes that the novel has been well loved.[57] If the novel had ceased to be read for its devotional value in Denmark, in Norway it seems to have retained some of its

[53] 'En af de allerældste Læremaader er at forestille Sandhed, ej alene i klare, tørre og nøgne Regler, men ogsaa, for det menneskelige Gemyts Skyld, under Exempler, Lignelse, Parabler og Fictioner': ibid. 6.

[54] 'Skriftets Paafund, Maade og Sammenhæng': ibid.

[55] 'Den er særdeles livfull og interessant og har derfor vært meget lest helt til vår tid … . Den innholder kristlige livsvisdom av blivende verd og er et smukt minnesmerke om pietismens rike åndsliv I dens blomstringstid': Erik Pontoppidan, *Menoza*, transl. Andreas Fleischer (Oslo, 1931), 5.

[56] '[I]midlertid er det en Selvfølge, at en Bog som den nærværende ikke paany udgives nærmest som Opbyggelsesbog for Nutids-Christne, men deels som et Mindesmærke om en historisk Personlighed og et bevæget Tidsrum i vor Kirke, deels som en nyttig og fornøjelig Læsning for Folk, som vide at sondre imellem fromme Betragtninger og Troesartikler': Pontoppidan, *Menoza* (Copenhagen, 1860), Preface, paragraph 5. Horstbøll describes some of the political and ecclesiastical tensions over the use of Pontoppidan's catechism, both when it was first published and in nineteenth-century Denmark. He also notes the differences in attitudes towards Pontoppidan in nineteenth-century Denmark and Norway: Henrik Horstbøll, 'Læsning til salighed, oplysning og velfærd. Om Pontoppidan, pietisme og lærebøger i Danmark og Norge i 17- og 1800-tallet', *Fortid og Nutid*, June 2003, 83–108.

[57] Pontoppidan, *Menoza* (1860), Preface, paragraph 7.

reputation for Christian insight. Pontoppidan himself certainly viewed his work as Christian pedagogy and his own foreword was included alongside that of later publishers. Moreover, both later forewords suggest that the novel remained well regarded and widely read.

Menoza, however, receives little attention in Danish literary or theological studies. This is unfortunate since the novel contains fascinating insights into how pietists spoke about and imagined conversion, besides its pages upon pages of contemporary cultural commentary. Discussing another edifying Scandinavian Christian novel, *Squire Adamson*, Mark Safstrom writes:

> The omission of Waldenström's most popular novel from Swedish literary history, as well as its neglect by historians, has much to do with the fact that it was embraced by the wrong public, i.e., lower- and middle-class church-goers, rather than the bourgeois class that was dominant at the turn of the century or the Social Democratic elite of the twentieth century.[58]

The later *Menoza* forewords hint at a similar reception and reading audience.[59]

Moreover, *Menoza* is significant because an understanding of the culture and roots of pietism has import beyond Scandinavian church and cultural history. Historians of anglophone evangelicalism, Mark Noll and Bruce Hindmarsh, have praised the work of the British historian W. R. Ward for rewriting the history of evangelicalism by attending to German history and historical scholarship, especially regarding pietism.[60] If Scandinavian pietism was not as influential on the British evangelical movement, the links between American evangelicalism and Scandinavian pietism via the Norwegian, Swedish and Danish immigrant communities nonetheless deserve to be explored more thoroughly.

[58] Mark Safstrom, *The Religious Origins of Democratic Pluralism: Paul Peter Waldenstrom and the Politics of the Swedish Awakening 1868–1917* (Eugene, OR, 2016), 32.

[59] The promotion of literacy and reading in nineteenth-century Norway has been examined more closely in relation to Hans Nielsen Hauge, a revival figure, who was certainly familiar with Pontoppidan. Haukland even writes that 'reading defined the Haugeans as a group': Linda Haukland, 'Hans Nielsen Hauge: A Catalyst of Literacy in Norway', *Scandinavian Journal of History* 39 (2014), 539–59.

[60] Mark Noll and Bruce Hindmarsh, 'Rewriting the History of Evangelicalism: W. R. Ward, 1925–2010', *Books and Culture: Christian Review* 17/2 (2011), 8, online at: <https://www.booksandculture.com/articles/2011/marapr/historyevangelicalism.html?paging=off>, last accessed 22 November 2018.

This article has touched only briefly on the way in which the fictional narrative offers a variety of lenses through which Pontoppidan's teaching on conversion can be viewed. A more in-depth study of *Menoza* might demonstrate more fully how Pontoppidan uses the novel to surpass the pedagogical limitations of his catechism, particularly regarding pietistic concerns about conversion or new birth. Might the narrative form be more fitting than a catechism to accomplish a pedagogical or edifying purpose?[61] In addition, although Pontoppidan's work is fictional, it might benefit from consideration in the light of recent scholarship on conversion narratives and autobiographies from the early modern era, particularly among English evangelicals, Moravians, and Dutch and German pietists.[62] Understanding how readers might have been expected to engage and learn from such narratives may offer insights into how *Menoza* as a narrative might have been received by its audience. On the fictional side, rather than comparing *Menoza* to Christian allegorical works such as Bunyan's *The Pilgrim's Progress* or P. P. Waldenström's *Squire Adamson*, its educational methods might be understood better when it is placed alongside other didactic novels. Pontoppidan owned a copy of the early modern French didactic novel *Les Aventures de Télémaque* (*The Adventures of Telemachus*), and a publication list from the 1880 Horsens edition of *Menoza* reveals numerous Norwegian translations of nineteenth-century Christian historical

[61] In reference to the pre-Cartesian conception of truth, Catherine Pickstock writes 'for as long as every thought had to be tested for its celestial or alternatively hellish origin, every thought was an act of ethical discernment, and "to be in the truth" was an act of ethical performance': Catherine Pickstock, *Repetition and Identity* (Oxford, 2013), 121. While certainly post-Cartesian, Pontoppidan and the pietists might have recognized the epistemologically complicated nature of truth (who is allowed to interpret the Scriptures, for example) and the linking of truth to ethical action. A narrative, which displays ethical action, is thus potentially more pedagogically appropriate than a catechism.

[62] See especially Bruce Hindmarsh, *The Evangelical Conversion Narrative: Spiritual Autobiography in Early Modern England* (Oxford, 2005); Christer Ahlberger and Per von Wachenfeldt, eds, *Moravian Memoirs: Pillars of an Invisible Church* (Skellefteå, 2017); Andreas Bähr, 'Fear, Anxiety and Terror in Conversion Narratives of Early German Pietism', *German History* 32 (2014), 353–70; Fred A. van Lieburg, *Living for God: Eighteenth-Century Dutch Pietist Autobiography* (Lanham, MD, and Oxford,. 2006); Barbara Becker-Cantarino, ed. and transl., *The Life of Lady Johanna Eleonora Petersen, written by herself: Pietism and Women's Autobiography in Seventeenth-Century Germany* (Chicago, IL, and London, 2005).

novels for children, for which there was clearly a demand.[63] Perhaps the publisher recognized that *Menoza* fitted within this category.

Edifying or devotional literature and reading ought not to be a pejorative label describing a genre which is often viewed as not deserving scholarly attention.[64] If *Menoza* has often been considered in this way, this article represents an attempt to rectify this by using the novel to open a window into the educational aspirations of pietism as a distinct cultural and religious movement. The novel has been seen to be, not *merely* an edifying work – as if edification was only a vapid sort of encouragement – but a work of education and formation. By reading *Menoza* as a catechetical work, the story operates on a meta-level: Menoza the character, on his quest for true Christians within the narrative, facilitates the building up of those who read the narrative as true Christians. Pontoppidan demonstrates for his readers an ideal process of catechesis for Menoza that mirrors his own catechism, but also introduces or reinforces the religious culture and emotionality of Danish pietism within a theological framework. The didactic sections of the novel are never devoid of certain fitting emotional responses, which are not themselves the purpose of the work, but rather witnesses to a changed life.[65] Read as a source of religious authority, the novel supplies both a 'how to' manual on becoming a true converted Christian for those not yet 'reborn' and encouragement for those who might see their own experiences mirrored in the characters. Given Pontoppidan's emphasis on daily renewal, it should not be surprising that *Menoza* can be positioned as a second catechism, a fictional account of a continuing process of education or re-education. Pontoppidan's audience (the children of God) always stand in need of such aids in this present life.

[63] These were authored by two British evangelical women, Emma Leslie and Charlotte Tucker. Potentially, the later reception history of *Menoza* enters into a milieu which is decidedly gendered: see especially Hilary Havens, ed., *Didactic Novels and British Women's Writing, 1790–1820* (Abingdon, 2016).

[64] 'Popular mischaracterizations of Christian readers as close-minded ignore the transformational presuppositions of devotional reading and its often unstated but crucial reliance upon the plenitude of meaning in a text': Liam Corley, 'The Jouissance of Belief: Devotional Reading and the (Re)Turn to Religion', *Christianity & Literature* 58 (2009), 252–60, at 255.

[65] See Pontoppidan's early work, *Troens-Speyl, forestillende Guds-Børns Kiende-Tegn* (Copenhagen, 1740); transl. Peter du Moulin as *The Mirror of Faith: By which the Children of God may be known* (Minneapolis, MN, 1927).

'The glory of the age we live in': Christian Education and Philanthropy in Eighteenth-Century London Charity Schools

W. M. Jacob*
Kings College London

This article discusses the Church of England's initiative in providing education for the children of the poor during the long eighteenth century with particular reference to London. Briefly it considers the religious, economic and social context and motives for this largely lay-led and lay-supported initiative in the 1690s and early 1700s to establish catechetical day elementary schools, which also taught reading and writing, for poor boys and girls. It focuses particularly on the extensive evidence available from schools in the growing suburbs of Westminster and Holborn and discusses the personnel involved with charity schools, as trustees, benefactors and teachers; how funds were raised and schools managed; and how children were managed, including the arrangement and oversight of apprenticeships. It demonstrates that the schools continued to be well supported, including financially, throughout the changing, economic, social, religious and political circumstances of the century, until most of them became associated with the National Society for the Education of the Poor in the Principles of the Established Church, founded in 1811.

The last years of the seventeenth century and the first decade of the eighteenth witnessed a burst of philanthropic energy on the part of Church of England laypeople to provide instruction in the Catechism and elementary education for children of the poor.[1] Most towns, many villages, and especially London saw the establishment of 'charity schools', most of which survived to become 'affiliated' after 1811 with the National Society for the Education of the

* 4 St Mary's Walk, London, SE11 4UA. E-mail: wmjacob15@gmail.com.

[1] A Dissenting charity school was established in Gravel Lane, Southwark, in the 1680s. Initially Dissenters supported charity schools, but, following the Sacheverell riots, they set up schools in Ratcliffe Highway in 1712, and in Horsely Down in Southwark, and Isaac Watts set up a charity school in Spitalfields. M. G. Jones noted five Dissenting charity schools in London: *The Charity School Movement: A Study of Eighteenth Century Puritanism in Action* (Cambridge, 1938), 131, 361.

Studies in Church History 55 (2019), 241–255
doi: 10.1017/stc.2018.30

Poor in the Principles of the Established Church. In London between 1699 and 1711 at least 112 schools were established in parishes within the area covered by the 'Bills of Mortality'.[2] Joseph Addison described them in 1713 as '[t]he glory of the age we live in'.[3] In 1719 it was estimated that £10,000 was raised annually in their support.[4] This article provides a case study of one association of such schools. It draws on the minute books of St Giles-in-the-Fields Charity Schools' trustees to explore the philanthropic attitudes of a school's trustees (men mostly of the better and middling sort) to educating children of poor parents in the faith, prayer and worship of the Church of England and to read, write and 'reckon', and, so far as can be discerned, the response of parents and children.

The context for the emergence of charity schools was the political and religious instability and moral anxiety following James II's removal, and the ambition to establish England as a godly nation and bulwark against the advancing Counter-Reformation in northern Europe. The English bishops developed a strategy, originating during the Restoration period, for further reformation of the church to establish a nation worthy of divine blessing in the wars against France and against sedition and rebellion at home.[5] The bishops sought to reinvigorate and pastorally reform the church, raising the standards, status and oversight of the clergy; their strategy included improving pastoral care and catechetical instruction and encouraging lay devotion, envisaging godly households as the basic unit of the church. There was also concern about London's dramatic population growth after the Restoration, caused by the migration of young, mostly poor, people into suburban districts. John Locke complained in a memorandum to the Board of Trade in 1698 about 'the relaxation of discipline and corruption of manners' which was leading to beggars swarming the streets. He recommended state-sponsored working schools teaching spinning and knitting for children aged three to thirteen, thus enabling them to earn their keep and to learn the discipline of

[2] That is, parishes in the cities of London and Westminster, Middlesex and Surrey making weekly returns of burials.

[3] *The Guardian*, ed. J. C. Stephens (Lexington, KY, 1982), 366 (no. 105, 11 July 1713).

[4] Craig Mark Rose, 'Politics, Religion and Charity in Augustan London *c.*1680–*c.*1720' (PhD thesis, University of Cambridge, 1988), 104.

[5] For the political and religious context, see Craig Rose, *England in the 1690s: Revolution, Religion and War* (Oxford, 1999).

work.[6] London's expanding economy required an articulate, literate, numerate, disciplined and moral workforce. In 1657 the lord mayor had wanted a 'charity school' in every ward, 'so that Christ's kingdom in little ones may more and more be advanced'.[7] Some individuals established schools for poor children, for example William Shelton at St Giles-in-the Fields in 1672, and in the 1690s 'corporations of the poor' were established in numerous towns to repress 'idleness and debauchery' and to catechize, educate and employ pauper children.[8]

Another philanthropic response to these concerns, largely the preserve of laypeople, was the Society for the Promotion of Christian Knowledge (SPCK), established in March 1699. Its purpose was defined by its members:

> whereas the growth of Vice and Immorality is greatly increased owing to the gross ignorance of the principles of the Christian Religion … [we] do agree to meet together once a week … to consult how we may (with God's blessing) be able to propagate Christian Knowledge by encouraging Charity Schools, distributing good books and by other such lawful means as shall be thought fit.[9]

They were anxious about the contagion of 'Popery' and about Quakerism, and so sought to inculcate in the children of the poor the teachings of the Church of England, their duties to God and their neighbours, and habits of industry. Later that month the SPCK approved a form for use by subscribers to charity schools, noting:

> whereas Christian virtue can grow from no other root than Christian Principles, we being touched with zeal for the honour of God, the salvation of souls of our poor brethren and the Promoting of Christian Knowledge among the Poor of this Parish do hereby promise … for the setting up of a School for teaching poor Children (whose parents

[6] M. G. Mason, 'John Locke's Proposals on Work-House Schools', *Durham Research Review* 13 (1962), 8–14.

[7] Paul Slack, *From Reformation to Improvement: Public Welfare in Early Modern England* (Oxford, 1999), 87.

[8] Ibid. 104–12; Michael Fitzgerald, *Ragged London: The Life of London's Poor* (Stroud, 2011), 140–1.

[9] Edmund McClure, ed., *A Chapter in English Church History: Being the Minutes of the Society for Promoting Christian Knowledge 1698–1704, together with Abstracts of Correspondence, Letters, etc* (London, 1888), 10.

are not able to afford them any education) to read and write and to repeat [and] understand the Church Catechism.[10]

The financial revolution arising from the war against France assisted the development of the SPCK and charity schools with the newly developed funding model of joint stock companies, enabling the middling sort and professional people to fund philanthropic projects with a sense of participation in those projects. The lapse of the Licensing Act in 1695 resulted in an explosion of printing and publishing, increasing the quantity of 'licentious literature', but also enabling the SPCK to commission tracts, booklets and books for schools and for distribution to the poor. There was also a general enthusiasm for establishing societies of like-minded people, for example the Society of Antiquaries, societies for the reformation of manners, and religious societies. Charity schools were the most numerous and successful such associational bodies.[11]

Richard Willis, dean of Lincoln, preaching at the first London Charity Schools Trustees' festival in 1704, reminded the estimated two thousand trustees, masters, mistresses, children and parents present: 'It is the Duty of every Master of a Family to keep up the Worship of God in it and to that end to have his Family frequently together, if it be possible every morning and evening.' For, he noted, '[e]very Family is a little Society and Congregation'. He added: 'Another duty is to instruct their Families in the principles of Religion from the cradle onwards, and to set them a good example, and to pray for their children'. Willis envisaged charity schools assisting poor parents 'to instruct [children] in Christian Religion and instruct them in things that will qualify them for work and to place

[10] Ibid. 18. For the SPCK's involvement with charity schools, see Jones, *Charity School Movement*; David Owen, *English Philanthropy 1660–1960* (London, 1965), 23–33; Robert Unwin, 'The Established Church and the Schooling of the Poor: The Role of the S.P.C.K., 1699–1720', in Vincent Allen McClelland, ed., *The Churches and Education: Proceedings of the 1983 Conference of the History of Education Society of Great Britain* (Leicester, 1983), 24–32; Rose, 'Politics, Religion and Charity'; idem, 'Providence, Protestant Union and Godly Reformation in the 1690s', *TRHS* 6th ser. 3 (1993), 151–70; idem, 'The Origins and Ideals of the SPCK 1699–1716', in John Walsh, Colin Haydon and Stephen Taylor, eds, *The Church of England* c.*1689*–c.*1833: From Toleration to Tractarianism* (Cambridge, 1993), 172–90.

[11] Michael J. D. Roberts, 'Head versus Heart: Voluntary Association and Charity Organizations in England *c*.1700–1850', in Hugh Cunningham and Joanna Innes, eds, *Philanthropy and Reform: From the 1690s to 1850* (Basingstoke, 1998), 66–86.

them in some Trade or other way of getting a living'.[12] Parents and apprentice masters and mistresses were expected to hear their children and apprentices repeat the Catechism at home, thereby refreshing their own memories, and also to hear them read (probably from the Bible or the Prayer Book), especially on Sundays. Children would thus evangelize their parents, and, in their turn, as parents (especially girls, as mothers), establish Christian households.[13] The SPCK commissioned *Prayers for the Use of the Charity Schools*, which included Prayer Book Morning and Evening Prayer, a 'short' (two-page) prayer and an evening prayer for children to use at home, prayers to be used when taking and leaving their seat in church, and graces before and after meals, as well as provisions for itemizing both sins and thanksgivings.[14] *Prayers for the Use of those who go from Charity Schools to an Apprenticeship or other Service* included similar sets of prayers, adding prayers to lead a virtuous life, thanksgivings for their parents and master and mistress, and prayers that they might be content with their lot.[15] The SPCK also sponsored booklets of prayers for use in people's subsequent working lives.[16]

Most studies of charity schools have focused on the early years of the eighteenth century. This article considers St Giles's schools throughout the century, in the context, especially for the earlier period, of other London charity schools, and also explores the apprenticeship of children beyond their schooling.[17]

[12] Richard Willis, *A Sermon preach'd in the Parish Church of St Andrew's Holborn, June 8th 1704 … at the first Meeting of the Gentlemen concerned in promoting the Charity Schools in and about the Cities of London and Westminster* (London, 1704). For 'household religion', see W. M. Jacob, '"Conscientious attention to publick and family worship of God": Religious Practice in Eighteenth-Century English Households', in John Doran, Charlotte Methuen and Alexandra Walsham, eds, *Religion and the Household*, SCH 50 (Woodbridge, 2014), 307–17.

[13] Leonard W. Cowie, *Henry Newman: An American in London 1708–1743* (London, 1956), 74. For mothers teaching children to read, see Margaret Spufford, 'Women teaching Reading to poor Children in the Sixteenth and Seventeenth Centuries', in eadem, *Figures in the Landscape: Rural Society in England 1500–1700* (Aldershot, 2001), XI, 47–62.

[14] *Prayers for the Use of the Charity Schools* (London, 1734).

[15] *Prayers for the Use of those who go from Charity Schools to an Apprenticeship or other Service* (London, 1715).

[16] See W. K. Lowther Clarke, *Eighteenth-Century Piety* (London, 1944), 17–22.

[17] Tim Hitchcock, 'Paupers and Preachers: SPCK and the Parochial Work-House Movement', in Lee Davison et al., eds, *Stilling the Grumbling Hive: Response to Social and Economic Problems in England, 1689–1750* (Stroud, 1992), 145–66; Clarke,

It is clear that there was considerable variety, perhaps depending on local circumstances, among the London charity schools in their governance, funding, entry requirements, provision of clothing for children, quality and levels of pay of teachers, and response to external pressures most notably in providing for children to work.[18] St Giles, situated between the cities of London and Westminster, was one of the largest and most multiply deprived newly populous London sub-urban parishes. Deserted by the rich for new developments in Mayfair and Bloomsbury, in 1711 it was identified by the Commission for Building Fifty New Churches as one of the populous and godless sub-urban parishes eligible for subdivision and a new church.[19] A work-house had been opened in the parish in 1695, also providing a school for children of people receiving poor relief. The St Giles trustees, unlike many others, therefore did not need to provide for the poorest children.

The rector, William Haley (also dean of Chichester) became a member of the SPCK in December 1699, and in April 1700 reported establishing a school for fifty girls.[20] In April 1705 Haley and twelve laypeople resolved to raise a subscription for a charity school

> to instruct the Children in the Principles of the Church of England … that they are Taught and Examined in the Church Catechism … [with] Prayers in the Schools morning and evening, and Sing Psalms morning and evening and [learn] to Pray at home on mornings as soon as they rise and evenings goeing to bed, and to use Graces before and after meat.[21]

Eighteenth-Century Piety, 78–9. Dianne Payne, 'London's Charity School Children: the "Scum of the Parish"?', *Journal for Eighteenth-Century Studies* 29 (2006), 382–97, focuses mainly on the early years of London charity schools. The same author's 'Children of the Poor in London 1700–1780' (PhD thesis, University of Hertfordshire, 2008) shows how charity schools were part of wider provision of education for poor children in London.

18 See Payne, 'London's Charity School Children'.

19 E. G. W. Bill, ed., *The Queen Anne Churches: A Catalogue of the Papers in Lambeth Palace Library of the Commission for building Fifty New Churches in London and Westminster 1711–1759* (London, 1979), 59.

20 McClure, ed., *A Chapter in English Church History*, 11, 40, 44, 59. See also *An Account of the Methods whereby the Charity Schools have been erected and managed and of the Encouragement given to them* (London, 1705), 8, which noted that the school had fifty girls and forty subscribers, with twenty girls already put out to apprenticeships.

21 London, LMA 4542/E/01/001, St Giles-in-the-Fields Parochial Schools Trustees' Minutes 1705–1712, 18 April 1705, 23 June 1709.

The first treasurer, Narcissus Luttrell, was a bencher of nearby Gray's Inn.[22] Thirty-five subscribers elected ten trustees to manage the schools. Haley and subsequent rectors seldom attended meetings, so management was largely in the hands of laypeople. By 1710 there were 240 subscribers supporting four schools with 100 boys clothed and thirty-five not provided with clothes, and 100 girls clothed, the second largest provision in London after St Andrew's, Holborn.[23]

The minute books suggest businesslike governance, with subscribers annually electing trustees, standing orders for weekly (later fortnightly) trustees' meetings, quarterly financial reports and regular reports from the master. Children's eligibility and suitability was ascertained; a subgroup regularly visited and inspected the schools, examining the children's work and their understanding of the Catechism.[24] They were represented on the Society of London Charity Schools Trustees, which organized the great annual festival service on Holy Thursday (then the conventional designation for Ascension Day) at St Sepulchre's, Newgate, and consulted other school trustees about good practice.[25] They advertised for, interviewed and elected masters and mistresses who were required to be 'such as frequent the Holy Communion, ... are of sober lives and conversations and ... well grounded in the Principles of Christianity'. In 1763 masters were also forbidden to follow any other business or occupation or teach other children or accept money or presents from parents; they must be under fifty and already a master or assistant, having taught reading and writing and arithmetic for at least twelve months, and 'of a good Temper'. The salary

[22] 'Narcissus Luttrell 1657–1732', in Eveline Cruickshanks, Stuart Handley and David Hayton, eds, *The History of Parliament: The House of Commons, 1690–1715*, 5 vols (Cambridge, 2002). He was also MP for Bossiney 1679–81 and Saltash 1691–5 in Cornwall, an active JP for Middlesex, a vestryman of St Giles, a book collector, diarist and commentator on his times.

[23] Trustees' Minutes 1705–1712; *An Account of the Methods whereby the Charity Schools have been erected and managed and the Encouragement given to them* (London, 1710), 10. Subscribers included Lord Chancellor Cowper, the duke of Newcastle, Dr Hans Sloane, and fifteen women. £140 was contributed in collections.

[24] Trustees' Minutes 1705–1712, 23 June 1709.

[25] For the London Charity Schools Trustees Society, see Rose, 'Politics, Religion and Charity', 104; Sarah Lloyd, '"Pleasing Spectacles and Elegant Dinners": Conviviality, Benevolence, and Charity Anniversaries in Eighteenth-Century London', *JBS* 41 (2002), 23–57.

was £50 a year plus apartment, coal and candles, which was above the going rate in other schools.[26]

Complaints against teachers, especially of unduly severe punishments, were investigated, and if found wanting teachers might be admonished, suspended or dismissed, for they were expected to set an example of Christian neighbourliness, and parents and children might be alienated if they did not. Complaints in 1718 of 'several neglects and misdoings' committed by Thomas Adge, a master, were investigated and he was 'expelled'.[27] In 1740 Mrs Griffiths was suspended because she 'cruely abused Sarah Dollson by giving her unwarranted Correction with an Unlawful weapon'. The trustees noted 'she did not behave with that respect to the Board as is due from a Mistress to the Trustees on her giving account of the above affair, Justifying herself rather than acknowledging her fault'.[28] In 1782–3 it was noted that discipline and cleanliness in the schools had become lax, and the trustees investigated the shortcomings, ensuring matters were put in good order.[29] They could be generous, granting £25 a year for life 'in consideration of his faithfulness' to a master resigning due to ill health in 1806, while a mistress who resigned for health reasons in 1807 received a gratuity of 15 guineas for 'her great attention and care of the children'.[30]

Fundraising for premises, teachers' salaries, books, children's clothing and apprenticeship premiums was a major concern in the context of the century's economic vagaries. From time to time, as in October 1739, when they reduced the master's salary, the trustees noted that expenditure had exceeded income. By 1806 expenditure was the significant amount of £1,309 *6s 9¾d*. It is unclear what the income was, but subscribers needed to be attracted. Distinguished preachers, including in 1786 John Wesley, were regularly invited to address special services at which collections were taken.[31] Both services and preachers made the case for the schools and for the importance of the Christian duty of generous philanthropy in educating the next

[26] Trustees' Minutes 1705–1712, 23 June 1709; LMA 4542/E/01/006, Trustees' Minutes 1762–1785, 16 June 1763; compare also Payne, 'London's Charity School Children', 399.
[27] LMA 4542/E/01/002, Trustees' Minutes 1712–1725, 15 October 1718.
[28] LMA 4542/E/01/004, Trustees' Minutes 1737–1747, 23 September 1740.
[29] Trustees' Minutes 1762–1785, January 1782 – August 1783.
[30] LMA 4542/E/01/007, Trustees' Minutes 1785–1807, 19 April 1806 – 27 May 1807.
[31] Ibid., 25 October 1785.

godly generation. Children, illustrating the fruits of charity and accompanied by the masters and mistresses, processed in their school clothes from school to church, and sang the psalms and anthem at the service.[32] Subscribers of 40*s* a year might nominate a child, aged eight and qualified by residence in the parish, for consideration for admission as a pupil. Later in the century the trustees, to encourage more subscribers, circulated printed subscription lists.[33] Donations and bequests, which were fairly frequent, were invested in property or stock, and a gold-lettered donors' board was provided for the schoolroom.[34]

As 'nurseries of piety', there were morning and afternoon prayers in the schools, probably based on Matins and Evensong in the Book of Common Prayer. For Sunday morning and afternoon services the pupils processed with the teachers to church, sitting in their own gallery, and in the afternoon boys and girls alternately were examined in church on their understanding of the Book of Common Prayer catechism as mediated through John Lewis's *The Church Catechism Explain'd and Confirm'd*.[35] Additionally, in 1727 trustees resolved that children must assemble in their schools every Sunday at 6 a.m. in winter and 5 a.m. in summer to hear a chapter of the *Whole Duty of Man*.

The curriculum comprised the Catechism, reading, and writing and arithmetic (for girls, only 'the first Rules … to enable them to keep Family Accounts'), and, for girls, also sewing and needlework. *The Christian Schoolmaster* outlined a four-year course with reading and the New Testament in the first year, reading and the Bible in the second year, beginning writing in the third year and arithmetic in the fourth year.[36] This strongly Anglican milieu was clearly acceptable to parents, for the schools were generally fully subscribed,

[32] For charity school sermons, see W. E. Tate, 'Church School Finance in the Reign of Queen Anne', *CQR* 159 (1958), 59–77; idem, 'The Charity Sermons 1701–1732, as a Source for the History of Education', *JEH* 9 (1958), 54–73; Donna T. Andrew, 'On reading Charity Sermons: Eighteenth-Century Anglican Solicitation and Exhortation', *JEH* 43 (1992), 581–91; Sarah Lloyd, '"Pleasing Spectacles and Elegant Dinners"'.

[33] Trustees' Minutes 1785–1807, 19 December 1787.

[34] Trustees' Minutes 1712–1725, 12 December 1716: 'no names be inserted but of such only who have given five pounds or more'.

[35] This had been written at the request of the SPCK, the author having reviewed thirty existing expositions; it was published in 1701 and sold at 3*s* a dozen.

[36] James Talbot's *The Christian Schoolmaster*, published under the auspices of the SPCK in 1707, for which see R. W. Unwin, *Charity Schools and the Defence of Anglicanism* (York, 1984), 25–30; Clarke, *Eighteenth-Century Piety*, 73–6. For catechetical teaching, see Ian

although from time to time there were vacancies in the girls' schools. Perhaps girls' help was more needed at home. The content and methods must have engaged children, as little disruptive behaviour and relatively little truancy were noted.[37] Nor does it seem that poor parents were deterred from sending children to school by loss of their earnings, for this was to some extent compensated for by children being clothed and shod.[38]

Trustees monitored attendance and discipline, requiring the master to report at every meeting 'the defaulters of ye Boys not coming to School and any crimes he shall find them guilty of'.[39] Children with 'the itch' or 'lousy' were required not to attend again until cured.[40] Children who truanted were summoned with a parent to give explanations to the trustees, and were expelled after a second or third incident. Truanting was taken seriously for it deprived another child of education. In 1785 boys accused of taking currants from a basket in Covent Garden were forbidden to be seen there without their parents, and in 1800 a boy was expelled for stealing a loaf.[41]

The trustees survived a number of crises precipitated by external circumstances. In the political and religious turmoil later in Queen Anne's reign school trustees were suspected of infiltration by extreme high church Jacobite sympathizers. Charity school children, including some from St Giles, were identified in 1710 amongst rioters following Dr Sacheverell's trial,[42] and in 1716 in pro-Jacobite riots.[43] The trustees forbade boys to become involved with 'Mobbs' on pain of expulsions, and required their 'Orders to be fairly Written in Large Hand and hung up in ye School Room'.[44] Bishop

Green, *The Christian's ABC: Catechisms and Catechizing in England* c.*1530–1740* (Oxford, 1996), 170–95, 249, 263.

37 At Greycoat Hospital in nearby Westminster the trustees recommended the master to 'win the love and affection of the children, and thereby invite and encourage them, rather than by correction to force them to learn': Payne, 'Children of the Poor', 103.

38 It is unclear whether much paid employment was available for children in London: see Patricia Crawford, *Parents of Poor Children in England 1500–1800* (Oxford, 2010), 180.

39 Trustees' Minutes 1705–1712, 1 August 1705.

40 Ibid., 17 April 1706.

41 Trustees' Minutes 1785–1807, 10 August 1785, 12 March 1800.

42 Trustees' Minutes 1705–1712, 17 May 1710.

43 Craig Rose, '"Seminaries of Faction and Rebellion": Jacobites, Whigs and the London Charity Schools', *HistJ* 34 (1991), 831–55; Cowie, *Henry Newman*, 87–9; Peter Maplestone, *St Clement Danes School: 300 Years of History* (London, 2000), 10.

44 Trustees' Minutes 1712–1725, 31 May 1716.

Edmund Gibson intervened in 1724, in a charge to London charity school masters and mistresses at St Paul's, to rehabilitate schools from allegations that 'Children are trained up to Disaffection to the Government' and 'Set above the lower and more laborious Stations and Offices of Life'. However, teachers, he observed, should 'do no more than to prepare Children to be good Christians and Servants', not teaching elaborate psalm settings or 'fine needlework'.[45] Social advancement was not encouraged.

It was also regularly claimed that charity school boys were numerous among convicted criminals. William Hogarth, a near neighbour in St Martin's Lane, in 1741 depicted his cruel apprentice wearing a St Giles cap. Subscribers were often criticized as self-interested and motivated by pride and profit, and schools for unfitting children for work as servants. Strong views were regularly expressed in the press, following Locke, that charity schools should train children for manual work and thus for their future position in life. Greycoat Hospital had introduced work into the curriculum in 1700, but abandoned it in 1734, and the response among London schools was very mixed, although the SPCK encouraged it.[46] Although St Giles girls made their own clothes in school, the trustees did not appoint a committee to consider work for boys until 1740, introducing knitting and silk-winding in 1744.[47] In 1750 another committee reviewed boys' work, visiting the Foundling Hospital and St George's, Hanover Square workhouse school to discover how they managed additional costs and poor returns on children's work. Another review in 1751 recommended introducing 'making Purses, Nett and Winding Silk for six Months' for four hours daily. The 1752 annual meeting ordered a detailed financial report, and subsequently a subscribers' meeting resolved that 'a proper Number of Boys be employed in the said manufactory', requiring a 'light building' costing £74 10*s*. Objections ensued to making 'Boys mere Slaves and Drudges' and to the capital expenditure, pointing out losses on the earlier 'Spinning Scheme'. Five people threatened to withdraw their

[45] *Directions given by Edmund Lord Bishop of London to the Masters and Mistresses of the Charity Schools within the Bills of Mortality and the Diocese of London, assembled for that Purpose in the Chapter House of St Paul's, November the 14th 1724* (London, 1724), 4–5.

[46] Payne, 'London's Charity School Children', 391. For a discussion of the provision of work as part of schools' curriculum, see Hugh Cunningham, *The Children of the Poor: Representations of Childhood since the Seventeenth Century* (Oxford, 1993), 25–35.

[47] Trustees' Minutes 1737–1747, 20 October 1740, 11 December 1744.

subscriptions. Another committee undertook a further review, and, despite noting losses of £10 10*s* in 1744, and £12 2*s* 6½*d* in 1751–2, recommended 'employing a part of the Boys' Time in useful Labour [which] will remove the great Objection of Idleness from this Institution'. The committee hoped also that the trustees 'will exert themselves in setting so Noble and useful precedent to the rest of the Charity Schools as the uniting of useful Labour and useful Learning as it bids fair to render these Boys better Members of the Community than if their whole Time was Employ'd in Learning only'.[48] By 1809, however, 'work' had ceased to be part of the curriculum.[49] Work was always a financial failure in schools: raw materials were expensive, and the children, being unskilled, produced poor-quality, unsaleable work.[50]

The final phase of a charity scholar's education was placement at the age of fourteen in a godly household as an apprentice or servant for seven years, to be fed and clothed and learn an occupation.[51] The SPCK recommended:

> Trustees shall see that the Masters to whom the children are apprenticed are persons of a sober and religious life and conversation who will cultivate and improve [an apprentice's] Christian disposition, Hear them read the Bible and some other good books, make them repeat what they have learned at school, see that they are constant in their morning and evening devotions, and not only carry them to church to be catechised there, but sometimes send or go with them to their minister to be catechised and instructed by him in private.[52]

[48] LMA 4542/E/01/005, Trustees' Minutes 1747–1762, July 1750, 6 August 1751, 28 May 1752, 12, 25 August 1752, 3 October 1752.

[49] *A Short State of the Charity Schools of St Giles in the Fields and St George Bloomsbury, with an Account of the Benefactions and Legacies and also a List of the Subscribers, July 1809* (London, 1809), 4.

[50] Jones, *Charity School Movement*, 93.

[51] On apprenticeships, see Christopher Brooks, 'Apprenticeship, Social Mobility and the Middling Sort 1550–1800', in Jonathan Barry and Christopher Brooks, eds, *The Middling Sort of People: Culture, Society and Politics in England, 1550–1800* (Basingstoke, 1994), 55–73, Joan Lane, *Apprenticeship in England* (London, 1996); Alannah Tomkins, *The Experience of Urban Poverty 1723–1782: Parish Charity and Credit* (Manchester, 2006), 179–87.

[52] *Circular Letter of the SPCK to its Clergy and Correspondents* (London, 1714), quoted in Jones, *Charity School Movement*, 49–50.

St Giles' trustees took great care over apprenticeships.[53] Two trustees inquired into the characters of masters before children were put out as apprentices.[54] Children were not apprenticed to 'any Person dissenting from the Church of England'. From 1784 only people renting property worth at least £10 a year were considered.[55] Parents might not take their own child as an apprentice, nor object to a trade or a master or mistress.[56] A child refusing an apprenticeship had to explain their reasons to the trustees and might be dismissed from the school. Sometimes children were apprenticed for a month 'upon tryall', and then 'upon their approbation and liking of each other' the apprenticeship was confirmed. In January 1780 Catherine Frazer 'absolutely refused to be bound at this time, to Richard West of Oxford Street, Breeches maker', but she agreed to go back for a further fortnight and 'upon further liking' was bound as apprentice to him.[57]

A £5 premium was provided for boys, reduced to £3 in 1728, and 40*s* [£2] for girls.[58] They received a Bible, Prayer Book, Psalm Book and *The Whole Duty of Man*;[59] and were required to come to the school 'once in halfe a year' for examination in the Catechism[60] and to take part in the Charity Schools Festival procession.[61] Although they had to return their school clothes, from 1740 masters or mistresses were provided with 40*s* to clothe girls, and girls received 10*s* after remaining in service for a year. Clothes must be returned if they stayed less than a year, but thereafter they might keep them.[62]

Apprenticeships were carefully monitored. In 1712 a boy complained that his master 'had used him hardly, and not allowed him Victuals'. The master was ordered to attend the next trustees' meeting.[63] When a mother complained that her son, apprenticed to Mr Watkins, a bricklayer, had been 'put away illegally to her great

[53] For a comparison with the apprenticeship of workhouse school children, see Lane, *Apprenticeship in England*, 85–90; Payne, 'Children of the Poor in London', 177–216.
[54] Trustees' Minutes 1737–1747, 19 June 1737.
[55] Trustees' Minutes 1762–1785, 17 June 1784.
[56] Trustees' Minutes 1705–1712, 18 September 1706.
[57] Trustees' Minutes 1762–1785, 12, 26 January 1780.
[58] Trustees' Minutes 1705–1712, 4 September 1706.
[59] Ibid., 19 March, 14 December 1707.
[60] Ibid., 14 December 1709.
[61] Ibid., 19 March 1707.
[62] Trustees' Minutes 1737–1747, 29 July 1740.
[63] Trustees' Minutes 1712–1725, 12 July 1712.

detriment' two trustees were appointed to make inquiries, who reported 'his Crimes were fully prov'd upon him' and referred the matter to a justice of the peace.[64] In 1733 when the trustees heard that a poor boy put out as apprentice was in the Bridewell, they agreed that the treasurer should pay the charge of 6*s* 4*d* for his release.[65] Apprentices from charity schools whose apprenticeship proved unsatisfactory may therefore have been in a better position than other apprentices, for their schools' trustees might take action on their behalf.

In 1809 an appeal for more subscriptions reported that 101 boys and seventy girls were being educated, including thirty-five girls boarded; that since 1700, 2,488 pupils had been apprenticed or 'taken out for service'; and that nearly as many had been 'taken out by their Relations or Friends'. The regime of teaching the Catechism and daily prayers and encouragement to household prayers continued. There had been 128 legacies and donations over 104 years (including 49 from women), and there were currently 425 subscribers.[66] This evidence, from one of the most populous and notoriously poor and criminal London parishes, demonstrates that for more than a century a succession of competent and generous laypeople efficiently and attentively provided and monitored education and apprenticeships, training selected poor children in the principles of the Church of England and in basic skills to enable them to earn a living. Artisans, as masters or mistresses of apprentices, also engaged with the project. As the schools, especially boys' schools, were usually full, it is apparent that parents of the poorer sort were keen to take up this provision, and that some former pupils, at least, prospered and were grateful. On 24 April 1775, the trustees must have felt gratified when 'three members of the Society of Persons educated in these Schools waited on the Board with a donation of £5 5s … as a token of their Gratitude for the Benefits received to them from the Charity'.[67]

While it is clear that the St Giles trustees, and the trustees of the fifty-eight other schools whose minute books survive in the London Metropolitan Archives, sustained their schools and protected the

[64] Ibid., 14 August 1717.
[65] LMA 4542/E/01/003, Trustees' Minutes 1726–1737, 14 March 1733.
[66] *Short State of the Charity Schools of St Giles*, 4–5, 8–9.
[67] Trustees' Minutes 1762–1785, 26 April 1775.

interests of children in them, it is noteworthy that they gave no consideration to increasing the provision for education in the face of the vastly increased population of the parish during the period. There is no evidence that in London Sunday schools provided from the 1780s an alternative and cheaper means of teaching children. From then on, there was national concern about lack of provision of elementary schools for poor children. Statistics were gathered about the number and efficiency of charity schools. Joseph Lancaster, a Quaker, and Andrew Bell, an Anglican, developed more economical monitorial systems for teaching children. Bell introduced his system at St Botolph's, Aldgate charity school in 1798. A number of new schools were also opened in and around London, for example at Limehouse in 1779 and Brentford in 1786, and a large parochial 'day school' in West Street, St Giles, by one of St Giles's clergy in 1802. Major initiatives included Lancaster's establishment of the British and Foreign Schools Society in 1808 to promote his system, largely supported by Dissenters, and in 1811, as part of a renewal of the SPCK, the establishment by some of its governors of the National Society, which aimed, using Bell's monitorial system, to support the provision of an elementary school in every parish.[68] Amongst these changes, St Giles's trustees continued charitable and compassionate, but cautious and conservative in their management of their charity to promote the education of poor children.

[68] See Henry James Burgess, *Enterprise in Education: The Story of the Established Church in the Education of the People prior to 1870* (London, 1958), 14–24.

Catechizing at Home, 1740–1870: Instruction, Communication and Denomination

Mary Clare Martin*
University of Greenwich

Catechizing played an important part in domestic religious education in Britain in the eighteenth and nineteenth centuries, as well as in the better documented early modern period. However, its significance has been neglected in comparison with family prayers (often deemed to be an expression of patriarchy), Sunday observance or even private prayers. This article analyses the incidence of catechizing across religious denominations in Britain from 1740 to 1870, and within selected overseas missionary families. Drawing on a wide range of personal memoirs, the article analyses the range of contexts and relationships within which catechizing could occur. These included not only household worship (which could be conducted by women) but also relationships between siblings. It demonstrates that catechizing could provide opportunities for asking questions and spending 'quality time' with parents and / or children, rather than embodying an alienating form of rote-learning. The article therefore challenges many stereotypes relating to family domestic education, relating to themes such as patriarchy, denominational difference and adult-child interaction.

The 'Catechism as set forth in the Book of Common Prayer' of 1549 was one of the, if not the, earliest forms of universal instruction in the reformed English church, intended to induce conformity. All 'youth and ignorant persons' were to go to church on Sundays to be instructed, while heads of household were instructed to catechize their dependants.[1] The simplest version, in the Book of Common

* University of Greenwich, Old Royal Naval College, 10 Park Row, London, SE10 9LS. E-mail: mm91@gre.ac.uk. I am grateful to members of the Education in the Long Eighteenth Century Seminar at the Institute for Historical Research, where this paper was first presented, on 4 November 2017, for their comments and questions, as well as to participants at the EHS Summer Conference.

[1] Ian Green, *Print and Protestantism in Early Modern England* (Oxford, 2000), 191–3. The Prayer Book Catechism of 1549 was enlarged in 1604 and revised in 1661–2: Ian Green, *The Christian's ABC: Catechisms and Catechizing in England, c.1530–1740*

Studies in Church History 55 (2019), 256–273
doi: 10.1017/stc.2018.31

Prayer, covered the Apostles' Creed, the Ten Commandments, the Lord's Prayer and the sacraments.[2] While the Church Catechism had similarities to those written by Luther and Calvin,[3] Dissenters also wrote their own versions, notably the Shorter or Westminster Catechism of the Westminster Assembly (1643–8), and others by Baptists, Quakers and Unitarians, as well as Roman Catholics.[4] Moreover, historians of the early modern period have argued that catechizing could involve informal questioning, facilitate the acquisition of literacy and promote more advanced intellectual engagement.[5]

However, the historiography of catechizing in the eighteenth and nineteenth centuries has been less positive. Although it has been recognized that catechizing was an important tool of the eighteenth-century church, and that most clergy were diligent about public catechizing, its frequent restriction to Lent reinforced older historiographies of eighteenth-century religious decline.[6] A strong strand in nineteenth-century educational history regarded catechetical teaching to labouring- or working-class children as a form of social control, at best tedious, at worst intended to reinforce Anglican hegemony.[7] A dominant historiography of family religion has associated the 'rise' of evangelical religion from the 1780s onwards with family prayers as

(Oxford, 1996), 71–4, 122–3; William Jacob, *The Clerical Profession in the Long Eighteenth Century, 1640–1840* (Oxford and New York, 2007), 236–41.

[2] Green, *Print and Protestantism*, 190; Scott Mandelbrote, 'The Bible as Didactic Literature', in Sara Pennell and Natasha Glaisyer, eds, *Didactic Literature in England, 1500–1800: Expertise Reconstructed* (Aldershot, 2003), 75–137, at 92.

[3] Charles Wallace Jr, 'Susanna Wesley's Child-rearing Letter', in idem, ed., *Susanna Wesley: The Complete Writings* (Oxford, 1997), 367–76, at 371–2, 378; Green, *Christian's ABC*, 17–21, 62, 71, 279.

[4] Green, *Print and Protestantism*, 191–3; idem, *Christian's ABC*, 43, 83–6.

[5] Green, *Christian's ABC*, 266–74; Mandelbrote, 'Bible', 92–4.

[6] Phillip Tovey, *Anglican Confirmation, 1660–1780*, Liturgy and Worship Series (Aldershot, 2014), 195–6, 230; Jacob, *Clerical Profession*, 237–42; Michael Snape, *The Church of England in an Industrialising Society: The Lancashire Parish of Whalley in the Eighteenth Century* (Woodbridge, 2003), 20–2.

[7] Philip McCann, 'Popular Education and Social Control: Spitalfields, 1812–1824', in idem, ed., *Popular Education and Socialisation in the Nineteenth Century* (London, 1977), 1–40, at 24; S. Frith, 'Socialisation and Rational Schooling: Elementary Education in Leeds before 1870', ibid. 67–92, at 78; Boyd Hilton, *The Age of Atonement: The Influence of Evangelicalism on Social and Economic Thought, 1795–1865* (Oxford, 1988), 33; Anna Davin, *Growing up Poor: Home, School and Street in London, 1870–1914* (London, 1996), 115; Pamela Horn, *The Victorian Country Child* (Kineton, 1974), 134–5.

the bedrock of domestic devotion, making no reference to catechizing.[8]

This article calls in question the frequent dichotomy constructed by literary scholars and historians of education between teaching of the Anglican catechism, which has been regarded as dull and restrictive, and other forms of more 'liberal', conversational domestic education allegedly practised by Dissenters.[9] Instead, it shows how all denominations had their own catechisms, and that pedagogy in Anglican households could include a questioning approach rather than mere rote-learning. While concurring with more recent authors that domestic religion persisted from the seventeenth century into the eighteenth, and that evangelical claims to have initiated the 'religion of the home' were exaggerated,[10] it demonstrates how domestic catechizing continued into the eighteenth and nineteenth centuries. Above all, it seeks to contribute to the history of children by recovering the perspectives of the young (however difficult the task) on a central aspect of eighteenth-century pedagogy. Gender issues are also considered: religious education has frequently been regarded as the preserve of females, while the respective roles of parents have also

[8] Christina de Bellaigue, 'Faith and Religion', in Colin Heywood, ed., *A Cultural History of Childhood and Family*, 5: *The Age of Empire* (Oxford and New York, 2010), 149–66, 306; John Tosh, *A Man's Place: Masculinity and the Middle Class Home, 1830–1914* (London and New Haven, CT, 1999), 37, 91–3, 147; Leonore Davidoff and Catherine Hall, *Family Fortunes: Men and Women of the English Middle Class* (London, 1987), 89, 109; Sean Gill, *Women in the Church of England from the Eighteenth Century to the Present* (London, 1994), 66; D. W. Bebbington, *Evangelicalism in Modern Britain: A History from the 1730s to the 1980s* (London, 1995; first publ. 1989), 66, 105.

[9] Aileen Fyfe, 'Reading Dissenting Children's Books in Late Eighteenth-Century England', *HistJ* 43 (2002), 453–73, at 470; Marion Amies, 'Amusing and Instructive Conversations: The Literary Genre and its Relevance to Home Education', *HE* 14 (1985), 87–99, at 91–2; Michele Cohen, 'The Pedagogy of Conversation in the Home: "Familiar Conversation" as a Pedagogical Tool in Eighteenth- and Nineteenth-Century England', *Oxford Review of Education* 41 (2015), 447–63, at 454.

[10] W. M. Jacob, '"Conscientious attention to publick and family worship of God": Religious Practice in Eighteenth-Century Households', in John Doran, Charlotte Methuen and Alexandra Walsham, eds, *Religion and the Household*, SCH 50 (Woodbridge, 2014), 307–17, at 312; Jeremy Gregory, *Restoration, Reformation and Reform, 1660–1828: The Archbishops of Canterbury and their Diocese* (Oxford, 2000), 238; Karen Harvey, *The Little Republic: Masculinity and Domestic Authority in Eighteenth-Century Britain* (Oxford, 2012), 46–7.

been regarded as significant in relation to ongoing debates about masculinity, motherhood and gender roles.[11]

How was childhood understood in this period? The age of majority for those who had resources to inherit was twenty-one,[12] yet pauper children as young as seven might be apprenticed. Anna Davin has noted, however, that children in service were likely to have been in a semi-dependent position: indeed, it has been argued that some people never attained full adult status.[13] No typology exists of commonly held Protestant understandings of the chronological development of children's spirituality. By contrast, seven as the age of first communion has been perceived as a landmark for Roman Catholic children.[14] Nevertheless, Protestant writers of catechisms and other devotional material for the eighteenth-century young showed an awareness of the differing cognitive and spiritual needs of children of different ages and, as discussed below, Isaac Watts and John Wesley adapted their catechetical materials accordingly, particularly for younger children. While a systematic analysis of catechisms published for different age groups and educational levels is beyond the scope of this article, analysis of domestic practice can contribute to a broader understanding of shared ideas about children's spirituality and religious development.

Sources

My primary aim here is to 'recover' family practices and children's experiences, rather than to document the content and production of texts. However, the problem with a routine practice such as catechizing is that it was frequently unrecorded.[15] The sources used cover many different parts of Britain, as well as English-speaking locations overseas, and include manuscript collections, home instruction

[11] Anthony Fletcher, *Growing up in England: The Experience of Childhood, 1600–1914* (New Haven, CT, 2008), 99–106, 245. For a reiteration of the 'separate spheres' thesis, see James Marten, 'Family Relationships', in Heywood, ed, *Cultural History*, 19–38, at 21.

[12] Roy Porter, *English Society in the Eighteenth Century* (London, 1988; first publ. 1982), 165–6.

[13] Anna Davin, 'What is a Child?', in Stephen Hussey and Anthony Fletcher, eds, *Childhood in Question: Children, Parents and the State* (Manchester, 1999), 15–36, at 22.

[14] Philippe Ariès, *Centuries of Childhood: A Social History of Family Life*, transl. Robert Baldick (Harmondsworth, 1973; first publ. 1962), 122–4.

[15] Jacob, '"Conscientious attention"', 307–12.

schemes and published editions of letters, diaries and childhood recollections. Many different Protestant denominations and types of Anglican churchmanship are represented, and the families of a number of clergy, ministers or missionaries are probably over-represented. Inevitably, memoirs and letters were more likely to survive from the middling and upper ranks, but collections of autobiographies have been particularly useful for accessing the experience of families in the labouring class.[16] These memoirs, like the descriptions of pious children in missionary and other memoirs, are subject to the problems of retrospective reconstruction and genre writing;[17] nonetheless, specific rituals and practices may provide a more definite focus for memory than more diffuse emotional experiences.

Background

The period between 1740 and 1870 witnessed many religious changes, notably the emergence of Methodism from the 1740s, the 'rise' of evangelicalism from the 1780s, the repeal of the Test and Corporation Acts in 1828 and the appearance of the Oxford Movement from 1833. Throughout the period, catechisms were a benchmark for maintaining orthodoxy and could have enormous political significance.[18] Controversies over the teaching of the Church Catechism have been regarded as crucial in the foundation of the National Society in 1811, and in preventing agreement about the nature of state-funded education until the 1870 Education Act forbade the teaching of any specific creed or formulary in state-funded schools.[19] There is evidence of catechizing throughout the period. In the early 1700s, clergy distributed catechisms to the labouring poor in Kent, Lincolnshire and Yorkshire, and reported

[16] For example, Thomas Jackson, *The Lives of the Early Methodist Preachers*, 6 vols (London, 1838–64).

[17] Ludmilla Jordanova, 'Children in History: Concepts of Nature and Society', in Geoffrey Scarre, ed., *Children, Parents and Politics* (Cambridge, 1989), 3–24, at 5; D. Bruce Hindmarsh, *The Evangelical Conversion Narrative: Spiritual Autobiography in Early Modern England* (Oxford, 2005), 293–319.

[18] See Robert Tudur Jones, *Congregationalism in England, 1662–1962* (London, 1965), 171; Robert G. Ingram, *Religion, Reform and Modernity: Thomas Secker and the Church of England* (Woodbridge, 2007), 81; Gregory, *Restoration*, 238; Green, *Christian's ABC*, 43.

[19] Eric Hopkins, *Childhood Transformed: Working-Class Children in Nineteenth-Century England* (Manchester, 1994), 144.

that some parents were catechizing their children at home.[20] Indeed, Michael Watts has argued that domestic catechizing in labouring and middling-sort families laid the foundation for many Methodist conversions.[21]

The first part of this article aims to establish basic patterns, such as the age of instruction, when catechizing occurred and by whom it was conducted. The second addresses children's responses, illuminating themes such as the relationship of catechizing to religious experience, parents as pedagogues and denominational difference. The focus throughout is limited to catechisms designed for a religious purpose.

Ages, Times and Catechists

Susanna Wesley (1669–1742) was accustomed to begin religious teaching soon after her children began to talk, starting just after 1690. The Wesley children were taught

> as soon as they could speak, the Lord's Prayer, which they were made to say at rising and bedtime constantly; to which as they grew bigger, were added a short prayer for their parents, and some collects; a short catechism, and some portions of Scripture … as their memories could bear … .[22]

Adam Clarke's family were taught 'with the earliest dawnings of reason' to commit to memory parts of the Church Catechism and the Shorter Catechism.[23] Four was frequently mentioned in life-story writing as a significant age.[24] Two early Methodist preachers, born in 1738, Thomas Taylor (the son of a Presbyterian tanner) and George Story, both from Yorkshire, later claimed that they had been able to recite the Shorter Catechism or the Church Catechism to their respective ministers aged four.[25] Thomas Priestley asserted the same of his brother Joseph (1733–1804) with reference to the

[20] Gregory, *Restoration*, 238; Jacob, *Clerical Profession*, 238; Green, *Christian's ABC*, 122.
[21] Michael Watts, *The Dissenters*, 1: *From the Reformation to the French Revolution* (Oxford, 1978), 423.
[22] Wallace, ed., *Susanna Wesley*, 371.
[23] James Everett, *Adam Clarke portrayed*, 2 vols (London, 1843–4), 1: 14–15, 38.
[24] Fletcher, *Growing up*, 99.
[25] Jackson, *Lives*, 5: 1–2, 218.

Shorter Catechism.[26] Other references to four- or five-year-olds learning the Church Catechism can be found in the 1740s, 1760s and 1840s.[27] The ages of six and seven were mentioned in the 1760s, the early 1800s and 1870.[28] However, Henry Venn, author of the popular *Complete Duty of Man* (1763), did not approve of teaching very young children and only started 'formal instructions' when they were eight.[29] Isaac Watts (1674–1748) also believed that content should be age-related, and very concrete for children under seven.[30]

Learning and performing the catechism could develop throughout the child's life-cycle, with differing levels of difficulty. On Sundays, in the 1820s, five of the six children of the high church Young family of Limehouse (born between 1815 and 1823), aged three to eight, had to learn or recite one of a series of catechisms, whilst the eldest, aged ten, had to learn or write the collect.[31] The younger children learned Watts's *First Catechism*, the Church Catechism, the *Mother's Catechism*, *Crossman's Catechism* and *Crossman's Questions*.[32] Mrs Young's schedule prescribed the most intensive weekday catechetical instruction (up to four or five times each week) for children between the ages of six and nine; her elder and younger children had less catechesis.[33] The diarist Emily Shore (1819–39) recorded how her mother taught her with her younger siblings, three girls and two boys, born between 1819 and 1825, when they were aged between

[26] *Memoirs of Dr Joseph Priestley to the Year 1795, written by himself, with a Continuation to the Time of his Decease, by his Son, Joseph Priestley, and Observations on his Writings, by Thomas Cooper … and the Rev. William Christie* (London, 1809), 5.

[27] Fletcher, *Growing up*, 249, 115, 117, for Hester Thrale's children; Manchester, JRL, Fletcher-Tooth Papers (hereafter: MAM, Fl), Box 23, manuscript autobiography of Mrs Mary Fletcher, Part 1, 1; Chester, Cheshire RO, Journals of William Charles Cotton, vol. 11, fol. 3, June 1846 (Microfilm 3).

[28] Francis Bamford, *Dear Miss Heber: An Eighteenth-Century Correspondence* (London, 1938), 2; Florence White, *A Fire in the Kitchen: The Autobiography of a Cook* (London, 1938), 43; Ernest Gray Sandford, ed., *Memoirs of Archbishop Temple by Seven Friends*, 2 vols (London, 1906), 1: 19.

[29] Henry Venn to Joseph Stillingfleet, 25 January 1785, in *The Letters of Henry Venn, with a Memoir by John Venn* (Edinburgh, 1993; first publ. 1835), 429.

[30] Green, *Christian's ABC*, 271–4.

[31] London, Museum of London (hereafter: MOL), Young Education Scheme (hereafter: YES), 48.85/6, Schemes of lessons, 1825–31.

[32] MOL, YES, 48.85/6, List of books; *The Catechism broke into Short Questions; to which is added an Explanation of some words, for the easier Understanding of it: Together with some Prayers for the Use of Charity Schools* (London, 1830 edn).

[33] MOL, YES, 48.85/6, Schemes of lessons, 1825, 1827.

six and twelve.[34] Catherine MacFarlane (1879–1946), who had been brought up in the Free Church of Scotland and lived in Glasgow, noted that 'thirteen was a serious age', at which she could 'recite the Shorter Catechism and chapters of the Old and New Testaments'.[35]

The Church Catechism had an end point and a purpose, as knowledge of it was a requirement for Anglican confirmation. While Phillip Tovey's case studies identify confirmation as usually taking place at the age of fourteen, the age could vary from ten to twenty-two.[36] In the diocese of London, fourteen was the expected age from the 1760s, rising to fifteen by 1798.[37] In the nineteenth century, fifteen to sixteen was a usual age. John Henry Newman (1801–90) recalled that 'of course I was word perfect in the Catechism at the age of fifteen'.[38] Fanny Keats was confirmed in 1819, aged fifteen,[39] and Charlotte Yonge was also fifteen when she was prepared for confirmation by John Keble by working through the Catechism and the communion service.[40] The high church Agnes Cotton was sixteen when she used her elder brother William's catechetical lecture cards.[41]

Unsurprisingly, catechizing is usually referred to across the period as a domestic devotional exercise on Sunday: for the 1750s, 1760s and 1770s, the early and late 1800s, and on Sunday evenings specifically in the 1740s and 1820s.[42] On weekdays, it might comprise part of schoolroom exercises, as with the Youngs in the 1820s, schoolmaster Roger Langdon's children in the 1860s and 1870s, and Lydia North Paget's domestic teaching in the 1850s and early 1860s.[43]

34 Margaret Emily Shore, ed., *The Journal of Emily Shore* (London, 1891), 27–8 (23 December 1832).

35 Catherine MacFarlane Carswell, *Lying Awake: An unfinished Autobiography and other Posthumous Papers* (London, 1950), 35.

36 Tovey, *Anglican Confirmation*, 199, 249, 257, 316, 334.

37 Mary Clare Martin, 'Children and Religion in Walthamstow and Leyton, 1740–1870' (PhD thesis, University of London, 2000), 358–66.

38 John Henry Newman, *Apologia pro Vita Sua* (London, 1890 edn), 1.

39 Marie Adami, *Fanny Keats* (London, 1937), 277–9.

40 Christabel Coleridge, *Charlotte Mary Yonge: Her Life and Letters* (London, 1903), 119.

41 Oxford, Bodl., MS Acland d.118, fol. 113, Agnes Cotton to William Charles Cotton, 1844.

42 Bamford, ed., *Dear Miss Heber*, 2; Everett, *Adam Clarke portrayed*, 1: 14–15; Almyra Gray, ed, *Papers and Diaries of a York Family, 1764–1839* (London, 1927), 21; Shore, ed., *Shore Journal*, 27–8 (1832).

43 MOL, YES, 48.85/6, Schemes of lessons, 1825–8; Langdon, *Life*, 67; Jeanne Peterson, *Family, Love and Work in the Lives of Victorian Gentlewomen* (Bloomington, IN, 1989),

Whereas Luther assumed that mothers would be teaching their children, Anthony Fletcher has argued that from the Reformation on, catechizing was the father's responsibility, and that many fathers were 'warm, intimate and caring', rather than harsh patriarchs.[44] There is some consensus that there was a transition from the educational importance of the father, with the mother supplanting the father by the mid- to late nineteenth century,[45] and some consider this led to a 'crisis' of masculinity.[46] However, family evidence is more complicated. A number of this article's eighteenth century subjects were catechized by their fathers, including Mary Bosanquet and also Faith Hopwood, whose mother was engaged in 'nursing the young ones' and 'left external matters' to their father.[47] The Free Church of Scotland Robert Haldane (1805–77), high churchman Bishop George Augustus Selwyn (1809–78) and low church London businessman Richard White (b. 1822) also catechized their children, from the 1830s to the 1870s.[48] Nevertheless, mothers might lead the process from the seventeenth century onwards.[49] These included the Presbyterian mother of Adam Clarke in the 1760s,[50] Frederick Temple's mother in the Ionian islands from 1821,[51] Sarah Selwyn in New Zealand during the 1840s and the Free Church Mary Ann MacFarlane in the 1870s and 1880s.[52] In the 1840s and 1850s, the Congregationalist Mrs Henderson of

36; Cambridge, Selwyn College Library, 'Reminiscences by Mrs S. H. Sarah Selwyn, 1809, 1867, with an Introduction and Notes by Edith Evans, typed from a Typescript held by the Library of the Auckland War Memorial Museum' (January 1892), 7, online at: <http://id.erudit.org/iderudit/037748>, last accessed 8 September 2018; Coleridge, *Yonge*, 96; White, *Fire*, 43; Fletcher, *Growing up*, 239, 228; Roger Langdon, *The Life of Roger Langdon, told by himself, with Additions by his Daughter Ellen* (London, 1909), 23–6, 67.

44 Fletcher, *Growing up*, 130.

45 Tosh, *Man's Place*, 90–3; Christina Hardyment, *Dream Babies: Child Care from Locke to Spock* (Oxford, 1984), 31–45; Leonore Davidoff, Janet Fink and Katharine Holden, *The Family Story: Blood, Kinship and Intimacy* (London, 1999), 125, 149.

46 Tosh, *Man's Place*, 90–3; Davidoff, Fink and Holden, *Family Story*, 125, 149.

47 Fletcher autobiography, Part 1, 1; Gray, ed., *Diary*, 21.

48 White, *Fire*, 43.

49 Mandelbrote, 'Bible', 94.

50 Everett, *Adam Clarke portrayed*, 1: 14–15.

51 Sandford, ed., *Temple Memoirs*, 18.

52 Eleanor Gordon and Gwyneth Nair, *Public Lives: Women, Family and Society in Victorian Britain* (New Haven, CT, and London, 2003), 140, 47; Cheshire RO, Cotton Journals, vol. 11, fol. 3, June 1846 (Microfilm 3).

British Guiana used to catechize her household on Sunday evenings on the sermon and their Sunday school lessons, as well as the schoolchildren who sat in the gallery in chapel.[53] Roger Langdon (b. 1829), the future scientist and stationmaster, learnt the catechism at a Sunday school run by his parents.[54] Governesses also acted as catechists, notably for Georgina Sitwell (b. 1824), the daughters of Lady Ilchester in Somerset, and the Strangeways children (aged ten, five and seven) from 1783.[55]

Siblings might also act as religious instructors.[56] In 1819, the poet John Keats sent his sister Fanny, aged fifteen, very detailed answers based on the Church Catechism to help her with her confirmation preparation.[57] By 1828, it was reported by Mrs Young of Limehouse that her daughter Emma (aged ten) 'assists in instructing the little ones in their Catechism and map of Canaan'. Horace (aged six) 'repeats his catechism with Lucy and Sidney' (aged seven and eight).[58] In the 1870s, Florence White's elder brother (aged fifteen) and his friend (aged fourteen) used to help her learn the catechism on Saturdays to recite on Sunday mornings, after which she received a cooked breakfast as a reward.[59] The catechism could also interest teenagers and adults. In 1846, Agnes Cotton wrote how, at prayers in Oxford, her brother-in-law, the future professor of medicine, Henry Wentworth Acland, 'talks about the catechism guided by an old Exposition by Wm Bishop of Gloster when I know not. We all take a turn, in reading the texts referred to.'[60] Catechism work could also form a part of sociability for younger children. In 1765, seven-year-old Mary Heber wrote to her father: 'Last Sunday afternoon I went to church and when we came home and was [*sic*] reading our books and saying our catechism, in came my aunt and cousin Glencowe.'[61] Grandparents might be involved. In 1858, Acland's

[53] Thomas Henderson, The *Missionary's Wife* (London, 1855), 99.
[54] Langdon, *Life*, 23.
[55] Fletcher, *Growing up*, 239, 222, 228.
[56] Linda A. Ryan, *John Wesley and the Education of Children: Gender, Class and Piety* (London and New York, 2018), 44.
[57] Adami, *Keats*, 71–2. The Keats siblings were orphans after the death of their father in 1804 and their mother in 1810.
[58] MOL, YES, 48.85/6, 1825.
[59] White, *Fire*, 43.
[60] Bodl., MS Acland d. 189, fol. 114, Agnes Cotton to William Charles Cotton, 7 February 1847.
[61] Bamford, *Dear Miss Heber*, 2.

daughter Sarah Angelina (1849–1930) reported: 'I am just going to say my catechism to Grandmamma.'[62] In the 1890s, the grandmother and aunt of Captain Edward Kenyon's children insisted on hearing them try to recite parts of it.[63] Ministers might come to teach it at home.[64] No clearly gender-differentiated pattern of catechizing emerges across the period.

Pedagogy and Children's Responses

Many historians and literary scholars have regarded catechizing as a routine practice of repetition in contrast to the more experimental educational approaches used, by, say, the Edgeworths.[65] Although catechisms were written in a question and answer format, and despite the recognition that much learning occurred through 'familiar conversation',[66] recent historians and literary scholars have represented Anglican catechizing as rigid. Aileen Fyfe, for example, argued that 'in the catechism the child had no flexibility or autonomy', whilst children had more freedom in Dissenting education.[67] Yet while the Shorter Catechism was taught by Dissenters, both Anglicans and Nonconformists argued for the importance of understanding.[68] Watts, who in 1730 produced a series of catechisms aimed at different educational levels, wrote: 'The business and duty of the teacher is not to teach words, but things. Words written in the memory, without ideas or sense in the mind, will never incline a child to his duty, nor save his soul.'[69] Watts 'thought catechizing was an ideal medium of instruction for the young', as it 'broke material into short segments,

[62] Bodl., MS Acland d.106, fol. 36, Sarah Angelina Acland to Mrs Sarah Acland, 2 May 1858.

[63] Taylor, 'Memoirs', 1: 23–5.

[64] Louisa Clara Meyer, *The Author of* The Peep of Day: *Being the Life Story of Mrs Mortimer* (London, 1908), 8; Green, *Christian's ABC*, 228.

[65] Alan Richardson, *Literature Education and Romanticism: Reading as Social Practice, 1780–1832* (Cambridge, 1994), 64–77.

[66] Cohen, 'Pedagogy as Conversation', 447–63.

[67] Fyfe, 'Reading', 470; Amies, 'Amusing and Instructive Conversations', 91–2.

[68] Mandelbrote, 'Bible', 92; Tovey, *Anglican Confirmation*, 197, 231.

[69] Isaac Watts, *Catechisms: Or, Instructions in the Principles of the Christian Religion and the History of Scripture, composed for Children and Youth, according to the different Ages. To which is prefix'd a discourse on the Way of Instruction by Catechisms, and the best Manner of composing them* (London, 1730), 17; Green, *Christian's ABC*, 271.

the questioning stimulated curiosity and a reply, and this to-and-fro was "familiar" like a conversation'.[70] Anglicans also produced differentiated texts: for example, John Lewis, whose catechism written specifically for the 'poor and unlearned' of Kent had gone into thirty-four editions by 1778.[71] John Wesley wrote a simpler version of the Church Catechism in his *Instructions for Children*, as he regarded the Church Catechism as too complex.[72] Clerics argued for the importance of understanding,[73] as did some parents,[74] although it was reported in 1704 that some thought rote-learning sufficed.[75] In what follows I will discuss these themes in relation to children's learning, notably the links between catechisms and religious experience, parents as pedagogues, and texts and denominationalism.

Religious Experience

Teaching the Church Catechism could provide an opportunity for religious experience, stimulated by personal interaction. Thus the Anglican Mary Bosanquet recalled: 'On Sabbath-evenings, my dear father used to instruct us in the Church catechism. At those seasons I can remember asking many questions … I wished to know whether anyone ever did love God with all their heart, and their neighbour as themselves.'[76] She recounted subsequently being converted to Methodism aged eight, with the assistance of a servant girl, but against the wishes of her family.[77] In this narrative, her early experience of learning the catechism was the starting point for her spiritual autobiography, not unlike the labouring-class examples cited by Watts.[78] Mary Bosanquet's concerns closely resembled those of Faith Hopwood, born in 1751 in York, who came from an

[70] Green, *Christian's ABC*, 272.There were no 'proofs' or Scripture references in his version for young children.

[71] Sylvia Stevens, *Quakers in Northeast Norfolk, 1690–1800* (Lampeter, 2012), 273; Wallace, ed., *Susanna Wesley*, 371; Gregory, *Restoration*, 273–8; Green, *Christian's ABC*, 228.

[72] [John Wesley], *Instructions for Children*, 4th edn (Dublin, 1744).

[73] Jacob, *Clerical Profession*, 237; William Wilson, *The Instructor: Conducted by the Parochial Ministers of Walthamstow* 1 (1836), 210.

[74] MOL, YES, 48.85/6, 1825, Rule 1.

[75] Green, *Christian's ABC*, 122, 228.

[76] Fletcher autobiography, Part 1, 1.

[77] Ibid. 4, 5.

[78] Watts, *Dissenters*, 1: 426–8.

evangelical background. Hopwood's diary recalled 'being required to repeat the catechism, collects and portions of Scripture', which 'occasionally led to serious examination whether I loved God with all my heart' as well as to fears about her future state.[79] Richard Hill (1732–1808), the first evangelical MP, was repeating the catechism one Sunday evening as a child of eight or nine, when 'I found my heart sweetly drawn up to heavenly objects'. The *Evangelical Magazine* of 1799 contained an 'Anecdote' in which a youth 'was convicted by being catechized'.[80] After learning the Westminster Assembly's Catechism in the 1850s, one seven-year-old Henderson child in British Guiana asked searching questions about the doctrine of assurance and God's love, which surprised her mother.[81] Thus asking questions or spiritual enlightenment could occur throughout the period as a result of catechetical engagement in different denominations, and could be perceived as assisting the spiritual development of adults.

Parental Engagement

Some parents were so dedicated to their task as religious educators that they wrote catechisms for their own children. Susanna Wesley wrote an exposition of the Apostles' Creed and the Ten Commandments.[82] The biographer of the nonjuror John Bowdler (1746–1823) recalled Bowdler's mother's 'peculiar turn for conveying instruction', and how she drew up a 'comprehensive' and 'plain' explanation of the Catechism that anyone could understand.[83] The Quaker Abiah Darby wrote an introductory catechism for her own children and those of her Quaker meeting in 1754, which was printed in 1763.[84] The father of Mary Elizabeth Haldane (1825–1925) 'wrote two catechisms for us, which we learned; one was on the

[79] Gray, ed., *Papers*, 21.
[80] Cited in Paul Sangster, *Pity my Simplicity: The Evangelical Revival and the Religious Education of Children, 1738–1800* (London, 1966), 41–2.
[81] Henderson, *Missionary's Wife*, 100.
[82] Wallace, ed., *Susanna Wesley*, 371.
[83] Thomas Bowdler, *Memoir of John Bowdler, Esq.* (London, 1825), 20.
[84] Stevens, *Quakers*, 273; Abiah Darby, *Useful Instruction for Children, by way of Question and Answer* (London, 1763), iii, v–vi.

Lord's Prayer, the other on the general doctrines of the Bible. I think now that both were rather beyond us.'[85]

Children's reactions and experiences clearly varied. Adam Clarke, son of a schoolmaster and small farmer in Ireland, whose mother started with the Apostles' Creed when he was six, recalled: 'I had a godly puritanic mother. For my mother's religious teachings, I shall have endless reason to bless my Maker.'[86] Emily Shore, a clergyman's daughter, recorded how every Sunday evening, after tea, they said 'some parts of the Catechism, mamma commenting as we go on in the simplest manner. I believe none of us are taught anything which is not thoroughly explained and I am afraid this is too unusual.'[87] By contrast, the children of Octavius Temple, commandant in the Ionian Islands and later lieutenant-governor of Sierra Leone, were expected to read the catechism with no explanation. Frederick (1821–1902), the future archbishop, recalled: 'My six year old birthday was a far more terrible day than the earthquake', as he and his siblings were all expected to say the Catechism by heart. 'I succeeded, and got what was then a large sum of money – sixpence.'[88]

Nevertheless, children might take control of the process. It was reported of Leslie Stephen that 'after one short struggle', he 'submitted with much docility to Watts' *Catechism*, but had a curious way of insisting on giving answers in his own words before he would give those that had been cut and dried'.[89] In 1846, Bishop Selwyn's son Willie, aged four or five, was 'saying his catechism to Mrs S.', and 'on the question being put, rehearse the Articles of thy belief, he wanted to open his prayer book and read the Athanasian creed instead of repeating the apostles' … he said the entire orders the former to be had [*sic*] on Trinity Sunday … he is never so happy as when reading the Prayer Book'.[90]

Not all children enjoyed learning the Catechism. Augusta Drane, a future Catholic convert and prioress, from a high church family, recorded how their religious education in the schoolroom was 'dry

[85] Elizabeth Sanderson Haldane, ed., *Mary Elizabeth Haldane (1825–1925): A Record of a Hundred Years* (London, 1925), 45.
[86] Everett, *Adam Clarke portrayed*, 1: 14–15.
[87] Shore, ed., *Shore Journal*, 27–8 (23 December 1832).
[88] Sandford, ed., *Temple Memoirs*, 1: 16, 19. There were eight surviving children, born between 1806 and 1823.
[89] Frederic W. Maitland, *Life of Leslie Stephen* (London, 1906), 25.
[90] Cheshire RO, Cotton Journals, vol. 11, fol. 3, June 1846 (Microfilm 3).

in the extreme': 'We said the Church Catechism, but I cannot call to mind any explanation ever being given on religious subjects.'[91] Although Charlotte Yonge claimed that '[i]n religious knowledge I was forward. We always said the Catechism every Sunday', she also 'always wished everything of the kind, except teaching the school children, to be over as fast as possible'. Nonetheless, she remembered being prepared for confirmation by Keble as 'an especial blessing'.[92] Captain Edward Kenyon (1854–1937), son of a Queen's Counsel, recalled: 'My mother used to teach us the catechism and read Sunday books to us, especially Miss Yonge's on the Collect, Catechism, etc.'[93] As a father, he did not wish to repeat this, but relatives insisted on hearing the children recite parts of the Catechism, to the children's dismay.[94]

Texts and Denominationalism

The Assembly or Shorter Catechism was taught throughout the period in Dissenting households.[95] Betsey Doddridge (1731–6), daughter of the prominent Nonconformist minister, was described as trying to teach a catechism to her dog, indicating this could be a child-initiated activity.[96] The Shorter Catechism contained a far greater number of biblical references, or 'proofs' supporting the statements of doctrine, than the Prayer Book Catechism of the Church of England.[97] Abiah Darby thought that the absence of these from her catechism would make it easier, although there were still 106 questions.[98] The future Unitarian minister Eliezer Cogan (1762–1855) learnt the Assembly's Catechism as a child, although 'its stern theology had by that time lost its hold of his father's mind, who told him,

[91] Bertrand A. H. Wilberforce, *A Memoir of Mother Frances Raphael, OSD (Augusta Theodosia Drane): Sometime Prioress Provincial of the Congregation of Dominican Sisters of S. Catherine of Siena, Stone; with some of her Spiritual Notes and Letters* (London, 1895), xx.
[92] Coleridge, *Yonge*, 17.
[93] Edward Ranulph Kenyon, 'Letter to my Grandchildren', 5, in private hands.
[94] Frances Margaret Taylor, 'Memoirs, Book I, 1894–1927', 23–5, in private hands.
[95] Walthamstow, Waltham Forest Archives, Acc. 10185, Joel Johnson memoir, 1731; Green, *Christian's ABC*, 80–3.
[96] Malcolm Deacon, *Philip Doddridge of Northampton, 1702–51* (Northampton, 1980), 67, 158 n. 67.
[97] Mandelbrote, 'Bible', 92.
[98] Darby, *Useful Instruction*, iii, v, vi.

"he need not learn the proofs"'.[99] Others considered them useful. In the 1810s, the Congregational minister George Collison wished the young Anglican Bevans, who attended his chapel in Essex, 'to learn this and called sometimes to hear them repeat it'. Their niece, the family biographer, later asserted: 'The Scripture proofs it contains were of great use to them.' Although their Anglican uncle George Bevan initially disapproved violently, he later relented.[100] Many Congregational missionaries' families, such as the Hendersons in the 1840s and 1850s, also learned the Shorter Catechism.[101] Annie Small (b. 1857), daughter of a Free Church of Scotland missionary in India, learned 'the first question and answer of the Shorter Catechism'.[102] However, by 1892 the Congregational missionary James Kennedy was regretting its 'setting aside' by families.[103]

There were sometimes surprising connections between the texts used by Anglicans and Dissenters. Since Adam Clarke's father was Church of England, and his mother Presbyterian, they were taught both the Church Catechism and the Shorter Catechism.[104] Although the Hackney Phalanx prevented the SPCK from publishing Watts's catechism in 1831,[105] it was used even in high church families, for instance by the Youngs, as well as by the evangelical Stephens.[106] Some Anglicans never learnt the Church Catechism, even when confirmed: the former evangelical G. W. E. Russell (1853–1919) was taught the Nonconformist Shorter Catechism instead; he suspected this was because the Church Catechism was 'too Sacramental'.[107]

Yet, other evidence indicates domestic instruction in the Church Catechism was still considered de rigueur by Anglicans. The religious education of William Sharpe in the early 1800s was influenced by his Unitarian relatives, and his Anglican schoolmaster felt his 'education

[99] *Memoir of the late Eliezer Cogan, from the* Christian Reformer *for April 1855* (London, 1855), 5; Priestley, *Memoir*, 5.
[100] Meyer, *Author*, 8–9.
[101] Henderson, *Missionary's Wife*, 100.
[102] Olive Wyon, *The Three Windows: The Story of Ann Hunter Small* (London, 1953), 10.
[103] James Kennedy, *Memoir of Margaret Stephen Kennedy* (London, 1892), 235.
[104] Everett, *Adam Clarke portrayed*, 1: 14–15.
[105] Edward Churton, *Memoir of Joshua Watson*, 2 vols (London, 1861), 2: 11–16.
[106] MOL, YES, 48.85, List of books, 1825.
[107] George W. E. Russell, *The Household of Faith: Portraits and Essays* (London, 1902), 240–1.

in church matters, catechism etc.' had been neglected.[108] When the Quaker Eliza Fox, at school in Chichester about 1800, explained: 'Please, ma'am, I never say catechism! ... the whole school turned their open eyes upon me', and the children asked questions such as 'What church did I go to on a Sunday? And did we say Catechism and the Belief?'[109]

Leslie Stephen's biographer claimed that 'his first days at Eton were made laborious by the Anglican catechism, as he had been brought up on Watts', again indicating that knowledge of the Church Catechism was an expectation in Anglican establishment circles. Stephen later wrote of its 'most irritating explanation of the Lord's Prayer'.[110]

Conclusion

This essay has explored an almost wholly neglected aspect of the churches and education in the modern era. It indicates that domestic catechizing could be a consistent aspect of family life in Anglican and Nonconformist households throughout the eighteenth and nineteenth centuries. Teaching of both the Church Catechism and Nonconformist Shorter Catechism frequently began by the age of four and could be extended through a developmental programme of catechetical learning. This might be promoted by parents creating schemes of instruction or writing catechisms themselves. Some memoirs indicate that catechetical learning could lead to spiritual experience, and that children might exercise active roles in asking questions or devising their own responses, rather than merely rote-learning.

The evidence supports a perspective which stresses continuity rather than abrupt change in family religious practice over the period from 1740 to 1870. Moreover, it suggests that the notion of a distinct shift in gender roles in relation to religious practice over the period 1740 to 1870 is problematic. While children might be catechized by fathers or mothers throughout the period, by the nineteenth century parental engagement was supplemented by governesses and siblings. Both sexes learnt one or more of the many available catechisms, with few references to gender difference, and elder brothers as well as

108 Kew, TNA, Sharpe Papers, Box 13/91, William Sharpe memoir, fol. 33.

109 E. J. Fox, *Memoir of Mrs Eliza Fox: To which Extracts are added from the Letters and Journals of her Husband W. J. Fox* (London, 1869), 8–9; Fletcher, *Growing up*, 254.

110 Maitland, *Stephen*, 25.

sisters might help younger siblings. Evidence from schools indicates that knowledge of the Anglican Church Catechism was expected in many quarters, while in many Nonconformist families the Shorter Catechism was learned. Domestic catechizing could constitute a form of familiar conversation, rather than being qualitatively different. While a quantitative assessment of its frequency is impossible to attain, given that such a routine practice may not have been recorded, this article has opened up possibilities for future study, such as how children actually learned their catechism. It also draws attention to the need for more studies of religious practice throughout the *longue durée*, to make it more feasible to assess continuities across the early modern and modern periods.

Saving Souls on a Shoestring: Welsh Circulating Schools in a Century of Change

Paula Yates*
St Padarn's Institute, Cardiff

This article examines the phenomenon of Welsh circulating schools from those of Griffith Jones in the mid-eighteenth century, which over nearly fifty years brought the basics of religious education to thousands of poor children and adults, to their successors later in the century under Thomas Charles and, in the nineteenth century, the Bevan Charity. It compares Jones's success with the relatively limited impact of the later schemes and seeks to demonstrate the importance of his flair for publicity, his connections, his use of Anglican networks and his organizational ability. The article considers how the changed political and social climate in the last decades of the eighteenth century and into the nineteenth affected the success of later schemes and describes how the schools had to adapt to changed expectations and new educational developments. It argues that the schools provide strong evidence against the view that the charity school movement was motivated primarily by the desire for social control.

In 1731 Griffith Jones, rector of Llanddowror in rural Carmarthenshire, established a scheme of circulating schools. Using the Welsh language, these temporary schools were intended to provide pupils with the rudiments of reading over a period of about three months before the instructor moved on to another parish. By the time of the scheme's collapse, some fifty years later, it had spread throughout Wales. This was not the only circulating system of education in the principality. A smaller-scale scheme of circulating schools in north Wales was organized by Thomas Charles from about 1785, which continued even after 1798, when Charles became the main agent for the Sunday School Society in North Wales and began founding the Sunday schools for which he is more famous. During the early nineteenth century, the scheme established by Griffith Jones re-emerged under the aegis of the Bevan Charity,

* 45 Glynne St, Cardiff, CF11 9NS. E-mail: pguleny@gmail.com.

Studies in Church History 55 (2019), 274–289
doi: 10.1017/stc.2018.32

but it now operated in a very different political and educational environment.

This article will analyse three aspects of the circulating school movement. Its main aim will be to consider why the schools founded by Griffith Jones were so much more successful than those of Thomas Charles and the Bevan Charity. It will explore how these schools were funded, and in particular the way in which their activities were publicized to raise charitable donations. It will argue further that the relationship between these school foundations and the Anglican clergy, at both parochial and diocesan levels, was also a consideration. Finally, it will reflect on the religious, political and educational climate in which these schools operated, as well as how both the environment and the schools changed over the period being examined.

Serious studies of the circulating schools are few and, in some cases, rather dated. Mary Jones's classic study of charity schools has a detailed section describing the circulating schools of Griffith Jones.[1] Geraint Jenkins's account of Jones's life and work paints a picture of a sickly but industrious figure, a powerful preacher and inspiration to the early Methodist leaders, although their excesses irritated him.[2] Jenkins's entry for Jones in the *Oxford Dictionary of National Biography* gives more detail on his relations with his Methodist friends and notes his equal dislike of Dissenters and Roman Catholics.[3] Gordon Wallace-Hadrill's series of four articles for *Pembrokeshire Life* follows the schools through to the nineteenth century but his findings have not been taken up by later scholars.[4] Roger L. Brown's study provides a detailed analysis of the testimonials provided by clergy and printed by Jones in his annual publication, *Welch Piety*.[5] Brown argues that Jones's connection with the early Methodist

[1] M. G. Jones, *The Charity School Movement: A Study of Eighteenth Century Puritanism*, 2nd edn (Cambridge, 1964; first publ. 1938), 297–314.

[2] Geraint H. Jenkins, '"An old and much honoured soldier": Griffith Jones, Llanddowror', *WHR* 11 (1983), 449–68.

[3] Geraint H. Jenkins, 'Jones, Griffith [*known as* Griffith Jones Llanddowror] (1684–1761)', *ODNB*, online edn (23 September 2004), at: <https://doi.org/10.1093/ref:odnb/15006>, accessed 9 June 2018.

[4] Gordon Wallace-Hadrill, 'An Experiment in Education: The Circulating Schools of South West Wales in the 18th and 19th Centuries', *Pembrokeshire Life*, September 1996, 26–7; October 1996, 14–15; November 1996, 14–15; December 1996, 14–15.

[5] Roger L. Brown, 'Spiritual Nurseries: Griffith Jones and the Circulating Schools', *National Library of Wales Journal* 30 (1997), 27–49. For the testimonials, see Griffith Jones [following Jones's death, Madam Bevan], *Welch Piety* (annually 1737–73). *Welch*

leaders in Wales has drawn attention away from his strongly Anglican credentials and the role of the parish clergy in the schools. Gareth Jones and Gordon Roderick accept the traditional belief that the success of the circulating schools created a literate nation but consider that the explanation of their success in terms of the failings of the established church over against the 'dynamic, inspirational, native Welsh-language' Methodist approach 'has long been shown to be more the product of Methodist hagiography than strict historical accuracy'.[6] William Jacob's account sets the schools in the context of eighteenth-century parish life and the church's wider role in education.[7]

Most recent studies have considered the schools mainly from the point of view of their contribution to the preservation of Welsh language and culture. Eryn White speaks of Jones's love of the Welsh language, albeit noting that its preservation was not part of his intention. She points out that by the 1740s he was under pressure to provide English-language schools in English-speaking areas, and that this had begun by 1747.[8] W. T. R. Pryce applies innovation and diffusion theory to the records of schools in *Welch Piety* and suggests the routes by which they might have spread.[9] He argues that the schools made an important contribution to the maintenance of Welsh identity. Wyn James maintains that the schools had a crucial role in making Christianity central to the lives of many Welsh people. He notes that Jones might have been surprised by, and possibly less happy about, some of the indirect results of his work, such as the

Piety, or a Succinct Account of the Rise and Progress of the Circulating Welch Charity Schools from the Year 1737, to the Year 1761 (London, 1761) announced Jones's death and contained details of the schools over the previous twenty-five years.

6 Gareth Elwyn Jones and Gordon Wynne Roderick, *A History of Education in Wales* (Cardiff, 2003), 37–43 (quotation at 40).

7 William Jacob, 'Part II: 1660–1780', in Glanmor Williams et al., *The Welsh Church from Reformation to Disestablishment 1603–1920* (Cardiff, 2007), 65–206, especially 158–64.

8 Eryn White, 'Popular Schooling and the Welsh Language 1650–1800', in Geraint H. Jenkins, ed., *The Welsh Language before the Industrial Revolution* (Cardiff, 1997), 317–47.

9 W. T. R. Pryce, 'The Diffusion of the "Welch Circulating Charity Schools" in Eighteenth-Century Wales', *WHR* 25 (2011), 486–519.

flourishing of Methodism and evangelical Nonconformity and the growth of radicalism.[10]

This present article takes the story of the Welsh circulating schools forward into the late eighteenth and early nineteenth centuries. It does not aim to advance the discussion of their contribution to the preservation of Welsh language and culture, but instead sets them in a wider context and considers how the schools were funded and managed and what factors, internal and external, contributed to the relative lack of success of all later attempts to set up such schools, compared with the extraordinary success of Jones's original project.

Griffith Jones was of relatively humble origin. He was educated at Carmarthen Grammar School and his lack of a university education may have contributed to some delay in his ordination. He was ordained priest in 1708 and presented to the rectory of Llanddowror in Carmarthenshire in 1716. He was an enthusiastic corresponding member of the Society for the Promotion of Christian Knowledge (SPCK) from about 1713,[11] and worked closely in the provision of schooling with his friend and patron Sir John Philipps, probably the most prolific provider of charity day schools in Wales during the earliest decades of the century.[12] In the summer of 1718 the two undertook a tour of the north of England and southern Scotland, visiting outposts of the SPCK. It may have been on this tour that Jones first came across the idea of temporary, mobile schools, in the shape of the ambulatory schools provided by the Scottish SPCK to teach the poor in remote parts of the Highlands. These schools were taught in English, which meant they had to stay longer in one place than Jones's circulating schools, so that the scholars could be taught English, but the model of funding and provision was very similar to that adopted by Jones in Wales: they were centrally funded and controlled but locally provided.

[10] E. Wyn James, 'Griffith Jones (1684–1761) of Llanddowror and his "Striking Experiment in Mass Religious Education" in Wales in the Eighteenth Century', in Reinhart Siegert, ed., *Volksbildung durch Lesestoffe im 18. und 19. Jahrhundert. Voraussetzungen – Medien – Topographie = Educating the People through Reading Material in the 18th and 19th Centuries: Principles – Media – Topography*, Presse und Geschichte, Neue Beiträge 68 / Philanthropismus und populäre Aufklärung, Studien und Dokumente 5 (Bremen, 2012), 275–89.

[11] Mary Clement, *The SPCK and Wales 1699–1740* (London, 1954), 22.

[12] Ibid. 102–4, 109, 111, 113, 120–1, 126–31, 137.

In many ways Wales and the Scottish Highlands shared similar problems of poverty and inaccessibility. Charity schools were costly to provide and Wales, like the Highlands, was poor. During this period, the Welsh economy was almost entirely based on agriculture and much of the land was too poor to sustain much more than the raising of sheep and cattle. There were few towns, and none of them large, so there were very few of the middling sort, and the poor were often very poor indeed. Wales had its noble and gentry families, many of whom set up charity schools in the early decades of the century, but, where this was not the case, individual clergy often struggled to raise funding and subscriptions to secure a building and a teacher. Parish incomes for Wales in this period show that it was not realistic to hope that parochial clergy could make large donations themselves.[13]

To address the problems of providing education in this context, Jones's idea was to avoid as many as possible of the common expenses of charity schools. His plan was to train teachers and then send them into a place, announcing in all the local churches that schooling would be provided for a short period of time, to teach children and older people to read. By 1738 about fifty teachers had been trained by Jones himself.[14] Attendance at the schools was free and costs were kept to a minimum. The schools used the language of the area (usually Welsh), so as not to waste time and effort teaching another language before scholars could begin learning to read. They taught only the essentials of religious literacy: reading the Bible and learning the Catechism, together with graces before and after meals and elements of Morning and Evening Prayer. There was no teaching of writing, needlework, reckoning or navigation as usually happened in charity schools. There was no long-term commitment to apprenticeships. There was no need to provide a building; schools were set up in any barn or outbuilding that could be spared for a few weeks and there was teaching during the day and in the evenings. After about three months, or sometimes longer, the teacher moved on elsewhere. With this pared-down approach, Jones reported in 1748 that 'about six poor people, or children, are taught for every twenty shillings'.[15]

[13] Rosemary O'Day and Felicity Heal, eds, *Princes and Paupers in the English Church 1500–1800* (Leicester, 1981), 243–4.

[14] Jacob, 'Part II', in Williams et al., *Welsh Church*, 160.

[15] *Welch Piety* (1747–8), 3.

It is not clear exactly when the schools started (probably in the early 1730s) but we know that by 1737, the year of Sir John Philipps's death, they had grown beyond the power of Jones to supply and control without much wider support.[16] In that year, he published the first of his annual reports on the progress of the schools, under the title *Welch Piety*. These were a crucial element in Jones's publicity system. They kept the schools repeatedly in the public eye in a form which reached potential donors across England and Wales and permitted Jones to respond to any criticisms, especially in the early years. Each edition contained details of the numbers of schools and scholars in the previous year, together with news of their good effects, gratitude to those who supported them and, in most years, testimonials from clergy who had had schools in their parishes; these spoke of the care and diligence of the masters, the extraordinary results (academic and spiritual) in those who attended the schools and the benefit to the neighbourhood of having had a school that year. The reports also show how the schools were organized and funded. Each year *Welch Piety* included a list of collectors willing to receive and pass on donations to the schools. The list varied from year to year, although there was a core of names which remained constant. They included clerics in several of the Welsh counties and (in different parts of England) members of the nobility and gentry, professional men and assorted clergymen. Jones himself was always on the list until his death, when he was replaced by Madam Bevan of Laugharne. Bridget Bevan was a committed educationalist, the heiress of John Vaughan of Derllys and widow of Arthur Bevan, an eminent lawyer and MP for Laugharne from 1727 to 1741. She had probably known Jones from her youth, when he had been the incumbent of Laugharne. She was certainly one of Jones's most long-standing patrons and advisers, and they carried on a voluminous correspondence, some of which has been published.[17] Although Madam Bevan is the only woman listed as a collector, donations would have come from women as well as men, as was common with

[16] Griffith Jones to Madam Bevan, 16 December 1736, in Edward Morgan, ed., *Letters of the Revd Griffith Jones, late Rector of Llanddowror, Carmarthenshire, Founder of the Welsh Circulating Schools, to Mrs Bevan, late of Llangharne* [modern Laugharne] *near Carmarthen* (London, 1832), 194.

[17] Morgan, ed., *Letters of Griffith Jones*.

philanthropic causes during the eighteenth century.[18] These collectors were part of a network of corresponding supporters set up by Jones. He asked supporters to promote and set up schools, to oversee schools in their locality, to pray for the project and to donate money if they could. However, he recognized that financial support was more difficult for the Welsh, acknowledging that without large donations from the English the schools could not survive.[19]

Jones maintained control over the funding himself, paid the teachers and made decisions about where to site the schools each quarter. The subjects dealt with in *Welch Piety* and the changing tone of the publication make clear that initially Jones had to defend his schools against accusations of Methodism and general suspicion from some fellow clergy. Gradually, however, they came to be seen as highly desirable and many parish clergy did all they could to encourage Jones to send them a school. By 1749 he could report his gratitude to 'our most Worthy and Right Reverend Diocesans, who are pleased to speak Kind Things, and approve of the Welch Schools, and recommend them'.[20] The support of the Welsh bishops was important for several related reasons: it helped to silence detractors and confirm that the schools were teaching sound religion, it gave strong local publicity to the schools and it encouraged clergy to support them. This was very important because the schools could never have extended so widely if Jones had not been able to draw on networks of Anglican clergy to find teachers and to set up and manage the schools. By 1749 the day-to-day management of the schools was effectively devolved or, as Jones put it, 'under the appointments and direction of the parochial clergy'.[21] The local clergy identified teachers, catechized the pupils, inspected the schools and reported each year on the master and the progress of the scholars. It also became common for the schools to be taught in the parish church itself: the proportion of schools taught in parish churches grew from none in 1739–40 to 52 per cent in 1751–2.[22]

[18] Women are frequently listed as donors by Jones, *Charity Schools*, and W. M. Jacob, *Lay People and Religion in the Early Eighteenth Century* (Cambridge, 1996).
[19] *Welch Piety* (1739–40), 11–14.
[20] *Welch Piety* (1748–9), 44.
[21] Ibid.
[22] Paula Yates, 'The Established Church and Rural Elementary Schooling: The Welsh Dioceses 1780–1830' (PhD thesis, University of Wales, Lampeter, 2007), 145.

In discussing the success of the schools, it is worth considering why *Welch Piety* was published. It was never a simple factual report but was essentially propaganda, aimed at encouraging donations from readers. Seen in those terms, Jones shines through as an expert publicist for the schools. *Welch Piety* emphasized the aspects most likely to encourage potential donors. It described the plight of the benighted poor of Wales and their desperate need for the gospel with all its benefits of salvation and right behaviour. Whilst good results in terms of behaviour were described, it left no doubt that it was the results in terms of salvation which were Jones's primary concern and which he expected to be that of his readers.

His urgent desire to spread the knowledge which would save people's souls (both those of the pupils and those of the donors) is manifest through all the issues of *Welch Piety* and his published letters about the schools. There are repeated references to Jones's intense gratitude – and that of the children and their parents – for the generosity of the English donors. The regularity and intensity with which the children pray for those who have given them the opportunity to learn about salvation is also stressed.[23] Testimonials from clergy bear witness both to the efficacy of the schools and to their freedom from any taint of Dissent.[24]

Jones's natural talent for fundraising propaganda was also helped by the fact that he was very well connected. Through his marriage to Philipps's sister Margaret in 1719, he was related to several of the leading families of south Wales and also to Sir Robert Walpole. Perhaps more importantly, through his membership of the SPCK he had access to many of the leading philanthropists of the day. His ill-health took him to Bath from time to time with Mrs Bevan, where he could meet his correspondents and encourage their support. This network of supporters was kept informed through his diligent letter-writing. *Welch Piety* is described as 'a letter to a friend', and he published other open letters explaining how the schools worked and showing their benefits and costs. It is hard to arrive at exact numbers of those educated in these schools: Jones himself admits that he

[23] Griffith Jones, *Welsh Piety or the Needful Charity of Promoting the Salvation of the Poor, being an account of the Rise, Method and Progress of the Circulating Welsh Charity Schools: With the Nature and Antiquity of the British Language, and Objections against continuing the Use of it considered. In Three Letters to a Friend by a Clergyman of Wales* (London, 1740), 26.

[24] Brown, 'Spiritual Nurseries', provides analysis and discussion of the testimonials.

cannot check the precise accuracy of the published figures and points out that some schools included scholars from previous years.[25] However, it is widely accepted that at least 200,000 children and adults were taught in the schools in the forty-five or so years of their existence and that they penetrated to virtually every corner of Wales. In 1764, a commissioner from Catherine the Great came to England to investigate education, and he took the trouble to visit Wales and report back on the circulating schools.[26]

The schools ended quite suddenly in 1779, by which time they had passed into the supervision of Jones's close friend, patron and collaborator, Madam Bevan of Laugharne. Laugharne was five miles from Llanddowror, and after his wife died in 1755, Jones went to live in her house to be cared for in his old age; he died there in 1761. Jones left Bevan the collected funds of the schools along with his private fortune of some £7,000, and under her management, the schools continued to prosper for a further eighteen years. On her death in 1779, Bevan left some £10,000 to trustees to maintain them for the future; however, her family had other ideas and contested the will. With neither central direction nor money, the entire system immediately collapsed, while the dispute spent twenty-eight years languishing in the Court of Chancery.

Although Jones's organization crumbled, the concept was by then so well known that it was taken up by others. For example, Dr Edward Williams, who taught the Dissenting academy at Oswestry, founded Sunday schools in north Wales from about 1789, and in about 1793 he converted them into circulating schools, using some older pupils as teachers.[27] There was also a group of parishes on the Llŷn peninsula which shared a circulating school funded by local giving, topped up from the Robert Owen charity. However, the most successful of these later circulating schools, albeit on a much smaller scale than Jones's schools, were those set up by Thomas Charles of Bala. Charles was an evangelical Anglican clergyman, born in Carmarthenshire in 1755 and ordained to a curacy in Somerset in 1778. He returned to Wales in 1783 to marry Sally Jones, whose mother was a shopkeeper in Bala. His attempts to find a local curacy failed after complaints from parishioners and local clerics and he

25 Jones, *Needful Charity*, 3.
26 Jones, *Charity School Movement*, 313–14.
27 Yates, 'Established Church', 163–4.

joined Sally's stepfather in preaching among the Methodists. Like Jones, he believed that the poor needed to be able to read to understand the Scriptures and be catechized, so he too set up a scheme of circulating schools. Beginning, probably in 1785, with one teacher whom he trained and supervised himself, by 1794, when the schools were probably at their largest, there were twenty teachers and Charles was using 'proper persons' as visitors to supervise the schools and catechize the pupils. The schools stayed in one place for six to nine months, teaching both rich and poor, and teachers were paid £10 a year. As well as holding the day schools, masters and mistresses were expected to teach 'on Sundays and as many nights in the week as convenient to instruct Young Persons grown up and in service'.[28] Charles visited the place chosen for the school in advance to discuss his plans with 'the principal inhabitants' and call a meeting of all the inhabitants to address them about the importance of teaching their children to read the word of God and to tell them he was sending a teacher. He then spoke informally to the parents and children 'and thus in general, we are kind friends ever after the first interview'. When the circulating school moved on, Charles visited again to catechize the children publicly and encourage the parents to support the Sunday school which would continue, taught by one of the successful pupils.[29] No record has survived of the numbers taught in each school, so comparisons are difficult, but Charles's network was clearly much smaller than Jones's. It never extended beyond north Wales and flourished for only about ten years, but nevertheless the impact of the schools must have been significant within that area.

Although Charles did not benefit from connections in the highest ranks of society as Jones had done, he did have access to wealthy evangelical networks, similar to those on which Jones had drawn. However, Charles produced nothing akin to *Welch Piety* and made little use of publications giving information about the value and expense of the schools. He raised money initially from voluntary subscriptions from Methodist societies in north Wales and from individual donations but, as the schools flourished, he turned to wealthier

[28] For a brief history of the schools and their rules, see a draft letter from Charles to an unnamed recipient (undated but 'near Ten Years' since the schools began), in Yates, 'Established Church', 156.

[29] Thomas Charles to Christopher Anderson, 4 January 1811, in D. E. Jenkins, *The Life of the Revd Thomas Charles, BA, of Bala*, 3 vols (Denbigh, 1910), 3: 365.

subscribers in London, where he stayed for several weeks most years to preach at the Countess of Huntingdon's chapel in Spa Fields. Subscribers included William Wilberforce and other members of the evangelical Clapham Sect. Charles also encouraged donations by writing occasional letters about the schools to publications such as the *Evangelical Magazine* and the *Gospel Magazine*, which tapped sources across denominations.[30] Possibly the most important difference between Charles's fundraising and that of Jones was that Charles did not establish a network of collectors and supporters to promote the schools across the country; neither did he follow Jones's example by devolving to others responsibility for setting up and managing the network of schools.

In 1796 Charles applied to the Sunday School Society in London for support, and in 1798 the society appointed a committee to raise subscriptions so that its work could be extended to Wales. From then on much of Charles's time was taken up by the Sunday schools for which he is famous but, although they declined gradually, the circulating schools continued, acting in support of the Sunday schools by revisiting them from time to time 'to revive them, and reanimate the teachers and people to carry them on; or else, in time, they gradually decline, in country places, where the children are scattered far from one another'.[31] However, Charles was not allowed to devote the funding he received for Sunday schools to the circulating schools and they continued to decline. In 1814, the year of his death, there were only three masters but nevertheless the schools struggled on, providing some day schooling in parts of Merionethshire until at least 1821, at which time they were being run by Revd Simon Lloyd, rector of Bala.[32] The fact that Charles's schools passed to the care of the local Anglican cleric rather than to the Calvinistic Methodists may seem curious and perhaps provides evidence for Charles's continuing sense of Anglican identity, long after he had thrown in his lot with the Methodists.[33]

[30] Yates, 'Established Church', 156.

[31] Thomas Charles to the *Evangelical Magazine*, 12 September 1808, in Yates, 'Established Church', 160.

[32] Aberystwyth, National Library of Wales (hereafter: NLW), Minor Deposit 728B (Church in Wales): Minute Book of the Trustees of the Bevan Charity, copy letter in minutes of 1821 meeting.

[33] For Charles's sense of Anglican identity, see Yates, 'Established Church', 154, 157.

Probably the most important factor in the relative lack of success of Charles's circulating schools was simply that he was working a generation after Jones, in very different circumstances. Writing in 1816, Lloyd accounted for the difficulties with funding in terms of 'the pressure of the times'.[34] The closing decades of the eighteenth century and the beginning of the nineteenth were a period of political and religious turbulence. The American colonies had been lost; the French Revolution had brought with it the spectre of a bloody revolution in Britain too; Thomas Paine had published *The Rights of Man* and *The Age of Reason* and there had been pamphlet wars, lasting longer in Wales than in other parts of Britain, advocating the downfall of the establishment in church and state.[35] In England and Wales, Methodism was in the process of splitting from the Church of England; a revitalized Dissent was beginning to be seen as a threat and the establishment was on the defensive. Education was becoming a focus for new interdenominational rivalries.[36] By 1817, Bishop Majendie of Bangor was of the opinion that the flourishing of Dissenting schools in the diocese would inevitably lead to 'the fall of the Constitution of this Country, both in Church and State, and probably at no distant period'.[37] Education itself had also moved on. A mixture of evangelical zeal and socio-political anxiety had prompted the spread of Sunday schools, an alternative solution to the problem of teaching large numbers of poor people with a minimal financial outlay. From 1811 the National Society would be offering support to parishes with the intention of achieving a school in every parish.[38] Charles's struggles to perpetuate Jones's legacy in north Wales were largely overtaken by these changes.

It was in this new and different context that circulating schools reappeared after the case of Madam Bevan's will was settled in

[34] Simon Lloyd to David Jones Charles, 8 August 1816, in Jenkins, *Life of Thomas Charles*, 3: 575.

[35] Marion Löffler with Bethan Jenkins, *Political Pamphlets and Sermons from Wales 1790–1806* (Cardiff, 2014), 11–12.

[36] See, for instance, Paula Yates, 'Drawing up the Battle-Lines: Elementary Schooling in the Diocese of Bangor in the Second Decade of the Nineteenth Century', in Nigel Yates, ed., *Bishop Burgess and his World: Culture Religion and Society in Britain, Europe and North America in the Eighteenth and Nineteenth Centuries* (Cardiff, 2007), 135–44.

[37] H. W. Majendie, *A Charge to the Clergy of the Diocese of Bangor, in the Month of September, 1817* (Bangor, 1817), 29.

[38] See, in this volume, Nicholas Dixon, 'The Political Dimension of the Education of the Poor in The National Society's Church of England Schools, 1811–37', 290–306.

1807. They were initiated by the newly established Bevan Charity, which existed to provide circulating schools, taught in Welsh, for children of the poor across Wales. In most ways, the charity replicated the aims and model of the original circulating schools, guarding against both Dissent and distrust by placing the schools very firmly under the control of the Church of England authorities in Wales. The rules insisted that teachers must be members of the Church of England and approved by the bishop or his representative. The placing of schools had to be approved by the bishop and visitors were to be appointed by him to visit each school in their area every six months and to report to him as well as to the trustees. These rules seem to have envisaged a much larger organization than ever actually developed. There could be several reasons for this: tighter regulation may have combined with poor communications to limit the expansion of the schools; in somewhat wealthier areas of north Wales there was a greater choice of schooling for the poor, and rival provision from established and Dissenting churches became a focus for conflict. In these circumstances, clergy may have been looking for a more stable and reliable education than an occasional visit from a circulating school could provide. There is evidence that some parents would have been happier if the schools had taught English.[39] It was only in St Davids, the poorest diocese and the one in which the charity was based, that the schools of the Bevan Charity had any great impact, and even here they were significantly more important in the three counties of the south-west, Pembrokeshire, Carmarthenshire and Cardiganshire, than in other parts of the diocese.

The surviving trustees' minute book for 1812–36 makes it clear that there was a thriving organization in the south-west corner of the diocese and also reveals that there were some schools in north Wales under the aegis of the charity.[40] Understandably, perhaps, the control of these northern schools by the trustees seem to have been rather limited. In 1812 the trustees wrote to the visitor for north Wales, pointing out that the use of clergy as teachers and teaching in English were both forbidden by the charity's rules and noting a little tetchily that 'not strictly complying with Trustees' Orders gives

[39] House of Commons, *Digest of Parochial Returns made to the Select Committee appointed to inquire into the Education of the Poor: Session 1818*, 3 vols (London, [1819), 3: nos 1205 (Aberporth), 1254 (Cilgerran).

[40] NLW, Minor Deposit 728B, Bevan Charity Minute Book.

much trouble and creates confusion'. In 1814 a bill for £36 was sent 'to pay the Masters Salaries in North Wales'. Schools in the north are rarely referred to in detail but in 1820 ten were listed; a copy letter to the visitor for north Wales is included in the minutes for 1832.

Although the terms of the charity suggest that it sought to set up schools which were very similar to those in Jones's organization, in practice they differed from their predecessors in three significant ways. First, they circulated less and taught for longer. Rather than moving on after one or two quarters, the Bevan schools stayed until the trustees decided to move the teachers on: two or three years in one place was not uncommon. They were also taught all year round apart from 20 August to 20 September and 24 December to 14 January.

Secondly, the charity soon decided to take advantage of the opportunities offered by the newly fashionable monitorial system to teach large numbers of children using one master. This system worked by using able children to teach their peers and was the brainchild of Dr Andrew Bell, a Scottish cleric and missionary, who had been inspired by watching children teaching each other in the streets of Madras. His system was promoted by the National Society, to which Bell acted as an advisor. In 1819, the Court of Chancery gave permission for the use of 'Dr Bell's system' in the Bevan Charity's schools and 'for that purpose to set up a central school' in Newport, Pembrokeshire. One of the masters, John Morgan, was sent to the National Society's school in Baldwin's Gardens, London, for a few weeks to learn the system and from then on new masters had, in their turn, to attend his central school in Newport for a few weeks to learn it from him. John Morgan continued to teach the central school until the middle of the century; he is commemorated with a window in St Mary's Church, Newport, and a plaque on the building thought to have housed the school.

Thirdly, possibly in response to pressure from parents ambitious for their children, the schools began to cover a somewhat wider range of subjects and include some teaching of English. In 1827, it was agreed that '[w]hen any shall have made a competent progress in the Welsh language, such scholars shall be placed in an English Class to be taught reading writing and Arithmetic.'

Overall, it is clear that the schools had to adapt themselves to a different culture and to different expectations from those for which their predecessors were designed. As the century moved on, they were overtaken by educational developments, first the National Society and later the succession of Education Acts. The National Society's schools were better funded and their teachers better paid. By 1850 the trustees, believing that the objectives of the charity could be better met by adapting to the times, petitioned to be permitted to give grants to the new National Schools; the resulting hearing found that the circulating schools were so unsatisfactory that they should be abolished, the teachers pensioned off and the funds used to support National Schools.[41] Gradually the charity, adapting to cultural change, changed completely from its original form, but it survived the disestablishment of the Welsh church and continues to provide funding for bilingual religious education in Wales. Today the Bench of Bishops of the Church in Wales meet annually as governors of the charity and amongst its most recent projects have been a collection of Welsh songs and a website for religious educational resources.[42]

This article has described three operational phases of the circulating school movement in Wales and has considered why the first, in the mid-eighteenth century, was the most successful in terms of finance and of geographical spread of the schools, and the length of time for which they continued to thrive. It has concluded that Griffith Jones's schools were much better funded than those of Thomas Charles; that a climate of suspicion, which affected many evangelical causes in the last decades of the century, seriously hindered Charles's fundraising efforts; and that the schools of the Bevan Charity, although well funded, were operating in a period when developments in education and changes in society had made their approach seriously outdated.

The reasons for Jones's superior funding and the greater spread and longevity of his schools were partly his approach to publicity and partly his structured network of supporters. Jones's series of publications, both *Welch Piety* and a series of pamphlets in letter form on subjects relating to the schools, provided far better publicity than Charles's occasional letters to evangelical magazines. The limited

[41] C. Morgan-Richardson, *History of the Institution once called 'The Welsh Piety' but now known as Mrs Bevan's Charity* (Cardigan, 1890), 8.

[42] I am very grateful to John Richfield of the Representative Body of the Church in Wales for this information. His role includes acting as clerk to the governors of the Madam Bridget Bevan Charity.

spread of Charles's schools was inevitable as long as he kept them under his own control, using 'proper persons' only as visitors for the schools. It was Jones's willingness to delegate the practicalities to parochial clergy, whilst maintaining control of the funding and monitoring the schools through reports from those clergy, which allowed his schools to spread far beyond his ability to supervise them himself. Most importantly, Charles never set up a system of corresponding members across England and Wales, as Jones had done, to promote and support the schools. This support system included the clergy who managed the schools but was much wider. Nourished by Jones's continuing supply of information about the schools, it was largely responsible for keeping the schools in the public eye and reminding the public of the need for funding.

The climate of fear and suspicion which developed in the final decades of the eighteenth century and continued into the nineteenth made many wealthier funders withdraw their support from causes which might encourage Methodism and Dissent, and Charles struggled to defend his schools against such accusations. At the same time, the rise of the Sunday school movement meant that what support remained in England for the education of the poor tended to be devoted to these schools and, although Charles used this funding to support his Sunday schools, it meant that his circulating schools continued to decline.

The political and religious climate also affected the schools of the Bevan Charity, although they did not rely on the financial support of individuals. Developments in education meant that clergy and funders could look to the National Society to support a more stable and effective form of education. Despite the Bevan Charity's decision to work with the National Society, it became clear that circulating schools no longer provided the best answer to the question of how to educate the poor. Jones's great project, which he had managed so successfully for so long in the middle decades of the eighteenth century, had been left behind by political, religious and educational change in the generations which followed.

The Political Dimension of the Education of the Poor in the National Society's Church of England Schools, 1811–37

Nicholas Dixon*
Pembroke College, Cambridge

One of the most important spheres of activity in the early nineteenth-century Church of England was the establishment and support of schools for the poor. The primary agent of such activity was the National Society. Founded in 1811 by clergymen and philanthropists, this organization aimed to maintain Anglicanism as the 'National Religion' by instructing as many poor children as possible in church doctrine under clerical supervision. By 1837, almost a million children across England were being educated in Anglican charitable institutions. This remarkable effort has largely been the province of educational historians. Yet it was also a political enterprise. The creation of a national system of education along exclusively Anglican lines represented an assertive intervention in the contemporary debate about the relationship between church and nation-state. Using a wide range of neglected sources, this article discusses how such political concerns were manifested at a local level in National Society schools' teaching, rituals and use as venues for political activism. It is argued that these aspects of the society's work afforded the church a powerful political platform. This analysis informs our broader understanding of the ways in which churches' involvement in mass education has sustained religiously inflected conceptions of nationhood.

In 1820, the Whig statesman Henry Brougham stated in Parliament that the clergy of the established church were 'not only teachers of religion, but, in the eye of the law, they were teachers generally'. In unsuccessfully proposing a comprehensive system of state-supported parish schools, he spoke of 'the infinite benefit that would arise from having the constant, the daily superintendence of such a character as a

* Pembroke College, Cambridge, CB2 1RF. E-mail: nad43@cam.ac.uk. The research upon which this article is based was funded by an Arts and Humanities Research Council Doctoral Training Partnership studentship, grant no. 1653413, supported by Pembroke College, Cambridge. I am most grateful to Andrew Thompson and Mary Clare Martin for their comments and suggestions.

Studies in Church History 55 (2019), 290–306
doi: 10.1017/stc.2018.33

well-educated and pious English churchman'.[1] That such a statement could be made by a rising star of the party of Fox and Holland, soon to denounce the chapter of Durham in a much-publicized libel trial, demonstrates the lack of controversy that attached to the proposition that the clergy should supervise the education of the English populace at this time. This proposition accorded with a general reluctance on the part of parliamentarians to sanction any state-maintained schooling and had a strong precedent in the church's canonical obligation to catechize children.[2] Even the Unitarian radical John Wade, in his *Extraordinary Black Book* (1831), conceded that '[p]ublic education is a subject that appears to have peculiar claims on the attention of the clergy', before castigating them for having 'generally neglected' their 'duty' as 'instructors of the people'.[3]

Wade's charge owed more to polemic than fact. The foundation by clergy, statesmen and philanthropists in 1811 of the National Society for Promoting the Education of the Poor in the Principles of the Established Church throughout England and Wales marked a watershed in popular elementary education. This institution existed for the establishment, improvement and homogenization of Anglican day schools under clerical supervision, for children whose parents could not afford to pay for their education. Although a not inconsiderable number of Anglican charity schools already existed and remained formally independent of the National Society, it was the principal motive force behind an Anglican educational revival of unprecedented scale.[4] By 1816, every diocese in England bar three had a local arm of the National Society.[5] In 1832, there were around

[1] HC Deb (2nd series), vol. 2, cols 73–4 (28 June 1828).

[2] Neil Smelser, *Social Paralysis and Social Change: British Working-Class Education in the Nineteenth Century* (Berkeley, CA, 1991), 66–75; W. M. Jacob, *The Clerical Profession in the Long Eighteenth Century, 1680–1840* (Oxford, 2007), 236.

[3] [John Wade], *The Extraordinary Black Book* (London, 1831), 6.

[4] On the early history of the National Society, see H. J. Burgess, *Enterprise in Education: The Story of the Work of the Established Church in the Education of the People prior to 1870* (London, 1958); Akira Iwashita, 'Politics, State and Church: Forming the National Society 1805–*c*.1818', *HE* 47 (2018), 1–17. This article concerns the National Society's operations in England; for its work in Wales, see H. G. Williams, '"Learning Suitable to the Situation of the Poorest Classes": The National Society and Wales, 1811–1839', *WHR* 19 (1999), 425–52.

[5] *Second Annual Report of the National Society, for promoting the Education of the Poor in the Principles of the Established Church* (London, 1814), 23–177; Mark Smith, ed., 'Henry Ryder: A Charge delivered to the Clergy of the Diocese of Gloucester in the year 1816', in idem and Stephen Taylor, eds, *Evangelicalism in the Church of England* c.*1790*–c.*1890:*

13,000 Anglican charitable schools throughout England and Wales, educating almost a million children.[6] Conversely, non-Anglican schools accounted for a relatively small share of educational provision. A parliamentary enquiry of 1833 found that only 2.2 per cent of daily schools in England were Dissenting institutions, accounting for 3.9 per cent of scholars.[7]

These statistics indicate that the clergy of the Church of England were widely shouldering the educational responsibilities which even Whigs and radicals conceded to them. The National Society's role in English society and politics was correspondingly vast. This article aims to demonstrate that the society's operations at a local level afforded the church a powerful political platform, and played a major role in the politicization of the English working class. This line of argument represents, in several respects, a departure from existing scholarship. National Schools have long been regarded as largely ineffectual and barely distinguishable from the free day schools of the British and Foreign School Society (BFSS), the National Society's principal rival, on account of similarities in teaching method. Frank Smith, writing in 1931, delivered a withering verdict on both societies' schools: 'Their emphasis on religious teaching (and in the Church schools on sectarian teaching), their meagre curriculum with reading as the chief accomplishment, their mechanical methods applied by unskilled assistants, and their cheapness and poverty, conspired to fossilise the elementary school'.[8] More recent studies have

A Miscellany, CERS 12 (Woodbridge, 2004), 51–108, at 75. The three exceptions were London, Rochester and Oxford, all of which had extensive provision of National Schools under non-diocesan auspices.

6 *Twenty-first Annual Report of the National Society, for promoting the Education of the Poor in the Principles of the Established Church throughout England and Wales* (London, 1832), 105–8, 123. This statistic resulted from a survey sent to parishes throughout England and Wales, in which approximately 83 per cent of parishes completed returns. The figures for the remaining 17 per cent were estimated on the basis of averages.

7 *Education Enquiry: Abstract of the Answers and Returns made pursuant to an Address to the House of Commons, dated 24th May 1833* (London, 1835), 1208. The proportion for Sunday schools was rather different as the church did not prioritize these, but nevertheless around two-thirds of English Sunday schools were Anglican, accounting for 55 per cent of scholars.

8 Frank Smith, *A History of English Elementary Education 1760–1902* (London, 1931), 80; cf. J. W. Adamson, *English Education 1798–1902* (Cambridge, 1930), 24–31; H. C. Barnard, *A History of English Education from 1760*, 2nd edn (London, 1961), 57; Mary Sturt, *The Education of the People: A History of Primary Education in England and Wales in the Nineteenth Century* (London, 1967), 34.

been less dismissive of the efforts of Anglican educationalists, but have remained focused on their contribution to education per se. Two institutional histories of the National Society draw attention to its achievements, relying largely on annual reports and the deliberations of its central committee in London.[9] Since the 1970s, a series of local case studies have also served to qualify conventionally negative assessments of the National Society, demonstrating its capacity to educate effectively.[10]

However, the political aspect of the National Society, though frequently remarked upon by contemporary observers, remains little explored. The epigraph of C. K. Francis Brown's 1942 study of *The Church's Part in Education 1833–1941*, a quotation from William Cowper-Temple, declared: 'In England popular education originated with no statesman, and was nurtured for no political end.' Instead, in Brown's view, the provision of schools for the poor was for 'sociological and religious reasons'.[11] Assessments of the National Society's purpose have remained largely in the realm of sociology, with occasional allusions to its desire to check political sedition.[12] Neil Smelser, for instance, maintains a sharp distinction between the political and religious contexts for the development of working-class education.[13] The only study to address the political aspect of such instruction at length is Philip McCann's case study

[9] Burgess, *Enterprise in Education*; Lois Louden, *Distinctive and Inclusive: The National Society and Church of England Schools 1811–2011* (London, 2012).

[10] Michael Sanderson, 'The National and British School Societies in Lancashire 1803–1839: The Roots of Anglican Supremacy in English Education', in T. G. Cook, ed., *Local Studies and the History of Education* (London, 1972), 1–36; Pamela Silver and Harold Silver, *The Education of the Poor: The History of a National School 1824–1974* (London, 1974); Marjorie Cruickshank, 'The Anglican Revival and Education: A Study of School Expansion in the Potteries 1830–1850', *North Staffordshire Journal of Field Studies* 20 (1980), 19–31; Mary Clare Martin, 'Church, School and Locality: Revisiting the Historiography of "State" and "Religious" Educational Infrastructures in England and Wales, 1780–1870', *PH* 49 (2013), 70–81.

[11] C. K. Francis Brown, *The Church's Part in Education 1833–1941, with Special Reference to the Work of the National Society* (London, 1942), title page, 3.

[12] John Lawson and Harold Silver, *A Social History of Education in England* (London, 1973), 243, 271; Thomas Laqueur, 'Working-Class Demand and the Growth of English Elementary Education, 1750–1850', in Lawrence Stone, ed., *Schooling and Society: Studies in the History of Education* (Baltimore, MD, 1976), 192–205, at 198; D. G. Paz, *The Politics of Working-Class Education in Britain, 1830–50* (Manchester, 1980), 4.

[13] Smelser, *Social Paralysis and Social Change*, 26–32, 70–90.

of schools in early nineteenth-century Spitalfields, in which this aspect is presented through the lens of sociological theories of 'socialization'. McCann sees the political dimension of the Anglican schools as paternalistic: 'Father, magistrate, monarch, deity, all Anglican and many other children who attended school at this period had their attention drawn to this omnipresent hierarchy, and few can fail to have absorbed some of its social significance.'[14]

However, the National Society's political dimension was much more varied and complex than this suggests, as appears when it is analysed in relation to contemporary political developments. It is with this dimension of the society's work, as opposed to the nature of its social function or role in furthering literacy, that this article is primarily concerned. Besides the society's controversial claim respecting what constituted 'national' education, political agendas were evident in three main areas: the National Schools' teaching, rituals and use as venues for political activism. This article will discuss each of these by reference to a variety of geographically dispersed examples, before considering their broader effect. It will do so principally by reference to contemporary newspaper accounts.[15] Such sources are to be treated with caution on account of their frequently partisan agendas, which could extend to education. In general, Tory-leaning newspapers celebrated the achievements of the National Society through fulsome descriptions of its commemorations, while Whig-leaning newspapers drew attention to the controversies in which the managers of National Schools became involved. But when considered together, items in newspapers of both persuasions present a convincingly mixed picture of the successes and difficulties of National Schools. Both the positive and negative press received by National Schools may have been susceptible to hyperbole, but it would be wrong to suppose

[14] Philip McCann, 'Popular Education, Socialization and Social Control: Spitalfields 1812–1824', in idem, ed., *Popular Education and Socialization in the Nineteenth Century* (London, 1977), 1–40, at 25. McCann also observed, however, that the contributions in this volume 'do not provide the basis for generalizations about popular education in the nineteenth century': 'Editor's Introduction', ibid. xii.

[15] The newspaper accounts were gathered by searching for references to the National Society and National Schools in newspapers digitized by the British Library in the British Newspaper Archive, online at: <https://www.britishnewspaperarchive.co.uk>. This database currently incorporates 147 English newspapers published during the period from 1811–37, from all regions of England and of a variety of political persuasions. It constitutes the largest and broadest sample accessible through digital resources of English local newspapers from this period.

that newspaper accounts are inadmissible as historical evidence in consequence. Most of the accounts presented here are of a primarily descriptive nature, concerning public events which would have been familiar to each newspaper's readership, and therefore unlikely to be wildly inaccurate. Furthermore, newspapers often give a more detailed and colourful view of the activities of the National Society than appears from more prosaic (but equally subjective) sources such as National Schools' annual reports and minute books, though these are nonetheless also important and complementary sources. In using newspapers as a basis for examining the early years of the National Society, a worthwhile and heretofore largely untapped avenue of enquiry is opened.

The political dimension of the National Society's operations was most obviously evident in its nomenclature. The creation of a system of 'national' education along specifically Anglican lines, and without state oversight, constituted a provocative intervention in the contemporary debate about the relationship between church and nation-state. Established at a time of significant Anglican revival, the National Society was the first society in Britain to use the appellation of 'national'.[16] As Joanna Innes has argued, its foundation represented a bold assertion of the Church of England's capacity to represent the nation at large.[17] Such exclusivity irked Dissenters, one of whom asked at a meeting in Lincoln in 1812, 'How can that be called a "National" School which is founded on a partial view of religions[?]'[18] Additionally, the church itself encompassed influential supporters of non-denominational education such as Henry Bathurst, bishop of Norwich, and Sydney Smith.[19] Opponents of Anglican exclusivity

[16] Bob Tennant, *Corporate Holiness: Pulpit Preaching and the Church of England Missionary Societies, 1760–1870* (Oxford, 2013), 152. On the revival of Anglicanism in this period, see Arthur Burns, *The Diocesan Revival in the Church of England,* c.*1800–1870* (Oxford, 1999); Stewart J. Brown, *The National Churches of England, Ireland, and Scotland 1801–46* (Oxford, 2001), 62–92.

[17] Joanna Innes, 'L'«Éducation nationale» dans les îles Britanniques, 1765–1815. Variations britanniques et irlandaises sur un thème européen', *Annales. Histoire, Sciences sociales* 65 (2010), 1087–1116, at 1103–4.

[18] *Stamford Mercury*, 31 January 1812, 4. The complaint that the National Society's title was a misnomer because of its religious exclusivity persisted throughout the period: see, for example, *Windsor and Eton Express*, 2 August 1818, 2; *Wolverhampton Chronicle*, 13 April 1831, 2; *Leeds Mercury*, 19 October 1833, 8; *Taunton Courier*, 27 January 1836, 9; *Yorkshire Gazette*, 22 October 1836, 2.

[19] Henry Bathurst, *Memoirs of the late Dr Henry Bathurst, Lord Bishop of Norwich*, 2 vols (London, 1837), 2: 69–70; Sydney Smith, 'Trimmer and Lancaster' (1806), in idem, *Works*, 3 vols (London, 1848), 1: 157–66.

generally supported the BFSS, which offered non-denominational religious education for the poor but failed to match its rival's financial and numerical strength.[20]

The teaching offered by the National Society was premised on the belief, proclaimed in its initial prospectus, that 'the National Religion should be made the first and chief thing taught to the Poor, according to the excellent Liturgy and Catechism provided by our Church for that purpose'.[21] The teaching methods used in the schools were drawn from *Elements of Tuition* (1808) by Andrew Bell, a Church of England clergyman from Scotland who had experimented with new modes of instruction as chaplain of an orphanage in Madras. Bell stipulated that schools should be divided into classes led by the more able pupils, who were made 'monitors', the whole being overseen by a single schoolmaster and a superintending visitor.[22] Such 'monitorial' methods were also used by the BFSS, in a permutation devised by the Quaker schoolmaster Joseph Lancaster.[23] But there the similarity ended. Whereas the BFSS taught children biblical passages without any doctrinal gloss, central to Bell's scheme was 'moral and religious Instruction' based on the Prayer Book Catechism, which was learned by rote.[24] Besides the inculcation of religious doctrine, the duty of civil obedience was strongly promoted, as is evident in a dialogue from the *National School Magazine* of 1824:

> Who placed our king over us?
>
> God.
>
> Prove this from Scripture.
>
> Rom. xiii. 1. 'Let every soul be subject unto the higher powers; for there is no power but of God; the powers that be are ordained by God.'
>
> Can a good Christian then, be a disloyal subject?
>
> No; for the Bible says, 'Fear God, honour the King.'[25]

[20] *Education Enquiry*, 1338; Henry Bryan Binns, *A Century of Education: Being the Centenary History of the British and Foreign School Society 1808–1908* (London, 1908), 55–7, 81, 103, 123–4.

[21] London, CERC, NS/2/2/1/1/1, National Society General Committee minute book, fol. 1r (16 October 1811).

[22] Andrew Bell, *The Madras School, or Elements of Tuition* (London, 1808), 15–17.

[23] Binns, *Century of Education*, 16–18.

[24] Ibid. 95–6; Bell, *Madras School*, 84–8.

[25] *National School Magazine*, 15 June 1824, 73–4.

Teaching personnel were both male and female and generally came from 'the middle class of society'.[26] They were carefully selected for their adherence to the established church, with Dissenters and Roman Catholics generally, though not uniformly, excluded.[27] Where the teachers' political opinions are recorded, these were consistently of a Tory or Conservative hue. William Lancaster, master of the National School of Market Rasen in Lincolnshire, was noted in 1821 for his 'attachment to Church & State in the good old fashioned way'.[28] At Warrington in 1836, it was reported that a National School master was the secretary of a local Conservative politician.[29]

The political content of National Society teaching was articulated at length at a dinner of Bath Church of England Lay Association in 1835 by the long-standing master of the town's National School, a Mr Browning. He explained that 'our motto is "the Bible and the crown – church and king – and may they never be separated"'. He added:

> We certainly do not instruct the children that they will be better sons, brothers, husbands, or fathers by becoming members of Political Unions; though that might be of great use in making them discontented, and *not* to do their duty in that state of life which it should please their Maker to call them.[30]

Nor did Browning intend to teach 'a blind obedience'. Instead, he aimed to defend 'the Protestant church' by 'handing down to our children the blessings that have descended to us from the piety and wisdom of our forefathers'.[31]

26 *Report from Select Committee on the State of Education* (London, 1834), 9.
27 Ibid. 11. On the training of National schoolteachers, see R. W. Rich, *The Training of Teachers in England and Wales during the Nineteenth Century* (Cambridge, 1933), 1–25. For exclusions, see, for example, Winchester, Hampshire RO, 128M84/2, Hampshire Society for the Education of the Infant Poor minute book, 44–5 (18 April 1816), 89 (1 December 1817). For isolated instances of non-Anglican teachers, see CERC, NS/2/2/1/1/3, National Society General Committee minute book, fol. 108^{r} (5 May 1819); Brighton, East Sussex RO, PAR 255/25/1/1, Brighton National Schools minute book, 271 (22 July 1835); Robert Southey and Charles Southey, *Life of Rev. Andrew Bell*, 3 vols (London, 1844), 3: 448.
28 Lincoln, Lincolnshire Archives, BNLW/3/10/1/10/2, John Robinson to Earl Brownlow, 3 March 1821.
29 Laqueur, 'English Elementary Education', 199–200.
30 *Bath Chronicle*, 3 December 1835, 4.
31 Ibid.

National Schools developed a number of rituals which reinforced this instruction. If most church services in this period were devoid of elaborate ceremonial, a National Society observance was seemingly incomplete without a procession of dignitaries and children, the carrying of colourful banners, the singing of hymns or patriotic songs and a dinner of roast beef and plum pudding. The frequency of these ceremonies challenges the conventional assumption that the Church of England was characterized by a relative absence of ritual in the early nineteenth century.[32] Furthermore, it demonstrates the centrality of a specifically Anglican agenda to many loyalist rituals, qualifying Linda Colley's argument that loyalists' use of religious terminology was a case of extravagant appropriation reflecting 'the spread of secular religion'.[33]

The monarchy, which in the person of George IV had supported the National Society from its foundation, provided a focal point for many of the occasions under discussion.[34] At Ipswich on the King's birthday in 1812, the National Schoolroom was festooned with 'a wreath of laurel, encircling "God save the King" handsomely gilt', while at an examination held on the Prince Regent's birthday in 1817 at Wendover National School, '[t]he festivities of the day were concluded by all the children drinking the health of his ROYAL HIGHNESS THE PRINCE REGENT, the firm friend and patron of the NATIONAL SOCIETY.'[35]

On occasion, royal observances assumed a positively antiquated character. From 1818, it was an annual custom for two boys and two girls from the Westminster National Schools selected for 'good conduct' to participate in the Royal Maundy ceremony.[36] For the

[32] See, for example, David Cannadine, 'The Context, Performance and Meaning of Ritual: The British Monarchy and the "Invention of Tradition", *c.*1820–1977', in Eric Hobsbawm and Terence Ranger, eds, *The Invention of Tradition* (Cambridge, 1983), 101–64, at 115; F. C. Mather, 'Georgian Churchmanship reconsidered: Some Variations in Anglican Public Worship 1714–1830', *JEH* 36 (1985), 255–83, at 261–2.

[33] Linda Colley, 'The Apotheosis of George III: Loyalty, Royalty and the British Nation, 1760–1820', *P&P* 102 (1984), 94–129, at 120–1.

[34] On monarchical patronage of the National Society in this period, see Nicholas Dixon, 'Church and Monarchy in England, 1811–1837' (MPhil dissertation, University of Cambridge, 2015), 81–5.

[35] *Ipswich Journal*, 13 June 1812, 2; *Cambridge Chronicle and Journal*, 22 August 1817, 3. See also the account of the royal birthday festivities at Canterbury in *Kentish Weekly Post*, 6 June 1817, 4.

[36] *Evening Mail*, 20 March 1818, 4; *Morning Post*, 20 April 1821, 3; 5 April 1822, 3; 28 March 1823, 1; *London Courier*, 16 April 1824, 2; *Bell's Life in London*, 3 April 1825, 3; *Morning Post*, 24 March 1826, 2; 13 April 1827, 3; 4 April 1828, 3; 17 April 1829, 3; 9

1820 anniversary of Charles II's restoration, schoolchildren in York attended the commemorative service prescribed in the Prayer Book at the cathedral and heard a preacher expound the text: 'My son, fear thou the Lord and the King, and meddle not with them that are given to change.'[37] As late as 1825, the schools under the auspices of the National Society in Rotherhithe were marking 'King Charles the First's Martyrdom', in addition to the Restoration and 5 November, with holidays.[38]

Yet supporters of the schools were also perfectly capable of inventing new observances as circumstances demanded. One of the most elaborate spectacles recorded was a procession of schoolboys in Norwich marking the peace of 1814:

> The head boys preceded the whole, carrying a banner with 'NATIONAL SCHOOL' inscribed upon it. Next followed a representation of a Bible and Crown, with the appropriate quotation of Scripture, 'FEAR GOD: HONOUR THE KING.' After which came the Book of Common Prayer, over which was written in large characters, 'Train up a Child in the Way he should go.'[39]

If the ties between monarch and subject were emphasized by such rituals, they also called to mind obligations to more immediate patrons. Sir John and Lady Shelley, benefactors of Maresfield National School in Sussex, gave an annual dinner on New Year's Day for the children of this institution in the servants' hall of their country seat, at which they distributed prizes and clothes.[40] Bonds of this kind were further expressed in the schoolchildren's participation in events of family significance. At Knaresborough in 1824, six hundred children processed from the National schoolroom 'headed by a band of music' to celebrate the birth of a son and heir to local worthy Sir William Slingsby, giving 'three cheers for the family of Slingsby'.[41] In 1832, the committee of Runcorn National School decided that, in recognition of 'the invariable attention paid by Sir Richard Brooke Baronet and

April 1830, 3; 1 April 1831, 3; W. J. Thoms, *The Book of the Court* (London, 1838), 314–15.

37 *Yorkshire Gazette*, 2 June 1820, 3.

38 *An Address to the Parents of Children, admitted into the Rotherhithe Charity and Amicable Society Schools, with the Rules and Orders to be Observed* (London, [1825]), 9.

39 *Norfolk Chronicle*, 9 July 1814, 2.

40 *Sussex Advertiser*, 4 January 1819, 3; *Public Ledger*, 4 January 1821, 3.

41 *Yorkshire Gazette*, 18 September 1824, 2.

his family to this Institution', the schoolchildren would attend the wedding of his daughter.[42] While such rituals would have required the co-operation of the schoolchildren's parents, they clearly also served a hierarchical social purpose. A Windsor clergyman named Allen suggested in 1835 that the foundation of a National School would 'if he might so express himself, be productive of great political advantages' in counteracting the 'disposition among the lower classes to regard not with proper feelings the higher class'.[43]

However, the encouragement of social deference was far from being the sole, or even the principal, priority of the organizers of National Society observances. More partisan political agendas were evident at the dinners of patrons and managers of the schools. The school anniversary at Thorpe-le-Soken, Essex, in 1814 was essentially a celebration of Napoleon's recent defeat. A toast was given to King Louis XVIII of France and a version of 'God save the King' was performed which included the lines:

If Statesmen dead can know,
What passes here below,
Pitt! how thy heart must glow,
God save the King.[44]

Such politicking was still evident in the 1830s. Shortly after the general election of 1835, a dinner to mark the anniversary of Deptford National School was presided over by Wolverley Attwood, the unsuccessful Conservative candidate for Greenwich. Attwood was eager to show magnanimity in defeat, telling diners that '[o]n all occasions like the present every feeling of political difference should be banished' and toasting the health of his victorious Whig opponents. This ploy fell flat, however, as the toast was given 'in any thing but a cordial manner, a great portion of the company being silent, and the cheers of a very faint description'.[45]

Anglican attempts to disclaim political partisanship therefore usually rang hollow. The early nineteenth century was a period

[42] Chester, Cheshire Archives, P95/3516/1, Runcorn National School minute book, 17 May 1832; *Gentleman's Magazine*, August 1844, 205.
[43] *Windsor and Eton Express*, 5 December 1835, 4.
[44] *Ipswich Journal*, 7 May 1814, 2.
[45] *Kentish Mercury*, 4 April 1835, 4. Attwood made another appearance at the school's anniversary in 1837 following the success of his second attempt at being elected an MP for Greenwich: *West Kent Guardian*, 28 October 1837, 8.

in which the Church of England was undergoing a thorough politicization, as the clergy and laity increasingly attempted to make their voices heard in national and local public debate. Political divisions consequently assumed a far greater significance than any variations in churchmanship. The National Schools, as a prominent sphere of Anglican activity, could hardly fail to be affected by this development, and soon became venues for political activism that was as multifarious as it was widespread. Especially formative in this regard was the Queen Caroline Affair of 1820, which split the church between the factions of George IV and his estranged wife Queen Caroline.[46] Some supporters of the National Society acted in accordance with its loyalist ethos. In Lambeth, a committee of seventeen met in private at the National School and issued a 'loyal declaration' on behalf of the parish's sixty thousand inhabitants.[47] At a meeting in Lancaster to frame a similar address, one speaker alluded to the 'exhibition' of 'that kind of education which combines piety to God with loyalty to the King' at the town's National School.[48] A chaplain of the archbishop of Canterbury, John William Whittaker, preached a sermon to aid the funds of the National School at Newington, Surrey, and was 'particularly thanked for some raps wh[ich] I gave to the Radicals, & the proselytes of Carlisle [*sic*] & Hone'.[49]

However, it was also possible for National Schools to be co-opted for more subversive demonstrations. The school at Alford, Lincolnshire, was lit in celebration of the dropping of the bill of pains and penalties which would have deprived Caroline of her rights as Queen had it been enacted.[50] In Limehouse, subscribers to the National School voted to allow their schoolroom to be used for a meeting to frame a supportive address to the Queen. This meeting was interrupted by the school's treasurer, Christopher Richardson, who protested that 'there were many Subscribers to the Charity who did not reside in the parish, and

[46] Dixon, 'Church and Monarchy', 49–52.

[47] *Evening Mail*, 25 December 1820, 2.

[48] *Westmorland Gazette*, 30 December 1820, 412.

[49] Cambridge, St John's College Library, Whittaker Papers, 2/16, John William Whittaker to Sarah Whittaker, [7 May 1821], quoted by permission of the Master and Fellows of St John's College, Cambridge. Whittaker was referring to the radical publishers Richard Carlile and William Hone.

[50] *Stamford Mercury*, 24 November 1820, 3.

who might, perhaps, withdraw their patronage if political Meetings were suffered there'. A Mr Fitch responded that the schoolroom 'could not be devoted to a more laudable purpose than the support of innocence against injustice and oppression. … [I]f the worthy Speaker thought otherwise, why did he not muster her Majesty's enemies, and oppose the proceedings?' At this point Richardson departed, and the address was carried.[51]

National Schools were further drawn into political debate by the proliferation of petitions against Catholic emancipation in the late 1820s. At Coventry in 1827, an anti-emancipation petition lay for signature 'for some days' at the city's National School.[52] An especially bitter dispute occurred in Norwich in 1829. The Whig *Norwich Mercury* sparked controversy when it reported that 'the Boys of one of the National Schools were marched up in procession … to a house near Fye-bridge, where all who could write set their signatures to the Petition against Catholic Emancipation preparing in this city'.[53] Henry Bathurst, archdeacon of Norwich and son of the bishop, asked that a 'satisfactory and public contradiction' of this report be given. Accordingly, a denial of the allegation was published by the trustees of the school. It then emerged that eight National schoolboys had signed the petition '*in a body*', but apparently without official encouragement.[54] In this instance, attendance at a National School appears to have been politically formative. In response, Bathurst argued that 'for children to take such a part in public matters, and especially where the subscribers to the charity are of different opinions as to the subject in question, is not only absurd in itself, but prejudicial to the character and interests of the institutions in which they are educated'.[55] The affair gained national attention when the duke of Sussex, patron of the BFSS, repeated a variant of the original report of the *Mercury* in the House of Lords, claiming that the schoolboys had been dismissed by their master early to sign the petition.[56] A

51 *Morning Chronicle*, 9 December 1820, 3. The National schoolroom in Greenwich was also used for a meeting to address the Queen: *Bath Chronicle*, 17 August 1820, 2.

52 *Northampton Mercury*, 29 December 1827, 4. The schoolroom was also the venue of a meeting to frame a clerical anti-emancipation petition in the same year: *Coventry Herald*, 29 June 1827, 2.

53 *Norwich Mercury*, 31 January 1829, 3.

54 Ibid., 7 February 1829, 2.

55 Ibid., 14 February 1829, 3.

56 HL Deb (2nd series), vol. 20, cols 940–1 (10 March 1829).

Reading newspaper predicted that anti-emancipationists there would 'attempt something of a "hole and corner" petition … and by the aid of a few "old ladies in breeches" and the little boys and girls of the National Schools obtain some signatures'.[57]

Although it remained possible for reformist gatherings to be held at National Schools, their overtly political function tended in the 1830s to assume a fixed form in their use as venues for meetings of working-class supporters of the nascent Conservative party, especially in industrial Lancashire.[58] At Chorley in 1836, the formation of an 'Operative Conservative Association' at a National School elicited a protest from local manufacturers.[59] In Liverpool, members of the Tradesmen's and Operative Conservative associations processed at the laying of the foundation stone of an Anglican school.[60] The following year, at a dinner in Wigan National School, local Conservative MP John Hodson Kearsley was feted by 'operatives', while at Rochdale 'a conservative tea party' was held in the National School.[61] A dinner of the Pilkington Operative Conservative Association held in a National schoolroom was the occasion of a speech by a curate named Sandford, who remarked to cheers that 'he trusted we should never look forward to the time when children would be taken from the care of the clergy in the national schools'.[62] It is not possible to determine how many members of these associations had attended National Schools, but such a correlation seems highly probable.

Godfrey Faussett, in urging the claims of the National Society on the University of Oxford in 1811, had preached that 'the defence of our Ecclesiastical Establishment is the defence of our Political Constitution'. Countering systems of non-denominational education was, in his view, 'manifestly the interest of the ecclesiastic and

[57] *Reading Mercury*, 9 February 1829, 3.

[58] For instances of reformist gatherings, see, for example, *Sheffield Independent*, 19 March 1831, 2; *Maidstone Journal*, 22 May 1832, 1; *Morning Advertiser*, 5 December 1834, 1. For an early example of a Conservative dinner, see *Morning Post*, 2 February 1833, 2. In Canterbury, the clergy used National schoolrooms for meetings to frame their responses to church reforms: *Kentish Gazette*, 29 March 1833, 3; 10 January 1837, 2.

[59] *The Standard*, 24 November 1836, 1.

[60] *Morning Post*, 7 September 1836, 3.

[61] *Durham County Advertiser*, 6 January 1837, 4; *Blackburn Standard*, 24 May 1837, 2.

[62] *Bolton Chronicle*, 25 November 1837, 3.

the statesman'.[63] During the succeeding quarter of a century, the National Society demonstrated its political potential. Although the principal aim of National Schools was to engender belief in Anglican doctrine and loyalty to the sovereign, the events of the 1820s and 1830s precipitated a broadening of this agenda to encompass the promotion of deference to the social hierarchy, opposition to Catholic emancipation and support for Peel's Conservative Party. Given the number of National Schools and the way in which they functioned as a point of contact between the poor and the church, the significance of their foray into the political sphere can hardly be underestimated.

In his recent comparative study of education and state formation, Andy Green suggests that '[t]he stultifying condescension of the Anglican schools, deriving from the ritual conservative belief in rank and status, no doubt did much to alienate the working class from education.'[64] In this schema, also discernible in the writings of Brian Simon and Thomas Laqueur, National Schools were a generally ineffective form of social control promoted by an unpopular Anglican elite.[65] The evidence brought forward here suggests an alternative interpretation. Not only did National Schools increase educational provision for the poor to an unprecedented degree; they also did so in a way which, far from alienating the working class, brought about a closer engagement with Anglican ideals.

This was strongly demonstrated by a survey conducted by the society in 1836, in which local committees were asked to provide information regarding 'the character and general conduct of young persons brought up in National schools'. The published results were no propaganda exercise; the society admitted that in some respects the

[63] Godfrey Faussett, *A Sermon on the Necessity of Educating the Poor in the Principles of the Established Church: Preached before the University of Oxford, at St Mary's, on Sunday, Dec. 1, 1811* (Oxford, 1811), 18–19; cf. Herbert Marsh, *The National Religion the Foundation of National Education: A Sermon preached in the Cathedral Church of St Paul, London: on Thursday, June 13, 1811* (London, 1811), 37–40; T. H. Lowe, *A Sermon, preached in the Parish Church of Tenbury, for the Benefit of the National School, established in that Town* (Ludlow, 1817), 14–16; Daniel Wilson, *The National Schools a National Blessing: A Sermon preached at Christ Church, Middlesex, on Sunday Evening, March 28, 1819* (London, 1819), 32–3.

[64] Andy Green, *Education and State Formation: Europe, East Asia and the USA*, 2nd edn (Basingstoke, 2013), 224.

[65] Brian Simon, *The Two Nations and the Educational Structure 1780–1870* (London, 1974), 132–3; Laqueur, 'English Elementary Education', 199.

information collected was 'exceedingly defective' and even detailed two National schoolboys' convictions for crimes.[66] Nevertheless, relatively reliable information was obtained regarding 24,466 scholars in 382 places.[67] The vast majority of this sample of pupils were said to be of good character.[68] Of 741 pupils educated in three schools in County Durham, it was claimed that all were 'regular in attendance at Church, and useful members of Society. They are distinguished by their good conduct, and are, in many instances … religious characters.'[69] Other responses remarked on noticeable increases in church attendance, the lack of criminality among former pupils and the number of pupils who had become teachers.[70]

The effect of such success for the Church of England was to render its political position more secure. A significant proportion of the labouring population were now becoming accustomed at an early age to a religiously inflected conception of nationhood, in which belonging to the established church and obeying the monarch were the twin cornerstones of a common identity. This was already apparent in 1833, when criticism of the National Society appeared in the *Bath Herald* newspaper. In response, an address containing '*spontaneous testimony*' from around seventy former pupils of Bath National School was presented to its committee:

> *From the extensive connection which we enjoy with those who were once our schoolfellows, and from information derived from others, there exists not among them, as far as we know, one solitary instance of a departure from the faith* … . We do most heartily and conscientiously express our firm and unshaken belief in those doctrines and precepts which were so indefatigably inculcated upon us by our excellent Master; and we hope that, in the practice of those duties, our employers would bear testimony to our zeal and industry.[71]

The National Society laid broad and permanent foundations for the maintenance and extension of the Church of England's influence.

[66] *Twenty-Fifth Annual Report of the National Society, for Promoting the Education of the Poor in the Principles of the Established Church throughout England and Wales* (London, 1836), 61, 86.
[67] Ibid. 94.
[68] Ibid. 61–90.
[69] Ibid. 69.
[70] See, for example, ibid. 72, 76, 79, 80, 82, 86.
[71] *Bath Chronicle*, 19 December 1833, 3.

This was primarily achieved through three means: the dissemination of a homogenous method for instructing the poor in Anglican doctrine and civil obedience, the development of rituals supportive of this agenda and the use of National Schools as venues for Anglican political activism. Even when considered in isolation from other areas of clerical activity, National Schools reveal the shakiness of the foundations upon which the notion of pre-Victorian Anglican lethargy was to be constructed later in the century.[72] Moreover, the success of the National Society's project surely reflects something of the dominance which the church exercised among a sizeable section of the English populace, despite the best efforts of Dissenters and radicals. The case of elementary education suggests the possibility that there was a wider Anglican socio-political dominance in England that, contrary to most standard accounts, may have persisted beyond the alleged displacement of the church's political hegemony in consequence of the legislative reforms of 1828–32. Further research concerning the National Society's operations beyond 1837 and Anglican associational activity throughout the nineteenth century will shed light on this larger question. Whatever the outcome of such enquiries, the contribution of National Schools to the mass politicization of the English populace in the early part of the nineteenth century is a historical factor which warrants recognition.

[72] See, for example, George Biber, *Bishop Blomfield and his Times: An Historical Sketch* (London, 1857), 1–25; William Nassau Molesworth, *History of the Church of England from 1660* (London, 1881), 308–9; R. W. Church, *The Oxford Movement: Twelve Years, 1833–1845* (London, 1891), 1–19.

Schools for the Poor in Mid-Nineteenth-Century Devon: Towards an Explanation of Variations in Local Development

Frances Billinge, Gail Ham, Judith Moss and Julia Neville*
Devon History Society

This article analyses elementary school development in three contrasting Devon communities during the mid-nineteenth century. This was a time of intense interest in the expansion of education amongst the labouring poor, but scholars have found it difficult to explain why schools were established in some places but not in others. With information from local sources, the authors have been able to identify the social context in which developments did (or did not) take place and the actions of the relevant interested parties. They argue that a significant variable accounting for success or failure is the availability of a local champion with the skills not only to persuade others of the merits of a school, but also to seize opportunities to further the project and manage the relationships necessary to assure its success.

The development of elementary schools between 1833 and 1870 has, by comparison with research on progress later in the nineteenth century, received little recent attention. The consensus is that what developed was haphazard or unpatterned, although sectarian rivalry is seen as a significant explanatory factor for school foundations. This article argues that close attention to what took place in individual localities can reveal patterns not otherwise detectable. Three case studies from communities of different kinds, all within the county of Devon, are discussed. These are Throwleigh, a small Dartmoor parish; Bovey Tracey, a market town with some industry; and Dartmouth, a historic seaport. Specifically, the article demonstrates the significance for school development of the availability of a local individual, whatever their background or religious persuasion, able to champion the establishment of a school. Such champions needed to be able to set out the

* Julia Neville, 18 Summer Close, Exeter, EX4 8BX. E-mail: j.neville@exeter.ac.uk. This article has been produced by members of Devon History Society undertaking a research project on early Victorian schools in Devon.

Studies in Church History 55 (2019), 307–323
doi: 10.1017/stc.2018.34

proposal, seize opportunities and manage relationships to deliver the change and to maintain the initiative. Where individuals lacked one or other of these attributes, the school might never be established, or might close prematurely.

A trio of studies of the development of education for the poor in England published between 1967 and 1971 set out a broad national narrative for the development of education.[1] This narrative posited that during the first half of the nineteenth century the traditional responsibilities of those fortunate enough to be well off for the welfare of the poor were challenged by mass industrialization and by new ideas which led to legal and constitutional reforms and to the wish to improve the 'condition of the labouring poor'. One result was the widening of access to elementary education and the growth of schools. Continuing tensions, both between religious denominations and within them, meant that a state system was slow to emerge. Even though the government undertook national surveys of education in 1818 and 1833, and allocated funds to support school building in 1833, it was not until 1870 that legislation mandating universal elementary education and the creation of schools by local boards was introduced. The establishment of a state system was strongly contested throughout by the National Society for Promoting the Education of the Poor in the Principles of the Established Church[2] and the British and Foreign School Society.[3]

[1] Mary Sturt, *The Education of the People: A History of Primary Education in England and Wales in the Nineteenth Century* (London, 1967); Gillian Sutherland, *Elementary Education in the Nineteenth Century* (London, 1971); John Lawson and Harold Silver, *A Social History of Education in England* (London, 1973).

[2] The National Society was established in 1811. At that time, whether religious education should be part of any school curriculum, and whether the poor should be educated, were hotly debated. In 1809 the perceived need for religious education of the urban and industrialized poor led to the funding of church schools through Queen Anne's Bounty. This, coupled with the interdependence of church and state, led some high church Tories to form a society 'to instruct and educate the Poor in suitable learning, works of industry and the principles of the Christian Religion according to the Established Church'. Schools in industrialized towns and teacher training were the initial priority. Grants to build schools were made available under strict conditions which necessitated part-funding by the local community: see Lois Louden, *Distinctive and Inclusive: The National Society and Church of England Schools 1811–2011* (London, 2012), 12–17; and, in this volume, Nicholas Dixon, 'The Political Dimension of the Education of the Poor in the National Society's Church of England Schools, 1811–37', 290–306.

[3] The British Society was established following publication in 1803 of Joseph Lancaster's *Improvements in Education as it respects the Industrious Classes of the Community*, drawing

Part of the prompt for these studies was the publication in the 1960s of a cluster of county histories of school development, including R. R. Sellman's *Devon Village Schools*.[4] Gillian Sutherland acknowledged these in her Historical Association pamphlet on *Elementary Education*: 'The interaction of educational provision and institutions with patterns of social mobility and political behaviour are [*sic*] fascinatingly complex.'[5] More recently, however, scholarship relating to the history of education has been dominated by studies of particular aspects of education such as the child's experience,[6] or the Victorian teacher,[7] or institutional histories such as that of the National Society.[8] The question of an explanation for what many scholars term the 'haphazard system'[9] of parish and private schools that developed before the 1870 Elementary Education Act requires further study. New tools such as online data collections, not available in the 1960s, can now facilitate detailed local research. This article uses three Devon case studies to examine how schools were developed in order to identify features that might explain success and failure.

---

on his practical experience of nondenominational teaching. Re-founded in 1814, it continued to promote the foundation of nondenominational schools: see Richard Aldrich, 'The British and Foreign School Society, Past and Present', *History of Education Researcher* 91 (2013), 5–12.

4 R. R. Sellman, *Devon Village Schools in the Nineteenth Century* (Newton Abbot, 1967). Sellman, who was interested in the role of local government, devotes significantly more attention to the period after 1870 than to earlier years.

5 Sutherland, *Elementary Education*, 46, refers to Rex C. Russell, *A History of Schools & Education in Lindsey, Lincolnshire, 1800–1902*, 3 parts (Lincoln, 1965), Parts 1 and 2; Brian Simon, ed., *Education in Leicestershire, 1540–1940* (Leicester, 1968); Marion Johnson, *Derbyshire Village Schools in the Nineteenth Century* (Newton Abbot, 1970); R. J. Smith, 'Education, Society and Literacy: Nottinghamshire in the Mid-Nineteenth Century' *University of Birmingham Historical Journal* 12 (1969), 42–56.

6 Pamela Horn, *The Victorian and Edwardian Schoolchild* (Stroud, 1989); Roderick Gordon, *Victorian Education and the Ideal of Womanhood* (Abingdon, 2016).

7 For example, Marianne Larsen, *The Making and Shaping of the Victorian Teacher: A comparative new Cultural History* (New York, 2011); Rowland William Rich, *The Training of Teachers in England and Wales during the Nineteenth Century* (Cambridge, 2015).

8 Louden, *Distinctive and Inclusive*.

9 This description appears to have first been used by Raymond Williams, *The Long Revolution* (London, 1961), 156.

The Case Studies

Empirical studies, or microhistories, of individual settlements use closely detailed observation to explore impact at a local level.[10] As Briggs noted,

> It was from the periphery not from the centre that English education developed. … It is … necessary to explore local economic, social (including religious) and political structures to understand why initiatives and activities in education varied as much as they did before the passing of the Education Act of 1870.[11]

Although Devon experienced little industrialization, the foundation of schools still proceeded apace in the mid-nineteenth century. Divergent beliefs about instruction in religion caused problems for school foundation and maintenance in Devon communities as they did elsewhere. The studies presented here illustrate that, while the circumstances in which the schools were or were not established were very different, taken together they illustrate the significance of the availability of individuals to 'champion' the foundation of particular schools.

Devon in the early nineteenth century had lost the prosperity generated by its pre-industrial wool trades and gained little in the way of other manufacturing processes. The livelihood of its inhabitants depended chiefly on farming and fishing, although the development of tourism had begun to provide alternative employment. Emigration kept population growth slow. The overall picture in the 1851 religious census suggests a rough division between Nonconformist strength in the west and Anglican dominance in the east.[12] The three communities under consideration, identified on the map (Fig. 1), are very different. Throwleigh is a small parish on the

[10] For a discussion of microhistorical techniques, see the early work of Barry Reay, *Microhistories: Demography, Society and Culture in Rural England, 1800–1930* (Cambridge, 1996), 259–62. More recent contributions include Matt Peltonen, 'What is Micro in Microhistory?', in Hans Renders and Binny De Haan, eds, *Theoretical Discussions of Biography: Approaches from History, Microhistory, and Life Writing* (Leiden, 2014), 103–18; Zoltán Simon, 'Microhistory: In General', *JSH* 49 (2015), 237–48.

[11] Asa Briggs, 'Select and Reject: Aspects of the Study of the History of Education', in idem, *The Collected Essays of Asa Briggs*, 3: *Serious Pursuits: Communications and Education* (London, 1991), 231–45, at 236.

[12] Bruce Coleman, 'The Nineteenth Century: Nonconformity', in Nicholas Orme, ed., *Unity and Variety: A History of the Church in Devon and Cornwall* (Exeter, 1991), 129–56.

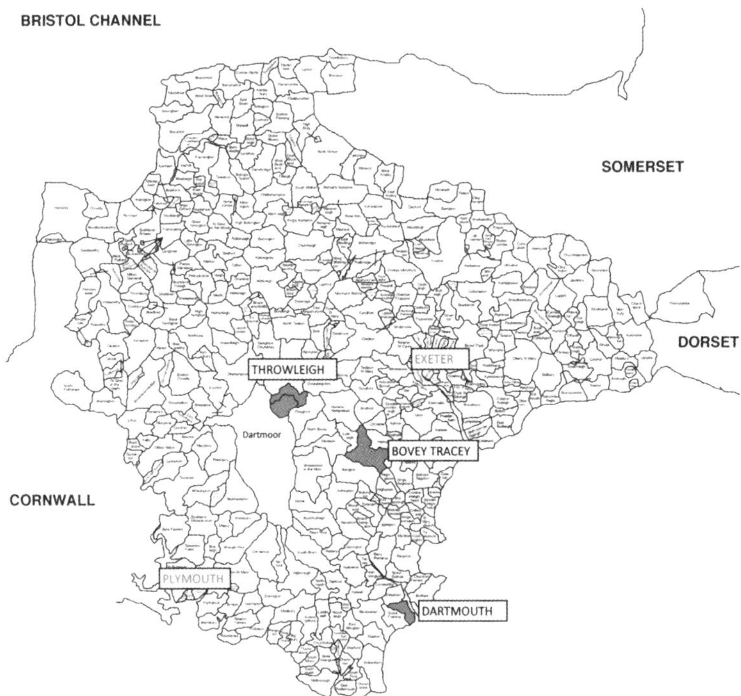

Fig. 1. Devon Historic Parishes Map (2002), adapted to show case study parishes. Reproduced by kind permission of Devon County Council.

north-east shoulder of Dartmoor, with a substantial proportion of the parish being common land on the moor. It is an area best described as dispersed settlement, with Throwleigh village and Murchington hamlet the only centres of population. The population in 1851 was 481. In the 1851 religious census the Anglican church recorded 100 people attending the principal service (with no Sunday school), while Providence Chapel, a Bible Christian establishment, recorded 112 (including a Sunday School). Bovey Tracey is a historic borough in rural south Devon, whose manor was held by the earls of Devon until they sold it in 1855. By the mid-nineteenth century its rural character was changing, with the development of a pottery industry from 1843. The population in 1851 was 2,086. That year's religious census found that attendance at the parish church (including Sunday school) was 515, at the Baptist chapel it was 368 and at the Methodist chapel 160. Dartmouth, on Devon's south coast, was a substantial port with a significant coastal carrying trade and shipbuilding industry. Tourism and leisure were increasing in importance, and the Royal Navy's new school for officer cadets moved to Dartmouth in 1863. The population in 1851 was 4,450. The religious census does not provide a full picture of church attendance here, as information for one Church of England congregation is missing, but the picture was more diverse, with Anglican, Independent, Wesleyan, Baptist, Particular Baptist and Brethren congregations all recorded. In 1833, 58 per cent of children attending Sunday school did so in the two Anglican parishes, while 42 per cent attended Nonconformist Sunday schools.[13]

Other sources used for these studies include two national education enquiries: the Digest of Parochial Returns made to the Select Committee appointed to inquire into the Education of the Poor in 1818,[14] the Education Enquiry: Abstracts of Answers and Returns in 1833[15] and the complementary local replies to the Bishop's Queries before Visitation in 1821.[16] The records of the National Society and the British Society provide some information for individual schools. The studies also draw on a wide range of local sources, such as parish histories, newspapers and family documents.

Throwleigh

The rural parish of Throwleigh lies about twenty miles west of Exeter. In the early nineteenth century, the rectors were mainly absent and

[13] 1833 data has been used as data is missing from the 1851 census: see *Education Enquiry. Abstract of the Answers and Returns made pursuant to an Address of the House of Commons, dated 24th May 1833. England*, 1: *Bedford – Lancaster* (London, 1833), 197 (St Petrox), 203, 209 (Townstal and St Saviour), online at: <https://parlipapers.proquest.com/parlipapers/result/pqpdocumentview?accountid=10792&groupid=105147&pgId=0c9056da-c0e3-43f7-ad19-a86ed9b2af3e>, accessed 12 May 2018.

[14] *Select Committee on the Education of the Poor (1818), Digest of Parochial Returns*, vol. 1, (London, 1819), online at: <https://parlipapers.proquest.com/parlipapers/result/pqpdocumentview?accountid=10792&groupid=105147&pgId=f37a4e0e-4727-4d1e-bafd-2d471908a719>, accessed 12 May 2018.

[15] *Education Enquiry 1833.*

[16] Michael Cook, ed., *The Diocese of Exeter in 1821: Bishop Carey's Replies to Queries before Visitation*, 2: *Devon*, Devon and Cornwall Record Society n.s. 4 (Exeter, 1960), 174.

the parish was in the hands of curates.[17] Although the parochial returns in 1818 reported a school attended by about twelve children, whose parents paid for their instruction,[18] in 1821 the responses to the Bishop's Queries before Visitation stated that no Anglican religious instruction was taking place, and that Methodist preachers were active in the parish.[19] In 1833 there was no school in Throwleigh.[20]

Between 1841 and the establishment of the board school in 1877, two successive rectors made efforts to establish a village school with the support of the National Society. Upon his appointment in 1841, Revd W. H. Schwabe immediately set up a Sunday School in the kitchen of his rectory. Within a month he was corresponding with, and applying to, the National Society for funding to build a two-storey school with classroom on the ground floor and teacher's accommodation above.[21] National Society documents record Schwabe's problems: in this poor rural parish there were no gentlemen farmers to offer financial support, and there was stiff competition from the Dissenting population:

> The parish has been much neglected, the late incumbent not having been resident, … and consequently dissent has spread … a sect presumptuous of arrogating to themselves the title of Bible Christians, have built a lay meeting house in the middle of my parish and lay schoolroom in connexion with it to which the children eagerly flock, both on Sundays and weekdays.[22]

Disappointed with the National Society's offer of only £20 towards his school, Schwabe left the parish for missionary work overseas, again consigning it to the hands of a curate.[23]

Revd S. H. Archer, appointed in 1852, initially incurred heavy expenses in restoring the church and building himself a new parsonage, while also personally maintaining a school in the old rectory. His

[17] Clergy of the Church of England Database, online at: <http://db.theclergydatabase.org.uk/jsp/locations/index.jsp>, Throwleigh, accessed 22 July 2017; London, CERC, National Society Operational Records, School Files, NS/7/1/12604, Throwleigh.
[18] *Digest 1818*, 187.
[19] Cook, ed., *Replies*, 174.
[20] *Education Enquiry 1833*, 208.
[21] CERC, NS/7/1/12604, Throwleigh.
[22] Ibid.
[23] Emmie Varwell, *Throwleigh: The Story of a Dartmoor Village* (Throwleigh, 1938), 132.

efforts to establish a purpose-built school are revealed in correspondence with the National Society commencing in January 1868.[24] Apart from his own support of the school, he was receiving £5 per annum from the Betton Charity.[25] The application to the National Society dated March 1868 estimated £134 to build the school, plus £8 13*s* professional fees. Archer asked for nothing for fitting out the school building, as he proposed to fund this himself. On the credit side, he had £20 from the diocesan board, and offered £22 13*s* of his own money. Having been led to believe that the National Society could offer £100 towards his school, he must have been disappointed when they offered him only £25 in April 1868. He returned the money in August, unable to raise the balance required. There were still no local landowners willing to provide financial support.

Schwabe's National Society correspondence provides evidence that the Bible Christians were running a successful day and Sunday School in the early 1840s, with about forty scholars attending the former.[26] The Bible Christians' records show that before Providence Chapel was built meetings took place in private houses: they were often hosted by Richard Dunning Gay and his mother at Coombe Farm, and an associated school for infants was run nearby.[27] Gay was a major landholder in Throwleigh parish and a significant person within the Bible Christian community. He built the chapel and domestic accommodation at Providence Place by 1839: the house there bears a date plaque, and a commemorative portrait inside the chapel also bears this date. From 1839 until a few years before his early death in 1859, he appears in the chapel's papers, fulfilling various roles. Gay is mentioned as a circuit steward and an elder for several years between 1839 and 1848;[28] he and his wife were attenders

[24] CERC, NS/7/1/12604, Throwleigh.

[25] The Ironmonger's Company managed a portion of Betton Charity funds to support Church of England charity schools. The funds were distributed through the dioceses, each chosen school receiving between £5 and £20. The company decided which schools should receive payment: City of London Livery Companies Commission, *Report on the Charities of the Ironmongers' Company, vol. 4* (London, 1884), 517–38, online at: <http://www.british-history.ac.uk/livery-companies-commission/vol4>, accessed 18 November 2015.

[26] CERC, NS/7/1/12604, Throwleigh.

[27] Throwleigh, Throwleigh Archive, 'Providence Methodist Church 1839–1989: Commemorative Programme celebrating 150 Years', digital copy.

[28] Exeter, Devon Heritage Centre (hereafter: DHC), 2200D/0/1, Chagford Methodist Circuit 1st Deposit, Circuit Stewards Account Book, 1827–48.

and class leaders throughout the 1840s; in 1849 he was the superintendent and his wife one of the teachers; and in 1851 he was on the School Teachers Committee, and his wife was continuing to teach.[29] This is evidence that a school was in operation at Providence before the school room itself was built. In 1858 Gay was one of the trustees for Gooseford, Chagford and Providence.[30] In the 1851 census he is described as schoolmaster. His wife and widowed sister Agnes continued to live at Providence Place after his death, and Agnes was recorded as schoolmistress in the 1861 census.[31]

From 1845 to 1855, minutes of the Sunday school teachers' meetings record purchases of quantities of reading books, Testaments, Bibles and reward books as teaching materials, providing evidence that children were being taught to read at Providence at that time.[32] *Kelly's Directory* for 1856 records a school for both sexes at Providence Place, supported by R. D. Gay Esq.[33] Expenditure on class books continued through to 1866.[34] The 1867 building accounts for the school room record the sources of funding, such as donations of the site and the cost of carriage of materials and funds raised by the opening tea in September 1868, as well as the amounts paid to particular builders. A deficit of £40 was covered by a single anonymous donation.[35]

The financing of the early education at Providence by chapel members with Gay's personal support and the Bible Christians' charitable funding of their school room offer a significant contrast to the experience of Archer and Schwabe, their difficulties in raising funding and the National Society's offers of only £20 and £25.

[29] DHC, 2200D/0/28, Chagford Methodist Circuit 1st Deposit, Minute Book of Elders' Meetings, 1842–55.

[30] DHC, 2200D/2/16, Chagford Methodist Circuit 2nd Additional Deposit, Chagford Chapel Account Book, 1842–46.

[31] 1851 Census, HO107/1885/477/5, Throwleigh; 1861 Census, RG09/1468/15/9, Throwleigh, 'Find My Past', online at: <http://www.findmypast.co.uk>, accessed 27 February 2017.

[32] Elders' Minutes, 1842–55, 28.

[33] *Kelly's Post Office Directory of Devonshire* (London, 1856), 298.

[34] DHC, 2200D/0/2, Chagford Methodist Circuit 1st Deposit, Circuit Stewards Account and Quarterly Minute Book, 1848–67.

[35] DHC, 2200D/6/2, Chagford Methodist Circuit 6th Additional Deposit, Providence Chapel Throwleigh, 1839–1917.

Bovey Tracey

In 1818 the *Digest of Parochial Returns* showed that there was one school in Bovey Tracey, an endowed school which offered just ten places to poor children. The claim of the *Digest* that 'the poor possess sufficient means of educating their children' was therefore inaccurate.[36] But the vicar also reported an endowed school in his 1821 responses to the Bishop's Visitation Queries, and referred to 'Anabaptist' and Methodist teachers in the town.[37] A National School was established by the Church of England in 1834, but the poorest families could not afford it and provision for them was only available in the three church Sunday Schools.[38]

In 1849 Revd the Hon. Charles Courtenay, a Queen's chaplain and brother of the earl of Devon, was appointed to the living of Bovey Tracey. This was no ordinary appointment for a small market town. Courtenay was married to one of the Queen's ladies-in-waiting, and his brother was Lord of the Manor.[39] As a supporter of the Oxford Movement, Courtenay pressed for the introduction of a more high church ethos in the parish church. Many of his parishioners disapproved, but he had the funds to put his vision into effect and built a new church, which was consecrated in 1853.[40] When it was dedicated, press reports complained about its 'Tractarian and popish nature'[41] and later the local surgeon, Dr Croker, wrote to the bishop criticizing the vicar.[42]

The local disputes against Tractarianism led one woman, Annie Croker, Dr Croker's daughter, to establish a nondenominational, coeducational school. She set up a British School in Bovey Tracey in 1861 and taught the children herself. In her words, the 'Romanizing character of the instructions [*sic*] imparted at some neighbouring schools makes the necessity to rescue the children

36 *Digest 1818*, 153; *Endowed Charities (County of Devon) Parish of Bovey Tracey, Charity Commission* (London, 1907), 3–5.
37 Cook, ed., *Replies*, 26–7.
38 *Education Enquiry 1833*, 172; *Charity Commission Enquiry*, 3–5.
39 *The Globe*, 6 June 1849, 3.
40 *Western Courier*, 22 June 1853, 8.
41 *Western Times* (hereafter: *WT*), 3 June 1854, 7.
42 *WT*, 24 June 1854, 7.

from error an imperative duty'.[43] She also wanted the poorest, mainly the children of the local pottery workers, to have access to education.

Opposition to Tractarianism continued, as illustrated by this press report from 1862:

> The tractarian priesthood, and the silly sheep who follow the tinkling of their bell, had a flowery holiday on Monday. The day was observed as the 'dedication' of St John's – what to [*sic*] may best be learned from the altars, super-altars, reredos, crosses, candles, flowers, and ecclesiastical millinery, offending protestant eyes at every turn.[44]

Courtenay then had another vision, to help so-called 'fallen' women. At his invitation the Clewer sisters of the Community of St John the Baptist, one of the most fashionable sisterhoods, set up a Devon House of Mercy in the parish in 1863.[45] The Clewer community had Tractarian leanings and now they effectively had a convent in Bovey Tracey. The local press criticized its popish nature and Annie Croker was angry that Clewer sisters taught in the National School. Despite Croker's antagonism, the history of sisterhoods shows that they were often pioneering women who escaped from female domesticity and trivial social activity, even taking their work to India.[46]

In 1865 Annie Croker complained that pauperized mothers were being offered an extra payment each year if they kept their children from Dissenting places of education.[47] Her school newsletter described her own success – 'The Puseyites … look jealously' on her work – and referred to the school 'stemming the tide of Tractarianism'.[48] She did not have the landed gentry as visitors or board members, but she did have the goodwill of the local pottery

[43] Uxbridge, Brunel University London Archives (hereafter: BULA), British and Foreign School Society Papers, BFSS/1/7/2/2/3/4, Annie Croker to Mr Wilkes (BFSS secretary), 30 December 1865. The authors are grateful to Jan Wood for drawing this reference to their attention.

[44] *WT*, 21 June 1862, 2.

[45] Valerie Bonham, *A Joyous Service: The Clewer Sisters and their Work* (Windsor, 1989), 10; Janice Wallace, 'The Devon House of Mercy, Bovey Tracey, 1863– 1940', *Transactions of the Devonshire Association* 133 (2001), 191–216, at 209.

[46] Susan Mumm, *Stolen Daughters, Virgin Mothers* (Leicester, 1999), ix–x, 4, 8.

[47] BULA, BFSS/1/7/2/2/3/4, Annie Croker to the secretary, 3 June 1865.

[48] Bovey Tracey, Bovey Tracey Heritage Trust, Anne Croker, 'Little Ones in Devonshire', articles from the *British School*, March and May 1866, pasted into Anne Croker's scrapbook, 1865–1900.

owner, John Divett, who employed most of her pupils' parents and provided the land for her to build a new school in 1866.[49]

Dartmouth

In 1818, Dartmouth had neither a National nor a British School, and both the historic charitable endowments in Dartmouth intended to provide free education had lapsed. Nonetheless, in the town's three administrative parishes there were twenty-three schools, attended by 453 children, perhaps a third to a half of all children in the town.[50] The 1833 *Education Enquiry* listed twelve 'daily schools' and two 'infant schools' across the three parishes, attended by 429 children.[51] Though not identified as such, there was by then at least one National School.[52] In 1823 John Seale (1752–1824) gave to the parish of St Petrox a site for a Sunday School building, and the gift was confirmed by his son, John Henry Seale (1780–1844).[53] Public subscriptions funded the building, and by 1831 a National School had been established.[54]

It is not unusual that a major landowner should provide a school in his parish, but philanthropy may not have been John Seale's only motivation. Dartmouth was controlled by the Holdsworth family; they managed the borough for the government, exercising extensive patronage.[55] Excluded from these advantages, John Seale became the leader of local political opposition to the Holdsworth regime, and enthusiastic for parliamentary reform.[56] The family's role in endowing the school site thus acquired political significance. The

[49] *WT*, 24 July 1866, 5.

[50] *Digest 1818*, 181 (St Petrox), 182 (St Saviour), 188 (Townstal). The Townstal return includes two 'classical schools' omitted from the summary table, presumably because they were considered not to be for poor children.

[51] *Education Enquiry 1833*, 203, 209. The apparent drop in provision may be misleading, as it is difficult to match the schools reported to schools recorded in other sources.

[52] Presumed to be the 'daily school' in St Petrox parish for '66 males and 59 females', as this closely matches the figures given for the St Petrox National School in 1831.

[53] A panel in St Petrox Church, Dartmouth, records the gift.

[54] CERC, NS 7/7/1/1, National Society Operational Records, Church School Inquiry, *c.*1831, 190.

[55] Terry Jenkins, 'Dartmouth', in D. R. Fisher, ed., *The History of Parliament: The House of Commons 1820–1832*, 7 vols (Cambridge, 2009), online at: <http://www.historyofparliamentonline.org/volume/1820-1832/constituencies/dartmouth>, accessed 11 May 2018.

[56] Ray Freeman, *Dartmouth and its Neighbours* (Dartmouth, 2007), 131.

Holdsworths were strongly against reform, and had little interest in education. The endowment may have helped to reinforce the Seale family's position as their opponents.[57] John Henry Seale finally became Dartmouth's MP after the 1832 Reform Act, and held the seat until he died in 1844. Politics certainly influenced the involvement of his son, Sir Henry Paul Seale (1806–97), in the development of Dartmouth's British School, although he did not go into Parliament himself. Sir Henry Paul Seale worked with Dartmouth's new Liberal MP, George Moffatt (1807–78),[58] and the Nonconformist communities to provide new buildings for the school.[59]

Both Moffatt and Sir Henry were keen supporters of education for the poor. Sir Henry was an Anglican, but disliked what he called 'the intolerant spirit of religious exclusiveness'; British Schools, he thought, were 'unsectarian', unlike National Schools.[60] But the project was not just about education. Moffatt thought the town he represented should have the prestige of 'large handsome schoolrooms', prominently positioned.[61] Narrower politics also applied. The British School building included a large room for political meetings because the Conservatives excluded the Liberals from other public venues. What the *Dartmouth Chronicle* called 'party spirit' was strong: 'the promoters [of the British School] being principally liberals, the conservatives, with but few exceptions, declined to assist, and in some instances, even opposed the scheme to the utmost'.[62] Moffatt's money and close involvement enabled the building to open in 1848.[63] However, in 1852 politics ended the partnership. Moffatt and Sir Henry disagreed over free trade; Moffatt resigned his seat and Sir Henry abandoned the Liberals.[64]

[57] According to Freeman (ibid. 139), John Seale also founded a school for the poor in Townstal in 1820. However, it does not appear in National Society records, and is not apparently included in the 1833 return.

[58] Moffatt, a wealthy London merchant, stood for Dartmouth in 1844, with Sir Henry's support, but narrowly failed to secure the seat. However, the incoming Conservative MP, Joseph Somes, died in 1845, and Moffatt won the resulting by-election.

[59] *List of British Schools (England and Wales), 1897* (London, 1897), 17; *Robson's Directory 1838* for Dartmouth shows the school in rented rooms in Coles Court.

[60] *WT*, 16 May 1846, 3.

[61] *WT*, 30 August 1845, 4.

[62] *Dartmouth Chronicle*, 24 March 1871, 2.

[63] *WT*, 22 July 1848, 7. George Moffatt contributed £400; Sir Henry laid the foundation stone.

[64] *Morning Chronicle*, 22 March 1852, 3; *Exeter and Plymouth Gazette*, 17 July 1852, 3.

Because the British School was closely linked to the Liberal cause, the new Conservative MP did not take on his predecessor's financial commitment.[65] Neither did Sir Henry or anyone else. The changing political climate led to a reduction in support; by 1855, twenty-five subscribers were supporting the British School, whereas fifty-one were supporting the National School.[66] The building closed temporarily, and although determined fundraising cleared the debt in 1856, the school never achieved its full potential.

However, the 1851 education census showed that many children in Dartmouth did not attend any school.[67] Richard Browne Cleland (1809–92), an ex-Cunard steamship captain, and mayor in 1860, set up an 'Evening Free School', offering free education to the poorest children.[68] The school was funded by donations and ran for at least three years; apart from the superintendent, teachers were unpaid volunteers. About seventy children attended each year.[69] In contrast to the British School, the initiative was supported across the political and religious spectrum. With the right leadership, therefore, people in Dartmouth could and did work together successfully.

CONCLUSION

The climate of the early Victorian period fostered the willingness to extend an elementary education to all children of the labouring poor. Development of appropriate schools was no longer exclusively the province of religious organizations; it attracted parliamentary attention and resources, and drew in employers as well as philanthropists.

[65] Rear Admiral Sir Thomas Herbert (1793–1861), MP for Dartmouth 1852–7.

[66] 'Notice of Subscribers to British School', *Dartmouth Chronicle*, April 1855, 4; 'Notice of Subscribers to National School Year commencing 1st January 1855', *Dartmouth Chronicle*, April 1856, 2.

[67] *Census of Great Britain, 1851: Education, England and Wales, Report and Tables* (London, 1854), cxciv–ccv (Table T), cxcvi–cxcvii (Dartmouth); this reported 286 children on the books of the two 'public' schools; 563 children on the books of fifteen schools in total. Dartmouth was reported upon as a municipal borough; the other communities in this study were not included in this exercise.

[68] Cleland himself once called this project a 'Ragged School', suggesting he may have been inspired by the ragged school movement (ragged schools were charitable organizations providing completely free education to the poorest children). Other than this reference, however, his initiative was not linked, so far as can be established, with the Ragged School Union, or with ragged schools elsewhere.

[69] *Dartmouth Chronicle*, 2 April 1861, 2; 1 April 1862, 4; 2 February 1863, 4.

However, the need to secure adequate local resources even when national grants were available meant that not all proposals succeeded.

The lack of schools in poor rural parishes was clearly not a priority for the diocese of Exeter at this period. The Diocesan Board of Education, established in 1839, worked through local boards set up within the archdeaconries. Their initial decision was to secure schools 'in the principal towns'.[70] On the Exeter Local Board, for example, to which Throwleigh was assigned, members were more concerned with sorting out Exeter's schools and creating a commercial school for the middle classes than with the needs of peripheral villages for elementary education.[71] Where there was a dynamic individual like Revd James Holman Mason of Widecombe, the 'Bishop of the Moor', and a wealthy inhabitant of a generous turn, like Mrs Larpent who paid for the school at Leusdon, provision could be made, even though the quality of the teaching in these tiny schools led one inspector to refer to them as 'hedge schools'.[72] In Throwleigh, however, where the Bible Christians had established a robust congregation capable of financing their children's education, the two successive Anglican rectors, whilst committed personally to developing a school, could not raise sufficient funds from the Diocesan Board, the Anglicans in the parish or the National Society to complement the money they were prepared personally to invest.

In Bovey Tracey the development of the National School might have proceeded on conventional lines, under a wealthy vicar willing not only to provide a subscription but subsequently to resource his preferred developments. However, doctrinal differences precipitated a split within his congregation, and abhorrence of his Tractarian views led to the emergence of an unlikely entrepreneur, Annie Croker. She was one of the unmarried, childless women of the 'middling sort' who had the time and could command the money to carry out her community vision. In this respect she was like other pioneering women in Victorian England.[73] Unlike Mrs Larpent, mentioned

[70] *Reports of the Exeter Diocesan Board of Education, 1839–1860, Preliminary Proceedings* (Exeter, 1839), 11; *Exeter and Plymouth Gazette*, 27 April 1839, 3.

[71] *Reports of the Exeter Diocesan Board of Education, First Annual Report* (Exeter, 1840), 24.

[72] Mary Stanbrook, *Old Dartmoor Schools remembered* (Brixham, 1991), 68, 87, 73.

[73] Susan Mumm, 'The Feminization of Nineteenth-Century Anglicanism', in Rowan Strong, ed., *OHA*, 3: *Partisan Anglicanism and its Global Expansion 1829–*c.*1914* (Oxford, 2017), 440–55, at 443.

above, Croker was not just a passive investor in good works but an actual agent of change. She reacted against Tractarianism and perhaps, as her work continued, she was also spurred on by the counter-example of the female leadership of the local sisterhood. Susan Mumm has suggested that because of the sisterhoods other laywomen found themselves able to expand their roles within Anglicanism with less opposition and less scrutiny. 'This can be seen as an example of how the advanced guard allows the centre of gravity to gradually shift; in this case to a more woman-oriented direction, although with great difficulty and considerable slowness.'[74]

Jennifer Ayto has argued that it was difficult to measure the contribution of Victorian women to the establishment of schools for the poor. In Bovey Tracey the evidence is clear: the children of the poor benefited from a female philanthropist with a great deal of drive.[75] This is a small town example of the evolution of feminization in Anglicanism which supports Mumm's view that a religious impulse such as the Oxford Movement could have positive effects upon the lives of women, even when they were opposed to what it represented, an argument which some historians have been slow to recognize.[76] Strong points out that Anglican diversity was not just about divisions, and that antagonism invigorated both sides.[77]

In Dartmouth, a community significantly larger than Throwleigh or Bovey Tracey, the development of both the National and the British Schools demonstrates a party political dimension absent from the other communities. Overt support for the National School may have been one tactic in the efforts of the Seale family to challenge the long-standing Tory control of the borough and build support for reform. The development of a British School for nondenominational teaching became a totemic Liberal cause to which both Sir Henry Seale and George Moffatt were attached. Their considerable influence gave momentum to the process, and when they fell out and removed their support from the school, it foundered. In contrast, Richard Cleland seems to have tried to

[74] Ibid.

[75] Jennifer Ayto, 'The Contribution by Women to the Social and Economic Development of the Victorian Town in Hertfordshire' (PhD thesis, University of Hertfordshire, 2012), 179.

[76] Susan Mumm, 'Lady Guerrillas of Philanthropy; Anglican Sisterhoods in Victorian England' (PhD thesis, University of Sussex, 1992), 31.

[77] Rowan Strong, 'Introduction' to idem, ed., *OHA* 3, 1–23, at 15.

overcome 'party spirit', and successfully involved leading members of Dartmouth's political and religious communities in his scheme. His success may have been because he was widely liked, or because the scheme was philanthropic, with no political dimension. However, the limited evidence suggests that the support he created for such a school evaporated soon after he ceased to lead it. It appears that without Cleland to champion it, the initiative could not survive.

The evidence from these studies suggests that inter- and intra-sectarian tensions were not the only explanatory factor for the haphazard pattern of elementary education provision before 1870. A further factor is the haphazard availability of local champions. It is unsurprising that so much of the development of schools for the poor in the early nineteenth century rested on the actions of individuals. Even when government grants were introduced, it remained the responsibility of local people to create and at least part-fund the premises and the teaching. A community leader or 'entrepreneur' was required, someone who could champion the idea that a school was needed, seize opportunities, such as the availability of premises or grants, and manage relationships to deliver the change.[78] These individuals can only be uncovered by detailed research at a local level: more local studies will surely identify similar community leaders elsewhere.

[78] Characteristics of 'policy entrepreneurs' described in John Kingdon, *Agendas, Alternatives and Public Policies*, 2nd edn (New York, 2003), 122–4.

They 'Come for a Lark': London Ragged School Union Teaching Advice in Practice, 1844–70

Laura M. Mair*
University of Edinburgh

Ragged schools provided a free education to impoverished children in the mid-nineteenth century. Inspired by religious fervour and presided over by Lord Shaftesbury, that figurehead of evangelical Anglicans, the schools taught the most destitute to read and write, as well as about the God who loved them. By 1870 the London schools alone recorded an average attendance of 32,231 children. The missionary aspect of the classroom shaped the recommended character of the teacher. Teachers were to be benevolent, while corporal punishment was discouraged. Teaching advice demonstrates that the classroom could prove difficult terrain and suggests that the respect of scholars was hard-won and highly valued. With children attending freely, it was necessary that they desired to return. The children were consumers whom teachers sought to please; their responses determined the success or failure of lessons. This article responds to recent scholarship that interprets the teachers as imposed and powerful agents. By focusing on advice given to teachers, it highlights both how the children were perceived and the impact evangelical theology had upon ideas regarding the teacher's character. Largely overlooked by church historians, the ragged school movement embodies the profound impact of evangelical Christians on popular education in the nineteenth century.

On Sunday 16 October 1853 Martin Ware III, the superintendent of Compton Place Ragged School's Sunday evening boys' class, sought God's blessing to 'accompany my labours' in his journal.[1] The ensuing entry, occupying just one side of a page, communicates the rewards and challenges ragged school teachers faced. After

* 33 Traquair Park West, Edinburgh, EH12 7AN. E-mail: laura.mair@ed.ac.uk. This article builds on the findings of my *Religion and Relationships in Ragged Schools: An Intimate History of Educating the Poor, 1844–1870*, forthcoming in Routledge's Studies in Evangelicalism series during 2019.

[1] Compton Place Ragged School was located in the borough of Camden in London. In 1855 the school moved to Brunswick Buildings, a five-minute walk from Compton Place. For simplicity, the institution is referred to as 'Compton Place' throughout this article.

Studies in Church History 55 (2019), 324–346
doi: 10.1017/stc.2018.3

invoking divine favour on the school, Ware detailed a recent visit from Alexander Patterson, a former scholar now in the navy. Ware noted that Patterson 'brought me an American Aloe', which he had purchased in the West Indies. Beneath this Ware recorded the recent sentencing of 'H. Evans' and 'J. Armstrong' to '2 yrs imprisonment for stealing a ~~Horse~~ Donkey & cart!', pointedly adding: 'They are each 9 yrs old'. At the foot of the page the entry closed with the news that young Ward, whose hardship Ware had cited before, had been discovered stealing. Ware's intense disappointment is evident in his bracketed '(alas, alas!)' and his closing, lament-laden sentence: 'he is a boy in whom I had the fullest reliance'.[2]

Hosted in haphazard classrooms, in barns and abandoned factories, or beneath railway arches, ragged children learned to read and write in spite of their poverty. Of most importance, however, was the communication of the gospel. God's love and saving work through Jesus Christ was at the core of a ragged school education. After the existing London ragged schools united under the London Ragged School Union (LRSU) banner in April 1844, they multiplied exponentially in the metropolis. By 1865 there were 613 schools in the capital alone. Moreover, although the LRSU played a crucial role in disseminating knowledge through its literature and public presence, ragged schools were not confined to London. Cities and large towns across England, Ireland, Scotland and Wales adopted the ragged school model, and unions similar to the LRSU were established in Liverpool and Manchester. The movement benefited from Lord Shaftesbury's 'child-championing prestige' and charismatic leadership following his appointment as LRSU president in November 1844, a title he held until his death over forty years later.[3]

Ragged schools were a crucial component of Britain's educational scene in the mid-nineteenth century, serving society's poorest children, who were precluded from learning elsewhere. Dame schools, or, as Gardner categorizes them, 'working-class private schools', provided an often progressive education in exchange for a small fee.[4] Such institutions, however, exceeded the modest means of the

[2] Woking, Surrey History Centre (hereafter: SHC) 1585/3, Martin Ware III, School Journal, 16 October 1853.

[3] Charles Montague, *Sixty Years in Waifdom, or, The Ragged School Movement in English History* (London, 1904), 164.

[4] Phil Gardner, *The Lost Elementary Schools of Victorian England* (London, 1984).

impoverished households for whose children ragged schools intended to cater. Although Sunday schools were free, they encouraged children to dress in their 'Sunday best' and often had little toleration for disruptive behaviour. In his study of working-class autobiographies, Burnett writes that destitute children were effectively excluded by their 'lack of suitable clothes, shoes or the "collection" penny'.[5] Even where Sunday schools did accommodate the most unkempt children, the discrepancy between their appearance and that of their classmates may well have dissuaded them from returning. The LRSU was keen to differentiate itself from the Sunday School Union (SSU) from the outset, making it clear that ragged schools were wholly separate from those institutions inspired by Robert Raikes and Hannah Ball. Accordingly, those present at a meeting of the LRSU in 1846 heard that ragged schools were for those 'whose abject wretchedness, or whose depraved character, precludes them from participating in the advantages of the Sunday schools'.[6]

The ragged school remit was a broad one. Most taught both boys and girls, separating the sexes during instruction. A wide range of ages were welcomed; in June 1846 one London school, 'a sample for all of the rest', taught those aged between five and seventeen.[7] As classes were arranged to fit the schedules of labouring children and volunteer teachers, evening and weekend classes were common. With growing numbers of scholars and teachers, the services offered by the schools increased also. Ragged churches, mothers' meetings, nurseries, penny banks, lending libraries and soup kitchens are a modest sample of the ventures that could stem from a single institution.[8] However, the LRSU was dealt a series of irreparable blows by the Education Acts of 1870, 1880 and 1891. These successively established board schools in regions deemed inadequately served, enforced attendance for children aged between five and ten years and instigated state provision for school fees up to ten shillings. Together these changes effectively eliminated the need for institutions specifically for poor children, and in consequence the number of ragged schools declined sharply. While the schools had counted 50,312 scholars in 1865, just a decade

[5] John Burnett, *Destiny Obscure: Autobiographies of Childhood, Education, and Family from the 1820s to the 1920s* (Harmondsworth, 1984), 143.

[6] 'The Ragged Schools', *Daily News*, 21 February 1846, 5.

[7] 'The Ragged School Union', *The Times*, 10 June 1846, 8.

[8] Kathleen Heasman, *Evangelicals in Action: An Appraisal of their Social Work in the Victorian Era* (London, 1962), 79–82.

later this number had been reduced to 'only about 7,000'.[9] Most ragged schools had made one of two choices by the close of the nineteenth century, either converting into board schools or disbanding altogether.

This article explores the guidance given to ragged school teachers by the LRSU in the light of the myriad challenges mentioned in newspaper reports, promotional literature and unpublished material relating to local schools. Of particular value is the LRSU's magazine, the *Ragged School Union Magazine* (hereafter: *RSUM*), which featured a regular 'Teachers' Column' offering advice and pedagogical guidance. 'On the ground' material offers access to the frustrations teachers experienced.[10] In detailing his encounters at Compton Place, Ware's journal provides a unique account of both the ragged school teacher's role and his reception by the scholars. Although access to the experiences of girls is limited by Ware's exclusive involvement with the boys' class, his journals nevertheless open up a new understanding of the ways in which faith shaped and inspired Victorian philanthropy. Because of the voluntary nature of these institutions, it was critical to their success that scholars not only attended but returned. To this end, lessons sought to engage and excite scholars while long addresses were condemned. By using ragged school teaching advice in conjunction with sources from local schools, this article explores the complex territory of the ragged school classroom. This approach enables our understanding to move beyond assumptions about the teacher's control and the scholar's obedience, shifting the focus towards the child's perception of, and participation in, the movement. More broadly, the interdenominational appeal of the schools offers important insights into the effectiveness of pan-evangelical initiatives in the mid-nineteenth century. Through focusing on the ragged schools, this article enhances our understanding of how the urban poor received and responded to evangelical teaching and middle-class philanthropic efforts. It enables us to rethink and reframe the relationships forged between evangelically motivated philanthropists and the children and families with whom they worked.

[9] 'The Twenty-First Anniversary of the Ragged School Union', *RSUM*, June 1865, 127; 'Proceedings of the Thirty-First Annual Meeting of the Ragged School Union', *RSUM*, June 1875, 133.

[10] The *RSUM* varies between 'Teachers' Column' and 'Teacher's Column'.

The ragged schools have received little concentrated attention from historians; however, the movement is regularly touched on by scholarship from an array of disciplines. Historians interested in nineteenth-century child poverty, such as Hugh Cunningham and Anna Davin, reference the schools in their studies of the portrayal and experiences of destitute children.[11] Although the movement is often cited in histories of education or evangelicalism, it rarely receives more than a cursory mention. Stephens's *Education in Britain* mentions the schools in its opening chapter, noting that the '1830s saw the beginnings of "ragged" or "industrial" schools, philanthropic endeavours aimed at saving vagrant and homeless children'.[12] Likewise, Sanderson states simply that ragged schools 'took the poorest, vagabond children for a basic education'.[13] Brown discusses the schools in relation to Shaftesbury's social action, as do Shaftesbury's biographers.[14] Heasman's *Evangelicals in Action* provides the most thorough account of the schools from an ecclesiastical perspective, dedicating a chapter to the movement and its achievements.[15] Given the large number of children who passed through the schools in London alone – the LRSU estimated upwards of 300,000 by May 1870 – the dearth of scholarship on the movement requires correction.[16]

The way in which poor children responded to religious teaching also remains under-researched. In her chapter on the moral instruction provided in late nineteenth-century English elementary schools, Wright examines the role that beliefs about poverty played in shaping moralistic teaching, concluding that existing evidence 'gives little agency or voice to the pupils themselves' and cannot 'tell us what

[11] Hugh Cunningham, *The Children of the Poor: Representations of Childhood since the Seventeenth Century* (Oxford, 1992); Anna Davin, *Growing up Poor: Home, School and Street in London, 1870–1914* (London, 1996).

[12] W. B. Stephens, *Education in Britain 1750–1914* (London, 1998), 10.

[13] Michael Sanderson, *Education, Economic Change and Society in England 1780–1870* (London, 1987), 24.

[14] Stewart J. Brown, *Providence and Empire: Religion, Politics and Society in Britain 1815–1914* (Harlow, 2008), 163; J. L. Hammond and Barbara Hammond, *Lord Shaftesbury* (London, 1923); J. Wesley Bready, *Lord Shaftesbury and Social-Industrial Progress* (London, 1926); Geoffrey Best, *Shaftesbury* (London, 1964); Georgina Battiscombe, *Shaftesbury: A Biography of the Seventh Earl 1801–1885* (London, 1974); Geoffrey B. A. M. Finlayson, *The Seventh Earl of Shaftesbury, 1801–1885* (London, 1981).

[15] Heasman, *Evangelicals in Action*, 69–87.

[16] 'Proceedings at the Twenty-Sixth Annual Meeting of the Ragged School Union', *RSUM*, June 1870, 130.

children thought'.[17] In relation to Sunday Schools, Laqueur argues that the religious teaching equipped children to face the very real challenges of bereavement and illness. Although Laqueur discusses conversions and revivals, his findings are limited by his focus on promotional material, which does not provide access to children's 'in the moment' responses to the Christian message.[18] In terms of how such teaching was imparted, Burnett observes that it 'was not, of course, supposed or intended that children should enjoy their schooling'.[19] This assertion may be applicable to many Victorian institutions; however, it cannot reflect the ragged schools.

Recent studies of nineteenth-century child-saving movements, of which the ragged schools formed a part, are dominated by narratives that cast the institutions as instruments of social control. According to such interpretations, predominantly middle-class teachers imposed their beliefs upon the children of the poor. According to Mahood and Littlewood, working-class children were subjected to the zealous and misguided fervour of evangelicals intent upon 'saving' their bodies and souls.[20] In their expansive study of evangelical child migration discourse, Swain and Hillel stress the invasive nature of such movements.[21] While providing valuable insights into the construction of child-saving discourse, Swain and Hillel do not assess how children reacted to, or interacted with, these organizations. Such scholarship focuses on the actions or attitudes of adults whose effects on children tend to be presumed, thus composing a picture of adult as agent and child as subject. The recent collection on child labour edited by Goose and Honeyman is of particular relevance here. Of especial value is their claim that '[a]lthough children have hitherto been silent,

[17] Susannah Wright, 'Moral Instruction, Urban Poverty and English Elementary Schools in the Late Nineteenth Century', in Nigel Goose and Katrina Honeyman, eds, *Childhood and Child Labour in Industrial England: Diversity and Agency 1750–1914* (Farnham, 2013), 277–95, at 294.

[18] Thomas Laqueur, *Religion and Respectability: Sunday Schools and Working-Class Culture, 1780–1850* (London, 1976), 160–9.

[19] Burnett, *Destiny Obscure*, 169.

[20] Linda Mahood and Barbara Littlewood, 'The "Vicious" Girl and the "Street-Corner" Boy: Sexuality and the Gendered Delinquent in the Scottish Child-Saving Movement 1850–1940', *Journal of the History of Sexuality* 4 (1994), 549–78.

[21] Shurlee Swain and Margot Hillel, *Child, Nation, Race and Empire: Child Rescue Discourse, England, Canada and Australia, 1850–1915* (Manchester, 2010). This study considers the *RSUM* alongside material from the Church of England's Waifs and Strays Society and Barnardo's Homes.

and historians frequently refer to the need to "strain" to hear their voices, in fact they can be clearly heard – both literally in protest, strikes, demonstrations and placards, and more figuratively in terms of direct action, including absconding, and breaking windows and machinery.'[22] Absence, interruptions, mockery, vandalism and actual or threatened violence may equally be interpreted as a means of protest in the ragged school classroom. It is less easy, however, to discern the motives or intentions underlying such behaviour.

When promotional literature is analysed in isolation, the conversation between teachers and children is silenced. This approach fosters a vacuum in which words and emotions are attributed to ragged school scholars, either as a positive and thankful chorus or a terrorized and tearful one. At the same time, such narratives often denigrate or belittle volunteer teachers, transforming them into (at best) misguided do-gooders or (at worst) domineering bullies. By bringing together promotional material with local documents, this article situates ragged school teaching advice within the context of the challenges teachers faced in practice.

Christianity and the Classroom

Determined to avoid the sectarian divisions that had plagued Sunday schools, ragged schools were emphatically interdenominational.[23] For the LRSU, 'oneness in Christ' was of greater value than 'oneness in church discipline'.[24] Although, to use Thomas Guthrie's words, the movement was founded 'upon a broad basis', it was nevertheless distinctly evangelical.[25] The schools were 'earnest, devoted, Evangelical, but not sectarian'.[26] According to the LRSU, those involved with the movement were 'members of a great evangelical alliance', who were 'working together in the schoolroom'.[27] Reflecting this principle, the schools were named after localities or streets rather than churches or individuals. In the hope of avoiding controversy, creeds were banished and the Bible was the central religious text permitted in the

[22] Goose and Honeyman, *Childhood and Child Labour*, 8.
[23] Laqueur, *Religion and Respectability*, 65–74.
[24] 'Our Principles: A Review', *RSUM*, January 1869, 2.
[25] 'Ragged Schools – Preliminary Meeting', *The Scotsman*, 24 March 1847, 3.
[26] 'Edinburgh City Mission', *Caledonian Mercury*, 25 January 1849, 3.
[27] 'Our Principles: A Review', *RSUM*, January 1869, 2.

classroom. As such, the 'Rules for the government' of Field Lane included 'VII. No Teacher shall be allowed to introduce any Catechism' and 'VIII. That the Bible shall be the principle Class Book'.[28] As far as possible, Christian teaching was to consist of simple biblical truths.

The ragged school mission and method therefore aligned with the four tenets of evangelicalism that Bebbington has identified: activism, biblicism, conversionism and crucicentrism.[29] The biblical message of Christ's salvation and the importance of conversion and the Christian's duty to 'go out into the highways and hedges, and compel them to come in' (Luke 14: 23) were at the heart of ragged school philosophy.[30] These identifying characteristics of evangelicalism can be seen in the LRSU's 1850 proclamation that:

> it was not merely with pens and primers they went down into the dark purlieus of misery and guilt, as if these could strike light into benighted minds … but they carried with them the Gospel – that only charter of human freedom – that only lever capable of elevating the morally depraved.[31]

Eight years later the *RSUM* encouraged those pioneering the recently established Liverpool schools to enter the city's 'dark recesses with the light of Evangelical Truth in their hand'.[32] It was only through the power of the gospel – and there 'was no instrument possessing so much power' – that impoverished and neglected children could be saved.[33]

[28] London, LMA 4060/A/01/001, Field Lane Ragged School Committee Minute Book, 1842–1846, 12 September 1843.

[29] David Bebbington, *Evangelicalism in Modern Britain: A History from the 1730s to the 1980s* (London, 2002), 3.

[30] This verse encompasses the ragged school message; it was quoted at the head of each LRSU *Annual Report*.

[31] *Crime and its Causes: A Reply to the Attacks of the 'Morning Chronicle' on the London Ragged Schools* (London, 1850), 3. The public meeting on which this pamphlet reports was convened in response to Henry Mayhew's accusations in the *Morning Chronicle* that 'institutions like the Ragged Schools, which seek to reform our juvenile offenders merely by instructing them, cannot be attended with the desired results': 'Labour and the Poor, Letter XLIV', *Morning Chronicle*, 25 March 1850, 5.

[32] 'Papers, Original and Selected: The Liverpool Ragged School Union', *RSUM*, March 1854, 64.

[33] 'Intelligence: St Giles' Ragged School', *RSUM*, January 1849, 18.

The movement's supporters deemed it part of a broader spiritual awakening, wherein God's people were no longer 'delegating their duties to priests, ministers, or missionaries, but themselves going'.[34] The role of the ragged school teacher was regarded as a calling, as encapsulated in the 1849 poem 'Unto this Work we are Called'.[35] Local prayer meetings invited God's Spirit into the classroom; the Field Lane Ragged School committee prayed for a 'pouring out of the Holy Spirit upon both Teachers & Taught'.[36] The *RSUM* featured reports of a 'spiritual awakening' among scholars and encouraged teachers to seek 'more abundant manifestation of Divine influence'.[37] Those teachers present at a meeting in St Giles's Refuge in November 1859 were roused by a spiritual call to arms: 'Let us then not rest till this Revival is experienced by ourselves; we shall then teach with a power that can be felt'.[38] With contemporaneous reports of revival breaking out across Britain, the ragged schools sought to share in this outpouring. Reflecting this evangelical fervour, not to mention the movement's financial constraints, the *RSUM* boasted an army of volunteers. By 1856, the LRSU's twelfth year, voluntary teachers numbered 2,118, compared with just 332 who were paid.[39] Two years later volunteers were commended because they had been, 'and are, and ever must be, the strength of the movement'.[40] It was not training that qualified individuals to teach; rather, teachers were to possess 'zeal, patience, and persevering energy'.[41] According to Shaftesbury, 'it was not necessary that [teachers] should pass an ordeal of examination … it was a knowledge of the Bible they ought to possess, and also an acquaintance with the human heart'.[42] Because of this reliance upon largely untrained volunteers, however, many adults working in the schools had little or no experience of teaching children.

34 'Spiritual Life and Ragged Schools', *RSUM*, November 1859, 217.

35 'Poetry: Unto this Work we are Called', *RSUM*, May 1849, 92.

36 LMA 4060/A/01/006, Field Lane Ragged School Committee Minute Book, 1858–1863, 18 January 1860.

37 'Spiritual Life and Ragged Schools', *RSUM*, March 1860, 62, 'Spiritual Life and Ragged Schools', *RSUM*, July 1858, 123.

38 'Spiritual Life and Ragged Schools', *RSUM*, January 1860, 17.

39 'Meeting of Paid Teachers', *RSUM*, January 1856, 10.

40 'Paid Teachers and their Annual Meeting', *RSUM*, May 1858, 92.

41 George Hall, *Sought and Saved: A Prize Essay on the Ragged Schools and Kindred Institutions* (London, 1855), 14.

42 'The Earl of Shaftesbury on Ragged Schools', *The Times*, 22 October 1859, 8.

The ragged school movement was one aspect of a larger evangelical picture. In her study of Anglican evangelicals, Heasman highlights their prominence within the LRSU, arguing that it 'was essentially an Evangelical organisation, its chairman being Lord Shaftesbury and its treasurer R. C. L. Bevan'.[43] Yet ragged school teachers were drawn from a variety of denominational backgrounds. The London City Mission, which Lewis calls 'the largest and possibly most enduring interdenominational mission in Britain', worked closely with the LRSU.[44] Drawn from across the evangelical spectrum, London City Missionaries frequently offered their services to ragged schools, participating in prayer meetings, speaking at assemblies and volunteering as teachers.[45] The scale of city missionaries involved with the movement is hinted at within a list of 1,704 London teachers that Alexander Anderson, a leading member of the LRSU, presented to Shaftesbury in 1867. Amongst the names are twenty-three London City missionaries. Although this figure may seem insignificant, it should be noted that 35 per cent – or 605 – of those named did not detail any occupation. Alongside a diverse amalgamation of trades, including 'cheesemonger', 'cow-keeper', 'fancy box-maker', 'pickle-filler' and 'surgeon', the title 'London City Missionary' recurs in various forms, including 'Frederick Cox, City missionary', 'Thos. Hazeldine, city missionary', and 'Thomas Salter, L. C. Missionary'.[46] The presence of city missionaries within this list demonstrates the movement's scope and reaffirms Anderson's claim that '[w]e belong to different evangelical denominations of Christians', which Shaftesbury labelled 'the safety and the purity of the system'.[47]

In undertaking his voluntary role at Compton Place alongside his primary occupation as a barrister, Ware was representative of those ragged school teachers who spent their evenings and weekends labouring in 'Christ's vineyard'.[48] Like Shaftesbury, Ware identified as an evangelical. Having been educated in a Baptist school, he

43 Heasman, *Evangelicals in Action*, 72.

44 Donald Lewis, *Lighten their Darkness: The Evangelical Mission to Working-Class London* (Carlisle, 2001), 49.

45 For more information on the connection between Scripture readers, London City missionaries, and the LRSU, see Lewis, *Lighten their Darkness*, 166; Heasman, *Evangelicals in Action*, 71.

46 'Presentation to the Earl of Shaftesbury', *RSUM*, August 1859, 162–75.

47 Ibid. 163, 166.

48 'Testimonials to Teachers and Scholars', *RSUM*, March 1860, 59.

became an Anglican as a young man.[49] His detailed school journals witness to the time their author invested in the institution and its scholars. In his later years he reflected in his memoirs that his active role at Compton Place had limited his professional achievements. It had, he wrote, 'interfered in some degree with my getting business'.[50] Ware volunteered at the school for approximately twenty-two years, seventeen of which are covered by his journals (1850–67).[51] Alongside the Sunday evening boys' class, of which he was superintendent from 1848 until approximately 1854, his weekly schedule featured home visits, committee meetings and prayer gatherings. Ware was also a part of the broader ragged school network, attending meetings or worship services for teachers in the Camden area. In addition to his involvement with the LRSU, he was actively involved with a number of other missionary societies, including the British and Foreign Bible Society, the China Inland Mission and the Church Missionary Society. The numerous obituaries that followed Ware's death, in publications such as *The Globe*, *The Guardian*, the *Pall Mall Gazette*, *The Record* and *The Times*, testify equally to his faith and to his prominence within philanthropic circles. He was, according to the Church of England's *Record*, an 'old and tried Evangelical' whose 'kindly presence will be missed at many council tables'.[52] Similarly, *The Globe* noted that Ware had been 'amongst the most active of London laymen'.[53] The *Yorkshire Evening Post* and the *Leeds Mercury* affirmed simply: 'the Evangelical party has lost a prominent layman in the person of Mr. Martin Ware'.[54]

They 'Come for a Lark'

Ragged school reports frequently described the crowds of excited children awaiting entry to their classroom. Henry Mayhew, the *Morning*

[49] SHC 1487/106/1, Memoirs of Martin Ware III.
[50] Ibid.
[51] This figure is given in a handwritten note from John Kirk, the secretary of the LRSU at the time of Ware's death in December 1895, enclosed in SHC 1585/7, Ware, Journal.
[52] Obituary in *The Record*, pasted ibid. While local newspapers presented versions of the same syndicated obituary, those published in major newspapers and evangelical journals were composed by different individuals and thus had different emphases.
[53] Obituary in *The Globe*, pasted ibid.
[54] 'Local Sport', *Yorkshire Evening Post*, 6 January 1896, 4, 'Births, Deaths, Marriages and Obituaries', *Leeds Mercury*, 7 January 1896, 8.

Chronicle journalist, expanded on this, telling how the children made much 'noise and ribaldry', causing grief to neighbours of the institutions.[55] As a site where children congregated with peers it is unsurprising that ragged schools were associated with play, or 'having a lark'. The difficult behaviour of ragged school children was, in Cunningham's words, 'a matter of notoriety'.[56] The notion of a ragged school was reportedly regarded with derision by many of the children. One commentator told how one group of ragged scholars were 'all in a state of frantic fun at the idea of any one schooling them'.[57] In 1850 the *Daily News* reported of Field Lane's earliest students that those 'who did attend came only for fun'.[58] Similarly, Ware often remarked on the insubordinate behaviour of his boys' class, describing it as 'difficult', 'noisy' and 'unruly'. On 8 and 15 December 1850 he labelled the boys' behaviour as 'turbulent'.[59] Within his journal, Ware noted his belief that some came 'only come for a lark' and expressed his frustration that one boy 'looks upon every thing as a lark – He seems to think it a lark to disturb the school'.[60]

As Ware's journal entries suggest, teachers were frequently interrupted by their scholars. In Ward's Place Ragged School one boy shouted 'clean your boots' whenever he felt the class was too quiet, while a companion 'perhaps thinking a variation in the performance desirable, would chime in with "ten a penny walnuts"'.[61] On other occasions, scholars mocked their teachers. When a Field Lane teacher told his class that 'the Lord is looking upon you; he is there above you', one boy 'put on a most ludicrous expression of incredulity, and standing up, proceeded to scrutinise the ceiling with a mock-critical air', after which he announced 'Blest if I see him'. According to the teacher, the boy's remark gave 'inexpressible delight' to his peers.[62] The singing of street-songs was an especially effective means of disrupting classes, allowing scholars to join in unison, singing lyrics

[55] Henry Mayhew, 'Labour and the Poor, Letter XVIII', *Morning Chronicle*, 19 March 1850, 5.
[56] Cunningham, *Children of the Poor*, 108.
[57] Untitled article, *Derby Mercury*, 24 January 1849, 2; 'Notes on Popular Movements', *Northern Star and National Trades' Journal*, 9 December 1848, 4.
[58] 'Visits to the London Ragged Schools', *Daily News*, 12 April 1850, 2.
[59] SHC 1585/1, Ware, Journal, 8 December 1850, 15 December 1850.
[60] SHC 1585/2, Ware, Journal, 16 November 1851.
[61] 'Ward's Place, Lower Road Islington', *RSUM*, January 1859, 10.
[62] 'Visits to the London Ragged Schools'.

unknown, and possibly offensive, to their teacher. By substituting the words of hymns with those of their own invention, the scholars of Lambeth Ragged School cast their teacher as an outsider within their classroom while simultaneously poking fun at the school's Christian message. These anecdotes demonstrate the scholars' quick wit, as well as the freedom with which they spoke (or sang) in the classroom.

It was not only the children's voices that interrupted teaching, however; some sought more physical means of disruption. Stones, mud and vegetables were smuggled into classrooms to be thrown at teachers or peers, while those denied entry launched makeshift missiles through the classroom windows. A letter signed 'S. R. S.', published in the *RSUM* in 1849, claimed that Field Lane teachers wore hats 'for protection' from the 'rotten vegetables and animal refuse' often thrown at them.[63] In January 1847 the *Daily News* told how 'books, slates, mud, and stones [were] flung at the teacher's head'.[64] In the same month *The Observer* quoted a Bristol teacher who had been 'pelted' with mud in the streets by the school's 'most unmanageable' boy.[65] Other supposed scholars went further still. One set a book on fire to show his feelings towards learning, while another utilized a heavy volume as a club-like weapon.[66] The *British Mothers' Magazine* recounted that children brought gunpowder into schools, lighting it and filling classrooms with smoke.[67] Fireworks appear to have been a popular means of wreaking havoc. Field Lane teachers described the 'delight of the pupils' when the superintendent attempted to 'quell an insurrection amidst the banging of crackers'.[68] Ware reported similar events, noting in November 1853 that the boys nearly 'set the place on fire with a Catherine wheel' and 'scared Mrs Ward out [of] her wits'.[69] Three years later Ware related how lessons were dramatically interrupted upon the discovery of a fire in the wash house. When the charred remnants of a firecracker were found, it was concluded to have been the cause. Such

[63] 'Correspondence', *RSUM*, March 1849, 55.
[64] 'Advertisements & Notices', *Daily News*, 11 January 1847, 2.
[65] 'Bristol Ragged School', *The Observer*, 25 January 1847, 3.
[66] 'Visits to the London Ragged Schools'; SHC 1585/7, Ware, Journal, anonymous letter, 18 June 1848.
[67] 'Ragged Schools of London', *British Mother's Magazine*, 1 February 1849, 48.
[68] 'Visits to the London Ragged Schools'.
[69] SHC 1585/3, Ware, Journal, 6 November 1853.

behaviour was undoubtedly entertaining to those involved. More than this, it was an assertion of the scholar's ability to direct the dynamics within the classroom. The throwing of objects, singing and impromptu interruptions all undermined the teacher's authority.

In literature intended for volunteers, as well as in that for the general public, ragged school teachers were regularly depicted as being at the children's mercy. Such accounts suggested that it was the children, not the teachers, who controlled the classroom. Upon first consideration such a portrayal may seem counterproductive for an institution seeking the public's financial support. Yet this narrative powerfully conveyed the teacher's heroism and the crucial role played by the movement in taming semi-delinquent children. Aspiring teachers were instructed that because of their wild nature, street-children 'could not be coerced, but must be persuaded'.[70] Teachers were reliant upon the children's cooperation, and reports of scholars refusing to follow instructions were numerous. Shaftesbury himself related an especially comic instance of mutinous children. He told how his good friend, the LRSU's secretary, Joseph Payne, that he entered a classroom to discover six scholars sitting on their long-suffering superintendent's back while singing 'Pop goes the Weasel'.[71] Thomas Guthrie recalled what happened when an inexperienced teacher in Edinburgh 'unfortunately closed his eyes' in prayer:

> For a moment his reverent attitude, and the voice of prayer, seemed, like the voice of Jesus on the stormy waters, to produce a great calm. But by-and-by I heard a curious noise, and I shall not forget the sight which met my eyes on suddenly opening them; there – and behind them a crowd of grinning faces, red with efforts to suppress their laughter – stood two ragged urchins, each holding a flaming candle under my friend's nose, and I could not help thinking that there was a wicked cleverness in this.[72]

It is more than possible that similar incidents occurred elsewhere, as in later years the *RSUM* instructed teachers to keep '*their* eyes fixed on the scholars' during prayer.[73]

[70] 'Westminster Ragged School', *The Times*, 24 April 1850, 5.
[71] Claire Seymour, *Ragged Schools, Ragged Children* (London, 1995), 22.
[72] Thomas Guthrie, *Out of Harness* (New York, 1867), 7–8.
[73] 'Teachers' Column: Rules for a Sunday Night School', *RSUM*, November 1870, 255.

In 1848 Shaftesbury affirmed the teacher's vulnerability in the classroom, asserting that the role was 'absolutely a service of danger'.[74] The *British Mother's Magazine* applied comparable terminology the following year, when it suggested that the opening of a school 'was often a curious scene' that was 'not free from danger'.[75] This language sensationalized and elevated the teacher's role, likening teachers to overseas missionaries. Although sparsely reported, there were numerous incidents of violence against teachers. The Bristol teacher who described the school's 'most unmanageable' scholar also told how the same child 'has kicked my legs', though adding '(happily he has no shoes)'.[76] When an array of 'juvenile "roughs"' congregated outside Harrow Street Ragged School and 'threatened to stone the master', they were unsurprisingly refused admission.[77] Two especially serious cases occurred at Field Lane and were detailed in the *Daily News*. In the first, a boy 'got a knife and attempted to *stab the superintendent*', while in the second a boy 'brought a large knife' with the intention, 'as he said, of sticking his teacher with it'.[78] The *RSUM* also reported an incident from Field Lane in which a group of boys planned to attend the school for 'a *lark*'; however, if any teacher intervened they would '*rip him up*'. In this instance, the boys' desire to have 'a lark' appears decidedly darker than those cases cited above. Since it was one of these boys who had previously attempted to '*stab the superintendent*', the threat was deemed serious.[79] In January 1863 the *RSUM* published a letter signed 'A Worker' entitled 'How to Treat the Roughs', which informed readers that 'within the last few days our Master has been assaulted' and the anonymous school in question had decided to press charges. The letter urged other institutions to prosecute violent children, suggesting that although 'this may appear very harsh … Some protection is required'.[80] However, such incidents were uncommon; one teacher was sufficiently confident in

[74] 'Ragged School Emigration', *The Examiner*, 10 June 1848, 374.
[75] 'Ragged Schools of London'.
[76] 'Bristol Ragged School'.
[77] 'School Agent's Work – West and South', *RSUM*, July 1869, 156.
[78] 'Visits to the London Ragged Schools'.
[79] 'Correspondence', *RSUM*, March 1849, 55. It is possible that the boy who attempted to '*stab the superintendent*' is the same boy mentioned in the *Daily News*, although this cannot be verified.
[80] 'Correspondence: How to Treat the Roughs', *RSUM*, January 1863, 20.

his scholars to suggest that they provide a knife-cleaning service to their communities.[81]

From Ware's journals it appears that one teacher, Mr Berrington, was regularly ridiculed by his class. Berrington complained to Ware of the tardiness and bad behaviour of his scholars; although Ware did not elaborate, such problems seem to have been more common under Berrington's supervision than his own. Ware recorded that one boy's father 'seemed to think Berrington a goose and complained of his bad management', again suggesting that Berrington had little control over the class.[82] On 6 January 1861 Ware recorded Berrington's 'trouble with Tom Ramsay', adding that he and another boy had 'knocked Mr Berrington's hat about'. The two boys had initially refused to apologize, only doing so immediately prior to the class treat. Two years later Berrington summoned another boy to court, charged with assaulting him.[83] By contrast, during his seventeen years at the school Ware never recorded any incidents of violence towards himself. The challenge Berrington faced when controlling the boys was further exemplified in May 1863 when Ware learned that he 'had beaten two of the boys very severely'. Violence, then, was not only meted out by the children to their teachers. After learning of Berrington's actions, Ware visited the mother of one of the boys and 'pacified her'.[84]

Historians including Gardner and Laqueur have recently contradicted traditional assumptions regarding the use of corporal punishment in nineteenth-century schools, arguing that it was often discouraged and deemed ineffective in the context of charity or voluntary schools.[85] It is not surprising, therefore, that corporal punishment was condemned by advocates of the ragged schools. Just as aggression in children was indicative of immoral influences, such behaviour in teachers was troubling. The *RSUM* made it clear that teachers should refrain from violence, advising that '*the teacher be deemed incompetent who cannot govern his school without the frequent use of the rod*'.[86] As early as 1847 Shaftesbury stressed that ragged

[81] 'Correspondence: Knife-Cleaning Brigade', *RSUM*, August 1865, 194.
[82] SHC 1585/7, Ware, Journal, 27 November 1864.
[83] SHC 1585/6, Ware, Journal, 6 January 1861, 23 August 1863.
[84] Ibid. 22 May 1863.
[85] Laqueur, *Religion and Respectability*, 17–18; Gardner, *Lost Elementary Schools*.
[86] 'Plans and Progress: Hints to Parties thinking about establishing Industrial Schools for the Outcast and Destitute', *RSUM*, July 1849, 128.

schools 'cannot operate by intimidation'.[87] George Hall, whose 1855 book on the schools was commended 'unanimously' by an LRSU committee including Ware, warned: 'Those who only know how to scold and drive … had better not enter our Ragged Schools'.[88] The *RSUM*'s 'Teachers' Column' told readers that '"Love begets love" and "Anger and hate beget anger and hate"'.[89] Such arguments attributed behaviour, for better or worse, to teachers. Drawing upon the educational concept of *tabula rasa*, or 'blank slate', championed by the influential eighteenth-century philosophers John Locke and Jean-Jacques Rousseau, it was argued that children reflected the environment to which they were exposed; born without preconceived knowledge, children were shaped by their surroundings. For this reason, teachers were to foster a sense of love in the classroom, rather than fear.

'The Happiest Portions of the Day'

The notion that children came to school freely, rather than in response to compulsion, was at the centre of the ragged school model.[90] Probably because of this, infrequent and sporadic attendance was a common problem. When discussing the challenges faced by teachers, Hall referred to those children 'whose attendance is so irregular as to do them but little good'.[91] He lamented the impact of infrequent attendance upon the schools' effectiveness: 'Whether it be reading, writing, sewing, tailoring, or shoemaking, the lesson is only half learnt'.[92] As Gardner has found regarding working-class private schools, many ragged schools experienced seasonal attendance: classrooms were filled in the cold winter months and left barren on long summer evenings.[93] This issue was addressed at a meeting of teachers in 1856. According to the report, it 'was

[87] *The Third Annual Report of the Ragged School Union, established for the Support of Free Schools for the Destitute Poor of London and its Suburbs* (London, 1847), 6.
[88] Hall, *Sought and Saved*, vii, 56.
[89] 'Teachers' Column: How to Win a Child's Heart', *RSUM*, February 1865, 43.
[90] Following the 1857 Industrial Schools Act, 'criminal' children could be committed by the order of a magistrate to attend an industrial school. As some ragged schools also qualified as industrial schools, they often received such children. Nevertheless, the focus of ragged school pedagogical advice was on those scholars attending voluntarily.
[91] Hall, *Sought and Saved*, 27.
[92] Ibid. 39.
[93] Gardner, *Lost Elementary Schools*, 174.

admitted by all' that attendance over the summer 'was very fluctuating'. Because of poor attendance, 'teachers felt discouraged', which was a contributory factor to many growing disillusioned with the ragged school movement and leaving.[94]

Ware's journals provide tangible evidence of the discouragement an empty classroom could cause. He reflected upon possible reasons for mass absences, regularly speculating on the impact of the weather on the turnout of scholars. On 11 July 1852 he noted: 'School rather empty probably from the heat of the weather'. At the close of the month the school was 'rather empty' again, this time 'in consequence of heavy storms – The rain comes through the roof terribly'.[95] The journals demonstrate that absent scholars were not only a problem during the summer. Four months after noting the 'heat of the weather', Ware recorded: 'Thin school for what reason I know not unless it was the rain'. The weather was not to blame on 26 December, however, when Ware concluded that the poor attendance was 'probably because of Xtmas festivities'.[96] The significance he attached to the number of children present is evident in his entry for 10 April 1853: 'Very thin school – the thinnest since Sept 1849. Alas! I fear without more exertion the school will go down more & more'.[97] It was in this context that Hall wrote that each school succeeded or failed according to its ability to attract scholars.[98]

The fact that many children came to school 'to have a lark' suggests that peer relationships had an important influence on school attendance.[99] Although Mayhew's *Morning Chronicle* articles, written in opposition to the movement, stressed the dangers of children being morally contaminated by delinquent or criminal classmates, the LRSU downplayed this risk. Instead, ragged school documents focused on the benefits to be reaped from establishing friendships and communities. Rather than preventing the children from interacting with one another, they aimed to create schools where positive and lasting relationships would be formed. The LRSU acknowledged that friendships were a vital component of the appeal; Christmas meals, entertainment evenings, days out and school reunions sought to

94 'The Teachers' Column: Delegates' Meeting', *RSUM*, June 1856, 122.
95 SHC 1585/2, Ware, Journal, 11 and 25 July 1852.
96 Ibid. 21 November, 26 December 1852.
97 Ibid. 10 April 1853.
98 Hall, *Sought and Saved*, 39.
99 Caroline Cornwallis, *The Philosophy of Ragged Schools* (London, 1851), 52.

knit school communities together and establish bonds both amongst scholars and between scholars and teachers. Although attendance for the sole purpose of socializing was discouraged, the LRSU nevertheless sought to utilize the children's love of play and create attractive environments. Organized trips to fairs and parks provided spaces in which the children could play together; thus on Good Friday 1857 Ware rewarded five scholars with a visit to the Crystal Palace. Tellingly, he noted afterwards that they 'seemed to enjoy playing about in the Park more than the interior of the Palace'.[100] Such accounts demonstrate that teachers recognized the significant role played by peer relationships in forming welcoming communities. Moreover, ragged school literature informed teachers that children learned more readily when lessons involved 'seeing, hearing, handling, or experimenting'.[101] Thus school trips were likewise valued as an opportunity to engage the children's senses. Both 'the countryside' and Regent Park's Zoological Gardens were common destinations for London's ragged school children. On 15 July 1851 Ware took forty boys to the Zoological Gardens. He later expressed his frustration in his journal, writing: 'We had some trouble in managing them. I do not much like it, as they get in other people's way'.[102] Despite Ware's embarrassment at the children's behaviour, such visits remained a regular feature of the school itinerary.

With regard to educational practice, teachers were advised against subjecting children to long addresses and sermons. Although moralistic and religious addresses were a key part of a ragged school education, it was seen as critical that they were given in a way that would have a positive impact. When detailing the most important principles to adhere to within the classroom, Hall recommended that teachers 'scrupulously avoid anything like an overtaxing of their small powers of endurance and attention'. Recognizing children's distinct intellectual needs, he critiqued systems according to which scholars were 'shut up – we might almost say, imprisoned' or 'kept in a most unchildlike quietness for three or four hours together'.[103] Similarly, in an 1849 article entitled 'Practical Suggestions', the *RSUM* stressed

100 SHC 1585/5, Ware, Journal, 10 April 1857.

101 'The Teachers' Column: Attention; or, Principles rather than Rules', *RSUM*, June 1864, 141.

102 SHC 1585/1, Ware, Journal, 15 July 1851.

103 Hall, *Sought and Saved*, 87.

the importance of sermons being delivered 'by some one capable of addressing and interesting children'. The same article specified with particular emphasis that addresses 'should not last above ten or fifteen minutes'.[104] Perhaps after reading the *RSUM*'s 'Practical Suggestions', Ware identified long addresses as a problem in his own school. He early learned the importance of speaking concisely as superintendent; in February 1850 he noted that the day had been challenging not only because of 'a lack of teachers', but also because he 'had kept them rather too long' during the address.[105] This extract demonstrates Ware's critical reflection on his own teaching practice and shows that he sought to tailor his lessons to the children's capacities. In later entries he critiqued the over-long addresses of his colleagues. In May 1858, after taking his class to an assembly at a neighbouring school, Ware recorded that it had 'lasted 1¾ [hours]', which he judged 'too long'.[106] When the teachers gathered to 'discuss the management of the school' in October 1864, it was decided that the address should not exceed fifteen minutes.[107]

The manner in which children were addressed was considered equally important. Teachers were to utilize topics that interested their scholars to engage them in the subject in hand. Hall advised that 'experience and study' would help the teacher 'to find that aspect of every subject which is most to the taste, and most within the comprehension of their infant minds'.[108] The ability to engage children in topics they might otherwise find uninteresting was an enviable gift among teachers. Ragged school publications made it clear that the most successful speakers were those who used terminology that their audience understood. In 1868 the Teachers' Column advised its readers to suit their words to the 'mental capacities' of children.[109] Given the centrality of the gospel to the ragged school mission, it was critical that children understood the phrases used when praying or singing. Shaftesbury evidently applied such ideals to himself, as *Punch* detailed how, during an assembly for ragged school children, 'Lord Shaftesbury, as is his wont, addressed the boys in words of

[104] 'Plans and Progress – Practical Suggestions: The Work, and how to do it', *RSUM*, February 1849, 33.
[105] SHC 1585/1, Ware, Journal, 17 February 1850.
[106] SHC 1585/5, Ware, Journal, 3 May 1858.
[107] SHC 1585/7, Ware, Journal, 22 October 1864.
[108] Hall, *Sought and Saved*, 49.
[109] 'The Teachers' Column: Prayer in Ragged Schools', *RSUM*, January 1868, 19.

kindness and affection', exhorting them with 'plain, impressive speech'.[110]

The way in which children received or responded to addresses was the primary factor under consideration when determining effectiveness. Accordingly, Ware was keenly perceptive regarding responses to his own talks. On 7 July 1850 he wrote that the scholars were 'not very attentive'; while three weeks later they were 'very attentive to [the] address', the subject of which he added in brackets: '(Jonah)'.[111] He reflected on the success of lessons in his journal, noting on 30 June 1850 that he had read the class a story 'as an experiment'. He deemed the venture a success, concluding that 'they seemed attentive & interested'.[112] Twelve years later, in November 1862, Ware's journal again conveys his perceptiveness regarding the mood in the classroom: he had decided 'not [to] give any address fearing a disturbance'.[113] This entry highlights how he responded to the children's behaviour and the classroom atmosphere; scholars influenced his plans, sometimes causing them to be postponed or cancelled altogether.

Conclusion

Prior to the increasing state intervention that followed the 1870 Education Act, ragged schools played an integral role in Victorian Britain. In London and across the nation, ragged schools went a considerable way to bridge gaps in the existing education systems, providing a place for those children whose appearance or want excluded them from other institutions. The interdenominational appeal of the schools brought together evangelicals from across Protestant denominations, generating a formidable response to child poverty. Middle-class individuals such as Ware lived out their social calling within ragged school classrooms in the evenings and over weekends, encountering children whose experiences were starkly different from their own. Ware's journals testify to the challenges he faced, highlighting the demanding nature of the role and the emotional and financial commitment that he made to the school. His detailed and

110 'The Shoeblack Brigade', *Punch*, 21 February 1857, 80.
111 SHC 1585/1, Ware, Journal, 7, 21 July 1850.
112 Ibid. 30 June 1850.
113 SHC 1585/6, Ware, Journal, 2 November 1862.

reflective entries provide a hitherto unseen insight into the anxieties experienced by ragged school teachers. The tension between Ware's religious motivation – his desire to share the gospel with impoverished children – and the reality he faced in the classroom is never far beneath the surface of his entries. Further, LRSU literature intended for teachers suggests that when Ware worried about his scholars' poor attendance, their unmanageable behaviour or their eternal souls he was not alone.

By contrast with the well-known Victorian idiom, children were both seen and heard in the ragged school classroom. Street culture, whether manifested in songs, theatrics or disruptive shouts, entered the schools with the children. In many cases children appear to have spoken freely and confidently in their classrooms, and anecdotal reports testify to their quick wit. Such disturbances were not only employed to entertain peers but to undermine teachers. In belting out street songs instead of hymns, children acted in unison, playfully excluding their teacher from the fun. Furthermore, children did not uniformly accept the religious teaching imparted. They asked questions, challenged their teachers and made light of the evangelical message on offer. By focusing on classroom dynamics and ragged school teaching advice, the complexity of the scholar-teacher relationship is demonstrated. This article calls into question the notions that the classroom was the teacher's dominion and that the children were victims of evangelical fervour. Ragged school children were by no means passive; they sought out the food, fun and friends these institutions offered.

Ragged school literature did not conceal the belittlement that teachers endured, which is also documented by local schools. On the contrary, the *RSUM* drew on such reports to convey the passion of their teachers and obtain the sympathy and support of its readers. Moreover, both ragged school literature and local accounts suggest that teachers could be vulnerable within their classrooms. Their intention may have been to share the gospel but, from flying objects to physical aggression, teachers had to be prepared for conflict. Ragged school accounts demonstrate that the respect of children was hard won and highly valued; the scholars' trust was earned through the teacher's kindness and patience. This aspect of the schools jars with the social control narratives that have dominated historical accounts of the movement. The interaction between ragged school children and their teachers, both as advised and in practice, facilitates a more nuanced interpretation of the nature and significance of the movement as a whole. The voluntary nature of attendance shaped the advice given to teachers. It was because of the children's freedom that a premium was placed upon the scholars' enjoyment. Teachers were advised to take advantage of the fact that children came 'for a lark', and peer relationships were interpreted as an asset rather than a danger. Day trips and events were used to promote friendships and enrich communities. Furthermore, lessons and addresses were evaluated on the basis of the children's responses. Dreary teaching, long sermons and incomprehensible terminology were the nemesis of the ragged school teacher. The happiness of scholars was the ultimate gauge of success in the classroom, effectively positioning the children as consumers the schools sought to please.

Despite the ragged school movement's pertinence to church historians, ragged schools have received limited attention. Although this article has gone some way to redress this oversight, the movement remains a fertile area of research. Scholars' understanding of the role played by Victorian evangelicals and their emphasis on familiarity with the Bible in championing education for the impoverished and improving literacy remains partial. With their pan-evangelical appeal, the ragged schools have the potential to generate important insights into interdenominational philanthropy and its impact on cross-class relationships.

Religious and Industrial Education in the Nineteenth-Century Magdalene Asylums in Scotland

Jowita Thor*
University of Edinburgh

The Magdalene Asylums were penitentiaries for 'fallen' women. A high percentage of such women had been involved in sex trade in some form; others were betrayed fiancées, unmarried partners or women with drinking problems. This article explores the Magdalene Asylums' education as a tool for reforming the inmates into women reflecting the managers' ideals of femininity and Christian virtue in nineteenth-century Scotland. The reports of these institutions describe their aims, quoting selected letters of former inmates, their parents and new employers. They give us an insight into how these Christian philanthropists imagined and applied educational programme for this group of women and girls. The two main areas of the asylums' education were religious teaching and instruction in a range of skills necessary for becoming a servant or a factory worker. Those who could not read and write also received basic literacy lessons. Magdalene Asylums in nineteenth-century Scotland offer a rich case study of a context in which education had a very narrow meaning and served a precisely defined purpose. They provided a broad spectrum of skills, although never at a comprehensive level. The article explores the managers' intentions and ideals by analysing the language they used to talk about 'successfully reformed' women.

In his book on Ireland's Magdalene Asylums, James M. Smith shows how these institutions exist 'in the public mind chiefly at the level of *story* (cultural representation and survivor testimony) rather than history (archival records and documentation)'.[1] In the case of Ireland, this is caused by very restricted access to the Catholic archives, which hold most of the materials, and a rich media and art response to them. In Scotland, by contrast, the archival documents are easily available but there is little interest in researching these institutions. This sometimes results either in a complete lack of knowledge

* New College, Mound Place, Edinburgh, EH1 2LX. E-mail: jo.thor@ed.ac.uk.

[1] James M. Smith, *Ireland's Magdalen Laundries and the Nation's Architecture of Containment* (Manchester, 2008), xvi.

Studies in Church History 55 (2019), 347–362
doi: 10.1017/stc.2018.4

about the Magdalene Asylums' historical presence in the country or in the assumption that they were the same as in Ireland. In the Scottish context, therefore, the asylums exist neither as story nor as history. This article will analyse the existing archival evidence in order to formulate part of these institutions' history. It will discuss the ways in which they saw themselves as places of education rather than penance for 'fallen' women in nineteenth-century Scotland.

The Magdalene establishments are usually understood as penitentiaries or houses of refuge for 'fallen women',[2] which subjected women to a harsh regime. This description, however, although true for some institutions, is one-sided. Whilst the infamous Magdalene Laundries in Ireland contributed to the belief that all Magdalene establishments were places of harsh punishment, abuse and forced incarceration, this image is not always accurate when considering the Scottish institutions, especially in their early stages. They form part of a long tradition of institutions dedicated to Mary Magdalene, whose particular missionary focus originally had been to help, or provide a refuge for, women involved in the sex trade, whether they had entered it voluntarily or were victims of poverty and sex trafficking. These institutions took nuanced and diverse forms in different national contexts across Europe, and changed enormously from their inception in medieval times to the closure of the last such institution in twentieth-century Ireland.[3]

In 1758 a new wave of Magdalene establishments in Britain and Ireland started with the London Magdalene Hospital and spread

[2] I try to avoid the word 'prostitute' as much as possible, despite its being a widely used term of the time. I prefer the term 'sex worker' to avoid sounding contemptuous towards the women described. Importantly, 'sex worker' in this article does not imply that all women under discussion had full agency when choosing this occupation (whether it was occasional or full-time). It merely indicates the method of earning money, and does not imply any assessment of women's agency. When a more inclusive category is called for, I refer to all women who were considered 'fallen' (which included any woman who had sex outside marriage or even women with drinking problems). I adopt the contemporary term 'fallen women' in quotation marks, to distance myself from the moral judgement of nineteenth-century philanthropists. Most twenty-first-century readers will understand 'prostitute' as referring to a sex worker; however, the nineteenth-century definition of the word was much broader.

[3] Vern Bullough and Bonnie Bullough, *Women and Prostitution: A Social History* (New York, 1987), 111, 130, 154, 185, 245–6, 274; Rebecca Lea McCarthy, *Origins of the Magdalene Laundries: An Analytical History* (Jefferson, NC, 2010), 73, 76.

slowly throughout the region.[4] The first Scottish establishment opened in 1797 in Edinburgh. Glasgow followed its example in 1815.[5] Aberdeen opened its first asylum around 1845, Dundee in 1848 and Greenock in 1853.[6] These were followed by additional asylums in these and other Scottish towns.[7] Scottish Magdalene Asylums became centres of education for women who sought a new start in their lives. They were part of growing efforts of social reform aiming to respond to social problems by considering their causes instead of punishing their victims. Scottish Magdalene Asylums became part of the wider 'social purity' movement, which attempted to eradicate prostitution and the sexual exploitation of women and children and became a major outlet for female philanthropy.[8]

Most of the asylums combined Protestantism, Magdalenism and lay charity. They were run by male and female committees consisting of middle-class philanthropists. Their main goal was to bring salvation to the 'fallen'. In Scotland most of them were lay, halfway reformatories, whose emphasis was on providing basic education, training in household duties and skills that were essential to find employment as a servant or in other occupations. At their inception, then, British Magdalene establishments were conceived as places of reformation and education, not of punishment, although some did later make penance and punishment a major part of their programmes, which could quickly lead to abuse. This was education conceived as the transmission of manual skills and knowledge of religious doctrine and practice, rather than education concerned with broadening of

[4] Herbert F. B. Compston, *The Magdalen Hospital: The Story of a Great Charity* (London: 1917), 15; James Hanway, *A Plan for establishing a Charity-house, or Charity-houses, for the Reception of repenting Prostitutes, to be called the Magdalen Charity* (London, 1758).

[5] Linda Mahood, *The Magdalenes: Prostitution in the Nineteenth Century* (London, 1990), 75.

[6] *The New Statistical Account of Scotland*, 12: *Aberdeen* (Edinburgh, 1845), 55; *The Dundee Directory for 1850* (Dundee, n.d.), 35; Lorraine Walsh, *Patrons, Poverty & Profit: Organised Charity in Nineteenth-Century Dundee* (Dundee, 2000), 49; *Rules of the Greenock House of Refuge, instituted 1853* (Greenock, n.d.), 2.

[7] The Magdalene Asylums in nineteenth-century Scotland have been a neglected topic in British history. While more has been published on the Magdalene Asylums in Ireland, especially in the twentieth century, the Scottish homes have received little attention. There are many relevant Scottish primary sources; some are used in this article, but many have yet to be studied.

[8] For more on the rescue movement, especially in the Irish context, see Frances Finnegan, *Do Penance or Perish: Magdalen Asylums in Ireland* (Oxford, 2001), 1–5; Jacinta Prunty, *The Monasteries, Magdalen Asylums and Reformatory Schools of Our Lady of Charity in Ireland, 1853–1973* (Dublin: 2017), 93–108.

the intellect.[9] The institutions' managers hoped that this would lead to the kind of reform they desired: formerly 'fallen' women were supposed to become humble, submissive and grateful for what God had given them. Their everyday life should be characterized by regularity, discipline, hard work, piety and (of course) acceptance of a strict sexual ethic.

Studying Magdalene establishments as places of education rather than oppression contributes to a deeper understanding of the agency of so-called 'fallen' women during the nineteenth century. It will add to the existing scholarship surrounding the Contagious Diseases Acts, passed in the 1860s to examine women for venereal disease and regulate prostitution. Debates over the morality of these acts provoked a public discussion on the agency of sex workers in England in the latter half of the century.[10] Scholarship on the Magdalene Asylums has centred around the agency of female residents and the negative manifestations of female managers' power. Learning more about the early Scottish Magdalene establishments can enhance and deepen our understanding. In particular, when seen from the more positive perspective of their aims and objectives, as places providing education and preparing women for independent lives, the Magdalene establishments take on a different complexion. In addition, the history of the Scottish Magdalene establishments reveals much about how Scottish Christian philanthropists, clergy and lay people envisioned suitable education for working-class women and especially 'fallen' women. As might be expected, it was an education that was intended to uphold the existing social hierarchy and shape working-class women into useful citizens, as defined by members of the middle and upper social orders.[11]

Discussing Magdalene establishments in this way has the further advantage of using 'gender as a theoretical category for religious history', as Sue Morgan has put it.[12] It seeks to avoid unnecessary

[9] D. C. Phillips and Harvey Siegel, 'Philosophy of Education', in Edward N. Zalta, ed., *The Stanford Encyclopedia of Philosophy* (Winter 2015 edn), online at: <https://plato.stanford.edu/archives/win2015/entries/education-philosophy/>, accessed 30 March 2018.

[10] See Francis Finnegan, *Poverty and Prostitution: A Study of Victorian Prostitutes in York* (Cambridge, 1979); Judith Walkowitz, *Prostitution and Victorian Society: Women, Class, and the State* (Cambridge, 1980).

[11] For a discussion on the influence of middle-class values and rejection of these norms by working-class Magdalenes of these institutions, see Mahood, *Magdalenes*.

[12] Sue Morgan, *A Passion for Purity: Ellice Hopkins and the Politics of Gender in the Late Victorian Church* (Bristol, 1999), 9.

polarization between religion and women's aspirations. An emphasis on religion as oppressive for women is an understandable approach when analysing later forms of Magdalene institutions, but it can lead to distortion when looking at the original ideals of the homes. This article will focus on education during the early years of each institution's existence, when they were relatively faithful to their set goals. For some asylums this means focusing on the first half of the nineteenth century; for others it means considering the 1850s and 1860s.

The Magdalene establishments during the nineteenth century can be described in a variety of ways, as reformatories, refuges, shelters or penitentiaries. Each institution had a different programme, focus and character. Existing scholarship reflects this plethora of different forms of institutions for 'fallen women'. Paula Bartley, Susan Mumm and Rene Kollar show how Magdalene establishments in England could resemble convents.[13] Unlike most of the Scottish Magdalene establishments, many of the English establishments were managed by religious, either Anglican sisters or Catholic nuns. By contrast, in Scotland most of the institutions were Presbyterian in orientation. They were subject to a complex administrative hierarchy. In many cases male directors and committees had executive powers. Female committees and workers were subordinate to these male structures, although they performed most of the work.[14] In Greenock, the president and vice-president were women, but its annual reports show that their male colleagues were in the positions of power.[15] An exception was Edinburgh's Female Shelter, whose committee consisted solely of 'ladies'.[16] In England's Anglican asylums, the class dynamic

[13] See Rene Kollar, 'Magdalenes and Nuns: Convent Laundries in Late Victorian England', *Anglican and Episcopal History* 73 (2004), 309–34, largely reproduced as idem, *A foreign and wicked Institution?: The Campaign against Convents in Victorian England* (Cambridge, 2011), 309–34; Susan Mumm, '"Not Worse than Other Girls": The Convent-based Rehabilitation of Fallen Women in Victorian Britain', *JSH* 29 (1996), 527–46; Paula Bartley, *Prostitution: Prevention and Reform in England, 1860–1914* (London, 2000).

[14] See, for example, *Rules of the Philanthropic Society of Edinburgh, 1st August 1797* ([Edinburgh, 1797?]).

[15] 40th to 43rd *Annual Reports of the Association of the Greenock House of Refuge or Shelter* (Greenock, 1894–7).

[16] *Ninth Report of the Female Shelter in Connection with the Scottish Ladies' Society for Promoting the Reformation of the most destitute of their own Sex, in Prisons and other Institutions* (Edinburgh, 1850).

was significantly different from that in Scotland. The background of the English sisters was mainly upper-class, while the residents came from working-class families. Those who were 'reformed' sometimes stayed at an institution for life as consecrated Magdalenes, choosing to live a secluded life of charity and prayer; however, they remained subordinate to the sisters.[17] In contrast, the Scottish asylums' main purpose was to educate and facilitate the women's return to society. The matrons, assistants and committee 'ladies' were mostly lay people and were usually married, and they saw the asylum as an intermediate state in their charges' path. The newspaper articles, regulations and annual reports of the Scottish institutions indicate that the members of their committees and the visitors were of middle- and upper-class background whilst the women working every day in the institutions were of lower social status.

There is an ongoing discussion regarding the extent to which Magdalene asylums incarcerated women. This is most pronounced in the research into the infamous Irish asylums, most of which were more similar to their English than to their Scottish counterparts. Mostly Catholic, run by nuns and highly valuing women's decision to stay in the institution as a religious, the Irish Magdalene Asylums have become a polarizing issue for scholars in the field. Finnegan, Luddy and Smith see these institutions as manifesting strong abusive tendencies, and describe them as places of incarceration and forms of social control.[18] In contrast, Prunty supports a more sympathetic view of the Irish asylums, seeing abuse as an exception rather than as the rule.[19] The truth probably lies somewhere in the middle. Kollar points to differences even within the same denomination, discussing two kinds of English Anglican asylums which differed significantly in the extent of the freedom they gave to women.[20] Studying Scottish asylums, which were very different from their English and Irish equivalents, helps us to see the Magdalene training in a more positive, but still critical, way. Possibly due to their decentralized character and complex management structures, they were less prone to abuse. Instead of seeing them as a means of oppression from the

17 Mumm, '"Not Worse than Other Girls"', 528.

18 See Finnegan, *Penance*; Maria Luddy, *Prostitution and Irish Society, 1800–1940* (Cambridge, 2007); Smith, *Laundries*.

19 Jacinta Prunty, *Our Lady of Charity in Ireland* (Dublin, 2017).

20 Kollar, *Magdalenes*, 320.

beginning of their existence, they can be seen as places of vocational training and religious education.

We turn now to consider what this education entailed. Considerable attention will be devoted to the letters and stories of individual occupants which the managers of the Magdalene establishments decided to publish in their reports. The article uses reports from several asylums, mainly in Edinburgh, which were of different sizes and set up for different kinds of women, but it will also consider institutions in Greenock. This sample presents a wide spectrum of such institutions, representative of those throughout the country. Edinburgh's homes show a variety that could be found in a bigger town where the numbers of 'fallen' women and their range of profiles met with an enthusiastic response from local philanthropists. Greenock, on the other hand, is an example of a small town where only one such charity existed and whose annual reports were regularly published in local newspapers. The Edinburgh Magdalene Asylum and Greenock's House of Refuge were each the main Magdalene asylum in their towns. They welcomed any woman who arrived at their door and who demonstrated her motivation by passing the probationary period. Edinburgh's Rescue and Probationary Home for Fallen Women represents a slightly different kind of Magdalene establishment: its purpose was mainly to provide temporary shelter for women coming there at night and only occasionally did it allow longer residence. Nonetheless, its managers still claimed to provide education intended to change their wards' lives. The St Andrew's House of Mercy, on the other hand, also located in Edinburgh, was a denominational institution under the patronage of the Scottish Episcopal Church. Another Edinburgh institution, the Reformatory Boarding-House for Higher Class Females, did not have a denominational affiliation but, as its name suggests, did not accept working-class women, who usually constituted the majority at other asylums.

Unfortunately, the sources that have survived are very intermittent. Of the institutions discussed here, the best-preserved documents are from the Edinburgh Magdalene Asylum, which produced annual – or triennial – reports, most of which have survived. These were mainly published and distributed among donors, subscribers and friends of the asylum. Their aim was to demonstrate that donors' money was being used effectively and in a worthy cause. Annual reports of the Greenock House of Refuge were published in local newspapers. Their extended readership meant that they must have increased the awareness in the town of the agency's activity; these reports sought to convince readers of its positive influence on the town.

The picture presented by these sources naturally reflects the managers' ideals and does not accurately portray the wide spectrum of different cases and women's feelings towards the institutions. It does, however, reveal the image that the institutions had carefully constructed. At the same time, the reports could be honest about failures and drawbacks. They admitted that some women fled the institutions, that the education offered in Magdalene Asylums did not always lead to a transformation in women's lives, and that many women managed to trick the directors in one way or another. In the reports, such stories were often intended to show the treachery, or even maliciousness, of 'fallen' women. Yet the stories also tell us much more.

It is clear that this type of source keeps us from seeing more disturbing aspects of the institutions and that these accounts should be read in a very critical way. The reports, for example, acknowledged that some women had 'escaped', but they usually did not explain why; nor did they recognize the tension between this language and the claim that women were allowed to leave if they wished so. While we cannot know how all the individual occupants viewed their Magdalene education, the reports indicate the middle-class philanthropists' goals. They show clearly that the philanthropists intended to transform those women whom they understood to threaten their ideals of harmonious society into productive members of the workforce.

William Tait, who was a physician at the Edinburgh Lock Hospital and who in that capacity worked with the Edinburgh Magdalene Asylum, described the institutions as

> established for the purpose of receiving such unfortunate females as appear to have experienced a conviction of the sinfulness of their conduct, and are willing to avail themselves of the advantages which they hold out to them. The object [is] to afford a temporary refuge … – to give them a religious and other necessary instruction, such as reading, sewing, washing … – to endeavour to effect a reconciliation with their friends, and restore the females to their status in society – or to procure for them such situations as they are qualified to undertake, after their residence for a certain period in the institution.[21]

[21] William Tait, *Magdalenism: An Inquiry into the Extent, Causes and Consequences of Prostitution in Edinburgh* (Edinburgh, 1840), 241.

In Tait's schema, the education provided at Magdalene establishments could be divided into three categories: religious, behavioural and industrial. These were perceived to be closely interconnected and all were essential for long-lasting reformation. They were also supposed to be universally applicable to all women, regardless of their specific environment.

The records of the Edinburgh Magdalene Asylum tell us that upon entering an asylum, the women's skills, education and religious knowledge varied substantially. It is very likely that other asylums were in the same position. The women came from many different social backgrounds, although probably the majority were from poor labouring families. Some were victims of domestic abuse. Some were orphans without even distant relatives or had families who never wanted to see them again; others had relatives who wanted to help them but for various reasons could not. The Female Industrial Home in Corstorphine, Edinburgh, was intended exclusively for women of the more 'respectable' social orders.[22] The Edinburgh Magdalene Asylum also had some also residents who came from better circumstances. 'E. H.', who lived there in the early 1830s, was 'respectably connected, and had received a liberal education'. Her 'fall' was attributed to pre-marital sex and her 'ungrateful' behaviour towards those who wished to help her.[23] 'E. F.' was similarly described as having good connections and great talents; she had been born abroad, where she received her education.[24] Another girl had attended an 'excellent school' sponsored by Lady Carnegie.[25] However, in the 1814 *Regulations* of the Edinburgh Magdalene Asylum it is suggested that only a minority of occupants had not been involved in sex trade at some point in their lives.[26] A similar suggestion was made by the Greenock House of Refuge.[27] Before the more widespread foundation of asylums across Scotland and the

[22] J. H. Maitland, *Female Industrial Home at Corstorphine, or Reformatory Boarding-House for Higher Class Females* (Edinburgh, 1864).
[23] *Report from the Directors of the Edinburgh Magdalene Asylum for 1830, 1831, & 1832* (Edinburgh, 1833), 12.
[24] Ibid. 14.
[25] *Report Read at the Annual Meeting of the Society for the Support of the Edinburgh Magdalene Asylum, December 7. 1835 … for 1833, 1834, & 1835* (Edinburgh, 1836), 10.
[26] *Regulations of the Society for Support of the Magdalene Asylum* (Edinburgh, 1814), 11.
[27] 'House of Refuge', *Greenock Advertiser*, 11 January 1866, 2.

rest of Britain, prospective residents travelled from nearby villages, other Scottish towns or even England to their chosen institution.[28]

The core of the Magdalene establishments' education was the intention to bring salvation to those whom society had abandoned to sin. Although a full conversion was not expected at the time of entering the institution, a woman was expected to confess her sin and to show her intention to live within the Christian faith.[29] Religious education was provided through daily prayers and through instruction given by the Ladies' Committee, the matron and the institution's chaplain or their equivalents, who spoke to women individually and in groups. Many of the Magdalene establishments provided worship twice a day, with a full service and religious lessons on Sundays. St Andrew's Home went beyond proselytizing its own Magdalenes and was also involved in very extensive missionary work in Edinburgh's Old Town, at that period the most impoverished and crime-ridden area of the city.[30] The managers and staff of the home were also involved in more traditional forms of education (ragged school and evening classes) which went beyond reforming 'fallen' women.[31]

The Magdalene establishments sought to transform the women into faithful Christians, who would trust God and treat the salvation of their souls as more important than any earthly needs or material aspirations. Revd James Peddie,[32] minister of the Bristo Street Secession Chapel in Edinburgh, in a sermon on behalf of the Edinburgh Magdalene Asylum in 1799, lamented that those not yet truly reformed would not 'be virtuous and starve' when faced with a choice between 'sin' or death.[33] A letter from a former occupant of the Edinburgh Rescue Home provided evidence of a successful conversion. She expressed her complete trust in God despite being

[28] *Report from the Directors of the Edinburgh Magdalene Asylum for 1827, 1828, & 1829* (Edinburgh, 1830), 16; *Report of the Society for the Support of the Edinburgh Magdalene Asylum, for 1843* (Edinburgh, 1844), 8.

[29] *Report from the Directors of the Edinburgh Magdalene Asylum for 1820* (Edinburgh, 1821), 6.

[30] Grant, *St Andrew's Home*, 3, 8.

[31] Ibid. 7.

[32] Kenneth B. E. Roxburgh, 'Peddie, James (1759–1845)', *ODNB*, online edn (23 September 2004), at: <https://doi.org/10.1093/ref:odnb/21753>, accessed 26 May 2018.

[33] James Peddie, *The Parable of the Lost Sheep explained and applied: A Sermon preached for the Benefit of the Edinburgh Philanthropic Society* (Edinburgh, 1799), 22.

anxious about her fate as she travelled to Australia: 'If we are right with God', she is said to have written, 'we do not need to care where we go, for He will take care of us. And now, dear Mr. and Mrs. Smith, I will bid you farewell. You will not hear from me till I get to the other side, that is to say, if spared.'[34] A Magdalene establishment was supposed to be, in the words of a former Magdalene, 'a door opened to me by the Lord'.[35] Indeed, it was sometimes literally a door to heaven. Some women were seriously ill when accepted to an institution and died during their stay, but it was said in the reports that they 'died in the placid hope of a joyful resurrection'.[36] A twenty-two-year-old woman was so weak that after being released from the Magdalene Asylum, she had to return to the institution after only six weeks of service in the countryside. Although she was facing death, it was reported that 'her conversations now breath the spirit of a true penitent and a genuine Christian … she is enabled to trust in [the] Saviour'.[37]

A truly converted penitent was supposed to blame herself for what she had gone through, even though the Magdalenes were simultaneously identified as passive objects rather than active agents in their fate and often described as 'poor' and 'unfortunate'. One former resident informed the committee in a letter from her new home in New York that she was 'ashamed of [her] past life'.[38] Another Magdalene wrote: 'O how I ought to bless the day, my footsteps were led to the Magdalene Asylum … . [It] has been the means, under God, of showing me my errors, and I humbly trust, of saving my precious soul!'[39]

The institutions' religious education was closely related to the behavioural education they offered. It is apparent from annual reports of the institutions examined in this article that their managers hoped that through developing habits of hard work in the laundry and sewing, and engaging in daily prayers and religious instruction, a 'fallen' woman could become a good domestic servant.

Humility and compliance were also seen as essential virtues to be learnt during the Magdalene training. They helped to avoid pride, one of the alleged causes of prostitution. One woman was sent

[34] *Rescue and Probationary Home for Fallen Women. Fourth Report* (Edinburgh, 1865), 4.

[35] *Report of the Edinburgh Magdalene Asylum 1830–2*, 13.

[36] Ibid. 16.

[37] *Report of the Edinburgh Magdalene Asylum 1833–5*, 11.

[38] *Report of the Edinburgh Magdalene Asylum 1830–2*, 11.

[39] Ibid. 15.

back to her parents in Aberdeen after the reformatory programme in Edinburgh. Her parents reported in their letter to the Magdalene Asylum that 'she appears very penitent, and that whereas formerly it was impossible to live with her, she is now as quiet and submissive as they could wish'.[40] The Canadian employer of a twenty-seven-year-old former Magdalene informed the Edinburgh Magdalene Asylum's matron that 'she has in every respect been what you or I could wish, and has on all occasions shewn herself most grateful and anxious to give satisfaction'; she asked whether the asylum could send her another such girl.[41] Including this story in a report acted as an encouragement for the readers to employ a Magdalene, who once reformed would be an ideal servant, grateful to work for a respectable family.

This submissive, acquiescent character was not, however, the only desirable educational outcome. It was hoped that women would also prove their independence and self-determination. St Andrew's Home reported that many Magdalenes were unwilling to enter domestic service and after the Magdalene training decided to return to their previous occupations as mill or factory girls.[42] This was not in line with the aims of the institutions, which saw domestic service, especially in the country, as more suitable for preserving a Magdalene's new-found morality. Some women continued to live and work within the institution. The Edinburgh Asylum related the story of a young woman, who after about a year of living in the asylum, was put in charge of the laundry and four years later was appointed a superintendent of the sewing section there. While visiting her family she met an old friend to whom she became engaged and, with the permission of the asylum's directors, they were married.[43] This young woman thus became an example for the Magdalenes and joined the circle of those who managed the institution.

Other women's stories were presented as successful, even when the women had left the institution against the directors' or matron's will. That was the case of E. F., who wrote to her matron:

[40] *Report* [from the Directors of the Edinburgh Magdalene Asylum for 1822?] (Edinburgh, [1823?]), 9.

[41] *Report of the Edinburgh Magdalene Asylum 1833–5*, 8.

[42] Grant, *St Andrew's Home*, 6.

[43] *Report by the Directors of the Edinburgh Magdalene Asylum, for the Year 1819* (Edinburgh, 1820), 8–9.

> I found from what you wrote, that you did not entirely approve of the step I was about to take. … It is now about four months since I left the Magdalene, and I am happy to inform you, that I have, in no instance, done any thing to incur the displeasure of the benevolent friends whom Providence has raised up for me.[44]

The institutions were supposed to teach 'habits of regularity and industry', as one of the Magdalenes described it, but these could be manifested in many ways.[45] The paths of the women after leaving the institutions varied. A successful education might sometimes lead to little more than reconciliation with friends and family or quitting an addiction. In 1822, the Edinburgh Magdalene Asylum accepted a woman who had been married twice and had several children; however, her second husband had abandoned them because of her drinking problem, and the children were taken care of by their maternal grandmother.[46] This woman spent around fifteen months in the institution and her mother took her back in October 1823 after receiving good reports of her behaviour.[47] Another widow, 'E. E.', 'fell into dissolute habits' after her husband's death. She spent two years in one institution, relapsed into her bad habits and was then taken in by the Rescue and Probationary Home. Two of her letters are quoted in the home's report. She wrote them from her new workplace, another Probationary Home, where she worked initially as a servant and later, having been promoted, was put in charge: 'Dear Friends, I think you will be pleased with my choice. I am safer here from many temptations than I would be out in a situation and I have it in my power to do a deal of good.'[48]

[44] *Report of the Edinburgh Magdalene Asylum 1830–2*, 14–15.

[45] *Report of the Edinburgh Magdalene Asylum 1833–5*, 12.

[46] What happened to 'fallen women' with dependent children is a topic that needs more research. At this stage, I have found no evidence that care for children was provided by the asylums, unless they were run by the Anglican sisters. It is important not to confuse the Scottish Magdalene establishments of that time with the later mother and baby homes which were created specially for pregnant women and had very different objectives to those of the Magdalenes. Later, in the twentieth century, some Magdalene Asylums changed their function (and name) and transformed into mother and baby homes. However, most women discussed here did not have children.

[47] *Report from the Directors of the Edinburgh Magdalene Asylum for 1823* (Edinburgh, 1824), 9.

[48] *Rescue and Probationary Home for Fallen Women. Fourth Report* (Edinburgh, 1865), 5–6.

In an earlier letter, E. E. confessed that her faith and self-discipline were not always exemplary.[49] Even though she experienced doubts and felt that she was not 'strong' enough to become a servant, the stability of her desire to change proved the Rescue's successful religious and moral education. Similarly, the Edinburgh Asylum's 1826 report admitted that 'a great proportion of the inmates' left against the director's will; yet, it reported, the asylum had accomplished its task: 'in many of these cases, the instructions they had received in the Asylums have been afterwards improved by them, and there is reason to believe that they had not returned to evil courses'.[50]

The religious and behavioural education offered by these institutions in turn formed an essential basis for effective industrial training. For all Magdalene establishments, it had 'always been considered a matter of the first importance to provide, so far as possible, for the future safety of those penitents who leave the Home'.[51] In order to do so, the establishments taught women skills that were essential for finding a job. Occupants were trained in the typical household duties required of a servant: sewing, laundry, cleaning, cooking and gardening. Louise Jackson, discussing twentieth-century English girls' homes, suggests that they acted as employment agencies that connected their wards with middle-class employers. The asylums discussed in this article similarly set as their goal the training of a reliable workforce. They can, therefore, be seen in the context of Prochaska's argument that the demand for servants was a contributing factor behind eighteenth- and nineteenth-century philanthropy of this kind.[52]

However, the aim of the industrial education seems to have been largely about self-discipline. Depending on the institutions women were employed in occupations which brought profit, such as calendaring, glazing fabric and (as already mentioned) sewing and laundry. In many instances, residents did not know how to undertake either basic household duties or perform typical working-class jobs such as sewing, working in a factory or a mill, and it was indeed crucial for

49 Ibid. 5.

50 *Report from the Directors of the Edinburgh Magdalene Asylum for 1824, 1825, & 1826* (Edinburgh, 1827), 14.

51 Grant, *St Andrew's Home*, 5.

52 Louise A. Jackson, '"Singing Birds as well as Soap Suds": The Salvation Army's Work with sexually abused Girls in Edwardian England', *GH* 12 (2000), 107–26, at 120–1.

them to learn these if they were to marry and have children or work. The Magdalene establishments, however, tended to emphasize training in laundry services and sewing, something that many residents had already been able to do before or would not need for future employment. Tait complained that the establishments were instructing women in precisely the trades that had led to their 'fall' in the first place, due to the low pay and high unemployment.[53] Unless we view this as managerial incompetence, it suggests that the key to Magdalene education was discipline and hard work, rather than a carefully designed 'professional training'. However, the often lengthy reformation time also served as an assessment period. Women had a chance to demonstrate their commitment to the establishments' values and thus earn merit to receive the letters of references essential to start their life anew. Thus it was not only a time of reformation but of continuous assessment of the institution's impact on a woman.

The Magdalene establishments' emphasis on occupying women with tasks in which they might have already been experienced and the very limited provision of intellectual education shows that the establishments conceived their educational role primarily as facilitating Christian conversion and providing moral training. Their aim was to shape the women into submissive workers, accustomed to a daily routine of hard work. In order to provide 'respectable' homes and pass on Christian values to their children, they needed to possess domestic skills, stay away from drinking and keep regular hours. The establishments were less concerned about teaching literacy and numeracy. It is likely that most of them provided lessons in reading, but classes in arithmetic or writing are very rarely mentioned. Even if these did exist, few hours were allocated for them, especially when compared to the time spent on manual tasks. Probably the women were taught as much as it was deemed necessary for them to be able to read the Bible and engage in religious devotion.

This educational approach certainly raises questions about the value of the Magdalene establishments' instruction. Even though many 'successfully reformed' occupants gained a degree of independence, it was limited. The institutions were concerned with training women of the lower social orders to be humble and efficient workers. They taught them to be content with their status in society and to know what this entailed. To be sure, a similar form of education

[53] Tait, *Magdalenism*, 245.

was being offered to most boys and girls of the labouring orders in Scotland at this time. Nonetheless, as the London Female Penitentiary put it, the institutions were, or sought to be, 'a school of virtue – [whose purpose is] to destroy the habits of idleness and vice, and to substitute those of honest and profitable industry, thus benefiting society whilst the individual is restored'.[54]

[54] Ibid. 246.

Scottish Presbyterianism and the National Education Debates, 1850–62

Ryan Mallon*
Queen's University Belfast

This article examines the mid-nineteenth-century Scottish education debates in the context of intra-Presbyterian relations in the aftermath of the 1843 'Disruption' of the Church of Scotland. The debates of this period have been characterized as an attempt to wrest control of Scottish education from the Church of Scotland, with most opponents of the existing scheme critical of the established kirk's monopoly over the supervision of parish schools. However, the debate was not simply between those within and outside the religious establishment. Those advocating change, particularly within non-established Presbyterian denominations, were not unified in their proposals for a solution to Scotland's education problem. Disputes between Scotland's largest non-established churches, the Free Church and the United Presbyterian Church, and within the Free Church itself over the type of national education scheme that should replace the parish schools severely hampered their ability to express common opposition to the existing system. These divisions also placed increasing strain on the developing cooperation in Scottish Dissent on ecclesiastical, political and social matters after the Disruption. This article places the issue of education in this period within this distinctly Dissenting context of cooperation, and examines the extent of the impact these debates had on Dissenting Presbyterian relations.

By the mid-nineteenth century, due to the growing political influence of organized religious Nonconformity and the pressure this group exerted on the church-state connection, the established churches' traditional monopoly over the educational provision for children in England, Scotland and Wales was waning.[1] The introduction in

* School of History, Anthropology, Philosophy and Politics, Queen's University Belfast, 25 University Sq, Belfast, BT7 1NN. E-mail: rmallon11@qub.ac.uk.

[1] D. G. Paz, *The Politics of Working-Class Education in Britain, 1830–50* (Manchester, 1980), 142–3; John Stevenson, 'Scottish Schooling in the Denominational Era', in Robert Anderson, Mark Freeman and Lindsay Paterson, eds, *The Edinburgh History of Education in Scotland* (Edinburgh, 2015), 133–52, at 135–40.

Studies in Church History 55 (2019), 363–380
doi: 10.1017/stc.2018.5

1831 of a state-run multi-denominational system of national education in Ireland weakened the Church of Ireland's position in society, and effectively led to its partial disestablishment through the 1833 Irish Church Temporalities Act.[2] As S. J. Brown has argued, the creation of a national and pluralist education scheme and the reduction of the established church in Ireland spelled the end of the Protestant establishment as 'a real force for the religious and moral instruction of the whole Irish people' and appeared to indicate that the position of the United Kingdom's other established churches, under pressure from the growth of militant Dissent, was also vulnerable.[3] Despite a brief yet significant revival of church schools in the late 1830s, the Whig government's attempts at reform from 1839 and the spectacularly successful Nonconformist opposition to Sir James Graham's 1843 Factory Bill dealt a serious blow to the prospect of a church-directed national education system and ensured that the tide appeared to be turning towards Dissent.[4] In essence, the education question formed part of the broader battle between the established churches and Dissent in the mid-nineteenth century.[5] Increasingly, debates on the future of national education in Britain were viewed as a struggle between the established churches, which were seeking to retain their statutory supremacy over the country's schools, and an apparently unified Dissenting interest growing in confidence and aiming to challenge the national churches' privileged position, both in education and in British society in general.[6]

In Scotland, this Dissenting interest was broadly represented by the National Education Association of Scotland (NEA). Formed in April 1850, the NEA was dominated by members of Scotland's two largest Dissenting Presbyterian denominations, the Free Church of Scotland and the United Presbyterian Church. The Free

[2] Donald H. Akenson, *The Irish Education Experiment: The National System of Education in the Nineteenth Century* (London, 1970), 113–22; John Coolahan, *Irish Education: Its History and Structure* (Dublin, 1981), 15–16.

[3] Stewart J. Brown, *The National Churches of England, Ireland, and Scotland, 1801–1846* (Oxford, 2001), 164, 169.

[4] Ibid. 213–15, 239–42, 341–4; Ian D. C. Newbould, 'The Whigs, the Church, and Education, 1839', *JBS* 26 (1987), 332–46; G. I. T. Machin, *Politics and the Churches in Great Britain, 1832 to 1868* (Oxford, 1977), 151–60.

[5] Machin, *Politics*, 165.

[6] Gerald Parsons, 'Reform, Revival and Realignment: The Experience of Victorian Anglicanism', in idem, ed., *Religion in Victorian Britain*, 1: *Traditions* (Manchester, 1988), 14–66, at 59–60.

Church had been formed in May 1843 following the Disruption, when four hundred and fifty ministers and almost half the laity seceded from the Church of Scotland in protest at the continued recognition of lay patronage and the state's perceived infringement of the Kirk's 'spiritual independence' and control over its own affairs. Founded in 1847, the United Presbyterian Church was an amalgamation of two older seceding groups, the United Secession and Relief Churches, which had split from the Kirk during the eighteenth century over the issue of patronage. These churches were represented in the NEA by leading figures such as the Free Church minister Thomas Guthrie, the Free Churchman and Liberal peer Fox Maule (later Lord Panmure) and John Brown, arguably the most influential minister in the United Presbyterian Church in this period.[7]

Unlike the Dissenting groups in England, which favoured full educational voluntaryism and opposed any plans for state intervention, the NEA proposed the creation of a comprehensive, non-denominational national education system, funded and organized by the state, and based on the opening up and extension of the existing parish school structure then under the sole authority of the Church of Scotland.[8] Replacing the church's ministers and heritors (landowners responsible for the upkeep of the parish church), they advocated the creation of local boards consisting of, and elected by, parents, ministers and ratepayers, and including members of all denominations. These boards would manage the schools, appoint teachers, determine the curriculum and be supervised by a central national board.[9] The first phase of the national education debates in Parliament, between 1850 and 1862, coincided with a period of transition in Scottish Dissent and in the relationship between the Free and United Presbyterian Churches. Although they had previously been bitter rivals, especially during the prolonged dispute over the church-state connection during the 1830s known as the 'voluntary controversy', by 1863 they had begun negotiations for formal ecclesiastical union. As Guthrie remarked, cooperation between the Free and United Presbyterian Churches in the NEA represented an 'auspicious

[7] *Report of the Proceedings of the Public Meeting of the Friends of National Education, in the Music Hall, Edinburgh, on Wednesday, January 24, 1854* (Edinburgh, 1854), 3–5.

[8] Timothy Larsen, *Friends of Religious Equality: Nonconformist Politics in Mid-Victorian England* (Woodbridge, 1999), 137–67.

[9] *The National Education Association of Scotland* (Edinburgh, 1850), 1–3.

omen' for the future union of Scotland's evangelical Dissenting churches.[10]

While Donald Withrington's excellent work on the divisions within the Free Church, and more recently John Stevenson's study on the Church of Scotland, have provided detailed insights into the key issues that underlay the debates, such as the contested role of religious instruction in schools, it is also important to place the education question in Scotland firmly within its religious context and to assess how the shifting mid-nineteenth-century Presbyterian landscape explicitly shaped the nature of the debates about education.[11] According to Stevenson, the Church of Scotland 'jealously guarded' both the historical link between the Kirk and Scottish education and its considerable powers over the supervision and inspection of the parish schools.[12] The impact of the Disruption, and the religious pluralism associated with Scottish society after 1843, heightened fears that the establishment would lose its privileged position with regard to parish schools and other public matters. This would especially prove the case after 1845, when the state took over administration of poor relief from the national church. The Poor Law Amendment Act removed yet another element of the established church's traditional control over Scottish society and fears that a similar change would occur in education resulted in a vigorous defence of the parish schools by the Kirk.[13] Drummond and Bulloch have argued that while Scotland remained overwhelmingly Presbyterian, the Disruption unleashed the same sectarian tensions that had gripped the education debates in England throughout the 1830s, with an increasingly powerful Dissenting group threatening the position of a debilitated and minority established church.[14] However, lingering divisions within Scottish Dissent, particularly between the Free and United Presbyterian churches, weakened attempts to create

[10] *Report of the Proceedings*, 56, 65–7.

[11] Donald J. Withrington, 'Adrift among the Reefs of conflicting Ideals? Education and the Free Church, 1843–55', in Stewart J. Brown and Michael Fry, eds, *Scotland in the Age of the Disruption* (Edinburgh, 1993), 79–97; John Stevenson, *Fulfilling a Vision: The Contribution of the Church of Scotland to School Education, 1772–1872* (Eugene, OR, 2012), 90–118.

[12] Stevenson, 'Scottish Schooling', 133.

[13] I. G. C. Hutchison, *A Political History of Scotland 1832–1924: Parties, Elections and Issues* (Edinburgh, 1986), 73.

[14] Andrew L. Drummond and James Bulloch, *The Church in Victorian Scotland, 1843–1874* (Edinburgh, 1975), 90–1.

a unified movement against the parish schools and, as Stevenson has claimed, prevented educational reform in Scotland until 1872.[15] By placing the Scottish education debates within the context of shifting Presbyterian relations, this article assesses the extent to which they can be viewed as a struggle between the establishment and Dissent, and whether a unified Dissenting voice against the state church, seemingly apparent in the NEA, actually existed in this period.

The Disruption, Presbyterian Relations, and the Parish Schools

To the Dissenters in the NEA, overhaul of the old parochial system was necessary to reinvigorate Scotland's withering educational provision. By the mid-nineteenth century, the Church of Scotland-run parish schools, intrinsically linked by supporters of the Kirk with Scottish national identity, had become antiquated, lacking in quantity and quality, and ill-suited to cope with the rapid societal changes associated with industrialization.[16] In the eyes of Dissenting critics, the parochial system was a grotesque illustration of the established church's 'supremacy' over Scottish education and indeed society in general.[17] These criticisms were exacerbated by the Disruption, a cataclysmic event that effectively split in two the national kirk, already weakened by the significant eighteenth-century secessions, and completely reshaped the Scottish religious landscape.[18]

The Disruption also effectively ended the Church of Scotland's claim to total control over education. As Callum Brown has argued, the parish school system traditionally formed an integral part of the Kirk's attempt to dominate all aspects of Scottish society. Whilst parish schools were open to all children regardless of denominational background, parochial teachers had to belong to the Church of Scotland and espouse its values.[19] However, despite the idealized vision of a 'school in every parish', the Church of Scotland was far

[15] Stevenson, 'Scottish Schooling', 148.

[16] George Lewis, *Scotland a Half-educated Nation, both in the Quantity and Quality of her Educational Institutions* (Glasgow, 1834), 75; Donald J. Withrington, 'The Free Church Educational Scheme, 1843–50', *RSCHS* 15 (1964), 103–15, at 104.

[17] David K. Guthrie and Charles J. Guthrie, *Autobiography of Thomas Guthrie, D.D., and Memoir by his Sons*, 2 vols (New York, 1875), 2: 291, 295.

[18] Brown and Fry, *Scotland*, viii–ix.

[19] Callum G. Brown, *The Social History of Religion in Scotland since 1730* (London, 1987), 98–9.

from exercising complete supremacy over Scottish education. In 1834, just over a fifth of Scotland's schools were part of the parish system.[20] A vast network of charity schools was provided in the Highlands by the Scottish Society for the Propagation of Christian Knowledge (which largely fell under the control of the Kirk) and the Edinburgh Society for the Support of Gaelic Schools, while by the 1850s nearly half of Scotland's schools were maintained by groups or private individuals with no formal attachment to any religious denomination.[21] Proliferation of Dissenting schools from the 1820s also led to increased denominational competition with the parish system, which would be intensified following the Privy Council Committee on Education's decision in 1846 to extend the system of grants to facilitate the building of schools by all Catholic and Protestant churches.

Nevertheless, it was the lingering perception of the educational supremacy of the established kirk, rather than the more complex reality, which fuelled Dissenting opposition to the parish system. The Reform Act of 1832 offered Scotland's Dissenters, mostly belonging to the urban middle class which benefited most from the extension of the franchise, a platform on which they could challenge the perceived hegemony of the religious and political establishment. Like the administration of poor relief, education was viewed within Scottish Dissent as another pillar of the old decaying order in which the established church exerted total dominance over Scottish society.[22] Constituting a minority of the Scottish population following the Disruption, the Church of Scotland's maintenance of its hitherto privileged position and control of the parish schools, compounded by its dismissal of over four hundred teachers who had sided with the Free Church, was condemned by its Dissenting opponents as 'the reverse of national – narrow, exclusive, and sectarian'.[23]

[20] Stevenson, 'Scottish Schooling', 137.

[21] Elizabeth Ritchie, '"Alive to the advantages of education". Problems in using the *New Statistical Account* to research Education: A Case Study of the Isle of Skye', *Northern Scotland* 7 (2016), 85–92, at 86; Withrington, 'Adrift', 80.

[22] This relationship between religious Nonconformity and political radicalism, and its challenge to the political and religious establishment, particularly regarding state education, was also a common feature in English Dissent: see, for example, Stephen Koss, *Nonconformity in Modern British Politics* (London, 1975); Larsen, *Friends*, 137–67.

[23] 'Scottish National Education', *North British Review* 12 (1849–50), 260–76, at 267; Joseph Fletcher, *Education: National, Voluntary, and Free* (London, 1851), 74.

Unsurprisingly, members of the established church were often openly critical of the NEA's motives, and very few supported the national education movement. In the eyes of the Kirk, Scotland's Dissenters were using education to reopen hostilities.[24]

The Disruption also had a significant impact on Dissenting relations in this period, as closer links were fostered between the Free Church and the United Presbyterian Church. Constituting roughly half the Scottish churchgoing population,[25] these two denominations forged a loose Dissenting alternative to the Church of Scotland through cooperation in the initial phases of the Evangelical Alliance (formed in 1846), territorial home mission work, and a highly successful electoral coalition based on shared opposition to the increased state endowment to the Roman Catholic seminary at Maynooth.[26] However, fundamental differences remained between the two churches, particularly regarding the church-state relationship. The United Presbyterians advocated the voluntary principle in religion and opposed the endowment of any religious denomination by the state. On the other hand, the Free Church, despite seceding from the established Church, retained the belief that the state should recognize and endow the national kirk, though without interfering in its internal affairs. The tension between the establishment and voluntary principles that had arisen during the 'voluntary controversy' of the 1830s occasionally plagued attempts at Dissenting cooperation after the Disruption. Nevertheless, the development of a Dissenting identity within the two churches after 1843 even stoked speculative attempts at union and the creation of a 'National Free Church' to rival and replace the state kirk. These attempts would lead to union negotiations from 1863 and culminated in the eventual creation of

[24] *A Voice from the Church, being a Review of the Resolutions and Speeches at the Public Meeting on National Education* (Edinburgh, 1854), 3.

[25] According to the 1851 religious census, the Free Church accounted for 32 per cent and the United Presbyterian Church 19 per cent of Scotland's churchgoing population. The established church also represented 32 per cent of Scots, while smaller Presbyterian denominations, such as the Reformed Presbyterian and Original Secession Churches, made up 2 per cent of churchgoers. The remaining 15 per cent comprised a growing Roman Catholic population, Episcopalians, Congregationalists, Baptists and Methodists: Brown, *Social History*, 61.

[26] For example, see the Dissent-dominated *Essays on Christian Union* (London, 1845); Thomas Chalmers, *Churches and Schools for the Working Classes* (Edinburgh, 1846); Gordon F. Millar, 'Maynooth and Scottish Politics: The Role of the Maynooth Grant Issue, 1845–1857', *RSCHS* 27 (1997), 220–79.

the United Free Church in 1900.[27] The emergence of the national education question after 1850 appeared to offer the two denominations another chance to work together under the umbrella of Dissent against the religious and political establishment. However, despite the movement's anti-establishment appeal, the alliance it created was very loose and exposed the limits and fragility of Dissenting unity in this period.

The debates and interests of this period must therefore be viewed in the context of Presbyterian relations after 1843, both between the establishment and Dissent, and within Dissent itself. While to some supporters the NEA represented an opportunity for Dissenting unity, for others denominational allegiances remained an integral part of the education debates. The Free Church minister and leading member of the NEA, Thomas Guthrie, argued that it was the 'duty' of Scottish Dissenters to cooperate to achieve reform. While the establishment's exclusive claim to the national schools presented an insurmountable 'barrier' to cooperation between all of Scotland's Presbyterians, Guthrie believed that the Free and United Presbyterian Churches were on a 'common path' regarding the future of Scottish education, and within the NEA could present a united front to the government.[28] However, this semblance of unity was dismissed within the Church of Scotland as hollow and a façade for underlying sectarian interests. According to one churchman, Scotland's Dissenters appeared to be 'willing to sacrifice the welfare of millions of their countrymen', so long as 'a Free Church can annoy an Established Church, or a voluntary procure a momentary triumph of his crotchety principle'.[29]

The first decade of the education debates in Scotland after 1850 needs to be viewed through the lens of these persisting sectarian tensions, perceived or otherwise, during the post-Disruption transition period. For instance, competing priorities and lingering divisions on principle within and between the Dissenting Presbyterian churches severely hampered any attempt at a unified national campaign for reform. Firstly, as the number of denominational schools grew considerably in this period, aided by the extended Privy

[27] George Sinclair, *A Letter addressed to the Non-established Presbyterian Communions of Scotland* (Edinburgh, 1854), 18–30.
[28] Guthrie and Guthrie, *Autobiography of Thomas Guthrie*, 2: 288–93.
[29] *The Education Question in Scotland* (Cupar, 1853), 5.

Council grants from 1846, the demand for a national education system was not even universal within Scottish Dissent.[30] After 1843 a large group led by Thomas Chalmers's heir-apparent, Robert Candlish, pursued the creation of a separate Free Church educational scheme designed to cater for the teachers dismissed following the Disruption, to rival the establishment's parish schools, and to support the new body's much-heralded claim to be the true Church of Scotland, with the status and obligations of a national kirk. Although the education scheme proved a qualified success, with 513 teachers and more than 44,000 pupils by 1847, it was opposed by a small but influential faction within the Free Church, led by Guthrie, James Begg and William Gunn. This faction believed that only a national, non-denominational system of education could fully reach the whole population, and dismissed Candlish's scheme as perpetuating sectarian conflict.[31] These divisions came to a head in a heated debate between Begg and Candlish at the 1850 Free Church General Assembly, which led both Guthrie and Gunn to resign from their posts on the Free Church's education committee.[32] As Withrington acknowledges, these disputes ensured that, within a decade of the Disruption, the Free Church was a 'house deeply, even irrevocably, divided against itself'.[33]

The Need for Reform

However, the increasing fragmentation of Scottish schooling documented in the 1851 census resulted in the realization within the main Dissenting churches that some kind of overarching reform was necessary to reverse the government's apparent acceptance of the institutionalized sectarianism of the denominational system and the Privy Council grants.[34] With the growing influence of the national education movement and the ever-increasing prospect of success in Parliament, the Free Church could not sit idly on the fence as Scotland's Dissenters debated their own vision of reform.

[30] Stevenson, 'Scottish Schooling', 138–41.

[31] For a detailed overview of the divisions within the Free Church, see Withrington, 'Free Church Educational Scheme', 103–15.

[32] *Elgin Courier*, 7 June 1850, 2; Guthrie and Guthrie, *Autobiography of Thomas Guthrie*, 2: 288; *Montrose, Arbroath and Brechin Review*, 5 July 1850, 7.

[33] Withrington, 'Adrift', 79–80.

[34] Stevenson, 'Scottish Schooling', 140–3.

A year after his confrontation with Begg, an ever shrewd and opportunistic Candlish, by now arguably the most prominent and influential Free Church minister, outlined proposals to the Privy Council on Education for his own national plan.[35] However, he asserted that any attempt at a national bill would not be at the expense of the maintenance of the Free Church's own denominational scheme. This rather tentative approval of reform failed to win over the Guthrie camp and bring about reconciliation between the church's conflicting parties.[36] Despite the opportunism of Candlish's decision, it at least ensured that by the early 1850s the majority of Presbyterian Dissenters were at least nominally in favour of some kind of national education system.

Nevertheless, divisions remained as to the details of any potential reform, and these would intensify as education became a central feature of parliamentary debates throughout the 1850s. Most of the divisions within the NEA and its membership centred on the disputed role of religious instruction, and its place or otherwise in any potential bill. Whilst a minority within the United Presbyterian Church sided with the secularists for the active exclusion of religion from any bill, the three major Presbyterian churches generally favoured some kind of religious influence in the schools. The majority in the Free Church, alongside their opponents in the establishment, believed that Scotland's schools should have an overtly religious character based on the teaching of the Bible and the Shorter Catechism. Unsurprisingly, Candlish advocated placing the reformed national schools under the management of the three main Presbyterian denominations, essentially replacing the existing Church of Scotland system with a broader Presbyterian one.[37]

The United Presbyterians and Guthrie's Free Church group, on the other hand, dismissed what they regarded as this outmoded connection between church, state and school, and argued that religious instruction, while an important element in the schools, should be separated from secular education. Concurring with the NEA's official stance, they proposed that while the state would solely administer secular education, the frequency and type of religious instruction should

[35] Education Commission (Scotland), *First Report by Her Majesty's Commissioners appointed to inquire into the Schools in Scotland* (Edinburgh, 1865), 107; 'National Education for Scotland', *Free Church Magazine* n.s. 2 (1853), 529–33.

[36] *Fife Herald*, 2 June 1853, 2.

[37] Robert Smith Candlish, *Letter to the Marquis of Lansdowne, on the Reform and Extension of the Parish School System of Scotland* (Edinburgh, 1851).

be decided by the popularly elected local boards and not by legislation. This proposal was aimed at finding common ground between Scotland's Presbyterians and was based on the assumption, scoffed at by Candlish, that the staunch Presbyterianism of the Scottish people would in any case safeguard the religious character of the school.[38] Advocating an even clearer distinction between religious and secular education, the United Presbyterians also called for separate stated hours for religious instruction, during which Dissenting or Roman Catholic parents could voluntarily withdraw their children, a proposal dismissed by the establishmentarian Free Churchman William Maxwell Hetherington as 'anti-theocratic'.[39] For their part, Guthrie and Begg were labelled 'atheists, deists, and infidels' by one Church of Scotland commentator.[40] While obvious differences on religious instruction exacerbated the conflict between the establishment and Dissent, the internal disputes within Dissent continued to threaten cooperation within the NEA. When the education question was put to Parliament after 1850, the policy of forbearance deployed in other areas of Dissenting cooperation after 1843 was deemed necessary to secure the success of such an uneasy coalition.

The National Education Bills

Between 1850 and 1862, seven major Scottish education bills were introduced into Parliament, six of which aimed to implement the aims of the NEA for a comprehensive state-funded education system. Predictably, the chief areas of distinction between these bills concerned the constituency of the proposed central board and, most significantly, the role of religious instruction in the national scheme. Despite the often confrontational character associated with the education debates, attempts at cooperation, especially among the non-established Presbyterians, were a central feature of the efforts to achieve a national system.

The introduction of Lord Melgund's national education bills in 1850 and 1851 thrust this apparent desire for Dissenting cooperation into the spotlight. These bills, focusing purely on secular education

[38] *Report of the Proceedings*, 46, 61, 64–5; *Caledonian Mercury*, 12 November 1849, 2–3.
[39] 'Scotland', *Christian Witness and Church Members' Magazine* 7 (1850), 186–8, at 187.
[40] 'Tests, or no Tests', *MacPhail's Edinburgh Ecclesiastical Journal and Literary Review* 11 (1851), 208–26, at 225.

and including no faith requirement for schoolmasters, left considerable power in the hands of the parish ministers and heritors. Despite this concession to the established church, the United Presbyterian Church expressed its 'strenuous' support for Melgund's proposals and called for unified Dissenting support.[41] The Free Church *North British Review* agreed and claimed that 'a union on the part of the great dissenting bodies of Scotland' was essential to the success of Melgund's bill. However, it also noted that the only difference between the Free and United Presbyterian Churches was the means by which this common object could be achieved, a view echoed by Melgund, who admitted that the issue of religious instruction presented the 'only difficulty in the way of a complete union betwixt the United Presbyterian Church and the Free Church' on education.[42] Despite the conciliatory stance offered by Begg and Gunn, the *Caledonian Mercury* claimed that Candlish's insistence on 'a distinct and direct recognition of religious instruction by the state' ensured that he and the Free Kirk majority were 'rowing in the same boat' as members of the established church, and 'on a tack the very opposite to the United Presbyterian Synod'.[43] This suspicion as to Candlish's motives would ultimately prove correct, as the Free Church leader skilfully undermined the NEA throughout the debates and persuaded home secretary Lansdowne to oppose Melgund's 'secular' measure in favour of an overtly religious system.[44] One Dissenter lambasted Candlish's somewhat Machiavellian opposition to Melgund's proposals, accusing the Free Church of acting as the 'self-elected patron and dictator of the education and religion of the youth of Scotland'.[45] The general hostility of the Free Church lobby, the obstinate attitude of the establishment and the lack of cohesion within the Dissenting churches in the NEA were an 'embarrassment' to Melgund and his supporters, and contributed to the narrow defeats of his bills in the House of Commons.[46] Guthrie condemned the continued partisanship of the debates, which he

[41] 'National Education', *United Presbyterian Magazine* 3 (1849), 20–2; *The Scotsman*, 6 October 1849, 2.
[42] 'Scottish National Education', 268; *Caledonian Mercury*, 5 November 1849, 2; ibid., 15 November 1849, 2–3.
[43] *Caledonian Mercury*, 12 November 1849, 2–3.
[44] Hutchison, *Political History*, 74.
[45] *Elgin Courier*, 14 March 1851, 4.
[46] Stevenson, 'Scottish Schooling', 144.

claimed saw the 'best interests' of the country and the churches, and the potential for a successful reform measure, 'sacrificed to extreme Establishment views on the one hand, and extreme Voluntaryism on the other'.[47]

The loss of momentum in the national education movement that coincided with Melgund's defeat did not last long. Within two years, the issue was taken up by the Lord Advocate and Free Churchman James Moncreiff, who would go on to introduce five education bills over the next decade. Moncreiff's zealous commitment to a national education system galvanized renewed calls for Dissenting cooperation, even from the most unlikely corners. At the Edinburgh Free Presbytery in late 1853, William Cunningham argued that 'a national system of education, based on right principles, could bring together the different evangelical denominations in friendly co-operation, and without compromise of their principles'.[48] However, critics within the Church of Scotland dismissed Cunningham's apparent olive branch to the voluntaries as a mere façade for denominational interests. This claim was criticized by the Free Church-supporting *Scottish Guardian* as an 'idle' attempt to sow the 'seeds of discord' among Scottish Dissenters.[49] Nevertheless, the occasional confrontation over religious instruction within the NEA, such as that between Cunningham and the United Presbyterian minister John Cairns at the society's Edinburgh meeting in January 1854, offered further evidence for the establishment's belief that the Dissenting alliance was 'an incongruous, dislocated mass' simply aiming at attacking the parish schools.[50] Support for the movement within the Free and United Presbyterian Churches and its attempt to foster Dissenting union were also questioned by the establishment. One Church of Scotland commentator noted the 'limited attendance' of Free Churchmen at a meeting in Glasgow and claimed that the United Presbyterian ministers who called the two meetings represented 'only a fraction' of the denomination. Candlish's 'careful' decision to avoid the Edinburgh event also implied to the writer that 'the clerical Pope of the Free Church' did

[47] Guthrie and Guthrie, *Autobiography of Thomas Guthrie*, 2: 298.

[48] 'National Education for Scotland', *Free Church Magazine* n.s. 2 (1853), 529–34, at 533.

[49] *Education Question*, 5; *Scottish Guardian*, 13 January 1854, 2.

[50] *Report of the Proceedings*, 72, 83–91; *Voice from the Church*, 3–5.

'not exactly agree' with the movement.[51] The Church of Scotland minister John MacDuff argued that there was a growing disparity between the Free Church membership and its leaders such as Guthrie, who were deemed to be needlessly perpetuating schism between the Free and established churches, and harming any 'dream' of reunion between the two denominations.[52] To the establishment, the coalition of Dissenters in the NEA represented 'no union' on Protestant principles.[53]

While differences certainly remained within the national education movement, the belief of the United Presbyterian minister John Harper that Scotland's Dissenters had a duty to set aside their smaller, seemingly surmountable differences for the common good of an improved education system was a common theme of NEA meetings in this period.[54] The perceived success of this reinvigorated Dissenting alliance was such that Guthrie viewed the Edinburgh meeting and the intended national system as a prelude both to Dissenting union and to Scotland attaining 'in the true sense of the expression, a National Church'.[55] The introduction of Moncreiff's bill coincided with a series of private conferences organized by George Sinclair and John Brown, which appeared to be 'preparing the way for union' between the Free and United Presbyterian Churches.[56] While the education question and its various disputes appeared to many as an 'obstruction' to such attempts to unite Scotland's Dissenters, Moncreiff believed that it instead 'prove[d] most forcibly the need for union' as envisioned by Brown and Sinclair, and 'demonstrate[d] the injury which the country and religion suffer from our divisions'.[57]

This optimism and desire for union would ultimately prove hollow when Moncreiff brought forward his first national education bill to the House of Commons late in February 1854. Generally, the bill built upon Melgund's earlier proposals, including the abolition of

[51] *Dundee Courier*, 15 February 1854, 4.

[52] *Aberdeen Press and Journal*, 15 February 1854, 7.

[53] *Voice from the Church*, 4.

[54] 'National Education', *United Presbyterian Magazine* 8 (1854), 141–4, at 142.

[55] *Report of the Proceedings*, 56, 65–7.

[56] 'Sir George Sinclair on Union between the Free and United Presbyterian Churches', *United Presbyterian Magazine* 8 (1854), 352–6, at 353–4; Robert Rainy and James Mackenzie, *Life of William Cunningham* (London, 1871), 259.

[57] Guthrie and Guthrie, *Autobiography of Thomas Guthrie*, 2: 300.

the confessional test for teachers and the creation of a system of local and national boards to replace the management and control of the establishment. However, as the English radical politician Richard Cobden noted in a letter to the Scottish lawyer George Combe, Moncreiff's desire to appease the various churches led to a disjointed and inconsistent bill that pleased no one.[58] Most significantly, his determination to secure the place of religious instruction in the national school curriculum hardened sectarian attitudes within the United Presbyterian Church, and led to a division within the NEA.[59] While the run-up to the bill had witnessed Scotland's evangelical Dissenters meeting on a united platform, an exclusive meeting of United Presbyterians was held in its aftermath to defend and reassert the church's denominational interests in the face of what they regarded as an unpalatable blueprint for national education. According to James Peddie and John Brown, clause twenty-seven of Moncreiff's bill, which stipulated that the state should legislate and pay for religious teaching in the schools, did 'violence to the religious convictions' of their fellow United Presbyterians and was 'at variance with the voluntary principle'. The United Presbyterian minister George Johnston also criticized Free Churchmen such as Candlish, Buchanan and Cunningham for infiltrating the NEA platform to 'advocate an opposite system' and thereby diluting and harming the influence and principles of the association and the United Presbyterian Church.[60]

This meeting provided the first indication that even those within the NEA most favourable towards united action were beginning to turn inwards and defend their own sectarian interests, neglecting the Dissenting label increasingly associated with the Free and United Presbyterian Churches after 1843. At a tense meeting of the NEA in Edinburgh two weeks later, the voluntary opposition to Moncreiff's bill was criticized by Fox Maule, who stressed the need for compromise to achieve reform.[61] The lack of cooperation associated with the bill was condemned by Moncreiff himself in a letter to Guthrie in the wake of the United Presbyterian meeting.

58 Richard Cobden to George Combe, 24 February 1854, in Anthony Howe and Simon Morgan, eds, *The Letters of Richard Cobden*, 3: *1854–1859* (Oxford, 2012), 16.
59 HC Deb (3rd series), vol. 130, col. 1167 (23 February 1854).
60 *The Scotsman*, 12 April 1854, 4.
61 *The Witness*, 29 April 1854, 5.

He wrote that he was 'thoroughly disgusted and sickened with the violence of the Established Church on the one hand, and of the extreme section of the voluntaries on the other'. Moncreiff also warned the United Presbyterians that unless they presented voluntaryism in a less offensive light it would 'put an end to all hope of union'.[62] The need for mutual forbearance was emphasized once again by Guthrie, who urged the supporters of national education to lay aside their denominational principles temporarily in favour of the national interest.[63] Despite Guthrie's best efforts, the open hostility within Presbyterian Dissent, combined with the surprisingly optimistic returns of the 1851 census on Scottish schooling and the opposition of English Tory MPs to any encroachment on the established schools in England or Scotland, ensured that Moncreiff's bill was defeated by nine votes in the House of Commons.[64]

The failure of two subsequent bills in 1855 and 1856 cemented the renewed sectarianism of the Dissenting churches and effectively killed off the anti-Maynooth electoral coalition that had dominated Scottish politics for over a decade.[65] The *Scottish Guardian* blamed the voluntaries, 'who have done nothing themselves for the education of the people', for persisting in 'obtruding their preposterous crotchets' in the way of a government 'desirous of supplying their deficiencies'. The demise of Moncreiff's national project saw a swift return to pre-existing denominational interests, with the *Guardian* calling on fellow Free Churchmen to fall back on their own education scheme with 'fresh ardour and success'.[66] This was echoed by Candlish, who urged them to renew their commitment to the Free Church scheme, which he felt had been held back for 'far too long' by the 'distraction' of national education.[67]

The increasing gulf between Scotland's Dissenters was exacerbated by the prospect, emanating from the Church of Scotland, of closer links between the Free and established churches, based on a common

62 Guthrie and Guthrie, *Autobiography of Thomas Guthrie*, 2: 299–300.
63 *The Witness*, 29 April 1854, 5.
64 *Glasgow Constitutional*, 28 March 1855, 4.
65 *Caledonian Mercury*, 20 March 1857, 2; *Paisley Herald and Renfrewshire Advertiser*, 4 April 1857, 1.
66 *Scottish Guardian*, 27 July 1855, 1.
67 *Proceedings and Debates in the General Assembly of the Free Church of Scotland, held at Edinburgh, May 1857* (Edinburgh, 1857), 255, 260–2, 266.

stance on education, and in particular the role of religion in the schools. At a Glasgow meeting in 1859, the established churchman and Conservative politician Archibald Orr-Ewing argued that while the Free Church appeared willing to work with the national kirk, the United Presbyterians presented the 'great difficulty' to Presbyterian cooperation. This claim was refuted by the United Presbyterian minister James Taylor, who maintained that it was the Church of Scotland's opposition to Moncreiff's proposals which prevented the passing of any national reform bill.[68] Despite some optimistic attempts to foster cooperation within the Presbyterian churches, such as the rather unrealistic 1857 public resolutions for Dissenting union by George Sinclair, by the early 1860s it had become clear to Moncreiff that educational reform could only be achieved 'bit-by-bit'.[69] The subsequent success of his 1861 proposal to simply abolish the religious tests for teachers in the parochial and burgh schools paid dividends for this more piecemeal plan, although the failure of a more extensive measure a year later proved that sectarian animosities remained a significant barrier to a fully national system.[70]

It is clear, then, that the first decade of the Scottish education debates after 1850 cannot be viewed as a simple conflict between the establishment and Dissent. While the Church of Scotland's continued claim to the national schools offered those outside the establishment a common platform on which to unite, the shifting and complicated nature of Dissenting relations ultimately scuppered the optimism and cooperation originally associated with the NEA. The Free Church's reluctance to support plans for a national system owed much to the belief that it represented the true Church of Scotland, with all the privileges such a position entailed. The insistence by Candlish and his supporters on the central role of religion in the proposed national schools, based on the Free Church's commitment to the church-state connection, was at odds with United Presbyterian voluntaryism. This difference in principle would impact on all Dissenting cooperation and would prove a significant barrier to union between the two churches for over half a century. The education debates also reignited hostilities between the major Presbyterian

[68] *Glasgow Herald*, 15 January 1859, 3.
[69] *Glasgow Herald*, 4 May 1857, 2; *John O'Groat's Journal*, 18 July 1861, 2.
[70] *Elgin Courier*, 26 April 1861, 5.

churches, proving a threat to Dissenting cooperation in other areas such as politics, while helping to cement the sectarian divisions associated with the Disruption era. The fundamental failure of the NEA in this period was its inability to reconcile these differences and offer a 'common path' for Scotland's Dissenters on which they, like fellow Nonconformists in Ireland, could adjust their relationships among themselves and with the evolving state to meet the changing circumstances of a society in which the churches appeared to have an increasingly loose hold.[71] Lingering denominational jealousies and the lack of a clear, united Presbyterian voice would ensure that no single church in Scotland had control of the education debates as they entered their second, conclusive decade.[72]

[71] Christopher F. McCormack, 'The Irish Church Disestablishment Act (1869) and the General Synod of the Church of Ireland (1871): The Art and Structure of Educational Reform', *HE* 47 (2018), 303–20, at 319–20.
[72] Stevenson, *Fulfilling a Vision*, 118.

Exporting Godliness: The Church, Education and 'Higher Civilization' in the British Empire from the late Nineteenth Century

Mark Chapman*
Ripon College, Cuddesdon

This article discusses the impact of the educational method pioneered in the English public schools on the development of education in Anglican schools in the British empire, with a particular focus on the Indian subcontinent from the turn of the twentieth century until the outbreak of the First World War. It discusses how the focus of missionary activity changed from a desire for overt evangelism into a sense of the transmission of moral and ethical values though a system of education in the Christian virtues. An educational understanding of salvation began to supplant the doctrinal. This is connected with the thinking on 'higher' and 'lower' civilizations of the period. A central focus is on the preparatory work for, and discussions around, the Pan-Anglican Congress of 1908 and the role played by Bishop H. H. Montgomery.

Religious revival in the nineteenth-century Church of England was, at least in part, centred on different understandings of what is inevitably the somewhat elusive idea of truth. While evangelicals and Tractarians both upheld very particular concepts of truth, which they identified in terms of their differing ecclesiologies, both parties agreed in locating truth within the confines of the Church, guaranteed by its Scriptures and tradition. A desire to share such Christian truth quickly provided a huge impetus for mission, including its educational work. Yet these partisan models were certainly not the sole expressions of Anglican understandings of truth, which some refused to locate within the confines of the visible church. For many – indeed, perhaps most – Anglicans, the idea that the Church was in exclusive possession of the truth was highly contested: a classical education revealed a far broader conception of truth. The paradigms of truth and, by extension, of salvation offered by the church parties were

* Ripon College, Cuddesdon, Oxford, OX44 9EX. E-mail: Mark.chapman@rcc.ac.uk.

Studies in Church History 55 (2019), 381–409
doi: 10.1017/stc.2018.6

far from dominant. For many in the Church of England, both at home and overseas, the Christian religion was but one expression of a wider understanding of truth, which was also to be found beyond the confines of the Church and which was to be acquired through education in the human virtues. On this model, Christianity was intimately connected with an educational model based on the idea of a growth into truth through the development of character. For many missionaries, the Christian religion was to be propagated through this educational paradigm rather than by dogmatic teaching. Indeed, many of those in the mission field, especially in those places where converts were few, soon began to realize that neither godliness nor civilization – the principal goals of education – were confined to Christianity. I would consequently suggest that Norman Etherington's statement that '[f]ew missionaries treated education as an end in itself; schooling was ancillary to the primary object of Christian evangelism' needs some nuancing.[1] While it may have been an accurate account of the impetus behind Christian mission in the first place, many missionaries through the nineteenth century came to see education rather than conversion as the primary means of Christian evangelism: an educational understanding of salvation began to supplant the doctrinal.

This article traces some aspects of this emphasis on education in the human virtues as it developed in missionary thinking in the British empire. Its time frame is limited to the late nineteenth and early twentieth centuries and its focus is on the Anglican Communion. Its main concern is with those churches that grew in places where there were already well-established world religions: in the deeply problematic racialist jargon of the time, I am interested in what were called the 'higher civilizations'. Evangelism, education and salvation, I would suggest, came to be understood as aspects of the same process, which did not necessarily require explicit acceptance of Christian doctrines.[2] These 'higher civilizations', which were normally identified with the societies of the East, especially those of India and Ceylon (Sri Lanka), China and Japan, were frequently understood as capable of expressing something of the virtues of Christianity as it was realized in universal human truths.

[1] Norman Etherington, 'Education and Medicine', in idem, ed., *Missions and Empire*, Oxford History of the British Empire Companion Series (Oxford, 2005), 261–84, at 261.
[2] See Hayden J. A. Bellenoit, *Missionary Education and Empire in Late Colonial India, 1860–1920* (Abingdon and New York, 2007).

The question of religion and the closely related theme of missionary education in the British empire are obviously hotly contested and complex,[3] not least when considering the developments at the turn of the twentieth century in Asia which form the main focus of this article. It is often difficult to extract missionary from imperialist goals: as Etherington suggests in the introduction to *Missions and Empire*, 'although missions and the official Empire were quite different operations, they play related parts in a larger drama – the spread of modernization, globalization, and Western cultural hegemony'.[4] At the same time, there was undoubtedly what Andrew Porter calls 'a subtle interplay of influences in missionary encounters with non-European peoples'.[5] Especially with reference to Asia, there was a complex set of interactions that make simple identifications of the Bible and the flag highly problematic. The impact of mission on the critique of the imperial project, as well as on the development of nationalism, and even in the formation of clearer non-Christian religious identities in British colonies is much contested.[6] In colonial Ceylon, for instance, there was even use of the concept of 'protestant Buddhism'.[7] What is undisputed, however, is that there is a close

[3] On this, see, for instance, Etherington, ed., *Missions and Empire*; Pieter N. Holtrop and Hugh McLeod, eds, *Missions and Missionaries*, SCH Subsidia 13 (Woodbridge, 2000); Steven S. Maughan, *Mighty England do Good: Culture, Faith, and World in Foreign Missions of the Church of England, 1850–1915*, SHCM (Grand Rapids, MI, 2014); Joseph Hardwick, *An Anglican British World: The Church of England and the Expansion of the Settler Empire,* c.*1790–1860* (Manchester, 2014); Hilary Carey, *God's Empire: Religion and Colonialism in the British World,* c.*1801–1908* (Cambridge, 2011); eadem, ed., *Empires of Religion* (New York, 2008); Andrew Porter, *Religion versus Empire? British Protestant Missionaries and Overseas Expansion, 1700–1914* (Manchester, 2004), especially 282; idem, ed., *The Imperial Horizons of British Protestant Missions, 1880–1914*, SHCM (Grand Rapids, MI, 2003); Brian Stanley, *The Bible and the Flag; Protestant Missionaries and British Imperialism in the Nineteenth and Twentieth Centuries* (Leicester, 1990). For a ground-breaking account which already pays attention to post-colonial issues, see Max Warren, *The Missionary Movement from Britain in Modern History* (London, 1965).

[4] Etherington, ed., *Missions and Empire*, 4.

[5] Porter, *Religion versus Empire?*, 321.

[6] Brian Stanley, 'Church, State and the Hierarchy of "Civilization"', in Porter, ed., *Imperial Horizons*, 58–84, especially 69–73.

[7] See, for example, Stephen C. Berkwitz, 'Hybridity, Parody, and Contempt: Buddhist Responses to Christian Missions in Sri Lanka', in Heather J. Sharkey, ed., *Cultural Conversions: Unexpected Consequences of Christian Missionary Encounters in the Middle East, Africa, and South Asia* (Syracuse, NY, 2013), 99–120; Elizabeth Harris, *Theravada Buddhism and the British Encounter: Religious, Missionary, and Colonial Experience in Nineteenth-Century Sri Lanka* (London, 2006). See also Shanthikumar Hettiarachchi, *Faithing the Native Soil: Dilemmas and Aspirations of post-colonial*

connection between the development of Christianity and the spread of empire, and that both were related to broader understandings of race and progress. What is striking about missions to Asia is the lack of success in conversions, especially among the cultural and social elite. While many might have been inspired by the great commission at the end of Matthew's Gospel to go out and baptize, there was very limited success. At the same time, however, missions became crucial in the establishment of educational institutions, which became increasingly respectful of indigenous religions and cultures. Indeed, although it falls outside the scope of this article, there was significant interest in categorizing and shaping the religions themselves, as C. A. Bayly has suggested in his lengthy discussion of religious encounter: 'the emerging world of print and the public sphere promoted religions as much as philosophical or political beliefs'.[8] Evolutionary ideas of religion, with the categorization of so-called 'advanced religions', along with related ideas of a hierarchy of races and higher cultures, all of which feature in the literature discussed here, are a key aspect of the imperial educational project which is particularly important in the Indian sub-continent, where many parallels were drawn between Western and Eastern religions, and where in the process the religions themselves were frequently reshaped.[9]

As they grew through the nineteenth century, educational missions became increasingly important as a key mechanism for carrying a set of ideas with an accompanying ethos across the British empire. In this they mirrored something of the domestic educational ideals of broad

Buddhists and Christians in Sri Lanka (Colombo, 2012). More generally, see Kenneth Cracknell, *Justice, Courtesy and Love: Missionaries and Theologians Encountering the World Religions, 1846–1914* (London, 1995), 181–260; Warren, *Missionary Movement*, 119–38.

[8] C.A. Bayly, *The Birth of the Modern World, 1780–1914: Global Connections and Comparisons* (Oxford, 2004), 325. See also Todd M. Thompson, 'Charles Malik and the Origins of a Christian Critique of Orientalism in Lebanon and Britain', in Charlotte Methuen, Andrew Spicer and John Wolffe, eds, *Christianity and Religious Plurality*, SCH 51 (Woodbridge, 2015), 350–65.

[9] Bayly, *Birth of the Modern World*, 332. For examples of cultural encounter, see Amiya P. Sen, ed., *Social and Religious Reform: The Hindus of British India* (Oxford, 2003); Peter van der Veer, *Imperial Encounters: Religion and Modernity in India and Britain* (Princeton, NJ, 2001); Justin Jones, 'Islam at Home: Religion, Piety and Private Space in Muslim India and Victorian Britain, *c.*1850–1905', in John Doran, Charlotte Methuen and Alexandra Walsham, eds, *Religion and the Household*, SCH 50 (Woodbridge, 2014), 378–404.

church Anglicanism as it had developed earlier in the century. The term 'broad church' itself emerged in the 1840s, supposedly in a sermon of 1847 by Arthur Penrhyn Stanley, the future dean of Westminster,[10] and was later used by W. J. Conybeare in his famous essay 'Church Parties', published in the *Edinburgh Review* during 1853.[11] Key to the broad church understanding of Christianity was a belief that it was not *sui generis* but was part of a shared human quest for truth. As many have observed,[12] there was an underlying Platonism to broad churchism: nothing could contain the whole of truth, since truth was ultimately to be found only with God. Such an understanding of Anglicanism was promoted by Thomas Arnold through his reforms at Rugby,[13] and quickly achieved dominance in the ethos which became established at the public schools. Many public school headmasters were appointed to the bench of bishops, including James Prince Lee of King Edward VI School in Birmingham, who became bishop of Manchester,[14] as well as Edward White Benson, first headmaster of Wellington College, and A. C. Tait and Frederick Temple, both headmasters of Rugby, all of whom became archbishops of Canterbury. The impact of the public school ethos spread far and wide: the vast majority of those entering colonial church leadership had passed through the public school system and had imbibed its educational ethos.

As they developed through the nineteenth century, boys' schools were to serve to help make boys into men through a combination of the practical with the intellectual.[15] This is what was meant by education in 'manliness' (*thymos*), which was closely related to the Greek aristocratic notion of *aretē*, a notion shared by the Romans, as well as Renaissance thinkers. This form of virtue ethics, as the practical expression of Christian truth, made an enormous impact on the

[10] See Owen Chadwick, *The Victorian Church*, 1: *1829–1859* (London, 1987), 544. There does not appear to be any record of the sermon itself.

[11] Reprinted and edited by Arthur Burns as 'Church Parties', in Stephen Taylor, ed., *An Anglican Miscellany*, CERS 7 (Woodbridge, 1999), 213–385.

[12] For a synopsis of broad church thinking, see Mark Chapman, 'Liberal Anglicanism in the Nineteenth Century', in Rowan Strong, ed., *OHA*, 3: *Partisan Anglicanism and its Global Expansion, 1829–c.1914* (Oxford, 2017), 212–31.

[13] See Eugene L. Williamson Jr, *The Liberalism of Thomas Arnold: A Study of his Religious and Political Writings* (University, AL, 1964).

[14] See David Newsome, *Godliness and Good Learning* (London, 1961).

[15] Girls' schools were to develop much later; as late as 1864 there were only twelve public secondary schools for girls in England.

development of the public school ethos, as well as that of the universities, through Arnold and many others. As Edward Thring, headmaster of Uppingham School from 1853 to 1887, put it: 'The whole efforts of a school ought to be directed to making boys manly, earnest and true. … First make them true, make them men, by the work and life in and out of school'.[16] The cultivation of what to future generations might have been considered an effete and perhaps even effeminate form of manliness was well expressed by B. F. Westcott, who would become not only bishop of Durham and one of the greatest Cambridge New Testament scholars of his generation, but also the father of four missionaries to India, two of whom will be discussed below. At the beginning of 1849, he wrote to his future wife:

> You have often heard my views of life, yet hear them once again … . To live is not to be gay or idle or restless. Frivolity, inactivity, and aimlessness seem equally remote from the true idea of living. I should say that we live only so far as we cultivate all our faculties, and improve all our advantages for God's glory. The means of living then will be our own endowments, whether of talent or influence; the aim of living, the good of man; the motive of living, the love of God.[17]

For Westcott, as for Arnold, all human faculties were to be improved for the glory of God.

While, for some, such an educational model of Christianity as growth into God's truth was disparaged as liberalism, it nevertheless had many advantages for Christian mission in places where there was little hope (or evidence) of mass conversion. In British India, for instance, as Etherington notes: 'When boarding schools sprang up, they acquired some of the characteristics of elite public schools in the British Isles.'[18] Indeed, 'in many places the term "native elite" was synonymous with "Christian-educated"'.[19] Where conversions were few, formation of character, rather than explicit evangelization, became central to the principles of missionary education. The reasons for this were simple: on the one hand, the instinct for Christian

[16] Edward Thring, *Education and School* (London, 1867), 269–70; see also H. D. Rawnsley, *Edward Thring: Teacher and Poet* (London, 1889), 12.

[17] Arthur Westcott, *Life and Letters of Brooke Foss Westcott*, 2 vols (London, 1903), 145.

[18] Etherington, 'Education and Medicine', 265. On missionary education in India, see Robert Eric Frykenberg, *Christianity in India: From Beginnings to the Present* (Oxford, 2008), 301–43.

[19] Etherington, 'Education and Medicine', 273.

survival in an often hostile environment meant that there was a need to respect pre-existing religious and cultural traditions. On the other hand, there was also a more positive sense in which the desire to educate people into a universal truth meant that missionaries were able to see aspects of this truth in non-Christian religious traditions. This allowed for a form of pluralism (which had already been tacitly recognized through a public school curriculum based on the pagan classics of Greece and Rome). Indeed, there were strong similarities between education in the classics of the Greco-Roman world, which dominated the syllabus of English further and higher education, and respect for the texts and traditions of the great world religions of the East.

Henry Hutchinson Montgomery

I begin my discussion of the shift in Christian missions towards a more educational ideal using the example of Henry Hutchinson Montgomery (1847–1932),[20] general secretary of the Society for the Propagation of the Gospel (SPG) from 1901, and previously bishop of Tasmania, who was to dominate early twentieth-century Anglican missionary thinking.[21] Despite the existence of the semi-official and partially established historic missionary societies, much Church of England mission had been something of a private enterprise, and was often dominated by enthusiasts from the different church parties.[22] However, by the turn of the century there was a degree of consolidation in Church of England missionary thinking. This was in part

[20] On Montgomery, see Steven Maughan, 'An Archbishop for Greater Britain: Bishop Montgomery, missionary imperialism and the SPG, 1897–1915', in Daniel O'Connor, ed., *Three Centuries of Mission: The United Society for the Propagation of the Gospel 1701–2000* (London, 2000), 358–70; idem, 'Imperial Christianity? Bishop Montgomery and the Foreign Missions of the Church of England, 1895–1915' in Porter, ed., *Imperial Horizons*, 32–57; idem, 'Montgomery, Henry Hutchinson (1847–1932)', *ODNB*; M. M., *Bishop Montgomery, with a Preface by the Archbishop of Canterbury* (London, 1933). For an insightful account of Montgomery's background, see Robert S. M. Withycombe, *Montgomery of Tasmania: Henry and Maud Montgomery in Australasia* (Brunswick East, Victoria, 2009).

[21] Henry H. Montgomery, *Foreign Missions*, 4th edn (London, 1909; first publ. 1904).

[22] For overviews, see Mark D. Chapman, *Anglicanism: A Very Short Introduction* (Oxford, 2006); W. M. Jacob, *The Making of the Anglican Church Worldwide* (London, 1997); Kevin Ward, *A History of Global Anglicanism* (Cambridge, 2006). Most comprehensive is now Maughan, *Mighty England*.

focused on the person of Montgomery, who proved more capable of working across the partisan divides than his more angular predecessor, H. W. Tucker. The SPG, after all, had been established in 1701, long before the creation of modern church parties.

Montgomery had been born in India, and had later imbibed something of the spirit of public school character formation at Harrow, even if he was somewhat better at games than the classics. As he wrote in his memoir: 'I think I learnt as much from games as from anything. They are a real education for life, helping to build up character, to endure adversity patiently, to fight uphill games, to keep one's temper, to practise unselfishness for a common object.'[23] This sense of a common ideal of character formation, of education for life, later shaped his approach to Christian mission, which he regarded as a form of education in the Christian virtues which was expressed most clearly in missionary educational establishments. On receiving news of his appointment as SPG general secretary, he wrote to his father-in-law, F. W. Farrar, dean of Canterbury, who had been one of his masters at Harrow:

> I can truly say that there is no post in all the world I would rather hold. To create a sort of foreign secretaryship of Anglican missions with a bishop at its head, to be a referee and guide in all Greater Britain questions. The outlook is terrifying in its possibilities. Had one the gifts, one could almost transform the general ideals of the Church and make them actually embrace the world. It strikes me at times as more Pauline in scope than that of any bishop in the Anglican Communion, and therefore most episcopal. This last point was the greatest difficulty at first, but I am clear about it now.[24]

Inevitably, the contested question in missionary thought concerned precisely what constituted such 'general ideals of the Church', as it sought to embrace the world through the work of Montgomery, who humbly saw himself as Anglican foreign secretary and modern-day St Paul.

It was also not clear about what Montgomery meant by 'Greater Britain'. This term was much used at the time. In his Donnellan lectures at Trinity College, Dublin, in 1900–1, G. Robert Wynne, archdeacon of Aghadoe in Ireland, had spoken of the church in 'Greater

[23] M. M., *Bishop Montgomery*, 8–9.
[24] Ibid. 49.

Britain'.[25] His principal concern had been the so-called 'settler empire', those churches which had simply transplanted English and sometimes Irish Anglicanism overseas to serve the white dominions. As has recently been documented by Joseph Hardwick, although they had their particular problems, these colonial churches shared much with the Church of England.[26] They usually lacked the privileges and burdens of establishment, there was often conflict over land, property and relations with colonial legislatures, and finance proved a perennial problem, as in Australia and Canada,[27] but the Anglican churches of the predominantly white dominions, most of which had developed systems of self-government by the twentieth century, retained much of the character of the Church of England, including its division into church parties.

Montgomery's concerns, however, went far beyond the settler churches. The role of religion in Greater Britain was not simply synonymous with '[t]he spiritual expansion of England', which had formed the subtitle to Tucker's book, *The English Church in other Lands*, published in 1886 as part of Mandell Creighton's series 'Epochs in Church History'.[28] Instead, Montgomery was concerned with the establishment of something different. While he remained an undoubted apologist for the British empire, regarding 'clergy as officers in an imperial army',[29] he nevertheless came to see a need for cultural sensitivity as he became increasingly aware of the complexity of the missionary context. At the same time, he also saw the importance of the reverse effects of overseas mission on the Church in England. He thus felt – somewhat in vain – that Christian mission within 'Greater Britain' might even help the Church of England overcome what he regarded as its petty domestic party squabbles.[30]

Montgomery's overall approach to mission is evident in his 1902 book, *Foreign Missions*, which is essentially a global survey of religions

[25] See G. Robert Wynne, *The Church in Greater Britain: The Donnellan Lectures delivered before the University of Dublin 1900–1901* (London, 1901); see also Carey, *God's Empire*.
[26] Hardwick, *Anglican British World*.
[27] See Hilary Carey, 'Gladstone, the Colonial Church, and Imperial State', in eadem and John Gascoigne, eds, *Church and State in Old and New Worlds* (Leiden, 2011), 155–82, especially 161–6.
[28] H. W. Tucker, *The English Church in other Lands, or, the Spiritual Expansion of England* (London, 1886).
[29] Montgomery, *Foreign Missions*, 2.
[30] Ibid. 10.

and cultures and the challenges they presented for Christian mission. While he shared many of the presuppositions about race and human development of his contemporaries, his general approach was nonetheless significant: as a key figure in Church of England mission he was beginning to pay what he regarded as due attention to the achievements of other religions and 'races' and trying to understand them in their own terms as best he could. As he wrote in the introduction:

> Signs, too, are discernible of an abatement of pride upon the part of the white races. It is beginning to be doubted whether after all God has given ten talents to them, and to yellow and black races only two and one. Bearing in mind, indeed, the lack of vision, of imagination, and of power to live in view of the spiritual, without great effort, among some of the leading Christian nations of to-day as compared with the more refined natural qualities of races still largely non-Christian, it is a question whether the work already done by the Gospel has not been more difficult than any task still left for it to do.[31]

While, hardly surprisingly, Montgomery saw Christianity as supreme and he retained a somewhat fanciful hope of mass conversions in India, he nevertheless placed great stress on the importance of the non-Christian world, and especially Asia, in the development of religion and human culture. He had even come to realize that Christianity was itself an Asian religion. Geographically, he claimed, 'all the great existing intellectual faiths of the world are Asiatic. Again, only in Asia have great sacred books been composed. … The Bible, Hindu, Arabic, Persian, and Chinese Scriptures close the list. The classical nations of Europe produced every branch of noble literature, except books of their religion.'[32] The missionary encounter with the non-Christian world raised significant questions about the European character of the Christian Church which meant that 'it is for her to welcome any race to a position of equality that is worthy of it; to revise her own opinions as to colour if those opinions need revision'.[33] He concluded:

> When the better spirit has become predominant, yellow and black perils will no more be discussed, and the great governments of the world

[31] Ibid. xvi.
[32] Ibid. 20.
[33] Ibid. xvii.

> will confess that in the deepest and most serious problems of life it is to the Church of God that men will have to turn for solutions achieved without bloodshed.[34]

Similarly, three years later, in a lecture given as part of a series which he shared with Eugene Stock of the Church Missionary Society, Montgomery noted the rise of the East:

> The twentieth century sees the general interest shift from Africa to Asia. The East awakes. For the first time in modern history the nations of the West have discovered that there is to be a limit to their conquests in Asia. Many are vexed, as though it were an unwarrantable impertinence upon the part of any race that is not white to have an independent existence.[35]

In 1907 Montgomery published an edited collection of seven essays, all by bishops, entitled *Mankind and the Church.*[36] The subtitle of the book is illuminating: it speaks of the *Contribution of Great Races to the Fulness of the Church of God.* Like Montgomery's earlier book on mission, the volume as a whole seeks to illuminate the context in which the 'great races' have developed, while at the same time discussing what they have given to human civilization. In the period of what was one of the high points of British imperial consolidation and despite frequent racial stereotyping, the book nevertheless displays a degree of openness towards other 'great races', especially those of the East. In his introduction, Montgomery raised the issue of what would later be called 'hybridity' in the relationship between missionary and imperial discourse and the categorization and development of the indigenous religions. He was especially concerned with the religions and cultures of the Indian sub-continent:

> India, so far as the educated class is concerned, is feeling the effect of Western ideas of liberty, and the Church has added its quota to the same movement. In religion observers tell us that there is among the same class a turning, albeit often unconscious, towards [an] atheistic attitude of mind. Perhaps, as part of the same effect, educated Indian

[34] Ibid. xvi–xvii.

[35] H. H. Montgomery and Eugene Stock, *Christian Missions in the Far East: Addresses on the Subject* (London, 1905), 6.

[36] H. H. Montgomery, ed., *Mankind and the Church, being an Attempt to estimate the Contribution of Great Races to the Fulness of the Church of God*, 2nd impression (London, 1909; first publ. 1907).

> thought certainly does not now adopt a contemptuous tone towards the Faith of the Gospel, but is just so much impressed by it as is shown by references in newspapers which praise the Christian standard of public life: and in their more religious writings the Indian is anxious to prove that Hinduism accepts all that is vital in the Christian Faith. History repeats itself. Nor can we doubt that the existence in India of men and women for centuries who have come to give their best and to take nothing must have had a deep effect. The growing wisdom of these men and women in their dealings with Hindus and Moslems, has mitigated a good deal of the veiled opposition to missions by English civilians which is one of the most strange phenomena of British Christianity.[37]

He regarded such an open Christianity as implicitly strengthening the ethical teachings of the major religions. The impact of other religions was also being felt nearer home:

> The effect of the Faith of Christ in quickening Hinduism and Mohammedanism into greater activity is paralleled by the same result on Buddhism in Ceylon and Burmah; for the missions of Christendom are no longer a negligible quantity anywhere. There is, of course, a certain reflex action on our own race. We hear of a Moslem mosque in Liverpool under the charge of an Englishman who has embraced Islam. We have Englishmen in Burmah and Ceylon who are preaching neo-Buddhism; and a certain section of English people play with Oriental cults as an improvement upon the Gospel message.[38]

On this account, the success of mission was being measured not simply in the numbers of converts, but through the ways in which Christianity had begun to reshape the indigenous religions and cultures themselves. There was a sense in which all people, regardless of religion, were capable of hearing and receiving the Christian ethos. Missionary educational institutions were to become central in this universalist and pluralist understanding of Christian truth which could be expressed in other religions and cultures. Education became one of the dominant themes at both the Pan-Anglican Congress held in London from 15–24 June 1908 and the Lambeth Conference of Anglican bishops from 5 July to 6 August that year.

[37] Ibid. xli–xlii.
[38] Ibid. xli–xlii.

THE PAN-ANGLICAN CONGRESS OF 1908

Montgomery's collection of essays was preparatory to the congress and conference. Montgomery, who was a close friend and confidant of Randall Davidson, archbishop of Canterbury from 1903, was the mastermind behind the congress, which proved to be the closest thing that Anglicans ever staged to a World's Fair. Over seventeen thousand people from across the Anglican world attended daily sessions in various London venues.[39] Unlike the Edinburgh Missionary Conference two years later, which followed similar methods and included questionnaires and reports,[40] it was not simply a gathering of missionaries: delegates also included a number (admittedly modest) of indigenous laity and clergy from the relatively new Anglican churches from across the world.

As part of the preparation for the congress, every bishop of the Anglican Communion was asked a number of simple questions about what they saw as the most important problems for the Church of God within and outside their own region, as well as what they saw as the 'chief corporate duty of the whole Anglican Communion at this time'.[41] Montgomery hoped not only that this fact-finding exercise might help clarify the distinctive challenges facing Anglicanism worldwide, but also that it might provide an impetus for renewal in the Church of England.[42] The congress itself was divided up into different sections and groups, each focusing on problems facing the Church in different parts of the world. Along with the subsequent Lambeth Conference, the congress offers a huge wealth of information about the changing presuppositions behind the Anglican missionary churches, which had grown exponentially in the previous sixty years or so.

Before the congress, very large numbers of preparatory papers were composed which offer important insights into the cultural assumptions of missionaries and, more generally, of Western perceptions

[39] See Alan M. G. Stephenson, *Anglicanism and the Lambeth Conferences* (London, 1978), 111–18.

[40] See Brian Stanley, *The World Missionary Conference, Edinburgh 1910*, SHCM (Grand Rapids, MI, 2009). On education, see Felicity Jensz, 'The 1910 Edinburgh World Missionary Conference and Comparative Colonial Education', *HE* 47 (2018), 399–414. Commission III of the conference was dedicated to 'Education in Relation to the Christianization of National Life'.

[41] George Bell, *Randall Davidson: Archbishop of Canterbury* (London, 1952), 568.

[42] Maughan, 'Imperial Christianity?', 40.

of other religions and cultures and, in the language of the time, other races. These papers, which were bound into the volumes of proceedings, are frequently highly informative and often betray the overwhelming recognition of the importance of missionary education as a means of expanding the influence of the Christian ethos. The preparatory papers and proceedings of the congress stretched to seven lengthy volumes.[43] The fifth was explicitly devoted to reports and debates on the church's missions in non-Christian lands. Although much of the discussion was practical and descriptive, many of the participants also addressed some of the wider issues in the relationships of missionaries with local cultures and religions.

The educational paradigm of Christianity shaped much of the discourse, and for many it was predicated on a hierarchy of races characterized through strong racial stereotypes. For instance, in his opening lecture, which introduced a rationale for mission to non-Christian lands, Stuart Alexander Donaldson (1854–1915), son of the first premier of New South Wales, and from 1904 until his death master of Magdalene College, Cambridge, clearly distinguished what he regarded as the higher civilizations from the lower. His language clearly illustrates the prejudices of Edwardian England and the shadow – and explicitly racist – side of missionary education in an imperial context:

> It is not only the acute intellect of the Hindu, or the practical industry of the Chinaman, or the marvellous adaptability of the Japanese which is feeling the birth-throes of a new life: the same is true of the degraded Australian aboriginal, of the ignorant Kaffir, of the licentious and blood-stained South Sea Islander, of the simple Eskimo, of the ignorant wild native of South America … . Never before in the history of the world has such an opportunity been offered for the permanent amelioration of the race. The responsibility is ours, ours of this generation.[44]

For Donaldson, Christian responsibility for the non-Christian was to be expressed chiefly through education. Indeed, he felt, education rather than conversion would become the means through which the moral values of Christianity were to be spread. In short, he claimed, the 'basis of missionary work' was 'education based on Christianity'. This attempt to work indirectly by establishing

[43] *Pan-Anglican Congress*, 7 vols (London, 1908).
[44] Stuart A. Donaldson, 'The Rationale of Foreign Missions', ibid. 5: 5–8, at 6.

institutions of education rather than through direct evangelization marked, he felt, a 'new departure for the development of Christian Missions'. This method was particularly applicable for the higher civilizations. Again using unfortunate language, he suggested that the educational method was 'certainly true already for China, Japan, and Ceylon. I think it is also true for races far less developed, and of a lower type of civilization. … . Our aim must be to strengthen the weak, so that they may be able to walk on their own legs, not on crutches.'[45] Perhaps with a degree of ironic foresight, given the educational background of many of the post-colonial elite, Donaldson consequently concluded that Christian education must become the crutch with the support of which other civilizations might be able to rise up to walk unaided.

Something similar, but without such explicit racist presumptions, was observed by many of those reporting on their experience in different missionary contexts. A good example is offered by two of the seven sons (and three daughters) of Brooke Foss Westcott. For them, education had offered an opportunity to help the population acquire the virtues of character that would allow them to express the ideals of Christian civilization even if they did not accept the faith itself. This would then be of benefit in the reshaping of Indian society. George Herbert Westcott (1862–1928), educated at, and subsequently assistant master of, Marlborough College, was an SPG missionary at Cawnpore (Kanpur) in Uttar Pradesh from 1889 to 1910 and afterwards bishop of nearby Lucknow. He was born while his father was a schoolmaster at Harrow, where he imbibed a strong sense of moral and social duty as well as a sense that all faculties are to be improved for the glory of God.[46] George's younger brother Foss (1863–1949), educated at Cheltenham, was bishop of Chota Nagpur in north-east India from 1905 to 1919 and bishop of Calcutta and metropolitan from 1919 to 1945.[47] Two other brothers also joined the work of the SPG in India. Foss had earlier been with George at Cawnpore, where they established industrial training. As bishop, Foss established schools that offered educational opportunities to about four hundred Anglo-Indian boys.

[45] Ibid. 6–7.
[46] See Gerald Studdert-Kennedy, 'Westcott, George Herbert (1862–1928)', *ODNB*.
[47] See idem, 'Westcott, Foss (1863–1949)', *ODNB*.

Foss and George Westcott, who remained extremely close until George's death, saw education as central to the missionary task. Both also retained an ideal of a non-dogmatic Christianity that was open to the influence of the wider culture and religious milieu (and which later paved the way for the development of Christian unity in South India). In this they clearly drew on their father's example. Brooke Foss Westcott offered his own thoughts on the role of the schoolmaster, which provided a model to his sons. He wrote of his time at Harrow:

> The frank questioning, the interchange of thought, the influence of personal enthusiasm, the inspiring power of living words, which come in the free intercourse of the class-room, give a force and a meaning to facts and theories which the book cannot convey. It is spiritual. The end of the teacher whose work we strive to follow is not fixed by the communication of his special lesson. He will seek, indeed, to do this as perfectly as possible, but he will at the same time suggest the vast fields which lie unexplored even in his own department; he will make clear the limitations and assumptions under which his results are obtained; he will add, if I may so express the truth, the symbol of infinity to the provisional statements which represent the actual attainments of man; he will use the most effective technical education as the vehicle of wider culture. Literature, art, and science will be for him partial revelations of a boundless life, and it will be his object to make the life felt through the least part with which he deals.[48]

Education was consequently an explicit invitation to explore the higher truth, which in turn relativized the provisional statements and partial revelations of human life. In this the influence of Plato is obvious. Brooke Foss Westcott wrote to his intimate friend F. J. A. Hort on 6 April 1859: 'Each Christian, so far as he is a Christian, is an ideal Christian, or rather is such by partaking in the *idea*. In "idea" he is one with Christ, and all that Christ did he did in Christ. But the work of all life is to realise this idea.'[49] It was through life rather than through doctrines that the Christian ideal was to be realized.

George Westcott drew on such ideas in the opening address of the Pan-Anglican Congress section on education on 16 June 1908. His

[48] Westcott, ed., *Life of Westcott*, 1: 190.
[49] Ibid. 235.

opening paragraph is explicit, and clearly expresses something of the public school ethos:

> We Christians believe in education, since through it are developed those powers which distinguish man from the lower animals; we believe in religious education, because we regard the spiritual faculty as the most precious of human possessions. Religious education is dependent upon direct teaching and personal influence. … Such personal influence makes itself felt, not only in the class-room, but in the teacher's study, in the playing field, and, above all, in the hostels or boarding houses which are now regarded as almost a necessary part of every school or college.[50]

In turn, he maintained, Christian teachers had generally stopped ridiculing popular religion, but instead preferred 'to emphasize the truths common to all religions … . They urge their pupils to be truthful, to be honest, to be loving, and to be pure; they help them to sympathize with all that is good, and to cultivate self-discipline and self-restraint.'[51] Although he regretted the fact that the number of converts was small, he nonetheless rejoiced 'that the Spirit of Christ is exercising so strong an influence upon those who consciously or unconsciously live as His disciples'.[52] While he admitted that some found the emphasis on education to be at the expense of evangelization, George Westcott felt it was the method Christ himself would have chosen had he come to cotemporary India. In subsequent discussion he repeated his point, at the same time emphasizing the importance of ensuring that missionary schools did not simply focus on educating the poor and dispossessed at the expense of the rich and influential. The reporter observed that George Westcott

> hoped that every one would applaud the proposal that it was necessary to preach to the educated classes as well as to the poor. The greatest danger before them at present was the risk of a boycott of Christianity in India, and it was therefore only wise that friendly relations with the educated classes should be cultivated. He thought the

[50] G. H. Westcott, 'General Statement, Missionary Methods (2) Educational 1', *Pan-Anglican Congress*, 5: 29–31, at 29.
[51] Ibid.
[52] Ibid. 30.

> time would come when the educated classes would move towards Christianity as the uneducated classes were doing at present.[53]

George Westcott clearly illustrates both the pragmatic need to maintain cordial relations with Indian culture, as well as a desire to use education to promote what he understood as the truths common to humanity.

In a similar manner to George Westcott, Henry Whitehead (1853–1947),[54] bishop of Madras and brother of the philosopher Alfred North Whitehead, highlighted the importance of educational work among both the higher and lower castes of India. Educated at Sherborne, Whitehead was the son of Alfred Whitehead (1827–98), headmaster of Chatham House School in Ramsgate, Kent. He went on to appoint the first Indian bishop, V. S. Azariah, as bishop of Dornakal in 1912. Like the Westcott brothers, Whitehead was to promote the scheme for reunion, also supporting a pluralist approach to revelation. In a short lecture on 'Village Populations versus Educated Classes', he was clear that there was a need to focus not just on lower castes and aboriginal tribal people but also on the higher castes. Despite the small number of converts, he held, Christianity had had a beneficial effect. It was crucial, he thought, to note that

> [the] effect produced by our educational work among the higher castes has been to spread among them a leaven of Christian ideas, to promote kindly feelings between the students and their Christian teachers, and to stimulate reform movements within Hinduism itself: but not, except in a few cases, to bring men to faith in Christ. These results have a very definite value, and I do not wish for a moment to depreciate them.

At the same time, however, he went on express a note of regret. 'After all,' he noted,

> the object of Christian Missions is not merely to Christianize men, but to make them Christians. It is possible, of course, that this educational work is gradually preparing the way for some great movement among the higher castes in the future. That, however, must of necessity be a matter of doubtful speculation. I heartily wish that I could think that

[53] *Pan-Anglican Congress* 5: 161.
[54] Jeffrey Cox, 'Whitehead, Henry (1853–1947)', *ODNB*.

> the educated classes are nearer to the acceptance of Christianity now than they were five-and-twenty years ago.[55]

Whitehead was also aware that the education of the poor and the education of the higher castes were closely related. It was, he maintained, the witness of Christian education of the poor that was 'the one thing that is capable of touching the hearts and consciences of thoughtful and educated men in India, and convincing them of the truth of Christianity. Let us exhibit Christianity to them in the future, not simply as a doctrine, but a life.'[56] Whitehead's words display a resemblance to the thought of Samuel Taylor Coleridge which is too close to be accidental. As Coleridge, who was one of the most important influences behind the formation of educational thinking in the early nineteenth century, put it in a famous aphorism in his most important work on pedagogy, *Aids to Reflection*: 'Christianity is not a theory or a speculation … but a life and a living process'.[57] For Whitehead, such a form of life was 'the most convincing proof to earnest and thoughtful men in India of the truth of Christianity'. It was to be found most clearly in 'the simple fact that it is indeed a gospel to the poor'.[58] Indeed, he felt, by raising up the poor and educating them, difference of caste might even begin to disappear, which would have a lasting effect on the people of India.

In much the same way, Foss Westcott, speaking on a similar theme, observed the success of missionary education in raising people from the lower castes. He noted:

> Some years ago I made a religious census of the clerks employed in the mercantile offices at Cawnpore, where I was then stationed, and I found that while from the proportion of the followers of the three great faiths Christianity, Hinduism, and Mohammedanism in the population of the city, we should expect to have found six Christians, the actual number was forty-two. Doubtless in some measure this excessive proportion was

[55] Henry Whitehead, 'Village Populations V. Educated Classes', in *Pan-Anglican Congress*, 5: 150–3, at 151.
[56] Ibid. 153.
[57] Samuel Taylor Coleridge, *Aids to Reflection in the Formation of a Manly Character on the several Grounds of Prudence, Morality and Religion, illustrated by select Passages from our elder Divines, especially from Archbishop Leighton* (London, 1825), 195 ('Aphorisms on Spiritual Religion').
[58] Bishop of Chota Nagpur [Henry Whitehead], *Pan-Anglican Congress*, 5: 153–7, at 153.

> due to the influence of missionaries in securing them appointments, but this does not wholly account for it. These men were not converts from the educated classes of India, but for the most part the sons of parents who had been won for Christ from the humbler castes.[59]

Foss Westcott went on to discuss the growth of the missionary schools which had succeeded in educating large numbers of boys and girls in his own diocese of Chota Nagpur, as well as in parts of South India. Most effective, he thought, were the boarding schools, 'because it is in these that Christian character is most surely built up when dealing with those who have been won for Christ from among the lower ranks of life in India'.[60] In turn, he felt that out of this might emerge a genuinely national expression of Indian Christianity:

> The desire for a really national Church is rapidly gaining strength. It seems to our Indian brethren intolerable that they should be taught to repeat the shibboleths of Western sectarian Christianity, or that a Church in which the universal faith is dressed in a Western garb should be reproduced in every particular in an Eastern country.[61]

In response, R. S. Copleston, bishop of Calcutta and metropolitan of India, also noted the delight of 'those of high station' at seeing the work of the churches in elevating the lower castes through education.[62]

Similar observations were made by Indian Christians themselves. An important preparatory pamphlet was written by Susil Kumar Rudra (1861–1925), a second-generation Christian and the first Indian principal of St Stephen's College, Delhi. With C. F. Andrews (1871–1940), he helped move the college away from its dependence on the Cambridge Brotherhood.[63] Rudra observed the interaction of Western and Eastern ideas that had been brought about by Christian education. Like Foss Westcott and Whitehead, he distinguished between work among the low-caste Hindus and aboriginal peoples and the higher-caste Hindus and Muslims. Even though there were far fewer converts among

[59] Ibid. 154.

[60] Ibid. 156.

[61] Ibid. 157.

[62] *Pan-Anglican Congress* 5: 158.

[63] On Andrews, see Philip Lockley, 'Social Anglicanism and Empire: C. F. Andrews's Christian Socialism', in Stewart J. Brown, Charlotte Methuen and Andrew Spicer, eds, *The Church and Empire*, SCH 54 (Cambridge, 2018), 407–21.

the latter, Christianity's influence had still been strongly felt through its social and ethical effects, rather than through conversion and the explicit acceptance of Christian doctrine. Rudra wrote:

> A high order of Western training is now open to educated Indians, and they are rapidly learning organized methods of life and action according to modern principles. If the Church loses touch with these new forces, she will be left 'high and dry'; as they sweep past her, cutting out their own channels. In order, therefore, to make the Church of India Catholic, to make it progressive, to fill it with power and spirit, to ensure its touch with the genius of the Indian mind, educational missionary work must be carried on among the higher castes with far greater determination than before.[64]

Rudra was clear that missionary societies should work together to achieve these goals, but he also stressed the need to ensure that they retained independence from the government, lest Christian institutes of education should lose their distinctive identity. According to Rudra, history had shown that it was all too easy to lose sight of the divine Master as the inspirer of their work.

Rudra went on to discuss other successes which had been brought about through education, even among Hindu reform movements such as the Brahmo Samaj:[65]

> Christian truths have been popularized; and though we cannot point to many remarkable baptisms of individuals, we can show a most remarkable baptism of thought. There has been a leaven of Christianity very widely spread over the country which has influenced each new indigenous religious movement in turn. The Brahmo Samaj, for example, has been influenced on every side by Christian ideas, and the same is almost equally true of other movements also. Still further, the very basis of the structure of Hindu society has been modified, and the constructive elements in this change have been unquestionably Christian.[66]

[64] S. K. Rudra, *Missionary Education in India*, Pan-Anglican Papers, Pamphlet S. D. 2(1) (London, 1908), 2.

[65] On Brahmo Samaj, see Kenneth W. Jones, *The New Cambridge History of India*, 3/1: *Socio-Religious Reform Movements in British India* (Cambridge, 1990), 30–9.

[66] Rudra, *Missionary Education*, 3.

However, despite such powerful examples, which showed how Christian ideals had been able to influence wider society, for the most part Christian schools had insufficient resources to ensure the persistence of the Christian ethos. Although many individuals continued to inspire, this was not the case with the institutions as a whole: 'Individual missionaries', Rudra wrote, 'have reflected that glory and have impressed individuals, but the living power of the body corporate is still wanting, and it is the witness of the Body of Christ which carries conviction.'[67]

Rudra's remedy was to expand the numbers of dedicated teachers, both lay and ordained, in order to increase what he called 'intensive influence'. At the same time, he claimed, it was important to ensure the indigenization of the gospel to enable the appropriate expression of theology. He went on:

> Christian thought, Christian ideals, have already been accepted as the highest in the land. The profoundest reverence is paid to Christ Himself. The Christian theology of the West, however, is often a very great intellectual stumbling-block. Can anything be done to present Christian truths in a form which will be acceptable to the Indian mind? Ought this not to be a special aim to be attained by Christian educationalists in India? Can Christian literature jointly undertaken by Eastern and Western Christians become a stepping-stone to Eastern theology?[68]

If such reforms could be brought about, this might then lead to a genuinely Indian church, which, he suggested, 'must be governed and moulded by Indian ideas and sentiments which are in accord with the spirit of Christ. For this Indian bishops are needed as well as an Indian Liturgy.'[69]

Others had made similar observations on the example of missionary education and the establishment of an Indian church. In a preparatory booklet on the *Equipment of Native Workers in India*, the CMS educator, Edmund Francis Edward Wigram (1864–1933),[70] warden

[67] Ibid. 3.
[68] Ibid. 6–7.
[69] Ibid. 7.
[70] On Wigram, see Ved Mehta, *Mahatma Gandhi and his Apostles* (New Haven, CT, 1976), 240. Returning to England, Wigram went on to become CMS secretary for India (1915–29) and CMS secretary (1929–32).

of St John's Divinity College in Lahore from 1896 to 1915, asked a simple question:

> How can our divinity schools, which are and must probably for a long time be manned chiefly by European teachers, turn out men fitted to present the truths of the Christian revelation in a manner that will not sound far off and foreign to their hearers[?] … We come with our English basis of training, and this is so strong on its own lines that it threatens to smother individuality and initiation on the part of our pupils.[71]

Whatever they did and however much they tried to assimilate, missionaries would always remain 'exotics to the last'. It was consequently impossible simply to graft 'on Western ideas and ideals to the Eastern stock'.[72] Instead, what seemed required was a 'nationalized Christianity', which alone would become the means by which India would 'most truly attain the goal of her newly born hopes and longings'.[73]

From a different perspective, Copleston,[74] who before his appointment as metropolitan of India had spent a lengthy time as bishop of Colombo from 1875 to 1902 in the predominantly Buddhist culture of Ceylon, also emphasized the importance of education. Copleston, a high churchman who resisted the appointment of CMS missionaries in Ceylon, had nonetheless become acutely aware of the problems of missionary arrogance and Western superiority.[75] In his presentation at the 1908 congress, Copleston noted that 'missionaries were too patronizing, and patronage was a thing people did not like. Missionaries must not be content with pity, with condescension, with patronage or even sympathy; they must go to the nations with reverence and respect. Persuasion was of little value in dealing with

[71] E. F. E. Wigram, *Equipment of Native Workers: India*, Pan-Anglican Papers, Pamphlet S.D. S (k) (London, 1908), 4–5.
[72] Ibid. 1.
[73] Ibid. 3.
[74] On Copleston, see Michael Laird, 'Copleston, Reginald Stephen (1845–1925)', *ODNB*. Copleston was married to Edith Chenevix Trench, whose father, Richard Trench (1807–86), archbishop of Dublin from 1864, had set up the first higher educational establishment for women in Ireland in 1866. From his Cambridge days, Richard Trench had been, and remained, a close friend of F. D. Maurice, another educational pioneer who displayed an interest in other world religions.
[75] See his Boyle Lectures, *The Religions of the World and their Relations to Christianity* (London, 1847).

the Buddhist.'[76] For Copleston, far more important than explicit evangelization was the need to detect a common ethical framework among those who practised other religions:

> Missionaries must address themselves to the Buddhist very much as they addressed themselves to any other sinful man. What the missionary had to do was to try and rouse his conscience and direct his thoughts to that which he did not deny, the evidences of the working of a living Creator in the world around him; to make him see that his conscience was naturally Christian; that he did call, in spite of all his atheistic profession, upon God in his time of need; and so to impress upon his prejudice-bound mind and sin-bound conscience the message of the goodness and love of Him in whose name he was seeking to win him.[77]

In his preparatory booklet on *The Missionary's Equipment: India*, Copleston had noted the importance of Indianization. Discussing what he called the missionary's 'intellectual outfit', he emphasized the importance of education in Indian culture and literature.

> There is a want of men who set themselves seriously to study the language, literature, and history of the peoples to whom they are sent. … There are two distinct uses of such knowledge, one of which is within the reach of comparatively few, while the other concerns all. Such knowledge, in the first use, qualifies a man to translate, to lecture and discuss, to debate and instruct; in the second use, which is even more important, it helps a man to cherish sympathy and respect for India and for Indians.[78]

Copleston detected what he felt to be an extraordinary ignorance of both the literature and history of India among missionaries. Yet, he felt, without an awareness of the indigenous culture there could be little sympathy with the Indian population. It was crucial to understand that 'much of what means most to him lie[s] in the privacy of his domestic religion and of his caste associations, but he is moulded, in some of his best and most intimate thoughts and desires, by the ancient ideals and traditions of his country'.[79] Copleston concluded:

[76] R. S. Copleston, 'Presentation of the Christian Faith to the Buddhist', *Pan-Anglican Congress*, 5: 177–81, at 178.
[77] Ibid.
[78] R. S. Copleston, *The Missionary's Equipment: India*, Pan-Anglican Papers, Pamphlet S. D. 5(a) (London, 1908), 1.
[79] Ibid. 3.

> let it be said, that a missionary to India can bring with him, as part of his equipment, few things more valuable than a certain humility in the presence of those among whom he is to work; a conviction that they have something which they do not owe to him, and which he could not have given them, but which is not altogether to be despised.[80]

In the discussion of Copleston's paper that followed, James Pereira, a lay representative from Ceylon, developed these ideas, even suggesting a Christianization of Buddhism. In Ceylon, as in India, there was, he claimed, a distinction between the educated and the uneducated:

> two classes of Buddhists had to be dealt with in Ceylon, the educated and the uneducated. The former were not true Buddhists, because they did not believe in the doctrines of Buddhism as laid down in the books, and they were largely influenced by people who had incorporated into Buddhism Christian ideas, thereby endeavouring to bolster up their faith. The ignorant Buddhists were superstitious, and had to be dealt with in another way. Christians should approach Buddhism with true sympathy, and point out that Buddhist doctrines had to be supplemented with something higher and nobler, namely, the essential principles of Christianity.[81]

Humility in the face of a higher truth, which shared much with the broad church ideal permeating the public schools, was thus clearly shaping missionary discourse.

Later, at the mass meeting in the Albert Hall on 18 June, A. G. Fraser (1873–1962), principal of the CMS Trinity College in Kandy from 1904 to 1924, spoke of the importance of educational missions and of moving towards a more culturally relevant curriculum, and the need to 'put the natives more and more into power – the men who knew the country and were less likely to make mistakes than the British'.[82] Fraser, who also served as CMS educational adviser in southern India, had supplied one of the preparatory papers, 'The Problem before Educational Missions in Ceylon',[83] where he

[80] Ibid.

[81] Copleston, 'Presentation', 181.

[82] Ibid. 274.

[83] A. G. Fraser, 'The Problem before Educational Missions in Ceylon', *Pan-Anglican Papers*, no. S. D. 2 (c). These are bound into volume 5. Fraser later chaired a commission on village education in India for the Conference of Missionary Societies in Great Britain

wrote of the national movement 'rooted in the very depths of Eastern religious patriotic feeling, … the expression of the growing self-consciousness of the peoples'.[84] He reported on a conference of Anglican missionaries the previous year in Ceylon, which had claimed:

> A college education divorces a young man from his own language, national traditions, and sympathy with his own people, and therefore greatly weakens his power for good among the race to which he belongs. … We recognize the fact, also, that our better educated Christians are so westernized by their education that they hold the Christian Faith too far apart from all mental comparison or contrast of its tenets with their old non-Christian faiths, and so are weak both for defence and for convincing those whom they ought to influence for Christ.[85]

According to Fraser, the result was that 'educated Christians and native clergy are too often only undeveloped Europeans, and they present the Gospel to their people in its foreign dress'.[86] The question was how to win the national movement for Christ. The solution, he felt, was that 'we must, in our educational missions learn to preach the Christ of India and Ceylon',[87] for 'Christ came not to destroy but to complete all that is best and truest in their ancient learning and faith, and we have the privilege of proving it. Only in the power of the risen Lord and Christ can a disciple fulfil the ethic of Buddha.'[88] This required schools to educate leaders so that 'natives are not only hewers of wood and drawers of water but brothers and men'.[89] His respect for the culture of Ceylon was deep:

> We are working amongst a people who, as a race, have a deeper spiritual genius, who have more gentleness and humility, a greater sense of discipleship and readiness to sacrifice themselves and their all, and it behoves us to walk reverently and with fear. They have a noble past, a profound philosophy, much that we have little time or opportunity

and Ireland: see A. G. Fraser, *Village Education in India: The Report of a Commission of Inquiry* (London, 1920).

84 Fraser, 'Problem', 1–2.
85 Ibid. 3.
86 Ibid.
87 Ibid. 4.
88 Ibid. 5.
89 Ibid. 7.

> to learn. Our ignorance in all that counts amongst them is almost boundless. But nowhere do humility and love, and kindly *camaraderie* meet a readier and more generous response than in India and Ceylon.[90]

A lasting tangible result of Fraser's time in Kandy was the magnificent chapel designed by his deputy Lewis John Gaster (1879–1939), modelled on Buddhist buildings in Polonnaruwa, an ancient capital of Sri Lanka, and later painted with striking images of an Asian Christ by David Paynter.[91] Here is an excellent example of the model of missionary education discussed here: a Christian school with a chapel built in a Buddhist vernacular style was educating predominantly Buddhist boys in the liberal virtues of the pursuit of truth and the acquisition of character as the fulfilment of the Christian ethos.

Conclusion

While it would obviously be wrong to assume that the approach exemplified by the missionaries presented in this article means that they were not interested in conversion, it is nonetheless the case that there was a tendency to see education as central to the missionary task, at least among the elites of India and Ceylon. It was through education that the Christian ethos was to function as a leaven for wider society and thus exert a powerful influence in social and political reform. In the hierarchy of races that continued to dominate Edwardian missionary thinking (and survived for much longer), it was accepted that the more 'developed' societies and thus the colonies of the East presented hugely different challenges for mission from those of other parts of the world. The concept of missionary trusteeship, which understood Christian missionaries as 'trustees' of a society until that society had reached a certain level of Christian civilization and which was widely shared among many missionaries at the time, simply did not hold: at least among the elite, the levels of education and civilization appeared to many missionaries to have reached levels comparable with those of the West.

[90] Ibid. 8.

[91] A description of the chapel can be found in 'Trinity College Chapel', online at: <https://www.trinitycollege.lk/chapel/>, and there are photographs in 'Building the Trinity College Chapel', at: <https://www.trinitycollege.lk/chapel/building-of-the-chapel/> both last accessed 20 November 2018.

This meant that the challenges of mission might best be met through education in the moral principles of Christianity, even where this did not lead to conversion, especially among this elite. Consequently, although few seemed prepared to acknowledge it at the time, there was in practice a recognition that the Christian Church would be likely to remain marginal to wider society and unlikely to make huge numbers of converts. As so many contributors observed at the 1908 congress, Eastern cultures simply did not seem to require the 'benefits' of Christian civilization in quite the same way as other parts of the world. While it is beyond the scope of this article, the language of racial hierarchy tended towards seeing African cultures as 'childlike' and innocent,[92] or as 'heathen' and in need of the light of the gospel.[93] Matters were usually understood quite differently in India, even if some missionaries derided Indian 'heathenism'.[94] In a non-Christian society which, as I have shown, many missionaries had come to see as of almost equal standing to those of the West, the sorts of moral responsibility that Christians felt for the wider society – and which the wider society might be persuaded to embrace – had to be exercised cautiously (and almost exclusively) through education and welfare. Only in this way, it was felt, would Christianity prove acceptable to the wider society. In the end, Christianity was forced to express itself more in terms of social and ethical mores and styles of behaviour than in doctrines and propositions to be accepted for salvation.

On this model, which might seem quite alien from much of the earlier rhetoric of Western mission and which remained quite different from other forms of evangelistic activity of the time which paid little attention to education,[95] churches had a particular role to play

[92] This understanding was even adopted in Article 22 of the League of Nations Covenant: Africa was now proclaimed to be a responsibility undertaken in the name of higher civilization, with 'the tutelage of such peoples … entrusted to advanced nations': R. F. Betts (rev. M. Asiwaju): 'Methods and Institutions of European Domination', in A. Adu Boahen, ed., *UNESCO General History of Africa*, 7: *Africa under Colonial Domination 1880–1935* (Berkeley, CA, 1985), 314.

[93] See also D. Chanaiwa, 'African Initiatives and Resistance in Southern Africa', ibid. 194–220, at 198; Wole Soyinka , 'The Arts in Africa during the Period of Colonial Rule', ibid. 539–64, at 563; R. D. Ralston, 'Africa and the New World', ibid. 746–81, at 780–1.

[94] See Esme Cleall's work on medical missions in India and the pathologizing of heathenism: *Missionary Discourses of Difference: Negotiating Otherness in the British Empire, 1840–1900* (Basingstoke, 2012).

[95] Etherington, 'Education and Medicine', 261.

in the development of Eastern societies, but through education rather than conversion. The idea of a culturally sensitive church which gradually came to dominate Anglican missionary thinking later in the twentieth century emerged from its role in shaping and guiding morals and education, which would ultimately exert an enormous influence. Although seldom explicitly stated, it would seem that the quest for conversion and recruitment was not the main focus of Church of England mission to India and most other Eastern societies. This recognition came less from the inner logic of Christian theology and more from the gradual realization that Christianity and civilization were not synonymous, and even that Christianity was a form of life concerned with truth rather than a set of doctrines. As Frykenberg observes, by the early twentieth century, the Christian task

> was not so much to convert peoples of India as to permeate Indian society with Christian values. In order to accomplish this, missionary scholars and thinkers needed to influence the elites who were taking to Western education in such droves. 'Conversion' as such was no longer deemed to be such a worthy goal.[96]

The broad church principle had consequently triumphed. As Frederick Temple noted in his contribution to *Essays and Reviews*, education of the human race was about growing up, about accepting that 'the mature mind of our race is beginning to modify and soften the hardness and severity of the principles which its early manhood had elevated into immutable statements of truth'.[97] This educational ideal was demonstrated perhaps most clearly in the mission field. While missionary thinking was predicated on the assumptions of imperialism with its often explicit racial stereotyping and cultural and economic domination, the examples of missionary education I have discussed marked a significant change. They may not seem to today's readers to have gone far, and some of the literature cited makes very difficult reading, but they did sow the seeds for questioning the assumptions of the superiority of Western civilization.

[96] Frykenberg, *Christianity in India*, 339.

[97] Frederick Temple, 'The Education of the World', in *Essays and Reviews*, 10th edn (London, 1862; first publ. 1860), 1–58, at 52.

Conversion and Curriculum: Nonconformist Missionaries and the British and Foreign School Society in the British West Indies, Africa and India, 1800–50

Inge Dornan*
Brunel University

This article examines the ways in which Nonconformist missionary societies worked hand in hand with the British and Foreign School Society (BFSS) to provide them with pedagogic training in the British System and BFSS teaching manuals and resources, as part of their evangelical mission of conversion in the British West Indies, Africa and India in the nineteenth century. The BFSS appealed to Nonconformist missionaries because it was based on unsectarian pedagogy, pioneered by the educationalist Joseph Lancaster. The article explores the various obstacles these missionaries faced, including the religious persecution they experienced in teaching an unsectarian system and the educational difficulties they experienced in persuading parents and local governments of the value of elementary education. It also draws attention to the ways in which they fought race and sex prejudice in the teaching of Africans, slaves and young girls. The current literature on missionary activities in the early nineteenth century pays scant attention to their role as educators: the article reveals the degree of their educational ambition and zeal and the lengths they went to in order to implement a progressive system of unsectarian elementary instruction in key parts of the British empire during the nineteenth century.

In 1826, Baptist missionary William Knibb sent the British and Foreign School Society (BFSS) samples of his pupils' handwriting and embroidery signed with their names, ages and status (slave and free) from the colony of Jamaica. The 'Slave Book'[1] (Figs 1–2; so named in the society's archives) is an extraordinary artefact, for slaves

* Politics and History, Brunel University London, Uxbridge, UB8 3PH. inge.dornan@brunel.ac.uk. I am extremely grateful to the BFSS archivists Mandy Mordue and Phaedra Casey for their assistance in cataloguing and making available for historical research the BFSS foreign correspondence collection.

[1] Uxbridge, Brunel University London Archives (hereafter: BULA), British and Foreign School Society Papers, BFSS/1/5/1/8/4/3, Slave Book. On Knibb and the role of the

Studies in Church History 55 (2019), 410–425
doi: 10.1017/stc.2018.7

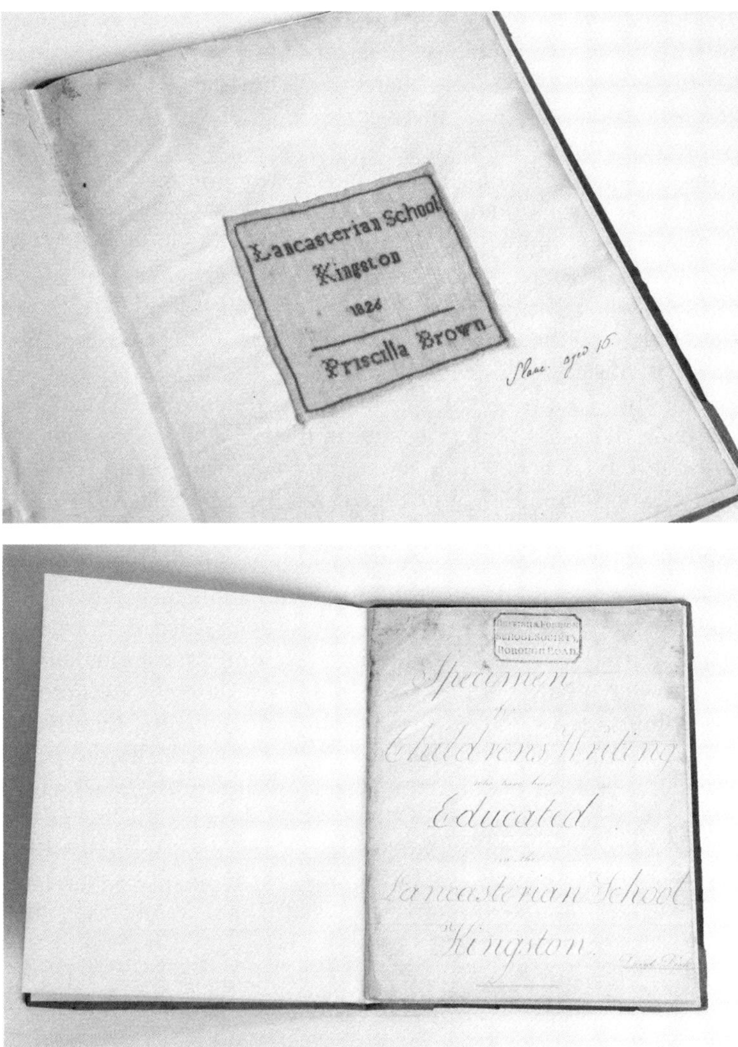

Figs 1–2: 'The Slave Book', ref: BFSS/1/5/1/8/4/3. Reproduced courtesy of Brunel University London Archives.

missionaries in the British West Indies, see Catherine Hall, *Civilising Subjects: Metropole and Colony in the English Imagination 1830–1867* (Cambridge, 2002).

in the British West Indies were customarily prohibited from learning to write, a fact that is poignantly illustrated by the dearth of written records by slaves in the colonial archives. The 'Slave Book' bears witness to the goals of Nonconformist missionaries such as Knibb who, before the Abolition Act (1833), challenged such long-standing planter prejudice by making religious instruction of the enslaved, based upon teaching slaves to read and in some cases also to write, an essential tool of Christian conversion. Furthermore, it testifies to the role of pedagogy in Nonconformist missionary education and in particular to Nonconformist missionaries' adoption of the Lancasterian method, also known as the British System, championed by the BFSS.

This study draws on the largely untapped and newly catalogued collection of foreign correspondence in the BFSS archive to establish how the BFSS operated hand in hand with Nonconformist missionaries to export the British System to Africa, India and the British West Indies in the first half of the nineteenth century, and to scrutinize how the British System functioned in each of these regions prior to 1850. Underlying both aspects is a concern to address two recognizable themes of missionary historiography, each related to the nature of missionary sources: first, the relatively limited engagement by scholars with archival records on missionary pedagogy;[2] and second, the dominance of the white male missionary voice in mission archives.[3] Nonconformist missionary correspondence to the BFSS provides a unique window on how Nonconformist missionaries sought to implement the British System in their schools, while the society's liberal and progressive education reform agenda, which saw it open its teacher training college to women teachers and

[2] See Patricia T. Rooke, 'Missionaries as Pedagogues: A Reconsideration of the Significance of Education for Slaves and Apprentices in the British West Indies, 1800–1838', *HE* 9 (1980), 65–79, at 75; eadem, 'The Pedagogy of Conversion: Missionary Education to Slaves in the British West Indies, 1800–33', *PH* 18 (1978), 356–74; Felicity Jensz, 'Missionaries and Indigenous Education in the 19th-Century British Empire. Part II: Race, Class, and Gender', *History Compass* 10 (2012), 306–17, at 310.

[3] On the dominance of the white male missionary voice and the marginal role of native voices in missionary archives and narratives, see Felicity Jensz, 'Non-European Teachers in Mission Schools: Introduction', *Itinerario* 40 (2016), 389–403. On recapturing the voices and influence of native missionaries, see Richard Hölzl, 'Educating Missions: Teachers and Catechists in Southern Tanganyika, 1890s and 1940s', ibid. 405–28; Hugh Morrison, 'Negotiated and Mediated Lives: Bolivian Teachers, New Zealand Missionaries and the Bolivian Indian Mission, 1908–1932', ibid. 429–49.

missionaries[4] as well as Indian, African and West Indian 'native assistants', gives a measure of visibility and voice to a cast of persons typically marginalized in early Nonconformist missionary archives. Finally, while this article offers a case study of Nonconformist missionaries' use and application of the British System, it also speaks to a wider scholarship on the relationship between missionaries, education and imperialism. Jean and John Comaroff's seminal two-volume study, *Of Revelation and Revolution* (a third volume on pedagogy is forthcoming), underlines the dual significance of literacy as a mutually constitutive instrument of Nonconformist evangelism and the European civilizing mission, which together, they argue, played an essential role in the 'colonization of consciousness' that underpinned European 'hegemony' in South Africa in the nineteenth century.[5]

The BFSS archive of foreign correspondence underscores the Comaroffs' emphasis on the importance of pedagogy as a tool of European hegemony, insofar as it documents why and how Nonconformist missionaries eagerly reached out to the BFSS to help establish Nonconformist mission schools in each of these three regions.[6] At the same time, however, this archive adds an important qualifier to the role of pedagogy as part of the apparatus of European hegemony and cultural imperialism by providing evidence of how pedagogy was actually implemented by Nonconformist missionaries before 1850. As this study argues, prior to 1850 the British System (where it was adopted) was far from consistently and rigorously applied in Nonconformist mission schools in the three regions

[4] The lines between 'missionary' and 'teacher' were frequently blurred. However, there were men and women who studied at the BFSS's teacher training college who taught in mission schools but were not evangelists, such as the prominent West Indian educational reformer and former BFSS pupil, John McSwiney.

[5] Jean and John Comaroff, *Of Revelation and Revolution*, 1: *Christianity, Colonialism and Consciousness in South Africa* (Chicago, IL, and London, 1991); eidem, *Of Revelation and Revolution*, 2: *The Dialectics of Modernity on a South African Frontier* (Chicago, IL, and London, 1997). For a critique of missionaries, cultural imperialism and the 'colonization of consciousness', see Ryan Dunch, 'Beyond Cultural Imperialism: Cultural Theory, Christian Missions, and Global Modernity', *History and Theory* 41 (2002), 301–25.

[6] For broad overviews of the operation of the BFSS in these regions, see George Bartle, 'The Role of the British and Foreign School Society in the Education of the Emancipated Negro, 1814–75', *JEAH* 15/1 (1983), 1–9; idem, 'The Role of the British and Foreign School Society in Elementary Education in India and the East Indies, 1813–75', *HE* 23 (1994), 17–33.

considered here. Pedagogy was certainly conceived of as a crucial component of Nonconformist evangelism and the European civilizing mission in this period, but its effectiveness as a tool of European hegemony must be weighed against the very real and concrete obstacles to its implementation in the British West Indies, Africa and India in the first half of the nineteenth century.

The BFSS owes its origins to Joseph Lancaster, a Quaker and educational pioneer, who in 1798 established the first Lancasterian school for the poor in Borough Road, Southwark, London, and in 1804 opened Britain's first teacher training institution, Borough Road College, also in Southwark.[7] Lancaster aimed to deliver a cost-effective system of elementary instruction that could be rolled out to the mass of Britain's poor and working classes, to which end he developed the Lancasterian monitorial method, whereby a master or mistress trained up a handful of talented older children to become monitors, who in turn instructed younger and less able pupils. In a context of increasing industrialization, Britain's political and social reformers cast a revealing spotlight on the manners and morals of poor and working-class children; as Michel Foucault argues in *Discipline and Punish*, they turned to elementary education, and to the Lancasterian system in particular, as a tool of social control and discipline.[8] Central to this was the inculcation of a moral code founded on Christian knowledge and instruction. In 1808, the Society for Promoting the Royal British or Lancasterian System for the Education of the Poor was formed; in 1814, signalling its transformation into an educational society with a global as well as a national agenda, it changed its name to the British and Foreign School Society.

The British System's strong Christian ethos was woven into the fabric of the BFSS and underlined the society's commitment to widespread social reform through moral and mental 'improvement' based on Christian education. The society's committee comprised prominent evangelicals, both Anglicans and Nonconformists, including renowned abolitionists, the MPs William Wilberforce and Henry Brougham, and its founders Samuel Whitbread and William Allen (its treasurer). After 1814, further leading lights of British abolitionism, Thomas Fowell Buxton and Zachary Macaulay, subscribed and donated to the society. Thomas Clarkson also gave his support to the

[7] George Bartle, *A History of Borough Road College* (Kettering, 1976).
[8] Michel Foucault, *Discipline and Punish: The Birth of the Prison* (London, 1977), 165–7.

BFSS and urged his contacts in Jamaica to adopt the British System.[9] It should come as no surprise that in the opening decades of the nineteenth century, evangelicalism conspired with the goals of abolitionism and social reform to direct the BFSS's overseas operations toward the slave societies of the British West Indies and Africa. It was a conviction, largely born of the British antislavery campaign, of the essential importance of Christian conversion and instruction to the 'improvement' and 'elevation' of West Indian and African slaves, which paired the BFSS with the Nonconformist missionary societies in a shared vision of a European Christian civilizing mission.

The British System's unsectarian pedagogy also aligned Nonconformist missionaries to the BFSS. As the BFSS manual stated, the British System 'exclude[d] the creed or catechism of any particular sect' so that 'all sects and parties' were encouraged to send their children to British Schools.[10] For this reason, the Bible was the only religious text on its curriculum. This corresponded with the approach of Nonconformist missionary evangelism that identified the word of God as the primary route to conversion and salvation, and helps to explain why Nonconformist missionaries were intent on teaching pupils to read, and why they looked to pedagogy to underpin their overseas mission in the first place: their pupils were to be enabled to access the Word of God first-hand through reading the Bible. The desire for printed texts, translations and teaching materials that accompanied Nonconformist expansion overseas is evidence of the centrality of pedagogy to Nonconformist evangelism.

It was through the society's teacher training college and its manual, distributed to all four corners of the globe during the nineteenth century, that Nonconformist missionaries sought to acquire knowledge of the British System. From 1810 onwards, Nonconformist missionary societies, namely the London Missionary Society (LMS), the Baptist Missionary Society (BMS) and the Wesleyan Methodist Missionary Society (WMMS), sent a steady stream of missionaries to the college, including, in 1824, William Knibb, who would later send the society 'The Slave Book'.[11] Via the Society's Ladies'

[9] BULA, BFSS/FC/Jamaica/123, Richard Taylor to James Millar, 18 August 1817.
[10] Joseph Stern, 'Introduction' to *Manual of the System of Teaching: Joseph Lancaster and the British and Foreign School Society* (Chippenham and Bristol, 1994), vi.
[11] BULA, BFSS/2/6/3/1, 'Borough Road Training College Male Students, 1810–1877', 1–26.

Department, the college also welcomed missionary wives as well as widows and single women keen to teach in overseas mission schools. When Nonconformist missionary societies approached the BFSS to recommend trained male teachers for their mission stations, they frequently expressed a preference for married men, often on the grounds that their wives might be profitably employed in delivering instruction, particularly to girls. The Ladies' Department's annual reports went so far as to single out missionary wives as valued conduits of the British System overseas.[12] Gendered European notions of female education accorded women a distinct role in delivering missionary pedagogy where parts of the curriculum were segregated: in the British System, needlework was taught exclusively to girls by female teachers (cf. Priscilla Brown's beautifully embroidered insignia of the Lancasterian school in Kingston, Jamaica, in the first image of 'The Slave Book' above). This was even more the case in India, where female teachers were employed exclusively in the all-female zenanas.[13] The BFSS collection of foreign correspondence testifies to the visible, valuable and frequently indispensable role of women in the field of Nonconformist missionary pedagogy and instruction, most especially in the delivery and promotion of overseas female education prior to 1850.[14] Employing men and women trained in the British System was a clear sign of the Nonconformist missionary societies' aspirations to situate Christian pedagogy at the heart of overseas evangelism. It was also a sign that when it came to education, Nonconformist missionaries were in broad alignment with the BFSS and current educational reforms in Britain in pursuing a commitment to expand education to girls as well as boys, and in so doing to open up the field of missionary instruction to women as well as men.

[12] *Seventh Report of the Ladies' Committee of the British and Foreign School Society* (London, 1821), 26.

[13] A zenana was a distinct and separate area of a Muslim household reserved solely for women, often known as a harem.

[14] See Regina Ganter and Patricia Grimshaw, 'Introduction: Reading the Lives of White Mission Women', *Journal of Australian Studies* 39 (2015), 1–6; Patricia Grimshaw, 'Rethinking Approaches to Women in Missions: The Case of Colonial Australia', *History Australia* 8 (2016), 7–24; Barbara Reeves-Ellington, Kathryn Kish Sklar and Connie A. Shemo, eds, *Competing Kingdoms: Women, Mission, Nation, and the American Protestant Empire, 1812–1960* (Durham, NC, 2010).

The BFSS's goal to effect the material and moral reform of Britain's poor and working classes through elementary education readily transformed into support for Nonconformist missionary efforts to expand pedagogic instruction to 'native teachers'. Over the course of the nineteenth century, Nonconformist missionaries from each of the regions under study dispatched a handful of their most talented students to Britain to study at the college. Joseph May, a former slave from Sierra Leone, trained at the college in 1840 and became a missionary, first in Freetown, Sierra Leone, then later in the Gambia. May studied alongside Charles Knight, also from Sierra Leone. Three years later, another Sierra Leonean, William Allen, trained at Borough Road.[15] In a letter to the BFSS, Revd Henry Badger wrote positively of the training these men received at the college and their role in introducing the British System to Sierra Leone:

> Your Society has done essential service to our schools here, in having taken Charles Knight, Joseph May, and William Allen into your Institution in the Borough-Road. They have acquired a great amount of information, and a good method of communicating it to the children of their own country. They have introduced the system with great success, and have been very diligent in its application. I know of nothing that has done more to raise the character of our schools.[16]

In a letter to the BFSS the following year, Badger lavished praise on the three Sierra Leonean missionaries, describing them as 'among the best teachers in the colony'.[17] The instruction these men had received at the college prepared them for a leading role in the implementation of the British System in Nonconformist mission schools in different areas of Africa and helped them secure a positive reputation among their European counterparts. In this respect they, as well as others who preceded and followed them at Borough Road, represent a notable counterpoint to studies that emphasize how 'native assistants' were commonly subordinated to, and typically derided by, European missionaries.[18]

[15] 'Borough Road Male Students', 1–26.

[16] *Fortieth Report of the British and Foreign School Society* (London, 1845), 27–8.

[17] *Forty-First Report of the British and Foreign School Society* (London, 1846), 29.

[18] On the tensions and ambivalent relations between 'native assistants' and European missionaries, see Comaroff and Comaroff, *Of Revelation and Revolution*, 2: 78–88; in contrast, for the close bonds that could form between European and non-European

Indeed, Nonconformist missionaries emphasized to the BFSS that creating a pool of 'native assistants' was essential to the survival of their mission stations, if for no other reason than to alleviate the financial pressure of employing costly European missionaries and teachers. To this end, missionaries were eager to establish overseas training schools. In the British West Indies, for example, four Normal Schools (teacher training institutions) were established in the immediate aftermath of the 1833 Abolition Act: all four adopted the British System and were overseen by the BFSS's former pupil, John McSwiney. Concerted efforts to increase the number of native teachers came to nothing, however, when in 1845 the British government terminated the Negro Education Grant, which had been introduced to help fund the creation of an elementary system in the aftermath of slavery, and two of the schools were forced to close. Thereafter, missionaries and education reformers consistently complained to the BFSS about the severe lack of well-trained local teachers in the former slave colonies. In Africa and India, 'native assistants' were even more instrumental in the running of mission schools in this period, for interpreters and translators were often essential to the delivery of instruction in the vernacular. In 1840, the LMS sent the BFSS a breakdown of its worldwide operations: it included '151 missionaries, 39 European and 382 native assistants', covering 554 stations and outstations.[19] The high proportion of native agency represented in these figures is striking, especially as it is unclear whether the figure of 151 missionaries included non-Europeans. Such evidence provides quantitative support to recent studies in missionary historiography which highlight the essential role played by 'native assistants' in Nonconformist evangelism.[20] It is, moreover,

missionaries, see David Maxwell, 'The Missionary Home as a Site for Mission: Perspectives from Belgian Congo', in John Doran, Charlotte Methuen and Alexandra Walsham, eds, *Religion and the Household*, SCH 50 (Woodbridge, 2014), 428–55.

19 *Thirty-Fifth Report of the British and Foreign School Society* (London, 1840), 118.

20 Esther Ruth Liu, 'The Nineteenth Century Missionary-Translator: Reflecting on Translation Theory through the Work of François Coillard (1834–1904)', in Simon Ditchfield, Charlotte Methuen and Andrew Spicer, eds, *Translating Christianity*, SCH 53 (Cambridge, 2017), 376–88; Bronwen Everill, 'Bridgeheads of Empire? Liberated African Missionaries in West Africa', *JICH* 40 (2012), 789–805; Jan Hüsgen, 'The Recruitment, Training and Conflicts surrounding "Native teachers" in the Moravian Mission in the Danish West Indies in the Nineteenth Century', *Itinerario* 40 (2016), 451–65.

in the context of such data and studies that the role and impact of African missionaries such as May, Knight and Allen ought to be read, for the very term 'native *assistant*' belies the leading role that they and other native missionaries played in the delivery of pedagogic and evangelistic instruction in mission communities.

The Nonconformist missionary practice of sending talented pupils to Borough Road and missionaries' subsequent positive reports on the accomplishments of these former pupils illustrates the way in which figures such as May, Knight and Allen represented proof both that 'elevation' and 'improvement' of Africans and emancipated West Indians was possible (and it was generally believed by both religious and secular reformers that such proof was needed) and that the synthesis between Protestant evangelism and education yielded favourable results. For the same reason, missionaries reported confidently on their pupils' capacity for progress and deployed an array of empirical and material evidence to show the strides taken toward their reformation. 'The Slave Book' that Knibb dispatched to the society is an example of this process. The exquisite handwriting and embroidery produced by slave and free children was consciously curated by Knibb so that the BFSS could witness with its own eyes the fruits of Christian instruction, quite literally, through the hands of the enslaved. As a further example, the Jamaica Education Society, which had adopted the British System in all its twenty-nine schools in the colony, sent the BFSS copies of its annual reports, documenting the numbers of pupils in reading, spelling and arithmetic classes as well as the numbers of pupils who were able to write on paper and who were studying English grammar, geography and needlework.[21] Missionaries also illustrated their pupils' abilities by drawing attention to the subjects and texts they studied. From Neyoor, India, Revd Frederick Baylis wrote in 1855 that pupils in his boys' boarding schools were 'taught in English as well as in their own language', studying '"Scripture Selections," the whole of Allen and Cornwell's "Grammar for Beginners," a part of the historical lessons in "Daily Lesson Book No 4," and the whole of a first geography, containing chiefly, the geography of India'.[22] In the girls' school, he observed, pupils had 'made considerable progress' in 'scriptural knowledge,

[21] BULA, BFSS/FC/Jamaica/44, 'Statistical Report of the Jamaica Education Society 1845'.

[22] *Fiftieth Report of the British and Foreign School Society* (London, 1855), 83–4.

geography, grammar, in their own language', which he judged to have a positive effect, adding the 'education thus given … will do much towards civilizing the Shanar people – once altogether sunk in the abominations of devil-worship, and in the grossest ignorance'.[23] Unmistakable here is the framing of missionary education as a civilizing mission. It was by transforming their pupils' progress into tangible evidence of missionary evangelism – samples of handwriting and embroidery, lists of books copied and memorized, performance data and tables of attendance – that Nonconformist missionaries hoped to secure the moral and material support of their home societies and educational and philanthropic institutions such as the BFSS in delivering the overlapping goals of Christian conversion and civilizing mission.

Indeed, the BFSS could be in no doubt that its moral and material support was desperately needed in the early decades of overseas evangelism. For although Nonconformist missionaries displayed considerable optimism regarding their pupils' aptitude for 'improvement', they also expressed considerable anxiety regarding the difficulties they faced in implementing the British System in their schools. For a start, trained missionary teachers from Borough Road were never sufficient in number to make up for the shortfall overseas of those suitably trained in the British System. Writing to the BFSS from South Africa in 1835, one missionary observed that pupils were 'instructed by means of lesson boards on the Lancasterian plan, in so far as I am acquainted with it'. He added: 'I have only to regret that I have not a more thorough knowledge of that system.'[24] At the same time, he praised the abilities of the native teachers working at the mission and the overall value of native agency in the colony. From Jamaica, Revd Jabez Tunley reported to the BFSS: 'those schools which are in opperation [*sic*], are not conducted so fully on the British System as one could wish the Masters of which schools, never having been in the "Normal Institution" except on a visit or so'.[25] Tunley's comments were not exceptional and support William Green's principal criticism of the monitorial system in the British West Indies that it was conducted by poorly trained monitors and teachers whose grasp of monitorial pedagogy was 'woefully

[23] Ibid. 84–5.

[24] *Thirtieth Report of the British and Foreign School Society* (London, 1835), 96.

[25] BULA, BFSS/FC/Jamaica/54, Jabez Tunley to the BFSS, 13 March 1847.

deficient in understanding'.[26] From the Cape of Good Hope, Revd Thomas Atkinson wrote: 'Of *system* I cannot say much. The entire want of monitors has occasioned much difficulty … I have often been obliged to act as monitor myself to the classes in succession.'[27] Similarly, LMS missionary Revd W. B. Addis, who studied at the college in 1827, wrote of his difficulties in securing suitable teachers in South India and confided that his mission schools were conducted on a 'modification' of the British System, which he justified by stating that 'anything complicated will not answer at present in our vernacular schools, for even our more simple method, based upon your system, takes a new schoolmaster some considerable time to learn – so utterly deficient in anything like order or regularity is the teaching of the schoolmasters of this country'.[28] Thomas Sturgeon, from the Baptist mission in Fernando Po in the Gulf of Guinea, admitted: 'We carry out the British system in this, and all our schools, as far as possible.'[29] From South Africa, Revd R. B. Taylor likewise acknowledged that he tried to 'follow the British system as much as possible'.[30] Where training in the British System was limited, among teachers as well as monitors, modification and adaptation of it was bound to occur, although missionaries were rarely inclined to disclose what this looked like in practice in their correspondence with the BFSS.

A severe shortage of teaching materials and sufficient funds further ensured that modification and adaptation of the British System was common. Pleas for teaching materials and complaints of missionary poverty pervade missionary correspondence to the BFSS. Missionaries at the LMS stations in Griqua Town, South Africa, wrote of their mixed fortunes in operating the British System in their schools. The day school at the head station was 'conducted according to the [British] system' and the new school room built in 1831 was 'completed, fitted up, and organized according to the Model School, Borough-road'. Notwithstanding, financial constraints prevented the LMS missionaries from introducing the 'excellent

[26] William A. Green, *British Slave Emancipation: The Sugar Colonies and the Great Experiment, 1830–1865* (Oxford, 1976), 334–5.

[27] *Thirty-Sixth Report of the British and Foreign School Society* (London, 1841), 114.

[28] *Forty-Fifth Report*, 86.

[29] *Fortieth Report*, 28.

[30] *Forty-Sixth Report of the British and Foreign School Society* (London, 1851), 100.

[British] system' into twelve new day schools.[31] In 1840, from the Cape of Good Hope, Revd Dr Philip begged the BFSS to send him whatever teaching resources it could spare: schools are 'generally destitute of lessons', he declared; '*you can be at no loss in sending us any quantity*, for the whole colony is a state of destitution … . *We have at this moment perhaps thirty stations all crying out for lessons.*'[32] In the British West Indies, missionaries routinely despaired at the scarcity of teaching resources. In 1844, the Baptist missionary Revd James Phillippo pleaded with the BFSS to send him school materials, explaining: 'some of the schools under my charge have been so destitute of every thing of the kind as to render them any thing but lancasterian [*sic*] schools', and in some 'scarcely a lesson of the british & foreign school society has been seen to adorn the walls, as I had not a spare sheet of them in possession'.[33] Rarely did Nonconformist missionaries in the British West Indies feel adequately provisioned in delivering elementary instruction in the colonies, and their letters ensured that the society was well aware of the considerable material difficulties under which they laboured.

Similarly, in Africa and India, where Nonconformist missionaries typically taught in the vernacular, the BFSS was informed of their struggles to source translations, particularly in the early days of mission work in these fields. Indeed, even as late as 1862, a report from the Christian Vernacular Society for India to the BFSS concluded: 'there is a lamentable deficiency of good Christian school books in many of the languages'.[34] In Bangalore, both Wesleyan and LMS missionaries were reported to be 'exceedingly anxious to see good school books translated into Canarese'.[35] At the LMS mission station in Kuruman, South Africa, missionaries printed their own translations via the local presses, in addition to applying to the BFSS to send translated books, paper and ink.[36] In 1834, it was informed that Revd Robert Moffat was in the process of printing a Tswana translation of the reading book used at Borough Road.[37]

[31] *Thirty-Third Report of the British and Foreign School Society* (London, 1838), 122.
[32] *Thirty-Sixth Report*, 49.
[33] BULA, BFSS/FC/Jamaica/14, James Phillippo to the BFSS, 11 February 1840.
[34] *Fifty-Seventh Report of the British and Foreign School Society* (London, 1862), 88.
[35] *Thirty-Eighth Report of the British and Foreign School Society* (London, 1843), 32.
[36] Stephen Volz, 'Written on our Hearts: Tsana Christians and the "Word of God" in the Mid-Nineteenth Century', *JRA* 38 (2008), 112–40, at 115–16.
[37] *Thirtieth Report*, 114.

Missionary complaints about the limited number of translated texts and references to the painstaking efforts of missionaries (and, we are typically left to presume, 'native assistants') to produce spelling books and texts in local languages – for example, Moffat's Tswana translations or, as another missionary reported, a translation into 'Tesuto dialect' (presumably Sesotho)[38] – simultaneously reflect the importance placed on vernacular instruction as a means to support conversion and the considerable lengths to which missionaries went, as well as demonstrating the difficulties they faced, in delivering vernacular instruction. Widespread evidence of lack of pedagogical training, combined with limited teaching resources and the difficulties of creating and obtaining translated texts, point to the challenges faced by missionaries in operating the British System in their mission schools. Moreover, their correspondence with the BFSS documents their struggles to deliver the British System in mission schools and thus cautions against over-emphasizing the widespread effectiveness of pedagogy as a tool of European civilizing mission before 1850.

While material difficulties challenged the full and proper implementation of the British System, the response of local populations also mitigated against its effectiveness as a tool of Nonconformist evangelism and improvement. From the British West Indies, the BFSS learned of extremely poor levels of pupil attendance in Nonconformist mission schools, which missionaries typically blamed on the combined effects of poverty, child labour and the failure of formerly enslaved parents to apprehend the value of education. From India, the society learned of the particular difficulties attending female instruction and the constraints imposed on the curriculum as a result of a clash over competing British, or missionary, and Indian views on education, gender and religion. From Bombay, Miss Richmond wrote of the 'insurmountable difficulties' that attended teaching girls, which included 'religious differences, early marriages, and intense dislike to the native women learning English … . We are not allowed to teach English, or give any kind of religious instruction.'[39] Laurence Kitzan argues that missionaries in India faced far more opposition than their counterparts in Africa, and directors of the LMS on more than one occasion issued warnings to missionaries not to interfere in India's political affairs and to steer clear of

[38] *Fifty-Second Report of the British and Foreign School Society* (London, 1857), 18.
[39] *Sixty-Fourth Report of the British and Foreign School Society* (London, 1869), 32.

condemning Hindu social customs, such as suttee, for fear of stoking up religious conflict.[40] From South Africa, the BFSS learned how the spread of English language instruction also provoked opposition. Revd S. Rolland, writing in 1851 from Beersheba, explained that at one of the national assemblies it was 'gravely proposed "to destroy all the missionaries", they having, it was alleged, shown the way for the other Europeans who are now taking possession of their country'. Highlighting local animosity toward the missionaries, he reported that a young man 'brought up in our schools proposed to destroy all the books and houses of the missionaries' and to 'kill all the whites'; however, he later 'abandoned' his plan.[41] In their correspondence, missionaries both wittingly and unwittingly revealed how local people were neither fully passive nor fully persuaded recipients of Christian instruction and pedagogy.[42] Hayden Bellenoit argues for the limitations of pedagogy in the case of India, concluding that 'rather than serving as a hegemonic colonial undertaking, mission schools were subject to Indian agency and contestation'.[43] Indeed, in all three regions considered here, even those parents who sent their children to mission schools did not shrink from pressuring missionaries to adapt their pedagogy in ways that aligned with the parents' interests, in some cases to such an extent that it undermined the ultimate goals of Nonconformist evangelism by insisting upon the omission of Christian instruction altogether.

As this study has argued, Nonconformist missionaries considered Christian pedagogy an essential instrument of evangelism in all three regions under study before 1850, and approached the BFSS to provide teacher training in the British System, via the college and the BFSS manual, along with much needed moral and material support. The BFSS's liberal and progressive education reform agenda resulted in an inclusive approach to teacher training that embraced the

[40] Laurence Kitzan, 'The London Missionary Society and the Problem of Authority in India, 1798–1833', *ChH* 40 (1971), 457–73, at 468.
[41] *Forty-Sixth Report*, 99.
[42] For further examples of local resistance to evangelism and pedagogy, see Volz, 'Written on our Hearts', 120; on the refusal of local peoples to passively accept the pedagogy practised by missionaries of the Church Missionary Society in Kenya see, Robert W. Strayer, 'The Making of Mission Schools in Kenya: A Microcosmic Perspective', *Comparative Education Review* 17 (1973), 313–30, at 321.
[43] Hayden J. A. Bellenoit, 'Missionary Education, Religion and Knowledge in India, *c.*1880–1915', *Modern Asian Studies* 41 (2007), 369–94, at 393.

instruction of women as well as men, and of non-European as well as European students and future teachers. Nonetheless, missionary correspondence with the BFSS suggests that adequately trained teachers were never sufficiently numerous in the mission field. Lack of training, funds and teaching resources contrived to hinder the proper operation of the British System, so that in all three regions 'modification' and 'adaptation' were common, particularly in the early decades of evangelism. If we add to this picture the varying degrees of local resistance to missionary instruction, as in the case of the disappointing pupil attendance in the British West Indies, widespread resistance to Christian instruction among communities in India and opposition to English language instruction in parts of Africa, we are left with the question of just how effective missionary pedagogy was as a tool of Nonconformist evangelism (or indeed of European hegemony) during the first half of the nineteenth century. To answer this satisfactorily, extensive research is now needed into how alternative pedagogies were practised by missionaries, how effectively they were implemented in mission schools and how they were adopted, adapted or opposed by local communities.

This study has suggested that in terms of the considerable range of challenges they faced in situating pedagogy at the heart of overseas evangelism and the sometimes insurmountable obstacles they experienced bringing about conversion through the curriculum, Nonconformist missionaries struggled to implement fully the British System in their schools in the British West Indies, Africa and India during the first half of the nineteenth century. The BFSS archive provides a unique perspective from which to examine the relationship between education and evangelism in these three regions and sheds light on what was actually taught and delivered in Nonconformist mission schools. This makes it possible to comprehend better the role and impact of pedagogy in overseas evangelism. Indeed, evidence from the society's interaction with missionaries suggests that the widespread difficulties they experienced operating the British System in their schools are a warning against over-emphasizing the power of British Protestant pedagogy to achieve the goals of European evangelism and a civilizing mission in Africa, India, and the British West Indies during the first half of the nineteenth century.

The Rise, Success and Dismantling of New Zealand's Anglican-led Māori Education System, 1814–64

Paul Moon*
Auckland University of Technology

Anglican missionaries, serving under the auspices of the Church Missionary Society (CMS), were the first Europeans to settle in New Zealand. Within months of arriving in the country in 1814, they began to convert the language of the indigenous Māori into a written form in order to produce religious texts that would assist with Māori education and conversion. The CMS missionaries also established schools for Māori which later grew into a de facto state education system until the colonial government accelerated its plans for a secular school regime from the mid-1840s. Despite the sometimes awkward religious and cultural entanglements that accompanied missionary proselytizing in this era, the mission schools established by the CMS flourished in the succeeding decades, elevating Māori literacy levels and serving as a highly effective tool of Anglican evangelization. This article traces the arc of the CMS mission schools from their inception in 1814 to their demise in the early 1860s, a period during which the British, and later New Zealand, government's stance towards the mission schools went from ambivalence, through assistance, to antipathy.

For the first half-century of European settlement in New Zealand, the CMS played a central part in Māori education. However, far from this role simply existing as an extension of the colonizing state, Anglican-led Māori schools experienced a rise and descent during this period, with teachers and leaders often finding themselves at odds with government policies in this area. This article traces the ascent and decline of the CMS Māori schools during this period, with a focus on the relationship between church and state, and the evolving educational and colonizing imperatives of these entities in this era.

It has been commonplace in recent historiography of nineteenth-century New Zealand to depict Anglican missionaries as agents of the

* Auckland University of Technology, Private Bag 92006, Auckland 1142, New Zealand. E-mail: paul.moon@aut.ac.nz.

Studies in Church History 55 (2019), 426–440
doi: 10.1017/stc.2018.8

British imperial state. Ballantyne makes this point explicitly, arguing that '[t]he Protestant tradition was a central element in British empire-building during the nineteenth century', and showing how the Protestantism of the era influenced official attitudes towards the providential nature of the British empire and its trusteeship role over colonies. Protestant evangelization (together with gender and race) was 'at the heart of imperial culture'.[1] This view is shared by a consensus of historians,[2] notwithstanding concessions to the contested relationships that sometimes existed between missionaries and colonial officials.

The self-imposed civilizing obligation of the British empire coincided with the conviction of some CMS missionaries (including, initially, Samuel Marsden, who founded the New Zealand mission) that British civilization ought to precede conversion.[3] Although British missionaries in this period were generally more concerned with securing souls than achieving the temporal objectives of colonial officials, the shared goal of spreading civilization has tended to be depicted as a facet of the overall process of British imperial expansion.[4] However, in New Zealand's case, the situation was in many cases more nuanced. While the CMS and colonial officials shared the desire for Māori to be 'civilized' throughout this period, the work of the CMS as the principal provider of schooling to Māori in the colony was initially independent of any direct British imperial control, and did not adhere to any imperial policy on the education of indigenous peoples outside the empire's administrative orbit. Indeed, far from

[1] Tony Ballantyne, *Webs of Empire: Locating New Zealand's Colonial Past* (Wellington, 2012), 137.

[2] Phillippa Mein Smith, *A Concise History of New Zealand*, 2nd edn (Cambridge, 2012), 43; James Belich, *Making Peoples: A History of the New Zealanders from Polynesian Settlement to the End of the Nineteenth Century* (Auckland, 1996), 187; Hilary M. Carey, *God's Empire: Religion and Colonialism in the British World,* c.*1801–1908* (Cambridge, 2011), 368.

[3] Kenneth Pomeranz, 'Empire & "Civilizing" Missions, Past & Present', *Daedalus* 134/2 (Spring 2005), 34–45; Hugh Carleton, *The Life of Henry Williams: Archdeacon of Waimate*, 2 vols (Auckland, 1874), 1: 89; Timothy Yates, *The Conversion of the Māori: Years of Religious and Social Change, 1814–1842*, SHCM (Grand Rapids, MI, 2013), 21–2; Andrew Sharp, *The World, the Flesh and the Devil: The Life and Opinions of Samuel Marsden in England and the Antipodes, 1765–1838* (Auckland, 2016), 704–18.

[4] John Darwin, *The Empire Project: The Rise and Fall of the British World-System, 1830–1970* (Cambridge, 2009), 9; Kate Darian-Smith, Patricia Grimshaw and Stuart Macintyre, *Britishness Abroad: Transnational Movements and Imperial Cultures* (Melbourne, 2007), 5.

being accomplices of British imperial expansion, the mission schools established by CMS missionaries were progressively undermined (among other circumstances) by New Zealand's colonial administration in favour of a secular educational system, which by the early 1860s had brought to an end the predominance of these schools.

The first half-century of the history of the CMS mission schools in New Zealand is surveyed here against the backdrop of an evolving and unequal relationship between church and state in the colony during this period, in which the work of the former eventually succumbed to the political preferences of the latter, and in which there were disparate objectives that increasingly overrode the common desire for Māori to become culturally, socially and religiously more like their European colonizers. From the arrival of the first European settlers in 1814 until 1832, there was no official British presence in the country. In 1833, New Zealand became a British residency, which was followed by the Treaty of Waitangi (1840), through which Britain claimed full sovereignty over the country. New Zealand's first parliament opened in 1854, and between 1860 and 1872 a series of wars were fought between some Māori tribes and the crown.

One of the axiomatic differences between the CMS and colony's government was the missionaries' insistence that all instruction in, and all reading materials provided for, the country's mission schools be in the Māori language. At the commencement of the mission in 1814 this was hardly of concern to British authorities, who had no presence in, nor authority over, New Zealand. However, by the mid-1850s the number of settlers exceeded that of Māori, and was growing rapidly, while the Māori population was in serious decline.[5] By that time, the colonial government (as well as many settlers) was becoming increasingly dissatisfied with aspects of CMS schooling in the colony, and particularly the continued emphasis on teaching in Māori in what was by then a majority-British country.

This article explores the ambivalent role of the CMS in Māori education in this era.[6] It also considers how the 'humanitarian narratives'

[5] Statistics New Zealand, *Principal Results for 1858 Census, Aboriginal Native Population – Appendix H* (Wellington, 2015), 1.

[6] Hugh Morrison, '"But we are concerned with a greater Imperium": The New Zealand Protestant Missionary Movement and the British Empire, 1870–1930', *Social Sciences and Missions* 21 (2008), 97–127.

of missionaries and officials, which Ballantyne has identified as a central influence on British colonial policy,[7] diverged increasingly from government policy. Māori Anglican mission schools went through four phases from 1814 to 1864: being set up, expanding, being cut back and then being discontinued. The transitions from each phase to the next tended to be more evolutionary than abrupt, and occurred at various rates in different parts of the country. Within each phase, consideration is given to the increasing role of officials in determining the fate of these schools, at the expense of the CMS objectives for them.

Setting up

Marsden, as the senior Anglican minister in New South Wales from 1800 to 1838, initially developed the plans to establish a mission in New Zealand in 1805.[8] After numerous delays, in 1814 the first three CMS missionaries, Thomas Kendall, William Hall and John King, arrived in the Bay of Islands, in the far north of New Zealand, to establish a mission there. Kendall was intent on learning the Māori language as a prelude to starting a school to teach Māori to read,[9] in accordance with instructions he had received from the CMS in London[10] and with practice in other CMS mission fields, particularly India.[11]

Within a year of arriving in the country, Kendall had written *A Korao no New Zealand, or, The New Zealander's First Book*, which contained in its fifty-four pages an alphabet, numbers, a basic

[7] Tony Ballantyne, 'Humanitarian Narratives: Knowledge and the Politics of Mission and Empire', *Social Sciences and Missions* 24 (2011), 233–64, at 237–42; Peter McKenzie, 'Public Christianity and Te Tiriti o Waitangi: How the "Clapham Sect" reached Down Under', *Stimulus: The New Zealand Journal of Christian Thought and Practice* 18/4 (2010), 23–31, at 23.

[8] John R. Elder, ed., *The Letters and Journals of Samuel Marsden, 1765–1838* (Dunedin, 1932), 39.

[9] Thomas Kendall to Josiah Pratt, 30 March 1814, in John R. Elder, ed., *Marsden's Lieutenants* (Dunedin, 1934), 49.

[10] Dunedin, Otago University, Marsden Archive, MS_0055_019, Josiah Pratt to Thomas Kendall, 16 August 1815.

[11] Brian Holmes, ed., *Educational Policy and the Mission Schools: Case Studies from the British Empire* (New York, 1967), 92–4; John Spencer, 'Colonial Language Policies and their Legacies in Sub-Saharan Africa', in Joshua A. Fishman, ed., *Advances in Language Planning* (The Hague, 1974), 163–76, at 163–4; Helen May et al., *Empire, Education, and Indigenous Childhoods: Nineteenth-Century Missionary Infant Schools in three British Colonies* (Farnham, 2014), 111–48.

vocabulary, some pronunciation suggestions and a few essential sentences. The work was deficient in many areas,[12] but in the absence of any alternative it became the main instructional text for the missionaries teaching the Māori people to read in the Māori language.[13] The issue of persuading Māori to conform to British ideals of civilization was also to some extent a consideration when the CMS began establishing schools for Māori, although the honorary secretary of the CMS, Revd Henry Venn, later warned that 'the European element in a native church' could be a 'great snare and hindrance to its growth', and could even lead to a 'collision of the races' in the mission field.[14] The approach taken by Venn and the CMS was in contrast to the more assimilationist approach to civilizing held by British officials.[15]

In August 1816, the first CMS school opened in New Zealand, with a roll of thirty-three. Within a decade, the size and number of these mission schools increased, and literacy soon began to expand into areas where no missionaries had been, a process that was made possible by Māori students in the CMS schools taking on the role of teachers in places where there were no European teachers.[16] By the late 1820s, the syllabus of the mission schools had become more standardized, by virtue of the circulation of a narrow range of standard texts on which literacy teaching was based. Māori parents were generally favourably disposed to their children attending these schools, often because they saw temporal as much as spiritual benefit in literacy.[17] As Christianity spread hand-in-hand with literacy in Māori communities at an accelerating pace from the 1830s (thanks to Māori as much as CMS missionaries)[18] two themes were becoming evident for the missionaries. Firstly, the preference of some

[12] Judith Binney, *The Legacy of Guilt: A Life of Thomas Kendall* (Wellington, 2005), 63, 175.

[13] William Knight, *Memoir of Henry Venn, BD: Prebendary of St Paul's, and Honorary Secretary of the Church Missionary Society* (London, 1882), 287.

[14] Birmingham, CRL, CMS Archive, CMS/B/OMS/C A2/L3, CMS Letter Book, 24 December 1860 – 23 September 1867, Henry Venn to Henry Townsend, 4 February 1862.

[15] Patrick Wolfe, 'Settler Colonialism and the Elimination of the Native', *Journal of Genocide Research* 8 (2006), 387–409.

[16] William Brown, *New Zealand and its Aborigines*, 2nd edn (London, 1851), 97–8.

[17] Elder, ed., *Marsden's Lieutenants*, 134.

[18] Raeburn Lange, 'Ordained Ministry in Maori Christianity, 1853–1900', *JRH* 27 (2003), 47–66, at 47.

missionaries for 'civilizing' Māori prior to converting them was regarded either as a slightly lower priority or as something that could occur simultaneously with conversion, as long as the current rate of conversions continued.[19] Secondly, from the missionaries' point of view, the decision to teach and publish only in the Māori language was clearly being vindicated.[20]

Expansion

Throughout the 1830s, the CMS continued to expand the number of mission schools in New Zealand. This expansion resulted in part from the peace-making roles played by many CMS missionaries during the period of social turbulence in much of Māori society brought about by the inter-tribal Musket Wars.[21] However, during this period, in contrast to the previous two decades, the British government was beginning to take an increasing interest in the fate of the country and its Māori population.

One of the incremental steps towards Britain's securing the sovereignty of New Zealand was the appointment of a resident – James Busby – to the country in 1833. As New Zealand's British settler population increased after this, a growing confidence emerged among colonial officials that this European presence would civilize the indigenous population.[22] This process was assumed to include the Māori acquiring the language of the colonizer, as had been the case with indigenous peoples in other parts of the empire.[23]

[19] Carleton, *Henry Williams*, 1: 42–3.

[20] Christopher J. Parr, 'A Missionary Library. Printed Attempts to instruct the Maori, 1815–1845', *Journal of the Polynesian Society* 70 (1961), 429–50, at 429–36; Stephen May, 'Language and Education Rights for Indigenous Peoples', *Language, Culture and Curriculum* 11 (1998), 272–96, at 284; Bernard Spolsky, 'Reassessing Māori Regeneration', *Language in Society* 32 (2003), 553–78, at 556. A similar pattern existed in other British mission fields: see Raeburn Lange, *Indigenous Leadership in Nineteenth-Century Pacific Islands Christianity* (Canterbury, 2006), 296.

[21] Jan Pilditch and Howard Staveley, 'Editing Waikato's Christian Missionary Journals', *Journal of New Zealand Literature* 23 (2005), 29–51, at 43.

[22] Richard Bourke to James Busby, 13 April 1833, in *Correspondence with the Secretary of State relative to New Zealand*, House of Commons Command Papers 238 (London, 1840), 6.

[23] See Stamford Raffles to Somerset, 12 June 1821, in Stamford Raffles, *Memoir of the Life and Public Services of Sir Thomas Stamford Raffles* (London, 1830), 498; Alastair Pennycook, *The Cultural Politics of English as an International Language* (Harlow, 1994), 76–7.

Missionaries in New Zealand were seen as fulfilling this civilizing role through their provision of education, albeit with the crucial exception that schooling was almost entirely in Māori. Nonetheless, Joel Polack, a Bay of Islands trader in the 1830s, noted a rapid increase in the number of Māori learning English at this time, and concluded that 'in the course of two or three generations, the native language will become obsolete, in favour of English'.[24] Despite this trend, CMS missionaries continued to adhere to their policy of teaching and publishing teaching resources only in Māori, and by 1840, the CMS had printed thousands of copies of the New Testament and other religious texts in Māori,[25] with demand for these texts continuing to outstrip supply.[26]

As British settlement in the country gradually increased to a white population of around two thousand by 1840,[27] the House of Lords convened a Select Committee on New Zealand, which reported back in 1838.[28] It considered that while all the schooling was presently undertaken in Māori, this was likely to be only a temporary arrangement. Nonetheless, in the first tangible indication of the intersection of imperial policy with the CMS mission schools in New Zealand, the committee resolved that the government should support the work of the missionaries in the hope of fostering civilization in the country.[29]

Cutting back

New Zealand became a British colony in 1840 through the conclusion of the Treaty of Waitangi. As settlers arrived in their tens of thousands during the two succeeding decades,[30] the colony's government became increasingly aware of, and responsive to, the attitudes of the immigrant population. Some colonists were openly hostile to the

[24] Joel S. Polack, *New Zealand: Being a Narrative of Travels and Adventures during a Residence in that Country between the Years 1831 and 1837*, 2 vols (London, 1838), 2: 280.
[25] Parr, 'Missionary Library', 436–7.
[26] Harrison M. Wright, *New Zealand, 1769–1840: Early Years of Western Contact* (Princeton, NJ, 1959), 162.
[27] John Jennings, *New Zealand Colonization* (London, 1843), 5, 11.
[28] *Report from the Select Committee of the House of Lords, appointed to inquire into the Present State of the Islands of New Zealand, and the Expediency of regulating the Settlement of British Subjects therein* (London, 1838).
[29] ibid. iii, 189, 191, 193, 200, 227.
[30] Statistics New Zealand, *New Zealand Long Term Data Series, Population* (Wellington, 2008), Table A 1.1.

CMS mission schools, seeing them as a barrier to the country's advancement. In 1843, the Auckland journalist Charles Terry insisted that 'the Government ... should enforce education of the native children, in English, as well as in their vernacular language'.[31] Another journalist was even more caustic, claiming that '[t]he missionaries have hitherto, with a most extraordinary and ignorant pertinacity, set their face against every attempt at teaching English to the natives, vainly endeavouring ... [to educate Māori] by lame translations of garbled extracts from the Scriptures'.[32]

Between 1840 and 1846, such views were counteracted by the office of Protector of Aborigines, a government department established in the colony with the express intention of bringing Māori 'within the pale of civilized life, and trained to the adoption of its habits'.[33] The protector was a CMS missionary, George Clarke, who worked to forestall the displacement of Māori by English in the mission schools. Until the disestablishment of the office in 1846, the CMS played a direct role in encouraging the state to retain Māori as the predominant language of instruction in schools for Māori.

During this period the CMS mission schools also became administratively more centralized and financially better coordinated.[34] However, shortages of funding and personnel from the mid-1840s led the government to begin assuming a degree of control over the provision and form of Māori education in the colony. Governor Robert FitzRoy's 1844 Education Ordinance was drafted explicitly to assimilate Māori by (among much else) creating schools 'for the instruction of the Native people in the English language'.[35] FitzRoy's governorship ended the following year without this

[31] Charles Terry, *New Zealand: Its Advantages and Prospects as a British Colony* (London, 1843), 188.

[32] Samuel M. D. Martin, *New Zealand; in a Series of Letters, containing an Account of the Country, both before and since its Occupation by the British Government* (London, 1845), 312.

[33] Normanby to William Hobson, 14 August 1839, in *Correspondence relative to New Zealand*, 39–41.

[34] Frances Porter, ed., *The Turanga Journals, 1840–1850: Letters and Journals of William and Jane Williams* (Wellington, 1974), 383–4; *Missionary Register* 36 (1848), 320, 322.

[35] *An Ordinance for appointing a Board of Trustees for the Management of Property to be set apart for the Education and Advancement of the Native Race* (Auckland 1844), preamble and §5, in Stephen May, 'Māori-Medium Education in Aotearoa / New Zealand', in James W. Tollefson and Amy B. M. Tsui, eds, *Medium of Instruction Policies: Which Agenda? Whose Agenda?* (Mahwah, NJ, 2008), 21–42, at 25–6.

ordinance having taken full effect, but his successor, George Grey, furthered this assimilationist policy with the introduction of his Education Ordinance in 1847, through which the government undertook to fund and oversee a state education regime in which 'instruction in the English language shall form a necessary part of the system'.[36] The stated intention of this ordinance was to improve the condition of Māori in the colony,[37] and it led to pressure on the CMS to begin training teachers, including Māori trainee teachers, to use only English as the language of instruction in their schools.[38] Importantly, the impetus for this shift to the use of English in mission schools came from colonial officials rather than the CMS, and Grey showed himself resolutely opposed to the CMS schools' continuing to teach in Māori.[39] At least some in the Anglican Church in New Zealand were beginning to share the governor's view: George Selwyn, New Zealand's first Anglican bishop, contributed to Grey's Education Ordinance, which he believed was in keeping with his desire for the amalgamation of the races.[40] Selwyn's position contrasted with that of some Anglican missionaries who continued to favour a more autonomous Māori education system.[41]

However, Māori were not merely passive participants in the mission school system.[42] By the 1850s the rate of growth in the number of Māori students had fallen, and there was no longer the willingness there had previously been among some Māori to travel long distances to attend the CMS schools.[43] One CMS missionary, Octavius Hadfield, implied that instruction solely in Māori was a policy with

[36] *An Ordinance for promoting the Education of Youth in the Colony of New Zealand* (Auckland, 1847), §3.

[37] Gilbert A. Wood, 'Church and State in New Zealand in the 1850s', *JRH* 8 (1975), 255–70, at 266–8.

[38] 'Rules for St John's Native Teachers' School', *The Calendar of St John's College New Zealand* (Auckland, 1846). 6–7.

[39] George Grey to Earl Grey, 24 December 1850, Appendix, in Great Britain Colonial Office, *Further Papers relative to the Affairs of New Zealand* (London, 1851), 95.

[40] Allan Davidson, *Selwyn's Legacy: The College of St John the Evangelist, Te Waimate and Auckland 1843–1993* (Auckland, 1993), 67; Neil Benfell, 'Politics and Puseyism: Bishop Selwyn and Education in New Zealand' (MEd thesis, University of Waikato, 1977).

[41] William Rolleston, 'Papers Relative to Native Schools', in *Appendices to the Journals of the House of Representatives* (hereafter: *AJHR*), Session I, A–03 (Wellington, 1867), 1–27, at 1–4; Martin, *New Zealand*, 312.

[42] Judith Simon and Linda Tuhiwai Smith, *A Civilising Mission? Perceptions and Representations of the New Zealand Native Schools System* (Auckland, 2001), 54–88.

[43] George A. Selwyn, *Annals of the Diocese of New Zealand* (London, 1847), 153–4.

which Māori themselves were finding less favour,[44] although the political and land issues affecting Māori probably played a more significant role.[45] In addition, while many CMS mission schools continued to instruct solely in Māori well into the 1850s, in places in New Zealand where there was a sizeable settler population, English was making its way into these schools. This was part of a process of linguistic acclimatization which accelerated the displacement of the Māori language by English, and which was consistent with the government's desire for Māori to become civilized though speaking English.[46]

Population shifts were also having a major bearing on the new policy of using English in all the country's schools, including the Māori mission schools. By 1858 the number of European settlers living in New Zealand had risen to 59,328 and was growing rapidly, while the Māori population had fallen to 55,336,[47] possibly less than half what it had been at the beginning of the century. The colonial government was becoming impatient with the slow pace at which the mission schools were supplanting Māori with English. 'A great duty rests with the General Government', an official, William Fitzherbert, wrote in 1858, 'to promote the education of Native and Half-caste children', and to this end, he concluded, 'English Masters and Mistresses should be invariably employed, and the teaching of the English language made the prominent feature of instruction'.[48] In a similar vein, the mission schools were increasingly making civilization a central aspect of their curriculum. As Hadfield expressed it: 'Native Schools...[are a] powerful and indispensable means for the true civilisation and advancement of the Maori population'.[49] By 1858, mission schools were regarded by one school inspector, William Russell,

[44] Donald F. McKenzie, *Oral Culture, Literacy and Print in Early New Zealand* (Wellington, 1985), 31.

[45] Judith Simon, 'Anthropology, "Native Schooling" and Maori: The Politics of "Cultural Adaptation" Policies', *Oceania* 69 (1998), 61–78, at 67.

[46] John M. Barrington and Timothy H. Beaglehole, '"A Part of Pakeha Society": Europeanising the Maori Child', in James A. Mangan, ed., *Making Imperial Mentalities: Socialisation and British Imperialism* (Manchester, 1990), 163–83, at 167; George Grey, 26 September 1851, *New Zealander*, 12 November 1851, 2.

[47] *Principal Results – Appendix H.*

[48] William Fitzherbert, in 'Reports on Native Schools 1858', *AJHR*, Session I, E–01 (Auckland, 1858), 1–77, at 55.

[49] Ibid. 12, 45.

as 'centres of civilization'.[50] Hugh Carleton, a member of the House of Representatives, emphasized to a receptive governor (Thomas Gore Browne):

> too much stress cannot be laid upon the acquirement of the English language. I believe that civilization cannot be advanced, beyond a very short stage, through means of the aboriginal tongue … . The Maori tongue sufficed for the requirements of a barbarous race, but apparently would serve for little more … .[51]

Language had come to be regarded as key to the emphasis on civilization.

At the same time, those mission schools which maintained instruction primarily in Māori were starting to see signs of decline. They faced many challenges, including difficulty in finding teachers, epidemics such as measles (which reduced student attendances for long periods), the decision by a growing number of Māori parents that their children were more productive working on farms than in classrooms, and a growing uncertainty among Māori parents at the purported benefits of schooling for their children.[52] Moreover, the demographic, cultural and social evolution of the country was encouraging the government to pursue a more assimilationist, English-based education system in the colony, and the CMS reluctantly acceded to these changes. However, the CMS could hardly be described as being 'to the fore' of British imperialism in the colony: its mission schools experienced setbacks in attendance, and its Māori-only language policy was steadily eroding in the face not only of government policy and but also of the evolving demands of Māori themselves.

Demise

The CMS mission schools were dealt a fatal blow in the early 1860s, when they fell victim to a drastically changing political environment.

[50] W. H. Russell, 'Report on Schools in the Province of Auckland', 16 February 1858, in 'Reports on Native Schools 1858', *AJHR*, Session I, E–01, 1–77, at 60.
[51] Hugh Carleton, 'Further Report on Schools in the Province of Auckland', in 'Reports on Native Schools 1858', ibid. 77.
[52] Octavius Hadfield, 'Report on the Otaki Industrial School, 1855', 13 January 1856, in 'Reports on Native Schools 1858', ibid. 33–4.

In March 1860, war broke out between the colonial government and Māori in Taranaki, a conflict which spread in 1863 to the Waikato region and then elsewhere. Within a few months of the commencement of the Taranaki conflict, Governor Gore Browne delivered a speech in which he linked the war with the challenges of a nation which was divided linguistically. This was another strident assertion of the government's assimilationist intent in the education field.[53]

By the mid-1860s, mission schools were increasingly complying with the government's wishes to teach either primarily or exclusively in English, partly as a response to the colony's changing demographics, but more directly in response to the fact that government funding for schools was based on English being the predominant language used in classes. Schools were also faced with declining Māori interest in schools which instructed only in the Māori language. The government's growing commitment to the removal of instruction in Māori from all schools encountered resistance from the early 1860s, with many Māori parents withdrawing their children from schools altogether. In some cases, the entire Māori student population of schools left; this was as much a sign of their dissatisfaction with the European world more generally as an indication of their views on the change in the language of instruction.[54] In addition, finding teachers prepared to work in mission schools where there was hostility between Māori and settlers was becoming increasingly challenging for the CMS.[55]

Moreover, the Kingitanga movement, a pan-tribal response to the incursions into Māori land by the colonial government, was inclined to cast the mission schools as obstacles to Māori self-determination.[56] As a consequence, by 1862 the education of Māori in those parts of the Waikato region under Kingitanga control was 'totally neglected', with mission school attendance overall having halved.[57] Ironically, many of these mission schools had been bastions of the Māori

[53] Thomas. G. Browne, 'Address of His Excellency the Governor to Maori Chiefs assembled at Waitemata on the 10th of June 1860', in 'Further Papers Relative to Native Affairs', *AJHR*, Session I, E–01 (Auckland, 1860), 1–40, at 34.

[54] John Morgan, in Benjamin Wells, *The History of Taranaki* (New Plymouth, 1878), 167–8.

[55] John E. Gorst, 'Report of J. E. Gorst, Esq., Inspector of Schools', in *AJHR*, Session I, E–04 (Auckland, 1862), 1–40, at 6–8.

[56] Ngapare K. Hopa, 'Land and Re-empowerment: The Waikato Case', in Angela Cheater, ed., *The Anthropology of Power* (London, 2005), 101–15, at 101; David McCan, *Whatiwhatihoe: The Waikato Raupatu Claim* (Wellington, 2001), 25–30.

[57] Gorst, 'General Report', 11.

language in a country where English had become the dominant language. Yet, although they received very little state funding, they were perceived as being state schools, and groups like Kingitanga viewed them with suspicion. The decline in mission school attendance was not limited to areas where Kingitanga had an influence, however. In other parts of the country, officials reported that 'with rare exceptions … [Māori] children are growing up unable to read and write, presenting in this respect a marked contrast to their parents, who almost without exception can read, write, and cypher with fluency'.[58] By the mid-1860s, most of the country's mission schools had ceased to operate, and even after the wars had ended, the majority of these schools remained closed, signalling the end of the era of the mission school in New Zealand.[59]

While the few remaining mission schools and the state education system remained divided by their language of instruction, the perception among some Māori was the exact opposite: that these schools were more obviously an agent of state in the 1860s than they had been at any previous time. Yet as early as 1844 the colonial government had initiated policies designed to marginalize the CMS schools especially, in favour of a more secular schooling system. Moreover, while it was the legislative actions of the colonial state which resulted in the loss of land in many Māori communities from the 1850s, and the loss of Māori lives as well during a succession of wars in the 1860s, it was the mission schools that suffered the backlash of boycotts and abandonment by Māori. This was despite the fact that the CMS missionaries (along with those of other denominations such as the Catholics and the Wesleyans) often spoke out in favour of their local Māori communities and against the actions of the New Zealand government.[60] The near-collapse of the country's Anglican-led Māori education system was the result, although in a few cases the CMS was able to maintain its support of Māori secondary education, notably Hukarere Native School for Girls, St Stephen's School, and Te

[58] George S. Cooper, 'Report from G. S. Cooper, Esq., Resident Magistrate, Napier', in 'Reports on the Social and Political State of the Natives in various Districts at the Time of the Arrival of Sir G. F. Bowen', *AJHR*, Session I, A–04 (Wellington, 1868), 1–39, at 13.

[59] Barrington and Beaglehole, '"Part of Pakeha Society"', 174.

[60] Marion Grau, *Rethinking Mission in the Postcolony: Salvation, Society and Subversion* (London, 2011), 226; Sarah Dingle, 'Gospel Power for Civilization: The CMS Missionary Perspective on Maori Culture 1830–1860' (PhD thesis, University of Adelaide, 2009), 131–48.

Aute College, the last of which provided much of the leadership for the early twentieth-century Māori renaissance.

Conclusion

While recent historiography has ascribed to Protestant missionaries, including CMS missionaries operating in New Zealand, a central role in British imperial expansion during the nineteenth century, such generalizations potentially mask what was a more intricate and at times ambiguous relationship. In New Zealand, this relationship evolved substantially from 1814 to 1864, making it even more difficult to characterize the CMS as an arm of British empire-building. On the one hand, CMS missionaries and British government officials pursued broadly similar objectives with respect to the perceived need to civilize Māori, through education and particularly religious instruction. In addition, until the mid-1830s CMS missionaries were one of the main sources of British intelligence on New Zealand, a role which unavoidably had an impact on the formation of British policy on the country. However, this analysis has shown that the relationship passed through various phases.

From 1814, when the CMS mission in New Zealand commenced, until the early 1830s, the work of the missionaries in the country was unobstructed by any direct official involvement, and took place with the tacit consent of colonial officials both in New South Wales and Britain. With the appointment of a resident to New Zealand in 1833, the country was drawn more closely into the orbit of the British empire, although it did not become a British colonial possession until 1840. From the early 1830s, the CMS mission schools grew dramatically in number, and spread throughout much of the country. By 1834, there were fifty-four of these schools north of Rotorua.[61] The consequence of this expansion was that the CMS mission schools emerged by the end of the decade as New Zealand's de facto state schooling system, a situation that was accomplished with no British government funding or administrative support. The objectives of the CMS in civilizing and educating Māori largely coincided with the findings of the 1838 House of Lords Select Committee on

[61] J. M. R. Owens, 'Christianity and the Maoris to 1840: A Comment', *New Zealand Journal of History* 3 (1969), 143–65, at 158.

New Zealand, but the direct influence of the committee's recommendations on the mission schools was negligible.

However, within four years of New Zealand becoming a British colony, the goals of the CMS mission schools and those of the country's colonial administration began to diverge. Ordinances issued by Governors FitzRoy and Grey in 1844 and 1847 respectively advanced the principle (which became a tenet of state policy for Māori education for the remainder of the century) that instruction in schools ought to be predominantly in English.[62] By the 1850s New Zealand's colonial government had become more strident in its demands for an assimilationist policy based on schools teaching only in English, a demand which went against the long-held practice and preference of the CMS to maintain Māori as the language used in its schools. The weight of popular opinion in the country, amongst settlers but perhaps also amongst Māori, was also shifting increasingly towards the government's stance on this matter. Gradually, the CMS acquiesced to the requirement that its schools deliver lessons mainly in English. Thus, from being at the forefront of the empire-building process, it lagged behind the assimilationist policies of the colonial state, a trait that was echoed in other parts of the empire.[63]

The outbreak of war in the colony in the 1860s effectively put the CMS mission schools in the position of fighting a metaphorical conflict on two fronts, facing on one side the government's insistence on assimilationist policies, and on the other contending with Māori communities which perceived the shift to an English-based curriculum as evidence that the mission schools were an agent of British colonial expansionism. By this time, though, the number of settlers in the country had exceeded that of the indigenous population, and the trajectory would see further growth of the former group and decline in the latter. Given these circumstances, missionaries themselves found it harder to justify maintaining the argument that Māori continue to be taught in their native language, and by the end of the century English had become the main or exclusive language of instruction in practically all the country's schools.

62 As examples, see the Native Schools Act (1867) and the Native School Code (1880).

63 Susan Thorne, '"The Conversion of Englishmen and the Conversion of the World Inseparable": Missionary Imperialism and the Language of Class in Early Industrial Britain', in Frederick Cooper and Ann Laura Stoler, eds, *Tensions of Empire: Colonial Cultures in a Bourgeois World* (Berkeley, CA, 1997), 238–62.

'The One for the Many': Zeng Baosun, Louise Barnes and the Yifang School for Girls at Changsha, 1893–1927

Jennifer Bond*
School of Oriental and African Studies

This article explores the role of Chinese Christian women in the internationalization of Chinese education in the early twentieth Century. In particular, it examines the changing relationship between Church Missionary Society (CMS) missionary Louise Barnes, and Zeng Baosun, the great granddaughter of Zeng Guofan. Zeng Baosun was born in 1893 in Changsha, educated at the CMS's Mary Vaughan School in Hangzhou, and became the first Chinese woman to graduate from the University of London, before returning to China to establish a Christian school for girls in Changsha (Yifang) in 1918. Although an extraordinary example because of her elite family background, Zeng's story highlights how Chinese women used the networks to which their Christian education exposed them on a local, national and international scale to play an important role in the exchange of educational ideas between China and the West during the early twentieth century. The story of the relationship between Zeng and Barnes also reveals the changing power dynamics between foreign missionaries and Chinese Christians in the process of indigenizing the church in China: the roles of teacher and pupil were reversed upon their return to Changsha, with Zeng serving as headmistress of her own school and Barnes as a teacher.

---

* 37 Darwin Rd, Wood Green, London, N22 6NS. E-mail: jenibond@gmail.com. I would like to thank Bill Lee for his kind assistance with my research and for allowing me to accompany his family and friends on a trip to Changsha in November 2015. I would also like to thank the President of the Yifang Girls' School Alumnae Association, Gong Anqi (龚安琪), for introducing me to the Changsha Tianjiabing Experimental Middle School (长沙市田家炳实验中学) and to Zeng Xianrong (曾宪蓉), a great-niece of Zeng Baosun in Taipei. I am grateful to Andrea Janku at SOAS for kindly reading a draft of the article and to the anonymous peer reviewers for their feedback. Finally, I wish to thank Queen Mary University of London Archives for providing the images used. This work was undertaken with the support of AHRC and Confucius Institute grants during my doctoral research in China.

Studies in Church History 55 (2019), 441–462
doi: 10.1017/stc.2018.9

On 24 June 1913, Louise Hester Barnes resigned her post as headmistress of the Church Missionary Society (CMS) Mary Vaughan High School in Hangzhou. Her resignation followed a dispute with the CMS about extending her furlough to enable her to support the higher education of a Chinese student who was studying in London under her care, Zeng Baosun (曾寶蓀; 1893–1978), the great-granddaughter of Zeng Guofan (曾國藩; 1811–72). Barnes explained in her letter to the society: 'It is with the very deepest regret that after a connection of almost twenty-three years with the beloved Church Missionary Society that I'm obliged to ask the committee to accept my resignation.'[1] She went on to explain her decision in a further letter dated 30 November 1913:

> I need hardly say I am not taking this serious step without much thought and waiting upon God. If I returned to China soon, it would have meant no college career for Miss Tseng, and that I considered very short sighted policy as I believe the time has come for us to give our very best efforts to the training of the Chinese or any other students, who are willing and capable of being trained.[2]

Barnes's decision to resign was indeed a 'serious step', as she had to forego her pension in consequence. As it turns out, her faith in Zeng's potential was justified. Zeng went on to become the first Chinese woman to earn an honours degree from the University of London, founded her own Christian school for girls in Changsha upon her return to China, and became a leading educator and political figure in republican China. She represented the Republic of China at the United Nations Commission on the Status of Women in Geneva in 1952 and at the Asian Anti-Communist League in Manila in 1956. Still, Zeng is little known in mainland China compared to her illustrious great-grandfather, Zeng Guofan, who is famed for his role in suppressing the Taiping rebellion (1850–64).

Zeng's story deserves greater historical scrutiny, not because she was the great-granddaughter of a famous Chinese general, but because her story throws light on the ways in which Christianity shaped the life of Chinese women at the turn of the twentieth

[1] Birmingham, CRL, CMS Archive, CMS/G1/CH2/O/1913/ 87, Louise Hester Barnes to Mr Bardsley, 24 June 1913.
[2] Ibid., CMS/G1/CH2/O/1913/121, Louise Barnes to CMS Committee, 30 November 1913.

century. The story of the relationship between Zeng and Barnes reveals the changing power dynamics between foreign missionaries and Chinese Christians in the process of indigenizing the church in China: the roles of teacher and pupil were reversed upon their return to Changsha, with Zeng serving as headmistress of her own school and Barnes as a teacher. Although an extraordinary example due to her elite family background, Zeng's life also highlights the important role played by Christian-educated Chinese women in the process of educational exchange between China and the West. Chinese Christian women such as Zeng could use the social networks to which their education gave them access on a local, national and international scale. Through their experiences of multiple educational systems, both Chinese and Western, they were active agents in the transfer of educational knowledge between China and the West in the early twentieth century, adapting, rejecting and assimilating different aspects as they saw fit.

Although much attention has been paid to the role of Western missionaries in the process of internationalizing Chinese education, the role of Chinese Christian women in the exchange has been understudied. There have been several explorations of the contribution of returning male Chinese overseas students who pursued degree studies in Japan, the UK and the USA at the turn of the twentieth century.[3] Hu Ying's examination of Ida Khan and Mary Stone has drawn attention to the role played by missionary-educated Chinese women who stepped outside the domestic sphere in the creation of the Chinese New Woman.[4] However, very little attention has been paid to their role in educational exchange, which has largely been dominated by studies of Western missionaries in their efforts to found and run universities in China.[5] Chinese women have been portrayed as passive recipients of a modernizing Western education, 'enlightening' and

[3] Stacy Bieler, *'Patriots' or 'Traitors': A History of American-Educated Chinese Students* (Armonk, NY, and London, 2009); see also her 'Zeng Baosun: Embracing Chinese Ideals and Christian Education', in Carol Lee Hamin and Stacey Bieler, eds, *Salt and Light*, 3: *More Lives of Faith that shaped Modern China* (Eugene, OR, 2011), 93–115.

[4] Hu Ying, 'Naming the First New Woman', *Nan Nu: Men, Women, and Gender in Early and Imperial China* 3 (2001), 196–231.

[5] Jessie Gregory Lutz, *China and the Christian Colleges, 1850–1950* (New York, 1971); Daniel H. Bays and Ellen Widmer, eds, *China's Christian Colleges: Cross-Cultural Connections, 1900–1950* (Stanford, CA, 2009); Ruth Hayhoe, *China's Universities 1895–1995: A Century of Cultural Conflict* (London, 1996).

'uplifting' them, unbinding their feet and freeing them from arranged marriages. Although there is a proliferation of English-language missionary writings, it is very difficult, due to a lack of sources in mission archives, to know how Chinese women themselves experienced and responded to missionary education. As Kwok Pui-Lan has highlighted, Chinese Christian women's voices were seldom recorded in conference reports or minutes of church meetings.[6] Better understanding of the role of Christian-educated Chinese women in this process of internationalizing Chinese education is vital for a fuller picture of the missionary enterprise in China and for putting the role of Western missionaries into clearer perspective.

Thomas Kennedy's translation of Zeng Baosun's memoir has made her story accessible to an English-speaking audience.[7] Zeng's memoir, originally published in 1970 when she was seventy-seven, is naturally influenced by loss of memory, nostalgia and the contemporary political situation, and therefore must be treated with caution. Zeng herself admits: 'All my diaries and records no longer exist. It has only been since I have enjoyed the peace and security of life here on Taiwan that I felt I could begin writing, but I have had to rely entirely on memory. Inevitably, this resulted in many errors and gaps.'[8] Although Kennedy's is a very close translation, I also draw upon the Chinese version for biographical and other information concerning her missionary school experience which he left out.[9]

Early Education and Conversion to Christianity

Zeng Baosun was born in the spring of 1893 into a wealthy family of the scholarly elite from Xiang Xiang (湘鄉), Hunan Province.[10] Her father, Zeng Guangjun (曾廣鈞), the eldest grandson of Zeng Guofan, was successful in the imperial examinations and in 1889,

[6] Kwok Pui-Lan, 'Chinese Women and Protestant Christianity at the Turn of the Twentieth Century', in Daniel H. Bays, ed., *Christianity in China: From the Eighteenth Century to the Present* (Stanford, CA, 1996), 194–208, at 196.

[7] Thomas Kennedy, *Confucian Feminist: Memoirs of Zeng Baosun 1893–1978* (Philadelphia, PA, 2002).

[8] Ibid. 157.

[9] Zeng's *Memoir* was originally published in 1970 by the Chinese Christian Literature Council in Hong Kong: 曾寶蓀 [Zeng Baosun], 曾寶蓀回憶錄 [*Zeng Baosun huiyilu*; *Memoirs of Zeng Baosun*] (Hong Kong, 1970).

[10] Ibid. 1.

at the age of twenty-three, became the youngest member of the Hanlin Academy, the highest academic institution for classical learning in China, sponsored by the emperor.[11] A friend and supporter of the reformer Liang Qichao (梁啟超; 1873–1929), he held progressive ideas on women's education.[12] He made sure his daughter's feet were not bound and did not arrange a marriage for her. He also did not object to Zeng's conversion to Christianity and allowed her to go abroad to study.[13]

As Susan Mann, Dorothy Ko and Ellen Widmer have shown, although there were many vocational avenues for female education in late imperial China, only the most privileged girls had a chance to receive a formal education.[14] Born into the wealth of the Zeng family, Zeng Baosun studied alongside her brothers and male cousins under tutors employed in the family school at the Zeng family home, Prosperity Hall, in Changsha. She was an unusually gifted scholar and an avid reader. Influenced by her reform-minded father, her tutors not only taught the Confucian classics, but also history, geography, modern languages and calisthenics.[15] Zeng was thus more than well prepared academically upon entering public education in missionary schools.

Zeng's varied formal educational experiences challenge us to rethink traditional interpretations, which place missionary education at the forefront of educational modernization in this period.[16] She found the academic standards at missionary schools disappointing compared to her rigorous training at home, and their heavily religious atmosphere restrictive. For example, Zeng recalled her disappointment at the curriculum when she entered the Baptist Eliza Yates Academy (晏摩氏女校) in Shanghai in 1904. Although she learned to play Western musical instruments (particularly the organ), which

[11] Kennedy, *Confucian Feminist*, 4.

[12] Ibid. 16.

[13] Ibid. 17.

[14] Susan Mann, 'The Education of Daughters in the Mid-Ch'ing Period', in Alexander Woodside and Benjamin A. Elman, eds, *Education and Society in Late Imperial China, 1600–1900* (London, 1994), 19–49; Dorothy Ko, 'Pursuing Talent and Virtue: Education and Women's Culture in Seventeenth- and Eighteenth-Century China', *Late Imperial China* 13 (1992), 9–39; Ellen Widmer, ed., *Writing Women in Late Imperial China* (Stanford, CA, 1997).

[15] Kennedy, *Confucian Feminist*, 21.

[16] John Cleverley, *The Schooling of China: Tradition and Modernity in Chinese Education* (London, 1985); Lutz, *China and the Christian Colleges*, 22.

was a novelty, the other subjects seemed of little use to her. Given her family background, she had little need for domestic education, which was designed to equip lower-class girls with the skills needed to make them useful Christian homemakers: 'I began to learn to do handicrafts, and to make garments, but there was no mathematics, history or geography.'[17]

Naturally academic and excelling in Chinese literature, Zeng found the academic environment of Wuben (務本女中), a Chinese-run private school for girls which she attended from 1905, much more amenable. In 1906 she transferred to Hangzhou Provincial Normal School for Women (杭州省立女子師範).[18] Recognizing her academic potential, the mathematics teacher Chen Boyuan (陳伯原) recommended that rather than becoming a primary school teacher, Zeng would do better to continue her studies at the newly opened Mary Vaughan High School (馮氏女校) in Hangzhou, where he was about to take up an appointment in 1909.[19]

The Mary Vaughan High School opened on 13 February 1909. It was named in honour of a CMS missionary who had donated two thousand dollars of her own money to build a school for girls in Hangzhou but had died shortly before it was finished. Her close friend and fellow CMS missionary, Miss Louise Barnes, was appointed as the acting principal for the school in 1909 and remained until 1912.[20] Louisa Hester Barnes was born on 14 January 1855, in Dorchester, Dorset.[21] In her modest family background, Barnes differed from the majority of CMS missionaries in this period, who tended, like Mary Vaughan, to come from the middle classes.[22] Her father, Peter Fredrick Barnes, was a bricklayer by trade.[23] It is difficult to ascertain Barnes's early educational background, but by 1881 she was a certified teacher living in Ryde on the Isle of Wight.[24] Her training and experience as a school teacher probably

17 Kennedy, *Confucian Feminist*, 23.
18 Ibid. 29.
19 Ibid. 30.
20 Arthur Elwin, *A Short Sketch of the Life of Mary Vaughan of Hangchow* (Oxford, 1909).
21 General Register Office, *England & Wales, Civil Registration Birth Index, 1837–1915*, Q1/1855/B, online at: FreeBMD, <https://www.freebmd.org.uk/>, last accessed 20 November 2018.
22 See Kenneth Scott Latourette, *A History of Christian Missions in China* (New York, 1929), 409.
23 Kew, TNA, WO 97/ 559, Royal Hospital Chelsea: Soldiers Service Documents.
24 Ibid., RG11/1179/58, Census Returns of England and Wales 1881, 13.

made her attractive to the CMS at a point when their educational activities were beginning to expand. In view of her humble family background, therefore, giving up her pension was a momentous decision. With no wealthy relatives to support her retirement, Barnes's decision to resign was a brave step which highlights how much potential she saw in her Chinese pupil.

The Mary Vaughan School was in many ways a new departure for the CMS in Zhejiang province. It was the society's first girls' school in East China to cater specifically for the upper classes. In a letter to the board, Barnes announced with great satisfaction that the school had been able to attract girls from 'High Class Families': 'Of the twenty-five pupils, eleven are the daughters of Christians; nearly all the remaining fourteen are from official families, three of their boarders are relatives of the Marquis Tseng. And one day scholar is a granddaughter of a late Prime Minister.'[25] Indeed, the fact that the Zeng family had signed up three of their daughters was very welcome advertising for the school, and enabled them to attract more upper-class pupils.[26]

Although the formal provision of women's education had been sanctioned in 1907 by the Qing government, when the Mary Vaughan High School opened there was no government school in East China which offered higher-level middle school training for girls. Prior to this a number of private schools for girls had been set up by Chinese reformers. In Hangzhou, Manchu noblewoman Hui Xing (惠興) established a school for girls, Zhenwen nüxue (貞文女學; later known as Huixing Girls' School; 惠興女子中學), as early as 1904. However, this school only offered a curriculum up to junior middle school level.[27] Therefore in the first decade of the twentieth century missionary schools were often the only places where elite girls could gain a higher-level middle school education. An advanced

[25] CRL, CMS/G1/CH2/O/1909/175, Louise Hester Barnes to Mr Baring-Gould, 19 August 1909.

[26] After Zeng entered the school, several more elite families signed up their daughters. On 13 September 1909, Barnes wrote: 'We are hoping to reopen the school tomorrow with a promise of several new scholars. All daughters of Mandarins': ibid., CMS/G1/CH2 /O/1909/186, Louise Barnes to Mr Baring-Gould, 13 September 1909.

[27] Huixing nüzi zhongxue, 'Ben xiao zhi lüe shi' ['A brief History of our School'], in 浙江杭州市私立惠興女子初級中學一覽 [*Zhejiang Hangzhou shi sili Huixing nüzi chuji zhongxue yilan*; *Catalogue of the Huixing Junior Middle School for Girls, Zhejiang, Hangzhou*] (Hangzhou, 1937), 1.

curriculum with English-language tuition and textbooks and plush new facilities help to explain why upper-class families such as the Zeng clan may have chosen the Mary Vaughan School. In November 1908, Barnes reported: 'On Saturday an educationalist lady from Shanghai asked to see over the building. She told me she had been engaged for six years in educational work in China, and had seen a great many schools, but never one quite like this – she quite envied me!'[28]

The strict discipline of missionary schools may have been another reason why elite reform-minded families such as Zeng's chose to send their daughters to missionary establishments in this period. By the turn of the century, education was becoming a class indicator for girls, and Zeng's was the first generation of her social class to receive a public education outside the home. As Joan Judge has explored, the moral ambiguity of female students, as the first category of 'respectable' women to step into the public sphere, was of deep concern in the print media discourse of the early twentieth century.[29] At Mary Vaughan, as at many missionary schools for girls in this period, conservative notions of female obedience and family loyalty were encouraged above all else, making it an attractive option for the upper classes and allaying parental concerns that a public education would give girls radical ideas and unfit them for their traditional roles as 'good wives and wise mothers'. Indeed Barnes stressed that the aim of female education in China was 'not only imparting intellectual knowledge, but of the training of these dear girls to be loyal, true and noble Chinese women'.[30]

In her memoirs, Zeng attributes her conversion to Christianity while studying at Mary Vaughan to three main factors. First was the influence of Miss Barnes, who forgave her after she led a short-lived rebellion against the school, sparked by the arrogance of a foreign teacher who, she felt, unfairly punished the whole class for one student's misdemeanour. Secondly, she cites the example of another teacher, Miss Stuart, who had returned to China as a missionary despite being crippled as a child and losing her parents during the

[28] CRL, CMS/G1/CH2/O/1908/198, Louise Barnes to Mr Baring-Gould, 30 November 1908.

[29] Joan Judge, *Republican Lens: Gender, Visuality and Experience in the Early Chinese Periodical Press* (Berkeley, CA, 2015), 56–7.

[30] CRL, CMS/G1/CH2/O/1909/177, Louise Barnes to Mr Baring-Gould, 23 August 1909.

Boxer Uprising of 1900. Finally, she was moved by her experience of attending revival meetings held at Mary Vaughan by Pastor Ding Limei (丁立美), one of the most influential Chinese preachers of the early twentieth century.[31]

Becoming the first Christian in her family was a challenge, as Zeng explained:

> … it was not easy to convert to Christianity at that time. In the first place my family had been followers of Confucianism for thousands of years … . None of our friends or relatives were followers of foreign religions. To have a young woman of the family become a Christian would simply make them a laughing-stock.[32]

While her grandmother was opposed to her conversion, her father was not, and gave his permission after asking Zeng to read texts which included Thomas Huxley's *On Evolution and Ethics*, Herbert Spencer's *The Study of Sociology*, Charles Darwin's *Origin of Species* and Adam Smith's *Wealth of Nations*, to ensure she was making an informed choice.[33]

The conversion of the daughter of such a family was the fulfilment of a female missionary educator's greatest hopes: to convert the upper classes to Christianity via their educated daughters. As her close relationship with Barnes developed and she continued to excel academically, Zeng accompanied Barnes back to England on her furlough in order to pursue a higher education, thus embarking on a new course of life on the eve of the 1911 revolution. Her family allowed her to pursue higher education in the UK on condition that she remain under Barnes's care at all times; if Barnes returned to China, so must Zeng.[34]

Higher Education in the UK

Zeng's educational experiences highlight the new networks for Chinese Christian women that were emerging on a local, national and international scale at the turn of the century. These networks provided women with unprecedented mobility and exposure to

[31] Kennedy, *Confucian Feminist*, 29.
[32] Ibid. 30.
[33] Ibid.
[34] Ibid. 35.

new experiences and life choices. Zeng, having already moved from Changsha to Shanghai and then to Zhejiang for her middle school education, now, under the protection of her teacher, Louise Barnes, studied in England. Zeng made use of these global missionary networks in seeking support to establish her own school for girls at Changsha.

Zeng studied at two girls' high schools in London, Worthing Church House School and Blackheath Girls' School.[35] She lived with Barnes, who rented small houses near to the schools, but also had the companionship of her cousin, Zeng Yuenong (曾約農), who was studying engineering at the University of London.[36] As Barnes devoted herself to Zeng's education, their relationship grew to resemble that of mother and daughter. As Jane Hunter has shown, it was not unusual for missionary women to adopt Chinese children, normally abandoned girls.[37] Zeng, from an elite family, was in no need of rescue or adoption; however, studying abroad in a foreign country, she was in need of a surrogate mother or mentor figure and Barnes fulfilled this role (Fig. 1).

In 1913, while Zeng was preparing to sit for the examination to enter Westfield College, Barnes had to make a life-changing decision: would she go back to China and continue her work as school principal or stay in England and support Zeng in her studies? After much reflection, and correspondence with the CMS, who refused to grant her an extension of her furlough, Barnes decided that her duty lay with her Chinese pupil.

> There are a few, who feel very strongly I am giving up the 'many for the one', and perhaps Miss Tseng might be strengthened if left alone; others … feel equally strongly I ought to remain in England at least for a time, and help the one who is capable, willing and ready to be trained … . There is a strong feeling we have been praying for such a one to come forward, and I can best help China and the work by remaining

[35] London, Blackheath Girls' School, Register 1912, no. 727.

[36] Zeng Baosun maintained a very close friendship with Zeng Yuenong throughout her life, and neither of them married. Zeng Yuenong was later instrumental in helping Baosun set up her school, Yifang Collegiate Girls' School (藝芳女子學院), where he acted as dean. He became a renowned educationalist in Hunan. As a man, he had access to important political and social networks in Changsha from which Zeng may have been excluded due to her sex: Kennedy, *Confucian Feminist*, 37.

[37] See Jane Hunter, *The Gospel of Gentility: American Women Missionaries in Turn of the Century China* (New Haven, CT, 1984), 192–4.

Fig. 1: Zeng Baosun with Miss Barnes on her graduation from London University, 1916. Image from *Beautiful China*, August 1970, 8. Queen Mary University of London Archives, Westfield College Archive, WFD-15-3-7.

> and that by so doing I am helping to prepare 'the One for the Many'. She will do more than twenty of me.[38]

Barnes felt strongly that the time had come for a self-supporting Christian church, and that with a college degree Zeng as a Chinese Christian could return to China and achieve far more than she, a foreign missionary, could ever hope to achieve.

In October 1913 Zeng entered Westfield College, one of the three women's colleges affiliated with the University of London, majoring in Biology and minoring in Mathematics.[39] Taking its inspiration from Mount Holyoke College in the USA, Westfield had been founded in 1882 with the goal of promoting women's higher education with a distinctly Christian ethos, as reflected in its original motto: 'Behold the Handmaiden of the Lord.' Evangelism both at

[38] CRL, CMS/G1/CH2/O/1913/121, Louise Barnes to Mr Bardsley, 20 May 1913.
[39] London, Queen Mary University of London Archives (QMA), Westfield College papers, WFD-10-1-3, Register, 102.

home and overseas remained at the heart of the college enterprise, with many of its graduates going on to work for the CMS.[40]

Zeng's experience of the English education system exposed her to new ideas which she would carry back to China and apply to her own school for girls in Changsha. Zeng provides a pertinent example of Chinese women's agency in the transnational circulation of educational ideas between China and the West in the early twentieth century. In her memoirs she stated frankly: 'Life at Westfield College, was filled with new experiences for me. The exposure to the way that students were treated at Westfield and the way they responded and conducted themselves afforded me important insights that influenced my direction of women's education in China.'[41] Zeng explained how the English trimester system would need to be adapted in China:

> This system of trimesters in the academic year would not work too well in China but the longer summer vacation would be an excellent idea to allow students to be out of classes during the extreme heat and have more time for review. It would also be suitable for schools in tropical Asia.[42]

She was also impressed by the trust and power afforded to the autonomous Student Association, which was self-governing and represented the interests of students to the college, and by the trust placed in students during examinations for which there was no proctor:

> I became familiar with a fine educational system. Later when I headed the Yifang School, I adopted many of the methods used at Westfield. Naturally, middle school students could not be given as much freedom as university students, but Yifang did not proctor examinations. It did not register de-merits; nor did we dismiss students for a certain number of demerits. These ideas I absorbed during my years at Westfield.[43]

Zeng's experience thus complicates the picture of a one-way flow of educational knowledge between China and the West. It shows that

[40] Janet Sondheimer, *Castle Adamant in Hampstead: A History of Westfield College 1882–1982*, (London, 1983), 7.
[41] Kennedy, *Confucian Feminist*, 52.
[42] Ibid. 54.
[43] Ibid. 55.

Chinese women were active agents in the dynamic flow of educational knowledge and expertise between China and the West, taking the best of two complementary systems and adapting it to a specific cultural setting, much as Chinese Christians were able to take and absorb aspects of Christianity, adapting it to Chinese culture.

During the First World War, Zeng was also deeply influenced by Quaker pacifism and by the social gospel, which was becoming popular in missionary circles. She joined the Westfield College branch of the Student Volunteer Movement, participating in small group discussions about religious and social problems. During this period of spiritual and intellectual growth, Zeng applied her Christian faith to the national situation in China, deciding that the best way for her to serve her country was to found her own Chinese-run Christian school for girls, and she started to use her own extensive networks in the UK to realize this dream.[44]

The Yifang School for Girls at Changsha

The Yifang Collegiate School for Girls (藝芳女子學院) was established by Zeng Baosun and Zeng Yuenong in Changsha in 1918. In evaluating Zeng's efforts, we must look beyond the self-congratulatory rhetoric of the missionary enterprise which praised her as the fruit of their labour, to examine how Zeng actively and resourcefully utilized the networks and connections which her Christian education opened to her, as well as her family's resources, and how she skilfully incorporated the best aspects of her international educational experiences into her own school for girls.

In spring 1915, during her third year of study at Westfield College, Zeng began to formulate plans for school. Although Barnes had originally conceived that Zeng would return to work as a teacher at the Mary Vaughan High School, Zeng was not convinced about this for several reasons. Zhejiang province, situated on the east coast of China, already had a number of schools for girls. She felt she could serve her country better by starting her own school for girls in the capital of her home province, Changsha, Hunan, where there were far fewer educational options available to girls of her class. In 1917 there was only one missionary middle school offering senior middle

[44] Ibid. 59.

school training to girls (jointly run by the American Presbyterian and United Evangelical Churches) and no higher-level government middle schools which could prepare girls for university.[45] The possibility of using family resources and connections to start her school was also an important consideration in Zeng's decision to return to Changsha.[46]

Using her own name and social position as a drawing point, Zeng's school was aimed at girls from elite families, who had previously been largely left out of the missionary school system. She hoped that her school might grow into a Central China Women's College, with a connection to a foreign university, along the lines of Ginling College in Nanjing.[47] By 1926 her school's curriculum offered a six-year middle school course, and four years of college-level education for girls which aimed at achieving university standard.[48] Enrolment grew steadily from eight pupils in 1918 to more than sixty by 1927, and the school expanded its buildings and facilities to meet this growing demand.[49]

A second important aspect of Zeng's decision was her conviction of the pressing need to indigenize the church in China. After the 1911 revolution, with the rise of Chinese nationalism, many missionaries (including Barnes) recognized the pressing need to establish a Chinese-controlled church. Zeng was also inspired by her uncle, Zeng Jirong, who had set up his own Chinese Christian church in Changsha, as she recalled in her memoir:[50]

> I wanted to start a Christian School run entirely by Chinese. Not that mission schools were not good but I felt that Christianity must be completely assimilated in Chinese society before the Chinese people would embrace it as their own religion, as they did Buddhism. Uncle Jirong had also felt this way and started an independent Christian

[45] *Educational Directory of China* (Shanghai, 1917), 19.

[46] Kennedy, *Confucian Feminist*, 57.

[47] QMA, WFD-15-3-2, Circulars relating to I-Fang, pamphlet entitled *A New School for China* (n.pl., *c.*1916).

[48] QMA, WFD-15-3-2, Winifred Galbraith, Circular letter, 'I fang Collegiate Girls School, Changsha, Hunan', March 1926.

[49] Winifred Galbraith, 'An Experiment in Chinese Education', *Chinese Recorder*, July 1927, 425-430.

[50] Zeng Jirong had been helped by Christian missionaries to recover from his addiction to opium and had been converted to Christianity at the same time as Zeng Baosun in December 1911: Kennedy, *Confucian Feminist*, 30.

> Church in Changsha. I would be very willing to accept foreign personnel and financial help, but unwilling to accept foreign control or foreign imposed conditions. Ms. Barnes agreed with this idea.[51]

Unlike some of her fellow CMS missionaries, Barnes herself had long been supportive of the principle of a Chinese-led Christian church.[52] Yifang thus became a remarkable early example of a Chinese-established Christian school in China. Another unusual aspect of the school for its time was the reversal of the power dynamics between missionary school pupil and teacher, as Zeng became headmistress of the school with Barnes as an English teacher under her (Fig. 2). As Zeng recalled, this was almost unheard of at the time in China: 'Ms. Barnes agreed to teach English but preferred that I serve as principal. I think this may have been a first in those days in China: an elderly foreigner working under a young Chinese, especially a Chinese who had formerly been her student.'[53] We can question whether this reversal of the power relationship between Western missionary and Chinese student was as dramatic as Zeng presents. The differences in both class background and financial resources may have made this power shift more natural. Barnes, conscious of her lowly class and educational background was both proud and in awe of her upper-class Chinese pupil. Zeng hints in her memoirs that she was aware of Barnes's very 'ordinary' background: 'I discovered that she was not extremely learned and articulate, simply an ordinary person.'[54] It is also possible that Barnes became financially dependent on Zeng after resigning from the CMS. The financial support that Barnes received from the wealthy family of Mary Vaughan, on which she lived for the rest of her life, was due partly to their friendship and partly to the prestigious Chinese student she had under her charge.[55]

[51] Ibid. 57.
[52] CRL, CMS/G1/CH2/O/1913/121, Louise Barnes to CMS Committee, 30 November 1913.
[53] Kennedy, *Confucian Feminist*, 76.
[54] Ibid. 29.
[55] According to Zeng, Barnes was given £8,000 by the family of Mary Vaughan shortly after her resignation from the CMS, to use at her discretion: Kennedy, *Confucian Feminist*, 48. This was a significant sum. According to Barnes's will, she had almost £2,000 left when she died in 1928: Principal Probate Registry. Calendar of the Grants of Probate and Letters of Administration made in the Probate Registries of the High Court of

Fig. 2: 'At the opening of the Yifang Girls school, August 10, 1918'; Louise Barnes sits on Zeng's right and Zeng Yueneng stands to her left. Image from *Beautiful China*, August, 1970, 8. Queen Mary University of London Archives, Westfield College Archive, WFD-15-3-7.

In establishing her school, Zeng drew upon the local, national and international networks to which her Christian educational background and her status as a member of the Zeng family gave her access. The principals of Westfield College, Agnes de Sélincourt and later Helen Richardson, were supportive of Zeng's idea for a girls' school in Changsha and were instrumental in securing donations towards the funds needed. After the school was established, Helen Richardson helped secure the appointment of three foreign teachers for Yifang: Miss Madge (1922–4), Winifred A. Galbraith (1925–7) and Violet C. Grubb (1925–7) were all 'Old Westfieldians' with degrees and educational experience.[56] In 1922 the school was by no means self-supporting, being mostly funded by the Zeng family, and therefore it was imperative to secure donations to support the

Justice in England. London, England, 1928, 172, online at: <http://www.ancestry.com>, accessed 5 May 2017.

[56] Kennedy, *Confucian Feminist*, 58.

cost of these foreign workers. Zeng Baosun, Zeng Yuenong and Barnes did not receive salaries.[57]

Lists of foreign and Chinese sponsors of the school also reveal the importance of the personal contacts that Zeng made during her studies in the UK in helping her secure the necessary funds. Using her CMS contacts, Barnes introduced Zeng to several prominent missionary families, Christian educators and churchmen, including the wealthy family of Mary Vaughan.[58] Zeng also recalls the invaluable help provided by Miss de Sélincourt: 'She sought out a number of prominent and zealous Englishmen who would give their support. Amongst them was Dr. W. Temple, later Archbishop of England. She also enlisted Ms. Richardson and Ms. McDougall to help me present my ideas to other educators. She considered this true missionary work.'[59] Zeng also made important contacts during her further studies in education at St Hugh's College, Oxford, and Newnham College, Cambridge, during the summers of 1916 and 1917.[60] On her way back to China in autumn 1917, Zeng travelled via the USA and Canada, where she advertised her new school, making valuable contact with leading Chinese intellectuals, including Hu Shi (胡適) and Chen Hengzhe (陳衡哲).[61]

Zeng's social position as a descendant of the famous Zeng Guofan no doubt facilitated her access to these intellectual contacts and social networks. Moreover, upon her return to Changsha, the Zeng family used its influence to secure the recovery of the Zeng Guofan ancestral temple as a site for the school, and to ensure the school's smooth registration with the Hunan provincial education authorities.[62] With the backing of her family proving a powerful asset (at least in its early days), the school was officially opened on 12 September 1918 with eight pupils. The school was named Yifang (藝芳), in memory of Zeng's grandmother's studio at Prosperity Hall.[63]

In establishing her school in Changsha, Zeng aimed to take the best of her Chinese and Western educational experiences and combine them into a unique formulation. She was aware of the advantages

[57] QMA, WFD-15-3-2, Pao Swen Tseng, Circular letter, 3 March 1922.
[58] Ibid., Circulars relating to I-Fang, 'List of donors 1917–1925'.
[59] Kennedy, *Confucian Feminist*, 57.
[60] Ibid. 63.
[61] Ibid. 70.
[62] Ibid. 75.
[63] QMA, WFD-15-3-5, Pao Swen Tseng to Dr Thwaites, 13 December 1971.

and pitfalls of each system and hoped to bridge the gap between Chinese government and foreign missionary education:

> The gulf separating Church-sponsored and secular education at that time was great … . The two educational systems, church and secular, rivalled each other but each had its forte. The church-operated universities inevitably stressed English, Western History and Geography, and Science. Although they made a considerable contribution in introducing new knowledge, they also missed a great deal concerning Chinese history, customs and the traditional culture.[64]

Zeng aimed to bridge the gap by drawing from both Chinese and English schools to fulfil what she perceived to be the needs of Chinese girls at Changsha. Her curriculum offered courses in the Chinese classics and history, geography, mathematics and science. Advanced mathematics courses included algebra, trigonometry, calculus and geometry. Students also benefited from the tuition of English by native speakers who taught texts ranging from Charles Kingsley's *Heroes* to Shakespeare. Zeng's curriculum was designed to outstrip both the Chinese government and Western missionary school curricula for girls at the middle school level.[65] Zeng reported proudly in 1948 the high college entrance rates of Yifang students: 'Our students have been uniformly successful in college entrance examinations: ninety per cent of our old students have university degrees. More than half of our students are in actual work outside the home.'[66]

Her educational plan had several distinguishing features, which made it both different from and similar to missionary schools in China. Perhaps recalling her own frustration at the strict atmosphere at missionary schools, Zeng was keen to stress student self-government and leadership in her school. A School Union was formed and all important decisions concerning the school were voted on by the students. Based on her experience of the student democracy and debating society at Westfield, Zeng also encouraged the students to practise debating issues of national concern. Sometimes she and Zeng

[64] Kennedy, *Confucian Feminist*, 71.

[65] QMA, WFD-15-3-2, Pao Swen Tseng, Circular letter, August 1921.

[66] QMA, WFD-15-3-5, Pao Swen Tseng to the principal of Westfield College, 5 April 1948.

Yunong would take opposite stances in the debate as an example for the students. Winifred Galbraith recalled:

> From the first the school has been self-governing; staff and students all belong to the students' union which settles all business of the school. … These meetings and decisions provide valuable training in public speaking, good temper, and for the foreigner at least, patience, since neither lessons, meals nor bedtimes are allowed to cut short the discussion.[67]

Several important and influential speakers came to Yifang in the period 1918–27, including the president of Peking University, Cai Yuanpei (蔡元培), who lectured on 'The Importance of Women's Education', and the former premier of China, Xiong Xiling (熊希齡), who spoke on 'Women's Work', as well as several YWCA secretaries and members of the Yale in China Mission.[68] This was policy, as Zeng explained:

> We also invited several well-known people to deliver lectures. Later, we established a regular practice of having someone from outside of the school speak on a specialized topic every Friday afternoon. On Saturday, I always had a one-hour talk on current events: world affairs or problems related to China, Hunan province or society at large.[69]

In its religious aspects Yifang differed from missionary schools in several ways. Although there were daily morning prayers and hymns led by Zeng, Sunday worship and Bible study classes, Yifang was not officially affiliated to any mission or denomination. Nor did Yifang require its students to attend chapel or Bible study, which until 1927 was usually compulsory at missionary schools. Indeed, Zeng was keen for girls to make informed decisions about their spiritual lives, and invited members of every missionary society in Changsha to give talks to the girls on Sundays. In her circular letter of 1922 Louise Barnes describes the open-minded interdenominational religious atmosphere at Yifang:

> Miss Tseng is one of those who look forward to the development of the native Christian church and she does not therefore ally herself to any

[67] Galbraith, 'Experiment', 427.
[68] QMA, WFD-15-3-2, Pao Swen Tseng, Circular letter, August 1921.
[69] Kennedy, *Confucian Feminist*, 76.

> missionary body, though living in sympathetic relationship with the various Christian communities represented in Changsha, a member from each of which is asked to give an address in the school each Sunday… . No pressure is put upon girls to become baptised, but when they do wish fully to accept the Christian faith, they are left entirely free to choose to which Christian church they wish to belong.[70]

In providing such an ecumenical atmosphere, Yifang was ahead of its time, foreshadowing the formation in 1922 of the National Christian Council of China (*Zhonghua quanguo jidujiao xiejinhui*; 中華全國基督教協進會), which sought to transcend denominational divides by establishing a Chinese-controlled church. Zeng's example as headmistress exerted a powerful influence, and many girls who came from elite non-Christian families became Christians through the exposure to the Christian atmosphere that pervaded Yifang.

There is not scope here to tell the story of Yifang itself, and the turbulent experience of its pupils, Chinese and foreign teachers during the social, cultural, political and intellectual outpouring of the May Fourth Movement in the 1920s,[71] the anti-foreign violence which accompanied the reunification of China under nationalist government during the Northern Expedition of 1926–7, and the war with Japan, events which led to the destruction and refounding of the school three times between 1918 and 1949. On 13 September 1927, Barnes died in Shanghai of a heart attack, which Zeng believed had been triggered by the strain of their escape from Changsha during the Northern Expedition.[72] During the 1930s Zeng was a YWCA delegate giving lecture tours across China, and represented China at the International Missionary Council at Tambaram, Madras (sometimes referred to as the World Christian Meeting) in 1938, before being elected to the national assembly in 1948. In 1949 she fled to Hong Kong and was then invited by the nationalist government to live in Taiwan, where she died in 1978. The legacy of

[70] QMA, WFD-15-3-2, Louise Barnes, Circular letter, 'An Outstanding Educational Enterprise', 1922.

[71] On the impact of this upon the Tientsin Anglo-Chinese College, see, in this volume, Marina Xiaojing Wang, 'Western Establishment or Chinese Sovereignty? The Tientsin Anglo-Chinese College during the Restore Educational Rights Movement, 1924–7', 577–92.

[72] Kennedy, *Confucian Feminist*, 93.

Zeng's work at Yifang is manifested in the generations of Chinese women whom she helped to educate. The strong Yifang alumnae association proudly carries on its school history though annual meetings and an annual magazine.[73] On today's Yifang campus (Changsha Tianjiabing Experimental Middle School; 长沙市田家炳实验中学), there is a monument celebrating the important contributions of Zeng Baosun, Zeng Guofan and Zeng Yuenong to modern Chinese education.

Zeng's life story, although an extraordinary one, highlights the dynamic role played by Chinese Christian women in the transfer of educational knowledge between China and the West during the early twentieth century. Their Christian status was essential in this process: Chinese women could use for their own ends the Christian networks to which their education and social status gave them access. Rather than being the 'passive recipients' or the 'fruits' of missionary labour, Chinese women were active agents in this exchange, appropriating, combining and rejecting different aspects of their educational experience as they saw fit. In Zeng's case, the result was a novel form of education that aimed to combine the best of the missionary, British and Chinese educational systems to form the next generation of Chinese women. This was an extremely pressing task, as both Chinese government and missionary educational initiatives in the first two decades of the twentieth century were focused primarily on the provision of boys' education, particularly at the middle school level. Moreover, while missionary colleges for women were opening on China's east coast from 1907, it was not until 1919 that Chinese government universities started to admit women.[74] Yifang was one of the earliest institutions offering college level training to women in inner China, and the first Christian women's college to be founded

[73] 長沙田家炳實驗中學主辦 [Changsha Tianjiabing Shiyan zhongxue zhuban; Tianjiabing Experimental Middle School], 藝芳晚晴 综合性年刊 [*Yifang Wanqing zonghexing niankan*; *Yifang School History Magazine*] (Changsha, 2006).

[74] The earliest missionary colleges for women were located in metropolitan eastern and coastal China, including North China Women's University in Beijing (1907), Huanan Women's College in Fuzhou (1909) and Ginling College in Nanjing (1915). In 1919 the government run Beijing Women's Normal University was established, following which government universities started accepting female students, the first being Peking University in 1920: see Cong Xiaoping, *Teachers, Schools and the making of Modern China* (Vancouver, BC, 2007), 93.

and led by a Chinese woman educator.[75] We can therefore draw wider parallels between Zeng's case and initiatives by highly educated pioneering women in other parts of the world to found colleges for women on their own terms, such as Emily Davis, who founded Girton College in Cambridge in 1869. In Zeng's changing relationship with Barnes, from pupil and teacher to headmistress and friend, we can see the changing power balance between missionaries and Chinese Christians in the early twentieth century. The school they established in mutual cooperation is an early example of the indigenization of the Chinese church, which in the 1920s and 1930s would become such a pressing task in the face of the rising tide of Chinese nationalism.

[75] The main mission-run university in Changsha, Yale-in-China, did not admit women until 1922: Bieler, 'Zeng Baosun', 102.

British World Protestant Children, Young People, Education and the Missionary Movement, *c*.1840s–1930s

Hugh Morrison*
University of Otago

This article considers the evolving relationship between Protestant children, pedagogy and the missionary movement across the British world. From the 1840s, children were a central focus of missionary society philanthropy. By the time of the 1910 World Missionary Conference, missionary and denominational thinkers were consistently highlighting their strategic importance and the need for clear policy that was focused on children's education. This article traces the ways in which this emphasis developed, and the impact that it had among the children involved. It argues that the children's missionary movement was educational at heart, wherein philanthropy and pedagogy went hand in hand. In particular, over the long nineteenth century all the players consistently emphasized the importance of nurturing a 'missionary spirit', a notion that was primarily religious in intent but which in practice moved from pragmatic philanthropy to a more formalized emphasis on education and identity formation. The article introduces representative ways by which this was articulated, drawing on examples from a range of British world contexts in which different communities of Protestant children were engaged educationally and philanthropically in very similar ways.

Looking back to his childhood in the 1870s, Harry Menzies nostalgically recounted his participation in events at Exeter Hall in London. Exeter Hall was the focal point for the great English evangelical gatherings of the nineteenth century. For youngsters, it was particularly remembered for the annual juvenile Protestant missionary rallies, begun as early as 1842 and soon replicated throughout Britain in other main centres.[1] There children were lauded as missionary

* College of Education, University of Otago, PO Box 56, Dunedin 9054, New Zealand. E-mail: hugh.morrison@otago.ac.nz.

[1] Brian Stanley, '"Missionary Regiments for Immanuel's Service": Juvenile Missionary Organizations in English Sunday Schools, 1841–1865', in Diana Wood, ed., *The*

Studies in Church History 55 (2019), 463–478
doi: 10.1017/stc.2018.11

supporters and exhorted to ever higher levels of commitment to the cause. Harry, however, remembered these meetings in a different light:

> Pleasanter in every way were the annual bus-rides … to Exeter Hall, where we invariably arrived early and occupied the front seat of the gallery. What if we didn't listen much to the speeches; what if now and then the loud popping of the cork of a ginger beer bottle interrupted the proceedings and drew shocked glances from our neighbours? [We were] no different from other children in their likes and dislikes, and authorities were tolerant, even though we made the annual meeting one long pic-nic.[2]

The intensity of these meetings notwithstanding, accounts of juvenile missionary support from across British world[3] settings highlight children's missionary support as a simultaneous site of philanthropic endeavour, intensive recruitment of hearts, minds and bodies for the missionary cause, socialization and great fun. The enduring image is that children primarily collected and gave money. Yet, as Francis Prochaska notes, Exeter Hall meetings were also a reminder that 'raising money and saving heathens was only one side of the children's missionary movement'. Equally important was the focus on the 'minds of the young' wherein '"training" became the watchword'.[4] A Baptist writer captured this dual philanthropic and pedagogical imperative when he argued that 'the passing of the missionary box must never be a mere formality. It should always be the occasion of some little word that shall increase knowledge, create enthusiasm, renew devotion, and stimulate generosity.'[5] Across the nineteenth and twentieth centuries, philanthropic ventures and movements were ubiquitous and complex sites of children's and young people's religious identity formation, as recent scholarship attests.[6] As Brian Stanley

Church and Childhood, SCH 30 (Oxford, 1994), 391–403, at 394–6; Francis K. Prochaska, 'Little Vessels: Children in the Nineteenth-Century English Missionary Movement', *JICH* 6 (1978), 103–18, at 111–12, 113; idem, *Women and Philanthropy in Nineteenth-Century England* (Oxford, 1980), 89–90.

2 *C.M.C.H. Old Members' Magazine*, February 1912, 87.

3 The term 'British world' refers to those countries or societies associated with Great Britain or the British empire, whether as constituents, associates or derivatives, or in some kind of formal arrangement.

4 Prochaska, *Women and Philanthropy*, 90.

5 Ernest Price, *Missionary Stories for the Juniors* (London, n.d. [post-1900]), v–vi.

6 Susan Ash, *Funding Philanthropy: Dr Barnardo's Metaphors, Narratives and Spectacles* (Liverpool, 2016); Shih-Wen Sue, '"Give, Give; Be Always Giving": Children, Charity

notes, however, over the longer term 'the allure of children's money-raising power' proved too powerful.[7] Consequently, both in historical and historiographical terms, the financial aspect has taken centre stage.

This article draws more explicit attention to the broader significance of children's missionary support, by focusing primarily on the ways that the relationship between children and young people,[8] pedagogy and missions emerged in Protestant rhetoric. It argues that the children's missionary movement was educational at heart, and that in it philanthropy and pedagogy went hand in hand. In particular, over the long nineteenth century all the players consistently emphasized the importance of nurturing a 'missionary spirit', a notion that was primarily religious in its intent but which in practice moved from pragmatic philanthropy to a more formalized emphasis on education and identity formation. The article introduces representative ways by which this was articulated, drawing on examples from a range of British world contexts in which Protestant children (white or settler and indigenous) were engaged educationally and philanthropically in very similar ways. It acknowledges that for these settings scholarship to date has tended to evaluate educational impact in terms of philanthropy, socialization, social class relations and the formation of racial or imperial attitudes.[9] By way of conclusion it also suggests that, looked at from a more specifically educational angle, children's missionary support fitted into particular national or denominational agendas, conflated civic and religious identity (especially in the context of empire and colonialism), and set children in imperial or quasi-global networks of information exchange.

---

and China, 1890–1939', *Papers: Explorations into Children's Literature* 24 (2016), 5–32; Henrietta Harrison, '"A Penny for the Little Chinese": The French Holy Childhood Association in China, 1843–1951', *AHR* 113 (2008), 72–92; Margot Hillel, '"Nearly all are supported by children": Charitable Childhoods in Late Nineteenth- and Early Twentieth-Century Literature for Children in the British World', in Hugh Morrison and Mary Clare Martin, eds, *Creating Religious Childhoods in Anglo-World and British Colonial Contexts, 1800–1950* (London, 2017), 163–80.

[7] Stanley, 'Missionary Regiments', 402.

[8] The main focus in this article is on Sunday school children up to about twelve years of age and Bible class young people up to about fifteen, from a range of settings including the USA, Canada, England, New Zealand and Scotland.

[9] Prochaska, 'Little Vessels', 113–15; Jeffrey Cox, *The British Missionary Enterprise since 1700* (New York and London, 2008); Hugh Morrison, '"Little Vessels" or "Little Soldiers": New Zealand Protestant Children, Foreign Missions, Religious Pedagogy, and Empire, *c.*1880s–1930s', *PH* 47 (2011), 303–21, at 312–21; Susan Thorne, *Congregational Missions and the making of an Imperial Culture in Nineteenth-Century England* (Stanford, CA, 1999).

Education and Children's Missionary Support: An Evolving Relationship

Children had been actively recruited as home-base supporters within the British missionary movement from the first decade of the nineteenth century, but especially from the 1840s onwards, with more systematic organization and the emergence of monthly periodicals. On the surface the financial element certainly dominated representations of the movement. In 1917 Constance Padwick,[10] a Church Missionary Society (CMS) missionary, writer and editor, noted in a historical review of British children and missions that this emphasis possibly dated back to the 1830s, which she labelled the 'decade of the discovery of children's halfpence'. She suggested that an 'examination of the story of the missionary societies during the [eighteen-] thirties leads to the conviction that missionary committees had discovered not children but a copper-mine'.[11] This motif has cast a long historical shadow, bolstered in part by extant financial statistics that indicate the relative importance of juvenile giving for English Protestant denominations in general, and missionary societies in particular.[12] Yet there was another dynamic at work. By the time of the 1910 World Missionary Conference, missionary and denominational thinkers had felt the need to re-emphasize the 'imperative importance of interesting the boyhood and girlhood of the churches in the work of foreign missions', lamenting that the 'present inability and ineffectiveness of the Church, in view of her great opportunities, is directly traceable to the lack of any policy of missionary education of her children in the past'. Therefore attention needed to be given to 'the study of the child and the laws of education'.[13]

Padwick was the first to stand back and assess the British movement over a longer historical trajectory. Her genealogy of juvenile

[10] Jocelyn Murray, 'Padwick, Constance Evelyn (1886–1968)', in Gerald H. Anderson, ed., *Biographical Dictionary of Christian Missions* (Grand Rapids, MI and Cambridge, 1998), 511.

[11] Constance Padwick, 'Children and Missionary Societies in Great Britain', *International Review of Missions* 6 (1917), 561–75, at 566.

[12] Prochaska, *Women and Philanthropy*, 81–3; Thorne, *Congregational Missions*, 126. A wide range of primary evidence suggests that children's money came from a combination of parents or family, from their own money-raising initiatives and as a result of increasing denominational children's charitable movements.

[13] Commission VI, 'Missionary Awakening', 20–1.

support is instructive for this article in terms of the ways that educational elements were implicitly, explicitly and continuously present (Table 1). Furthermore, educational and religious developments from the late eighteenth century onwards together acted as important precursors for the juvenile moment of the 1830s and 1840s. In particular, Padwick referenced new educational philosophy and practice, represented by the early Madras and Lancasterian schooling systems, by Rousseau and by Pestalozzi, as well as contemporary evangelical revivalism's emphasis on childhood as the key developmental stage for taking 'increased responsibility … for [the] personal use of privileges'.[14] She finished with a pointed observation, reflecting the same concerns expressed by the report of Edinburgh's Commission VI on the 'Home Base of Missions':

> So we stand in 1917, heirs of the past with its triumphs and its mistakes, and we look for the next step in the way of God. … And we missionary folk stand convinced that Christianity, as taught to the children and as practised in the nation, has been robbed of force and motive power by the strangely general omission of its missionary bearing, its missionary ideals and its missionary demands.[15]

In Padwick's estimation, education was central for the relationship between children and missions. Beyond her analysis, a longer and wider reading of the movement reveals that this was in fact acknowledged throughout the nineteenth century. In the first instance the responsibility for this was often more located in the Christian home, where parents, not clergy or teachers, were expected to take primary responsibility. North American Baptist Revd Dr Smyth argued vociferously in 1846 that the 'missionary spirit of a family, and through it of the church, (which is composed of families,) is the greatest moral agent, under God, by which the Gospel is to be diffused'. Parents should be exemplars to their children in both what they believed about and what they did for missions, especially through their 'example, reading, conversation, prayers, and conduct'.[16] This was a long-lived sentiment, which constituted an ongoing point of tension between those who saw the home as the centre of

[14] Padwick, 'Children and Missionary Societies', 563–4.
[15] Ibid. 575.
[16] 'Train the Children', *Baptist Missionary Magazine* 26 (1846), 154.

Table 1. Genealogy of British Children's Missionary Support to 1917

Period	Development
1816	A Wesleyan Methodist 'Juvenile Missionary Society' formed (Leeds).
1827	*Baptist Children's Magazine & Sabbath Scholars' Reward,* containing missionary articles.
1830s	'the decade of the discovery of children's halfpence'.
1830s/1840s	Emergence of children's missionary magazines,[17] e.g.: 1839: *Missionary Repository for Youth* (London Missionary Society) 1842: *Juvenile Missionary Instructor* (CMS) 1844: *Wesleyan Juvenile Offering* (Methodist) 1845: *Juvenile Missionary Herald* (Baptist) 1849: *Parochial Missionary Magazine* (Society for the Propagation of the Gospel).
1850s	A focus on 'pity' as a motive, prevalent across mid-nineteenth-century literature, depicting the heathen as benighted; criticized by Padwick for exploiting children's feelings and for the ways that it possibly led to apathy or culturally superior attitudes among the young.[18]
1860s	Emerging focus on 'heroism' and on fiction.
Late 1800s – early 1900s	The 'new educational policy of the societies': 'the provision of graded lessons' (age-specific pedagogy) and 'provision for the children's activities' (more child-centred, interactive learning).
By 1917	Need for missionary educators to take seriously the importance of professional schooling and national curricula approach.

Source: Padwick, 'Children and Missionary Societies in Great Britain'.

informal education and those who emphasized an institutional approach. As the century progressed however, this latter conviction prevailed, as church-based education for the young became

[17] Other British Protestant children's missionary magazines began in Scotland (1840s) and Ireland (1850s).

[18] See Felicity Jensz, 'Hope and Pity: Depictions of Children in Five Decades of the *Evangelisch-Lutherisches Missionsblatt*, 1860–1910', in Judith Becker and Katharina Stornig, eds, *Menschen – Bilder – Eine Welt. Ordnungen von Vielfalt in der religiösen Publizistik um 1900* (Göttingen, 2018), 259–81, at 259 n. 3, in turn referencing Marianne Gullestad, *Picturing Pity: Pitfalls and Pleasures in Cross-Cultural Communication: Image and Word in a North Cameroon Mission* (New York and Oxford), 2007.

formalized and professionalized through the Sunday school movement in particular.[19] By the first decade of the twentieth century, in many Protestant contexts the Sunday school and the youth-orientated Bible class had become the expected institutional homes for missionary support. Edinburgh's Commission VI, referring to various North American settings, noted that the Sunday school movement offered a 'unique opportunity' in terms both of 'what it can do for missions' and of 'the effect of this work of education on the Church of the future'.[20] Moreover, by the early 1900s Anglo-American Sunday schools were well established as 'primary sites for missionary propaganda' and as 'an important source of missionary funding'. Indeed, across nineteenth-century British world settings they had become the 'single largest source of information about what foreign people were like'.[21] As such, they were important sites of attitudinal formation with respect to the wider world, albeit increasingly supplanted by state-run schools in this respect from the early 1900s, with the implementation of compulsory education and its attendant pedagogical paraphernalia.[22]

Fostering a 'Missionary Spirit'

A long-running historical and pedagogical motif was that of fostering a 'missionary spirit' among children and young people. Although Padwick did not explicitly use this phrase, she alluded to it, suggesting that early nineteenth-century writers had missed a vital connection: 'what is absent to an astonishing degree is the connexion between the child's gift and the Lord. The giving of the missionary penny seems hardly ever treated as an act of worship, a personal transaction between the little child and God.' She went on to suggest that this

[19] For an introduction to this movement in the British context, see Stephen Orchard and John H. Y. Briggs, eds, *The Sunday School Movement: Studies in the Growth and Decline of Sunday Schools* (Milton Keynes, 2007).

[20] Commission VI, 'Missionary Awakening', 22–3.

[21] Cox, *British Missionary Enterprise*, 100, 101; see also Susan Thorne, 'Religion and Empire at Home', in Catherine Hall and Sonya Rose, eds, *At Home with the Empire: Metropolitan Culture and the Imperial World* (Cambridge, 2006), 143–65, at 144; Christine Weir, '"Deeply Interested in these Children whom you have not seen": The Protestant Sunday School View of the Pacific, 1900–1940', *Journal of Pacific History* 48 (2013), 43–62.

[22] On educational developments, see Bengt Sandin, 'Education', in Colin Heywood, ed., *A Cultural History of Childhood and Family in the Age of Empire* (London and New York, 2014), 91–110, at 104–8.

had changed: 'we to-day must be grateful to the Sunday school reform movement for making the child's offertory a great moment with its song and prayer'.[23] The notion of fostering a missionary spirit was in essence an educational ideal, indicating that missionary support was primarily a spiritual act, but one that needed adult intervention and support. Three examples drawn chronologically from the period are indicative of how this idea became wedded to institutional expressions of religious childhood, and more specifically to children's education and the formation of juvenile identity.

In the first instance, missionary spirit was a concept applied equally to Protestants of all ages, as made abundantly clear by Revd T. B. Whiting (CMS) at the 1860 Liverpool Missionary Conference.[24] He held that having a missionary spirit transcended 'that cold acknowledgment of the duty which unlocks the purse at stated intervals'; rather, it marked out individuals who took 'such an interest in the cause as will ensure self-denial in its behalf'.[25] This could only be the profound product of 'divine grace'. As such, the existence of a missionary spirit depended upon 'the number of truly converted hearts' and therefore upon the degree to which 'true religion' (that is 'all that tends to excite and maintain a spirit of vital godliness and living faith') gripped those in the churches.[26] One state of being could not exist without the other. At the same time, as with 'every other Christian grace', he also argued that the missionary spirit needed 'to be fostered in the hearts of God's people'.[27] To achieve this, he presented a twenty-point strategy, which included gaining information; subscribing to and studying newspapers, periodicals, books and pictures; attending meetings and lectures; and belonging to organized groups.[28] Whiting noted briefly that 'Juvenile Associations are especially important, not only on account of the large sums they produce, but also because they early enlist the sympathies of the heart.'[29] In these terms, while there was in the 1860s a clear association between children's support and institutional

[23] Padwick, 'Children and Missionary Societies', 568.
[24] T. B. Whiting, 'On the Best Means of exciting and maintaining a Missionary Spirit', in *Conference on Missions held in 1860 at Liverpool* (London, 1860), 58–64.
[25] Ibid. 58.
[26] Ibid. 59.
[27] Ibid. 58–9.
[28] Ibid. 59–63.
[29] Ibid. 63.

organization, more important was the conviction that genuine juvenile engagement should be predicated on an internal dynamic that was both intellectual and emotional. Reference to the 'sympathies of the heart' presumed a prior reorientation of that 'heart' away from self and towards a higher set of priorities, nurtured through organizational involvement, among other things.

While Sunday schools were not specifically referenced in this rhetoric, by the 1880s they were clearly on the agenda (reflecting their increasingly important presence across British world settings), and their role in nurturing a changed juvenile 'heart' was more clearly delineated. This is evident in the second example, drawn from an address by the Northern Irish Presbyterian minister Rutherford Waddell to southern New Zealand Sunday school teachers in 1883.[30] Talking on 'The Sabbath-School and Missions', he laid out a strong case for the Sunday school as a prime site of missionary spirit formation. By this stage, across the British world, Sunday schools were a well-established component of colonial Protestant religion, drawing on increasing numbers of settler children across the denominations as well as being a key tool in missions among indigenous children.[31] Yet Waddell suggested that missions were not yet seriously on Sunday school agendas, a situation he viewed critically, making clear that this had to change. Reflecting a commonly held view, he argued that Sunday school children were the church of the future; they would 'take our place and carry on Christ's work when we are gone', including the primary task of missions which lay at the

[30] Rutherford Waddell, 'The Sabbath-School and Missions', *New Zealand Missionary Record*, February 1884, 44–9.

[31] John Webster Grant, *The Church in the Canadian Era*, rev. edn (Vancouver, BC, 1988), 58–9; Robert Handy, *A History of the Churches in the United States and Canada*, OHCC (Oxford, 1976), 281–2; Frank Hanson, *The Sunday School in New Zealand Methodism* (Auckland, 1998); David Stuart Keen, 'Feeding the Lambs: The Influence of Sunday Schools on the Socialization of Children in Otago and Southland, 1848–1901' (PhD thesis, University of Otago, 1999); Hugh McLeod, *Religion and Society in England, 1850–1914* (Basingstoke, 1996), 78–82; Hugh Morrison, 'Service, Sacrifice and Responsibility: Religion and Protestant Settler Childhood in New Zealand and Canada, *c*.1860–1940', in Morrison and Martin, eds, *Creating Religious Childhoods*, 241–60, at 242–5; Neil Semple, '"The nurture and admonition of the Lord": Nineteenth-Century Canadian Methodism's Response to "Childhood"', *Histoire sociale / Social History* 14 (1981), 157–75; Geoffrey Troughton, 'Religion, Churches and Childhood in New Zealand, *c*.1900–1940', *New Zealand Journal of History* 40 (2006), 39–56; Weir, 'Deeply Interested in these Children', 44–5.

heart of the church's identity and purpose.[32] Therefore shaping young minds and lives was a foundational task. Like Whiting, Waddell perceived that a 'missionary spirit' could not be imposed but instead emanated from a more profound formation of Christian character, best done during childhood. He remonstrated that:

> We know the truth of this in regard to everything else – in regard to conversion, to virtue, &c. We know the value of teaching youth to be truthful, honest, pure. We know that if childhood is allowed to pass without its being taught these cardinal virtues, it is vain to begin it when character is formed. And so of the missionary spirit. Do we believe that a missionary spirit is an essential element of Christian character? Then the time, and I would say the only time, to create such a spirit is in youth. It is perfectly futile to expect a missionary spirit in the Church, if the seeds of it have not been sown in the Sabbath-schools, which are the nurseries of the Church. Hence the duty and responsibility of giving missions a prominent place in Sabbath-school teaching.[33]

Waddell did not presume to delineate or impose a curriculum. However, he strongly suggested that for a missionary spirit to be awakened, there were some key provisos. Firstly, teachers themselves needed to be thoroughly 'possessed' with this same missionary spirit, so that children would imbibe their teachers' 'enthusiasm' for missions.[34] Secondly, financial considerations must be secondary at best. Through their own enthusiasm teachers should focus on 'filling the child's soul with the Spirit of Christ. If you can do that, then the rest will follow as certainly as the waters pour out when you lift the sluice; but if you do not do that … you degrade the great principle of Christian liberality.' Finally, teachers should do two things: 'teach the children to have wide sympathies' and 'teach them the joy and heroism of doing good'.[35] Sunday schools were free to implement all manner of strategies, projects and plans, but needed to be shaped by, or based upon, a more profound rationale.

Waddell's speech was made in the context of a missionary movement full of late nineteenth-century bravado, yet to sense any crisis

[32] Waddell, 'Sabbath-School and Missions', 45.
[33] Ibid.
[34] Ibid. 45.
[35] Ibid. 46.

looming on the horizon, and it was directed at a burgeoning children's religious movement still edging its way towards organizational sophistication. The third and final example, drawn from the early twentieth century writing of American missionary statesman John R. Mott, indicates that by then the connection between missions and Sunday schools had become much more finely drawn. Writing in 1904, foreshadowing issues to be raised again at the 1910 conference, Mott sketched out programmatically a systematic educational schema for fostering a juvenile missionary spirit.[36]

Like Waddell, Mott understood the imperative importance of engaging childhood and youth as key stages of faith and character formation, arguing that if 'for twenty or even fifteen years the young people of Christendom could be interested and properly instructed in missions the whole Church would be filled with the missionary spirit'.[37] Sunday schools were pivotal sites from which this 'spirit' could have an increasingly pervasive influence, both on other church-centred juvenile or youth organizations and on individuals as they developed in their faith. Drawing on contemporary Canadian and American examples, Mott focused pragmatically on appointing Sunday school missionary 'officers', systematic planning, structured programmes with children and young people's different developmental stages in mind, regularly timetabled missions-focused slots, manuals and training for teachers and collections of missionary-focused books in Sunday school libraries.[38] At the same time these elements could not be separated from the wider life of the church. Clergy should play a pedagogical role by emphasizing two things. Firstly, preparing children and young people for communicant membership (a 'serious and impressive occasion') was strategically significant, for during this preparation the minister could exert 'a deep missionary influence on young people', complementing what had been learnt and imbibed through both their formal and informal education.[39] Secondly, Mott suggested that the minister should also 'seek to influence parents … to be willing to facilitate their children devoting themselves to the service of Christ either at home or abroad'. In

[36] John R. Mott, *The Pastor and Modern Missions: A Plea for Leadership in World Evangelization* (New York, 1904).
[37] Ibid. 74.
[38] Ibid. 75–6.
[39] Ibid. 78–9.

particular, 'the spirituality of the home' remained central to the 'development of missionary spirit and purpose in children'.[40] In both cases Mott drew upon his broad reading of missionary and other Christian exemplary biographies. Overall, he saw home and Sunday schools together as critical for forming young Christians characterized by 'right habits of giving to missions, praying for missions, and working for missions'.[41]

From the 1900s onwards, although the home remained important, missions were systematically and more comprehensively built into Sunday school and Bible class syllabi and programmes. Informed missionary support (financial and emotional) effectively became institutionalized across a broad range of British world and American settings. National denominational and international transdenominational teaching materials included a regular and carefully thought out regime of mission-oriented lessons, ideas and resources. Denominational magazines likewise carried regular missionary-focused materials and reports, supported in most cases by dedicated missionary magazines for the young, published by missionary or women's committees, which often acted as proxy curriculum resources, drawn upon by Sunday school teachers and missionary group leaders alike. These were not one-offs; rather, as for example in the case of the late 1920s American Southern Baptist magazine *World Comrades*, they provided week-by-week programmes of teaching and learning that potentially eased the load of teachers.[42] While the focus was on offering systematic pedagogical materials, the underlying concern of fostering a missionary spirit remained central. As Southern Baptist children were reminded at Christmas 1927:

> China is but one of the nations of the world and there are millions of people who cannot keep Christmas because they have not heard the announcement of the angels. … Let us be so full of Christ in our hearts at Christmas that we will care about all the others in the world and will love them and pray for them. CHRIST-MAS – cherish the day, Comrades, slip away from the tissue paper and tinsel, the new toys

[40] Ibid. 167.
[41] Ibid. 76–7.
[42] For example, 'Girls' Auxiliary Programs' and 'Royal Ambassadors', *World Comrades*, January 1928, 10–16, 17–22.

and the frolic and tell Jesus you are grateful for Christmas, pledge him all the room in your heart that he wants and needs.[43]

Historicizing Children's Religion

The relationship between children and religion is currently opening up as an important area of scholarly interest and public debate, with dual attention given to constructions or representations of childhood and to children as religious actors or agents.[44] The historical question of children's religion is a complex subject in which we find 'complex counterpoints of ecclesiastical prescription and practice, of parental love and fear, and … on the part of children themselves, of passivity and active appropriation'.[45] For the nineteenth and twentieth centuries, education and philanthropy were key sites wherein Protestant children imbibed, responded to and acted out religious beliefs and ideals, and children as 'missionary supporters' were an important expression of this. As has been seen here, moreover, the result was more than the finances raised. As previewed in Prochaska's writing during the 1970s and 1980s,[46] educational intent is an important lens through which to achieve a more nuanced understanding of juvenile religious philanthropy. Missionary philanthropy was certainly a prominent extrinsic activity that highlights the progressive ways in which the churches' young were increasingly seen as strategic religious and public actors. Philanthropy was therefore significant for juvenile religious and identity formation and helped in their integration into emotional-theological communities that valued participation and service,[47] albeit for reasons that varied across time and place. At the same time, as exemplified in the example of Rutherford Waddell, these communities emphasized broader notions of children as pre-adults; missionary support helped to orient their thinking towards the kinds of

[43] The Comrade, 'World Comrade Comments', *World Comrades*, December 1927, 1.
[44] See further Don S. Browning, and Marcia Bunge, eds, *Children and Childhood in World Religions: Primary Sources and Texts* (New Brunswick, NJ, 2009); Anna Strhan, Stephen G. Parker and Susan B. Ridgely, eds, *The Bloomsbury Reader in Religion and Childhood* (London and New York, 2017).
[45] Janet L. Nelson, 'Introduction' to Wood, ed., *Church and Childhood*, xix–xxiv, at xx.
[46] See n. 1 above.
[47] See further Hugh Morrison, 'Settler Childhood, Protestant Christianity and Emotions in Colonial New Zealand, 1880s–1920s', in Stephanie Olsen, ed., *Childhood, Youth and Emotions in Modern History: National, Colonial and Global Perspectives* (Basingstoke, 2015), 76–94.

citizens they might be as adults and, specifically, encouraged them to think about future missionary service as a vocation and career.

This focus on the centrality and intentionality of the educational factor therefore helps to take us beyond mere pounds, shillings and pence (as important as these were), to tease out the wider significance of the children's missionary support movement across Protestant settings. To date, perhaps, this has been best done for English contexts. Prochaska, for example, helpfully suggests that the nineteenth-century children's missionary movement opens up the opportunity to think further about changing conceptions of childhood, the nature of children's recreation and 'the power of the missionary societies to form racial and cultural attitudes in the young'.[48] Likewise, we now have a very clear sense of the ways in which Sunday schools and missionary education were important for working-class religion and imperial engagement.[49] However, these remain somewhat speculative or are limited to particular denominations, leaving room for more finely grained and comparative research. Moreover, they are English- or British-centred and thus reflect specificities of time and place that may or may not pertain more broadly.

By way of conclusion, when the wider British world is considered from an educational angle, at least two further observations can be made that indicate fruitful avenues for further thinking. Firstly, this approach provides an interesting opportunity to consider the connections between children as missionary supporters and as consumers of material culture. Across the spectrum of national contexts, children, through the missionary movement and Sunday schools, interacted with a range of material culture in a way that was broadly educative and significant up to the late nineteenth century, when compulsory schooling was introduced more comprehensively. Periodical literature emerges as a significant element in this process and was, by the early 1900s, a well-entrenched element of children's missionary support. This too can be approached from two angles. On the one hand missionary magazines for children can be considered as part of a wider global or imperial circulation of goods, ideas and information, through which children were informed and developed ideas about the wider world

[48] Prochaska, 'Little Vessels', 110, 113–14.

[49] Thorne, *Congregational Missions*, 6, 114–18; Hugh McLeod, 'New Perspectives on Victorian Class Religion: The Oral Evidence', *Oral History Journal* 14 (1986), 31–49.

from shared texts.[50] On the other hand this literature gave power to children's agency as interactive readers and missionary participants.[51] Periodicals called for a response from juvenile readers, provided a vehicle for them to participate in missionary support, gave them a public voice, helped to develop the emotional-theological communities noted above and possibly bolstered hierarchical views of their relationship to other children (especially in non-European or non-Christian settings).

Secondly, an educational focus highlights how the children's missionary movement was constitutive of juvenile citizenship, variously defined as religious, civic and imperial. This, while focused on the 'religious', often in reality led to the conflation of imperial and religious identity for children and young people, possibly reinforcing identities predicated on dualistic notions of 'them' and 'us' in terms of attitudes toward non-Western children. Heavenly citizenship was a consistent thread across the decades under study, but how that was conflated with other civic notions changed noticeably. In essence children might be seen as 'global citizens', but what that meant changed over time. Up to and including the First World War, such notions were demonstrably connected to imperial citizenship and varying notions of the 'nation', although this connection was accentuated more in some settings (Canada and Scotland) than in others (New Zealand). Missionary rhetoric and pedagogy also helped to cement stronger and more cohesive denominational identities and loyalties. In the inter-war decades, however, that began to change. Imperial and wartime language was co-opted within the religious discourse of a 'higher *imperium*' involving a primary allegiance to God. Furthermore, citizenship was reconstructed in the light of peace movements and the League of Nations, with a more pronounced emphasis on the 'brotherhood of man'. In the longer term, in the years immediately following the Second World War, upholding democracy became an important motif, as missions began to be constructed more in terms of partnership than of paternalism. Thus the missionary movement that embraced and activated large numbers of British world children and young people contributed to collective and individual identities as much as it became a treasure trove of the

[50] See Isobel Hofmeyr, 'Introduction: World Literature and the Imperial Textual Commons', *English Studies in Africa* 57 (2014), 1–8.

[51] See Michelle Elleray, 'Little Builders: Coral Insects, Missionary Culture, and the Victorian Child', *Victorian Literature and Culture* 39 (2011), 223–38.

church. Character and identity formation, spirituality, finance and citizenship emerge as significant outcomes of an enduring feature of juvenile Protestant religion spanning the late nineteenth and early twentieth centuries.

'In perfect harmony with the spirit of the age': The Oxford University Wesley Guild, 1883–1914

Martin Wellings*
Oxford

From the middle of the nineteenth century, educational opportunities at the older English universities were gradually extended beyond the limits of the Church of England, first with the abolition of the university tests and then with the opening of higher degrees to Nonconformists. Wesleyan Methodists were keen to take advantage of this new situation, and also to safeguard their young people from non-Methodist influences. A student organization was established in Oxford in 1883, closely linked to the city centre chapel and its ministers, and this Wesley Guild (later the Wesley Society, and then the John Wesley Society) formed the heart of Methodist involvement with the university's undergraduates for the next century. The article explores the background to the guild and its development in the years up to the First World War, using it as a case study for the engagement of Methodism with higher education in this period.

In Michaelmas Term 1882 a small group of undergraduates at the University of Oxford were encouraged by the Wesleyan superintendent, Hugh Price Hughes, to undertake a mission in the eastern suburb of St Clement's.[1] Hughes opened a rented mission room in Catherine Street on 18 January 1883, and it became the base for weekly services, a Sunday School, a Band of Hope and a programme of tract distribution. In the face of competition from other evangelistic agencies in the neighbourhood, the Catherine Street Mission proved to be short-lived, closing by the end of the year,[2] but the student group that had gathered to undertake the project became the nucleus of the Oxford University Wesley Guild, a society which endured under different names into the twenty-first

* 26 Upland Park Rd, Oxford, OX2 7RU. E-mail: martin.wellings@oxfordmethodists.org.uk.

[1] Oxford, Oxfordshire History Centre (hereafter: OHC), Oxford Methodist Circuit Archives, NM5/F1/A1/1, Minutes of the Wesley Guild (hereafter: WGM 1, and similarly books 2–4; books 1–3 are unpaginated), preceding minutes for 10 February 1883.

[2] Ibid., 24 November 1883.

Studies in Church History 55 (2019), 479–493
doi: 10.1017/stc.2018.36

century.[3] The early history of the guild offers significant insights into Methodist engagement with higher education, illustrating the church's perception of the opportunities and challenges presented by the repeal of the university tests and showing how far hopes and fears about retaining the loyalty of university-educated Methodists were realized in the ultimate destinations of guild members. The extant minutes of the guild, supported by membership lists and term cards, make it possible not only to offer a narrative of the history, but also to analyse the personnel and fluctuations in membership, the evolving purposes of the group, and the strength or otherwise of denominational commitment among Methodist undergraduates at Oxford in the decades leading up to the First World War.

Although the Wesleys' Methodism began with the Oxford 'Holy Club' in the 1720s and 1730s, Methodism in all its varieties was largely excluded from the university by the middle of the eighteenth century, and the Methodist mission in Oxford thereafter focused on the resident population, not the undergraduates. The university tests ensured that Wesleyan and Nonconformist families were unable to send their sons to Oxford; social expectations, too, helped to keep Methodists out. When Benjamin Gregory arrived in the city as the Wesleyan minister in 1857, he found that '[w]ith the University the one unpardonable sin was attendance at a Nonconformist church. Dog-fighting, all sorts of loose escapades and low habits might be condoned, but the line must be drawn somewhere, and it was drawn – at the Methodist chapel.'[4]

By the late 1850s, however, the situation was changing, as Oxford's traditional identity as a bastion of the Church of England came under attack from the long-running agitation for the relief of Dissenting disabilities and from pressure for reform from within the university.[5] Some relaxation of the tests was achieved in 1854, opening the BA degree to Nonconformists, and seventeen years later the Universities Tests Act (1871) enabled them to proceed to higher degrees and fellowships.[6]

[3] Robert D. Simonson, *A History of the John Wesley Society, 1883–1983* (Oxford, 1983).

[4] Benjamin Gregory, *Autobiographical Recollections* (London, 1903), 407.

[5] W. R. Ward, 'From the Tractarians to the Executive Commission, 1845–1854', in M. G. Brock and M. C. Curthoys, eds, *The History of the University of Oxford*, 6: *Nineteenth-Century Oxford, Part 1* (Oxford, 1997), 306–36, at 332–6.

[6] M. G. Brock, 'A "Plastic Structure"', in idem and M. C. Curthoys, eds, *The History of the University of Oxford*, 7: *Nineteenth-Century Oxford, Part 2* (Oxford, 2000), 3–66, at 22–4.

The counterpoint to parliamentary and university negotiations over reform was the expansion of Nonconformity, and especially of Wesleyan Methodism, in mid-Victorian England, and the social aspirations which accompanied numerical growth. The Wesleyans were the largest Protestant community outside the Church of England in this period, claiming a membership in excess of 347,000 in 1871; this had risen by almost 50,000 a decade later.[7] Although the Wesleyans' core constituency in the latter part of the nineteenth century comprised the households of skilled manual workers, artisans and those engaged in routine non-manual labour, with a leavening of clerks in the urban areas and labourers in the countryside,[8] there were plenty of Methodists with educational ambitions. Some were members of the Wesleyan lay elite, while others were drawn from an intellectual aristocracy, closely tied to the ministry. Wesley's insistence that the Methodists should be 'a reading people'[9] and his persistent efforts to educate his preachers made many Methodists aspire to learn, and kindled a thirst for knowledge, encouraging Methodists to take the opportunities offered by the educational reforms of the era.

Until the mid-1860s, official Wesleyan educational endeavour focused on Sunday Schools and elementary schools. John Scott led the initiative to establish Wesleyan elementary schools from 1843, with an ambitious programme to build 700 schools in seven years.[10] Although achievement fell short of aspiration, with the assistance of government grants from 1847–8 the Wesleyans were able to reach a total of 743 schools by 1870.[11] Secondary provision, however, was very sparse. The Connexion maintained subsidized boarding schools at Kingswood and Woodhouse Grove for the sons of ministers, but the only other schools formally linked to the denomination were Wesley College, Sheffield (1838), and the Wesleyan Proprietary Grammar School, Taunton (1843; renamed Queen's College in

[7] *Minutes of the Methodist Conference* 1871, 356; ibid. 1882, 180.

[8] Clive D. Field, 'The Social Structure of English Methodism: Eighteenth – Twentieth Centuries', *British Journal of Sociology* 28 (1977), 199–225, at 206–7.

[9] John Telford, ed., *The Letters of John Wesley*, 8 vols (London, 1931), 8: 247 (Wesley to George Holder, 8 November 1790).

[10] John T. Smith, *Methodism and Education 1849–1902* (Oxford, 1998), 12.

[11] F. C. Pritchard, *Methodist Secondary Education: A History of the Contribution of Methodism to Secondary Education in the United Kingdom* (London, 1949), 176.

1887), each operating under the direction of a private company.[12] These schools looked to the University of London for the external academic accreditation of matriculation and for bachelors' degrees, although by 1868 they were also taking advantage of the Oxford Local Examinations and achieving considerable success.[13] Connexional policy, however, meant that most boys were required to leave Kingswood and Woodhouse Grove at the age of fifteen, which precluded preparation for university admission.

The work of the Schools Inquiry Commission (1864–8) prompted the Wesleyans to re-examine their secondary schools.[14] The commission's categorization of schools according to leaving age ranked the Wesleyan schools embarrassingly in the 'third grade'. The Wesleyan leadership was well aware of its own burgeoning middle-class constituency, and was fearful that a lack of Methodist provision might encourage parents to send their children to rival schools, with the inexpensive and determinedly high church Woodard schools being a particular source of concern.[15] In the wake of the Schools Commission's report, and with university reform on the political agenda from 1868, plans for a comprehensive system of Wesleyan schools, reaching from the elementary level to admission to Oxford and Cambridge, were developed by Henry French, mathematics master at Taunton. French set out his plans in a series of letters to the heavyweight Wesleyan weekly newspaper, the *Watchman*.[16] Henry Hartley Fowler, rising to prominence in the denomination and in the Liberal party, persuaded the connexion to institute its own schools inquiry in 1871.[17] Meanwhile, Richard Bell, superintendent minister in Oxford, made an appeal for support for a major extension of Wesleyan work in the city, urging 'the commanding claims of the educational centres of this country' on connexional funds.[18]

[12] Ibid. 136–45, 166–7; H. J. Channon, *History of Queen's College, Taunton* (Taunton, n.d.).

[13] *The Times*, 31 August 1868, 6.

[14] Pritchard, *Methodist Secondary Education*, 211–20.

[15] Ibid. 188–92; Channon, *Queen's College*, 63.

[16] 'XYZ' [Henry French], 'Middle-Class Education', *Watchman and Wesleyan Advertiser* (hereafter: *WWA*), 6 January 1869, 6; 20 January 1869, 24; 17 March 1869, 86; 19 May 1869, 161.

[17] Pritchard, *Methodist Secondary Education*, 243–4.

[18] Richard Bell, 'Methodism in the University Towns', *Methodist Recorder* (hereafter: *MR*), 2 December 1870, 656.

The flurry of letters and reports in the late 1860s and early 1870s resulted in piecemeal changes. French's comprehensive system was not adopted, although Wesleyan districts were encouraged to set up new 'middle-class' schools. Kingswood and Woodhouse Grove were amalgamated in 1875, forming one institution with two centres, and by concentrating the older pupils at Kingswood a stronger upper school was created. A new 'first grade' school, The Leys, was opened in Cambridge in 1875. As significant as these developments, perhaps, was the role of particular headmasters in encouraging applications to Oxford and Cambridge: Thomas Sibly at Taunton,[19] T. G. Osborn at Kingswood[20] and W. F. Moulton at The Leys.[21]

The universities of Oxford and Cambridge, however, remained a cause of concern to Wesleyans. William Arthur, past president of the Wesleyan Conference, warned in July 1870 that 'whilst many members of the Wesleyan Methodist Society had gone into Oxford, they had not in any part of the kingdom a member of the Methodist Society who had come out of Oxford'.[22] Henry Young, superintendent when Alfred Gregory arrived to begin his studies at Brasenose, recalled that 'there were a few sons of Methodists in various colleges', but 'there was no undergraduate attending our chapel'.[23] One response to this was to conclude that Wesleyans should avoid the university at all costs. Samuel Romilly Hall, delivering the ex-president's charge to newly ordained Wesleyan ministers in 1869, warned them not to jeopardize their children's spiritual welfare for the sake of worldly advancement, and not to send their sons to Oxford or Cambridge.[24] George Lidgett, responsible for the education of his orphaned nephew, John Scott Lidgett, denied him the opportunity of going to Oxford or Cambridge as his father had intended, and sent him to University College, London, instead. Scott Lidgett reminisced that his uncle thought the older universities were 'not likely to strengthen, and perhaps likely to undermine, my Methodist

[19] Channon, *Queen's College*, 69–71; Pritchard, *Methodist Secondary Education*, 168–71.
[20] A. G. Ives, *Kingswood School in Wesley's Day and Since* (London, 1970), 165–76.
[21] Derek Baker, *Partnership in Excellence* (Cambridge, 1975), 121–36.
[22] *WWA*, 26 July 1870, 243.
[23] Benjamin Gregory, *Consecrated Culture: Memorials of Benjamin Alfred Gregory* (London, 1885), 77.
[24] Samuel Romilly Hall, *A Charge Delivered to Forty-Three Junior Preachers, on their Ordination to the Christian Ministry and their Admission into Full Connexion with the Wesleyan Conference* (London, 1869), 27, 34–5.

convictions and sympathies'.[25] However, Lidgett's frustration and annoyance at this decision demonstrated that a policy of avoidance would not work, and that Wesleyans needed to make provision for undergraduates at Oxford and Cambridge. This encouraged the construction of new and fashionably Gothic chapels in Hills Road, Cambridge (1870–1) and New Inn Hall Street, Oxford (1877–8), and pressure on the Stationing Committee to appoint suitably qualified ministers to appeal to cultured students.[26] Cambridge led the way in instituting a regular gathering 'of a social character' for undergraduates in 1873, and, with W. F. Moulton's support, this evolved into the Wesley Society.[27]

The traditional method of Wesleyan pastoral care and spiritual nurture was the weekly class meeting, where members gathered to share Christian experience, insight and admonition. Alfred Gregory persuaded two other Methodist undergraduates to form a designated university class in Oxford, and this met during term-time, under the guidance of the superintendent.[28] The class was a very small group, with membership in single figures through the 1870s,[29] but it was from the university class, in the winter of 1882, that the idea of a new venture emerged.

As originally conceived, the Wesley Union or Wesley Guild was designed to be ecumenical in membership and evangelistic in focus. In this way it complemented both the university class, which was already meeting the spiritual needs of committed Wesleyans, and the recently-formed Nonconformist Union, which offered a social and intellectual programme to 'remove the feeling of isolation which Nonconformists experience on entering the University'.[30] Membership of the guild was not confined to members of the

[25] J. Scott Lidgett, *Reminiscences* (London, 1928), 13; Alan Turberfield, *John Scott Lidgett. Archbishop of British Methodism?* (Peterborough, 2003), 17.

[26] 'New Chapel at Hills Road Cambridge', *MR*, 27 May 1870, 285; Martin Wellings, 'The Building of Wesley Memorial Church, Oxford', *Chapels Society Journal* 2, *Building the Church* (2016), 21–35.

[27] *WWA*, 9 April 1873; W. Fiddian Moulton, *William F. Moulton. A Memoir* (London, 1899), 151.

[28] Gregory, *Consecrated Culture*, 77.

[29] Bell, 'Methodism in the University Towns', *MR*, 2 December 1870, 656. Class lists survive in OHC, Oxford Methodist Circuit Archives, NM5/A/A2/6–8, Circuit Schedule Books. The designation 'university class' first appeared in the schedules in 1876.

[30] Oxford, Mansfield College, Oxford University Nonconformist Union Minute Book 1881–6, 'Rules of the Oxford University Nonconformist Union', 75; Robert Forman Horton, *An Autobiography* (London, 1917), 52–4.

Wesleyan Society: it was open to 'any member of the University being a regular communicant of some Christian Church',[31] and the principal objective of the group was to run the Catherine St Mission. Most of the early meetings were concerned with the practical organization of the mission: devising a preaching plan for the Sunday and midweek services, furnishing the mission room, providing refreshments and raising funds. Several visiting speakers came to address the guild, and most offered guidance on Christian life and witness, although in May 1883 W. H. Dallinger, Methodism's leading scientist, spoke on science and religion.[32] With the demise of the mission towards the end of 1883, the guild needed a new purpose. Price Hughes suggested 'some definite work' in another part of Oxford, perhaps running a Sunday School at New Hinksey, where the circuit had opened a new chapel in July 1882,[33] but the option of 'meeting for social purposes, for hearing papers read &c' was also tabled.[34] With Hughes's departure from Oxford in the summer of 1884, the guild soon abandoned the challenge of 'definite work' and settled into a rhythm of two or three meetings a term, gathering in members' rooms to read papers, debate issues or listen to invited speakers. Meetings were structured around 'private business' – amending and approving minutes, admitting new members, electing officers, changing the rules of debate – and the 'public business' of papers and discussions. The rules specified that the host could spend up to *7s. 6d.* entertaining the guild, but that the cost of providing tobacco could not be claimed as an expense.[35]

The guild's programme included some high-profile speakers: presidents and past presidents of the conference such as E. E. Jenkins, Frederic Greeves, Robert Newton Young and T. B. Stephenson;[36] Wesleyan theological college tutors such as F. W. Macdonald, W. T. Davison and J. A. Beet;[37] and (occasionally) prominent lay

[31] WGM 1, 24 November 1883.

[32] Ibid., 19 May 1883.

[33] 'Alterations and Improvements in Oxford', *Jackson's Oxford Journal*, 14 October 1882, 7.

[34] WGM 1, 24 November 1883; 2 February 1884.

[35] WGM 2, 1 May 1891, Rule 13.

[36] WGM 1, 24 February 1883, 20 February 1886; WGM 2, 11 May 1890, 11 June 1893.

[37] All three were frequent visitors, and Beet was elected a vice-president in Michaelmas Term 1891.

Methodists such as S. D. Waddy, QC, MP.[38] Some came to Oxford to preach on Sunday at the New Inn Hall Street chapel, and met the guild on the preceding Saturday evening: Charles Garrett, ex-president, was due in October 1883, but arrived late after a 'tedious' train journey, and sent apologies; Hughes improvised an address on 'the state of the lower classes and the great need of social reform'.[39] Hughes returned to Oxford in January 1891, 'asserting his right to be honoured as the founder of the Guild'[40] and came back in subsequent years. There were non-Wesleyan speakers too. In March 1890 Canon Fremantle spoke on 'bringing Christ into all our daily works and pursuits',[41] while A. M. Fairbairn, principal of Mansfield College, was a regular speaker at, and host of, guild meetings, and an early vice-president. Recurring themes for speakers were apologetics, particularly approaches to biblical criticism;[42] consistent Christian living at and after university; and fidelity to Methodism, suggesting that invited speakers were perhaps unaware of the 'unsectarian' strand in the guild's rules, and thought that their brief was to strengthen denominational loyalties.

The suggestion that guild members might read papers was canvassed as early as November 1883, but the first undergraduate to address the guild seems to have been E. E. Kellett, who spoke on 'Robertson of Brighton' in December 1885.[43] Thereafter members addressed a range of subjects, religious, ethical, literary, philosophical and occasionally political. Kellett discussed 'Tennyson's Vision of Sin' in February 1887;[44] T. C. Piggott, whose father was the senior Wesleyan missionary in Rome, spoke on 'The Liberation of Italy' some months later;[45] A. E. Taylor, honing his skills as a critical thinker, offered 'An Apology for Wesleyanism' in November 1894, prompting the superintendent, Enoch Salt, to hail it as the most remarkable paper he had ever heard.[46] In June 1898, F. E. Corley's paper on 'Christianity and Social Problems', supported by references

[38] WGM 1, 23 May 1885.
[39] Ibid., 27 October 1883.
[40] WGM 2, 31 January 1891.
[41] Ibid., 8 March 1890.
[42] For instance, 23 May 1891 (Davison) and 5 November 1892 (W. F. Moulton).
[43] WGM 1, 5 December 1885.
[44] Ibid., 23 February 1887.
[45] Ibid., 28 May 1887.
[46] WGM 2, 11 November 1894.

to Ruskin's *Unto this Last* and Edward Bellamy's *Looking Backward*, provoked members to disagree with 'some of his seemingly strongly Socialist contentions'.[47] Serious papers were leavened with debates in which members took sides at random: thus the guild voted to 'approve the aims and tendencies of the new journalism' and agreed 'that the present position of the Socialist leaders is indefensible' but rejected a motion that 'the tone of modern Oxford is deplorable', declaring: 'We are young men … we need athletics.'[48]

The legacy of the Catherine Street Mission lived on in the guild's connections with the development of the Wesleyan Settlement in Bermondsey. The guild had begun in the era of concern for 'outcast London', and in November 1883 Samuel Barnett, vicar of St Jude's, Whitechapel, came to address a meeting at St John's College on 'Settlements of University Men in Great Towns'.[49] One outcome of Barnett's initiative was Toynbee Hall, established in 1884, and this was the model for the Wesleyan Settlement created in Bermondsey by Scott Lidgett. Sanctioned by the Wesleyan Conference in 1889 and opened in 1892, the Bermondsey Settlement followed Barnett's example of placing university and professional men alongside a large working-class population, seeking to strengthen understanding across classes, to offer opportunities for education and to address social ills.[50] Lidgett came to Oxford in February 1889, accompanied by J. H. Moulton and W. P. Workman, both on the staff of The Leys School, and Percy Bunting, barrister and editor. The deputation shared the vision of the settlement, and the guild carried unanimously a resolution welcoming the scheme.[51] Thereafter the guild was represented on the committee of the settlement, and Lidgett visited Oxford regularly to report on progress. Several members of the guild moved to Bermondsey after graduation, including W. F. Lofthouse[52] and J. B. Eames, who returned to describe to the guild in June 1897 how he was running a class for the study of literature, observing

47 Ibid., 10 June 1898.

48 Ibid., 28 May 1892, 11 March 1892, Summer 1891 (n.d.).

49 Anne Ockwell and Harold Pollins, '"Extension" in all its Forms', in Brock and Curthoys, eds, *History of the University of Oxford*, 7: 661–88, at 670–5.

50 W. F. Lofthouse, 'The Warden of the Bermondsey Settlement', in Rupert E. Davies, ed., *John Scott Lidgett: A Symposium* (London, 1957), 52–6.

51 WGM 1, 22 February 1889.

52 Lofthouse, 'Warden of the Bermondsey Settlement', 60.

cheerfully that 'it appeared that even if the class failed to fully understand Browning, they at all events were not without a lively affection for him'.[53] Guild members were encouraged to visit the settlement; two years later the guild agreed to host a Whit Monday excursion to Oxford from Bermondsey, and to provide guides and tea.[54]

It has already been seen that the guild began with a commitment to be 'unsectarian'. F. W. Macdonald, addressing the founding meeting in February 1883, endorsed the choice of the name 'Wesley Union' on the grounds that 'the name had nothing unworthy or sectarian about it, but was in perfect harmony with the spirit of the age'. The first members included one Anglican (R. T. Talbot of Exeter) and two non-Wesleyan Methodists, W. P. Orme of Lincoln and H. W. Horwill of Wadham, sons respectively of New Connexion and Bible Christian ministers.[55] Hughes quickly recruited the Congregationalist Joseph King (Trinity), secretary of the Nonconformist Union, onto the guild's committee, and brought R. F. Horton, founder of the union and fellow of New College, to lead a discussion on 'Mission Work in Oxford'.[56] Several of the guild's founding members were already active in the Nonconformist Union, and the union's rules made provision for denominational representation on its committee.[57] The change from running the Catherine Street Mission to meeting for papers and discussion brought the programmes of the two societies into close resemblance. In the early part of 1884 it was suggested that 'closer contact' with the Nonconformist Union would be desirable, and a guild meeting adjourned early so that members could attend a gathering of the union.[58] The two groups maintained a separate existence, however, with the guild becoming more definitely Methodist and the union more Congregationalist. In 1898 the guild's rules were revised, striking out the 'unsectarian' clause and replacing it with a new Rule 2: 'That any Member of the University, being also a Member or adherent of any Methodist Church, be eligible for membership'.[59] Hints in the minutes suggest that the mid-1890s were

[53] WGM 2, 18 June 1897.
[54] Ibid., 10 February 1899.
[55] WGM 1, 10 February 1883.
[56] Ibid., 10 February 1883; 28 April 1883.
[57] Minutes of the Nonconformist Union, 3–5, 17 May 1881.
[58] Ibid., 26 January, 1 March 1884.
[59] WGM 2, 2 December 1898.

difficult years for the guild, and that a new start came with the arrival of W. J. Hutton as superintendent in 1896. It is possible that the stronger Methodist emphasis in the rules was part of Hutton's attempt to reinvigorate the guild after a period of 'drift'.

The guild did not keep consistent records of membership or attendance, particularly in the early years, and membership lists in the minute books were annotated working documents, marking admissions, resignations and changes of residence as they occurred rather than tabulating statistics. Those who stayed on in Oxford after graduation retained membership, but were not clearly distinguished from undergraduates until a category of 'Life Members in Residence' was created; similarly, local ministers were included in the lists until separately designated as 'Honorary Members'. It is possible, however, to take soundings across the years between 1883 and 1914 and to assess the size, strength and composition of the guild. Membership tripled in the first decade, from an initial sixteen in 1883 to forty-eight in Michaelmas Term 1892. Thereafter a steep decline set in, so that in Hilary Term 1898 there were just sixteen members again. Numbers recovered slowly: there were twenty-five undergraduate members in the autumn of 1900, twenty-nine in 1904 and thirty-seven in 1905, and up to the First World War undergraduate membership remained in the thirties, with typically ten new members elected each Michaelmas Term to replace the leavers of the previous summer. There was a wide representation from the colleges, unsurprisingly with clusters at particular times: Balliol, Merton, Christ Church, Jesus, Wadham and Corpus Christi were consistently well represented, and the guild also attracted non-collegiate students, who comprised a significant and distinctive element of the university's population.[60] Taking Michaelmas Term 1891 as an example,[61] the guild claimed thirty-three undergraduate members, drawn from eleven colleges and with five non-collegiate students. Seven had matriculated from Kingswood School, five from Taunton and three from Rydal School, Colwyn Bay – all Wesleyan institutions – but there were also representatives of St Paul's School, Manchester Grammar School, the City of London School, Dulwich College

[60] Alan Bullock, '"A Scotch University added to Oxford"? The Non-Collegiate Students', in Brock and Curthoys, eds, *History of the University of Oxford*, 7: 193–208, especially 201, 207.

[61] WGM 2, Term Card, Michaelmas Term 1891, listing members and their colleges.

and several other provincial grammar schools, as well as two from the Wesleyan School, Oxford, the brothers Albert and Gilbert Richardson, sons of the local Wesleyan schoolmaster.

Attendance at guild meetings rarely exceeded twenty, and for a long period through the 1890s it was regularly in single figures. High-profile speakers sometimes attracted better audiences, including visitors and guests: among the best-attended gatherings of the period were Price Hughes's 'earnest address urging on the aristocracy of learning a deep and real sympathy with the poor and helpless' in June 1894 and W. T. Davison's careful summary of recent developments in biblical criticism in November 1899.[62] Conversely, attendance in May 1892, when Revd Nehemiah Curnock spoke about religious journalism, was 'scanty', due to the proximity of Eights Week, while the meeting on 19 May 1900 was abandoned due to the imminent celebration of the relief of Mafeking.[63] When W. F. Moulton queried the programme of two or three meetings a term, urging the advantages of the Cambridge pattern of a weekly gathering, A. E. Taylor replied that Oxford undergraduates were too busy with 'hard reading' for additional activities.[64]

It remains to be asked whether the Wesley Guild fulfilled the hopes of its founders and promoters. Hugh Price Hughes's initial scheme to recruit an interdenominational group of students to staff a mission room in the expanding working-class suburbs of East Oxford soon petered out, but commitment to a broadly based approach to evangelism and social concern endured, both in the guild's long-term support for the Bermondsey Settlement and in the subsequent careers of guild members such as W. F. Lofthouse, a founder member of the Wesleyan Methodist Union for Social Service,[65] and E. E. Genner, who represented the university on the Oxford Board of Guardians for more than twenty years.[66] A much more general statement of purpose – that the guild 'has been formed to afford Members of the University an opportunity of mutual intercourse'[67] – was certainly fulfilled by the meetings, but did the guild

[62] Ibid., 2 June 1894, 21 November 1899.
[63] Ibid., 21 May 1892, 19 May 1900.
[64] Ibid., February 1891 (no date in the minutes).
[65] D. J. Carter, 'Lofthouse, William Francis', in John A. Vickers, ed., *A Dictionary of Methodism in Britain and Ireland* (Peterborough, 2000), 210.
[66] 'The Late Mr E. E. Genner', *Oxford Times*, 9 January 1931, 15.
[67] Printed on the front of the 1891 term card.

succeed in sustaining the denominational identity and loyalty of Methodist undergraduates in the face of competition from other churches and world-views?

Looking first at the sixteen founding members, R. T. Talbot came from an Anglican background and became an Anglican priest. Six of the others, all from Methodist backgrounds, took Anglican orders, some entering parish ministry and others pursuing careers in education.[68] Five definitely remained in Methodism: J. J. Findlay, headmaster first of Queen's College, Taunton, and subsequently of Wesley College, Sheffield, and then professor of education at Manchester;[69] H. W. Horwill, who followed his father into the Bible Christian ministry and then became a journalist;[70] E. E. Kellett, schoolmaster at The Leys;[71] A. F. Kerry, who stayed in Oxford as organist at New Inn Hall Street and headmaster of the City Technical School; and Sidney Vanes, who was an active lay Methodist and schoolmaster in Adelaide until his death in 1901.[72] Others went on to careers in the home civil service,[73] in India[74] or in politics,[75] but their later religious allegiance is unclear.

This pattern persisted. Some guild members entered the Wesleyan ministry, including W. F. Lofthouse, J. H. Ritson and R. N. Flew, all later presidents of the conference, and A. J. Costain, headmaster of Rydal Mount School. Others were active as lay Methodists, like F. E. Corley, who taught at the Madras Christian College from 1906–36,[76] and E. E. Genner, fellow of Jesus College, Oxford, and then of Oriel. A. S. Peake, of Primitive Methodist stock, was a member of the guild before leaving Oxford in 1892 for his life's work of training ministers at Hartley College, Manchester, where he did much to establish the university's faculty of theology. Others joined

[68] W. E. Humphreys, W. E. Colegrove, J. A. Forrest, Samuel Jackson, T. W. Moulton and W. J. Ward.

[69] Ron Brooks, 'Findlay, Joseph John (1860–1940)', *ODNB*, online edn (2004), at: <http://www.oxforddnb.com/view/article/46690>, accessed 23 May 2017.

[70] *MR*, 13 March 1952, 7. Horwill gave up pastoral work because of ill-health, but remained in the ministry.

[71] Brian Harrison, 'Kellett, Ernest Edward (1864–1950)', *ODNB*, online edn (2004), at: <http://www.oxforddnb.com/view/article/75374>, accessed 24 May 2017.

[72] 'The Late Mr Vanes, MA', *The Advertiser* (Adelaide), 14 October 1901, 4.

[73] J. G. Willis: *The Times*, 20 May 1924, 19.

[74] W. E. Hoare: *London Gazette*, 11 October 1929, 6521 (grant of probate).

[75] S. S. Savery: *The Times*, 28 December 1938, 12.

[76] *MR*, 22, 29 July 1937.

the Church of England, such as A. E. Taylor, philosopher and Gifford Lecturer,[77] and A. E. Hillard, later high master of St Paul's,[78] or moved away from denominational loyalties and faith commitments altogether, like W. P. Crozier, later editor of the *Manchester Guardian*.[79]

Although each biography has its own unique blend of influences and experiences, the haemorrhage of Oxford-educated young men from Methodism in this period is striking. The jeremiads of the 1870s had warned that Oxford and Cambridge were unconducive to the maintenance of Methodist loyalties, and the history of the Wesley Guild seems to show that these fears were not unfounded. Methodist and free church students remained a minority in the university, and although there was no coercion, social and cultural pressures to comply with an Anglican norm were very present. Graduates seeking careers in education had limited opportunities in Methodist schools: a significant number of those who entered Anglican orders became schoolmasters. Although by the end of the nineteenth century the Wesleyans had many imposing city centre and suburban chapels, with affluent middle-class congregations, most Wesleyans still worshipped in small chapels or places with a working-class majority. There were serious scholars in the Wesleyan ministry, but only a small number of graduates, and swathes of the connexion remained suspicious of academic expertise. A combination of personal circumstances, career opportunities and cultural affinities may help to explain the departure of Wesley Guild members from Methodism.

In November 1899 W. F. Lofthouse, by now tutor at the Wesleyans' Handsworth College, returned to the guild to open a debate on the topic 'Wesley College, Oxford'. Plans for a Methodist college in Oxford were under discussion, its advocates hoping perhaps to emulate the Congregationalists' Mansfield. Lofthouse was sceptical, reflecting that many of 'our men' in the theological colleges 'have not much education', and that it would not work to bring them 'straight from the plough or desk to Oxford'. Furthermore, 'the chief need of our ministers was not academic

[77] Donald M. MacKinnon, 'Taylor, Alfred Edward (1869–1945)', rev. Mark J. Schofield, *ODNB*, online edn (2008), at: <http://www.oxforddnb.com/view/article/36426>, accessed 18 June 2017.

[78] *The Times*, 11 November 1935, 14.

[79] A. J. A. Morris, 'Crozier, William Percival (1879–1944)', *ODNB*, online edn (2004), at: <http://www.oxforddnb.com/view/article/32651>, accessed 30 June 2017.

culture'. William Bradfield, the superintendent, strongly disagreed, declaring that 'we owe it to the world to rear scholars'.[80] These tensions and realities were played out in the early history of the Wesley Guild, illustrating the social and academic aspirations of Methodism in the late nineteenth century, and also its fears of cultural assimilation and denominational extinction in a milieu dominated by other traditions and values. Despite its beginnings in ecumenical cooperation and evangelism, the guild soon became a safe and supportive community for a small group of Methodist undergraduates. Exposed to the challenges and opportunities of an Oxford education, some were able to combine professional success and Methodist loyalty, while others found different paths as their careers unfolded. Access to Oxford and Cambridge certainly brought the advantages and status long denied to Nonconformists, but, in spite of the best efforts of groups like the Wesley Guild, sustaining Methodist identity in the university and thereafter proved a very tall order.

[80] WGM 2, 4 November 1899.

Churches and Adult Education in the Edwardian Era: Learning from the Experiences of Hampshire Congregationalists

Roger Ottewill*
Southampton

Through their enthusiastic embrace of the doctrine of the 'institutional church', late Victorian and Edwardian Congregationalists demonstrated their commitment to, inter alia, *the intellectual development of church members and adherents. Many churches, large and small, sponsored mutual improvement societies, literary and debating societies and programmes of public lectures, as well as ad hoc talks, covering every conceivable subject from the natural sciences to contemporary social and political issues. What motivated Congregationalists to engage in activities of this kind, and to what extent were they seen as an integral part of their religious vocation? In considering these questions, evidence is drawn from initiatives of two Congregational churches in Edwardian Hampshire: London Street, Basingstoke's Mutual Improvement Society and Avenue, Southampton's annual programme of lectures. What emerges is an approach to ministry that blurred the boundary between the sacred and the secular and a gradual weakening of commitment as churches were superseded by secular providers. In reviewing an under-explored aspect of the relationship between religion and education, the article serves as an addition to the limited literature on this subject.*

During the nineteenth and early twentieth centuries, many churches in Britain made a notable contribution to the education not only of children but also of adults. Although the activities of Sunday schools are well known and reasonably well documented, those of parallel organizations for adults – mutual improvement societies, programmes of public lectures, literary and debating societies and adult Sunday schools – have attracted less attention. That said, Simon Green and Stephen Yeo, in their studies of religion in West Yorkshire and Reading respectively, do highlight the contribution of churches and chapels to adult education in the second half of

* 15 Atherley Court, Southampton, SO15 7NG. E-mail: rogerottewill@btinternet.com.

Studies in Church History 55 (2019), 494–510
doi: 10.1017/stc.2018.20

Victoria's reign and the Edwardian era.[1] Likewise, from a more secular perspective, Roger Fieldhouse, in his history of modern British adult education, gives due recognition to the involvement of churches in collaboration, or competition, with non-religious providers such as mechanics' institutes, working men's institutes, women's colleges and university extension classes.[2] This was undoubtedly a crowded field of activity, with many nineteenth-century initiatives paving the way for those of the twentieth.

For Nonconformist churches and chapels, adult education provision was one of the most conspicuous manifestations of the doctrine of the 'institutional church', that is, the belief that church premises should be social centres as well as places of worship.[3] This had a pervasive influence as the nineteenth century gave way to the twentieth. As Keith Robbins observes, 'the "institutional church", as a notion, with variants, was widely taken up … [with] the result … [being] a formidable array of activities and organizations conducted under church auspices'.[4] In his history of Congregationalism, Tudur Jones comments that application of the institutional principle 'had been growing in popularity during the last quarter of the nineteenth century and reached its high-water mark in the early years of the twentieth'.[5] Indeed, it was the 'ecclesiological phenomenon' of the age.[6]

For Michael Watts, the institutional church was

> the practical expression of the theological liberalism of the late nineteenth century: of the emphasis on the immanence of God and the

[1] Simon Green, 'Religion and the Rise of the Common Man: Mutual Improvement Societies, Religious Associations and Popular Education in three Industrial Towns in the West Riding of Yorkshire *c.*1850–1900', in Derek Fraser, ed., *Cities, Class and Communication: Essays in Honour of Asa Briggs* (London, 1990), 25–43; Stephen Yeo, *Religion and Voluntary Organisations in Crisis* (London, 1976).

[2] Roger Fieldhouse et al., *A History of Modern Adult Education* (Leicester, 1996).

[3] More formally: 'The institutional church … was a practical experiment … [which] aimed at bridging the gulf between the Sunday School and the Church; … ministering to the development of man's all-round nature; … [and] making such provision as is necessary under social conditions which make true home-life impossible': C. Silvester Horne, 'Institutional Church', in James Hastings, ed., *Encyclopaedia of Religion and Ethics*, 13 vols (Edinburgh, 1914), 7: 362–4. See also Robert Tudur Jones, *Congregationalism in England 1662–1962* (London, 1962), 315, 318.

[4] Keith Robbins, *England, Ireland, Scotland, Wales: The Christian Church 1900–2000*, OHCC (Oxford, 2008), 55.

[5] Jones, *Congregationalism*, 315.

[6] Ian Sellers, 'Liverpool Nonconformity: 1786–1914' (PhD thesis, Keele University, 1969), 118.

> incarnation of Christ, which saw … the goal of the Christian not so much [as] the attainment of eternal life in heaven but the establishment of the kingdom of God on earth … .[7]

In a chapter devoted to the subject, he demonstrates the many ways in which Nonconformist churches contributed to every aspect of the 'social and intellectual well-being' of their members and others who came within their sphere of influence.[8] Advocates of the institutional doctrine argued that it was 'the Church's duty to teach by practice as well as by precept, that religion covers the whole of life'.[9] Such a holistic approach to ministry inevitably led to a weakening of traditional theological dichotomies, such as body and soul or mind and spirit, and blurred the boundary between the sacred and the secular. As Peter Yalden points out, one of the foremost champions of the institutional church, the influential Congregationalist, Revd Sylvester Horne, believed that churches should aim to 'help people develop all their capabilities, not only the soul but the mind and body as well'.[10] In so doing, enhancing the intellectual prowess of members and adherents had a high priority.

For Richard Mudie Smith, the journalist and editor of *The Religious Life of London*, the institutional church was 'the centre of active, aggressive, social work. Open seven days a week, it … aim[ed] at the redemption and development of body, mind and soul'.[11] In this way, it embodied the business-like and hard-headed approach which, as David Bebbington argues, was one feature of the Enlightenment which profoundly influenced evangelicals. It was a 'significant expression … of their pragmatic temper'.[12]

Involving extensive lay participation in establishing and sustaining 'a wide variety of subsidiary associations and activities', it was hoped

[7] Michael Watts, *The Dissenters*, 3: *The Crisis and Conscience of Nonconformity* (Oxford, 2015), 170.

[8] Ibid. 168–90.

[9] Bertram Smith and Francis Wrigley, 'The Church's Week-Night Programme: I. A Defence of Church Activity', *The Examiner*, 6 June 1901, 190.

[10] Peter Yalden, 'Association, Community and the Origins of Secularisation: English and Welsh Nonconformity, *c.*1850–1930', *JEH* 25 (2004), 293–324, at 310.

[11] Richard Mudie Smith, ed., *The Religious Life of London* (London, 1904), 9.

[12] David Bebbington, 'Evangelicalism and British Culture', in Stewart J. Brown, Frances Knight and John Morgan-Guy, eds, *Religion, Identity and Conflict in Britain: From the Restoration to the Twentieth Century. Essays in Honour of Keith Robbins* (Farnham, 2013), 105–19, at 108.

that these 'would help to attract people' of many different backgrounds into the churches.[13] From an evangelistic perspective, these can be seen as a counterbalance to the aggressive campaigns of the first half of the nineteenth century, those of Moody and Sankey in the 1870s, and the simultaneous Free Church missions of the early months of 1901. In other words, the institutional church was seen as a form of outreach more in keeping with the less emotional and more cerebral spirit of the age symbolized by improvements in the provision of educational opportunities for all. However, as Jeremy Morris observes in a study of religion and urban change in nineteenth- and twentieth-century Croydon, while reinforcing 'the ties between church membership and the wider circle of potential church members', church-based organizations were not 'very effective in recruiting from outside this periphery'. This was partly because they were not sufficiently proactive, relying 'on some initial interest in the life of the church', but also, and pertinently, because they required 'some level of educational and intellectual attainment as well'.[14] Moreover, as Dominic Erdozain has cogently argued, in pursuing pleasure and recreation in its many forms, including adult education, churches risked undermining their primary rationale, the saving of souls.[15] Indeed, at the time some shared these concerns.[16]

Nevertheless, the institutional church can be seen as a rational response to the increased leisure time and proliferation of secular pastimes enjoyed by many in society at large. Churches felt they had to compete and offer their members something similar, thereby cementing their loyalty by meeting most of their needs 'from the cradle to the grave', fearing that if they did not do so they would lose support. Activities intended to be more edifying than many offered by secular providers were embedded within the life of most Edwardian churches, echoing the call to 'seriousness and high

[13] Yalden, 'Origins', 310.

[14] Jeremy Morris, *Religion and Urban Change: Croydon 1840–1914* (Woodbridge, 1992), 80.

[15] Dominic Erdozain, *The Problem of Pleasure* (Woodbridge, 2010).

[16] For example, in a later article than the one cited in n. 9 above, Smith and Wrigley expressed the view that '[t]he week-night Programme should be designed primarily not to attract outsiders to religion, but to provide for those already within the Church's sphere of influence. … It would be a fatal error to attempt to substitute the concert for the Cross': 'The Church's Week-Night Programme: III. The Church and the Programme', *The Examiner*, 20 June 1910, 222.

mindedness' that had invigorated the evangelical Christianity of the Victorian age.[17] Green, discussing what he refers to as the 'associational ideal', argues that this held out 'the genuine possibility of meaningful self-improvement', coupled with 'divine social activity' and 'the ultimate sacred goal of personal salvation'.[18]

Furthermore, by this stage church premises were often extensive, incorporating, in addition to the main worship area, schoolrooms and spaces for larger gatherings. It was often felt, from both moral and economic points of view, that they were a valuable resource, the potential of which needed to be fully realized by utilizing them throughout the week and not simply on Sundays. Their use for adult education was seen as one means by which churches could respond to the interests – and the needs – of the community more widely.

This article examines the character and format of adult education provision on the basis of the experiences of two Congregational initiatives in Edwardian Hampshire: the London Street Mutual Improvement Society and a public lecture programme, the Avenue Lectures. Their contribution to what today is known as 'lifelong learning' is assessed. From surviving evidence, found mainly in church magazines and local newspapers, what emerges is a gradual weakening of their commitment as churches were superseded by secular providers. By concentrating on the Congregationalists of Hampshire it is not intended to imply that they were unique as adult education providers. Indeed, as Green, Yeo and Watts illustrate, members of other denominations were also involved in such programmes. However, Congregationalists developed a particularly high profile in this respect and arguably exerted an influence beyond their denominational boundaries. Similarly, while this is primarily a local, 'microscopic', study, engagement with secondary sources enables a number of broader, 'microcosmic' points to be made, particularly with regard to the changing environment within which churches were operating as facilitators of adult education and in relation to the doctrine of the institutional church.[19]

[17] Ian Bradley, *The Call to Seriousness: The Evangelical Impact on the Victorians* (London, 1976).

[18] Simon Green, *Religion in the Age of Decline: Organisation and Experience in Industrial Yorkshire, 1870–1920* (Cambridge, 1996), 182.

[19] For the distinction between 'microscopic' and 'microcosmic' studies, see Michael M. Postan, *Fact and Relevance: Essay on Historical Method* (Cambridge, 1971), 20–1.

London Street Mutual Improvement Society

In promoting adult education, some of the larger Congregational churches in Hampshire formed mutual improvement societies. As their title suggests, these were intended to be, as Fieldhouse puts it, a 'collective form of … self-education'.[20] This was to be achieved through the presentation of papers to stimulate debate and constructive criticism. Although such societies were by no means the exclusive preserve of churches,[21] they were often, as Watts and others attest, a key feature of the institutional church.[22]

In the north-east Hampshire market town of Basingstoke, London Street Congregational Church ran, for approximately fifty years from the mid-Victorian era,[23] a well respected Mutual Improvement Society (LSMIS). Unlike the position in Croydon, where Morris indicates that 'mutual improvement societies … have left behind too little evidence to merit much more than a passing reference', primary source material for the LSMIS has survived.[24]

Although the precise origins of the LSMIS are unknown, it seems likely that it was a successor organization to Basingstoke Literary Association (1859–64), in which a leading figure was London Street's minister, Revd John Mark Wilks.[25] In 1889, the aim of the LSMIS was 'to turn out its members as genuine, frank and free members of society – worthy to be equal to other people and able to win that position'.[26] Underlying this aspiration was the notion of

[20] Fieldhouse, *Modern Adult Education*, 14.

[21] C. J. Radcliffe, 'Mutual Improvement Societies in the West Riding of Yorkshire, 1835–1900', *JEAH* 18/2 (1986), 1–16; M. I. Watson, 'Mutual Improvement Societies in Nineteenth-Century Lancashire', *JEAH* 21/2 (1989), 8–17.

[22] Watts, *Dissenters* 3, 168–90.

[23] In 1890, a contributor to one LSMIS debate, Mr Reavell from Aldershot, 'expressed his pleasure at being … afforded the opportunity of revisiting the Society of which he had been a member thirty years [previously]': *Hants and Berks Gazette* (hereafter: *HBG*), 22 February 1890.

[24] Two minute books have survived and are lodged with the Hampshire RO in Winchester. They cover the years 1889–1894 (8M62/5) and 1900–11 (23M72/G1).

[25] Wilks was minister of London St Congregational Church between 1858 and 1862. From Basingstoke he moved to London, where he became a prominent educationalist as well as an eminent preacher. For further information about the Basingstoke Literary Association, see Diana Macmarill, 'A Society of Literature 1859–1864', *Basingstoke Archaeological and Historical Society Newsletter* 146 (1999), 7–12.

[26] Winchester, Hampshire RO, LSMIS Minute Book 1889–94.

what Anne Rodrick has characterized as 'citizenship by debate'.[27] Through participation in LSMIS activities, members would gain self-confidence as their knowledge increased and their analytical and oral communication skills developed, thereby helping them to become better informed and more engaged citizens. Such hopes echoed those of 'a pedagogic and ethical' nature highlighted by Green, with 'public-speaking, collective discipline and individual seriousness' being to the fore.[28]

The LSMIS was still flourishing at the beginning of the twentieth century, as a reference to it in a local newspaper of 1902 indicates: 'this excellent society … has behind it a record in which it might take pride, and before it, we hope, a career of further usefulness in the stimulation of … [members] to improve their powers of thought and of speech'.[29] Taking these comments at face value, it would seem that the goal of self-improvement and, by implication, a more active mode of citizenship had been achieved.

By 1902 the LSMIS was open to people of both sexes and all ages. This contrasts markedly with the societies studied by Green which were exclusively male and targeted at young people. Indeed, for Watts, they were part of the attempt 'to retain the interests of young people … once they became too old for Sunday school'.[30] Although there is no direct evidence, this may have been an earlier aim of the LSMIS. However, by the early twentieth century, it had a broader purpose.

There was 'an annual subscription', one shilling for the 1901–2 session, 'payable in advance by each member', which secured admittance to 'all ordinary meetings'.[31] The rules specified how debates were to be conducted and listed the officers. Although all office holders were men, seven of the ten committee members for the 1901–2 session were single women and nearly two-thirds of the 69 members were women.[32] This calls into question the accuracy of Barry Doyle's assertion, based on his study of Congregationalism in Edwardian

[27] Anne Rodrick, *Self-Help and Civic Culture: Citizenship in Victorian Birmingham* (Aldershot, 2004), 113–23.

[28] Green, 'Religion and the Rise of the Common Man', 39.

[29] *HBG*, 1 November 1902, 5.

[30] Watts, *Dissenters* 3, 175.

[31] Hampshire RO, 23M72/G1, LSMIS Membership Card for 1901–2.

[32] For the 1902/3 session, 47 of the 88 members were women: *HBG*, 28 March 1903, 6.

Norwich, that 'in most churches female members were offered little in the way of literary, civic or political education'.[33]

In Basingstoke, the minister took a leading role in the LSMIS, serving as its president. London Street's well-respected minister from 1887 to 1907, Revd Capes Tarbolton, was ideally suited to this role since he maintained a lively 'intellectual interest in modern movements of thought … and had considerable literary gifts of which he was most modest … [and] as … [a] speaker he was original and incisive'.[34] Additionally, other Congregational ministers often made a contribution, as can be seen in the programme of lectures for 1904–5 (Table 1). Comprising an eclectic mix of topics and incorporating various pedagogic techniques, such as experiments, visual aids, illustrative readings and lantern slides (seen as 'adding interest' and immediacy to the proceedings), the programme was designed to have widespread appeal.[35]

However, the LSMIS faced a number of challenges. At the opening soirée in 1902, 'even under the influence of music and refreshments, the company did not altogether relax its stiffness, and seemed strangely shy of one another'.[36] More seriously, two years later it was reported:

> Some members might be disappointed that they had not got more debates – in fact they had none. For that the members themselves were to be blamed entirely. The Secretary would have only been too pleased if the members had been willing to come and scratch [out] each other[']s eyes, but they all seemed to be blessed with such unanimity that they could not even get up sufficient differences of opinion for a debate. They might have amongst them budding orators … but at present they were practising in private. Perhaps at some future time they would resume those debates which in the past had been found to be so interesting and exciting.[37]

The absence of debates clearly undermined a key principle of mutual improvement societies which was, as Green puts it, 'for members to seek to teach each other to the mutual advantage of all'.[38]

[33] Barry Doyle, 'Gender, Class and Congregational Culture in Early Twentieth-Century Norwich', *JURCHS* 5 (1992–7), 317–35, at 325.
[34] *Congregational Year Book* 1926, 183.
[35] *Hampshire Independent* (hereafter: *HI*), 9 February 1907, unpaginated.
[36] *HBG*, 1 November 1902.
[37] Ibid. 5 November 1904, 6.
[38] Green, 'Religion and the Rise of the Common Man', 35.

Table 1. London Street Congregational Church Mutual Improvement Society Programme of Lectures, 1904–5

Date	Speaker	Subject
15 Nov. 1904	Revd Herbert Arnold [retired Congregational minister]	'The Portrait of Oliver Cromwell as painted by himself'
22 Nov. 1904	Revd F. W. R. Dorling [Minister, Castle St Congregational Church, Reading, 1899–1905]	'Henry Drummond'
29 Nov. 1904	Mr Sidney Rossiter	'Flame and Combustion' with experiments
6 Dec. 1904	Revd R. B. Brindley [Minister, George St Congregational Church, Croydon, 1901–8]	'Some Clerical Celebrities of my Youth'
13 Dec. 1904	Mr W. H. Hunt	'A Colony of Mercy' with lantern slides
17 Jan. 1905	Mr G. Gage	'Tibet and the Tibetans'
24 Jan. 1905	Revd A. Clegg [Minister, Berkhamsted Congregational Church, 1902–10]	'Edgar Allan Poe' with illustrative readings
31 Jan. 1905	Revd R. Dobbie [Minister, Crondall Congregational Church, 1903–7]	'Tennyson's In Memoriam'
7 Feb. 1905	Revd Capes Tarbolton [Minister, London St Congregational Church, Basingstoke, 1887–1907]	'Peerless Pepys'
14 Feb. 1905	Revd H. P. Slade, FRAS [Minister, Holderness Rd Presbyterian Church, Hull, 1887–1908]	'The Wonders of the Heavens' with lantern slides
21 Feb. 1905	Revd G. Freeman [Minister of Newhaven Congregational Church, 1902–5]	'Thrift'
28 Feb. 1905	Revd R. Teasdale [Minister of Gosport Congregational Church, 1902–8]	'Thomas Chatterton, the Marvellous Boy'
7 Mar. 1905	Mr. J. A. Simes	'Some Impressions of Italy from a Naturalist's Point of View' with lantern slides
14 Mar. 1905	Mr. Leslie B. Hall	'The Life of a Moss' with lantern slides and specimens

Source: *HBG*, 5 November 1904, 6.

For reasons which are unclear, the LSMIS went into hibernation during the middle years of the decade, being successfully resuscitated for the 1907–8 session. As it was put in the January 1908 issue of the church magazine: 'One hundred and sixty-three persons of both sexes have been candid and true enough to come out boldly and say they mutually desire to be improved!'[39] There was also renewed emphasis on appealing to the young: '[the LSMIS] is practically the only means of mental culture and improvement that is easily accessible to young people and while the style of meeting aims at more than amusement only, yet it is by no means of the dry as dust variety'.[40] To this end, as the 1909–10 programme indicates (Table 2), the academic components were supplemented with regular social evenings and a recital. Moreover, the inclusion of discussions, some in the form of mock parliaments, suggests that the earlier appeal had borne fruit.

Thus, by the end of the first decade of the twentieth century the LSMIS was still very much alive and served as an exemplar of London Street's embrace of the doctrine of the institutional church and its desire to reach out to the community at large. For the 1909–10 session, twelve of the twenty-three committee members were women, eight single and four married. However, since details of the membership are unknown, it is not possible to determine whether it had any success in drawing in those who had no other connection with the church, or the age and gender balance at this time.

In early 1910 it was reported that the LSMIS had 'well sustained its reputation during the past few weeks in the variety and interest of its meetings'.[41] A year later, however, it is clear that all was not well. As reported in the *Church Manual*,

> at the commencement of Session 1911/12 it was thought advisable to bring the Society into line with kindred organizations by changing its old title of 'Mutual Improvement' … [to that of 'Literary Society'] and to hold meetings fortnightly instead of weekly as a concession to the increased multiplicity of 'full' evenings.

[39] *Basingstoke Congregational Magazine* (hereafter: *BCM*) n.s. 1/1 (January 1908), unpaginated. Unlike some of the earlier years, the gender mix of the membership at this time is not known.

[40] Ibid. n.s. 2/10 (October 1909), unpaginated.

[41] Ibid., n.s. 3/1 (January 1910), 8.

Table 2. London Street Congregational Church Mutual Improvement Society Programme of Events, 1909–10

Date	Speaker	Subject
19 Oct. 1909	---	Social Evening
26 Oct. 1909	---	Mock Parliament
2 Nov. 1909	Professor Andrews	Lecture 'The Puritan Ideal'
9 Nov. 1909	Mr J. Froome	Discussion 'Do modern amusements make for wholesome recreation?'
16 Nov. 1909	Revd N. Richards [Minister, Winchester Congregational Church, 1907–10]	Lecture 'In Memoriam'
23 Nov. 1909	Mr Bird	Discussion 'Is compulsory Military Training desirable?'
30 Nov. 1909	Mr Higgs	Lecture 'A Cruise in the North Sea'
7 Dec. 1909	–	Mock Parliament
14 Dec. 1909	Mr Shrubsole, FGS	Lecture 'Holiday Rambles in Hungary'
21 Dec. 1909	Mr F. G. Harrisson	Discussion 'Will Airships benefit Mankind?'
11 Jan. 1910	–	Social Evening
18 Jan. 1910	Revd A. Clegg [Minister, Berkhamsted Congregational Church, 1902–10]	Recital
25 Jan. 1910	Mr T. K. Phillips	Discussion 'The Daylight Saving Proposal'
1 Feb. 1910	SPCA	Lecture 'Ants, Bees and Wasps'
8 Feb. 1910	–	Mock Parliament
15 Feb. 1910	Revd F. W. R. Dorling [Minister, Shanklin Congregational Church, 1908–24]	Lecture 'The Grand Old Man'
22 Feb. 1910	Mr Howell	Book Evening
1 Mar. 1910	Dr Ahrens	Lecture 'Women'
8 Mar. 1910	Mr Gregory	Discussion 'Is the Socialist State Possible?'
15 Mar. 1910	Mr Rossiter	Lecture 'Comets'
22 Mar. 1910	–	Impromptu speaking
29 Mar. 1910	–	Social Evening

Source: LSMIS Membership Card, 1909–10.

Furthermore, membership and attendance were 'not as good as the interest and high quality of the programme' deserved. Thus, the question arose as to whether the society had 'finally fulfilled the need it was originally started to meet'.[42] Although it struggled on until 1914, it would seem to have been but a shadow of its former self.

In seeking to explain the LSMIS's demise, a key consideration concerns competition from other adult education providers. Basingstoke had a very active Mechanics Institute and although this had coexisted with the LSMIS for many years, it appears to have sustained a higher level of interest in the years leading up to the outbreak of the First World War.[43] In addition, the first decade of the twentieth century saw the emergence of new adult education providers, one of the most significant being the Workers' Educational Association (WEA) founded in 1903. As recounted by Yeo, the branch of the WEA in Reading, only fifteen miles from Basingstoke, was 'proud of its … pioneer status'.[44] Its formation was emblematic of the 'shift in the centre of gravity of activities away from churches and chapels into the town'.[45] Thus, in the field of adult education, churches can be seen as victims of their own success, laying foundations on which secular providers could build. Put a little differently, it seems likely that the LSMIS and similar societies stimulated a thirst for 'lifelong learning' within the community at large which outgrew the confines of a particular church. Indeed, through the attention the LSMIS received in the local press, its impact on the intellectual life of the community may well have extended beyond the membership.

One final consideration concerns the extent to which adult education had to contend with newer leisure pursuits, particularly the cinema. As McKernan highlights, film was 'an entertainment form of unprecedented social impact'.[46] It is perhaps no coincidence that Basingstoke's first purpose-built cinema, the Electric Palace, opened in October 1910.[47]

[42] *London Street Congregational Church Basingstoke Manual* (Basingstoke, 1912), 50.

[43] Founded in 1841, the Mechanics Institute moved into purpose-built premises in 1869: 'Mechanics Institute, Basingstoke', online at: <https://www.victoriacountyhistory.ac.uk/explore/items/mechanics-institute-basingstoke>, accessed 7 February 2018.

[44] Yeo, *Religion and Voluntary Organisations*, 235.

[45] Ibid. 169.

[46] Luke McKernan, 'A Fury for Seeing: Cinema, Audience and Leisure in London in 1913', *Early Popular Visual Culture* 6 (2008), 271–80, at 272.

[47] For a detailed discussion of the origins of the cinema in the town, see Mervyn Gould, *Basingstoke Entertained* (Wakefield, 2007), 7–10.

Avenue Lectures

Within Hampshire, arguably the most distinguished Congregational adult education initiative was the very popular annual programme of lectures arranged by Southampton's Avenue Congregational Church. This was somewhat different from a mutual improvement society in that all its events took the form of lectures, with eminent speakers imparting their knowledge of specialist subjects to a relatively passive audience. There was no attempt to inject any element of mutuality, as Avenue also sponsored a Literary and Debating Society for this purpose.

Founded in 1892, the Avenue Congregational Church was located in a newly developed 'select suburb' for the middle classes.[48] Responsibility for organizing the lecture programme was exercised by the church's Lectures and Entertainments Committee, which was set up in 1895. The aim was to 'deal principally, with some of those problems – National, Social, Literary, which at the present time are prominently engaging public attention'.[49] Lectures were held monthly between September and March, there was an admission fee and tickets were initially sold at a number of outlets in Southampton.

As the church magazine commented regarding the 1902–3 programme:

> For many years Southampton has not had such men as Dr Dallinger and Dr Andrew Wilson on the lecture platform and although the privilege of hearing these and other front rank men in their various special subjects entails considerable expense, yet we understand the Committee are fully confident that as long as a first-class series of Lectures is provided they will have the cordial support of the Congregation and also of the outside public.[50]

Thus there was a desire to provide opportunities for Southampton residents to learn directly from those at the forefront of their area of expertise. In this respect, the approach was unapologetically elitist; in putting together such an illustrious programme, Avenue can be said to have followed in the footsteps of the Institute attached to

[48] Dora Caton, 'Century of Change for Avenue Congregational Church', *Hampshire* 22/8 (1992), 40.

[49] *Avenue Record* 1895, 14.

[50] *Avenue Free Churchman* (hereafter: *AFC*) 5/8 (1902), vi.

Westbourne Park Baptist Church. As Watts records, for twenty years around the turn of the century,

> [this] institute's public lectures attracted large audiences and an impressive array of distinguished speakers: H. M. Stanley described his African travels, Professor Flinders Petrie talked about Egyptology, Fridtjof Nansen spoke of his pioneer journey across the Polar ice cap, and Winston Churchill related his experiences in the Boer War. The world of science was represented by Oliver Lodge and the astronomer Sir Robert Ball; that of music by Sir Hubert Parry; and literature by Arthur Conan Doyle and Jerome K. Jerome.[51]

Although not as well known or of quite the same calibre as the Westbourne Park lecturers, something of the standing of those who contributed to the Avenue Lecture series and the variety of topics covered can be gained from the programmes for 1901–2 and 1913–14 (Tables 3 and 4).

Avenue's lecture programme received considerable publicity in the local press, thereby keeping the church in the public eye.[52] This undoubtedly helped to broaden the programme's appeal well beyond the congregation and to maximize the audience. While such a venture was in keeping with the spirit of the institutional church, it would have been seen by critics as a distraction from the spiritual aspects of church life. Moreover, as with mutual improvement societies, competition from other providers could not be ignored. Indeed, during the early months of 1914, Avenue's lecture hall was hired by Hartley University College as the venue for its extension lectures, with Professor G. K. Sutherland giving a series of three talks on evolution.[53] The hall was also used by Southampton Literary and Philosophical Society.

Nonetheless, following their suspension during the war, lectures were resumed from the 1919–20 session and initially the demand for tickets exceeded the availability of seats.[54] Their popularity

[51] Watts, *Dissenters* 3, 169.

[52] For example, a report of the Carruthers Gould's lecture appeared in *HI*, 24 January 1914, 1; of Frederick Christian's lecture in *HI*, 21 February 1914, 1; and of Walford Davies's 'melodious lecture' in *Southampton Times and Hampshire Express* (hereafter: *STHE*), 28 March 1914, 16.

[53] See, for example, a report of Professor Sutherland's first lecture in *STHE*, 24 January 1914, 16.

[54] Throughout the war, the hall 'served as a venue for "the comfort and welfare of the soldiers and sailors who in great numbers passed through" Southampton to and from

Table 3. Avenue Congregational Church Programme of Lectures, 1901–2

Date	Speaker	Subject
2 Oct. 1901	Sir George Robertson	'Chitral, and the Story of the Siege'
23 Oct. 1901	Mr Ernest Denny	Elocutionary recital
20 Nov. 1901	Revd J. M. Bacon	'Voyages in Cloudland'
11 Dec. 1901	Mr E. T. Read of *Punch*	'Caricature in and out of Parliament'
15 Jan. 1902	Revd Charles Clark	'Lord Macaulay: Historian, Poet, Statesman'
19 Feb. 1902	Madame Bertha Moore	'Three Centuries of English Song'
19 Mar. 1902	Revd A. B. Boyd-Carpenter	'Stephen Langton: Archbishop and Patriot'

Source: *AFC* 4/7 (1901), vi.

Table 4. Avenue Congregational Church Programme of Lectures, 1913–14

Date	Speaker	Subject
8 Oct. 1913	Sir Harry Johnston, GCMG, KGB, DSc	'The Peoples of Central Africa.' Fully illustrated
29 Oct. 1913	Miss Kate Malecka	'My Experiences of Russian Poland.' Fully Illustrated
26 Nov. 1913	Prof. Silvanus P. Thompson, FRS, DSc	'The Magic Mirror of Japan.' Specially Illustrated
17 Dec. 1913	Mr Alexander Watson	Dramatic Recital
21 Jan. 1914	Sir F. Carruthers Gould	'A Chapter in Animal Symbolism.' Fully Illustrated
18 Feb. 1914	Frederick W. Christian, BA	'Robert Louis Stevenson in Samoa and his Native Friends in the South Seas.' Fully Illustrated
25 Mar. 1914	Dr H. Walford Davies, LLD, ARCM, FRCO	'On Melody.' Illustrations by the Templars Quartette

Source: *AFC* 16/9 (1913), 4.

continued until the mid-1920s, when 'there was a serious falling off of patrons' from both the congregation and the public at large. This was attributed to the keenness of the 'competition … [from] the

their way to the Front': Roger Ottewill, 'The Avenue Quarter: Exemplars of Edwardian Congregationalism', *JURCHS* 9 (2014), 227–47, at 235–6.

entertainment and scholastic world', with free lectures at the University College and Celebrity Concerts at the Central Hall, but also the advent of the wireless, being specifically mentioned.[55] Indeed, the organizers may have had in mind the emergence of radio listening groups as a contribution to adult education.[56] Concern was also expressed over the cost of the lectures. In 1929, it was decided not to organize them for the following season, with what proved to be the forlorn hope that they would be revived the following year with 'great enthusiasm'.[57]

Conclusion

In many respects, locally based adult education provision of the kind offered by Congregational churches and those of other denominations reflected the *Zeitgeist* of Victorian and Edwardian Britain. Encapsulating notions of intellectual curiosity and self- improvement, participation by the churches reflected a desire not to be left out, and a reluctance to cede to the secular world a monopoly in this sphere. If Christianity was to apply to the whole of life then it was essential to respond to an increasing demand for cerebral pursuits arising from improvements in education more generally. As Jones has observed, 'the progressive and successful Congregational church of the early twentieth century was a community in which the creation of a bright and happy fellowship had first priority'.[58] For many churches, it was also one in which the pursuit of intellectual fulfilment was a critical ingredient of the mutually supportive fellowship to which they aspired.

Nevertheless, although both understandable and laudable, neither the concept of the institutional church in general nor adult education provision in particular were unproblematic. For churches there were

[55] The British Broadcasting Company was founded in 1922, with the number of radio licences increasing from 200,000 in 1923 to 2.6 million in January 1929: 'The History of the UK Radio Licence', online at: <http://www.radiolicence.org.uk/licence1920s.html>, accessed 6 April 2018.

[56] For a discussion of the role of listening groups as 'a significant part of the adult education programming' in the early decades of radio, see David Goodman, 'A Transnational History of Radio Listening Groups, I: The United Kingdom and United States', *Historical Journal of Film, Radio and Television* 36 (2016), 436–65, at 439.

[57] *AFC* 32/9 (1929), 2.

[58] Jones, *Congregationalism*, 318.

risks attached to being stallholders in the market place of secular pursuits, and in many instances they were, in competitive terms, ultimately the losers. Moreover, as some argued at the time, such activities undermined the principle of being *in*, but not *of*, the world.

That said, in the sphere of adult education churches can take credit for, and perhaps some comfort from, helping to lay foundations on which other generalist and specialist bodies have subsequently built. Today, these include the University of the Third Age, book groups, local history societies and a myriad of voluntary organizations catering for particular interests, with church members often contributing time, energy and expertise. In addition, many churches maintain a commitment to adult education through the running of courses, albeit with a strong religious orientation, of which Alpha and Christianity Explored are the best known. Here there are echoes of the adult school movement which, as Mark Freeman observes, managed with some success during the inter-war years to merge evangelism with education.[59] Furthermore, although the doctrine of the institutional church waned after the First World War, 'the idea that the successful church … [was a] busy church' continued to hold sway.[60] The fact that mutual improvement societies and lecture programmes disappeared from a busy church's programme of activities by no means diminishes their valued and valuable contribution to adult education during the Victorian and Edwardian eras.

[59] Mark Freeman, 'The Decline of the Adult School Movement between the Wars', *HE* 39 (2010), 481–506.
[60] Jones, *Congregationalism*, 297.

'The catechism will save society, without the catechism there is no salvation': Secularization and Catholic Educational Practice in an Italian Diocese, 1905–14

Fabio Pruneri*
University of Sassari

Compulsory public education in Italy came into being almost simultaneously with the process of national unification. From the outset, the liberal ruling class was faced with the old-established educational tradition of the church, and historians of education have explored the process of the secularization of education. This article sheds light on how decisions of the hierarchy and the pope, especially during the early twentieth century, were translated into practical pastoral action, noteworthy in some cases for a surprising modernity in the means used. The article focuses on the dioceses of northern Italy and in particular that of Bergamo, a populous agricultural centre then undergoing rapid industrialization. Using diocesan archive materials and the press of the period, it focuses on new forms of pastoral work, particularly those directed at teaching the catechism by means of societies for children and young people, catechism competitions and slide shows. The results obtained using this approach challenge the perception of Catholicism as intransigent on this issue.

This article will explore the effects of anti-Catholic ideology in the diocese of Bergamo during the early twentieth century, considering the reactions of Christian communities to the process of secularization of education. There is a large body of research related to the history of the Italian Catholic Church in the late nineteenth and early twentieth centuries, including studies by Arturo Carlo Jemolo and Silvio Tramontin, the six-volume encyclopaedia on the *History of the Catholic Movement* edited by Francesco Malgeri, and more

* Piazza Conte di Moriana, 8, 07100 Sassari, Italy. E-mail: pruneri@uniss.it. I would like to thank Geert Thyssen, Maria Patricia Williams and the anonymous readers for their helpful comments on this article. I am also grateful to Jane Price for proofreading and to Alessandro Persico and the staff of the Diocesan Archive of Bergamo for allowing access to archival material.

Studies in Church History 55 (2019), 511–529
doi: 10.1017/stc.2018.21

recently the studies of Alberto Melloni.[1] However, relatively little has been written about the relation between church and education, and even less adopting a methodology that uses local sources.[2] The first part of this article discusses in general terms the relation between state and church with regard to education; the second focuses on the action taken by the bishop of Bergamo, Giacomo Radini-Tedeschi (1905–14), to undermine the ubiquity of secular culture and to root Christians in the faith, starting from childhood.

During the period covered by this study, the long-standing conflict that saw the nascent Italian state opposed to the church was not resolved, but rather in some respects accentuated. The clash between the Catholic Church and Italian nationalism derived from the church's hostility towards the Kingdom of Italy and its refusal to recognize the kingdom's legitimacy, which was perceived by Pius IX initially as a threat to temporal power of the papacy and later (after the end of the Papal State in September 1870) as a danger also to its spiritual power. The tension between Catholicism and liberal-national principles, which would not be resolved until 1929, was accentuated by the spread of socialist ideas, especially among the working classes. Marxist ideologies were considered particularly dangerous by the Catholic Church because they gained a consensus not just among the urban proletariat but also amongst peasants, who had traditionally shown themselves receptive to Catholic doctrine. In addition, the attempt to reject and control the errors of so-called 'modernism' was a constant concern during the pontificate of Pius X (1903–14). Fear of being perceived as hostile to the traditional faith – for example, by fostering a rationalist approach to the Scriptures or encouraging a clear separation of church and state – restrained the actions of many lay people and priests. However, at the same time, anxiety to determine the authentic meaning of sacred Scripture and the dogmas

[1] Arturo Carlo Jemolo, *Chiesa e stato in Italia negli ultimi cento anni* (Turin, 1948); Silvio Tramontin, *Profilo di storia della Chiesa italiana dall'Unità ad oggi* (Turin, 1980); Francesco Malgeri, ed., *Storia del movimento cattolico in Italia*, 6 vols (Rome, 1981); Istituto della Enciclopedia Italiana and Alberto Melloni, eds, *I Cristiani d'Italia* (Rome, 2012). For Italy as a case study, see Frank Coppa, 'Italy: The Church and the Risorgimento', in Sheridan Gilley and Brian Stanley, eds, *CHC*, 8: *World Christianities* c.*1815*–c.*1914* (Cambridge, 2005), 233–49.

[2] Giovanni Vian and Luciano Caimi, eds, *La religione istruita nella scuola e nella cultura dell'Italia contemporanea* (Brescia, 2013).

of the Christian faith led the ecclesial authorities, from the cardinals and bishops to local parish priests, into vigorous educational effort that reached the seminaries, the Catholic associations and the faithful in general.[3]

This article examines these phenomena from the bottom up, starting from local sources such as diocesan archives, bishops' bulletins, correspondence with priests and associational activity in parishes. It seeks to move away from the stereotype of a church of the faithful separate from the church of the hierarchy, instead contributing to a new genre of studies which illustrate the contribution of Christianity to the growth of Italy as a nation. The results of this research make it possible to counter a historiographical tendency to position the conflict between church and state within an over-simplified political and ideological perspective, a point of view that tends to consider the reaction of the papacy against the Kingdom of Italy's political power, consigning questions of pastoral action to the background. Instead, it is suggested that both the hierarchy and the parish priests found themselves in a field of experimentation and innovation in a world anchored to a traditional faith.

Secularization of Schools after Italian Unification

The Casati Act of 13 November 1859 laid out the public education system of the nascent Kingdom of Italy in three hundred and eighty articles.[4] It marked an important (and transient) moment that constituted a point of equilibrium between two developments. The first was the introduction of direct state control over the entire chain of studies from the university to elementary school. Article 3 of the Casati Act stated: 'The Ministry of Public Education governs public education in all branches and promotes their development: it oversees private instruction to protect morality, hygiene, state institutions and public

[3] Annibale Zambarbieri, 'Rinnovamento spirituale e cultura nell'Italia del primo Novecento', *Annali di Storia dell'Educazione e delle Istituzioni Scolastiche* 16 (2009), 15–39.

[4] Gabrio Casati (1798–1873) was an Italian politician, a supporter of Camillo Benso, count of Cavour and his moderate party. He was appointed as minister of education in the government of La Marmora, which lasted from 19 July 1859 to 21 January 1860. His name is linked to the law establishing the public school system in unified Italy: see Luigi Ambrosoli, 'Casati, Gabrio', *DBI* 21: 244–9. For the full text of the Casati Act, see *Legge e decreti sulla Pubblica Istruzione* (Palermo, 1860), 3–110.

order.'[5] This act brought universities almost entirely under government control, and all educational initiatives by private individuals were carefully scrutinized by the new state apparatus. High schools (*liceo*)[6] and grammar schools (*ginnasio*)[7] were carefully placed by the state to ensure an appropriate geographical spread, while elementary schools across the kingdom were entrusted to the care of municipal administrations but made subject to a national inspection system.[8]

The second development stressed the need to preserve the liberal character of the nascent Kingdom of Italy. Accordingly, the state was to avoid monopolistic excesses in education; thus, for example, the act safeguarded the freedom of families to choose the kind of compulsory education to be undertaken by their children in the early years.[9] The opportunity to open an institution of secondary education was granted to 'every citizen who had reached the age of 25 and met the necessary moral requirements'.[10] Freedom of teaching was granted to all university professors except those who through their writings, their teaching, or both had contradicted 'the truths on which religious and moral order rests'.[11] The rights of religious minorities were also recognized,[12] although the constitution of the Kingdom of Piedmont-Sardinia (1848), later effectively the Italian Constitution, did not explicitly permit religious freedom but rather identified Catholicism as the only state religion.[13]

Within this general framework, it is not surprising that religion was a compulsory subject in elementary schools, designated the first branch of learning both in the lower and higher grade of compulsory

[5] 'Il ministro della pubblica istruzione governa l'insegnamento pubblico in tutti i rami e ne promuove l'incremento: sopravveglia il privato a tutela della morale, dell'igiene, delle istituzioni dello Stato e dell'ordine pubblico': Regio Decreto no. 3725, 13 November 1859, 'Legge sul Riordinamento dell'Istruzione pubblica', in *Legge e decreti*, 9; Luciano Pazzaglia, 'Educazione e scuola nel programma dell'Opera dei Congressi (1874–1904)', in idem, ed., *Scuola e società nell'Italia unita. Dalla Legge Casati al centro-sinistra* (Brescia, 2001), 87–126.

[6] Casati Act, §§189, 194, 197.

[7] Ibid., §§199, 201.

[8] Ibid., §§312, 325 (elementary schools), 332 (examination of primary school teachers).

[9] Fathers were obliged to provide elementary education for their children, either by sending them to municipal schools or by organizing lessons privately: ibid., §326.

[10] Ibid., §246.

[11] Ibid., §106.

[12] Ibid., §222.

[13] The constitution of Piedmont (the Statuto Albertino) was extended to all states joining the Kingdom of Italy, and lasted until the birth of the republic.

elementary education (comprising four school years), where it was taught by the 'ordinary teachers'. In secondary schools, the subject had to be delivered 'by a spiritual director [*direttore spirituale*], appointed by the Minister of Public Education'.[14] However, practising Catholics, who at the time represented the majority of Italians, regretted that priests were not responsible for the teaching of religion in elementary schools, and that the 'spiritual director' who presided over religious education in high schools was appointed by the ministry and not by the local diocese.[15]

Without doubt, the separation of public education from religious authority was greater after Italian reunification; in Lombardy, for example, priests had previously been accustomed to being appointed to school leadership roles. The position of school director now became a civil rather than an ecclesiastical one.[16] Nonetheless, the process of secularization was less pronounced in Italy than in France. In Italy, members of governments and, more generally, the political elites who had led the laborious process of unification, who were often representatives of the secular bourgeoisie and the enlightened aristocracy, put in place a number of arrangements intended to secure a Catholic consensus and obtain wider support for the liberal cause.[17]

From the Catholic point of view, the situation deteriorated after the passing of the Coppino Act on 15 July 1877, as a result of which religion was replaced by 'elementary notions of the duties of man and the citizen' in the compulsory school curriculum.[18] The act's main purpose was to combat illiteracy, but it was named for Michele Coppino, a left-wing parliamentarian and minister of education, known for his membership of the Freemasons. Signs of the decline of Catholic influence had been apparent since 20 September 1870, when Rome was conquered, as the long process

[14] Casati Act, §193.

[15] For these divergences, see Fabio Pruneri, 'L'insegnamento religioso nella scuola elementare', in Giovanni Vian and Luciano Caimi, eds, *La religione istruita nella scuola e nella cultura dell'Italia contemporanea* (Brescia, 2013), 27–41, at 32–5.

[16] Coppa, 'Italy', 240.

[17] Luciano Pazzaglia, ed., *Cattolici, educazione e trasformazioni socio-culturali in Italia tra Otto e Novecento* (Brescia, 1999).

[18] For the text of the act, see Regio Decreto no. 3961, 15 July 1877, Michele Coppino, 'Legge sull'obbligo dell'istruzione elementare', §2, *Gazzetta Ufficiale del Regno d'Italia*, no. 177 (30 July 1877), 3057–8.

of Italian unification and the final defeat of the Papal States under Pius IX were largely realized. These events had far-reaching effects on education. For example, the circular issued by Cesare Correnti, minister of education, in 1870 made the teaching of religion in schools optional rather than compulsory; in 1873 theology faculties were abolished in state universities; and spiritual directors were removed from secondary schools in June 1877.[19]

Bishop Radini-Tedeschi of Bergamo and Education

Building on this general background, we turn now to our case study, to analyse on a small scale the effects of the government's education policies and the church's reactions. Bergamo in northern Italy offers a useful case study of the effects of nineteenth-century secularism during the early twentieth century. It was a densely populated agricultural centre in the process of rapid industrialization, and had a strong Catholic tradition. The Opera dei Congressi, a body of clergy and priests which sought to defend the position of the Catholic Church against government policy, was very active in promoting economic and social activity through agricultural loan provision, mutual aid societies and cooperatives. The diocese of Bergamo was led by a bishop who would leave a rich legacy of pastoral activity: Giacomo Maria Radini-Tedeschi had been appointed by Pius X in 1905.[20] His biography provides insights into the special connection he had with the field of education.

Two experiences prior to his nomination as a bishop seem to have been particularly formative for his understanding of the difficulties encountered by practising Catholics in a society in process of secularization. Born in Piacenza in 1857, two years before the Casati Act was passed, Radini-Tedeschi attended *ginnasio* and *liceo* in Bergamo from 1870 to 1874, experiencing some of the problems faced by colleges and boarding schools with a religious affiliation. He attended the College of St Alexander, which in March 1872 was placed

[19] See Regio Decreto no. 3918, 23 June 1877, Michele Coppino, 'Legge che modifica l'ordinamento dei licei, dei ginnasi e delle scuole tecniche, ed accresce di un secondo decimo lo stipendio dei presidi, direttori ed insegnanti', *Gazzetta Ufficiale del Regno d'Italia*, no. 160 (10 July 1877), 2761–2.

[20] Francesco Vistalli, *Monsignor conte Giacomo Maria Radini Tedeschi vescovo di Bergamo* (Milan, 1935); Angelo Roncalli, *Mons. Giacomo Maria Radini-Tedeschi vescovo di Bergamo* (Rome, 1963; first publ. 1916).

under observation and then suppressed by the authorities of the Kingdom of Italy because it was accused of 'instilling into the soul of the pupils' the 'clerical spirit'. The replacement of the rector, Alessandro Valsecchi, who had been accused of 'anti-national sentiment', made possible its reopening, but the threat of closure caused students to transfer to other institutions in 1872 and 1873.

Secondly, in 1889, at the Catholic congress of Lodi, Radini-Tedeschi, together with a lawyer from Brescia, Giuseppe Tovini, contributed to the drafting of the programme of the Pia Opera for preserving faith in Italian schools, as part of the third section of the Opera dei Congressi, dedicated to education. The Pia Opera was an attempt to curb the power of those opposed to Catholic initiatives and to build networks among lay people engaged in the development of educational institutions not hostile to the clergy.

From 1890 Radini-Tedeschi lived in Rome, where he began his diplomatic career at the Vatican Secretariat of State under Cardinal Mariano Rampolla. He carried out some missions abroad but continued his relationships with the Opera dei Congressi and the Catholic associations; for example, he was involved in organizing pilgrimages to the Holy Land from 1896 to 1905.[21]

By the time of his appointment as bishop, two largely incompatible positions had emerged within the Opera dei Congressi. On one hand some, defined as 'intransigent' Catholics (*Cattolici interansigenti*), asserted the exclusive responsibility of the clergy to lead the Christian populace. These ultramontane Catholics, or *Integristes*, hoped to restore the past, in which the hierarchy was respected and feared; they sought to counter the separation of church and state. Catholic Action groups, on the other hand, believed in cooperation between clergy and laypeople, both in defence of the church and in political action, although at this stage they did not support any specific political party. They undertook initiatives such as the establishment of male and female associations, support of the Catholic press, workers' organizations, welfare initiatives for immigrants and, last but not least, the defence of education,[22] recognizing that education could offer an ideal terrain on which to cultivate

[21] Giuseppe Battelli, 'Radini Tedeschi, Giacomo Maria', *DBI* 86: 116–18.

[22] Gianluigi Della Valentina, 'Dal mutualismo al sindacalismo. Il movimento sociale cattolico a Bergamo', *Ioannes XXIII: Annali della fondazione Papa Giovanni XXIII* 5 (2017), 44–77.

de-Christianization and that it was being so used by the new ruling class which was ideologically in favour of a secular state.

Anti-clericalism reached even the conservative and disciplined diocese of Bergamo during the first decade of the twentieth century. The city was less exposed than some others to the process of secularization, because the mayor and the municipal and provincial councils embraced Catholicism. Since the early 1880s, the Opera dei Congressi had been active in this area. Of particular importance was the local Catholic press: the weekly *Il Campanone* and the newspaper *L'Eco di Bergamo*, both of which had a significant influence on the laity of the province. Catholics also worked to establish the bank of the Piccolo Credito Bergamasco (1891) and to organize the electorate in local and national elections, and it was in this province that the first 'Catholic deputy', Agostino Cameroni, was elected to the Italian parliament in 1904. Cameroni could not be part of a Catholic party since the *non expedit*, the Catholic hierarchy's policy of non-cooperation in elections, was still in force.[23] However, these restrictions could be avoided in specific cases, such as when it was necessary to defeat a candidate viewed as an 'expression of Masonic and socialist arrogance', such as Adolfo Engel, Cameroni's adversary. Cameroni's election offered hope to those who were attempting to increase Catholic influence on society.

The working classes in northern Italy were affected by illiteracy and widespread poverty, two factors which were also at the root of an alarming migratory phenomenon. At the same time, vocations to the priesthood were flourishing, as attested by the large number of seminarians, four hundred at the bishop's arrival. The ratio of

[23] This expression was used within the church to denote abstention from the polls, whether as a voter or a candidate. The papacy effectively refused to recognize the legitimacy of the Liberal state by forbidding participation in one of its higher political expressions, the vote. Pius IX's *Non expedit* was converted into a prohibition that lasted until the beginning of the twentieth century, when Catholics were tacitly allowed to support candidates who might stem the advance of the Italian Socialist Party. Only with the 'Gentiloni pact' of 1913 did the ban cease, at least partially, leading to the election of Giolitti's Liberal candidates (Catholic deputies), who promised to support Catholic policies: Frank J. Coppa, *Politics and the Papacy in the Modern World* (Westport, CT, 2008); Gabriele De Rosa, *Storia del movimento cattolico in Italia* (Bari, 1966); Guido Formigoni, *I cattolici-deputati (1904–1918). Tradizioni e riforme* (Rome, 1988); John Pollard, *Catholicism in Modern Italy: Religion, Society and Politics since 1861* (Abingdon, 2008); Andrea Tornielli, *Pio IX* (Milan, 2011).

clergy to inhabitants placed the diocese of Bergamo in first place amongst the dioceses of Lombardy.

Radini-Tedeschi's pastoral approach gave primacy to the energy of the Catholic associations, as a reaction to growing anti-clericalism. The bishops and parish priests believed that scepticism undermined the very roots of human experience. The abandonment of the faith was particularly serious and visible in the educational field. A pastoral letter issued by the nine bishops of the highly populated dioceses of Lombardy in 1910 highlighted the risks of abandoning young people, 'tyrannized by their own unbridled passions and surrounded in every part, in every way, by every kind of incentive to evil, [to] run carefree on the path of error and vice'. The bishops were concerned about '[i]nfamous novels, schoolbooks stained with errors and mockery of religion, atheistic and materialistic teachers, obscene photographs, sensuous scenes in cinemas and theatres, [and the] absolute lack of religious instruction in many schools and in many families'.[24] Likewise, they identified a worrisome spread of sports, designed not as a tool to provide strength but to foster 'the inhuman courage of the Gladiator'.[25] Last but not least, they expressed their anxiety about the abandonment of churches, catechesis and the sacraments by many children in the years immediately following their first communion.[26]

The Lombard bishops believed that it was pointless to complain about the moral crisis while appealing to the remedies suggested by secular forces. The fining of parents who failed to allow their children to attend school, the establishment of leisure centres, and calls for decorum, patriotic sentiment and honour all mattered very little if the moral perversion of teenagers was not counteracted by religion. 'The catechism will save society, without the catechism there is no salvation', the bishops asserted. The duty of all parents was therefore to provide education regarding the truths of religion, but also to demand that this teaching be given in elementary schools. This renewal of catechesis, seen as a bastion against socialist propaganda, was to bring with it the reward of a restoration of Christian life.[27]

[24] 'Lettera Pastorale dell'Episcopato Lombardo. I mali moderni e il loro rimedio', *La vita diocesana* 2 (1910), 220–5, at 221.

[25] Ibid.; Giacomo Maria Radini-Tedeschi, 'A proposito di società ginnastiche e sportive. una lettera di Mgr. Vescovo', ibid. 3 (1911), 258–9, at 258.

[26] 'I mali moderni', 221.

[27] Ibid. 223.

At the same time, a process of disciplining the clergy was under way, with a constant insistence upon respect for the authority of the pontiff and bishops in line with the anti-modernist sentiments of Pius X's encyclicals *Pascendi Dominici Gregis* (8 September 1907) and *Motu proprio Sacrorum Antistitum* (1 September 1910).[28] The implications of this ecclesiastical policy were far-reaching: for example, in seminaries, 'the reading of any newspaper or periodical' was prohibited, a harsh restriction that also applied 'outside the seminary, during the vacations'.[29] Careful control was exercised over teaching programmes aimed at aspiring priests. The return to the foundations of Catholic tradition was also reaffirmed through the requirement that priests, parish priests, confessors and preachers take an anti-modernist oath.

In his pastoral letter of 1910, Radini-Tedeschi upheld vigilance as one of the virtues of a bishop. This would be given expression during his second pastoral visitation of the diocese, during which he visited villages and observed the activities of the local clergy, seeking to verify how the pontiff's prescription was being applied. The bishop was committed to providing for the spiritual needs of the people; he also carried out confirmations.[30] He consistently encouraged the faithful to respect orthodoxy, for example, in his recommendation that lay people might observe a season of penance and recollection in Lent by not attending shows and theatre spectacles, which were, he warned, accompanied by promiscuity amongst the audience and the actors.[31] On the political side, in line with the encyclical *Rerum Novarum* issued by Leo XIII in 1891, Radini-Tedeschi affirmed his right to make pronouncements on social issues against the excesses of capitalism. In autumn 1909, he expressed support for the workers of the Zopfi cotton mill in Ranica, a village near Bergamo, justifying the six-week strike which had been

[28] Pius X, *Sacrorum antistitum* (1910), online at: <https://w2.vatican.va/content/pius-x/la/motu_proprio/documents/hf_p-x_motu-proprio_19100901_sacrorum-antistitum.html>, accessed 19 October 2018; Ermenegildo Camozzi, ed., *'Il caso Mattiussi La Chiesa di Bergamo tra modernismo e conservazione agli albori del ventesimo secolo (Archivio Segreto Vaticano, 1911)* (Bergamo, 2015).

[29] 'Cautele sapienti contro il Modernismo', *La vita diocesana* 2 (1910), 274–81, at 280–1; 'Catechismo con proiezioni', ibid. 3 (1911), 78; 'Ancora il Catechismo con proiezioni. L'esempio di Brescia', ibid. 123–6.

[30] Giacomo Maria Radini-Tedeschi, 'Lettera Pastorale di S. E. M. Vescovo', ibid. 2 (1910), 317–28, at 321.

[31] Idem, 'Atti Vescovili. Teatrini e Spettacoli in quaresima', ibid. 60.

called by the Catholic-inspired trade union in the quest for a decent wage and the right of workers to organize themselves.[32]

Speaking in Nembro in 1910 at the twenty-third Federal Feast of the Catholic Associations, Radini-Tedeschi directed the attention of the Catholics of Bergamo to the serious problems in the educational realm. In particular, he stressed the danger of schooling without the catechism and without God and urged families to support a series of projects that the diocese was initiating to 'save the rights of the Christian school'.[33] He reminded the clergy, and above all their lay followers, of the need for humility: 'Too many want to be captains, too few want to become soldiers.'[34] This entailed sincere obedience by individual members of every Catholic association to their leaders, for submission to one's superiors was the indispensable condition for fighting the enemy effectively.

In his pastoral letter 'Mali e Rimedi' ('Diseases and cures'), presented on the first Sunday of Advent in 1910, Radini-Tedeschi also noted deficiencies in education. He claimed: 'Education has lost its guiding light, its crucifix, its discipline, its catechism, its high ideals, its missionary purpose; and schooling has become [an opportunity] to attack young souls, to assault the truth, [to work] against science, against true civilization, against man, society, Church and God.'[35] This pessimistic tone pervaded the entire document: for Radini-Tedeschi, 'apostasy', in the sense of the complete negation of the transcendent, seemed the best definition of this terrible time.[36]

Many concerns troubled the diocesan clergy and increased the bishop's anxiety: the spread of modernism, even among the flock of believers, the spread of rationalism in the study of Scripture, the emergence of new understandings of obedience and discipline amongst clergy and laity, the spread of a 'worldly' conception of life, and a feeling of hostility towards the hierarchy and the authority of the pope.[37]

[32] Della Valentina, 'Dal mutualismo al sindacalismo', 70–3. The strike involved many female workers.

[33] 'La festa federale di Nembro', *La vita diocesana* 2 (1910), 300–3, at 300.

[34] Ibid. 301.

[35] 'La scuola ha smarrita la sua luce, il suo, il suo crocifisso, la sua disciplina, i suoi alti ideali, la sua missione educativa, ed è venuta ad essere un attentato alle anime giovani, un attentato contro la verità, contro la scienza, conto la civiltà verace, contro l'uomo, la società, la Chiesa, Iddio': Giacomo Maria Radini-Tedeschi, 'Lettera Pastorale di S.E.M. Vescovo al Clero ed al Popolo. Mali e Rimedi', ibid. 353–75, at 355–6.

[36] Ibid. 356.

[37] Ibid. 357–8.

For Radini-Tedeschi, the causes of the diocese's afflictions were to be found in three separate but related factors: the increase of humanitarian and apolitical associations supported by Freemasonry, the dissemination of the anti-clerical press and the secularization of education.[38] With the removal of the crucifix, the catechism, the gospel and compulsory religious instruction, the school, he claimed, was no longer a temple of knowledge, but 'a den of iniquity' (*una tana*).[39] The remedies he proposed were, inevitably, the exact opposites of the evils. Catholic associations must oppose atheist societies; for this reason, the bishop encouraged the presence of Catholic Action in every parish. Many parishioners expressed scepticism: they did not understand the reasons for this novelty, but Radini-Tedeschi countered their hesitancy: 'These associations were not present in the villages in the past, as once there was no railway, telegraph, the use of electricity', but the church must keep up with the new challenges presented by modernity. Priests who were slow to establish groups in defence of religion posed problems as serious as those posed by sceptical priests. Radini-Tedeschi warned that while the priests 'slept', trusting in the orthodoxy of their flock, liberal or socialist societies, supported by the anti-clerical press, fuelled the fires of rebellion. The slowness of many dioceses to grasp the situation had allowed the growth of anti-clericalism to the point that the 'serpent' of atheism was already biting the heel of 'dormant Christians'. Lastly, he replied to the objection of some parishioners that 'we are parishes for all' and who did not favour creating associations that they feared would divide the people into parties and foster discontent. 'Better divided than completely disorientated', was Radini-Tedeschi's response.[40]

[38] Ibid. 362.

[39] In the context of the battle against impurity, we must note the warnings sounded regarding female conduct. The first national congress of Italian women was held from 23–30 April 1908. *La Civiltà Cattolica*, in a long article on this meeting, appreciated that 'women [had] also act[ed] collectively ... to [have] their rights recognized and respected', but warned against feminism inspired by 'anti-clerical foolishness inspired by laicism' and the 'indecent ravings of the new sexual morality': 'Il primo congresso delle donne italiane', *La Civiltà Cattolica* 2 (1908), 513–32, at 517. In contrast to these symbols of 'decadence and death', it was necessary to return to 'the old morality, based on catechism and defence of modesty': ibid. 532. Warnings about women's modesty, reserve and self-possession would become common during the first half of the twentieth century in clerical sermons and episcopal pastoral letters.

[40] 'Mali e Rimedi', 365.

Education and catechesis were key to the defence of lay people's interests, which, in line with the instructions given by Pius X in the encyclical *Acerbo Nimis* (*On teaching Christian Doctrine*) of 15 April 1905, had to begin during the early years of children's lives; as much as possible must be done to prevent children and young people from joining groups not authorized by the church. The bishop suggested setting up a *società tra i fanciulli* (society for work with young boys), to support boys who had recently made their first communion.[41]

Catechism and Catechism Competitions

The attention to catechesis was related to several factors: the National Catechetical Congress held in Piacenza in 1889, with further catechetical congresses taking place in Milan in 1910 and Brescia in 1912, the requirement of *Acerbo Nimis* for religious education through catechesis, and the lowering of the age for first communion to seven in the papal decree *Quam Singulari* (8 August 1910). One consequence of the catechetical congresses was the birth of schools of religion aimed at the laity, and particularly young people. These schools spread throughout the Italian peninsula, offering religious education to young Catholics attending high schools and universities. They were intended to provide an answer both to the abolition of theological faculties in state universities and to the removal of religious education from the secondary school curriculum. This was a difficult task. *Acerbo Nimis* instructed that the catechism had to be imparted to one and all 'in a plain and simple style adapted to the intelligence of the hearers'.[42] Each parish was meant to have a special confraternity intended to improve the knowledge of the catechism; this would only be possible with the help of Catholic Action combined with the efforts of lay people under clerical guidance.

The educational dimension, including the strategies used to attract the interest of children and young people and the organizational and pastoral aspects of widespread catechesis aimed at consolidating the faith of children at an early age, deserves attention. As noted above,

[41] Giacomo Maria Radini-Tedeschi, 'Catechismo e scuola', *La vita diocesana* 2 (1910), 401–9, at 401.

[42] Pius X, 'On Teaching Christian Doctrine', online at: <http://www.papalencyclicals.net/Pius10/p10chdoc.htm>, accessed 19 October 2018.

Pius X had lowered the age of first communion 'in order … to help children even at a tender age to be united to Jesus Christ, live his life, and obtain protection from all danger of corruption'.[43] Some scholars consider that the pope's intention was also to impress the solemnity of the rite on the sensitive and innocent minds of children, so that it would have a lasting effect, even into adolescence. In addition, he wanted to encourage the religious supervision of children by their parents.[44]

In response, Radini-Tedeschi launched a series of initiatives, congresses and publications relating to catechesis. He maintained contact with the parish priests of his diocese through correspondence and by means of a monthly bulletin, *La Vita Diocesana*. The bishop invited the clergy to set up committees of fathers for the study of the catechism, arguing that 'the apt study of catechism, properly taught' was 'one of the most important marks of the Christian life'.[45] In the seminary, the formation of ordinands and young clerics was to be based on the Roman Catechism; they would then implement what they had learned in their parishes. Catechesis should be given not only to children but also to adults; special attention was to be given to young people and families who, for reasons of poverty, were migrating to other continents.[46] Guidelines and practical advice were offered to catechists in a list of seventy points divided into various topics. Under surveillance, he explained how to keep order in class, how to prevent chaos, how to enforce discipline, how to place students on school benches and how to maintain 'detachment' from students. The rules to be followed during the lesson included punctuality, gentleness and balance; threats, reprimands, rebukes and punishments, especially if they caused humiliation, should be avoided. There were some points about preparation and a discussion of how the adults were supposed to behave before and during the lesson. Priests were invited to prepare lessons well; to encourage timid children to take part in the discussions and not to reward arrogant pupils; they should 'never reproach the children for their ignorance';

[43] Pius X, 'Quam Singulari', online at: <http://www.papalencyclicals.net/pius10/p10quam.htm>, accessed 19 October 2018.

[44] Steven M. Avella and Jeffrey Zalar, 'Sanctity in the Era of Catholic Action: The Case of St Pius X', *US Catholic Historian* 15 (1997), 57–80, at 75.

[45] Giacomo Maria Radini-Tedeschi, 'Catechismo e gare catechistiche', *La vita diocesana* 3 (1911), 427–9, at 427.

[46] Idem, 'Il Vescovo al suo clero', ibid. 198–218, at 211–12.

in their teaching, they should offer examples taken from everyday life. Finally, the teacher should lead the pupils in prayer, and priests should also entrust their pupils to God through prayer.[47]

Although he tailored the message of the catechism to an audience of male and female pupils[48] – boys and girls were taught in the same context, but in separately timetabled classes – Radini-Tedeschi's priority was to reclaim children from religious ignorance. Curates and parish priests were to spend Thursday mornings on male catechism classes and Thursday afternoon on female classes.[49] Sundays should also be devoted to making religion accessible to children. The early age of children making their first communion became an opportunity to influence not only their 'tender souls' but also the souls of their parents on the 'happiest day of their life', as the day of the children's first communion was described.[50]

The bishop's efforts were successful, as indicated by the catechism competitions.[51] These had a history dating back to the sixteenth century, but had been suspended in 1700 due to violent altercations.[52] The renewed competitions began in 1909 within the Diocesan

[47] 'Consigli pratici al catechista. Tolti dalla "Guida Pratica all'insegnamento del Catechismo" compilato per cura di un Fratello delle Scuole Cristiane', ibid. 88–91, at 88.

[48] For example, since 1908 the bishop had planned a special course for the religious training of future primary female teachers. Through the Scuola Magistrale di Religione, girls attending boarding schools could follow courses leading to a licence allowing them to propagate the faith to schoolchildren: 'Scuola Magistrale di Religione e Seconda Gara Catechistica Femminile', ibid. 181–3, at 181.

[49] Thursday was not a school day during this period.

[50] This phrase, which became popular during the nineteenth and twentieth centuries, originated in Napoleon's answer to a question about what had been his happiest day. As Joyce depicted it, 'once a lot of generals had asked Napoleon what was the happiest day of his life. They thought he would say the day he won some great battle or the day he was made an emperor. But he said: Gentlemen, the happiest day of my life was the day on which I made my first holy communion': James Joyce, *A Portrait of the Artist as a Young Man* (London: 2005; first publ. 1916), 52.

[51] Giacomo Maria Radini-Tedeschi, 'Circolare ai MM. RR. Parroci della Città e Diocesi. Catechismo e Gare Catechistiche', *La vita diocesana* 3 (1911), 426–9.

[52] See 'Scuole, Gare e Feste Catechistiche d'una volta', ibid. 4 (1912), 126–31. Schools for Christian doctrine had been present in Bergamo since the mid-sixteenth century, introduced by Bishop Carlo Borromeo, in part to counter the spread of Protestantism. By 1611, there were 93 schools in the city of Bergamo and 400 throughout the diocese, providing catechesis for over 40,000 children. Competitions were selective, and the bishop and nobility attended a formal award ceremony. The winner was acclaimed with the title of king, and his court of parishioners was rewarded with refreshments. In 1700, rivalry between schools degenerated into violence and murder; the costs of the processions accompanying the awards had also become prohibitive, putting an end to the

Federation of the Church Male Youth Centres and the Diocesan Union of Daughters of Mary. Resuming the academic competitions represented a 'return to the old system of public disputations',[53] but under Radini-Tedeschi, these competitions lost their link with the young people's associations and were drawn into the work of the diocese. The available data, though incomplete, shows their success: 157 participants took part in the Bergamo competitions in 1909; in 1911 there were 282; a year later there were 330; and in 1913 the number of participants reached 1,762, with 451 participants in the competitions for boys and young men, and almost three times as many in those for girls and young women.[54] However, given that the province of Bergamo had a population of about 520,000 in 1911, the numbers of youngsters involved in the competitions represented a tiny minority. Moreover, although an increasing number of children participated, catechism contests were limited in that they were only accessible to the best students of each parish or diocese. These competitions must have enlivened the teaching of catechism, and they became public festivals. Similar initiatives were organized in other parts of Italy. In Bologna, Bishop Della Chiesa suggested a competition for the publication of a catechism book that would attract children's interest.[55] In Rome, priests gave the children bread, stationery or little pictures of saints to encourage attendance at catechism.[56]

Over time, the catechism competitions came to be carefully structured, according to regulations approved in December 1911.[57] Three levels were established: parish, 'vicariate' or deanery and diocesan. Selection took place in front of a jury chaired by the parish priest (for parish competitions), the dean (for vicariate competitions) or the bishop (for diocesan competitions). Each participant could

competitions. From then until the early twentieth century, they were limited to a celebration on 11 June.

53 Ibid. 131.

54 Giacomo Maria Radini-Tedeschi, 'III Gara Catechistica Maschile', ibid. 4 (1912), 131–3, at 131; 'Gare Catechistiche Diocesane', ibid. 6 (1913), 202–9, at 208–9.

55 John F. Pollard, *Il papa sconosciuto. Benedetto XV (1914–1922) e la ricerca della pace* (Cinisello Balsamo, 2001); Antonio Scottà, *Giacomo Della Chiesa, arcivescovo di Bologna, 1908–1914. L'"ottimo noviziato' episcopale di papa Benedetto XV* (Soveria Mannelli, 2002), 134–5.

56 Fortunato Iozzelli, *Roma religiosa all'inizio del Novecento* (Rome, 1985), 285.

57 Giacomo Maria Radini-Tedeschi, 'Comunicazioni d'urgenza a tutti i Parroci per l'insegnamento del catechismo', *La vita diocesana* 3 (1911), 426–9, at 426–7.

choose between the recitation competition, which required the 'literary recital of a part of the Catechism', which in practice meant answering the catechism questions correctly, or an 'intelligence competition' with a written examination.

The recitation competition was divided into sections for boys and girls between the ages of nine and twelve and young men and women aged twelve to twenty. Contestants were placed in a semicircle and interrogated; those who made mistakes were eliminated; and the prize was awarded only to those who answered ten questions correctly from memory and three more by insight. The intelligence competitions took place only at diocesan level and involved the writing of an essay on a section of the catechism, for those aged between twelve and fourteen, or an apologetic theme, for those aged between fourteen and twenty-five years. There were different tests for male and female students at elementary, middle and high schools, and for workers, shop assistants and artisans; for young women a distinction was made between aspiring teachers, students of technical and commercial schools and workers. The diocesan competitions were particularly solemn and ended with communion. Arising from the competitions, an account was sent to the Congregazioni Primarie Diocesane della Dottrina Cristiana (Primary Congregation of Diocesan Christian Doctrine), which monitored the spread of catechesis in the parishes of the diocese.

These events offered an opportunity for different social classes to meet, being attended by university students, teenage members of church groups, workers and young Catholics; the festival also brought together the inhabitants of city and countryside, with lay people coming from villages, towns and cities to receive their awards from the bishop's hands.[58] These awards, inscribed with the winners' name, were doubtless displayed at home.

Conclusion

The diocese of Bergamo experienced, and had to respond to, many aspects of the Italian state's secular vision. Radini-Tedeschi defended the Catholic community against these dangers by reproducing the clerical and hierarchical character of the church of Pius X. The bishop

[58] 'Regolamento per le gare catechistiche', ibid. 4 (1912), 271–5.

took full control of the activity of laity and diocesan clergy, but at same time, he knew how to dialogue with the people and how to focus on warning the faithful about the risks of immorality, vice or blasphemy rather than political struggle. This explains, for example, the commitment to both religious education at school and catechesis in the parish. As demonstrated in recent research,[59] Radini-Tedeschi's episcopate could be linked with the group known as Integralists, but it diverged from their approach in two respects: the organization of the laity for close collaboration in the church's apostolic work, especially in pastoral action, and his commitment as a socially concerned Christian, championing workers' rights in one of the first great strikes in 1909.

This article underlines the first aspect, the multi-faceted 'care of souls', and particularly the educational question, which certainly also had political implications. The bishop's initiatives indicate his desire to control the flock, but also his concern about their piety and his desire to foster catechesis, knowledge of doctrine and forms of popular devotion such as prayer, pilgrimage and processions.[60] Radini-Tedeschi promoted the formation of committed lay people, aware of, and able to respond to, the spiritual needs of their families. He no longer saw piety exclusively in terms of the liturgy and the activities of traditional confraternities. He endorsed pilgrimages to the Holy Land, in search of the foundations of the Christian faith.[61]

Although the conflict between church and state was strong, attention to the catechism allowed the introduction of interesting novelties. For example, in 1911, a priest of Brescia, Angelo Zammarchi (1871–1958), a co-founder of the Catholic publishing house Editrice La Scuola, presented the advantages of catechesis using new means such as lantern slides, missionary films and popular newspapers.[62] This opened the way to the use of mass media. Radini-Tedeschi would not see this, for he died on 22 August 1914, just weeks after the outbreak of the First World War.

[59] See *'Un uomo di genio, un vescovo apostolico'. Formazione e governo pastorale di G. M. Radini Tedeschi*, special issue of *Ioannes XXIII: Annali della fondazione Papa Giovanni XXIII* 5 (2017), 1–147.

[60] Ermenegildo Camozzi, ed., *Visite ad limina apostolorum 1854–1921* (Bergamo, 2004), 587–684.

[61] Angelo Roncalli, *Viaggio in Terra Santa, 1906. Il diario di un 'giornalista' diventato Papa* (Milan, 2016).

[62] 'Catechismo con proiezioni'.

The activity of parishes and the mobilization of Catholics against the loss of the social and cultural significance of religion could be interpreted in different ways. This article has shown that Radini-Tedeschi was careful to remain within the parameters of the theology of Pius X and that his pastoral education, aimed at the simplest people, sought to preserve an ideal of purity and refusal to compromise with the secularized world. However, it has also shown that the response of families and young people highlighted the inescapable need for the faithful to compromise with that world, and Catholic ability to pursue spiritual, cultural and political growth through diocesan initiatives. Catechetical education utilized popular religion for pedagogical purposes, employing popular rites and practices in the service of the anti-modernist principles that were currently fashionable. Training people in proper devotional practices became the means to achieve religious 'purity', that is, orthodox adherence to the teachings of Pius X. In this way, the effort went beyond simply defending the faith to constructing cohesive communities whose members shared the same values. In Radini-Tedeschi's thinking, the only way to survive the temptations of the secular world was to strengthen the bonds between the faithful and the Christian community; this accounts for his focus – and that of his clergy – on catechism and religious education, and on the sacrament of first communion. One of the results of this new focus on education was the use of practices such as the teaching of religion in school and the catechism competitions.

At the beginning of the twentieth century, secularization was an unquestionable fact in Italy, but Catholic education nonetheless continued to constitute one aspect of Italian collective identity. The Catholic Church had not lost its disciplinary power, but at the same time its hierarchies demonstrated their ability to dialogue with, negotiate with, or confront social actors and political decision-makers in responding to the problems of daily life, especially in local pastoral work. Radini-Tedeschi's initiatives in Bergamo left a legacy in the work of Fr Angelo Roncalli, who had been his secretary and was later his biographer. In 1958, Roncalli became Pope John XXIII. The question of Radini-Tedeschi's influence on John XXIII's pontificate remains to be explored.[63]

[63] Marco Roncalli, *Giovanni XXIII. Angelo Giuseppe Roncalli, una vita nella storia* (Turin, 2012): 104–44.

‘War to the knife’? The Anglican Clergy and Education at the End of the First World War

Mark Smith*
Oxford University

In 1918 Charles Gore, the bishop of Oxford, issued queries preparatory to an episcopal visitation, including a series of questions about the future of church schools and religious education more generally. Coming some sixteen years after the restructuring of the dual system of state- and church-supported education by the Balfour Education Act of 1902, this material yields valuable insights into the views of approximately six hundred clergy regarding the successes and dysfunctions of the system at parish level. Set within the context of recent historiography on the trajectory of English Christianity in the1920s, this article uses this material to discuss the clergy's views on the value and purposes of school-based religious education, the prospects for sustaining these after almost four years of war and the compromises that might be required in order to preserve them.

In March 1918, the bishop of Oxford, Charles Gore, issued a set of queries prior to his final visitation. For the most part, his questionnaire followed the standard format established since the mid-eighteenth century, seeking details about the condition of the six hundred parishes comprising his diocese which might subsequently be used to address issues of organization or pastoral concern. When it came to the subject of education, however, his approach was rather different, asking not for information but rather for the views of his clergy on how best to proceed. Another move to address the educational issues facing both church and state in the early twentieth century was in the offing. Gore had already engaged publicly with the question in a speech in the House of Lords, reprinted for the benefit of his local audience in the pages of the *Diocesan Magazine*, in the debate around the proposals for what eventually became the Fisher Education Act of 1918. Here he contended that educational reform should proceed without reference to religious controversy, principally because the bulk of public opinion was exasperated by it.

* 106 Victoria Rd, Oxford, OX2 7QE. E-mail: mark.smith@conted.ox.ac.uk.

Studies in Church History 55 (2019), 530–544
doi: 10.1017/stc.2018.22

Nevertheless, once the reform was enacted, 'the country must reconsider the question of religion and its position in education on a new basis'. In particular, he argued, 'I am quite sure it is impossible that we could go forward for ten years without something approaching total reconstruction of the position which religion must occupy in the training of teachers.'[1]

Informed by his experience of parliamentary debate, Gore's questionnaire addressed the issue of 'Single School Areas',[2] asking his clergy whether they thought the current status of church schools ought to be retained or whether there might be compromises to be made in the make-up of management committees, the appointment of head-teachers and the character of religious teaching. Then, moving to a more general issue about the place of religion in education, Gore enquired whether his clergy might think such compromises might be worth making in exchange for more satisfactory conditions of religious teaching in state-provided elementary schools. Framed as a series of short sentences at the head of a blank foolscap page, these queries invited discursive answers. Many of the clergy duly obliged. Taken together, the responses to the questionnaire provide an excellent basis on which to evaluate a considerable body of Anglican clerical opinion on the state of religious education in their parishes and its prospects for the future.[3]

Although rich in studies of individual schools, the more general historiography of the relationship between religion and elementary education in the first two decades of the twentieth century remains relatively slender. There is no full-length study of the topic, which therefore tends to receive a few pages of coverage in more general works on the history of religion – in which the topic of education is only of passing interest[4] – or in general social histories or histories

[1] *Oxford Diocesan Magazine* 12 (1918), 89.

[2] These were parishes in which there was no alternative elementary educational provision to that provided by the Church of England.

[3] The surviving returns to the survey are collected in three bound volumes held in the Oxfordshire History Centre (hereafter: OHC) within which each return has been assigned an individual serial number. The returns for the Oxford archdeaconry, essentially coterminous with the pre-1974 county, are at Oxford, OHC, MSS Oxf. Dioc. c.380.

[4] See, for example, Callum G. Brown, *Religion and Society in Twentieth-Century* The 1914 and 1918 visitation returns for the archdeaconry of Oxford will be published in the Oxfordshire Record Series in 2019. *Britain* (Harlow, 2006); Keith Robbins, *England, Ireland, Scotland, Wales: The Christian Church 1900–2000*, OHCC (Oxford, 2008), 65–9; Stewart J. Brown, *Providence and Empire 1815–1914* (Harlow, 2008), 412–23.

of education which, especially after 1914, have tended to discard religion as a major concern.[5] Even where the relationship between religion and education has been at the centre of historical attention, the early twentieth century has tended to receive relatively little coverage, especially in comparison with the struggles of the nineteenth century or the consequences of the Second World War and the Butler Education Act of 1944, recently described by Simon Green as 'an instrument of Christian stewardship'.[6] Only the politics and policies of education in this period have attracted sustained attention from historians: Ian Machin and others have provided a high-level view of the fortunes of parliamentary attempts to address educational problems in the nineteenth and early twentieth centuries.[7] However, a consequence of the focus on politics has tended to be a preoccupation with conflict as the primary lens through which education is viewed, especially in the period between the passage of the Balfour Education Act in 1902[8] and the First World War. In his work on the 'Nonconformist Conscience', for example, David Bebbington stressed the significance of Nonconformist resistance to rate-supported denominational education, the introduction of which provoked 'a classic crusade of unprecedented proportions', which

[5] Pamela Horn, *Education in Rural England 1800–1914* (New York, 1978); W. B. Stephens, *Education in Britain 1750–1914* (Basingstoke, 1998); Gillian Sutherland, 'Education', in F. M. L. Thompson, ed., *The Cambridge Social History of Britain 1750–1950*, 3: *Social Agencies and Institutions* (Cambridge,1990), 119–69; Martin Daunton, *Wealth and Welfare: An Economic and Social History of Britain 1851–1951* (Oxford, 2007), 488–510.

[6] S. J. D. Green, *The Passing of Protestant England* (Cambridge, 2011), 213. See also Priscilla Chadwick, *Shifting Alliances: Church and State in English Education* (London, 1997); John T. Smith, *Methodism and Education 1849–1902* (Oxford, 1998); Lois Louden, *Distinctive and Inclusive: The National Society and Church of England Schools 1811–2011* (London, 2012).

[7] G. I. T. Machin, *Politics and the Churches in Great Britain 1832 to 1868* (Oxford, 1977), 151–60; idem, *Politics and the Churches in Great Britain 1869–1921* (Oxford, 1987), 31–40, 260–73, 284–93. See also E. R. Norman, *Church and Society in England 1770–1970* (Oxford, 1976), 262–6; Tony Taylor, 'Lord Cranbourne, the Church Party and Anglican Education 1893–1902: From Politics to Pressure', *HE* 22 (1993), 125–46; Geoffrey Sherington, *English Education, Social Change and War 1911–20* (Manchester, 1981).

[8] The 1902 Education Act allowed Local Education Authorities to give financial support raised from the rates to voluntary denominational schools, including those of the Church of England and the Roman Catholics, without taking them under state control (although they would have the right to appoint two of the managers) or supervising the religious teaching given in the schools.

generated sustained resistance for over a decade.[9] Nonconformity, Bebbington notes, 'was stirred more deeply and more unanimously on a public issue than ever before or since'.[10] Searches for a compromise thereafter were frustrated by the incompatible views of, and the mutual distaste between, Nonconformist Protestants and Anglo-Catholic Anglicans, compounded by an increasingly assertive Roman Catholic interest given additional weight by the parliamentary influence of Irish nationalism.[11]

This article uses as its sample the 234 returns made by Oxfordshire parishes. The material is given additional interest by being drawn from the largest diocese of the Church of England, headed by a bishop who was centrally concerned with educational issues. Oxford diocese provided a mainly rural setting particularly rich in single-school areas (where those issues were potentially at their most acute), but also including a range of market towns and more substantial urban settlements such as Banbury and the city of Oxford itself.[12] Attending to the words of the Oxfordshire clergy themselves provides an opportunity to move away from the preoccupations of the current historiography and to take a fresh look at the issues surrounding education from the point of view of men on the ground in the parishes. It also opens a window onto the shift in balance of clerical opinion on the matter in the light of a decade-and-a-half's experience of the Balfour Act in operation and the impact of three-and-a-half years of war.

Three central themes emerge from a review of this material. First is considerable evidence of a growing détente between Anglicans and Nonconformists in the field of religious education. While perhaps surprising, given the historiographical prominence of the notion of conflict following the 1902 act, a substantial number of Oxfordshire incumbents reported an absence of tension and occasionally the increasing growth of friendly relationships. At Steeple Barton, for example, the incumbent remarked on 'events which

[9] D. W. Bebbington, *The Nonconformist Conscience: Chapel and Politics 1870–1914* (London, 1982), 142.

[10] Ibid. 143; see also D. R. Pugh, 'English Nonconformity, Education and Passive Resistance 1903–6', *HE* 19 (1990), 355–73.

[11] Bebbington, *Nonconformist Conscience*, 143–52; Machin, *Politics and the Churches 1869–1921*, 284–93.

[12] For another study of church schools in part of the diocese, see, in this volume, Grant Masom, 'Fighting the Tide: Church Schools in South Buckinghamshire, 1902–44', 545–60.

point to vast improvement to the better in the relations of the Church and Nonconformist [*sic*]'.[13] Clear evidence of mellowing on the part of the parish clergy can be found in their response to the thought of compromise in the area of school management. While some were determined to strive to keep day-to-day control of church schools entirely in church hands, a majority were happy to contemplate the inclusion of Nonconformists on their management committees and several had positive experience of mixed management committees already in operation, often in cases where managers appointed by the local education authority (LEA) were Nonconformists.[14] This applied even in small parishes where the Church of England might have expected to enjoy a monopoly: in the tiny seigneurial village of Asthall the incumbent reported that his management committee of six had for many years included two Nonconformists and that 'all the Managers have worked together in perfect harmony'.[15]

A similar attitude marked clerical responses to the possibility of modifying religious teaching in church schools. Many of the clergy felt that no changes need be made. In some parishes, this was the result of an entire absence of Nonconformity, as at Bucknell and Harpsden,[16] but more usually it was because, at least from the perspective of the clergy, the Nonconformists resident in their parishes appeared to be content with the existing arrangements. Thus the vicar of St Clement's in Oxford commented:

> No demand has ever been made in my hearing for any alteration … as to the character of the religious teaching. So far as the last mentioned point is concerned we have a number of children of Nonconformist parents in the schools who regularly attend Wesleyan Sunday Schools but no request has ever been made to withdraw any children from religious instruction.[17]

Occasionally, clergy also testified to their willingness to promote the effective operation of the conscience clause when Nonconformist parishioners had expressed concerns. At Asthall, for example,

[13] OHC, MSS Oxf. Dioc. c.380, 18.
[14] LEAs replaced the earlier school boards as the state providers of elementary education following the Education Act of 1902. They were essentially committees appointed by county and county borough councils and some larger urban districts.
[15] OHC, MSS Oxf. Dioc. c.380, 7.
[16] Ibid. 37, 93.
[17] Ibid. 151.

> In this Parish there has never been any desire on the part of Nonconformist parents to withdraw their children from Religious Instruction as given in the School: the only objection ever made was by Baptist parents who objected to their children being made to say the answers to the first portion of the Church Catechism, which was only natural and their wishes were at once complied with.[18]

An overwhelming majority of those who did recommend change supported the admission of Nonconformist ministers or other qualified teachers into church schools to teach groups of Nonconformist children at the request of their parents, as at South Banbury and St Frideswide in Oxford.[19] A few of the clergy, though, suspected that their Nonconformist colleagues were unlikely to rise to the challenge. As the vicar of Swalcliffe reported, 'I would be prepared to allow nonconformists to give their particular teaching to their children in Church Schools. But I doubt very much whether they would avail themselves of the privilege'.[20]

In only a handful of parishes does conflict seem to have remained high on the clerical agenda: notably at Piddington, where, perhaps giving evidence of the persistence of Anglican hauteur, the incumbent complained of 'a nonconformist element of an ignorant and therefore narrow and bigoted type'.[21] However, even in the view of the Anglican clergy themselves, the most significant threat to the progress of détente in the Oxford diocese came less from the Nonconformist side than from the increasingly assertive Anglo-Catholicism evident in some of its parishes. Several of the clergy pointed to the risks: the incumbent of Holton, for example, suggested that in some parishes free churchmen 'resent the religious teaching which in many cases approximates to Roman teaching'. The curate of Ducklington

[18] Ibid. 7.

[19] Ibid. 16, 154.

[20] Ibid. 202; cf. ibid. 42, 104a.

[21] Ibid. 166. He was probably referring to the Independents / Congregationalists, who were present in some strength in the Oxfordshire parishes along the Buckinghamshire border and had established a chapel in Piddington by 1848: Kate Tiller, ed., *Church and Chapel in Oxfordshire 1851: The Return of the Census of Religious Worship*, Oxfordshire Record Society 55 (Oxford, 1987), 82; Mary D. Lobel, ed., *A History of the County of Oxford*, 5: *Bullingdon Hundred*, VCH (London, 1957), 258. A comparably dismissive attitude, in this case to Baptists, was exhibited by the vicar of Littlemore: OHC, MSS Oxf. Dioc. c.380, 123.

expressed the view that '[i]t is the very extreme views of some which have alarmed even moderate nonconformists.'[22]

A prominent example of this tendency was Nicholas Poyntz, vicar of Dorchester on Thames, whose response to the bishop's options for compromise was characteristically uncompromising: 'If the Church believes in Herself she cannot recognise other forms of religion, or make any compromise with them. In Baptism She becomes the Spiritual Mother of the Baptized and cannot rightly hand them over to another form of religion.'[23] Poyntz was an unusually vigorous and pugnacious Anglo-Catholic whose interventions in his local schools, especially his teaching the schoolgirls to say the Hail Mary, had caused some embarrassment to Bishop Paget as a member of the Ecclesiastical Discipline Commission in the previous decade. Poyntz had also been conducting a campaign of attrition against local Nonconformists for years, culminating in his purchase in 1908 of the site of the recently closed Baptist chapel and the application to the land title of a restrictive covenant preventing its use in future by any Nonconformist group. He had sought, without success, to use the same tactic ten years previously in relation to the site of the former Primitive Methodist chapel subsequently acquired by the Salvation Army.[24]

The second theme to emerge from the Oxfordshire clergy's responses to their bishop was a strong commitment to the retention and, if possible, extension of the denominational principle in education. As the incumbent of Milton-under-Wychwood explained, 'I believe in denominational schools, first, last, and all the time.'[25] In consequence, while content to accommodate Nonconformists in management and teaching, they were much less happy to compromise on the appointment of head teachers. Here the bishop's question was adverting not just to the concerns of the Nonconformists but also those of the National Union of Teachers (NUT), which was campaigning against religious tests in relation to teaching appointments. In the responses, as compared to the more relaxed position on school management, the proportions opposing and supporting compromise were reversed, with only 22 incumbents even tentatively in favour of

22 Ibid. 109, 69.
23 Ibid. 66.
24 K. Tiller, ed., *Dorchester Abbey: Church and People 635–2005* (Stonesfield, 2005), 76–83.
25 OHC, MSS Oxf. Dioc. c.380, 131.

the move, compared to 110 resolutely opposed. Most of these contented themselves with simply stating that the head teacher should be a churchman or woman or that it would be inappropriate for a Nonconformist to head a church school. Some, however, expressed their position with considerable force, as in the case of the incumbent of Pyrton who reported: 'I feel very strongly that we must never surrender the appointment of the Headteacher, nothing will compensate us for such a loss.'[26] Where extensive negative comment was provided, it tended to be the NUT rather than Nonconformists which provided the target. The vicar of Blackbourton, for example, confided to his bishop: 'I have no faith in the "scraps of paper" of the N.U.T. Socialist and nonconformist ideas are too prevalent for us to give an inch which would mean in the end the N.U.T. taking the ell.'[27]

Several incumbents made a comprehensive defence of the current arrangement precisely on the grounds that it was essential to the preservation of denominational education. For instance, the vicar of Chipping Norton proposed:

> I think we should seek by all means to retain our Church Schools in single-school areas. Neither the management, appointment of head teachers or the character of religious teaching should be altered lest it should interfere with the 'atmosphere' of the school. It is this 'atmosphere' that is so tremendously important. So many children have no real homes and a school under proper management and loyal Church Teachers with no vagueness of undenominationalism can be made a real home and 'mother' to teach them devotion and in addition one has to remember there is such a thing as teaching secular things religiously. The sense of Church membership too can only be fostered by attendance at such a school. I venture to think that the sad lack of sense of membership, and ignorance generally of their own Church, revealed by so many soldiers at the front (we are told) is arising [from] attendance at Council Schools or Church Schools compromised out of all character.[28]

The necessity for 'definite' church teaching was a commonplace in the clergy's responses to their bishop's enquiries[29] and their welcome

[26] Ibid. 168.
[27] Ibid. 26.
[28] Ibid. 49.
[29] Ibid. 1, 123, 143.

to Nonconformist teachers was intended to promote parallel denominational teaching. The aim was not to water down the teaching of the church but rather to permit its intensification, as the vicar of Sandford St Martin explained:

> My own view is, that … it would be worthwhile and fair to give Nonconformity the privilege of teaching their own children in Church Schools in single-school areas: that it would be better to teach a few church children definitely than a large number indefinitely or whose church teaching is counteracted at home – and that it would make for Christian fellowship and charity.[30]

The corollary of the clerical commitment to denominational education was a deep scepticism about the utility of undenominationalism and a general hostility to the principle. At Brize Norton, for example, the vicar reported on the unsatisfactory nature of the undenominational religious teaching at the local LEA-provided school, in consequence of which '[o]ur Children are absolutely heathen and ignorant of the simplest facts even of the Patriarchs, or of our Lord's Life. In many cases, as here, if the clergy have no voice in the teaching, the Bible is a dead letter.'[31]

Similarly, the perpetual curate of Claydon noted that a 'Council School, humanly speaking renders it impossible to hope for the spread of any religious feeling among the people – it practically kills religion'.[32] To clergy like these, the idea of a more satisfactory version of the terms currently in operation in LEA-provided schools was a contradiction in terms and the only proper course was resolute opposition to the spread of these schools and an energetic attempt to render it unnecessary. As the vicar of Fritwell put it, '"Compromise may act in politics but concentration is needed in wars" and this is war to the knife against the hideous monster of "undenominationalism".'[33]

The final theme to emerge from a review of the clergy's response to the bishop's enquiry, somewhat less overt than the other two, offers both an insight into their view of the purpose of religious education at the elementary level and, in some cases, evidence for an underlying

[30] Ibid. 175.
[31] Ibid. 34.
[32] Ibid. 51.
[33] Ibid. 84.

anxiety about its usefulness. A handful commented warmly on the value of church schools in laying the foundation on which the clergy could build the church in the next generation. The vicar of Sydenham, for example, thought his school should be retained in its current status because 'the influence over the children and through them over the parish generally is very great'.[34] Similar views were expressed, both in urban benefices like St Barnabas in Oxford and village parishes throughout the county.[35] The warmest endorsement, however came from the perpetual curate of Holy Trinity, Henley:

> As one who has given religious instruction in Church day-schools for 20–5 years regularly once or twice a week, and continues to do so, I am profoundly convinced of the necessity of doing our utmost to maintain their definite status as far as possible. I find the School to be the invaluable nursery of the Church. It is through teaching and knowing the children that I find doors open to me in houses which would be otherwise, in a sense, closed.[36]

It was this sense of the continuing potential of church schools that encouraged the clergy to be so tenacious of the denominational principle. Indeed, there was, despite the different inflections of church party, a broad agreement across the range of responses about the essentials of religious education. The vicar of Faringdon wanted 'truly Gospel teaching in education'.[37] His colleague at St Frideswide in Oxford asserted that 'the whole training and development of the child should be based on a religious ideal, and that the Catholic ideal, and should be religious in aim and in method'.[38] They would have agreed, however, that such education must be a genuine expression of the faith rather than merely formal. As the vicar of Shirburn put it, 'real religious education should be given in all elementary schools',[39] and for the incumbent of Fritwell, '[t]he Head teacher <u>must</u> be a consistent Churchman or Church woman, believing and living the Catholic faith … they cannot teach what they do

[34] Ibid. 205.
[35] Ibid. 150, 197, 198, 224.
[36] Ibid. 98.
[37] Ibid. 75.
[38] Ibid. 154.
[39] Ibid. 183.

not believe and practice themselves.'[40] The unusually irenic rector of Swerford reported:

> If such a thing were possible, I should like to see a system under which (with safeguards against bitterly controversial teaching such as would justly be offensive to consciences on the one side or the other) we could all agree to encourage the individual teachers, High, Low or Broad, to teach what they themselves really feel most strongly and with most conviction. This does not seem to me impossible. But I am … assured that your Lordship will regard me as an enthusiastic dreamer. [41]

Nonetheless, not all the clergy were equally convinced that that the schools were realizing their potential and the returns are marked by a strong undercurrent of disquiet. For some this was simply a question of viability: they feared their preferred model of denominational instruction would be overwhelmed by state-backed undenominationalism underpinned by the power of the purse, reflected in better equipped schools and higher salaried teachers, and reinforced by the support of the teachers' union.[42] For others, though, even denominational education had produced such disappointing results that it seemed hardly worth persisting with. The rector of Rotherfield Peppard reported:

> There has been a Church School in this Parish for close upon 50 years, but I cannot find that it has been instrumental in building up convinced Churchmen. Practically all the men of the artisan and labouring classes in the Parish have been educated at the School, and yet it is a rare exception to find among them a Communicant. A Church School which produces a beggarly harvest of this kind is certainly not worth retaining, if in doing so we are standing in the way of a really efficient National System of Education.[43]

To some extent attitudes like this reveal heightened expectations on the part of an increasingly Anglo-Catholic clergy, especially with respect to producing congregations of communicants rather than the kind of results produced by the school at Sandford St Martin: 'though there is perhaps no very deep or definite Church membership realised, it is peculiarly a parish of men and women of goodwill to the

[40] Ibid. 89.
[41] Ibid. 212.
[42] Ibid. 50, 57, 107.
[43] Ibid. 172.

church'.[44] However, the responses adduced a range of reasons for educational failure. Some were disappointed by the material with which they had to work. One or two expressed concern about the children. At Newington, for example, the incumbent contrasted his previous charge in the north of England which had two large schools 'with effective church teaching of very intelligent children' with his country cure in Oxfordshire, where 'I realise how much there is of the very first rudiments of religion which has constantly to be taught and which we do not seem to get beyond'.[45] Others were concerned about the indifference of the parents which undermined attempts at religious formation.[46] Given the emphasis on 'reality' in religious instruction, however, the most frequently expressed anxieties were about teachers who were churchmen or women in name only and did not therefore deliver the teaching with conviction.[47] This was supplemented by a serious concern within the clerical body that not all of their number gave a high enough priority to involvement with the school. At Cowley, for example, the vicar warned that 'the real danger is that my brethren the Clergy do <u>not</u> visit the Schools enough and that they do not look upon them as one of the most important branches of their work'.[48] Moreover, even those who did engage were not always a success. As the rector of Drayton St Leonard, himself married to a certificated teacher, put it, 'the clergy, if <u>they</u> teach must <u>learn to teach scientifically</u>'.[49]

A few of the responses suggested that the problems lay deeper in the system. The incumbent of Shipton-on-Cherwell thought the system was too 'examinational', tending to treat religion like any other subject,[50] and given this situation, his colleague at Nuffield felt that elementary schools should focus on moral instruction: 'A knowledge of certain parts of Bible history either of the old or n[ew]. Testament will not save children from lying and stealing and foul speech.' He suggested reserving more definite church teaching for the Sunday school.[51] At Swerford, the rector thought the structure of religious

[44] Ibid. 175.
[45] Ibid. 137.
[46] Ibid. 1, 77, 182.
[47] Ibid. 42, 68, 194.
[48] Ibid. 57.
[49] Ibid. 68.
[50] Ibid. 181.
[51] Ibid. 144.

education for mixed school communities militated against 'reality' in the teaching:

> What I feel most strongly is that the present system tends to make each teacher present to the children a minimum of his or her ... religious convictions. They say to themselves 'I must not say this, or I shall not be dealing fairly with the children of dissenters: I must not say that, or I shall not be dealing fairly with the children of strong churchmen.'[52]

The vicar of Goring felt the church school system was flawed by its failure to pursue a sufficiently holistic view of religious education: 'I do not think our Church Schools have stood to their ideal. The sacred and the secular are almost as sharply separated in them as in Council Schools.'[53] The rector of Witney, on the other hand, thought there was probably too much religious teaching in the schools already: 'I am sure the children are fed up with religious lessons – five days every week and twice on Sundays. I take great care that my own children are not surfeited as the elementary school children are. Religion is to them knowing facts not living a life.'[54]

Whatever their qualms, however, only a tiny minority of the Oxfordshire clergy favoured any kind of major reconstruction; unsatisfactory though many of them felt the system might be, they were determined to stick with it for fear of something worse. This view had, if anything, been deepened by the experience of war. As the incumbent of St Peter in the East, Oxford, put it, the reports of misconduct by German troops provided 'an object lesson in the necessity of religious teaching'.[55]

Given the clear views expressed by his clergy, the bishop's own policy as enunciated in the charge he delivered on his visitation tour in May and June 1918 must have come as something of a bombshell. Gore began with a gloomy analysis of the prospects for the present system. The existing provision of church schools would be impossible to maintain, he argued, because of a lack of resources and the tendency of the new central schools to be established under the forthcoming education act to displace them in importance, making the district rather than the parish the natural unit of education. The

52 Ibid. 212.
53 Ibid. 88.
54 Ibid. 226.
55 Ibid. 162.

increasing proportion of teachers trained in undenominational state colleges would further weaken the influence of the church,[56] and if the issue were left unaddressed would ensure the eventual general triumph of undenominational education which, he contended, 'rests on no intelligent principle and provides no sound basis for training in religion'.[57] Thus far, Gore's attitudes were in line with Oxfordshire clerical opinion. However, in the light of the developments he foresaw, Gore suggested a series of radical responses.

Rather than capitalizing on the new spirit of compromise evident in the returns, Gore rejected the option of parallel denominationalism favoured by the vast majority of his clergy in favour of a third way – a new interdenominationalism. Optimistic about the prospects for improved relations with the Nonconformist churches already developed during the war, he proposed statutory interdenominational councils which LEAs could ask to direct the religious instruction in their schools and which could also oversee training in state colleges leading to a certificate of competence in religious instruction. Such certified teachers could then be given primary responsibility for the delivery of religious instruction in state-provided schools.[58] In areas with multiple schools, Gore proposed that church schools could continue to operate on their existing basis. In single school areas where the only school was a LEA 'provided school' it should make facilities available for denominational education as requested by groups of parents. His most radical proposals, however, were reserved for the single-school areas most prevalent in his own diocese – those where the school was provided by the Church of England. These schools, he argued, must become 'provided schools' during school hours, with head teachers appointed not by the managers but by the LEA. Religious instruction would be given on an interdenominational basis as in other local education authority schools, although facilities for Anglican denominational teaching would also be made available. Any other approach, he concluded, especially an attempt to retain the system of elementary education in its present form, would be to embark on a losing battle, leading to the marginalization of religious education however conceived.[59]

[56] Charles Gore, *Dominant Ideas and Corrective Principles* (Oxford, 1918), 52–9.
[57] Ibid. 55.
[58] Ibid. 60–3.
[59] Ibid. 63–6.

Consideration of the clerical responses to bishop Gore's visitation queries demonstrates the capacity of attention to the views of men on the ground to refocus the historiography of the relationship between religion and education in the early twentieth century. Of particular importance here, is the evidence of growing détente around issues of school management and the admission of Nonconformist teaching into church schools, despite the longevity of a few ecclesiastical warriors. This development suggests that the paradigm of conflict in the relationship between religion and education in the early twentieth century, still dominant in the historiography, requires modification. The central issue in the minds of the Anglican clergy was no longer *whether* to accommodate the scruples of Nonconformist parents, but *how* to do so without compromising the principle of denominational education. This principle was maintained with such tenacity not because of ecclesiastical competition with, or theological animus against, Nonconformity, but because they believed it to be the only sure foundation for a system of education in which religion could be a living reality. In some respects, this was a debate stretching back to the rivalries of the early 1800s, but it was, by 1918, inflected by a century of experience and given new urgency by wartime conditions. The solution supported by the vast majority of clerical opinion in Oxfordshire – a sort of mutually assured denominationalism – was fundamentally different from the model of interdenominational agreement espoused by their diocesan. The difference in view between the bishop and his clergy was perhaps mainly one of perspective: on the one hand, that of Anglican ministers working in the harvest fields of rural Oxfordshire and on the other, an ecclesiastical statesman deeply involved in debates over the government's educational proposals for months. However, the challenges they faced accelerated with the social and demographic changes of the post-war years, as declining rolls and restricted finance undermined the viability of village schools and the church's educational efforts in the towns were swamped by the rising tide of urban population growth. In this context, the degree of divergence between the two visions of the future for Anglican schools represents all too clearly the difficulty the church was to face in developing any educational policy capable of addressing the challenges of the succeeding decades.

Fighting the Tide: Church Schools in South Buckinghamshire, 1902–44

Grant Masom*
Kellogg College, Oxford

In 1902 elementary school provision in Oxford diocese – England's largest – reflected the national picture: 72 per cent were church schools, with total rolls of 54 per cent of school-age children. The bitterly contested 1902 Education Act apparently protected the future of church schools, but in practice its provisions severely undermined them, particularly in growing areas of the country. By 1929, Oxford's assistant bishop reported the schools' situation as 'critical'. This article examines the impact on the church schools of one rural deanery in South Buckinghamshire, between the 1902 and 1944 Education Acts. Several schools found themselves under threat of closure, while rapid population increase and a rising school leaving age more than quadrupled the number of school-age children in the area. Closer working with the local education authority and other denominations was one option to optimize scarce resources and protect the Church of England's influence on religious education in day schools: but many churchmen fought to keep church schools open at all costs. This strategy met with limited success: by 1939 the proportion of children in church schools had decreased to 10 per cent, with potential consequences for how religion was taught to the other 90 per cent of children.

The debate about secularization focuses, *inter alia*, on changes in the nature of religious belief, the social influence of religion and the influence of, and adherence to, religious institutions.[1] Most explanations focus on external factors – modernization of thought, urbanization, increasing leisure alternatives and so on – in which churches and other institutions can appear passive and lacking agency.[2] As

* 6 Hill Place, Farnham Common, Bucks, SL2 3EW. E-mail: grant.masom@gmail.com.

[1] After Bryan Wilson, as quoted in J. C. D. Clark, 'Secularization and Modernization: The Failure of a "Grand Narrative"', *HistJ* 55 (2012), 161–94, at 178.

[2] For reviews of the historiography, see Jeremy Morris, 'The Strange Death of Christian Britain: Another Look at the Secularization Debate', *HistJ* 46 (2003): 963–76; idem, 'Secularization and Religious Experience: Arguments in the Historiography of Modern British Religion', *HistJ* 55 (2012), 195–219; Clark, 'Secularization and Modernization'.

Studies in Church History 55 (2019), 545–560
doi: 10.1017/stc.2018.23

Jeremy Morris has noted, relatively neglected are approaches which 'assume no significant change in religious need, but instead locate the causes of church decline in the various strategies adopted (or refused) by churches themselves'.[3] Morris referred to these as 'supply side' arguments; others, such as Dominic Erdozain, have referred to 'internal secularisation'.[4]

Churches have long seen the religious socialization of children as a key part of their ministry; and historians likewise have identified this as a crucial factor in church adherence.[5] Church deficiencies in the religious socializing of children could be seen as a form of 'internal secularisation', therefore. The primary focus of historians studying the religious education of nineteenth- and twentieth-century children has been on Sunday schools.[6] However, in the early twentieth-century Anglican mind, the primary means by which religious education was delivered was church day schools, not Sunday schools: as one rural dean put it, 'of the agencies engaged in instructing and educating the young, the Day schools are the most important, for there the foundations of the faith are laid'. Consequently, for church people, 'after the Church, the Day schools should be next in importance'.[7] Philip Eliot, bishop of Buckingham, saw day schools as a key part of institutional Christianity, with its 'visible society, ministry, episcopate, sacred books, sacraments, schools etc, all necessary for her existence'.[8] Hubert Burge, bishop of Oxford, emphasized their importance when addressing his clergy in 1922: 'If a Parish Priest has a Church school in his parish, I hold that it is as much a matter of obligation upon him to give religious instruction in that school as it is to say his daily offices and to visit his people, and to tend the sick and dying.'[9]

[3] Morris, 'Strange Death', 964–5.

[4] Ibid. 965 n. 8; Dominic Erdozain, 'The Secularisation of Sin in the Nineteenth Century', *JEH* 62 (2011), 59–88.

[5] Robert Currie, Alan Gilbert and Lee Horsley, *Churches and Churchgoers: Patterns of Church Growth in the British Isles since 1700* (Oxford, 1977), 6, 118, explicitly links church attendance to 'endogenous' factors, that is, the handing down of Christian faith from one generation to the next.

[6] Philip Cliff, *The Rise and Development of the Sunday School Movement in England, 1780–1980* (Redhill, 1986); Stephen Orchard and John Briggs, eds, *The Sunday School Movement: Studies in the Growth and Decline of Sunday Schools* (Milton Keynes, 2007).

[7] 'Church Conference at Slough', *Slough Observer* (hereafter: *SO*), 20 May 1922, 3.

[8] 'The Bishop of Buckingham and the Growth of Slough', *SO*, 19 May 1933, 10.

[9] Hubert Murray Burge, *A Charge given at his Primary Visitation to the Clergy and Churchwardens of the Diocese of Oxford* (Oxford, 1922), 45.

These were not isolated comments. The triennial visitation return questionnaires issued by successive bishops of Oxford during the inter-war years showed the same priorities: a section of five or six questions (out of around twenty-five covering all aspects of the incumbent's ministry) focused on day schools, with an assumption that these would be church schools, whereas typically just half a question related to Sunday schools.[10]

This may have been the contemporary focus, but it is not one reflected in the historiography. Lois Louden's history of the National Society, the Church of England's agency responsible for its schools, is comprehensive but inevitably somewhat partisan.[11] Simon Green has referred to the 'abject failure of the various churches' to deliver satisfactory religious education 'to many English boys and girls' in the early twentieth century, due to theological divisions between the established and free churches, but his primary focus was on the 1944 Education Act.[12] Otherwise, church schools are often mentioned, but rarely seen as worthy of specific focus.[13]

This article argues that the failure to engage with church schools is a significant omission in understanding the trajectory of decline in affiliation and adherence to organized religion. Specifically, it contends that the Church of England's strategies regarding its day schools in the period following the 1902 Education Act had a significant impact on the religious education of millions of children in the twentieth century, including those who did not attend a church school; those strategies weakened the institutional strength not only of church schools but also of the churches themselves, by dissociating religious education (RE) from Christian formation within the body of faith. The focus is on the period between the 1902 and 1944 Education Acts. The challenges faced by church schools in South

[10] For example, Oxford, Oxfordshire History Centre (hereafter: OHC), MS Oxf. dioc. c.384, 'Buckingham Archdeaconry Clergy Answers 1924'.

[11] Lois Louden, *Distinctive and Inclusive: The National Society and Church of England Schools 1811–2011* (London, 2012).

[12] S. J. D. Green, *The Passing of Protestant England: Secularisation and Social Change, c.1920–1960* (Cambridge, 2012), 220.

[13] For example, Adrian Hastings, *A History of English Christianity 1920–2000*, 4th edn (London, 2000). Elsewhere in this volume, Mark Smith makes a similar point, with other examples: '"War to the knife"? The Anglican Clergy and Education at the End of the First World War', 530–44.

Buckinghamshire, one of the most rapidly growing areas of the country, and the responses of clerical and lay leaders will be examined.

Church day schools were not only significant as religious institutions, but also socially: in 1902, 3.1 million children, or 57 per cent of England's children, attended one of 14,275 voluntary schools, which comprised 71 per cent of the national total. Of these, 83 per cent were Church of England schools.[14] These schools were typically older than the council, or board, schools; their buildings were increasingly costly to keep in good repair, let alone to adapt to meet increasing statutory requirements. In addition, central funding for voluntary schools was significantly less, and the corresponding financial squeeze became a national problem: as Louden laments, 'in effect, elementary schools dragged the whole educational system down because the denominations were incapable of making necessary improvements'.[15] This situation led to revised funding arrangements under the 1902 Education Act, whereby teachers in voluntary schools would be funded by a local education authority (LEA) but appointed by local managers (that is, the churches); the LEA would also fund 'fair wear and tear' and purely educational operating costs. The churches would be responsible for repairs, statutory improvements (monitored by the LEA) and costs for non-school use.[16]

The inter-war period saw a significant shift in the industrial centre of gravity of Britain from the north and Wales towards the south-east. Older heavy industries (coal, iron and steel, shipbuilding and textiles) experienced recession, while newer, growth industries (motor vehicles, aircraft and light engineering) were drawn to the Midlands and south-east, closer to markets rather than to sources of energy and raw materials. Such industries also tended to be located close to, but not in the centre of, the major conurbations, notably London, stimulating 'urban sprawl' and suburbanization.[17]

Substantial inter-regional economic migration resulted, with an estimated 1.1 million people moving away from the north and Wales towards the south-east, as well as out-migration from the

[14] Louden, *Distinctive and Inclusive*, 52.
[15] Ibid.
[16] Ibid. 52–64, 'Rescue for the Voluntary Schools 1900–1945'.
[17] For a contemporary analysis, see *Report on the Location of Industry* (London, 1939), produced by an independent consultancy, Political and Economic Planning.

centres of the major cities.[18] There was rapid population growth, particularly in the ring of counties around London, including Buckinghamshire, the southern part of which is the focus of this study.[19] The area classified as South Buckinghamshire by the Registrar General was in Church of England terms the Burnham rural deanery, a group of eighteen parishes with the rapidly growing town of Slough at its heart.

Figure 1 shows the population growth of South Buckinghamshire in the first half of the twentieth century, with a clear acceleration after the Great War due to inward migration. The solid line normalizes the data against general population growth: in this period, the population grew more than twice as fast as the national average, from 47,000 to 114,000. Such demographic changes posed significant challenges for all institutions.[20] The churches were no exception, and the Church of England, as the national church, was affected most of all. As Archbishop Lang told the Church Assembly in 1935:

> This problem of making spiritual provision for the populations of the new districts which were being formed in many parts of the country was the greatest that had been presented to the Church in our generation. It might almost be said to be one of the greatest ever presented to the Church of England in the course of its long history … some dioceses … were almost breaking down under the magnitude of the problem.[21]

Oxford was one of 'a dozen or more' such dioceses, although not the most severely affected.[22]

In addition to the challenge of general population growth, the school leaving age was progressively raised from 10 to 15 years of age between 1880 and 1947, with provision for part-time education beyond this age. Figure 2 shows the impact: the number of children

[18] David Feldman, 'Migration', in Martin Daunton, ed., *The Cambridge Urban History of Britain*, 3: *1840–1950* (Cambridge, 2001), 185–206.

[19] *Census 1951 England and Wales: County Report, Buckinghamshire* (London, 1954), xii. From 1921 to 1951, the three fastest growing counties were Hertfordshire, West Sussex and Buckinghamshire.

[20] A. D. K. Owen, 'The Social Consequences of Industrial Transference', *Sociological Review* 29 (1937), 331–54.

[21] 'Church Assembly: Problems of the New Areas', *The Times*, 19 June 1935, 9.

[22] 'Seventeen Million English "Pagans"', *SO*, 1 November 1935, 6.

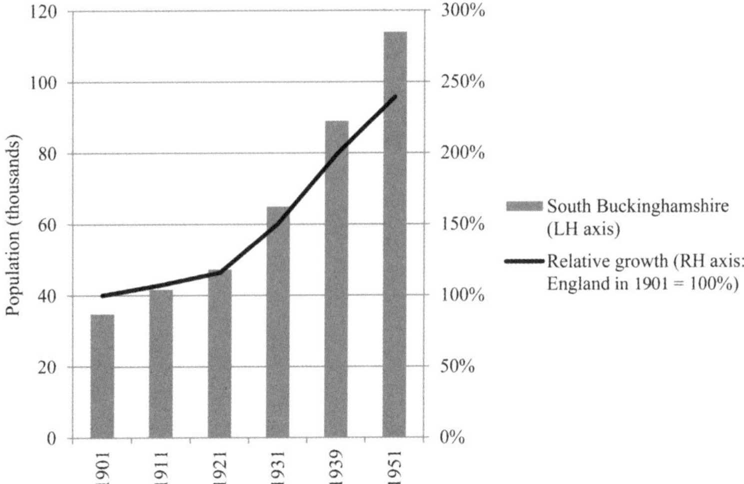

Fig. 1. South Buckinghamshire population growth 1901–51. Sources: *Census 1921 England and Wales: County of Buckingham* (London, 1924), 1, Table 2; *Census 1951 England and Wales: County Report, Buckinghamshire* (London, 1954), xiv, Table A.

of compulsory full-time school age in Slough rose from 1,200 to 9,000 in the fifty years up to the Second World War, again accelerating in the inter-war years.

As noted, the Church of England saw the provision of RE in day schools, and specifically church day schools, as a high priority. Facing the huge increase in schoolchildren in growing areas, there were three general directions open to the church: to maintain and expand existing church schools, to build new schools, or to be actively engaged in providing RE in council schools.

The default position – maintenance of the status quo – was outlined to Slough churchgoers in 1921 by a representative of the National Society. It was churchgoers' 'bounden duty' to preserve the church schools endowed by their forefathers; without them, 'all continued security for the teaching of Christian faith to the children of the parish disappears'.[23] While acknowledging that it was 'often the case [that] fairly good religious teaching [was] given in Council Schools', he maintained that in some, no religious instruction at all

[23] 'The Church Schools', *SO*, 3 September 1921, 2.

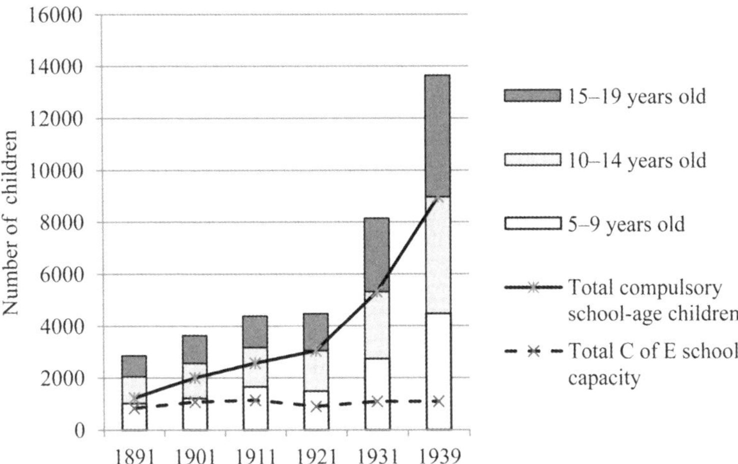

Fig. 2. Church of England school provision in Slough measured against total school-age population, 1891–1939. Sources: *Kelly's Directory of Buckinghamshire*, 1891, 1899, 1903, 1911, 1915, 1920, 1924, 1928, 1931, 1939; http://www.visionofbritain.org.uk/unit/10032751/cube/AGESEX_85UP>, accessed 4 August 2013.

was given; in any case, it was only in church schools that the Catechism was taught. This argument fell on willing ears; so too did the oft-repeated injunction that all true education must be based on a sound religious foundation.[24] However, events would show this to be an expensive strategy which failed to cater for the vast majority of Slough's children.

At first sight, the position was reasonably healthy. Oxford diocese claimed that 528 out of 730 elementary schools were church schools in 1929, with 49,300 children out of a total of 90,600 on their rolls.[25] In Buckinghamshire in 1920, there were 152 church schools and 82 council schools.[26] However, on closer examination, the position was much weaker, and in 1929 was described by Bishop Shaw, the diocese's assistant bishop, as 'critical'.[27] There were several challenges: apart from population growth and the rising school leaving age, these included the pattern of urbanization, the financial

[24] For example, 'Church Conference at Slough', *SO*, 1 May 1920, 3.
[25] 'The Church Schools', *SO*, 15 November 1929, 10.
[26] 'Church Conference', *SO*, 1 May 1920.
[27] 'The Church Schools', *SO*, 15 November 1929.

provisions of the 1902 Education Act, and the question of whether, in parents' minds, church schools offered something more than the free schooling provided through council schools.

Table 1 shows the distribution of population and church schools across the Burnham rural deanery. The pattern of urbanization meant that the twelve church schools were poorly located in the historic parishes rather than situated according to population. The early growth of Slough had created a significant mismatch between population and parishes even in 1912; by 1939, rapid urbanization had accentuated this still further, and the largest parish in the deanery had eighty times the population of the smallest. In two smaller, rural parishes, pupil numbers fell to unviable levels as couples with children moved away, probably to jobs in Slough, and these parishes' schools were closed in the 1920s. Elsewhere, some church schools found themselves well away from the new housing estates: in the largest parish the church school was two miles north of the major new developments; but in any case it offered only 195 places for over 2,000 school-age children.[28] This meant that the church could not provide enough places even for the children of churchgoing Anglican parents: in 1923, before the great population expansion, it was estimated that nationally two-thirds of such children attended council schools, for lack of sufficient church school places.[29]

The 1902 settlement had been intended to protect the future of church schools; in practice, it simply deferred tackling the fundamental underlying problems. Repairing existing church schools involved substantial costs. In addition, the churches were responsible for any alterations and enhancements to church schools to meet rising standards: for example, providing additional floor space per pupil or enabling the serving of school meals. In 1920, it was estimated that £400,000 was needed simply to bring church schools in Buckinghamshire up to the statutory level: a sum that, addressing the Burnham rural deanery, a senior layman described as 'perfectly impossible … for churchpeople … to find'.[30] Even this would do nothing to increase capacity to meet the rapidly increasing demand in the larger parishes, illustrated in Table 1.

[28] OHC, MS Oxf. dioc. c.393, 'Farnham Royal Clergy Answers 1936'.
[29] 'Church Unity', *The Times*, 14 June 1923, 9.
[30] 'Church Conference', *SO*, 1 May 1920.

Table 1. Burnham Rural Deanery Church Schools

	1912			1939		
	Population		**schools**	**Population**		**Schools**
Smallest 6 parishes	1,907	6%	4	3,384	4%	2
Middle 6 parishes	7,485	22%	4	16,517	17%	5
Largest 6 parishes	25,222	73%	4	75,377	79%	3
			12			10
Smallest parish	147			262		
Largest parish	10,000			20,000		

Sources: *Crockford's Clerical Directory*, 1912, 1939; *Kelly's Directory of Buckinghamshire*, 1911, 1939.

Ultimately, the church had a choice about how to direct its energies and the financial contributions of its committed supporters. For example, in Datchet, just south of Slough, 'saving our school' cost £6,500, raised locally after much effort by the church.[31] In practice, the school was too large and well attended to have been allowed to close, with a capacity of 320 and attendance of 280 in 1931.[32] The alternative was to transfer ownership to the LEA, with the corresponding responsibility for maintaining the school fabric, but at the cost of loss of church control over the RE syllabus. However, the £6,500 needed to 'save' the school as a church institution could otherwise have funded much-needed church extension – for example, a 250-seat church on a nearby estate cost £1,600 – or additional clergy.[33]

Even where funds for church schools were found, it was usually to upgrade schools to meet minimum standards, and the newer council schools were better equipped, as clergymen recognized.[34] In Datchet, there was no alternative to the church school; but parents in central Slough could choose between church and council schools. Even church parents were torn: in 1922, Slough's rector complained they 'failed to realise the far more vital importance of sending their children to Church schools than of securing for them more luxurious

[31] 'Rural Deanery of Burnham', *SO*, 12 November 1926, 8.
[32] OHC, MS Oxf. dioc. c.390, 'Datchet Clergy Answers 1931'.
[33] 'New Church at Manor Park', *SO*, 8 June 1934, 4.
[34] 'Chalvey Schools: To the Parents of the Scholars', *SO*, 30 May 1914, 8.

surroundings elsewhere', and that this was resulting in low rolls at the church infant school.[35]

Perhaps parents 'failed to realise' because the church could not make a sufficient case for preserving church schools. The line of argument had not changed since the battles over the 1902 act. Firstly, it was argued that these schools offered the best way to guarantee that children would be given a sound religious education; secondly, that this was the essential foundation for a wider education; and thirdly, that RE needed to involve induction into the Church of England, including its denominational practices and teaching.[36] Winning the argument centrally was one test of whether the case had been made; raising sufficient money locally to upgrade existing church schools, and to build new ones, was another test of public opinion. During the 1920s and 1930s the church struggled both nationally and locally to win the argument.

This was, not least, because it was hard to maintain that religious instruction was not being given in council schools. In Buckinghamshire, the LEA's policy was 'that definite instruction in the principles and practice of the Christian faith shall be systematically given in every [council] school'.[37] Fifteen years before the provisions of the 1944 Education Act, this included beginning the day with a hymn, the Lord's Prayer and other prayers, an optional Scripture reading, followed by twenty to thirty minutes of religious instruction.[38] In 1931, one senior churchman conceded that 'the religious teaching in some of the [Council] schools was extraordinarily good'.[39] Despite church concerns that it might be seen as an optional extra, 'less important than arithmetic or geography', a local council school headmaster took the opportunity of the annual prize-giving to emphasize the value placed on RE.[40] 'The curriculum is comprehensive and the children seem to realise very fully the significance of this part of our work', he maintained. Parents might therefore ask

[35] 'Slough Church Schools', *SO*, 8 July 1922, 4.
[36] For a detailed review of the 1902 debate , see D. R. Pugh, 'The Church and Education: Anglican Attitudes 1902', *JEH* 23 (1972), 219–32.
[37] 'Religious Instruction in Elementary Schools', *SO*, 31 May 1929, 5.
[38] 'Religious Instruction in Schools', *SO*, 24 April 1931, 8.
[39] 'Oxford Diocesan Conference: Educational Problems in Schools and Parishes', *SO*, 1 May 1931, 8.
[40] 'The Church Day Schools', *SO*, 4 September 1931, 5; 'Religious Instruction in Schools', *SO*, 24 December 1937, 4.

how this differed from what was being offered in church schools. The headmaster went on to emphasize that the purpose of RE was to give children 'a thorough training in citizenship', presumably of a 'Christian country'.[41] This was non-denominational RE delivered by teachers, and induction into local churches – of whatever denomination – formed no part of it. In church schools, the clergy's involvement in teaching was often on a daily basis, as witnessed by the visitation returns. But in council schools the clergy's role was limited to being a 'manager', or governor, with no day-to-day involvement. Over time, it appears that fewer parents cared: in Colnbrook, after another intensive 'save our school' campaign, the vicar remarked of local parents: 'it is questionable whether if the [church] schools were surrendered [to the LEA] they would be much upset'.[42]

As shown in Figure 2, the number of children of compulsory full-time school age in Slough had risen from around 1,200 in 1891 to around 9,000 in 1939. In 1891, there were 837 Church of England school places in the town, which accounted for 68 per cent of the number of children in school; by 1939, given the funding challenges it faced, the church had been unable to do more than grow capacity to 1,094 places, which now accounted for just 12 per cent of the total number of schoolchildren.[43] A strategy of protecting existing church schools at all costs had not prevented school closures in two smaller parishes or a massive dilution of provision in the growing parishes. Within forty years, the clergy had moved from being a daily part of the education of the majority of Slough's children to exercising this role for a fairly small minority. In consequence, they lost the link schools created with the parents. Church schools had lost significant traction, and with it, certainly in many Anglican churchmen's minds, one of the main ways in which the church engaged with its parishioners.

This might be seen as an inevitable consequence of 'the shift from religious to secular control of various of the erstwhile activities and functions of religion'.[44] However, the church had had opportunities to secure a very different outcome to the teaching of RE, not just for

[41] 'Religious Instruction [1937]'.

[42] OHC, MS Oxf. dioc. c.384, 'Colnbrook Clergy Answers 1924'.

[43] *Kelly's Directory of Berkshire, Bucks and Oxon, 1891* (London, 1891), 437; *Kelly's Directory of Buckinghamshire, 1939* (London, 1939).

[44] Part of Bryan Wilson's definition of secularization: Clark, 'Secularization and Modernization', 178.

the declining number of children in church schools, but for the millions of children attending council schools (the third option highlighted above).[45] In many communities, the church owned the only school; in other areas, church schools were a key part of a mixed landscape of voluntary and provided schools. In 1920, the value of church school buildings was put at £40 million and they formed a substantial part of the nation's schools stock.[46] Recognizing the financial unsustainability of the status quo, as the First World War ended Archbishop Davidson proposed a cooperative approach on RE in all schools, 'while there were still school buildings to bargain with'.[47]

Over the next few years, general agreement was reached with the government and the free churches, whereby all church schools would come under the control of LEAs, thus relieving churches of the burden of maintenance and improvement; in return, the teaching of RE in all council schools would be strengthened by the provision of properly trained RE teachers, emphasis on setting RE within the context of the church, and cooperation with local clergy of all denominations.[48] The money saved would be directed towards teacher training colleges, which according to the archbishop were 'the key to the whole situation', to provide 'qualified teachers … thoroughly grounded in … imparting to little children the truths of their Holy Faith'.[49] The discussion took place at all levels of the Church of England; in 1921, the bishop of Oxford recommended to his clergy that in return for strong cooperation from all denominations in RE teaching, 'all schools would be provided by the public authority'.[50] The proposals were recommended to a Burnham deanery conference by a senior layman, who described them as 'very promising indeed' and observed that 'churchpeople would save money' by accepting the offer. A motion commending the proposals was passed unanimously.[51]

It was not only the financial unsustainability of the status quo that was understood. At the Church Assembly in 1924, two of the dioceses highlighted by Lang ten years later as those most affected by

[45] See p. 550 above.
[46] 'Future of Church Schools', *The Times*, 17 June 1920, 16.
[47] Louden, *Distinctive and Inclusive*, 59.
[48] 'Church Problems', *The Times*, 18 June 1923, 13.
[49] 'Church Unity', *The Times*, 14 June 1923.
[50] Burge, *Primary Visitation*, 44–5.
[51] 'Church Conference', *SO*, 1 May 1920.

south-eastern urbanization pleaded the case of those unserved by church schools. The bishop of Chelmsford referred to Dagenham, then growing even faster than Slough: 'it was impossible for the Church to provide religious education in these populous new areas where there were no Church schools. The social upheaval was going to produce these districts everywhere'. In Islington, Revd H. W. Hinde, the rural dean, noting that only 5,020 out of 60,000 school-age children were in church schools, asked for a solution to 'the whole problem; not making Church schools their first concern, but adequate religious instruction in all schools'.[52]

However, as noted above, some rank and file members of the National Society were against this approach, and they found open ears, particularly in rural communities, 'where the country parson looked upon the school as his greatest asset in the management of the parish'.[53] After the Church Assembly approved Davidson's approach, Dean Gamble of Exeter warned against 'the assumption … that because the Church Assembly may have passed a resolution … therefore the whole Church accepts it. Those who think so will find they have deceived themselves.'[54] In 1923 the National Society AGM voted against its leadership and against Davidson's proposals, calling on church authorities to abandon any policy of negotiating 'the surrender of Church schools'.[55] Vainly did the archbishop of York warn that 'maintaining Church schools as they are was not a policy that had any future' and that it risked making 'the Church, which had done so much for education, seem to be perpetually blocking the way to educational progress'.[56] A vocal minority maintained that church schools should not only be retained but should be as fully funded by the state as council schools, and that denominational teaching should be allowed in council schools, a throwback to arguments put forward in 1902. *The Times* observed that any solution must recognize that even within a Christian consensus there was a wide variety of religious life and experience; but some churchmen 'forget that those outside have convictions and claims no less real than their own'.[57]

52 'Church Assembly', *The Times*, 22 November 1924, 8.
53 'Women's Ministry', *The Times*, 17 February 1922, 12.
54 'Dual Control in the Schools', *The Times*, 11 January 1923, 6.
55 Louden, *Distinctive and Inclusive*, 59.
56 'Church Assembly', *The Times*, 22 November 1924.
57 'Religion in the Schools', *The Times*, 24 November 1924, 13.

Despite five years of debate, continuing resistance meant that the opportunity for a new settlement passed; but educational change continued. During 1924 and 1925, the Board of Education 'black-listed' hundreds of church schools that required urgent repairs or faced closure. In 1925 Bishop Shaw proposed to the Oxford Diocesan Conference that church schools be retained, but accepted that 'some Church schools were quite unfit for their purpose', with 91 schools on the 'black lists'.[58] By 1929, as we have seen, he was reporting a 'critical situation' whereby, despite expenditure of £91,000 to resolve problems over the last three years, and the closure of some schools, looking forward it was 'impossible to state what sum would be required, but it must be large'; no solution was offered for the expanding populations.[59]

These financial pressures ultimately led to more cooperation centrally on the syllabus to be used in council schools within the Oxford diocese, following the example of other dioceses which had proactively sought local solutions in the absence of a national settlement.[60] As noted above, this meant that council schoolchildren experienced a daily act of worship with a non-denominational focus.

Visiting the rural deanery conference in 1934, Buckinghamshire's education secretary emphasized the considerable level of cooperation with the churches centrally, but noted the predictability of local opposition, including the dislike of change, particularly when involving religion and schools.[61] Some arguments seemed to reflect less a concern about a reduction in church influence than opposition to any broadening of the provision of education. Thus, commenting on the education secretary's visit, the churchgoing *Slough Observer* editor condemned 'the extravagant, needless faddisms of the Hadow Report … a mass of pseudo-psychological twaddle', maintaining that 'the sound, simple education of the past, such as the Church of England has invariably provided in its schools, is all that is needed by the average child'.[62] The education secretary also noted, however, that 'in the long run, education, like all public services,

[58] 'Diocesan Conference: Resolution to retain Church Schools', *SO*, 13 November 1925, 2.
[59] 'The Church Schools', *SO*, 15 November 1929.
[60] 'Religion in Slough Schools', *SO*, 18 September 1931, 5; Louden, *Distinctive and Inclusive*, 60–2.
[61] 'County Education Secretary on the Hadow Scheme', *SO*, 30 November 1934, 4.
[62] 'The Church and Hadow', *SO*, 30 November 1934, 7.

follows public opinion' and normally 'a long way behind'.[63] Public opinion had left the church and its schools behind on the question of religious education, if nothing else.

In summary, we have seen that the 1902 settlement had changed little in terms of the first two options open to the church in responding to the huge increase in the numbers of schoolchildren in growing areas. Maintaining existing church schools became increasingly difficult, and thoughts of increasing the provision of church schools were generally illusory. Nationally, by 1939 'the voluntary schools were again in a parlous state', according to Louden.[64] In Slough, any funds raised had been consumed by repairs, and it had been impossible to fund expansion, so that the absolute number of Church of England school places had remained roughly constant. However, population growth had reduced this number from 68 per cent to 12 per cent of Slough's schoolchildren by 1939. We have seen from the contemporary national debate that Slough was but one example of such challenges faced by the Church of England in the rapidly expanding towns of the south-east.

These challenges had led the church's senior leadership to conclude, in the archbishop of York's words, that 'maintaining Church schools as they are was not a policy that had any future'.[65] In the years following the Great War, there seemed widespread agreement on an approach which would have traded the church's substantial stock of schools for a much greater role in the religious education of the majority of schoolchildren, the training of teachers and the placing of true religious education firmly in the context of membership of the wider church family.[66] Apart from funding the training of teachers in RE, the church would also have released substantial funds to be utilized in other parts of its mission, such as building new churches and funding new clergy. However, internal resistance meant the proposals did not proceed, and a different settlement was reached in 1944.

For Simon Green, 'the abject failure' of the churches to agree on the content of RE in state schools meant that during the inter-war years, with Sunday school enrolments also declining, many children received little or no religious education; this was a failure to which

[63] 'County Education Secretary', *SO*, 30 November 1934.
[64] Louden, *Distinctive and Inclusive*, 65.
[65] 'Church Assembly', *The Times*, 22 November 1924.
[66] 'Church Unity', *The Times*, 14 June 1923.

the 1944 act brought a solution.[67] This article has argued that the failure had another consequence. In Buckinghamshire at least, comprehensive RE education in state schools was county policy well before the 1944 act, with the danger that RE could be seen as a 'subject', to be adequately learned outside the body of faith.

Matthew Arnold's receding tide of faith has proved a popular analogy in the debate on secularization.[68] However, if there was a clear opportunity for the churches – of all persuasions, but led by the Church of England – to reaffirm that true religious education involved induction into the church, then it is arguable that, by failing to negotiate a new settlement, the churches themselves contributed to secularization in Britain. Perhaps this was not so much a failure to address the receding tide of faith as a lack of attention to the advancing tide of demographic, economic and educational change.

[67] Green, *Passing*, 219–21. On the fortunes of Sunday schools during this period, see, in this volume, Caitriona McCartney, 'British Sunday Schools: An Educational Arm of the Churches, 1900–39', 561–76.
[68] Morris, 'Strange Death', 963.

British Sunday Schools: An Educational Arm of the Churches, 1900–39

Caitriona McCartney*
University of Durham

Throughout much of the twentieth century, Sunday schools in Britain played a significant role, both disseminating and forming Christian faith. There was near universal attendance at the schools, and as a result there was widespread exposure to Christian teaching and hymnody. Despite this, their role as an educational arm of the churches is under-researched. This article considers the experience of the schools from the beginning of the century until the outbreak of the Second World War. It examines how and what Sunday schools taught during this time, and the extent to which they adopted pedagogical developments. The article also considers the responses of the schools to the various education acts passed in this period. In addition, it examines what the schools themselves, their scholars and the churches thought of their effectiveness, and reflects upon the tensions that arose between the schools and the churches. The article concludes that Sunday schools were an integral part of the churches' educational reach in society and therefore deserve much more thorough examination by historians.

British Sunday schools were a significant tool of religious socialization and education, particularly in the first half of the twentieth century. Thomas Laqueur's foundational work, *Religion and Respectability* (1976), demonstrated their significance in working-class communities. He argued that 'the period 1780–1850 witnessed the birth of a working-class culture that was deeply rooted in that ethic of education, religion and respectability which was embodied in the Sunday school'.[1] Likewise, Hugh McLeod concluded that 'the overwhelming majority of working-class children went to Sunday school … [and] … many middle-class children attended Sunday school too'.[2] A Gallup

* 67 Rykneld Rd, Littleover, Derby, DE23 4BH. E-mail: caitriona.m.mccartney@durham.ac.uk.

[1] Thomas Laqueur, *Religion and Respectability: Sunday Schools and Working Class Culture 1780–1850* (London, 1976), 245.

[2] Hugh McLeod, *Religion and Society in England, 1850–1914* (London, 1996), 78.

Studies in Church History 55 (2019), 561–576
doi: 10.1017/stc.2018.24

poll conducted in 1957 found that 90 per cent of participants had attended Sunday school as a child, 73 per cent regularly.[3] Likewise, research conducted by Hugh McLeod (1996), Sarah Williams (1999), Dorothy Entwistle (2001) and others has demonstrated that a majority of those interviewed had attended Sunday school at some point in their lifetime.[4] The importance of Sunday schools can be also attributed to the role they played in educating the masses. Before the passing of the Education Act in 1870, Sunday schools were one of the few options children had to receive some form of education. As Frank Prochaska has observed, 'without the Sunday schools and charity schools, millions of children would have grown up without any formal instruction'.[5] From 1870 they were increasingly freed from the burden of teaching scholars to read, and emphasis shifted to helping form faith in their scholars and directing them into the churches.

However, the experience of Sunday schools from 1900 to 1939 is under-researched by historians of religion. For instance, Philip Cliff's study, while informative, has just two brief chapters concerning the period.[6] Laqueur's work only examines the work of the schools until around 1850.[7] Additionally, his conclusion that the Sunday schools were largely the domain of the working classes has been challenged by Malcolm Dick and Keith Snell. Dick argued that teachers at the schools did not come from a working-class background.[8] Likewise, Snell concluded that while some teachers were drawn from the working classes, most were drawn from higher social classes.[9] These studies provide useful insights into the social conditions within which the

[3] Clive Field, *Secularization in the Long 1960s: Numerating Religion in Britain* (Oxford, 2017), 45.

[4] McLeod, *Religion and Society in England*, 36; Sarah Williams, *Religious Belief and Popular Culture in Southwark, c.1880–1939* (Oxford, 1999), 142; Dorothy Entwistle, '"Hope, Colour, and Comradeship": Loyalty and Opportunism in early Twentieth-Century Church Attendance among the Working Class in North-West England', *JRH* 25 (2001), 20–38, at 24.

[5] Frank Prochaska, *Christianity and Social Service in Modern Britain: The Disinherited Spirit* (Oxford, 2006), 41.

[6] Philip Cliff, *The Rise and Development of the Sunday School Movement in England 1780–1980* (Redhill, 1986), 205–18, 219–37.

[7] Laqueur, *Religion and Respectability*.

[8] Malcolm Dick, 'The Myth of the Working-Class Sunday School', *HE* 9 (1980), 27–41, at 36.

[9] Keith Snell, 'The Sunday-School Movement in England and Wales: Child Labour, Denominational Control and Working-Class Culture', *P&P* 164 (1999), 122–68, at 133.

schools operated, but they do not detail the experiences of those involved with these institutions. More recent publications by Mark Griffiths and Naomi Stanton (now Thompson) have examined the work of the schools during the twentieth century.[10] However, Griffiths focused upon the origins of the schools in the eighteenth century in relation to the outreach work of the churches with children in the twenty-first century.[11] Stanton's research highlighted the challenges the schools faced from the 1940s onwards in regard to the emerging emphasis upon youth work in Britain.[12] Only briefly did either consider the history and experience of the schools between 1900 and 1939.

Many scholars have attributed great significance to the schools, yet do not provide evidence for their conclusions.[13] Additionally, when Sunday schools are discussed by historians, however briefly, they are often heavily critiqued. For instance, Jeffrey Cox concluded that the schools were an ineffective tool for imparting religious knowledge, because of large classes and a lack of discipline.[14] Likewise, Simon Green asserts that the teaching at the schools was 'of course … rarely sophisticated'.[15] These judgements have led many other scholars simply to paint all Sunday schools with the same broad brush. Historians have failed to explore or challenge these conclusions. This is a significant oversight in the historiography of the religion of this period. This

[10] Mark Griffiths, *One Generation from Extinction: How the Church connects with the Unchurched Child* (Oxford, 2009); Naomi Stanton, 'From Raikes' Revolution to Rigid Institution: Sunday Schools in Twentieth-Century England', in Ruth Gilchrist et al., eds, *Reflecting on the Past: Essays in the History of Youth and Community Work* (Lyme Regis, 2011), 71–91; Naomi Thompson, *Young People and Church since 1900: Engagement and Exclusion* (London, 2017).

[11] Griffiths, *One Generation*, 23–48, 57–61.

[12] Stanton, 'Raikes' Revolution', 77–89.

[13] For example, see Richard Schweitzer, *The Cross and the Trenches: Religious Faith and Doubt among British and American Great War Soldiers* (London, 2003), 6; Alan Wilkinson, *The Church of England and the First World War* (London, 1996), 239; James Kitchen, *The British Imperial Army in the Middle East: Morale and Military Identity in the Sinai and Palestine Campaigns, 1916–18* (London, 2014), 75. For a reassessment of the importance of Sunday school education during the First World War, see Caitriona McCartney, 'British Sunday Schools and the First World War', *Kirchliche Zeitgeschichte / Contemporary Church History* 31/1 (2018), 107–17.

[14] Jeffrey Cox, *English Churches in a Secular Society: Lambeth 1870–1930* (Oxford, 1987), 95–7.

[15] S. J. D. Green, *Religion in the Age of Decline: Organisation and Experience in Industrial Yorkshire, 1870–1920* (Cambridge, 1996), 215.

article aims to demonstrate the important role Sunday schools played in exposing, educating and forming the Christian faith of much of the British population. It also shows that the schools attempted to professionalize their work and that they were more sophisticated than some historians have previously suggested. To explore these themes, I have consulted the records of individual Sunday schools, often held in local record offices, as well as local newspapers. Additionally, the records of the National Sunday School Union (NSSU), an interdenominational organization formed to support the work of Sunday school workers and teachers, and of denominational Sunday school organizations have been utilized. These sources, taken together with other publications, give a fuller picture of Sunday school life in early twentieth-century Britain.

Teaching at Sunday Schools

Before the passing of the 1870 Education Act, Sunday schools were one of the few forms of education open to many children. The idea of the Sunday school was not new. During the eighteenth century many individuals set up small Sunday schools, such as Miss Harrison in 1765 in Bedale, North Yorkshire and Miss Ball in 1768 in High Wycombe, Buckinghamshire.[16] The institution grew under the influence of Robert Raikes in the 1780s,[17] who formalized and popularized the Sunday school concept.[18] Raikes's inspiration came from observing poor children misbehaving in Gloucester on Sundays.[19] For him there was a simple solution: he appealed for women to teach children to read and to instruct them in the Church Catechism, in order to keep them off the streets.[20] Cliff asserts that from the outset the schools aimed to provide education for the masses.[21] Griffiths argues that Sunday schools started primarily as Bible teaching institutions, and also suggests that the purpose of child evangelism emerged as an unintended consequence of

[16] W. H. Watson, *The First Fifty Years of the Sunday School* (London, 1862), 6.
[17] Cecil Northcott, *For Britain's Children: The Story of the Sunday Schools and of the National Sunday School Union* (London, 1952), 13.
[18] Griffiths, *One Generation*, 43.
[19] Northcott, *Britain's Children*, 13.
[20] Ibid. 14.
[21] Cliff, *Rise and Development*, 2.

Raikes's work in Gloucester.[22] It appears that the schools fulfilled an array of purposes. This is perhaps why they were so popular: they could respond to a range of different needs. By 1787 Raikes claimed that more than a quarter of a million children were attached to the institution.[23] Attendance peaked during the late nineteenth and early twentieth centuries.[24]

With the passage of the 1870 Education Act, Sunday schools increasingly became about religious education rather than secular education.[25] This, however, did not diminish their important educational role in working-class communities. John MacKenzie suggests that Sunday school libraries and prizes provided poor children with access to literature they otherwise would not have had.[26] In 1923 David Lloyd George argued in the *Sunday School Chronicle* (an interdenominational magazine for Sunday school teachers) that 'the university of the people is the Sunday School. Think of what they learn there. The quality of the knowledge is higher and better than anything they get elsewhere.'[27]

Sunday school workers aimed to introduce their scholars to the Bible, Christian doctrine and hymnody. Curricula throughout the period between 1900 and 1939 appear to have remained consistent in content. Schools that were affiliated with the NSSU worked through different books of the Old and New Testaments over a period of six years, to cover most of the Bible using the 'British Uniform' or 'International Lessons'.[28] These were produced by the British Uniform Lesson Committee which was associated with the World Sunday School Association and the NSSU.[29]

22 Griffiths, *One Generation*, 37.

23 Northcott, *Britain's Children*, 17.

24 Stanton, 'Raikes' Revolution', 74.

25 Stephen Orchard, 'Introduction' to idem and John Briggs, eds, *The Sunday School Movement: Studies in the Growth and Decline of Sunday Schools* (Bletchley, 2007), xiii–xix, at xvii. The impact of the Education Acts on the Sunday schools will be explored further below.

26 John MacKenzie, *Propaganda and Empire: The Manipulation of British Public Opinion 1880–1960* (Manchester, 1984), 206.

27 'The Sunday School: The People's University', *Sunday School Chronicle* (hereafter: *SSC*), 10 May 1923, 286.

28 Albert Dunning, 'Report of the International Lesson Committee', in *The World's Third Sunday School Convention: Held in London, July 11th to July 16th, 1898* (Chicago, IL, 1898), 137–40, at 137.

29 Gerald Knoff, *The World Sunday School Movement; The Story of a Broadening Mission* (New York, 1979), 35.

Denominations and organizations were encouraged to adapt the courses to suit their scholars and theological positions.[30] It is difficult to gage numerically how widely these lessons were used, although records of individual schools from across the country indicate that a wide range of schools did so.[31] Church of England Sunday schools, however, followed schemes developed by their own Sunday School Institute, not those provided by the NSSU. The Sunday School Institute voted annually on which books of the Bible would be taught, and prepared lesson material accordingly.[32]

Teachers were also encouraged to include lessons on missionary work.[33] The Sunday School Institute encouraged its schools to teach their scholars about the Prayer Book and catechisms. For instance, in 1905 it began to devise a four-year curriculum which included teaching from the Bible alongside catechisms, the Prayer Book and church seasons for schools to use.[34] The NSSU, through its publication, the *Sunday School Chronicle*, strongly encouraged workers to give lessons on temperance.[35] After the First World War, schools were provided with suggested lessons for Remembrance Sunday.[36] Sometimes, however, the curricula were not well received. In 1919 the Wesleyan Methodist Sunday School General Committee recorded that there had been dissatisfaction with the content of the morning sessions, which appeared to be nearly identical to the afternoon sessions. This was felt to be too repetitive for some scholars who might attend twice on a Sunday.[37]

[30] Cliff, *Rise and Development*, 230.

[31] Barrow-in-Furness, Barrow Archive and Local Studies Centre, BDFCBWM/11/7/1, Vickerstown Sunday School Teacher's Minute Book 1908–1922, 73 (5 February 1913); London, LMA, ACC/1361/05/002, Ferme Park Baptist Church, Sunday School Minute Book 1912–1918, 13 January 1912; Edinburgh, National Records of Scotland, CH11/21/10, Roxburgh Primitive Methodist Church, Sunday School Teacher's Minutes 1907–1916, 5 December 1912.

[32] London, CERC, SSI/2/1/10, Sunday School Institute General Committee Book 1914–1922, 384 (1 July 1919).

[33] *Church Missionary Society, Sunday School Missionary Lessons* (London, 1900), 1–7.

[34] CERC, SSI/2/1/8, Sunday School Institute General Committee Book 1900–1907, 412 (7 February 1905).

[35] 'Temperance Notes', *SSC*, 4 January 1900, 13; 'A Pledge Signing Campaign', *SSC*, 29 May 1924, 330.

[36] 'How to celebrate Armistice Sunday in the Sunday School', *SSC*, 30 October 1930, 842.

[37] Manchester, JRL, Methodist Archive, DDEy/7/1, Wesleyan Methodist Sunday School Department General Committee Minutes 1908–24, 270 (9 October 1919).

During the twentieth century, Sunday school organizations increasingly sought to improve their work by embracing developments in the fields of pedagogy and child psychology. Prominent members of the NSSU such as George Archibald Hamilton and Emily Huntley gave lectures and wrote articles which encouraged teachers to take the 'study of the child' seriously.[38] Hamilton was inspired by the work of Friedrich Froebel, whose father and uncle had both been both Lutheran pastors.[39] As Meike Baader has argued, Froebel's research, published in the late nineteenth century, 'laid chief emphasis upon the importance of the child, upon self-activity as the basis of the method of all instructions, upon natural interests as the initial point of all instruction'.[40] Froebel recalled memorizing Bible texts, hymns and the Catechism.[41] Despite the important role they had played in his life, however, he believed that 'church songs are not adapted to the understanding of children'.[42] Archibald Hamilton seems to have popularized the use of Froebel's methods amongst Sunday school and church workers.[43] He and other prominent members in the Sunday school movement argued that the most effective way to embrace the findings of child psychology studies was introduce a system of 'grading'.[44] Known as 'the Graded Movement', this method of organization argued that children should no longer be taught lessons as a whole school. Psychological research had found that children moved through distinct stages during their childhood. Children aged five and aged ten were very different; therefore, they needed lessons which were tailored to their age group.[45] Scholars were to be separated into smaller classes by age. The integration of

[38] Birmingham, CRL, National Christian Education Council (hereafter: NCEC), Part 1, D10, Volume containing annual reports for 1906–7 to 1909–10, report for 1907–8, 40; 'Studying the Child', *SSC*, 7 January 1904, 18; Miss Huntley, 'Sunday-School Work', in *Mundesley: Verbatim Report of Sermons and Lectures* (London, 1910), 185–286, at 189–99.

[39] M. Smith, 'Froebel and Religious Education', *Early Child Development and Care* 12 (1983), 303–17, at 303.

[40] Meike Baader, 'Froebel and the Rise of Education Theory in the United States', *Studies in Philosophy and Education* 23 (2004), 427–44, at 431.

[41] Smith, 'Froebel', 311.

[42] Ibid. 312.

[43] Sang-Wook Lee, Roy Evans and Peter Jackson, 'Froebel in the Sunday School Movements of England and the USA', *Early Child Development and Care* 110 (1995), 89–99, at 97.

[44] 'Studying the Child', *SSC*, 7 January 1904, 18; Miss Huntley, *Sunday-School Work*, 199–214.

[45] *The Manual of the Wesleyan Methodist Sunday School* (London, 1912), 35–6.

such methods into the life of the Sunday schools suggests that they were not as unsophisticated as some historians have suggested.

Schools gradually adopted this new system of organization.[46] By 1907, the Church of England Sunday School Institute was encouraging all its schools to teach children in accordance with their age rather than having one lesson for the whole school.[47] In later years they also provided advice as how to split the school and what should be taught in each age group.[48] Grading, however, was not taken up by all schools and some protested at its introduction. Cliff has suggested that the introduction of grading contributed to the splitting of the committee which wrote the 'British Uniform Lessons'.[49] Letters to the *Sunday School Chronicle* in 1932 complained that the system was causing decline.[50] Less experienced teachers may have felt uncomfortable with taking smaller classes by themselves, in contrast to the old system which had offered them an opportunity to learn from more experienced volunteers.[51] Additionally, during the first half of the twentieth century, Sunday school attendance was in decline.[52] Clive Field estimates that there were 6,978,159 scholars in 1901,[53] but that by 1939 this number had fallen to 4,177,000.[54] The introduction of grading in 1906 made it an easy scapegoat for some teachers.

Alongside these developments, there was also an increased emphasis on teacher training. Stanton argues that in the face of declining attendance, Sunday school organizations became preoccupied with training their workers.[55] Leaders within the Sunday school movement feared that professionally trained day school teachers would

[46] Cardiff, Glamorgan Archives, DECONG10/23, Windsor Road Congregational Church, Sunday School Teacher's Minutes 1907–28, 13 February 1907; 'The Graded Sunday School: Need for Teachers', *Burnley Express*, 23 October 1912, 6.

[47] CERC, SSI/2/1/8, General Committee Book 1900–7, 549–50 (6 November 1907).

[48] Ibid., SSI/2/1/9, General Committee Book 1907–14, 365–7 (5 December 1911).

[49] Cliff, *Sunday School Movement*, 230.

[50] Ibid. 231.

[51] Griffiths, *One Generation*, 231.

[52] Stanton, 'Raikes' Revolution', 75.

[53] Clive Field, '"The Faith Society"? Quantifying Religious Belonging in Edwardian Britain, 1901–1914', *JRH* 37(2013), 39–63, at 58.

[54] Clive Field, 'Gradualist or Revolutionary Secularization? A Case Study of Religious Belonging in Inter-War Britain, 1918–1939', *CHRC* 93(2013), 57–93, at 86.

[55] Stanton, 'Raikes' Revolution', 75.

be compared to their untrained workers.[56] It was suggested by the NSSU that all teachers should be trained in how to use the Bible in their lessons as well as in the principles of pedagogy and child psychology, so that their teaching would be more effective.[57] The NSSU founded a training college for teachers, Westhill in Selly Oak, Birmingham, in 1907 and the Church of England Sunday School Institute soon followed, opening St Christopher's College in Blackheath in 1909. Increasingly, some Sunday schools started to offer training classes for their teachers, and sought to make attendance at these classes compulsory for all teachers.[58] However, it was recognized that not all teachers could attend these lectures or classes, and Sunday school organizations and the schools themselves provided alternatives for those unable to participate. For instance, the NSSU offered a correspondence programme, with different courses for teachers to study, which culminated in an examination.[59] Likewise, the Sunday School Institute also offered correspondence courses to their teachers, including options on Sunday school organization, practical teaching and child study.[60] These attempts to educate and equip teachers demonstrate the Sunday schools' attempt to professionalize their work, suggesting that the schools were not as stagnant as some historians have argued them to be.

Sunday Schools and Education Acts

The responses of Sunday school organizers and teachers to the passage of the education acts during the first half of the twentieth century have been overlooked. Rather, historians have tended to explore the responses of church leaders and politicians.[61] During the period between 1900 and 1939 some in the Sunday school movement

[56] 'The Sunday School Teacher's Turn', *SSC*, 9 November 1922, 277.
[57] 'Sixteen Years of Sunday School Leadership', *SSC*, 12 July 1923, 431.
[58] Barrow Archive and Local Studies Centre, BDFCBWM/1/4/1, Barrow Wesleyan Methodist Circuit Sunday School Council Minute Book 1912–48, 2–3 (3 June 1912); BDFCPM/1/6, Barrow-in-Furness Primitive Methodist Circuit Sunday School Committee Minutes 1900–17, 1 September 1900.
[59] NCEC report for 1907–8, 37–9.
[60] Sunday School Institute General Purposes Committee 1907–14, 278 (6 December 1910).
[61] For example, see James Murphy, *Church, State and Schools in Britain, 1800–1970* (London, 1971); N. R. Gullifer, 'Opposition to the 1902 Education Act', *Oxford Review of Education* 8 (1982), 83–98.

expressed their displeasure at the passing of the series of education acts. This arose in part from long-standing tensions between the established and non-established churches. Nonconformists had been forced until 1868 to pay tithes and contribute to church rates.[62] However, the provision and oversight of education, including the licensing of teachers, had remained under the control of the established church.[63] James Munson has contended that by this time the Nonconformists were strongly committed to the school board system. The boards had educated many Nonconformists and given ministers opportunities to engage in political work in their towns.[64] Any change to this system was not going to be well received in Nonconformist circles. The 1902 act dissolved school boards and created local education authorities, which would be managed by county councils and county borough councils.[65] Nonconformists and others also opposed proposals, such as one which would give rate aid to all denominational schools, which was viewed as offering a permanent subsidy to the established churches in England and Wales and to the Roman Catholic Church.[66] Some Sunday school teachers viewed this provision as nothing other than an attempt to reinforce the Church of England's control of education. For example, an article in the *Sunday School Chronicle* argued that 'all who have studied the Government Bill must be aware that this principle has shaped it from beginning to end. It is in truth a Bishops' Bill.'[67] Likewise, some individual Sunday schools voiced their dissatisfaction at the act. Teachers at Splott Road Baptist Sunday school in Cardiff objected that those not belonging to the established church had not been given a voice or a vote concerning the act; they felt that it would hinder their scholars from entering the teaching profession.[68]

Other education acts, such as those passed in 1918 (raising the school leaving age to fourteen) and 1921 (consolidating previous acts), were similarly unpopular with many involved in Sunday school work, especially those who felt that their work was being

[62] Murphy, *Church, State and Schools*, 2.
[63] Ibid. 1.
[64] James Munson, *The Nonconformists: In Search of a Lost Culture* (London, 1991), 246.
[65] Murphy, *Church, State and Schools*, 92.
[66] Ibid. 90.
[67] 'The Rights of the Child', *SSC*, 5 June 1902, 397.
[68] Glamorgan Archives, DBAP49/3/1, Splott Road Baptist Church, Sunday School Minute Book 1896–1911, 30 September 1902.

undermined. Indeed, Prochaska has argued that the expansion of the government into education, traditionally provided by the churches, contributed to Christian decline through a dilution of religious teaching as the state encroached upon the monopoly of Sunday schools regarding religious education.[69] Day school teachers with professional training were increasingly set against Sunday school teachers who were volunteers. State provision of education could be blamed for the decline in Sunday school and church attendance. In 1918, the *Sunday School Chronicle* published an article in which an interviewee expressed the fear that 'the new education act will tend to empty Sunday School and Church still further'.[70] In 1922 another article argued that with the introduction of compulsory education, Sunday school teachers 'felt sorely handicapped in the competition with the standard set by the professional teacher, and not unnaturally felt ill at ease when their pupils were comparing their Sunday treatment with the precision of day school manipulation'.[71] As Stanton suggests, the education provided (or subsidized by) by the state surpassed what the Sunday schools could offer. Moreover, most parents were satisfied with the religious education their children received at day school.[72] The provision of religious education in day schools in part explains why the influence of the Sunday schools declined in twentieth-century Britain. The state had simply put them out of a job.[73]

However, not all those involved in the Sunday school movement saw the 1902 act in so bad a light. Rather, some saw it as providing an opportunity to provide their scholars with a better education. Revd Allan Cameron concluded:

> Their Sunday school teachers and their churches were much indebted to the work done by the teachers in our public schools. The great aim of Sunday school work was not so much to fill the minds of the children with learning as to make them grow up good, Christian young men and women and good citizens.[74]

[69] Prochaska, *Christianity and Social Service*, 150.
[70] 'The Education Act: Are the Churches Preparing', *SSC*, 5 December 1918, 583.
[71] 'The Sunday School Teacher's Turn', *SSC*, 9 November 1922, 277.
[72] Stanton, 'Raikes' Revolution', 75.
[73] On the interplay between church day schools and Sunday schools, see, in this volume, Grant Masom, 'Fighting the Tide: Church Schools in South Buckinghamshire, 1902–44', 545–60.
[74] 'Sunday School Convention', *Aberdeen Press and Journal*, 19 September 1910, 6.

Others felt that the schools could support the work of the state. Ernest Hayes, a prominent member of the NSSU, argued in 1930 that:

> To-day the State has rightly assumed the responsibility of the education and physical care of the child, and helps him in adolescence in vocational and recreative directions. But what the State is doing would be much better done, and a great deal added to it, if those carrying on Raikes's work in the Sunday schools took a zealous and well-informed interest in these so-called secular matters.[75]

Even the *Sunday School Chronicle* embraced the opportunities that came with these changes for Sunday schools. One writer remarked:

> When the State has definitely and finally placed the sacred duty of the religious training of the young upon the Home and the Churches, … [they] will be required to make more of their Sunday Schools, financing them and equipping them with greater liberality, supplying them with more teachers, and contributing of their best to their best investment.[76]

There was thus a feeling amongst some Sunday school workers that the education acts made their work more important, not less. In turn they hoped that this would mean that the churches would put more effort and resources into the schools.

The Churches and Sunday Schools

During the period between 1900 and 1939 relationships between the Sunday schools and the churches were not always harmonious. The archbishop of Canterbury's Committee on Sunday Schools in 1912 concluded: 'the last reflection suggested by the returns is that Nonconformists are making their Sunday schools a success because they believe in them while amongst our clergy a large number regards them as a necessary evil, and perhaps the majority have no ideals whatever in connection with them'.[77] Some in the Sunday school movement also believed that the churches were not doing enough

[75] Ernest Hayes, *Raikes the Pioneer: Founder of Sunday* Schools (London, 1930), 122.

[76] 'The Education Bill: The Opportunity of the Sunday School', *SSC*, 11 December 1902, 851.

[77] London, LPL, Davidson papers, vol. 496, fol. 165.

to support the work of the schools. For instance, a NSSU publication claimed:

> we still find the Sunday school movement despised and neglected by Christian people who ought to know better. Too often Church officials and members are absolutely indifferent to the work being done among the children and it is customary to regard the Sunday school as beneath the support of respectable middle-class people.[78]

Those in leadership positions in the churches did not always appreciate or value the work of the schools.

Some of these tensions may have arisen from the fact that running a Sunday school was a costly venture. Sunday school prizes and gifts were the some of the biggest financial drains on the schools. Revd A. Lawley told one of Charles Booth's researchers that he valued Sunday schools, but when he had first taken the church over it was £3,000 in debt because of the spending on treats and prizes.[79] However, the main source of tension was control. As Stanton and Griffiths highlight, the schools had started as a venture that was independent from the churches.[80] Some were concerned that children would attend Sunday schools rather than church services, and, as the bishop of Exeter, Archibald Robertson, argued, 'it would be looking for far too much from the Sunday school to expect of it any kind of substitute for Church going'.[81] It was only in 1918 that Easter Day communicants surpassed Sunday school attendance in the Church of England,[82] and until the mid-twentieth century Sunday school attendance generally surpassed church membership in most Nonconformist denominations.[83] Moreover, although it was not

[78] CRL, NCEC, Part 1, D157, Guidance Leaflet for the Sunday School Advance Campaign (*c.*1930s), 'Sunday School Advance: The Adolescent Campaign, Your Sunday School Job: A Survey and a Challenge', 4.

[79] London, London School of Economics, Booth/B350, 'George H. Duckworth's Notebook: Police and Publican District 7 [Mile End Old Town and Spitalfields], District 8 [Aldgate, St George's in the East, Shadwell], District 9 [Bethnal Green, North and South], District 10 [Bethnal Green East], District 11 [Poplar and Limehouse]' (online edn, 2016), 122, at: <http://booth.lse.ac.uk/notebooks/b350#?cv=61&c=0&m=0&s=0&z=-18.679%2C0%2C2493.358%2C1483>, accessed 29 December 2016.

[80] Stanton, 'Raikes' Revolution', 78; Griffiths, *One Generation from Extinction*, 268.

[81] 'Sunday Schools Conference at Exeter', *Exeter and Plymouth Gazette*, 10 April 1913, 4.

[82] Robert Currie, Alan Gilbert and Lee Horsley, *Churches and Churchgoers: Patterns of Church Growth in the British Isles since 1700* (Oxford, 1977), 128–9, 167.

[83] Ibid. 133–4, 169–70, 172–3, 142–3, 178–9, 149–50, 181–90.

the intended purpose of the schools, Griffiths has suggested that they became indirect recruiters for church membership,[84] and Thompson and Doreen Rosman indicate that there was an increasing expectation from the churches that Sunday schools would provide them with new members.[85] As Rosman has highlighted, however, many of those who passed through the Sunday schools did not become regular worshippers.[86] When scholars did not transfer into membership, frustration was expressed in the churches. Thompson's analysis strikingly inverts this problem: 'the fact was that the Sunday schools were successfully engaging large numbers of young people well into the twentieth century – but the churches were failing to attract them into Church membership'.[87]

There was, nonetheless, an improvement in relations during this period. In 1903, Randall Davidson, the archbishop of Canterbury, wrote a glowing review of the work of the Church of England's Sunday School Institution:

> I have no hesitation in saying that I regard the work promoted by the Institute as of absolutely paramount importance at the present moment. … knowing as I do how faithfully and effectively the Institute has laboured for many years past in facilitating that work, and providing help to teachers and scholars alike, I shall be thankful to know that it is now obtaining the increased support and encouragement which it eminently deserves.[88]

The Church of England's Church Assembly Report on Religious Education in 1929 concluded: 'The Sunday School has sometimes been regarded as a necessary but burdensome and expensive part of the organisation of a self-respecting parish. It is coming to be used and enjoyed as an opportunity for one of the most effective kinds of service.'[89] Similarly, also in 1929, the Wesleyan Methodist Church praised its Sunday Schools, affirming that 'we have

[84] Griffiths, *One Generation*, 46.
[85] Thompson, *Young People*, 32; Doreen Rosman, 'Sunday Schools and Social Change in the Twentieth Century', in Orchard and Briggs, eds, *Sunday School Movement*, 149–60, at 151.
[86] Rosman, 'Sunday Schools', 151.
[87] Thompson, *Young People*, 44.
[88] LPL, Davidson papers, vol. 88, fol. 57 (18 February 1903).
[89] *Church Assembly Report of the Commission on Religious Education appointed by the Archbishops of Canterbury and York* (London, 1929), 18.

wonderfully efficient organizations and institutions in the Sunday School … . The influence of all this work is magnificent'.[90] Slowly throughout this period Sunday schools, rather than being on the periphery of the churches, became central to their work. These examples also illustrate that the churches believed the work of the schools to be effective.

Conclusion

This article has argued that Sunday schools played a significant role as the educational arms of the churches. The statistics concerning the schools at the beginning of the twentieth century demonstrate how widely children attended the schools. This was where many children were exposed to Christian hymnody and doctrine. The article has argued that rather than being unsophisticated, the education offered at the schools attempted to expose scholars to the Bible, Christian faith and doctrine and missionary work. Sunday school curricula were produced for teachers to help guide their scholars through the Bible and included lessons about other themes, such as missionary work. In the early twentieth century, these curricula were adapted according to developments in pedagogy and child psychology, and scholars were separated into age groups. Moreover, Sunday schools did not remain stagnant in their methods: Sunday school unions and associations (and to some extent their teachers) were prepared to experiment to provide the most effective education for their scholars. However, these changes were not always greeted with enthusiasm.

Sunday schools saw their monopoly on education, especially religious education, challenged with the introduction of a more comprehensive system of compulsory schooling. Some teachers felt that this would benefit their work as they could focus on providing children with a religious education. Some also believed that these changes would result in more support from the churches. The article has also considered some of the tensions that arose between the churches and the schools. There were issues regarding the cost of the schools but also regarding their control. Nevertheless, during the first half of the twentieth century the churches increasingly supported the work

[90] H. J. Holloway, 'The Church's Attitude to the Youth of To-Day', in *Methodism: Its Present Responsibilities. The Proceedings of the Methodist Church Congress* (London, 1929), 111–15, at 112.

of the schools and believed it to be an important part of their work rather than a burdensome venture. Sunday school teachers and those within the churches felt that the schools were offering a good religious education to their scholars. The evidence presented challenges the widely held assumption by historians that the schools were ineffective tools of religious socialization. Sunday schools played an integral role in educating a large proportion of the British population in the tenets and language of Christianity. They deserve a more thorough appreciation by historians of religion.

Western Establishment or Chinese Sovereignty? The Tientsin Anglo-Chinese College during the Restore Educational Rights Movement, 1924–7

Marina Xiaojing Wang*
Chinese University of Hong Kong

The 1920s were a vital period for the evolution of Christianity in China, during which the Anti-Christian Movement of 1922–7 brought Christianity under serious attack. A new conception of nationalism, influenced by Lenin's theory of imperialism, dramatically changed the way in which Christianity (and especially mission schools) was regarded, from being viewed as a positive factor in China's modernization to being seen as a hated cultural imperialist invasion. The period from 1924 to 1927 featured the demand for the restoration of educational rights, during which the identity of mission schools was used to stir up nationalist hatred. This article takes Tientsin Anglo-Chinese College (TACC) of the London Missionary Society (LMS) as a case study. It examines how the TACC missionary authorities responded to nationalistic sentiments emerging within the college and in society, and how they reacted towards the compulsory registration and consequent abolition of compulsory school religious education. It explores key issues behind the interaction between mission schools and the socio-political context, such as how TACC reconstructed its identity during the process of school registration, and how it negotiated with the Ministry of Education under the tension between two divergent approaches of Christianizing and nationalizing mission schools, a tension which became acute as a consequence of the application of regulations making school religious education and practice optional.

In 1922, the Committee of Reference and Counsel of the Foreign Missions Conference of North America published a detailed report based on a survey of Christian education in China, which strongly urged mission schools in China to become 'Chinese' as soon as possible:

> The Christian schools must also as rapidly as possible divest themselves of their foreign character … . It must be remembered that Chinese Christians are Chinese as well as Christian, and that the very patriotism

* Divinity School of Chung Chi College, Chinese University of Hong Kong, Shatin, N. T. Hong Kong. E-Mail: marina.xj.wang@gmail.com.

Studies in Church History 55 (2019), 577–592
doi: 10.1017/stc.2018.25

> which Christianity tends to produce will draw them away from a school whose atmosphere is foreign and to one that is Chinese. It is not wise to compel them to choose between these alternatives … .
>
> Thoroughly Christian in its character and thoroughly Chinese in its atmosphere, raised to a high level of efficiency, it can render a service which a school lacking any of these characteristics cannot at all perform.[1]

In the same year, the Anti-Christian Movement broke out in response to a conference of the World Student Christian Federation on 4 April at Tsinghua University, Beijing. This movement brought Christianity under serious attack. Provoked by political disintegration resulting from conflict between warlords, and by the unfavourable position of the country internationally, a result of Western interference, a new ideological conception of nationalism arose among Chinese intelligentsia and soon spread nationwide. Under the influence of Lenin's theory of imperialism, this modern nationalism dramatically changed the image of Christianity: from being viewed as a positive factor in China's modernization, it began to be rejected as a hated cultural imperialist encroachment.[2] The period from 1924 to 1927 featured demands for the restoration of educational rights as well as customs rights and extraterritorial rights, and the identity of mission schools began to fuel the hatred of nationalists in republican China. In its survey of Christian education and the socio-political context in China, the American Committee of Reference and Counsel seems already to have sensed the uneasy tension between mission schools and Chinese nationalists, and its recommendation can be seen as an attempt to turn the tide before the conflict was exacerbated still further.

This article takes Tientsin Anglo-Chinese College (TACC) of the London Missionary Society (LMS) as a case study.[3] It examines how

[1] Committee of Reference and Counsel of the Foreign Missions Conference of North America, *Christian Education in China: A Study made by an Educational Commission representing the Mission Boards and Societies conducting Work in China* (New York, 1922), 14.

[2] Daniel H. Bays, 'Foreign Missions and Indigenous Protestant Leaders in China, 1920–1955: Identity and Loyalty in an Age of Powerful Nationalism', in Brian Stanley and Alaine Low, eds, *Missions, Nationalism, and the End of Empire*, SHCM (Grand Rapids, MI, 2003), 144–64, at 146; R. Po-Chia Hsia, 'Christianity and Empire: The Catholic Mission in Late Imperial China', in Stewart J. Brown, Charlotte Methuen and Andrew Spicer, eds, *The Church and Empire*, SCH 54 (Cambridge, 2018), 208–24, at 223.

[3] This article uses the Pinyin system to spell the names of Chinese persons, places and church organizations, but keeps Wade-Giles spellings for those fixed as historical terms, such as Tientsin Anglo-Chinese College.

the TACC authorities responded to nationalist sentiments emerging during this period, and how they reacted to the forced registration of schools and the subsequent removal of compulsory religious education. Particular attention is paid to the tension between the identity of mission schools and the quest for strong national sovereignty in Chinese society, and to the conflict between two divergent trends of Christianizing and nationalizing education in early twentieth-century China. The college self-identified as the representative of British education in China; its image as foreign, together with that of other Christian colleges and schools, became one of the major sources of Chinese nationalist resentment. This article argues, however, that other factors, such as the college's location, its local social network and the composition of its student body, also played a part in the college's negotiations with the nationalist government. The case of TACC reflects the complexity of the experiences of Christian schools in the midst of nationalist challenges. This has not been thoroughly explored in scholarship on the interaction between Christian schools and Chinese nationalism.[4]

British Identity meets Chinese Sovereignty: TACC during the Anti-Christian Movement

A by-product of the LMS's mission work in north China, the forerunner of TACC was founded by Jonathan Lees (1835–1902) in Tianjin in 1863, under the name 'Theological Institute in Tianjin' (天津養

[4] Studies on the topic of Christian schools and Chinese nationalism include Jessie Gregory Lutz, *China and the Christian Colleges, 1850–1950* (New York, 1971); eadem, *Chinese Politics and Christian Missions: The Anti-Christian Movement of 1922–1928* (Notre Dame, IN, 1988); Yip Ka-che, *Religion, Nationalism and Chinese Students: The Anti-Christian Movement of 1922–1927* (Washington DC, 1980); Daniel H. Bays and Ellen Widmer, eds, *China's Christian Colleges: Cross-Cultural Connections, 1900–1950* (Stanford, CA, 2009); 胡衛清 [Hu Weiqing], 普遍主義的挑戰： 近代中國基督教教育研究 (1877–1927) [*Pubian Zhuyi de Tiaozhan: Jindai Zhongguo Jidujiao Jiaoyu Yanjiu (1877–1927)*; *The Challenge of Universalism: A Study of Modern Christian Education in China*] (Shanghai, 2000); 尹文涓 [Yin Wenjuan], ed., 基督教與中國近代中等教育 [*Jidujiao yu Zhongguo Jindai Zhongdeng Jiaoyu*; *Christianity and Modern Secondary Education in China*] (Shanghai, 2007); 徐以驊 [Xu Yihua], 中國基督教教育史論 [*Zhongguo Jidujiao Jiaoyu Shilun*; *A History of Christian Education in China*] (Guilin, 2010); 周東華 [Zhou Donghua], 民國浙江基督教教育研究 [*Minguo Zhejiang Jidujiao Jiaoyu Yanjiu*; *A Study of Christian Education in Zhejiang in the Republican Era*] (Beijing, 2011).

正聖經學院), with the purpose of training native Christian workers.[5] During the 1890s, it underwent a process of reconstruction and enlargement under Samuel Lavington Hart (1858–1951), and developed into a college equipped with advanced Western facilities.[6] When it reopened in 1902 after the Boxer Uprising, the college adopted the name 'Tientsin Anglo-Chinese College' (天津新學書院) in response to Hart's vision. It aimed 'to meet the desire for Western Learning' and 'to give a liberal education, based on Christian principles, to the class of Students who would otherwise be out of touch with ordinary Missionary effort'.[7] TACC was opened up to large numbers of non-Christian families and moved towards becoming a college of higher education. It thus differed from most Christian universities and colleges in republican China, which had their origins in nineteenth-century mission schools aiming to provide students with both knowledge of the Bible and a general education. The college's development from a theological seminary, whose specific purpose had been to train native church workers, to a modern college reflects an exceptional case in the history of Christian education in China.[8] In 1918, however, the collegiate department of TACC, which offered degree courses in arts, science and engineering, was transferred to the newly established Yenching University in Beijing. From that point on, TACC existed as a middle school.[9] During the 1920s, when the Anti-Christian Movement broke out,

[5] Jonathan Lees, 'The Tientsin and Peking Missions', in *The China Mission Hand-book*, 2 parts in 1 vol. (Taipei, 1973; first publ. 1896), part 2, 18–20, at 20.

[6] When the renovation work was completed in 1898, the college had a museum and several laboratories, as well as a good range of scientific equipment, such as a telescope, telephonic and telegraphic instruments and X-ray apparatus: London, School of Oriental and African Studies Library (hereafter: SOAS), Special Collections, Council for World Mission (hereafter: CWM), China, Personals, Box 11, S. Lavington Hart, 'Looking Back Seventy-Five Years'; CWM, LMS, North China Reports, Box 3 (1892–7), no. 5809, Arrival no. 8623, S. Lavington Hart, Tientsin, 14 March 1898; 'The Walford Hart Memorial College', *Chronicle of the London Missionary Society* (1898), 209–13.

[7] North China Reports, Box 8 (1915–21), The Tientsin Anglo-Chinese College, 1902–1921.

[8] For the early history of the Theological Institute in Tianjin and its transformation into TACC, see Marina Xiaojing Wang, 'The Best Method of selecting and training Native Preachers: A Study on the Evolution of the Theological Institute in Tianjin (1863–1902)', *Sino-Christian Studies: An International Journal of Bible, Theology and Philosophy* 23 (2017), 7–40.

[9] North China Reports, Box 11 (1932–6), Memorandum on the Work, Policy and Future of the Tientsin Anglo-Chinese College, 1936, 4.

TACC ranked prominently amongst the educational institutions in Tianjin, with an enrolment of 555 students.[10] Its graduates proved competitive in the job market, and a considerable number worked in the customs service, in the postal service, on the railways and in the bureau of mines in Tianjin and elsewhere, while others pursued further study overseas or taught in TACC and other Christian schools and colleges.[11]

Hart successfully turned the institute into a modern college of higher education. However, faced by the appeal to all Christian schools in China to 'become as rapidly as possible thoroughly Chinese',[12] the TACC authorities seem to have failed to meet this call. The origins and development of the college, for Hart and other TACC missionary staff, had given it a symbolic significance, and in particular a 'unique position' as representing British education:

> The TACC … stands alone as the representative of *British* education in the North of China, excluding Peking and Mukden … .
>
> Returning to the unique position which the TACC must take up as the representative of *British* Education, the need to increase the present diminished staff is evident.[13]

Twenty years after its establishment, therefore, the college was still proudly emphasizing its British identity.[14] This contradicted the increasingly nationalist tone of Chinese society, and would be seriously challenged by the Anti-Christian Movement.

[10] In Tianjin, there were Peiyang University, which was established by the government, with 150 students of college grade, the Technological College (300), the Naval Medical College (60), the Law School (150) and Nankai University, with 1,200 students of all grades: North China Reports, Box 9 (1922–7), Newsletter from Dr and Mrs E. J. Stuckey, Tientsin, 1923, 12.

[11] 張紹祖 [Zhang Shaozu], 天津新學書院簡史 ['Tianjin Xinxue Shuyuan Jianshi'; 'A Brief History of TACC'], 天津和平區文史資料選輯 [*Tianjin Heping Qu Wenshi Ziliao Xuanji*; *A Collection of the Historical Sources of the Heping District in Tianjin*] 2 (1989), 49–62, at 55, 61–2; 涂培元 [Tu Peiyuan], 天津新學書院的形形色色 ['Tianjin Xinxue Shuyuan de Xingxingsese'; 'A History of TACC'], in 文史資料存稿選編 [*Wenshi Ziliao Cungao Xuanbian*; *A Collection of the Available Historical Sources*], 26 vols (Beijing, 2002), 23: 477–88, at 479.

[12] Foreign Missions Conference, *Christian Education in China*, 14.

[13] North China Reports, Box 9, S. Lavington Hart, Report for the Year 1922, 1–2 (my emphasis).

[14] Ibid., Box 10 (1928–31), S. Lavington Hart, Report for the Year 1928, 2.

During its first stage in 1922, this movement developed into a broader campaign to oppose all religions and to achieve social progress through the advancement of science.[15] According to A. P. Cullen, a member of the TACC staff, in this period there were elements 'distinctly hostile to Christian influences' among the students.[16] A magazine was issued, in which students criticized foreign missionaries as being 'Government propagandists' of the West, whose intention was the 'ultimate enslavement and destruction' of China.[17] Nonetheless, for Cullen and other TACC missionary staff, this anti-Christian tide seemed to have died down very quickly.[18] It thus attracted little of their attention.

A sudden change of circumstances occurred after 1924, when churches and mission schools were denounced as agents of foreign cultural aggression. According to Hart's annual report to the LMS, not only students but also staff and teachers in several schools in Tianjin became 'active agents' during the disturbance. A good number of them were influenced by Soviet propaganda on imperial cultural aggression, as well as Sun Yat-sen's nationalist cry, 'China for the Chinese'.[19] Christian school authorities and their Christian influences became the main targets of challenge and resistance.[20] Statements made during a number of meetings of Chinese educational institutes criticized Western 'interference' in China's educational policy. Some of the institutes passed resolutions attempting to condemn missionary educational methods and to abolish religious instruction in schools. Even at a conference of Christian educators in Beijing in 1924, criticism of Western education and mission schools in China could be heard.[21]

The Anti-Christian Movement was pushed to its climax by the 'May Thirtieth Incident' in 1925, the death of thirteen Chinese

[15] Lutz, *Chinese Politics*, 281–2; Jonathan T'ien-en Chao, 'The Chinese Indigenous Church Movement, 1919–1927: A Protestant Response to the Anti-Christian Movement in Modern China' (PhD dissertation, University of Pennsylvania, 1986), 170; 張欽士 [Zhang Qinshi], 國內近十年來之宗教思潮 [*Guonei Jin Shinian Lai zhi Zongjiao Sichao*; *Religious Thought Movements in China during the Last Decade*] (Beijing, 1927), 193–6.

[16] North China Reports, Box 9, A. P. Cullen, Annual Report 1922, 4.

[17] Ibid. 6.

[18] Ibid. 7.

[19] North China Reports, Box 9, S. Lavington Hart, Report for 1924, 1–2.

[20] Ibid. 2.

[21] Ibid. 3–4.

students fired on by British policemen in Shanghai.[22] This sparked off the spread of anti-foreign sentiment throughout the country. While students and other young people became increasingly politicized after the incident, leftists successfully transformed the anti-Christian sentiment into an anti-imperialist one. Chinese nationalists turned their attention to the issues of the unequal treaties between China and its international partners and to the educational rights of mission schools. A large number of urban Chinese Christians, particularly mission school students, took part in patriotic campaigns and protests.[23] Hart regarded 1925 as 'the most anxious of all the years in the history of the College'.[24] There were strikes at TACC in June, when students refused to take classes and demanded that the college authorities issue a statement expressing solidarity with the Chinese. Some students left to join Li Ming (Dawn) School, a newly established college in Beijing, which took an oppositional stance against TACC and other Christian schools.[25] TACC, like all other Christian schools and churches in China, experienced an identity crisis in the face of these nationalist challenges.

During this period, Christian education was condemned as an intrusion on 'national sovereignty' and religious freedom.[26] In October 1923, the Young China Association, a key promoter of nationalist campaigns, issued a declaration advocating 'nationalist education' aimed at fostering patriotic sentiments amongst the Chinese. Christian education was rejected as a type of cultural invasion or 'de-nationalization', leading to the loss of national consciousness and identity among students.[27] Education was thus viewed as an inseparable aspect of 'national sovereignty'. Jessie Lutz argues that a fundamental factor behind this mentality was the concept that the main function of education, including Christian education, was to

[22] For details of the 'May Thirtieth Incident', see Hung-Ting Ku, 'Urban Mass Movement: The May Thirtieth Movement in Shanghai', *Modern Asian Studies* 13 (1979), 197–216.
[23] Lutz, *Chinese Politics*, 160–5, 170–3.
[24] North China Reports, Box 9, S. Lavington Hart, Report for 1925, 1; ibid., C. H. B. Longman, Report for 1925, 3–4.
[25] Hart, Report for 1925, 2–4; Zhang, 'Jianshi', 59–60.
[26] Lutz, *China and Christian Colleges*, 232–3.
[27] 陳啟天 [Chen Qitian], 新國家主義與中國前途 ['Xin Guojia Zhuyi yu Zhongguo Qiantu'; 'New Nationalism and China's Future'], 少年中國 [*Shaonian Zhongguo*; *Young China*] 4/9 (1924), 1–13, at 8–9.

'serve the state'.[28] Christian education, therefore, needed to be under Chinese control in order to serve national purposes. To reclaim educational rights from foreign educational establishments was, in nationalist thinking, equivalent to defending national sovereignty. They began, therefore, to call for Christian schools to be registered with the government.

Sinicization and De-Christianization: TACC's Process of School Registration

On 16 November 1925, the Beijing Board of Education issued 'Regulations Governing the Recognition of Educational Institutions Established by Funds Contributed from Foreigners'. This required mission schools to be registered: to do so, they had to have Chinese principals or vice-principals; the curriculum must conform to Ministry of Education standards; there should be no compulsion to attend religious ceremonies; and no course in religion should be included amongst the compulsory subjects.[29]

The attitude of the TACC authorities in 1925 remained very suspicious towards registration, and the college seemed sceptical about the process and reluctant to engage with it:

> Will there be room for a College such as ours when the Chinese take full control of the education in their country? There will not be room for many of our institutions; they will have to be absorbed in the general national scheme of education. First may come the necessity to undergo Registration, with such safeguards as can be agreed upon. Then will come the rivalry of Government institutions, and the favour shown to those who are learning in them. The next phase may be the difficulty in making ends meet, and finally the closing down of many of the schools that have done splendid work up to the present.[30]

The college authorities were aware, however, of the fact that there would be a heavy price to pay for non-registration: 'If the power of the Cantonese spreads northwards, we may have to face the alternative as to whether we accept the principles of Sun Yat Sun [Sun

[28] Lutz, *China and Christian Colleges*, 232.

[29] SOAS, Conference of British Missionary Societies 348, National Christian Council (hereafter: NCC) Annual Report 1925–6, 196–211.

[30] North China Reports, Box 9, S. Lavington Hart, Report for 1926, 7.

Yat-sen] and are willing to place him in the highest pinnacle of honour, or close our College for good.'[31]

During the North Expedition of 1926–8, large numbers of Christian schools and colleges came under serious nationalist attack, and the government continued to urge schools to register in accordance with the regulations. At the 1926 annual conference of the National Christian Council of China (NCC), the committee on religious education emphasized the need for school registration:

> The disadvantages of non-registration will be so serious for middle schools and colleges that every effort must be made to retrieve whatever loss in opportunity for religious education may be involved in registration. Manifestly an added responsibility will fall on the Church to meet this loss by providing a more adequate programme of religious education.[32]

Under these circumstances, TACC was obliged to take action to prepare for registration. Its first step, in 1927, was to draft a new constitution, according to which the college was placed under control of a court of governors, consisting of prominent Chinese and British residents of Tianjin.[33] The court of governors then elected a management board to administer college affairs; this was composed of six Chinese and five British members.[34]

Anti-Christian sentiments lessened in intensity during 1927–8. However, measures to ensure state control over education had just begun. The National Government of the Republic of China in Nanjing, established in 1927, and the Chinese Educational Bureau, established in 1928, both made school registration mandatory and accelerated its pace. Although in the early 1920s there had been strong nationalist appeals for mission school registration and

[31] Ibid. 6.

[32] NCC Annual Report 1925–6, 151–2.

[33] The court of governors included three times as many Chinese as British, amongst them Yan Huiqing [顏惠慶], ex-premier of the Republic; Liang Ruhao [梁如浩], ex-minister of foreign affairs; Huang Rongliang [黃榮良], formerly minister to New Zealand, Australia and Austria; an ex-chancellor of the exchequer, possibly Zhou Xuexi [周學熙]; and James William Jamieson, the British consul-general; as well as British bank managers and the chairman and members of the British Municipal Council: North China Reports, Box 10, A. P. Cullen, Decennial Review 1920–1930, 17; Tu, 'Xingxingsese', 483.

[34] North China Reports, Box 9, C. H. B. Longman, Report for 1927, 3; ibid., A. P. Cullen, Report for 1927, 3.

two separate governments to apply this policy, in the north (the Beiyang Government) and the south (the Guomindang [GMD] Government), there was no centralized governmental authority which could have enforced a unified implementation of registration.

One of TACC's chief concerns in 1928 was its application for registration. The new government regulations had made it impossible for the college to send graduates to Yenching University unless it was registered with the Chinese Educational Bureau.[35] The process of registration as reported by Hart was not pleasant. The Chinese Educational Bureau was determined to force the college to change some of its educational methods and amend a number of its regulations. Above all, it demanded that the college abandon its 'foreign headship', a requirement of all mission school registration.[36] Nationalists intended to use school registration to achieve the twin goals of the 'sinicization' and 'de-Christianization' of mission schools.[37] Ideological control over mission schools was high on the agenda. Hart reported that the Educational Bureau required full information about all teaching members of the college, including information about where they had been trained, and whether they had been trained according to the principles of the GMD, the 'Three Principles of the People'.[38] It also assigned teachers who had been trained under the 'Three Principles of the People' to teach in the college, and Chinese drill sergeants to provide students with military training.[39]

Registration only proved possible after Hart's retirement, which obliged the college to find a successor and enabled it to appoint a Chinese principal, thus fulfilling the registration requirements. However, Hart and other TACC missionary staff believed that the principal should be a 'British-trained' Christian, who would preserve the college's British traditions and spirit.[40] Moreover, the TACC missionaries were convinced that to 'take the place of Dr. Hart was

[35] Hart, Report for 1928, 1.
[36] Ibid. 1.
[37] Zhou, *Zhejiang Jidujiao Jiaoyu*, 82.
[38] The 'Three Principles of the People', also known as Sanmin Zhuyi (三民主義), refer to the principles of *Minzu* (nationalism, 民族), *Minquan* (popular sovereignty / democracy, 民權) and *Minsheng* (people's livelihood, 民生). These were developed by Sun Yat-sen to express his revolutionary ideas and served as the fundamental doctrines of the GMD: Sun Yat-sen, *San Min Chu I: The Three Principles of the People* (Shanghai, 1927).
[39] Hart, Report for 1928, 1–2.
[40] Ibid. 4.

a manifest impossibility'. They therefore intended to 'satisfy Chinese feelings' by appointing an honorary principal or president, who would have no share in the ordinary internal affairs of the college, but would be held in high esteem by society.[41] In 1929, after Hart's retirement, Huang Rongliang (Y. L. Hwang, 黃榮良) accepted the invitation to serve as honorary principal. According to Cullen, Huang had not only been educated in universities both in China and overseas, but had also served since 1909 as the Chinese minister (equivalent to ambassador) to New Zealand, Australia and Austria.[42] There can be no doubt that Huang's experience met the criteria set by the TACC missionaries. The college's registration was completed in April 1930, soon after Huang took up the position of honorary principal at the beginning of the 1929–30 academic session.[43] However, Huang tendered his resignation in September 1930, only a few months after registration was completed. The college failed to find 'another gentleman willing to act' as honorary principal, and Ma Shanggong (S. K. Ma, 馬尚功), the vice-principal, was appointed acting principal of the college.[44] It was not until 1942, after the outbreak of the Pacific War, when foreigners were interned by Japanese troops, that the Chinese principal really took charge of college affairs.[45] The exact reason behind Huang's resignation remains unclear from the available sources. According to C. H. B. Longman, a LMS missionary and a member of the TACC staff, the position of honorary principal 'demands more time and attention than Mr. Hwang [Huang] felt able to give, if he is to be well acquainted with the working of the College and have real authority'.[46] However, Cullen's confidential report to the LMS in 1929 may reveal Huang's real concern:

> He [Huang] is not altogether satisfied with the arrangement … . He feels that he is not sufficiently 'Principal' to be in a position to cope with these things [knotty college affairs], and not sufficiently 'Honorary' to be able to disregard them or delegate them to those

[41] Ibid. 4–5; North China Reports, Box 10, A. P. Cullen, Report for 1928, 5; idem, Report for 1929, 2.
[42] Zhang, 'Jianshi', 51.
[43] North China Reports, Box 10, C. H. B. Longman, Report for 1930, 1.
[44] Ibid. 2.
[45] Tu, 'Xingxingsese', 486.
[46] Longman, Report for 1930, 2.

more intimately acquainted with the ordinary methods of procedure.[47]

One alumnus recalls that Huang's resignation was rather a response to a contretemps with Longman.[48]

As discussed above, besides the aim of sinicizing Christian schools, the other important objective of the nationalist government was to de-Christianize them through forbidding compulsory religious activities and classes. According to the report of the China Christian Educational Association in 1926, Christian school authorities and Chinese Christian educators generally agreed that schools should accept the regulations and register with the government. However, they had deep reservations about the regulation which made religious education and practice optional in schools.[49] The cost of acceptance was that the distinctively Christian characteristics of the schools would be much weakened and even lost. It therefore became a central concern for Christian educators.

In this area, however, TACC seems not to have encountered as many obstacles as most other Christian colleges and universities, for most of its religious activities had been on a voluntary basis for some time.[50] Hart had reported that voluntary 'Bible Circles' (Bible classes) were held in almost all year groups, with a total enrolment of 173 students. The daily assembly for morning prayers was voluntary in theory, but had full attendance in practice. As a college open to non-Christians, in 1930 the percentage of Christian students in the college was recorded as 10.4 per cent. In some year groups, however, the percentage of Christian students was as high as 46 per cent.[51]

On the whole, TACC's registration, although undertaken reluctantly, met no major obstacles. The college was not as seriously affected by the anti-Christian campaigns as other Christian schools and colleges, some of which – such as Nankai University in Tianjin, St John's University in Shanghai and Holy Trinity College

[47] Cullen, Report for 1929, 5.

[48] According to Tu Peiyuan's account of the history of TACC, the dispute between the two occurred when Longman had the minutes of one of the college's board meetings published in *The Times*. Huang quarrelled with Longman after he discovered that Longman had removed Huang's address to the meeting from the published version. This may have triggered Huang's resignation: Tu, 'Xingxingsese', 484.

[49] NCC Annual Report 1925–6, 201.

[50] Hart, Report for 1925, 2–4.

[51] North China Reports, Box 10, A. P. Cullen, Annual Report 1930, 8–9.

in Guangzhou (Canton) – found themselves the targets of nationalist attack. Even in 1925 when the Anti-Christian Movement was at its peak, the majority of TACC's graduating students attended the diploma and university entrance examination. When the September semester started that year, an enrolment of 350 was recorded. By March 1927, the total enrolment had reached 500, its maximum capacity.[52] One reason for this may have been the college's location in the French concession, where the power of the Chinese authorities and nationalists was more limited, and certain liberties were guaranteed.[53] Within the college, apart from the discord between Huang and Longman noted above, a friendly relationship between missionaries and Chinese staff generally manifested itself, even during this time of trial. Longman and Hart both affirmed their Chinese colleagues' 'magnificent loyalty'.[54] This may have reflected the homogeneous nature of the college staff, but also the fact that many Chinese members of staff were recruited from the college. According to the records, TACC's first five graduates all stayed to take up positions as college faculty members.[55] Two-thirds of the Chinese staff were college alumni and were therefore likely to have similar views and values to their missionary colleagues.[56] In addition, and perhaps even more importantly, the social network which TACC developed in North China greatly aided the college in its negotiations with the educational authorities. A good number of prominent politicians and businessmen, both Chinese and foreign, had been closely related to TACC since its establishment. Some served as its sponsors or belonged to the court of governors, others sent their children to the college, such as Yuan Shikai (袁世凱), former president of the Republic of China, and Liang Yanqing (梁燕卿), Comprador (Chinese manager) of Jardine Matheson Holdings Limited in Tianjin.[57] A large number of TACC students came from the more

[52] Hart, Report for 1924, 1–2; idem, Report for 1925, 2–4; North China Reports, Box 10, C. H. B. Longman, Report for 1926, 1–3; ibid., Newsletter from Dr and Mrs E. J. Stuckey, January 1928, 7; Lutz, *China and Christian Colleges*, 239–49.
[53] Hart, Report for 1924, 4–5; Longman, Report for 1925, 6; Hart, Report for 1928, 2.
[54] Longman, Report for 1925, 5–6; North China Reports, Box 9, S. Lavington Hart, Report for 1927, 9.
[55] Zhang, 'Jianshi', 55, 61–2.
[56] Tu, 'Xingxingsese', 482.
[57] Ibid. 478.

'wealthy and influential' classes of Chinese society,[58] while most of its graduates were recruited by commercial associations, banks, customs offices and the railways, all key to the region and vital to China's modernization. Situated in Tianjin, one of the major commercial ports in modern China, TACC's strong 'foreign' identity and educational features may to some extent have been 'tolerated' by a good number of students and the social elite, owing to the pragmatic benefits it brought them.

Conclusion

The competitiveness of TACC graduates in the job market demonstrates that in general, Christian education in China had played a positive role in spreading Western learning and technology in China and contributing to the construction of a modern society. However, questions may be raised as why, during the 1920s, Christian schools were regarded rather as an obstacle to China's modernization. The tension between Christian education and Chinese nationalism reveals a number of issues which Christianity – and with it Christian education – was facing in the semi-colonial Chinese context.

Firstly, Christianity in China had failed to respond adequately to China's desire for national unity, strength and sovereignty. One of the most important themes in modern Chinese history was the desire to seek a path towards 'national salvation' (Jiu Guo, 救國). Yip Ka-che identified two dimensions of 'national salvation': the ending of foreign domination in China and the establishment of a strong centralized state equipped to facilitate socio-economic modernization.[59] Christianity was unable to offer solutions for the first dimension owing to its apparently inseparable relationship with foreign countries.[60] In the quest to establish a powerful state, the possibility of establishing a liberal Western social and political model for Christian China was discredited when China's interests were neglected at the Paris Peace Conference of 1919.[61] In addition, with the widespread introduction of Western

[58] Cullen, Report for 1927, 4.

[59] Yip Ka-che, 'China and Christianity: Perspectives on Missions, Nationalism, and the State in the Republican Period, 1912–1949', in Stanley and Low, eds, *Missions*, 132–43, at 134.

[60] Lutz, *Chinese Politics*, 288.

[61] Ryan Dunch, *Fuzhou Protestants and the Making of a Modern China 1857–1927* (New Haven, CT, 2001), 185; Lutz, *Chinese Politics*, 2–3, 49–50, 57–8. During the Paris Peace

science, technology, thought and learning into Chinese society, the majority of Chinese intellectuals and the social elite increasingly distinguished Christianity from Western civilization, considering it irrelevant to the process of modernization.[62]

Secondly, a new type of nationalism matured in the 1920s; influenced by Lenin's theory of cultural imperialism, it relocated Christianity on the political map of China.[63] Education came to be viewed as a vital part of national sovereignty, as a means of instilling a sense of national identity and ideals, and control over the educational rights of Christian schools was thus brought onto the agenda of the nationalist campaigns. The case of TACC reveals the twofold approach of the nationalist government to national education during the first half of the twentieth century: nationalization (sinicization) and secularization (de-Christianization) of mission schools. It further demonstrates that the nationalization of Christian education took priority. TACC was regarded by missionaries as a key representative of British education in China. This, to some extent at least, validated the intent of the Chinese nationalists to make mission schools Chinese by appointing Chinese heads: the sinicization of Christian schools could never be fully realized as long as school affairs remained in the hands of missionaries. The case of TACC also reflects the complexity and ambiguity of the interaction between Christian schools and Chinese society, in which its practical role and its local social network had an important effect. Mission schools did not all share the same fate during the Anti-Christian Movement. This complexity deserves closer examination.

The nationalist government endeavoured to de-Christianize mission schools through enforcing patriotic education ('party

Conference of 1919, instead of granting Chinese delegates' immediate request for direct restitution of German-leased territory and other rights in Shandong, the Western Allies in general agreed to hand former German interests to Japan. China's failure to regained Shandong and Western powers' neglect of China's sovereignty led to the outburst of nationwide resentments and sparked student demonstrations in Beijing, known as the May Fourth Movement of 1919. The movement marked the rising tide of modern Chinese nationalism and stimulated Chinese intellectuals to search for China's own way to become a strong nation: Xu Guoqi, *Asia and the Great War: A Shared History* (Oxford, 2017), 153–84, 'China and Japan at Paris: Old Rivalries in a New World'.

[62] Lutz, *China and Christian Colleges*, 514.

[63] Bays, 'Foreign Missions', 146.

transformation education').[64] Military training was made compulsory in all registered middle schools, replacing compulsory classes in religion, where they existed.[65] The tension between Christian education and nationalist education or, to put it more precisely, the process of incorporating Christian education into the national educational system in order to serve the parties' political purposes, continued throughout the 1930s, 1940s and 1950s. It led ultimately to the demise of Christian schools in communist China in 1952, when foreign missions were expelled from the mainland.[66]

[64] Susan Rigdon, 'National Salvation: Teaching Civic Duty in China's Christian Colleges', in Bays and Widmer, eds, *China's Christian Colleges*, 193–217, at 202–6.

[65] North China Reports, Box 11, Eric H. Liddell, Report for 1934, 1.

[66] By 1952, Christian schools had either been closed down or taken over by local governments. Christian universities ceased to exist both as institutions and as names at the same time, when the government launched a campaign for the institutional reorganization of higher education: Lutz, *China and Christian Colleges*, 473–84.

The British Council of Churches' Influence on the 'Radical Rethinking of Religious Education' in the 1960s and 1970s

Jonathan Doney*
University of Exeter

It is widely accepted that during the later 1960s, Religious Education (RE) in English state-maintained schools underwent a significant transition, moving from a Christian 'confessional' approach to an academic study of world religions. A detailed examination of the activities of the British Council of Churches' Education Department during the period reveals examples of an active promotion of this study of world religions, something that hitherto has been absent from the historiography of RE. For example, the department organized key conferences, meetings and consultations, at which future directions for RE were considered and discussed. A research project undertaken for the department in the later 1960s, which led to the 1968 report Religion and the Secondary School, *was prompted by the identification that '[t]oday the needs of children and young people demand a radical rethinking and reshaping of the purpose and method of religious education'. This report included a statement specifically encouraging the study of non-Christian religions, which was repeated in later key documents. This article shows how the British Council of Churches' Education Department played a role in the development of the 'non-confessional' study of world religions in English state-maintained schools from as early as the late 1940s.*

The 1944 Education Act made the provision of Religious Education (hereafter: RE) compulsory in all state-funded schools in England, a status that the subject retains today. Having developed at a particular intersection of educational, ecclesiastical and societal influences, RE thus holds a unique position in the curriculum of English schools,

* University of Exeter, St Luke's Campus, Heavitree Rd, Exeter, EX1 2LU. E-mail: J.Doney@exeter.ac.uk. I am grateful to Annmarie Valdes, Rob Freathy and the anonymous peer reviewers for their helpful comments on an earlier version of this article.

Studies in Church History 55 (2019), 593–608
doi: 10.1017/stc.2018.26

and as a consequence it has a religious, educational and political importance.[1]

In terms of the subject's history, there is a general consensus amongst scholars that during the 1960s and 1970s, a new chapter in the history of English RE began; consequently, the period is highlighted as one of great transformation. Between the post-war introduction of compulsory RE and the mid-1960s, most RE in English publicly-funded schools was delivered through a confessional, often proselytizing, pedagogy, whereby children were nurtured in, and encouraged to adopt, the beliefs and practices characteristic of the Christian faith.[2] During the mid-1960s this Christian confessionalism was swept aside and replaced by a 'post-confessional, multi-faith', phenomenological and liberal study of world religions,[3] with the publication in 1971 of the *Schools Council Working Paper 36: Religious Education in Secondary Schools* often being situated as the locus of transformation.[4]

[1] L. P. Barnes, 'The Misrepresentation of Religion in Modern British (Religious) Education', *British Journal of Educational Studies* 54 (2006), 395–411; Department for Children, Schools and Families, *Guidance on the Duty to promote Community Cohesion* (London, 2007); idem, *Religious Education in English Schools: Non-Statutory Guidance 2010* (Nottingham, 2010).

[2] For example, L. P. Barnes and A. Wright, 'Romanticism, Representations of Religion and Critical Religious Education', *BJRE* 28 (2006), 65–77; R. Jackson and K. O'Grady, 'Religions and Education in England: Social Plurality, Civil Religion and Religious Education Pedagogy', in R. Jackson et al., eds, *Religion and Education in Europe: Developments, Contexts and Debates* (Münster and New York, 2007), 181–201.

[3] For example, L. P. Barnes, 'Ninian Smart and the Phenomenological Approach to Religious Education', *Religion* 30 (2000), 315–22; idem, 'Developing a new Post-liberal Paradigm for British Religious Education', *JBV* 28 (2007), 17–32; Barnes and Wright, 'Romanticism'; L. P. Barnes, 'An Alternative Reading of Modern Religious Education in England and Wales', *British Journal of Sociology of Education* 30 (2009), 607–19; idem, 'Developing a new Post-liberal Paradigm'; Kevin O'Grady, 'Professor Ninian Smart, Phenomenology and Religious Education', *BJRE* 27 (2005), 227–37; G. Teece, 'Too many competing Imperatives? Does RE need to rediscover its Identity?', *JBV* 32 (2011), 161–72; Stephen Parker and Rob Freathy, 'Context, Complexity and Contestation: Birmingham's Agreed Syllabuses for Religious Education since the 1970s', *JBV* 32 (2011), 247–63; eidem, 'Ethnic Diversity, Christian Hegemony and the Emergence of Multi-Faith Religious Education in the 1970s', *HE* 41 (2012), 381–404.

[4] *Schools Council Working Paper 36: Religious Education in Secondary Schools* (London, 1971). For an example of the situating of this paper as transformational, see L. Phillip Barnes, 'Working Paper 36, Christian Confessionalism and Phenomenological Religious Education', *Journal of Education and Christian Belief* 6 (2002), 61–77.

There has been a great deal of historical analysis of this change, mostly undertaken through the lenses of pedagogy, curriculum theory and national policy.[5] However, much of this has been reliant on analyses of a restricted range of policy documents (at local and national levels), with certain highly problematic assumptions made about policy implementation, including the notion that these documents are *descriptive* of classroom practice, when in reality, they were and are *prescriptive* (Parker and Freathy in particular highlight examples of these prescriptions' not being followed).[6] This has led to the development of a dominant historiography which constructs a narrative of rapid change in the nature and purpose of RE while failing to differentiate adequately between policy and classroom practice.[7] Review of a wider body of material shows that the widespread adoption of the study of world religions in English schools became possible as a result of a series of complex, concurrent, interlinked and networked changes which took place over a longer period than has previously been described, being more evolutionary than sudden and revolutionary;[8] changes in classroom practice became widespread, eventually creating circumstances in which a change in policy at both national and local levels became possible.[9]

Furthermore, these developments appear to have been driven by a complex combination of educational, theological and socio-political changes. These changes not only fuelled the furnace in which modern English RE was forged, but were significantly affected by, and affected, race and community relations as well as by the advance of interfaith dialogue and partnerships. Technological developments in communication and worldwide travel made it possible to learn

[5] Rob Freathy and Stephen Parker, 'The Necessity of Historical Enquiry in Educational Research: The Case of Religious Education', *BJRE* 32 (2010), 229–43; see also Dennis Bates, 'Christianity, Culture and Other Religions (Part 2): F. H. Hilliard, Ninian Smart and the 1988 Education Reform Act', *BJRE* 18 (1995–6), 85–102; Penny Thompson, *Whatever happened to Religious Education?* (Cambridge, 2004); Barnes and Wright, 'Romanticism'; Terence Copley, *Teaching Religion* (Exeter, 2008).

[6] See, for example, Parker and Freathy, 'Context, Complexity and Contestation'; Jonathan Doney, '"That would be an Ecumenical Matter". Contextualizing the Adoption of the Study of World Religions in English Religious Education using "Statement Archaeology": A Systematic Operationalization of Foucault's Historical Method' (PhD thesis, University of Exeter, 2015), 84–7.

[7] For a more detailed discussion, see Doney, '"Ecumenical Matter"'.

[8] For more detail on this contrast, see ibid. 66–9.

[9] Ibid. 111–12.

about and experience other cultures and countries in ways previously unimaginable. Increasingly, such encounters were not just happening overseas.

Immigration was a significant political and social issue. Racially motivated riots in Nottingham and Notting Hill in 1958[10] triggered a national debate over immigration control,[11] but although immigration control may have reduced numbers, it did not reduce tensions.[12] The controversial election of Peter Griffiths as MP for Smethwick in 1964, the formation of the National Front in 1967 and Enoch Powell's 'rivers of blood' speech given in Birmingham in 1968 all attest to the complex and dynamic state of race and community relations during this period.[13] However, discussion of immigration has been insufficiently nuanced; tending to focus on colour and / or country of origin, issues of religious affiliation have been marginalized.[14] Whilst Peter Webster highlights the fact that children growing up in the 1950s and 1960s were the first generation that 'had widespread experience of having neighbours who practised other faiths',[15] the extent to which, during the earlier part of this period at least, many of the families settling from overseas were Christian has been

[10] R. Karapin, 'The Politics of Immigration Control in Britain and Germany: Subnational Politicians and Social Movements', *Comparative Politics* 31 (1999), 423–44, at 429. Similarly motivated riots took place in Middleborough (1961) and St Helens (1963): Dominic Sandbrook, *White Heat: A History of Britain in the Swinging Sixties* (London, 2007), 665.

[11] Economic factors were already moderating immigration, which was rising and falling in line with the British economy, with a three-month time lag: Paul Rich, 'Black People in Britain: Response and Reaction, 1945–62', *History Today* 36 (1986), 14–20. See Karapin, *Politics of Immigration Control*, for a detailed discussion; note, however, that Karapin erroneously claims that the 1958 riots 'put the issue of immigration control on the political agenda for the first time since World War II': ibid. 429. This overlooks a House of Commons debate of 5 November 1954: HC Deb, vol. 532, cols 821–32; see also Grosvenor, *Assimilating Identities*, 19.

[12] Karapin asserted that 'Black immigration dropped from 85,000 per year in 1960–2 to 40,000 per year in 1963–66': R. Karapin, 'The Politics of Immigration Control in Britain and Germany: Subnational Politicians and Social Movements', *Comparative Politics* 31 (1999), 423–44, at 441; Zig Layton-Henry, *The Politics of Immigration* (Cambridge, MA, 1992), 13.

[13] On the election of Griffiths, the formation of the National Front and Powell's speech, see Sandbrook, *White Heat*, 661–83.

[14] See, for example, Grosvenor, *Assimilating Identities.*

[15] Peter Webster, 'Race, Religion and National Identity in Sixties Britain: Michael Ramsey, Archbishop of Canterbury and his Encounter with Other Faiths', in Charlotte Methuen, Andrew Spicer and John Wolffe, eds, *Christianity and Religious Plurality*, SCH 51 (Woodbridge, 2015), 385–98, at 385.

overlooked. A survey by the Schools Council, circulated to a sample of 213 schools in 1969, requested information about 'Christian immigrant children' and 'non-Christian immigrant children'; it reported that numbers within each category were very similar, but small in comparison to non-immigrant children (97%), 1.3 per cent of children being 'non-Christian immigrant children' and 1.8 per cent being 'Christian immigrant children'.[16]

Against this complex backdrop, there was a rise in interest in non-Christian religions and their practices, perhaps influenced by the Beatles phenomenon and the growing influence of teachers such as the Maharishi Mahesh Yogi.[17] All this took place in the context of reduced interest in institutional Christianity, arguably contributing to a further reduction of interest.[18] There was an expansion of ongoing discussions under the aegis of the Roman Catholic Church and the World Council of Churches (WCC) between Christians and those of other worldviews, both religious and non-religious. Increasingly such activities were seen as a legitimate activity of the Christian Church, especially in the light of *Nostra Aetate*, the 'Declaration on the Relation of the Church with Non-Christian Religions' of the Second Vatican Council, promulgated in 1965, and the work of the WCC.

Whilst highlighting the change in English RE during the 1960s and 1970s, existing historiography fails to attend to the context in which these developments took place, despite the dominance of the church in both the provision and the development of RE.[19] Specifically, the role of the British Council of Churches (BCC) has hitherto been overlooked. This article emerges from a three-year project which considered the influence of the ecumenical movement, globally and locally, on the development of the classroom study of world religions, focusing particularly on the role of the British Council of Churches' Education Department (BCCED).

[16] *Schools Council Working Paper 44: Religious Education in Primary Schools* (London, 1972), 78, Table 9.

[17] See, for example, Terence Thomas, *The British: Their Religious Beliefs and Practices* (London, 1988), 103–55.

[18] Freathy and Parker, *Secularists*, 225–7, where the authors make a robust argument for using the term 'de-Christianization' rather than 'secularization'.

[19] Terence Copley, 'Is UK Religious Education failing to address its own Cultural Context?', in Rune Larsson and C. Gustavsson, eds, *Towards a European Perspective on Religious Education* (Skellefteå, 2004), 80–9; Freathy and Parker, 'Necessity'.

The Role of the BCCED in encouraging the Study of World Religions

In contrast to earlier attempts at formal ecclesiastical co-operation in Britain, the BCC, formed in 1942, was both successful and fruitful. It soon established effective departments for Youth and Publications, developed work in Scotland and by 1949 had established over 170 local councils of churches.[20] In 1946 the BCC set up an Education Committee, formally constituting the Education Department in 1951, some seven years after the provisions of the 1944 Education Act had come into force.[21]

A detailed examination of the work of the BCCED during the 1960s, the period in which RE in schools was undergoing the change from Christian confessionalism, reveals a number of examples of its active promotion of the study of world religions. Against the backdrop of increasing opportunity for engagement between Christians and those practising other faiths, the examples that follow relate to the expansion of the concept of RE, seeing this expansion not only as facilitating discussion but as a matter of seeking to encourage the involvement of non-Christian faiths.

In 1961 the BCCED was made aware of a 'Conference on Teaching about World Religions in Schools', through an invitation issued by the organizers.[22] The programme included sessions on 'knowing about religions', 'teaching about world religions in the secondary school' and 'report on work done with junior school children'.[23] The organizers expressed the hope that an observer from the BCCED would be able to attend, stressing that the conference

[20] On unsuccessful earlier attempts, see, for example, Stephen Charles Neill, 'Plans of Union and Reunion', in Ruth Rouse and Stephen Charles Neill, eds, *A History of the Ecumenical Movement 1517–1948* (London, 1954), 484–95.

[21] London, CERC, BCC/ED/2/3/3, Correspondence and papers concerning the formation of the Committee on Christian Education and its subsequent development, 1939–55, Meeting of the committee, 4 November 1944. On the formation of the Education Department, see BCC/ED/2/1/10, Representation on the Education Department, 1951–8 (correspondence concerning membership of the committee).

[22] The conference was held at the University of London Institute of Education under the chairmanship of Professor W. R. Niblet, then the dean: BCC/ED/7/1/7, School-church relationships: papers and correspondence, 1953–65, 'Programme of, and letters relating to, Conference on Teaching about World Religions in Schools, Saturday 9th December, 1961'.

[23] These sessions were to be delivered by E. G. Parrinder, F. H. Hilliard and B. Cousin respectively: ibid., 'Programme of Conference on World Religions in Schools, 1961'.

was 'the first of its kind'.[24] The acting secretary of the BCCED responded to this invitation positively, undertaking to 'let other members of the Department know about this', but no record has been found of who attended the event, or of their reactions.[25]

Eight years later, in 1969, a Consultation on Religious Education in a Multi-Religious Society, convened by the BCCED in collaboration with the Community Relations Committee (later to become the Race Relations Board) was held at Harrogate.[26] It brought together those 'who were in some way concerned to take advantage of the possibilities of educational enrichment offered by the presence of considerable number of children of non-Christian faith in our schools', and included 'representatives of the Islamic, Sikh, Hindu and Christian communities'.[27] One outcome of this consultation was an expressed desire to consider how 'non-Christian religions could form a significant part of RE syllabuses'.[28]

Running parallel to preparations for this consultation, a working party had been established in May 1969 by the BCCED to consider the issue of 'Recruitment, Employment and Training of Teachers Concerned with Religious Education in Schools'.[29] Evidence was invited from the Council of Christians and Jews, the 'Immigrant Communities, and Denominational education representatives'.[30] Responses were received from the Indian High Commission,[31]

[24] Ibid., B. Cousin to Revd E. D. G. Stanford, 22 November 1961.

[25] In the absence of Stanford, the outgoing secretary, Nina Borelli (acting secretary) replied: ibid., Nina Borelli to B. Cousin, 28 November 1961.

[26] BCC/ED/2/1/2, Education Department Minutes November 1963–January 1972, 13 February 1969. A press release circulated after the event claimed this meeting to be 'the first of its kind to be held in this country': BCC/ED/7/1/58, 'Immigrants / Interfaith – West Yorkshire Consultation 1969: Various Papers and Correspondence', BCC press release, 4 March 1969.

[27] BCC/ED/7/1/58, Executive minutes, 21 May 1969; item 69/13 records the debate about the positioning of the BCC in relation to the event and ensuing publication, concluding: 'It would not be a BCC publication but reference would be made to the fact that BCCED had been responsible for convening the consultation'.

[28] Ibid., Report on the consultation, 5.

[29] BCC/ED/2/6/2, Various papers submitted to the Working Party on Recruitment, Employment and Training of Teachers.

[30] BCC/ED/2/6/1, Various papers including evidence, reports, etc. submitted to the Working Party on the Recruitment, Employment and Training of Teachers together with copies of unsigned minutes, 1969–70, Minutes of First meeting of Working Party on Recruitment, Training and Employment of Teachers concerned with Religious Education in Schools, 27 May 1969.

[31] Ibid., Enclosure G.

the Sikh community,[32] the Hindu community,[33] the Community Relations Council[34] and the National Secular Society.[35] Compilation of the submitted material resulted in a suggested list of elements that should be included in RE at secondary level, including 'a knowledge of other religions and philosophies of life combined with a tolerance for those who hold other beliefs'.[36]

A seminar on 'Religious Education in a Multi-Religious Society', organized by the BCCED, took place in September 1970, in London.[37] The event demonstrates that the pattern of involving representatives of a variety of faith communities was becoming routine, or normalized.[38] Participants were asked to discuss a list of ten questions relating to the place of Christianity and other religions in RE. One of the questions asked was: 'In multi-racial county schools, is a totally Christian syllabus of religious education justified?'; the recorded answer was an emphatic 'no'.[39]

Finally, from 10–14 July 1972 a Conference on 'Interfaith Dialogue in Education', organized by the BCCED in collaboration with the Office of Education at the WCC and the government's Department of Education and Science (DES), took place at Stamford Hall in Leicester.[40] This not only demonstrates the

[32] Ibid., Enclosures H and I.
[33] Ibid., Enclosure J.
[34] Ibid., Enclosure K.
[35] National Secular Society publications included Maurice Hill, *Surveys on Religion in Schools* (London, [1969?]); Margaret Knight, *Morals without Religion, and other Essays* (London, 1954); *Submissions for a new Education Act* (London, [1969?]); William McIlroy, *Educational Reform: Story of a Campaign* (London, 1968); David Tribe, *Religion and Human Rights* (n.pl., n.d.).
[36] BCC/ED/2/6/2, Compilation of material gathered, 11 February 1971, 18–19.
[37] BCC/ED/7/1/57, 'Immigrants and Education – Various Papers'.
[38] The meeting was attended by about forty people, including school inspectors, university tutors, members of the BCC and the Free Church Federal Council, and representatives of other Christian groups and of the Hindu, Islamic, Sikh and Jewish communities: ibid., Seminar attendance list, 15 September 1970.
[39] BCC/ED/7/1/57, 'Religious Education in a Multi-Religious Society', 15 September 1970, Working Party Paper I. Further questions focused on the relationship between child development and the benefits to the pupil of being 'exposed to religious material from faiths other than his own', and an evaluation of 'how newer techniques of teaching religious education help or hinder in a multi-religious approach'.
[40] BCC/ED/2/1/2, Education Department minutes, 14 May 1971, item 71/9 (10) (Conference on Religious Education in a Multi-Religious Community, 3–5 May 1971); ibid., 25 January 1972, item 71/9 (8) (Joint WCC/BCC Conference on Interfaith Dialogue in Education, 1972); BCC/ED/2/1/11, BCC, Autumn 1971

establishment of a tripartite link between the department, the WCC and the DES but, taken with the other events organized and supported by the BCCED, it suggests that the BCCED had a positive orientation towards interfaith dialogue within education generally, and within RE specifically.

In different ways, these examples demonstrate a focus on resolving the tension between the teaching of non-Christian worldviews (initially other faiths but increasingly non-religious viewpoints too) and the dominance of Christianity in the curriculum. Key to achieving a balance was the expressed desire to justify RE on 'valid educational grounds'.[41] This expressed itself in the enthusiasm expressed at Harrogate in 1969 for ensuring that the study of world religions would not merely be a response in areas with a high proportion of immigrants, but 'educationally beneficial' on a much wider scale. This approach was further illustrated at the London conference, where the relationship between up-to-date scholarship on child development and teaching methods was explored. In summary, these events and discussions demonstrate that the BCCED was actively involved in promoting the study of world religions at a time when RE was changing in classrooms across England.

Radical Rethinking of Religious Education and the Alves Report

But from where and when did these ideas emerge? An exploration of the wider discourses of the BCCED reveals that during the period leading up to the late 1960s there had already been an expressed desire for change, which found particular expression through two calls, about a decade apart, for a radical rethinking of RE. In 1963, prompted by the upcoming twentieth anniversary of the passing of

---

Meeting, Education Department Report, 10 (WCC / BCC Conference on Interfaith Dialogue in Education, 10–14 July 1972, Stamford Hall, Leicester, Paper M).

[41] The study groups which met in preparation for the 1972 Leicester conference had as their terms of reference 'to consider some of the issues that emerge in trying to provide a religious education *valid on educational grounds* in a multi-faith society, and having theological cohesion acceptable to Christian people': BCC, Autumn 1971 Meeting, Education Department Report, 10 (WCC/BCC Conference on Interfaith Dialogue in Education, 10–14 July 1972, Stamford Hall, Leicester, Paper M; emphasis in original). The term was also used a number of times as an underpinning principle within *Working Paper 36* (e.g. ibid. 16, 37).

the 1944 act, a campaign was launched, calling for 'the full implementation of the 1944 Education Act'.[42] In 1962, the BCCED had initiated a discussion of its frustration regarding the lack of success in RE (even though the success criteria were disputed), which observed that 'from neither the statutory nor the independent stream do we find an influx of committed Christians commensurate with the effort made in schools. Is it a possible task?'[43] The BCCED agreed that a review of the religious provisions of the 1944 act was necessary, concluding: 'Today the needs of children and young people demand a *radical rethinking* and reshaping of the purpose and method of religious education, both in the material itself, in the manner of presentation, and the way in which it is related to life in the school and beyond it.'[44]

However, the phrase 'radical rethinking' did not originate here. It is first found in the discourse of the BCCED in 1958: discussing the period since the 1944 act, and considering the future of RE, the BCCED Executive 'took the view that what was required … was a radical re-thinking of the purpose of Religious Instruction'.[45]

This attempt to rethink religious education led to the establishment of a special committee of the BCCED in 1963. This committee set in motion a detailed research project, funded by the Gulbenkian Foundation (Lisbon), which offered funding of £5,000 over two years.[46] Colin Alves, who was lecturer in divinity at King Alfred's College, Winchester, was seconded to the BCCED to act as investigating officer for the duration of the project.[47] Unlike some other projects at the time, which focused on local policy documents, Alves's work centred on issues arising from classroom practice. He deployed a large-scale survey questionnaire, undertaken during 1965–6 with secondary school pupils and focusing almost entirely

[42] BCC/ED/7/1/40, 1963 Campaign for Education: Various papers and correspondence, 1963 Campaign for Education flyer.

[43] BCC/ED/2/1/1, Education Department minutes, 21–22 June 1962, Report on the Nature of Religion and Religious Instruction; ibid., BCC, 12 March 1964 Meeting, Appendix 1, 'Spring 1964. Programme of Investigation into the Nature and Future Needs of Religious Education in Schools'.

[44] Ibid. (emphasis added).

[45] Ibid., Executive Committee minutes, 27 October 1958, item 225.

[46] Ibid., Education Department minutes, 12 November 1963, item 64/2 (Research on nature and future needs of Religious Education).

[47] BCC, 12 March 1964 Meeting, Appendix 1, item 64/12 (appointment of Alves as investigating officer); Colin Alves, *Religion and the Secondary School* (London, 1968).

on biblical knowledge, Christian religious practice (including personal Christian affiliation) and Christian morality.[48] The final report, *Religion and the Secondary School*, was published in 1968; however the status of this report is complex.[49]

In mid-1967, a draft report was considered by the BCCED, with the status of the report in relation to the BCC being a focus of some discussion.[50] As the 'main body of the report was to the Gulbenkian Foundation', it was 'agreed that a factual statement that [the report] had been presented to the BCC would be adequate'.[51] Consequently, the foreword in the published report, written by the then general secretary of the BCC, opened with the emphatic statement: 'THIS IS not an official Report of the British Council of Churches, but the Council is glad to have been able, through its Education Department, to initiate the research project it describes'.[52] The foreword also suggested that '[Alves's] conclusions should be assessed on their own merits and not necessarily as representing the views of the British Council of Churches'.[53] However, the published report also incorporated a 'Report of the Special Committee appointed by the Education Department of the British Council of Churches', which introduced Alves's work, reflected on its findings and suggested courses of action.

This later section appears to have had a more authoritative status within the BCC; it is the 'Report of the Special Committee' that sets out a proposed 'New Deal' for RE.[54] The report discussed 'limiting factors which are within the power of the educational system to change', including the restricted supply of suitably trained teachers, the unsuitability of many public examinations and qualifications that were available to students, the lack of timetabled periods for RE and the loading of 'the scales of professional advancement … against religious education specialists'.[55] In addition, this part of

[48] Alves, *Religion*, especially 36, 129 (Survey 65, 66 respectively).

[49] BCC/ED/7/1/46, Papers and correspondence relating to the investigation into the nature and future needs of religious education primarily in county schools, working party, 1963–6; see also BCC/ED/2/1/1.

[50] BCC/ED/2/1/2, Education Department minutes, 14 July 1967.

[51] Ibid.

[52] Alves, *Religion*, 11, emphasis original.

[53] Ibid., Foreword by Kenneth Sansbury, dated October 1967.

[54] Ibid. 13 (Special Committee Report, §1).

[55] Ibid. 16–18 (Special Committee Report, §9).

the report included an explicit encouragement of the study of non-Christian religions: 'We can, and should, learn from men of other faiths theistic and non-theistic and they from us'.[56]

The study of non-Christian religions in RE in English schools, as called for in the 1968 report, was not novel, however. Evidence from elsewhere testifies to this. For example, the evidence provided to the Durham Commission during 1968 in response to the question 'Should provision be made … where circumstances appear to justify it, for religious education other than Christian education?'[57] shows that a number of respondents believed that the case had already been made,[58] and in some schools the practice was already established.[59] Similarly, the evidence submitted by the Church of England's National Society for the Promotion of Religious Education commented not only that the practice was already established, but that representatives from non-Christian traditions were involved in the Agreed Syllabus Committees that set out the content and aims for RE teaching in county schools.[60] This claim is corroborated by contemporaneous agreed syllabus documents from a number of local education authority areas.[61]

Indeed, looking further back, there is evidence that the study of non-Christian worldviews was taking place in schools as early as the 1920s, even if it was at that point limited to some schools, and in them restricted to later phases of schooling.[62] There are also examples of the study of other religions during the post-war period – following the provisions of the 1944 Education Act – suggesting an openness towards the study of non-Christian worldviews. Even before

[56] Ibid. 15 (Special Committee Report, §7).
[57] CERC, NS/7/8/1/14, Questionnaire (question 6).
[58] Ibid., Paper 16, Response from County Councils Association.
[59] For example, ibid., Paper 15, Evidence from Girl's Public Day School Trust.
[60] NS/7/8/1/18, National Society proposed evidence to Commission on Religious Education.
[61] For more analysis of this, see Doney, '"Ecumenical Matter"', 51–115.
[62] Terence Copley, 'Rediscovering the Past: Writings on Religious Education in Religion in Education Quarterly, 1934–39, raise some Questions for Today's Religious Educators', *BJRE* 20 (1998), 80–9; see also G. E. Phillips, 'The Study of Other Religions in Schools', *Religion in Education* 6 (1939), 221–6; A. Mayhew, 'The Comparative Study of Religions in Schools', *Religion in Education* 4 (1937), 14–21. *Religion in Education* was the professional journal for RE teachers; on its history, see Stephen G. Parker, Rob Freathy and Jonathan Doney, 'The Professionalisation of Non-denominational Religious Education in England: Politics, Organisation and Knowledge', *JBV* 37 (2016), 201–38.

the establishment of the BCCED in 1951, there are indications that the study of religions other than Christianity was being discussed by some within the ecumenical movement. A sequence of letters in 1946 between Tissington Tatlow, director of the Institute of Christian Education, an ecumenical group established in 1935 and concerned with engendering cooperation between 'Christianity and Education … at home and overseas',[63] and Sir Walter Moberly, then chairing the BCC's Committee on Christian Education, the forerunner of the BCCED, provides evidence of this.[64] Tatlow and Moberly objected to the age group for which such material was included rather than to its inclusion per se: it was studied only by students who had reached the age of fifteen, thus excluding the vast majority of students, who would leave school at that age.[65] However, it is clear that teaching material dealing with other faith traditions was available, that the BCC Education Committee was aware of this material, and that the committee was involved in actively promoting it. For example, one list circulated in 1948, headed 'Publications [that] can be ordered from BCC', included Marcus Knight, *The Mind of Japan* (n.d.); S. S. Milford and W. R. Garrad, *Ancient Faiths and Lore of India* (1947); Frank A. Smalley, *Chinese Philosophy and Religion* (1947); and Mabel C. Warburton, *The Mind and Ways of Islam* (1947).[66] These examples support the claim that including the study of world religions alongside the study of Christianity in the RE classrooms of England, while perhaps still unusual and not widespread, was not entirely novel, even in the late 1940s.

Encouragement to Study non-Christian Faiths in English RE

Whilst Alves's *Religion and the Secondary School* does not appear to have been widely circulated, perhaps because it considered RE only in relation to county schools,[67] the recommendations themselves became influential through repetition.[68] The recommendation that the study of other religions and belief systems should be encouraged

63 For a historical account of the Institute of Christian Education, see ibid.
64 BCC/ED/7/1/3, Tatlow to Moberly, 28 November 1946.
65 Ibid.
66 BCC/ED/2/3/3, List of publications available from the BCC, 1948.
67 Alves, *Religion*, 13.
68 For more on the authoritative nature of repeated statements, see Doney, '"Ecumenical Matter"', 141–9.

was repeated in *The Fourth R* (1970), often known as *The Durham Report*,[69] which was circulated more widely, perhaps because it considered RE in both county and church schools.[70] In this way the recommendation became established in church discourse.

The encouragement to study world religions was further repeated in *Working Paper 36*, which quoted directly from *The Fourth R*.[71] Thus the recommendation was introduced to educational discourse. The Schools Curricula and Examination Council (generally known as the Schools Council) had been launched in March 1964 as a representative body to monitor curriculum and examinations in England, taking over responsibility from the Secondary Schools Examinations Council (formed in 1958) and the Curriculum Study Group (formed in 1962).[72] The Schools Council was seen as an authoritative body, looked to by local and national government, as well as by the inspectorate and individual teachers.[73] Consequently, publications under its banner, particularly its series of working papers, were considered as having some degree of authority or 'official' sanction.[74]

There are strong textual similarities between Alves's report to the BCCED, *The Fourth R* and *Working Paper 36* with regard to learning from non-Christian faith communities, demonstrated by the repetition of a key statement which had first appeared in the Report of the Special Committee: 'We can, and should, learn from men of other faiths theistic and non-theistic and they from us'.[75] This statement is repeated in *The Fourth R*, in a chapter that Alves was involved in

[69] Ian Ramsey, ed., *The Fourth R: The Durham Report on Religious Education* (London, 1970), §216.

[70] Ibid. 94–152, 'Religious Education in Schools with Special Reference to County Schools', 205–72, 'Church Schools'.

[71] *Working Paper 36*, 19; see Doney, '"Ecumenical Matter"', 159–214.

[72] P. Gordon, 'The Schools Council and Curriculum: Developments in Secondary Education', in R. Lowe, ed., *The Changing Secondary School* (London, 1989), 52–71; P. Fisher, 'Curriculum Control in England and Wales: The Birth of the Schools Council, 1964', *JEAH* 16/2 (1984), 35–44; R. Manzer, 'The Political Origins of the Schools Council', *Secondary Education* 4/2 (1974), 47–50.

[73] *Working Paper 36*; Doney, '"Ecumenical Matter"', 159–214.

[74] Manzer states: 'Almost everyone admitted that the bulletins and working papers which the Council's secretariat soon began to produce were useful and even influential documents': *Political Origins*, 50; see also Gordon, *Schools Council*, 56–7, 68. Stewart highlights the influence of Schools Council publications overseas, linking its influence and authoritative standing to its role in regard to examinations: M. Stewart, 'The Growth of the Schools Council 1966–1973', *Secondary Education* 4/2 (1974), 51–3.

[75] Alves, *Religion*, 15 (Special Committee Report, §7).

drafting,[76] and again in *Working Paper 36*. The historiography of English RE has generally presumed that Ninian Smart had authorial responsibility for *Working Paper 36*, but archival evidence indicates that final editorial control was actually vested in the hands of Alves: publication was agreed by the relevant committee, 'subject to any amendments being referred to Mr Alves'.[77] Whilst it would not be true to claim that Alves was solely responsible for the repetition of the statement, his involvement in all three reports is evident, although his contribution has hitherto been unacknowledged.

Thus, although Alves's recommendation in the BCCED report cannot be claimed as the moment at which everything changed in English RE, it can be considered a watershed in the process of the legitimization, normalization and (eventually) widespread adoption of the study of world religions as the dominant approach to RE in English schools in the later 1960s. His report marked a point at which the practice is identifiable as distinct from existing practice within national ecumenical discourse, positively articulating an emerging classroom approach for the first time. This approach in RE, supported by the BCCED, became widespread. By the mid- to late 1970s it was reflected in national and local policy documents.[78]

Conclusion

This exploration of archival material from the BCC reveals that the BCCED played a hitherto unreported role in the adoption of the study of world religions as a dominant approach to English RE. Two calls by the BCCED, a decade apart, for the radical rethinking of RE led ultimately to the 1968 report *Religion and the Secondary*

[76] CERC, NS/7/8/1/7, '[Durham] Commission on Religious Education', Draft for discussion, ch. 4, 'Religious Education in County Schools'.

[77] Kew, TNA, EJ 1/210, RE Committee minutes, 28 October 1970. Neither the files of the Consultative Committee nor those of the Religious Education Committee of the Schools Council include drafts of *Working Paper 36*, so it is currently impossible to ascertain the exact nature and extent of Alves's editorial work.

[78] For a detailed analysis of this process, as traced through the contents of the main professional journal for RE teachers of the time (*Learning for Living*), see Doney, '"Ecumenical Matter"', 66–81. Regarding policy change, see TNA, ED 135/35, HMI Memos 1975, Memo 3/75, discussed in detail in Doney, '"Ecumenical Matter"', 78–9; also the Swann Report: Department of Education and Science, *Education for All: The Report of the Committee of Inquiry into the Education of Children from Ethnic Minority Groups* (London, 1985); Education Reform Act 1988, ch. 40, §8(3).

School, edited by Colin Alves. Alves's encouragement of the study of non-Christian religions in the RE classrooms of England was repeated, and thus imbued with authority, in two spheres. Firstly, it entered the ecclesiastical sphere through being taken into *The Fourth R*. Secondly, it entered the educational sphere via *Working Paper 36*. Alongside this, there is evidence of the BCC's active promotion of the study of world religions in the classroom, shown in its encouragement of cooperation with other religions in a series of conferences and meetings in the late 1960s and in the inclusion of, and consultation with, representatives of faith communities beyond Christianity.

The tracing of the BCCED's active encouragement of the expansion of RE in English schools beyond the boundaries of Christianity shows that this was not, as previous studies have suggested, a novel development in the later 1960s; nor did the practice originate with Alves. The beginnings of the practice of studying non-Christian religions in the English RE classroom date back to the inter-war period. From the late 1940s onwards, the BCC was making available materials to support the teaching of non-Christian religions.

It is therefore clear that during the later 1960s the BCCED's radical rethinking of religious education led to practical engagement with non-Christian faiths, together with an explicit call to study these faiths in the RE classroom. In this way, the department's work gave some legitimacy to the study of non-Christian faiths, and it played a role in the normalization and eventual widespread adoption of the study of world religions in English RE classrooms.[79] This adoption took place at a time when national policy was generally silent on this question and local policy was often constrained to confessional Christianity, and at a time of growing interaction between different religions as immigration began to change the demographic of local communities. However, as normalization of the study of world religions and the impact of immigration took place at different speeds in different areas, there were undoubtedly parts of Britain where school students experienced a shift to the study of world religions in RE classrooms earlier than the expansion of their own inter-religious experience.

[79] For more detailed analysis of this process of normalization, see Doney, '"Ecumenical Matter"', 66–81.